Full Disclosure

Combating Stonewalling and Other Discovery Abuses

ATLA PRESS

Published by
ATLA Press
1050 31st Street NW
Washington, DC 20007

Cover Design by
Marcella Kulchitsky

Library of Congress Catalog Number 94-21124
ISBN 0-941916-70-7

2nd Printing, 1995

© 1994 Association of Trial Lawyers of America

Full Disclosure

Combating Stonewalling and Other Discovery Abuses

Francis H. Hare, Jr.   James L. Gilbert   Stuart A. Ollanik

SUMMARY CONTENTS

About the Authors xxiii
Acknowledgments xxv
Foreword xxvii
Introduction
    The Whole Truth xxxi

Part One: Discovery Obligations

Chapter One
    Right of Access to Relevant Information 3

Chapter Two
    Proper Discovery Response 25

Chapter Three
    Policy Choices Represented by the Federal Rules 47

Part Two: Stonewalling

Chapter 4
    Stonewalling in Products Liability Litigation 73

Chapter 5
    Common Tactics for Evading Disclosure 81

Chapter 6
    Dump Truck Discovery 117

Chapter 7
    Document Destruction and Other Spoliation of Evidence 141

Chapter 8
    Confidentiality Orders—The Stonewaller's Shield 157

Chapter 9
    Turning the Tables on Stonewallers 181

Chapter 10
    Sanctions 189

Appendix 1
    Discovery of Particular Topics 219

Appendix 2
    Authorities Regarding the Benefit of Information Sharing.............327
Appendix 3
    Summary of Authorities for Discovery Abuse Sanctions 383
Bibliography..387
Index by Jurisdiction...425

DETAILED CONTENTS

About the Authors xxiii
Acknowledgments xxv
Foreword xxvii
Introduction:
    The Whole Truth xxxi

PART ONE: DISCOVERY OBLIGATIONS

Chapter One: Right of Access to Relevant Information 3
  I. Purposes of Discovery 3
  II. Scope of Discovery 5
    A. Broad, Liberal Construction of the Rules 5
    B. Discovery Relevance 6
      1. Subject Matter of Any Claim or Defense 7
      2. Reasonably Calculated to Lead to Admissible Evidence 10
    C. Uncertainty Resolved in Favor of Discoverability 11
  III. Limitations on Discovery 12
    A. Privilege 12
      1. Claiming Privilege 12
      2. Attorney-Client Privilege 13
      3. Work-Product Doctrine 14
    B. Trial Preparation: Experts 16
      1. Testifying Experts 17
      2. Nontestifying Experts "Retained or Specially Employed in Anticipation of Litigation or Preparation for Trial" 18
      3. Experts Informally Consulted for Trial but Not "Retained or Specially Employed" 19
      4. Experts Who Are Regular Employees or Fact Witnesses 20
    C. Court's Discretion 20

    IV. Discovery of Computerized Information 22

    V. Conclusion. 24

Chapter Two: Proper Discovery Response 25

    I. General Rules Governing the Response 25

    II. Duty of Inquiry. 27

    III. Duty to Supplement Responses 33

    IV. Burden on Party Resisting Discovery 39

    V. Specific Objections 40

        A. Relevance Objection. 40

        B. Burden Objection 41

        C. Vagueness Objection 43

    VI. Conclusion 45

Chapter Three: Policy Choices Represented by the Federal Rules 47

    I. Use of the Rules to Balance Conflicting Values 48

        A. Utility of Discovery: Full Disclosure vs. Cost Savings 48

        B. Concern with Discovery Overuse vs. Concern with Evasion 49

        C. Counsel as Advocate vs. Counsel as Officer of the Court 50

        D. Judicial Intervention vs. Judicial Laissez-Faire 53

        E. Prefiling Proof of Liability vs. Proof Obtained by Discovery 54

        F. Who Pays: Discovering Party vs. Disclosing Party. 55

    II. History of the Rules Governing Discovery Conduct—
1937 through 1983. 56

        A. Adoption of the Federal Rules of Civil Procedure. 56

        B. 1970 Amendments 57

        C. 1980 and 1983 Amendments. 58

    III. 1993 Rule Amendments—From Discovery to Disclosure 60

        A. Requirements of the Amended Rules 60

            1. Automatic Disclosures 61

            2. Presumptive Limits on Discovery 64

            3. Discovery Planning and Scheduling 64

            4. Sanctions for Deposition Conduct 64

        B. Policy Choices Reflected in the New Amendments 65

            1. Utility of Discovery. 65

            2. Adversarial Character of Discovery. 66

            3. Overuse vs. Stonewalling 66

            4. Utility of Judicial Intervention 66

  5. Prefiling Proof of Liability 66
  6. Cost-Shifting.. 67
 C. Effects of the 1993 Amendments................................. 67

Part Two: Discovery Evasion

Chapter Four: Discovery Evasion in Products Liability Litigation 73
 I. Evasion Denies Plaintiffs Access to Justice 73
 II. Abusive Request vs. Stonewalling Response 77
  A. Causes.. 77
  B. Means of Detection and Prevention............................. 79
  C. Consequences 79
 III. Need for Deterrence 79

Chapter Five: Common Tactics for Stonewalling Disclosure 81
 I. Overview: Patterns of Deception 81
 II. Boilerplate Objections 83
 III. Use of Semantics 85
 IV. Unilaterally and Subjectively Limiting the Scope of Relevance 86
 V. Evasive, Misleading, or False Responses............................ 88
 VI. Delay.. 94
 VII. Shell Game 101
 VIII. Stonewalling in Depositions 103
 IX. Stonewalling Concerning Expert Witnesses 106
 X. Probing Plaintiff's Knowledge of Manufacturer's Documents
  to Facilitate Stonewalling.. 109
  A. Request Exceeds the Scope of Discovery....................... 110
  B. Information Available from Another, More Convenient Source 111
  C. Information Protected by Work-Product Doctrine..................111
  D. Allowing Beneficial Collaboration vs. Enabling Evasion 114
 XI. Conclusion 115

Chapter Six: Dump Truck Discovery 117
 I. Overview: Dump Trucks, Shuffled Decks, and Needles in Haystacks.... 117
 II. Intended Use of the Business Records Option 119
  A. Objectives of the Business Records Option....................... 120
  B. Prerequisites to Invoking the Business Records Option 122
   1. Burden of Response.. 122

  2. Information Contained in the Records. 125
  3. Duty to Specify **125**
 C. Application of the Business Records Option to
  Rules 34(b) and 45(d). **128**
III. Abuse of the Business Records Option in Recent Practice 130
 A. Central Document Repositories Operated by Defendants. 130
  1. Honda's ATV Repository **131**
  2. Reading Rooms **132**
 B. Abusive Use of Computers. **133**
IV. Preventing Abuses of the Central Document Repository. 133
 A. Proper Procedures for Business Records Options 133
  1. Prior Court Approval. **133**
  2. Assurance of Full Disclosure **134**
  3. Assistance in Obtaining Answers or Locating
   Requested Documents. **134**
  4. Logistics of Access and Use **134**
 B. Examples of Proper Use of the Business Records Center 135
  1. On-Site Inspection **135**
  2. Court-Operated Repository **136**
  3. Plaintiff-Operated Central Document Repository. **138**

Chapter Seven: Document Destruction and
Other Spoliation of Evidence **141**

I. Magnitude of the Problem **141**
II. Duty to Preserve Evidence **144**
 A. Nature and Scope of the Duty **144**
 B. Document Retention Policies **146**
 C. Destructive Testing. **149**
III. Remedies for Evidence Destruction or Spoliation. **150**
 A. Traditionally Available Penalties and Remedies **150**
  1. Discovery Sanctions **150**
  2. Unfavorable Inference **151**
  3. Criminal Penalties. **152**
  4. Professional Discipline. **152**
  5. Traditional Negligence Claims **152**
 B. Evolving Remedies **153**
  1. Intentional Spoliation. **153**
  2. Negligent Spoliation. **154**

  3. Fraudulent Concealment of Evidence 155
  4. Contract Actions for Spoliation 156
 IV. Conclusion 156

Chapter Eight: Confidentiality Orders—The Stonewaller's Shield 157
 I. Isolating Plaintiffs... 157
  A. Purported Grounds for Confidentiality......................... 158
  B. Defendants' True Motivation 159
 II. Value of Information Sharing 162
  A. Leveling the Playing Field.................................... 163
  B. Benefits of Information Sharing by Plaintiffs 165
   1. Justice... 165
   2. Efficiency... 165
   3. Reduced Expense.. 165
  C. Verification of Full Disclosure................................. 166
 III. Combating a Motion for a Restrictive Confidentiality Order 167
  A. Voluntary Agreement Trap 167
  B. Defendant's Legal Burden of Proof 169
   1. Manufacturer's Heavy Burden of Proof...................... 169
   2. Standard of Particularized Proof............................ 169
   3. Probability and Quality of Alleged Harm 170
   4. Character of Alleged Harm 170
   5. Weighing Countervailing Interests 170
  C. Requirements for Trade Secret Protection 170
   1. Competitive Use... 171
   2. Matters of General Knowledge 172
   3. Matters in the Public Domain 173
   4. Sale of a Product... 173
  D. Documents Obtained Outside of Discovery 174
  E. Identical Discovery Requests 174
  F. Interrogatories to Identify Disputed Documents................... 175
  G. Deposing the Manufacturer's Affiants 175
  H. Counter Affidavits 175
  I. Proposed Alternative Order 176
 IV. Public Access to Discovery Information 176
  A. Constitutional Basis for Public Disclosure 177
  B. Legislation and Court Rules 178
  C. Privacy and Property Rights as a Bar to Public Disclosure 179

Chapter Nine: Turning the Tables on Stonewallers 181

   I. Using Discovery to Flush Out Evidence Destruction 181

      A. Interrogatories and Requests for Production 182

      B. Depositions...184

      C. Finding Proof of Suppression or Spoliation 184

   II. Embracing Your Opponent's Discovery Misconduct 185

Chapter Ten: Sanctions...189

   I. Purposes of Sanctions 189

   II. Sanction Authorities 190

      A. Fed. R. Civ. P. 37 191

         1. Sanctionable Conduct 191

         2. Sanctionable Entity 192

         3. Authorized Sanctions 192

         4. Procedures...192

      B. Fed. R. Civ. P. 26(g)...194

         1. Sanctionable Conduct 194

         2. Sanctionable Entity 196

         3. Authorized Sanctions 196

         4. Procedures...196

      C. Fed. R. Civ. P. 16(f) 196

         1. Sanctionable Conduct 196

         2. Sanctionable Entity 196

         3. Authorized Sanctions 197

         4. Procedures...197

      D. Fed. R. Civ. P. 30(d)(2) 197

         1. Sanctionable Conduct 197

         2. Sanctionable Entity 197

         3. Authorized Sanctions 197

         4. Procedures...197

      E. Fed. R. Civ. P. 30(g)...197

         1. Sanctionable Conduct 198

         2. Sanctionable Entity 198

         3. Authorized Sanctions 198

         4. Procedures...198

      F. 28 U.S.C. § 1927..198

         1. Sanctionable Conduct 198

         2. Sanctionable Entity 199

   3. Authorized Sanctions 199
   4. Procedures 199
  G. Inherent Power of the Court 199
   1. Sanctionable Conduct 200
   2. Sanctionable Entity 200
   3. Authorized Sanctions 200
   4. Procedures 201
 III. Types of Sanctions 201
  A. Awarding Attorney Fees and Costs 202
  B. Imposing Fines 203
  C. Precluding Issues or Evidence 203
  D. Deeming Facts Established 204
  E. Striking Pleadings 204
  F. Ordering Default or Dismissal 204
  G. Charging Contempt 207
  H. Removing Counsel 208
 IV. Appellate Review 209
  A. Reviewability 209
  B. Standard of Review 210
  C. Review of Magistrate's Determination 210
 V. Role of Sanctions in Countering Stonewalling 211
 VI. Conclusion 216

Appendix 1: Discovery of Particular Topics 219
 § 1 Jurisdiction 219
 § 2 Fact/Law Distinction 220
 § 3 Opinions/Conclusions 221
 § 4 Contentions 221
 § 5 Impeachment 222
 § 5.1 Generally 222
 § 5.2 Surveillance Films 224
 § 6 Identification of Persons Participating in Response 225
 § 7 Insurance/Indemnity Information 226
 § 8 Tax Returns 226
 § 9 Medical Records 227
 § 9.1 Generally 227

§ 9.2 Plaintiff's Medical Records...228
§ 9.3 Defendant's Medical Records 229
§ 9.4 Court-Appointed Physician or Other Expert.............................229
§ 9.5 Plaintiff's Medical Records in Possession of Defendant 230
§ 10 Identification of Parties 230
§ 11 Defendant's Organizational Structure...................................230
§ 12 Membership in Trade Organizations....................................231
§ 13 Identity of Competitors and/or Members of the Industry..............232
§ 14 Corporate Record Retention/Destruction Program 232
§ 15 Identification of Nonexpert Witnesses..................................232
§ 15.1 Generally..232
§ 15.2 Identification of Blood Donors and Other Related Situations 234
§ 15.3 Anticipated Trial Witnesses 236
§ 16 Expert Witnesses...236
§ 16.1 Generally..236
§ 16.2 Fact Witness Experts 239
§ 16.3 Trial Experts 240
§ 16.4 Consulting Experts 242
§ 17 Identification of Documents 247
§ 17.1 Generally...247
§ 17.2 "Trade Secrets" and Other Claims of Privilege......................248
§ 17.3 Translation of Foreign Language Documents 250
§ 17.4 List of Documents or Bibliography................................251
§ 17.5 Index of Documents 251
§ 17.6 Abstracts or Summaries of Documents 252
§ 17.7 Statistics..252
§ 18 Documents in Computer Form.....................................252
§ 18.1 Generally..252
§ 18.2 Facts/Information in Computer Format 255
§ 18.3 Use of Computer in Litigation Support 257
§ 19 Defendant's Relationship with the Government......................259
§ 20 Defendant's Assets/Net Worth 261

§ 21 Minutes of Corporate Meetings. 263
§ 22 Trial Preparation 264
§ 22.1 Generally 264
§ 22.2 Statements 264
§ 22.3 Course of Business Materials 266
§ 22.4 Investigative Materials. 268
§ 22.5 Litigation Testing 272
§ 23 Technical Literature. 275
§ 23.1 Generally 275
§ 23.2 Statutes and Regulations. 276
§ 23.3 Standards (Government, Industry, Foreign, In-House) 276
§ 23.4 Patents 277
§ 23.5 Authoritative Publications 278
§ 24 Contractual Provisions 278
§ 25 Environment of Use. 278
§ 26 Hazard Identification 279
§ 27 Design Objectives 279
§ 28 Specifications/Formulae/Ingredients 280
§ 29 Production Records. 281
§ 30 Quality Assurance Records 281
§ 31 Packaging 281
§ 32 Path of Distribution. 282
§ 33 Warnings and/or Instructions. 282
§ 34 Materials Produced in Other Cases 283
§ 35 Transcripts of Testimony in Other Cases 285
§ 36 Other Similar Incidents (Including Adverse Reaction Reports). 286
§ 37 Other Complaints and/or Lawsuits. 292
§ 38 Tests/Studies 295
§ 38.1 Generally 295
§ 38.2 Other Year or Model Types 297
§ 38.3 Alternative Designs 300
§ 38.4 Research and Development. 302

§ 39 Examinations and/or Testing (Including Destructive Testing) of Subject Product...304
§ 39.1 Generally...304
§ 39.2 Plaintiff's Right to Be Present at Test/Examination..................306
§ 40 Subsequent Remedial Measures in General............................307
§ 41 Post-Sale Notification, Warning, Recall and/or Modification..........308
§ 42 Warranties 309
§ 43 Advertising and Other Representations 309
§ 44 Marketing Information 310
§ 45 Discovery Misconduct 311
§ 46 Documents Reviewed by Deponent Before Testimony................311
§ 47 Deposition of CEO or Opposing Attorney 314
§ 48 Reports by Third Parties Including Government Agency 317
§ 48.1 Generally...317
§ 48.2 Nongovernmental Entities 318
§ 48.3 Governmental Entities 320
§ 49 Identification of Defendant's Own Documents 322
§ 50 Coordination of Defense 324

Appendix 2: Authorities Regarding the Benefit of Information Sharing 327
   A. Treatises 327
   B. Reported Cases..349
   C. Unreported Cases..372

Appendix 3: Summary of Authorities for Discovery Abuse Sanctions 383

Bibliography..387
   I. Discovery, General..387
     A. Treatises 387
     B. Law Review Articles..387
     C. Other Legal Periodicals 390
     D. Annotations...392
   II. Discovery Abuse 395
     A. Articles 395
     B. Annotations..402
   III. 1993 Amendments 402

    IV. Confidentiality Orders 404
        A. Anti-Secrecy Legislation and Court Rules........................ 404
            1. Legislation 404
            2. Court Rules.. 404
        B. Congressional Materials... 404
            1. Floor Statements 404
            2. Committee Hearing Statements 404
            3. Committee Prints.. 405
            4. Congressional Research Service 405
        C. Books.. 405
        D. Periodicals.. 406
        E. Looseleaf Services 415
        F. Annotations 416
        G. Newspapers 416
        H. ATLA Convention and Seminar Materials 422
        I. Miscellaneous Materials.. 423

Index by Jurisdiction.. 425
    Index to Chapters 425
    Index to Appendices 434

ABOUT THE AUTHORS

Francis H. ("Brother") Hare, Jr., is of counsel with the firm Hare, Wynn, Newton & Newell in Birmingham, Alabama, and also serves as chief legal officer of the Attorneys Information Exchange Group, Inc. He received his undergraduate degree from the University of Alabama and his J.D. from the University of Virginia. For the last 15 years, he has served as an adjunct professor at the Cumberland School of Law. Mr. Hare is a member of the International Academy of Trial Lawyers, the International Society of Barristers, the American Board of Trial Advocates, and the Inner Circle of Advocates, and he is a past president of the Alabama Trial Lawyers Association. He has written four books and more than 50 articles in legal publications. Mr. Hare is a frequent speaker at legal seminars.

James L. Gilbert heads the firm James L. Gilbert & Associates, P.C., in Arvada, Colorado, emphasizing products liability litigation dealing primarily with automotive products. He received his undergraduate degree from Colorado State University and his J.D. from New York University Law School. Mr. Gilbert is a frequent lecturer and has authored numerous articles as well as a book, *Confidentiality Orders*. He received the 1990 Citation of Excellence Award from the Association of Trial Lawyers of America and has chaired numerous ATLA committees, including the Discovery Abuse Committee and the Committee on the Courts, and served on the executive committee of the Litigation Group Leaders' Council. Mr. Gilbert is a fellow in the International Society of Barristers, is the national chairperson of the Attorneys Information Exchange Group, Inc., and has been a member of the Board of Directors of the Colorado Trial Lawyers Association since 1981.

Stuart A. Ollanik currently practices with James L. Gilbert & Associates, P.C., in Arvada, Colorado. After receiving his bachelor's degree from George Washington University and his J.D. from Georgetown University, Mr. Ollanik moved to Anchorage, where he clerked for the Alaska Court of Appeals and practiced with a litigation firm. He relocated to Colorado, and as an assistant attorney general, he represented Colorado in environmental litigation, including the state's natural resources damages action at the Rocky Mountain Arsenal. Mr. Ollanik has spoken at various seminars for the National College of Advocacy and the Attorneys Information Exchange Group, Inc., and he co-authored a chapter in the book *Excellence in Advocacy*.

ACKNOWLEDGMENTS

We offer our sincere thanks collectively to our many colleagues who, by keeping us informed of their battles with stonewalling manufacturers, have allowed us a wider perspective on the growing threat to the civil justice system described in this book.

Special thanks are due to Sharon Kiker, Tanya Neumeier, and Pat Austin, who typed the manuscript, and to Lou Leto of ATLA Press, who oversaw production of the book. The folks at ATLA Press, including our editors Cathy Kruvant, April Gustafson, and Laura Rucker, former editors Rich Page and Lisa Benshoff, and law clerk Kathleen Maguire, showed great patience in working with us—their consummate professional competence improved the final product immeasurably. This book would not and could not have been written without the invaluable assistance of Cathy Kruvant, who somehow maintained not only her sanity but a wonderful sense of humor despite the numerous and thorny "obstacles" placed in her path by the authors. Others at "team ATLA" have been an ongoing source of important information, including Sharon Goins of Membership, Lauren Larson and Dan Cohen of Public Affairs, Madelyn Appelbaum of Communications, and Ned Miltenberg and Jim Rooks of the Office of the General Counsel.

Our colleagues on the Committee on the Courts and former Discovery Abuse Committee, including Dianne Jay Weaver, Russ Smith, Leonard Schroeter, Mark Mandell, Jojene Mills, Paul Stritmatter, and many others, have provided both information and insight in committee gatherings and brainstorming sessions. Dianne Jay Weaver's foreword captures the spirit of the issues presented here perfectly. Richard Whitworth, Carrie Frank, Bruce McKee, Kit Belt, and Phil Jauregui contributed legal scholarship. Russ Langley and the staff and directors of the Attorneys Information Exchange Group were an invaluable source of information supporting this project.

Discovery abuse issues are most often handled by the trial court and frequently do not, for a number of reasons, become the subject of a reported decision. In our effort to verify the facts of individual instances of stonewalling, we directly contacted scores of plaintiffs' attorneys with requests for supporting information. Although we have almost certainly omitted the names of people who provided valuable assistance, the following is a list of lawyers who faithfully responded to our pleas for help:

Ted Allen; Tom Anderson; Scott Baldwin, Sr. and Scott Baldwin, Jr.; Danny Becnel; Randall Bono; David Boone; Turner and Margaret Branch; Frank Branson; Arthur Bryant; Jim Butler; John Cabaniss; Elizabeth Cabraser and Andy Lamis; Rex Carr; Bob Cheeley; Stanley Chesley and Dianna McBride; Larry Coben; Russ Cook; Phil Corboy; Lennie Decof; Foy Devine; Mike Eidson; Rich Ellis; Kendall and John Few; Joel Fogel; Roe Frazer; Mike Gallagher; Wendell Gauthier and Scott LaBarre; William Gaylord; Bob Gibbins; Vince Glorioso; Robert Gordon; Browne Greene; Steve Heninger; Ben Hogan; Mike Hugo; Mark Hutton; Tim Knight; Ralph Knowles and Leslie Bryan; Fred Levin; Arnold Levine; Jack Liber; Sal Liccardo; Sue Lister; Paul Luvera; Mick McBee; Joe McCray; Richard Miller; Bob Montgomery; John E. Morton; Ron Motley; Dianne Nast; Peter Chase Neumann; Murray Ogborn; John Overchuck; Jerry Palmer; Peter Perlman; David Perry; Darrel Peters; Vern Petri; Neal Pope, Tim Morrison and Bill Cornwell; Jim Pratt; Leonard Ring; Mark Robinson, Jr.; John Romano; Ed Rubinoff; Harold Sakayan; Nicole Shultheis; Don Slavik; Howard Specter; Barbara Stevens; Raymond Thomas; Gayle Troutwine and Mike Williams; Lanny Vines; Ted Warshafsky; Ralph Wegis; Marti Wivell; and John Younger.

Many of these lawyers not only furnished the limited information we specifically requested but took extra time to provide additional materials such as relevant motions, briefs, and the like. A special thanks to Kendall and John Few, who invariably made sacrificial efforts to respond to the authors' inquiries.

Brother Hare thanks his wife, Sue, for her loving support and encouragement.

Jim Gilbert thanks his wife, Mary Ann, and children, Micky and Kristine.

Stuart Ollanik thanks Wendy Block, Adam, and Tyler for their indulgence, support, and inspiration. He also thanks Jordan and Joan Ollanik for his law degree.

FOREWORD

I began practicing law in 1970 and almost immediately gravitated to products liability litigation. Since the first 10 years of my practice were confined to insurance defense work, I defended a large number of corporations in products liability litigation that addressed a wide variety of consumer goods.

The 1970s was the decade when consumers began to understand their rights and to seek redress when those rights were ignored by product manufacturers. As an insurance defense lawyer, I witnessed the responses of corporations to the claims of injured consumers.

I can tell you from firsthand experience that 15 to 20 years ago, corporations were, for the most part, responding honestly (though conservatively) to discovery requests. I can also tell you that the litigation greatly benefited not only individual plaintiffs but also the general public: Many manufacturers quickly addressed hazards associated with the use of their products.

The decade of greed, the 1980s, dramatically changed that type of response. Instead of properly responding to discovery requests and the need to correct product hazards, most corporations turned their energy and efforts to *stonewalling* discovery. The response to a consumer claim became standard: Make this litigation so difficult and so expensive that most plaintiffs' attorneys will be overwhelmed, abandon the claim, and never try this kind of litigation again; make the discovery process extremely time-consuming for the parties and the court; encourage the courts to deny discovery requests by suggesting that this will "move the case along," "avoid tiresome arguments between lawyers about interrogatories and requests for production," and "free up the court's time to handle more cases instead of spending so much time on discovery disputes"; and, of course, argue that products liability cases are "frivolous" suits that destroy the competitive spirit of "altruistic" corporate leaders.

The ingenuity of stonewallers in the 1990s is unparalleled and limited only by their economic resources. They justify protective orders by claiming that protective orders keep trade secrets from competitors, and that sharing of information among consumer attorneys increases litigation (if consumers find out about their rights they might enforce them). They use the misnomer "document retention programs" for what are actually document destruction programs, and keep records in such a manner that all discovery can be labeled burdensome. They even claim English language difficulties by pretending not to understand what their opponents are requesting.

The techniques and arrogance of the professional stonewallers are boundless. In a recent products case that my office prosecuted, we asked for the engineering drawings of certain component parts of the rifle. The response was a multipage affidavit from the defendant's "Consumer Relations Director" (also known as a corporate claims decliner) describing a complex set of mazes that constituted the manner in which the company stored its records. The affidavit asserted that producing these drawings would require several hundred hours and thousands and thousands of dollars. The task was alleged to be at worst "overwhelming"; at best, it was too burdensome to undertake.

We then requested production of the parts catalog provided to gun dealers. With that, we could request the engineering drawings by part number as listed in the catalog. This approach produced the drawings in less than ten minutes (we timed it), yet the court refused to impose sanctions.

Judicial hostility toward plaintiffs' discovery efforts in products liability cases is unfortunately more common than not. As attorneys for consumers, we cannot simply bemoan this situation among ourselves. We have an obligation to take affirmative steps to educate the court on the justness of our requests. We cannot hope to succeed at this task until we have educated ourselves thoroughly on the subject.

We must then educate the court as to the significant advantages the defense has over the plaintiff. For example, the defendant is able to provide the defense counsel with in-depth knowledge of each of the disciplines of technology involved in the case. In fact, many major manufacturers have resorted to retaining the services of one or two law firms so that teams from these firms can assist local counsel nationwide in providing an experienced, sophisticated defense. The defense counsel is given all of the relevant technological information and other internal documents reflecting the basis for corporate decisions concerning the design, development, manufacture, marketing, and distribution of the product. And, of course, the defense has far superior economic resources.

An understanding of the relevant technology is essential to bringing a defective products case; nevertheless, the plaintiff's counsel is often precluded from ever sharing information with other consumer attorneys prosecuting similar claims. The contents of the defendant's documents are relevant to every issue in any products liability case; without these documents, the plaintiff's attorney cannot adequately prepare the client's case.

The defendant knows that the likelihood of winning a trial is greatly increased if these documents and their contents are withheld from the jury's consideration. Additionally, without these documents on which the plaintiff's case hinges, the plaintiff may be forced to settle the claim for less than its fair value. These are powerful incentives motivating the defendant to resist or withhold disclosure of relevant information. Stonewalling discovery is often the final nail in the coffin of consumer rights: It destroys the ability of the victim to pursue legal remedies.

The plaintiff's counsel finally has a highly effective weapon to combat stonewalling—the most thorough, in-depth work that has ever been published on the subject. No attorney should undertake the prosecution of a products liability case without the help of this book. Even the most seasoned products liability attorney will find *Full Disclosure* to be an invaluable resource.

The authors of this book are not merely veterans in the field of products liability litigation, they are recognized nationwide as five-star generals in the war against corporate giants who profit by ignoring the safety and welfare of the consumer. In this book, the authors provide you with the insight, strategies, and ammunition you need to successfully overcome the many roadblocks that manufacturers will throw in front of you. Protecting the rights of the consumer truly is an ongoing war against powerful enemies who would destroy those rights. This book must be your arsenal.

Dianne Jay Weaver

INTRODUCTION

THE WHOLE TRUTH

A great deal of legal literature in recent years has been devoted to the topic of discovery abuse. The overwhelming majority of these articles focus on the misuse or overuse of discovery *requests* and ignore the flip side of the coin: "stonewalling" or responses that evade or suppress the disclosure of relevant information. This book addresses the latter type of abuse, particularly as it arises in complex tort cases such as products liability litigation.

Stonewalling is simply the failure or refusal to provide discoverable information properly requested by the opposing party. It occurs in many forms, ranging from groundless objections to the actual destruction of evidence. Unfortunately, this type of abuse has reached epidemic proportions in complex tort cases. Practitioners have observed this trend. It also is apparent from the marked increase in reported cases imposing sanctions for various forms of stonewalling.

We examine stonewalling by defendants in complex tort cases, focusing particularly on products liability litigation. As in many kinds of tort cases, products liability litigation presents a tremendous temptation to defendants to conceal information. The product manufacturer alone possesses evidence that can be used against it. In discovery, the manufacturer is asked to hand that evidence voluntarily to its litigation adversary. It is a lot to ask a corporate employee or counsel to turn over the "smoking gun" memo or the testing results proving that the defect was recognized before or during manufacture. Our justice system, of necessity, asks and demands no less.

Unfortunately for trial lawyers and their clients, in an alarming (if not surprising) number of instances, a manufacturer's defensive instinct prevails over its legal and ethical duties. While it would be unfair to assert that every manufacturer cheats in litigation, the list of discovery abusers includes leading manufacturers whose behavior by example shapes American corporate culture. Ford Motor Company,[1]

---

[1] *See* Rozier v. Ford Motor Co., 573 F.2d 1332 (5th Cir. 1978); Parrett v. Ford Motor Co., 52 F.R.D. 120 (W.D. Mo. 1969); Buehler v. Whalen, 374 N.E.2d 460 (Ill. 1978); Haumersen v. Ford Motor Co., 257 N.W.2d 7 (Iowa 1977); Rock Island Bank & Trust Co. v. Ford Motor Co., 220 N.W.2d 799 (Mich. Ct. App. 1974); Babb v. Ford Motor Co., 535 N.E.2d 676 (Ohio Ct. App. 1987).

General Motors,[2] International Harvester,[3] Honda Motor Company,[4] and other giants of commerce in the United States and abroad[5] have been taken to task by courts for stonewalling discovery.[6]

Similar problems afflict other kinds of litigation in which (1) injured individuals sue entities with greater information and resources, (2) liability is based on technical subject matter, and (3) the defendant initially possesses the bulk of the relevant infor-

---

[2] Sellon v. Smith, 112 F.R.D. 9 (D. Del. 1986); Sellers v. General Motors Corp., 40 Fed. R. Serv. 2d (Callaghan) 590 (E.D. Pa. 1984); Carlson v. General Motors Corp., 289 N.E.2d 439 (Ill. App. Ct. 1972); *see also* Noone v. Oldsmobile Div. of Gen. Motors Corp., No. 85-68704 (Harris County, Tex. Dist. Ct. Nov. 21, 1988).

[3] Ostendorf v. International Harvester Co., 433 N.E.2d 253 (Ill. 1982); Maietta v. International Harvester Co., 496 A.2d 286 (Me. 1985).

[4] Fjelstad v. American Honda Motor Co., 762 F.2d 1334 (9th Cir. 1985), *order on remand*, No. CV81-227-BLG-JFB (D. Mont. May 23, 1986); Honda Motor Co. v. Salzman, 751 P.2d 489 (Alaska), *cert. dismissed*, 487 U.S. 1260 (1988); American Honda Motor Co. v. Votour, 435 So. 2d 368 (Fla. Dist. Ct. App. 1983), *order on remand*, No. 794686CA (l) 01 B (Palm Beach County, Fla. Cir. Ct. Sept. 7, 1983); *see also* Weathers v. Honda Motor Co., Nos. 8:89-1371-17 and Hammond v. Honda Motor Co., 8:88-3435-17 (D.S.C. Feb. 14, 1990); Perez v. American Honda Motor Co., No. 87-1969-CIV (S.D. Fla. Aug. 17, 1988); Menlo v. American Honda Motor Co., No. 87-2102 (E.D. Pa. Mar. 30, 1988); Braun v. American Honda Motor Co., No. CV 86-337-BLG-JFB (D. Mont. Sept. 4, 1987); Brandt v. R.L. Atwood, Inc., No. 85-6366-H (Nueces County, Tex. Dist. Ct. Mar. 30, 1987); Samples v. R.L. Atwood, Inc., No. 84-6496-H (Nueces County, Tex. Dist. Ct. Feb. 5, 1987).

[5] *See, e.g.*, Craig v. A.H. Robins Co., 790 F.2d 1 (1st Cir. 1986); Weiss v. Chrysler Motors Corp., 515 F.2d 449 (2d Cir. 1975); Thomas v. Hoffman-LaRoche, Inc., 126 F.R.D. 522 (N.D. Miss. 1989); Stengel v. Kawasaki Heavy Indus., 116 F.R.D. 263 (N.D. Tex. 1987); Altschuler v. Samsonite Corp., 109 F.R.D. 353 (E.D.N.Y. 1986); Carlucci v. Piper Aircraft Corp., 102 F.R.D. 472 (S.D. Fla. 1984), *aff'd in part, rev'd in part*, 775 F.2d 1440 (11th Cir. 1985); In re "Agent Orange" Prod. Liab. Litig. (Diamond Shamrock Corp.), 98 F.R.D. 558 (E.D.N.Y. 1983); In re Air Crash Disaster Near Chicago, Ill. (Am. Airlines, Inc.), 90 F.R.D. 613 (N.D. Ill. 1981); Kozlowski v. Sears, Roebuck & Co., 73 F.R.D. 73 (D. Mass. 1976); Bollard v. Volkswagen of Am., Inc., 56 F.R.D. 569 (W.D. Mo. 1971); West v. Johnson & Johnson Prods., Inc., 220 Cal. Rptr. 437 (Ct. App. 1985), *cert. denied*, 479 U.S. 824 (1986); Rockwell Int'l. Corp. v. Menzies, 561 So. 2d 677 (Fla. Dist. Ct. App. 1990); Hense v. G.D. Searle & Co., 452 N.W.2d 440 (Iowa 1990) (en banc); McInnes v. Yamaha Motor Corp., U.S., 659 S.W.2d 704 (Tex. Ct. App. 1983), *aff'd*, 673 S.W.2d 185 (Tex. 1984), *cert. denied*, 469 U.S. 1107 (1985); Taylor v. Cessna Aircraft Co., 696 P.2d 28 (Wash. Ct. App. 1985); Gammon v. Clark Equip. Co., 686 P.2d 1102 (Wash. Ct. App. 1984), *aff'd en banc*, 707 P.2d 685 (Wash. 1985).

[6] Our practice experience is consistent with that of one federal judge who observed that "for some reason . . . defendants in motor vehicle products liability cases based upon defects in design and workmanship have been unusually evasive and loathe to make discovery." Bollard v. Volkswagen of Am., Inc., 56 F.R.D. 569, 583 n.4 (W.D. Mo. 1971) (W. Becker, C.J.) (citing Parrett v. Ford Motor Co., 52 F.R.D. 120 (W.D. Mo. 1969)).

mation regarding liability. These circumstances are presented in a broad range of cases as disparate as toxic torts, employment discrimination, medical negligence, securities fraud, and premises liability actions. While we frequently use products liability actions as examples and speak in terms of defective products and manufacturers, the points made have a much broader applicability. Cases cited come from all sorts of litigation.

Stonewalling affects not only individual litigants, but the consuming public at large as well. In an opinion ordering disclosure of cigarette manufacturing industry documents, Judge H. Lee Sarokin decried the practice of protecting profits by hiding product dangers. While Judge Sarokin was ultimately removed from the case because of his frank words, and his order reversed, his sentiments remain valid:

> In light of the current controversy surrounding breast implants, one wonders when all industries will recognize their obligation to voluntarily disclose risks from the use of their products. All too often in the choice between the physical health of consumers and the financial well-being of business concealment is chosen over disclosure, sales over safety, and money over morality. Who are these persons who knowingly and secretly decide to put the buying public at risk solely for the purpose of making profits and who believe that illness and death of consumers is an appropriate cost of their own prosperity.[7]

We hope this book will serve two purposes. First, we aim to assist the bench and bar, as well as academia, in understanding the nature, pervasiveness, and means of remedying this type of discovery abuse, which has received disproportionately little attention. Practitioners and the judiciary must recognize stonewalling and be aware of the substantial body of case support for thwarting it if this pernicious form of litigation abuse is to be curtailed. Second, we hope this book will help readers quickly identify authorities that are useful in countering discovery abuse by manufacturers in products liability and other complex tort cases.

This book is organized in two parts. Part one, including the first three chapters of the book, addresses discovery obligations. It sets out the requirements against which the discovery misconduct described in part two can be measured.

Chapters 1 and 2 address general principles governing the right of access to relevant information through the discovery process, including rules governing discovery requests and responses. Chapter 3 examines policy choices affecting discovery abuse made by the Federal Rules of Civil Procedure. We look at policy choices represented by the initial adoption of the Federal Rules of Civil Procedure, and policy shifts reflected in rule reform efforts over the years. This chapter includes an analysis of the 1993 rule amendments and their likely impact on stonewalling.

Part two includes the remainder of the book. It examines stonewalling in its many forms and discusses causes, effects, and cures. Chapter 4 focuses specifically on

---

[7] Haines v. Liggett Group, Inc., 140 F.R.D. 681, 683 (D.N.J. 1992), *rev'd* 975 F.2d 81 (3d Cir. 1992), *later proceedings* 814 F. Supp. 414 (D.N.J. 1993).

the impact of stonewalling on products liability and other complex tort litigation. The causes, means of detection and prevention, and effects of stonewalling on products cases are examined.

Chapters 5 through 8 examine in detail the most common stonewalling tactics and how to counter them. Chapter 5 identifies many evasion maneuvers and analyzes the case law rejecting these tactics. Chapter 6 examines the "dump truck" discovery strategies designed to bury the litigation opponent in irrelevant information and thus make important documents difficult to identify. Chapter 7 looks at issues surrounding document destruction and alteration, including the emerging use of tort and contract actions for spoliation of evidence. Chapter 8 is devoted to confidentiality orders and their misuse by manufacturers to prevent plaintiffs from uncovering discovery evasion. Also discussed in chapter 8 are legal arguments plaintiffs' attorneys can use to overcome successfully a defendant's motion for a restrictive confidentiality order that would prevent plaintiffs in similar cases from sharing information.

Chapters 9 and 10 focus on how to combat stonewalling tactics. Chapter 9 reveals ways plaintiffs can use discovery to detect and prove stonewalling, and then how to "turn the tables" on the discovery abuser by making the stonewaller bear the consequences of its improper conduct. Chapter 10 addresses the law of sanctions—available under the rules, by statute, or pursuant to the inherent power of the court—that may be brought to bear to redress stonewalling. Finally, three appendices contain reference materials that should be useful to plaintiffs' attorneys facing stonewalling defendants.

This book focuses principally on discovery conducted under the Federal Rules of Civil Procedure. The authorities that construe these rules will be persuasive if not controlling in most state court jurisdictions.[8] Indeed, most states have adopted rules of discovery similar to the federal rules.[9]

As this book goes to press, major amendments to the federal rules governing discovery have just gone into effect. The amendments require the disclosure of specified basic information by each party without the need for discovery requests. Further discovery by interrogatory or deposition is limited. These amendments faced stiff political opposition. Though they were not killed or changed by Congress prior to their December 1, 1993, effective date, there has been talk of Congress modifying or suspending the new provisions by legislative action in 1994. As of December 16, 1993, 38 of the 94 district courts in the federal system had expressed an intention to opt out of revised rule 26(a)(1).

We discuss the new rules and their effect on the phenomenon of stonewalling in detail. However, practice under the prior rules is also discussed, for several reasons.

---

[8] *See, e.g.,* AMERICAN LAW OF PRODUCTS LIABILITY 3D § 53.1 n.12 (1987 & Supp. 1992).

[9] *See* MARK A. DOMBROFF, DISCOVERY app. I (1986); JACK H. FRIEDENTHAL ET AL., CIVIL PROCEDURE § 7.1, at 379 n.8 (2d ed. 1993); FLEMING JAMES, JR. & GEOFFREY C. HAZARD, JR., CIVIL PROCEDURE § 5.2, at 230 (3d ed. 1985); Note, *Discovery Abuse Under the Federal Rules: Causes and Cures*, 92 YALE L.J. 352, 354 n.11 (1982).

First, most discovery principles remain unchanged. The amendments neither altered the broad scope of discovery nor eliminated procedural means to obtain discovery. Second, it is unclear how the new amendments will be amended in the near future. Third, most state rules are more similar to the former federal rules than they are to the amended rules. This may change if the federal amendments remain in effect, as states move to conform their discovery procedures to federal practice.

While this book relies principally on published opinions for support, the reader should be aware that only a small percentage of the cases in which discovery abuse occurs result in published opinions. The vast majority of stonewalling conduct probably goes undetected; even where detected, most abuses are handled without a published order, especially in the state court systems, and most do not surface on appeal. Therefore, unreported cases are occasionally cited or discussed in this book. While some jurisdictions restrict the precedential value of unpublished opinions, they are of value here for illustrative purposes or as documentation of stonewalling conduct. Unreported cases can also be used as evidence of the willingness of a particular defendant to engage in stonewalling.[10]

Although this book is written from the perspective of the plaintiff's lawyer, it is intended to appeal to a higher objective than gaining tactical advantage. The parties on both sides of the "v."—and society as a whole—have an important stake in the success of the discovery process: If discovery does not serve to bring forth the truth, the whole truth, and nothing but the truth, our system of civil justice cannot function.

---

[10] We have attempted to verify that unpublished opinions referenced here have not been reversed or withdrawn, by writing to attorneys familiar with the cases. Not all inquiries have been answered. Because there is no national system for checking the subsequent history of unreported cases, and because it would be impractical to check the case files of each unreported opinion cited here, the authors cannot guarantee the continued viability of any unpublished opinions.

PART ONE:

DISCOVERY OBLIGATIONS

CHAPTER ONE

RIGHT OF ACCESS TO RELEVANT INFORMATION

I. PURPOSES OF DISCOVERY

To understand the purposes of modern discovery, we must consider the problems discovery rules were intended to remedy.[1]

> Under the prior federal practice, the pre-trial functions of notice-giving, issue-formulation and fact-revelation were performed primarily and inadequately by the pleadings. Inquiry into the issues and the facts before trial was narrowly confined and was often cumbersome in method.[2]

This practice gave rise to what became popularly known and criticized as the "sporting theory of justice," where the outcome of a case depended "on the fortuitous availability of evidence or the skill and strategy of counsel."[3] The result of such limited discovery was that judicial proceedings became "a battle of wits rather than a search for the truth."[4]

The shift in the federal rules to a notice-giving function for pleadings had the effect of investing the discovery process with the vital role of providing the parties with the information necessary to prepare for trial.[5] As the United States Supreme Court observed in *Hickman v. Taylor*, almost ten years after adoption of the discovery rules, "[m]utual knowledge of all the relevant facts gathered by both parties is essen-

---

[1] A select bibliography of scholarly materials dealing with discovery generally appears in the Bibliography to this book.

[2] Hickman v. Taylor, 329 U.S. 495, 500–01 (1947).

[3] 8 CHARLES ALAN WRIGHT & ARTHUR R. MILLER, FEDERAL PRACTICE AND PROCEDURE § 2001, at 18–19 (1970 & Supp. 1992). For discussion of the origins of discovery under the federal rules, see chapter 3.

[4] 8 WRIGHT & MILLER, *supra* note 3, at 14.

[5] Hickman v. Taylor, 329 U.S. 495, 501 (1947).

tial to proper litigation."[6] The modern discovery rules adopted the basic philosophy that "prior to trial every party to a civil action is entitled to the disclosure of all relevant information in the possession of any party, unless the information is privileged."[7] As noted in *Hickman v. Taylor*, this approach was adopted precisely for the purpose of eliminating the inadequacies of the former system:

> The various instruments of discovery now serve (1) as a device, along with the pretrial hearing under Rule 16, to narrow and clarify the basic issues between the parties, and (2) as a device for ascertaining the facts, or information as to the existence or whereabouts of facts, relative to those issues. Thus civil trials in the federal courts no longer need be carried on in the dark. The way is now clear, consistent with recognized privileges, for the parties to obtain the fullest possible knowledge of the issues and facts before the trial.[8]

On the twentieth birthday of the federal rules, the Court again recognized the contribution of the discovery provisions to truth-based judicial decision making.

> Modern instruments of discovery serve a useful purpose, as we noted in *Hickman v. Taylor*. . . . They together with pretrial procedures make a trial less a game of blind man's buff and more a fair contest with the basic issues of facts disclosed to the fullest possible extent.[9]

The discovery procedures established by rules 26 through 37 may be the most important provisions of the Federal Rules of Civil Procedure. Embodied in these rules are philosophical implications essential to the broad objective of the American civil justice system: to provide for the meaningful expression of a citizen's right to redress for wrongs done to person or property. These rules were founded on the premise that access to knowledge is necessary to ascertain the truth.[10] The outcome of a dispute cannot be based on the truth unless all relevant facts are available to both parties.

---

[6] *Id.* at 507.

[7] 8 WRIGHT & MILLER, *supra* note 3, at 15.

[8] Hickman v. Taylor, 329 U.S. at 501.

[9] United States v. Procter & Gamble Co., 356 U.S. 677, 682 (1958).

[10] *See, e.g.*, Tiedman v. American Pigment Corp., 253 F.2d 803, 808 (4th Cir. 1958) ("discovery is founded upon the policy that the search for truth should be aided"); Cox v. E.I. DuPont de Nemours & Co., 38 F.R.D. 396, 398 (D.S.C. 1965) ("in search for the ultimate, TRUTH, the Federal Courts [are] blessed with the rules of discovery"); De Seversky v. Republic Aviation Corp., 2 F.R.D. 113, 114 (E.D.N.Y. 1941) (purpose of discovery is "to get the truth" for trial preparation and trial); Martinez v. Pfizer Lab. Div., 576 N.E.2d 311, 315 (Ill. App. Ct. 1991) ("[t]he objectives of pretrial discovery are: (1) the enhancement of the truth-seeking process; (2) the improvement in preparation by attorneys for trial; (3) the elimination of unfair surprise; and (4) the expeditious and final determination of controversies in accordance with the substantive rights of the parties"); State v. Lowry, 802 S.W.2d 669, 671 (Tex. 1991) ("[d]iscovery is . . . the linchpin of the search for truth"); Jampole v. Touchy, 673 S.W.2d 569, 573 (Tex. 1984) ("the ultimate purpose of discovery is to seek the truth, so that disputes may

Discovery under the federal rules has four distinct but interrelated purposes, as follows:[11]

- to narrow and clarify the issues;
- to identify potentially relevant information and the persons who might possess such information, and to ascertain how and from whom it may be procured in order to assist the parties in preparing for trial;
- to eliminate unfair surprise; and
- to promote the expeditious, just, and final resolution of disputes in accordance with the substantive rights of the parties.

Although the 1993 amendments to the discovery rules[12] alter the form and method of conducting discovery, the amended rules preserve these traditional discovery objectives.

The procedures set out in rules 26 through 37 are intended to function as an integrated mechanism to enable a party to prepare its case for trial in a manner that advances the overriding purpose of the federal rules as a whole: to "promote the just, speedy, and inexpensive determination of the action."[13]

II. SCOPE OF DISCOVERY

A. Broad, Liberal Construction of the Rules

The express language of the rules clearly establishes a strong policy favoring full disclosure. Rule 26(b)(1), which defines the scope of discovery, provides the following:

> *In general.* Parties may obtain discovery regarding any matter, not privileged, which is relevant to the subject matter involved in the pending action, whether it relates to the claim or defense of the party seeking discovery or to the claim or defense of any party. . . . It is not ground for objection that the information sought will be inadmissible at the trial if the information sought

---

be decided by what the facts reveal, not by what facts are concealed"), *overruled in part on other grounds*, Walker v. Packer, 827 S.W.2d 833, 842 (Tex. 1992); *see also* John J. Kennelly, *Discovery as to Products, Premises, Documents and Persons—Part I*, 20 TRIAL LAW. GUIDE 152, 152–53 (1976) (quoting Underwood, J., Ill. Sup. Ct.).

[11] For authorities supporting the stated purposes, see DISCOVERY PROCEEDINGS IN FEDERAL COURT §§ 1.1, 6.1, 9.2 (Shepard's eds., 2d ed. 1991 & Supp. 1992); MARK A. DOMBROFF, DISCOVERY §§ 1.01–1.08 (1986 & Supp. 1990); ROGER S. HAYDOCK & DAVID F. HERR, DISCOVERY PRACTICE § 1.1 (2d ed. 1988 & Supp. 1992); TERRENCE F. KIELY, PREPARING PRODUCTS LIABILITY CASES § 5.1 (1986 & Supp. 1989); 4 JAMES W. MOORE ET AL., MOORE'S FEDERAL PRACTICE ¶ 26.02 (2d ed. 1991 & Supp. 1992); JAMES L. UNDERWOOD, A GUIDE TO FEDERAL DISCOVERY RULES § 1.01 (2d ed. 1985); 8 WRIGHT & MILLER, *supra* note 3, §§ 2001, 2101, 2162, 2201, 2252.

[12] The recently adopted amendments to the discovery rules are discussed in chapter 3, section III.

[13] 8 WRIGHT & MILLER, *supra* note 3, at 17.

appears to be reasonably calculated to lead to the discovery of admissible evidence.

The rules governing production requests, interrogatories, and requests for admissions specifically refer to and incorporate the scope of discovery set forth in rule 26(b)(1).[14]

If the discovery rules are to accomplish their intended purpose, the courts must give them a liberal construction.[15] Courts have uniformly held that the scope of discovery contemplated by the rules should be broadly and liberally construed to achieve full disclosure of all potentially relevant information.[16] As the Supreme Court stated in *Hickman v. Taylor*,

> We agree, of course, that the deposition-discovery rules are to be accorded a broad and liberal treatment. No longer can the time-honored cry of "fishing expedition" serve to preclude a party from inquiring into the facts underlying his opponent's case.... To that end, either party may compel the other to disgorge whatever facts he has in his possession.[17]

Under this policy, the party who opposes discovery carries a "heavy burden" of showing why discovery should be disallowed.[18] As noted in regard to the objectives of discovery, the 1993 amendments do not alter the rule of construction that courts should accord discovery requests.

B. Discovery Relevance

The scope of discovery contemplated by the rules revolves around the meaning of "relevance" as that term is used in rule 26(b)(1). As with the scope of discovery in general, the courts have held that the meaning of relevance for discovery purposes

---

[14] FED. R. CIV. P. 33(c) (interrogatories); Fed. R. Civ. P. 34(a) (requests for production); FED. R. CIV. P. 36(a) (requests for admission).

[15] United States v. McWhirter, 376 F.2d 102, 106 (5th Cir. 1967); United States v. AT&T Co., 461 F. Supp. 1314, 1341 (D.D.C. 1978); United States v. National Steel Corp., 26 F.R.D. 599, 600 (S.D. Tex. 1960); *see also* Ex parte Dorsey Trailers, 397 So. 2d 98, 103 (Ala. 1981); Cornet Stores v. Superior Court, 492 P.2d 1191, 1193 (Ariz. 1972). *See generally* DISCOVERY PROCEEDINGS IN FEDERAL COURT, *supra* note 11, §§ 1.3, 6.2, 7.2, 9.1, 14.1–14.78; 8 WRIGHT & MILLER, *supra* note 3, at 17, § 2007, at 37 n.94, § 2008, at 45 n.21.

[16] *See* numerous cases cited in the following treatises. AMERICAN LAW OF PRODUCTS LIABILITY 3d § 53:5, at 14 (1987 & Supp. 1992); DISCOVERY PROCEEDINGS IN FEDERAL COURT, *supra* note 11, §§ 1.3, 6.2, 7.2, 9.1, 14.1–14.7; DOMBROFF, *supra* note 11, § 1.09; 10 FEDERAL PROCEDURE, LAW. ED., DISCOVERY AND DEPOSITIONS § 26.2 (1988 & Supp. 1992); HAYDOCK & HERR, *supra* note 11, § 1.4; KIELY, *supra* note 11, § 5.2, at 142–44, § 7.3, at 202, app. at Supp. 99; 4 MOORE ET AL., *supra* note 11, ¶¶ 26.55–26.56; 8 WRIGHT & MILLER, *supra* note 3, § 2001, at 17 n.15, § 2007, at 37 n.94, § 2008, at 45–46 n.21, §§2165–2167, 2206, 2254–2256.

[17] 329 U.S. 495, 507 (1947).

[18] *See* Blankenship v. Hearst Corp., 519 F.2d 418, 429 (9th Cir. 1975). This burden is discussed in chapter 2, section IV.

should be broadly construed.[19] As one court ordering discovery noted, "[f]ortunately, in the search for the ultimate, TRUTH, the Federal Courts, blessed with the rules of discovery, are not shackled with strict interpretations of relevancy."[20] Two phrases in the rule provide the criteria for establishing the scope of this term: (1) "relevant to the subject matter involved in the pending action, whether . . . claim or defense" and (2) "the information sought appears reasonably calculated to lead to the discovery of admissible evidence."

1. Subject Matter of Any Claim or Defense

By linking relevance to the "subject matter" of the case rather than to the issues presented by the pleadings, the drafters of the rule created a much broader ambit for the discovery process.[21] As one treatise explains, "The term subject matter relates to any matter in a case; it does not limit itself to the merits of a case nor does it distinguish between substantive concerns and procedural matters."[22] Shortly after adoption of the federal rules, a federal district court clarified how this formulation furthers the purposes of discovery.

> To limit an examination to matters relevant to only the precise issues presented by the pleadings, would not only be contrary to the express purposes of rule 26 . . . but also might result in a complete failure to afford plaintiff an adequate opportunity to obtain information that would be useful at the trial.[23]

Significantly, the rule specifically provides that the relevant subject matter includes not only the claim involved but also the defenses,[24] which may in some cases be more important than the subject matter of the claim. In ruling on a relevance or a "burdensome" objection by a defendant, it is entirely appropriate for the court to consider whether the plaintiff's discovery request seeks information about facts that have been alleged as a defense.

Because one of the purposes of discovery is to clarify the issues, limiting the scope of discovery to the subject matter of the issues presented in the original plead-

---

[19] *See generally* DISCOVERY PROCEEDINGS IN FEDERAL COURT, *supra* note 11, § 14.4; HAYDOCK & HERR, *supra* note 11, § 1.48; 4 MOORE ET AL., *supra* note 11, ¶ 26.56; 8 WRIGHT & MILLER, *supra* note 3, § 2008.

[20] Cox v. E.I. DuPont de Nemours & Co., 38 F.R.D. 396, 398 (D.S.C. 1965).

[21] *See* Duplan Corp. v. Deering Milliken, Inc., 397 F. Supp. 1146, 1187 (D.S.C. 1974); United States v. IBM Corp., 66 F.R.D. 180, 182 (S.D.N.Y. 1974); La Chemise Lacoste v. Alligator Co., 60 F.R.D. 164, 170–71 (D. Del. 1973); Triangle Mfg. v. Paramount Bag Mfg., 35 F.R.D. 540, 542 (E.D.N.Y. 1964).

[22] HAYDOCK & HERR, *supra* note 11, § 1.4, at 16; *see also* 4 MOORE ET AL., *supra* note 11, ¶ 26.56[1], at 26–101.

[23] Stevenson v. Melady, 1 F.R.D. 329, 330 (S.D.N.Y. 1940) (citations omitted).

[24] FED. R. CIV. P. 26(b)(1).

ings has been criticized as counterproductive.[25] The statement of specific claims and issues may, however, broaden the scope of discovery in some instances.[26]

Discovery in complex cases often discloses to the plaintiff new issues and facts that may or may not relate directly to the underlying merits of the case. This result is, of course, a perfectly appropriate function of the discovery process.[27] "Indeed," notes one treatise, "one of the benefits resulting from a broad scope of discovery is this opportunity to explore, discover, and establish new information which supports another theory or which bolsters a previously unsupported allegation."[28] The courts have often noted that discovery should be permitted as to matters that are or "may become" relevant to the subject matter in dispute.[29] Justice Powell, speaking for a unanimous Supreme Court, observed

> The key phrase in this definition—"relevant to the subject matter involved in the pending action"—has been construed broadly to encompass any matter that bears on, or that reasonably could lead to other matter that could bear on, any issue that is or *may be* in the case. Consistently with the notice-pleading system established by the Rules, discovery is not limited to issues raised by the pleadings, for discovery itself is designed to help define and clarify the issues. Nor is discovery limited to the merits of a case, for a variety of fact-oriented issues *may arise during litigation* that are not related to the merits.[30]

---

[25] *See* 8 WRIGHT & MILLER, *supra* note 3, § 2008, at 41–42.

[26] For example, the financial status of the defendant may not be discoverable in the absence of a specific claim for punitive damages. *See, e.g.*, Moran v. International Playtex, Inc., 480 N.Y.S.2d 6 (App. Div. 1984). *See generally* AMERICAN LAW OF PRODUCTS LIABILITY 3D, *supra* note 16; HAYDOCK & HERR, *supra* note 11, § 1.4, at 20–21; D.E. Evins, Annotation, *Pretrial Discovery of Defendant's Financial Worth on Issue of Damages*, 27 A.L.R. 3D 1375 (1969 & Supp. 1992). It should be noted that under the 1993 amendments to rule 26, automatic disclosures are required of information regarding disputed facts alleged "with particularity" in the pleadings. *See* FED. R. CIV. P. 26(a)(1)(A) and (B), Amendments to the Federal Rules of Civil Procedure and Forms, approved by the United States Supreme Court (Apr. 22, 1993), *reprinted in* 146 F.R.D. 401 (1994) [hereinafter 1993 Amendments].

[27] *See, e.g.*, Oppenheimer Fund, Inc. v. Sanders, 437 U.S. 340, 351 (1978); Patterson Oil Terminals, Inc. v. Charles Kurz & Co., 7 F.R.D. 250, 251 (E.D. Pa. 1945); HAYDOCK & HERR, *supra* note 11, § 1.4, at 20; 8 WRIGHT & MILLER, *supra* note 3, § 2001, at 17–18, § 2008, at 41 n.10 & 43 n.13.

[28] HAYDOCK & HERR, *supra* note 11, § 1.4, at 22.

[29] Oppenheimer Fund, Inc. v. Sanders, 437 U.S. 340, 351 (1978); Wauchop v. Domino's Pizza, Inc., 138 F.R.D. 539, 544 (N.D. Ind. 1991); United Nuclear Corp. v. General Atomic Co., 629 P.2d 231, 250 (N.M. 1980), *cert. denied*, 457 U.S. 901, *reh'g denied*, 452 U.S. 932 (1981). *See generally* DISCOVERY PROCEEDINGS IN FEDERAL COURT, *supra* note 11, § 14.4, at 221; 8 WRIGHT & MILLER, *supra* note 3, § 2008, at 41–45.

[30] Oppenheimer Fund, Inc. v. Sanders, 437 U.S. 340, 351 (1978) (citations omitted; emphasis added); *see also* Avianca, Inc. v. Corriea, 705 F. Supp. 666, 676 (D.D.C. 1989).

Thus, discovery may properly be used to uncover "potential" issues, to "ferret out . . . possible claims or defenses,"[31] and to support a claim that is being challenged by the defendant as insufficient.[32]

The breadth of discovery relevance is reflected by courts ruling that discovery should be permitted as to matters that "'might conceivably have a bearing' on the subject matter"[33] and holding "that a request for discovery should be considered relevant if there is any possibility that the information sought may be relevant to the subject matter of the action."[34]

The issue of relevance to the subject matter in a products liability case typically revolves around the defect alleged to have caused the plaintiff's injury. Many cases have noted that, for discovery purposes, the court should not adopt a legal standard of relevance that is more restrictive than the standard ordinarily applied by technical experts in the field.[35]

For instance, in *Fireman's Fund Insurance Co. v. ECM Motor Co.*,[36] the plaintiff's subrogee alleged that a fire had been caused by a 24-volt surveillance camera motor.

---

[31] HAYDOCK & HERR, *supra* note 11, § 1.4, at 19.

[32] *See* 8 WRIGHT & MILLER, *supra* note 3, § 2008, at 44.

[33] United Nuclear Corp. v. General Atomic Co., 629 P.2d 231, 250 (N.M. 1980), *cert. denied*, 451 U.S. 901, *reh'g denied*, 452 U.S. 932 (1981).

[34] 8 WRIGHT & MILLER, *supra* note 3, § 2008, at 47 n.23; *see* Wauchop v. Domino's Pizza, Inc., 138 F.R.D. 539, 544 (N.D. Ind. 1991); Snowden v. Connaught Lab., Inc., 137 F.R.D. 336, 341 (D. Kan.), *aff'd*, 136 F.R.D. 694 (D. Kan. 1991); HAYDOCK & HERR, *supra* note 11, § 1.4, at 17 n.9. *See generally* DISCOVERY PROCEEDINGS IN FEDERAL COURT, *supra* note 11, § 14.4, at 220–21.

[35] *See, e.g.*, Lohr v. Stanley-Bostitch, Inc., 135 F.R.D. 162 (W.D. Mich. 1991) (permitting discovery regarding other types of tools that discharge projectiles using "contact trip method"); Hess v. Pittsburgh Steel Foundry & Mach. Co., 49 F.R.D. 271, 272–73 (W.D. Pa. 1970) (in determining relevance judge should view matter from perspective of what specialists trained in the field would consider to be relevant); Hindelang v. R.D. Werner Co., 469 N.W.2d 2 (Mich. Ct. App. 1991) (permitting discovery regarding other ladders with similar foot design); Valet v. American Motors, Inc., 481 N.Y.S.2d 364 (App. Div. 1984) (plaintiff alleging instability of Jeep CJ-7 vehicle could discover accident information about CJ-5 model, which was "sufficiently similar in regard to center of gravity and track width"); Johantgen v. Hobart Mfg. Co., 407 N.Y.S.2d 355 (App. Div. 1978) (permitting discovery regarding other products utilizing identical allegedly defective component); *cf.* Jackson v. Firestone Tire & Rubber Co., 788 F.2d 1070 (5th Cir. 1986) (evidence regarding other multipiece truck wheel rims admissible); Trevizo v. Astec Indus., 751 P.2d 980 (Ariz. Ct. App. 1987) (evidence regarding other instances of polyurethane expanding when heated admissible); Gowler v. Ferrell-Ross Co., 563 N.E.2d 773 (Ill. App. Ct. 1990) (evidence of accidents due to unprotected nip point at other cracking mills admissible), *appeal dismissed per curiam*, 571 N.E.2d 148 (Ill. 1991). *See generally* AMERICAN LAW OF PRODUCTS LIABILITY 3D, *supra* note 16, §§ 53:41–53:43; HAYDOCK & HERR, *supra* note 11, § 1.4, at 19–22; KIELY, *supra* note 11, §§ 5.2–5.7, 7.3. See additional authorities cited in appendix 1, §§ 36–38.

[36] 132 F.R.D. 39 (W.D. Pa. 1990).

The court permitted discovery of information regarding a 120-volt motor also manufactured by the defendant, since it "may lead to admissible evidence concerning defects in the design of the motors, or dangerous characteristics associated with the impedance protection."[37] In support, the court noted,

> In *Bowman v. General Motors Corp.*, 64 F.R.D. 62 (E.D. Pa. 1974), the court permitted discovery of subsequent models of the same automobile in litigation. In response to GM's contention that the fuel tank assembly of the later models was substantially different from that of the subject model, the court noted that "identity is a function not only of component parts, but also of engineering principles." The court refused to adhere to a narrow construction of the notions of similarity and identity, for to do so would have foreclosed meaningful discovery.[38]

The court in *Fine v. Facet Aerospace Products Co.*,[39] made the same point:

> In product liability actions it is frequently difficult to judge which of a manufacturer's products are sufficiently similar to the alleged defective product to be subject to discovery. Generally, different models of a product will be relevant if they share with the accident-causing model those characteristics pertinent to the legal issues raised in the litigation.[40]

2. Reasonably Calculated to Lead to Admissible Evidence

Admissibility at trial under the rules of evidence is not the test for the discoverability of information under the Federal Rules of Civil Procedure.[41]

> Whether . . . information is found to be admissible at trial has little bearing on the issue of discoverability. Rule 26(b) makes a clear distinction between information that is relevant to the subject matter for pretrial discovery and the ultimate admissibility of that information at trial. Admissibility at trial is not the yardstick of permissible discovery.[42]

The test for relevance in the context of discovery is considerably less stringent than the relevancy requirements that govern admissibility of evidence at trial.[43] Dis-

---

[37] *Id.* at 41.

[38] *Id.*

[39] 133 F.R.D. 439 (S.D.N.Y. 1990).

[40] *Id.* at 441. The court in Baine v. General Motors Corp., 141 F.R.D. 328, 330 (M.D. Ala. 1991) followed a similar analysis. *See also* General Motors Corp. v. Lawrence, 651 S.W.2d 732 (Tex. 1983).

[41] FED. R. CIV. P. 26(b) 1946 advisory committee's note; *see also* DISCOVERY PROCEEDINGS IN FEDERAL COURT, *supra* note 11, §§ 14.5–14.6; HAYDOCK & HERR, *supra* note 11, § 1.4, at 17; 8 WRIGHT & MILLER, *supra* note 3, § 2008, at 47–51.

[42] Chubb Integrated Sys. v. National Bank, 103 F.R.D. 52, 59 (D.D.C. 1984) (citation omitted).

[43] Liew v. Breen, 640 F.2d 1046, 1049 (9th Cir. 1981); Snowden v. Connaught Lab., Inc., 136 F.R.D. 694, 698 (D. Kan. 1991); Schaap v. Executive Indus., 130 F.R.D. 384, 386 (N.D. Ill. 1990); Jenson v. Boston Ins. Co., 20 F.R.D. 619, 622 (N.D. Cal. 1957). *See generally* DISCOVERY PROCEEDINGS IN FEDERAL COURT, *supra* note 11, § 14.6; 8 WRIGHT & MILLER, *supra* note 3, § 2008, at 48 n.29.

covery may properly be had of information inadmissible at trial so long as there is a reasonable possibility that the information sought may lead to other evidence that *will* be admissible.[44] For example, inadmissible hearsay may be discoverable,[45] as well as information concerning subsequent remedial measures[46] and other similar incidents,[47] regardless of their admissibility at trial.

Of course, if the information sought is potentially admissible, then it is almost certainly subject to discovery.[48]

The 1993 amendments to the federal rules require the parties to meet and make a good-faith effort to voluntarily refine the subject matter on which discovery is required.[49]

C. Uncertainty Resolved in Favor of Discoverability

If the court is uncertain as to the relevance of a particular request, there are compelling reasons to allow discovery. Judge Irving Kaufman opined that generally the court should initially order the request to be answered, subject to a later finding of irrelevancy.[50] Judge Kaufman aptly noted that the wisdom of this approach is based on the clear policy of the rules, which favor full disclosure. He observed that in "the early stages of the litigation, it is rare that a showing can be made that a particular item of requested information is not 'relevant' under the broad definition given that word in Rule 26."[51]

---

[44] Avianca, Inc. v. Corriea, 705 F. Supp. 666, 676 (D.D.C. 1989); 8 WRIGHT & MILLER, *supra* note 3, § 2008, at 49–50; *see also* Stanzler v. Loew's Theatre & Realty Corp., 19 F.R.D. 286, 288 (D.R.I. 1955).

[45] FED. R. CIV. P. 26(b) 1946 advisory committee's note; *see* 8 WRIGHT & MILLER, *supra* note 3, § 2008, at 49 n.30.

[46] Culligan v. Yamaha Motor Corp., U.S., 110 F.R.D. 122, 124–25 (S.D.N.Y. 1986); Bowman v. General Motors Corp., 64 F.R.D. 62, 69 (E.D. Pa. 1974); *see also* AMERICAN LAW OF PRODUCTS LIABILITY 3D, *supra* note 16, §§ 53:37–53:39; appendix 1, § 40.

[47] Kozlowski v. Sears, Roebuck & Co., 73 F.R.D. 73, 75 (D. Mass. 1976); Mendelowitz v. Xerox Corp., 573 N.Y.S.2d 548, 552 (App. Div. 1991); *see also* AMERICAN LAW OF PRODUCTS LIABILITY 3D, *supra* note 16, §§ 53:41–53:43; V. Woerner, Annotation, *Pretrial Discovery to Secure Opposing Party's Private Reports or Records as to Previous Accidents or Incidents Involving the Same Place or Premises*, 74 A.L.R. 2D 876 (1960 & Supp. 1992); appendix 1, §§36–37.

[48] *See, e.g.,* American Benefit Life Ins. v. Ille, 87 F.R.D. 540, 542 (W.D. Okla. 1978); *see also* SCOTT BALDWIN ET AL., THE PREPARATION OF A PRODUCT LIABILITY CASE § 7A.3.2, at 572 (2d ed. 1993); 8 WRIGHT & MILLER, *supra* note 3, § 2008, at 48 n.27.

[49] *See* 1993 Amendments, *supra* note 26, FED. R. CIV. P. 26(f). See discussion of the 1993 Amendments in chapter 3.

[50] Irving R. Kaufman, *Judicial Control over Discovery,* 28 F.R.D. 111, 119 (1961).

[51] *Id.*

This approach is widely accepted in practice:

> If the court is uncertain as to the relevance of a discovery request, a response is generally ordered since it may be difficult to determine from the pleadings all of the issues which will be developed at trial, and if the discovered matter is offered at trial, an objection may be raised at that time.[52]

Haydock and Herr make the same observation and offer the following practical explanation:

> Most judges, when confronted with the issue of whether to allow something to be discovered, permit such discovery—for several reasons. One, the rules clearly favor liberal disclosures, and judges like to follow the rules. Two, reported opinions allowing discovery outnumber cases prohibiting discovery, and judges like to go with the numbers. Three, an attorney who takes the time and effort to prepare a motion, memorandum, and proposed order, all for some bit of information, must be convinced that he or she is right and must really want the information. Judges will respect that conviction and may not want to second-guess that judgment. Four, courts recognize that the value of the information sought usually outweighs the burden discovery places on the responding party, and courts like to weigh things. Five, there is less likelihood of being reversed on appeal if discovery is permitted than if it is not permitted, and judges do not like to think themselves wrong.[53]

The wisdom of allowing discovery where there is some doubt as to relevancy is supported also by the fact that any potential for harm to the responding party from the use of the information can be better handled by a protective order or by leaving the question of admissibility to the trial judge.[54]

III. LIMITATIONS ON DISCOVERY

A. Privilege

1. Claiming Privilege

Rule 26(b)(1) specifically excludes privileged matter from the scope of discovery. A detailed discussion of types of privilege that might justify limiting the discovery process is beyond the scope of this book,[55] but some important privilege principles follow.

---

[52] DISCOVERY PROCEEDINGS IN FEDERAL COURT, *supra* note 11, § 14.7, at 223; *see* United States v. AT&T Co., 461 F. Supp. 1314, 1341 (D.D.C. 1978); Duplan Corp. v. Deering Milliken, Inc., 397 F. Supp. 1146, 1188 (D.S.C. 1974); Patterson Oil Terminals, Inc. v. Charles Kurz & Co., 7 F.R.D. 250, 251 (E.D. Pa. 1945); Grinnell Co. v. National Bank, 2 F.R.D. 116, 116–17 (E.D.N.Y. 1941); *cf.* Avianca, Inc. v. Corriea, 705 F. Supp. 666, 676 (D.D.C. 1989).

[53] HAYDOCK & HERR, *supra* note 11, § 1.4, at 24–25.

[54] 8 WRIGHT & MILLER, *supra* note 3, § 2008, at 47, 50–51.

[55] *See* AMERICAN LAW OF PRODUCTS LIABILITY 3D, *supra* note 16, §§53:6–53:13; DISCOVERY PROCEEDINGS IN FEDERAL COURT, *supra* note 11, ch. 15; DOMBROFF, *supra* note 11, §§ 2.01–2.148; HAYDOCK & HERR, *supra* note 11, §§ 2.1–2.9; 4 MOORE ET AL., *supra* note 11, ¶¶ 26.60–26.61; 8 WRIGHT & MILLER, *supra* note 3, §§ 2016–2020.

Facts do not become privileged merely because they are reflected in a privileged communication or work-product document. Even though the document is privileged, the underlying factual data or information may be discoverable.[56] Therefore, a conclusory statement that production of the requested information would violate a privilege is not sufficient to avoid disclosing that information.

As in the case of other objections, the party resisting discovery on the ground of privilege has the burden of proof.[57] The objecting party must not only identify the specific documents to which the claim of privilege applies but also allege facts demonstrating that the privilege has been properly asserted.[58] The 1993 amendments to the Federal Rules of Civil Procedure require a party claiming privilege to "describe the nature of the documents, communications, or things not produced or disclosed in a manner that, without revealing information itself privileged or protected, will enable other parties to assess the applicability of the privilege or protection."[59]

2. Attorney-Client Privilege

The attorney-client privilege provides protection to the client for refusing to disclose—and prevents any other person from disclosing—confidential communications made between the attorney and the client for the purpose of rendering legal services.[60]

For the privilege to exist, the following prerequisites must be met:

- The party for whom the privilege is invoked either is a client or seeks to become a client.

- The attorney or a representative is engaged in the relationship for the purpose of rendering legal services to the client.

- The information is confidential and not intended to be disclosed to third parties for the purpose of obtaining either an opinion on legal services or assistance in a legal proceeding.

---

[56] Bradley v. Melroe Co., 141 F.R.D. 1 (D.D.C. 1992) (ruling that factual data contained in work-product documents were discoverable; manufacturer permitted to redact "all mental impressions, opinions, evaluations, recommendations, and theories").

[57] *See, e.g.,* United States v. Bump, 605 F.2d 548, 551 (10th Cir. 1979).

[58] *See, e.g.,* King v. Conde, 121 F.R.D. 180, 189 (E.D.N.Y. 1988); Meyer v. Citizens & S. Nat.l Bank, CA No. 84–103-C02 (M.D. Ga. Sept. 24, 1986) (refusing to consider claims of privilege for defendant's failure to adduce support for validity of claims; opinion carefully analyzes nature of burden on party asserting privilege). *See generally* DISCOVERY PROCEEDINGS IN FEDERAL COURT, *supra* note 11, § 15.2; EDNA SELAN EPSTEIN & MICHAEL M. MARTIN, THE ATTORNEY-CLIENT PRIVILEGE AND THE WORK-PRODUCT DOCTRINE 10–13, 107–09 (2d ed. 1989).

[59] 1993 Amendments, *supra* note 26, FED. R. CIV. P. 26(b)(5).

[60] *See generally* DISCOVERY PROCEEDINGS IN FEDERAL COURT, *supra* note 11, § 15.19, at 261; HAYDOCK & HERR, *supra* note 11, § 2.5.3, at 135; 4 MOORE ET AL., *supra* note 11, ¶ 26.60[2], at 26–163 to –168; 8 WRIGHT & MILLER, *supra* note 3, § 2017, at 133.

- The privilege has not been waived by the client.[61]

The attorney-client privilege was founded on the public concern for open and frank communication between attorney and client to enable the attorney to render sound legal advice. For an attorney to determine solutions and advice in the most effective manner, he or she must be fully informed of the reasons the client has sought representation.[62] Both the client's communication and the attorney's response and advice are protected by the attorney-client privilege.[63]

Once a communication is deemed privileged, it is immune from discovery. Unlike the work-product doctrine, undue hardship will not overcome the attorney-client privilege. However, the privilege protects only the confidential communication itself, not the disclosure of underlying facts by those who communicated with the attorney: It is the process rather than the factual content that is protected.

The privilege exists to protect the client, not the attorney, so it is the client who determines whether to claim or waive the privilege. Only the client, or the attorney acting on behalf of the client (with the client's consent), may waive all or part of the attorney-client privilege. The privilege over a confidential communication can be waived if the information is communicated directly to a third party, communicated in the presence of a third party, or otherwise disclosed voluntarily. Generally, where disclosure is inadvertent rather than voluntary, it does not constitute a waiver of the privilege. In deciding whether an inadvertent disclosure waived a document's confidentiality, a court must consider the reasonable precautions that were taken to maintain the confidentiality of documents.[64]

3. Work-Product Doctrine

Rule 26(b)(3) codifies the work-product doctrine originally set forth in *Hickman v. Taylor*.[65] The doctrine protects the attorney's files from intrusion by opposing coun-

---

[61] *See generally* DISCOVERY PROCEEDINGS IN FEDERAL COURT, *supra* note 11, § 15.20, at 263; HAYDOCK & HERR, *supra* note 11, § 2.5.3, at 143; 4 MOORE ET AL., *supra* note 11, ¶ 26.60[2], at 26–167; 8 WRIGHT & MILLER, *supra* note 3, § 2017, at 133.

[62] *See generally* DISCOVERY PROCEEDINGS IN FEDERAL COURT, *supra* note 11, § 15.19, at 261; HAYDOCK & HERR, *supra* note 11, § 2.5.3, at 133; 4 MOORE ET AL., *supra* note 11, ¶ 26.60[2], at 26–163.

[63] *See generally,* DISCOVERY PROCEEDINGS IN FEDERAL COURT, *supra* note 11, § 15.19, at 262; HAYDOCK & HERR, *supra* note 11, § 2.5.3, at 140; 4 MOORE ET AL., *supra* note 11, ¶ 26.60[2], at 26–167 to –168; 8 WRIGHT & MILLER, *supra* note 3, § 2017, at 133.

[64] *See generally* DISCOVERY PROCEEDINGS IN FEDERAL COURT, *supra* note 11, § 15.26, at 270; HAYDOCK & HERR, *supra* note 11, § 2.5.3, at 136–37; 4 MOORE ET AL., *supra* note 11, ¶ 26.60[2], at 26–176.

[65] 329 U.S. 495, 510–12 (1947); *see* FED. R. CIV. P. 26(b)(3) 1970 advisory committee's note. *See generally* AMERICAN LAW OF PRODUCTS LIABILITY 3D, *supra* note 16, §§ 53:14–15:21; DISCOVERY PROCEEDINGS IN FEDERAL COURT, *supra* note 11, §§ 16.11–16.18; DOMBROFF, *supra* note 11, §§ 2.14–2.258; HAYDOCK & HERR, *supra* note 11, § 1.6; 4 MOORE ET AL., *supra* note 11, ¶¶ 26.63–

sel unless special circumstances are present. For the doctrine to apply, the material must be a document or a tangible item otherwise discoverable under rule 26(b)(1), that was prepared in anticipation of litigation or for trial by or for a party or its representative.[66]

The work-product doctrine was created to assure a certain degree of privacy to each attorney's evaluation of his or her own case when assembling information and preparing strategy, and it reflects the perception that opposing counsel should not receive the benefits of another's work.[67]

Like the attorney-client privilege, the work-product doctrine does not protect the underlying facts discovered in preparing work-product documents, the identity of the parties from whom the facts were obtained, or the fact of the existence of the work-product documents. Selection of nonprivileged documents deemed relevant or important is protected from discovery because selection may be a crucial part of the trial preparation and may reveal the attorney's strategy.[68]

Materials classified as work product may be discoverable if the party seeking discovery proves a substantial need for the materials in preparation of its case and proves that it is unable to obtain the substantial equivalent of the material by other means without experiencing undue hardship. Courts have demonstrated wide discretion in determining whether circumstances justify discovery in these cases.[69]

Some materials protected by the work-product doctrine reflect mental impressions, conclusions, opinions, or legal theories. This type of protection is sometimes labeled "opinion work product" and cannot be overcome by a showing of substantial need and inability to obtain the equivalent without undue hardship.

26.64; 8 WRIGHT & MILLER, *supra* note 3, §§ 2021–2028. Authorities differ as to whether the work-product doctrine is properly considered a privilege, or an independent source of immunity from discovery. The work-product doctrine is covered by rule 26(b)(5) in the 1993 amendments to the federal discovery rules. Rule 26(b)(5) requires a description of information withheld as privileged or protected. *See* 1993 Amendments, *supra* note 26.

[66] *See generally* DISCOVERY PROCEEDINGS IN FEDERAL COURT, *supra* note 11, § 16.11, at 317; HAYDOCK & HERR, *supra* note 11, § 1.6.1, at 30–31; 4 MOORE ET AL., *supra* note 11, ¶ 26.64[1], at 26–287; 8 WRIGHT & MILLER, *supra* note 3, § 2024, at 196–97.

[67] *See generally* DISCOVERY PROCEEDINGS IN FEDERAL COURT, *supra* note 11, § 16.11, at 317; 4 MOORE ET AL., *supra* note 11, ¶ 26.63[1], at 26–284; 8 WRIGHT & MILLER, *supra* note 3, § 2022, at 186.

[68] *See generally* DISCOVERY PROCEEDINGS IN FEDERAL COURT, *supra* note 11, § 16.12, at 320; 4 MOORE ET AL., *supra* note 11, ¶ 26.64[1], at 26–289 to -290; 8 WRIGHT & MILLER, *supra* note 3, § 2023, at 194.

[69] *See generally* DISCOVERY PROCEEDINGS IN FEDERAL COURT, *supra* note 11, § 16.15, at 325; HAYDOCK & HERR, *supra* note 11, § 1.6.4, at 43; 4 MOORE ET AL., *supra* note 11, ¶ 26.64[3.–1], at 26–300; 8 WRIGHT & MILLER, *supra* note 3, § 2025, at 214.

"Only in rare and extraordinary cases, will opinion work-product be discoverable."[70] Disclosure of protected information by statements or conduct of the client, or by the attorney acting on behalf of the client, will result in a waiver of the protection in some cases. If materials are made known to third parties and the "disclosure substantially increases the possibility that an opposing party could obtain the information," then the disclosure may constitute a waiver.[71]

B. Trial Preparation: Experts

Discovery regarding experts was severely limited[72] until 1970, when the Federal Rules of Civil Procedure were amended to permit broader pretrial discovery of expert opinions.[73] The federal rules seek a balance between allowing a party to evaluate and effectively challenge an opposing expert's opinion and guarding against the danger that one party will unfairly use another party's experts to prepare its own case.[74]

The scope of discovery regarding experts and consultants, and the procedures to be followed, are set forth in new rule 26(a)(2) (disclosure of expert testimony) and rule 26(b)(4) (expert discovery) and parallel state rules. The 1993 amendments significantly changed rule 26(b)(4) and added an expert disclosure requirement, as discussed in chapter 3, section III. Many states, however, follow the old rule. Under the former federal rule, different requirements apply to four classes of experts and consultants, as follows:[75]

- testifying experts,
- nontestifying experts retained or specially employed in anticipation of litigation or in preparation for trial,

---

[70] DISCOVERY PROCEEDINGS IN FEDERAL COURT, *supra* note 11, § 16.17, at 328. *See generally* HAYDOCK & HERR, *supra* note 11, § 1.6.3, at 40; 4 MOORE ET AL., *supra* note 11, ¶ 26.64[3.-2], at 26–314; 8 WRIGHT & MILLER, *supra* note 3, § 2026, at 229.

[71] DISCOVERY PROCEEDINGS IN FEDERAL COURT, *supra* note 11, § 16.18, at 329. *See generally* HAYDOCK & HERR, *supra* note 11, § 1.6.3, at 42; 8 WRIGHT & MILLER, *supra* note 3, § 2024, at 209–10.

[72] *See generally* 8 WRIGHT & MILLER, *supra* note 3, § 2029, at 240–50; Thomas R. Trenknet, Annotation, *Pre-Trial Discovery of Facts Known and Opinions Held by Opponent's Experts Under Rule 26(b)(4) of Federal Rules of Civil Procedure*, 33 A.L.R. FED. 403, 409–14 (1977 & Supp. 1992); *see also* appendix 1, § 16. For a discussion of the defendant's tactics to evade or preclude discovery of expert testimony, see chapter 5, section IX.

[73] FED. R. CIV. P. 26(b)(4) 1970 advisory committee's note cites favorably three sources advocating broader expert discovery: Knighton v. Villian & Fassio, 39 F.R.D. 111 (D. Md. 1966); Jack H. Friedenthal, *Discovery and Use of an Adverse Party's Expert Information*, 14 STAN. L. REV. 455, 485–88 (1962); Jeremiah M. Long, *Discovery and Experts Under the Federal Rules of Civil Procedure*, 38 F.R.D. 11 (1965).

[74] *See* FED. R. CIV. P. 26(b)(4) 1970 advisory committee's note.

[75] 8 WRIGHT & MILLER, *supra* note 3, § 2029, at 250; *see also* Ager v. Jane C. Stormont Hosp. & Training Sch. for Nurses, 622 F.2d 496, 500–01 (10th Cir. 1980). The 1993 amendment to this rule is discussed in chapter 3, section III.

- experts informally consulted but not retained or specially employed, and
- experts who are regular employees or fact witnesses.

1. Testifying Experts

Former rule 26(b)(4)(A)(1) provides that

> [a] party may through interrogatories require any other party to identify each person whom the other party expects to call as an expert witness at trial, to state the subject matter on which the expert is expected to testify, and to state the substance of the facts and opinions to which the expert is expected to testify and a summary of the grounds for each opinion. (ii) Upon motion, the court may order further discovery by other means, subject to such restrictions as to scope and such provisions, pursuant to subdivision (b)(4)(C) of this rule, concerning fees and expenses as the court may deem appropriate.

In jurisdictions using the former federal scheme, an interrogatory seeking the information specified in the rule should be propounded early in every case. If the responding party has not yet selected testifying experts or selects additional experts at a later date, the party is required to supplement any incomplete earlier response.[76]

A proper response must adequately set forth the facts and opinions the expert is expected to present, as well as the grounds for each opinion.[77] Failure to fully provide grounds for opinions can lend support to an opposing party's motion for summary judgment or motion in limine to exclude an expert's opinion.[78] However, the rule applies only to experts expected to testify. There is no need, early in the case, to provide this information for an expert who merely *may* testify.[79]

The 1993 rule amendments permit depositions of testifying experts, as discussed in chapter 3, section III. In jurisdictions operating under rules based on former federal rule 26(b)(4), however, further discovery as to testifying experts is available only on motion and order and is subject to such restrictions and conditions as to scope, fees,

---

[76] 8 WRIGHT & MILLER, *supra* note 3, § 2049, at 323 n.89; *see, e.g.*, Weiss v. Chrysler Motors Corp., 515 F.2d 449 (2d Cir. 1975) (reversing judgment for products liability defendant where defendant manufacturer failed to supplement discovery regarding expert opinion); Tabatchnick v. G.D. Searle & Co., 67 F.R.D. 49 (D.N.J. 1975) (duty to supplement when new expert identified); Williams v. Union Carbide Corp., 734 S.W.2d 699 (Tex. Ct. App. 1987) (same); *see also* Voegeli v. Lewis, 568 F.2d 89 (8th Cir. 1977) (medical malpractice plaintiffs entitled to new trial when unfairly prejudiced by inadequacy of discovery responses regarding defense experts); *cf.* Grimes v. Haslett, 641 P.2d 813 (Alaska 1982) (finding duty to supplement when expert significantly changes opinions between deposition and trial). See generally chapter 5, section IX.

[77] *See* Rupp v. Vock & Weiderhold, Inc., 52 F.R.D. 111, 113 (N.D. Ohio 1971) (answers setting forth subject matter of expected testimony without substance of facts and opinions and summary of grounds for each insufficient).

[78] *See* LeBarron v. Haverhill Coop. Sch. Dist., 127 F.R.D. 38, 41 (D.N.H. 1989) (excluding expert for inadequate disclosure).

[79] Hoover v. United States Dep't of the Interior, 611 F.2d 1132, 1141 n.12 (5th Cir. 1980).

and expenses as the court may deem appropriate. While the rule provides no standard by which courts may evaluate a motion for further discovery, courts generally permit broad and liberal discovery from expert witnesses.[80] Discovery is routinely permitted of experts' reports, notes, drafts, work papers, source data, and communications with counsel, and depositions are routinely allowed.[81]

Courts differ on the issue of whether attorney work product given to an expert is discoverable. Some courts have allowed broad discovery of anything an expert has reviewed in connection with the case.[82] Other courts have held that the mere transmittal of attorney work product to an expert does not waive the limited work-product protection provided by rule 26(b)(3).[83]

Where further discovery is permitted, the court should require the party seeking discovery to pay the expert, pursuant to rule 26(b)(4)(C). However, because courts liberally approve further discovery, parties frequently agree to schedule depositions and exchange experts' reports without resort to court order. These agreements typically include terms of compensation for time spent by an expert in deposition or responding to discovery. Frequently, each side will agree to bear its own experts' costs.

2. Nontestifying Experts "Retained or Specially Employed . . . In Anticipation of Litigation or Preparation for Trial"

As provided by former rule 26(b)(4)(B),

> [a] party may discover facts known or opinions held by an expert who has been retained or specially employed by another party in anticipation of litigation or preparation for trial and who is not expected to be called as a witness at trial, only as provided in Rule 35(b) [medical examination] or upon a showing of exceptional circumstances under which it is impracticable for the party seeking discovery to obtain facts or opinions on the same subject by other means.[84]

The post-1993 amendment rule provision is similar, as discussed in chapter 3, section III.

---

[80] 8 WRIGHT & MILLER, *supra* note 3, § 2031.

[81] *See generally* Steven K. Sims, Note, *Treating Experts Like Ordinary Witnesses: Recent Trends in Discovery of Testifying Experts Under Federal Rule of Civil Procedure 26(b)(4)*, 66 WASH. U. L.Q. 787 (1988).

[82] *See* Boring v. Keller, 97 F.R.D. 404, 407–08 (D. Colo. 1983); James Julian, Inc. v. Raytheon Co., 93 F.R.D. 138, 145–46 (D. Del. 1982).

[83] Bogosian v. Gulf Oil Corp., 738 F.2d 587, 594–95 (3d Cir. 1984); North Carolina Elec. Membership Corp. v. Carolina Power & Light Co., 108 F.R.D. 283 (M.D.N.C. 1985); Baise v. Alewel's, Inc., 99 F.R.D. 95, 97 (W.D. Mo. 1983). *See generally* Bryan Lewis, Note, *Discovery Under the Federal Rules of Civil Procedure of Attorney Opinion Work Product Provided to an Expert Witness*, 53 FORDHAM L. REV. 1159 (1985).

[84] *See also* Timothy L. James, Comment, *Protecting the Non-Testimonial Expert*, 33 S.D. L. REV. 303 (1988).

Courts differ on whether to permit discovery of the identity of an expert specially consulted but not expected to testify, without a special showing.[85] Exceptional circumstances might be found in the rare instance "where the field of experts is limited and the other side has retained all of the experts in that field."[86] The requisite showing may also be made where an expert has unique access to factual information. He or she may have performed tests, for example, on an item or material of limited quantity which was consumed or destroyed in the test. In one federal case, a party was required to produce the reports of its nontestifying experts who were present when allegedly defective piping was removed.[87] Discovery from nontestifying experts has also been permitted where their findings or reports are relied on by testifying experts.[88]

3. Experts Informally Consulted for Trial but Not "Retained or Specially Employed"[89]

Under former rule 26(b)(4), "discovery of expert information acquired in anticipation of litigation or for trial 'may be obtained only' as set out in that rule." Because the rule does not address experts who were informally consulted but never retained, neither their identities nor their opinions are discoverable.[90] In *Ager v. Jane C. Stormont Hospital & Training School for Nurses*, the court discussed the difficulty of determining whether an expert is "retained" or merely "informally consulted." The court suggested consideration of factors such as the following:

---

[85] *See, e.g.*, In re Folding Carton Antitrust Litig., 83 F.R.D. 256, 259–60 (N.D. Ill. 1979) (identity discoverable); Baki v. B.F. Diamond Constr. Co., 71 F.R.D. 179, 181–82 (D. Md. 1976) (same). *But see* FED. R. CIV. P. 26(b)(4)(B) 1970 advisory committee's note ("a party may on a proper showing require the other party to name experts retained or specially employed"); Cox v. Piper, Jaffray & Hopwood, Inc., 848 F.2d 842, 845 (8th Cir. 1988) (Beam, J., dissenting) (identity not discoverable without showing of exceptional circumstances); Ager v. Jane C. Stormont Hosp. & Training Sch. for Nurses, 622 F.2d 496, 503 (10th Cir. 1980) (same).

[86] Debbie Brower Cannon, Note, *Federal Discovery Practices Concerning Expert Witnesses*, 14 OKLA. CITY U. L. REV. 391, 403 (1989).

[87] Sanford Constr. Co. v. Kaiser Aluminum & Chem. Sales, Inc., 45 F.R.D. 465, 466 (E.D. Ky. 1968); *see also* Colden v. R.J. Schofield Motors, 14 F.R.D. 521 (N.D. Ohio 1952) (where vehicle disassembled in course of expert's inspection, report of inspection ordered produced).

[88] *See* Delcastor, Inc. v. Vail Assocs., Inc., 108 F.R.D. 405, 408 (D. Colo. 1985); Heitmann v. Concrete Pipe Mach., 98 F.R.D. 740, 742 (E.D. Mo. 1983).

[89] *See generally* Sheila E. McDonald, Comment, *The In-House Expert Witness: Discovery Under the Federal Rules of Civil Procedure*, 33 S.D. L. REV. 283 (1988).

[90] 8 WRIGHT & MILLER, *supra* note 3, at § 2033, at 257; *see* FED. R. CIV. P. 26(b)(4)(B) 1970 advisory committee's note; Ager v. Jane C. Stormont Hosp. & Training Sch. for Nurses, 622 F.2d 496, 501 (10th Cir. 1980); Baki v. B.F. Diamond Constr. Co., 71 F.R.D. 179, 182 (D. Md. 1976).

(1) the manner in which the consultation was initiated; (2) the nature, type and extent of information or material provided to, or determined by, the expert in connection with his review; (3) the duration and intensity of the consultative relationship; and (4) the terms of the consultation, if any (e.g., payment, confidentiality of test data or opinions, etc.). Of course, additional factors bearing on this determination may be examined if relevant.[91]

4. Experts Who Are Regular Employees or Fact Witnesses

By its terms, former rule 26(b)(4) applies only to expert information "acquired or developed in anticipation of litigation or for trial." The discovery limitations of this rule do not apply to regular employees of a party not specially employed for a case, or to experts who were also actors or viewers of the occurrences resulting in litigation. Such experts are treated as ordinary witnesses, subject to the ordinary broad scope of discovery.[92] Thus, "a doctor who performed an operation that gave rise to a malpractice claim . . . [or] an actuary who witnessed an automobile accident" is subject to discovery as a fact witness, without regard to the limitations of former rule 26(b)(4) or the requirement that the party seeking discovery pay experts' fees and expenses.[93]

C. Court's Discretion

Although the discovery rules were intended to be liberally construed, the scope of discovery is not unlimited. The ambit of relevance does not extend to information "that has no conceivable bearing on the case."[94] Prefacing the general statement of the scope of discovery contained in rule 26(b)(1) is the qualification "Unless otherwise limited by order of the court in accordance with these rules. . . ." Thus, the rules clearly contemplate that the court may, on a proper showing, exercise its discretion to limit the scope of discovery. The court's authority to limit discovery is found in rule 16; rule 26(b)(2), and (c); and rule 37.[95]

The court should begin its consideration of a request to limit inquiry with a presumption in favor of discovery.[96] The court should exercise its judicial discretion so as to limit discovery only where the "interests of justice require such action."[97]

> Whether the matter is brought to the attention of the court by a motion for a protective order under Rule 26(c) or by a motion under Rule 37(a) to compel answers to interrogatories that have been objected to, discovery will be allowed unless the

---

[91] 622 F.2d 496, 501 (10th Cir. 1980).

[92] *See* FED. R. CIV. P. 26(b)(4) 1970 advisory committee's note; 8 WRIGHT & MILLER, *supra* note 3, § 2033, at 258.

[93] Keith v. Van Dorn Plastic Mach. Co., 86 F.R.D. 458, 460 (E.D. Pa. 1980).

[94] 8 WRIGHT & MILLER, *supra* note 3, § 2008, at 45–46 n.22.

[95] See discussion of these provisions in chapter 3.

[96] *See* Berkley v. Clark Equip. Co., 26 F.R.D. 153, 154 (E.D.N.Y. 1960).

[97] *Id; see also* DISCOVERY PROCEEDINGS IN FEDERAL COURT, *supra* note 11, § 6.2, at 309.

court is satisfied that the administration of justice will be impeded.[98]

When a defendant attempts to persuade the court to restrict the scope of discovery to prevent discovery of internal documents, the court should consider the following points:

- whether the documents contain vital evidence, without which the plaintiff cannot adequately prepare its case;
- whether the disputed documents are exclusively in the possession of the defendant;[99]
- whether the plaintiff cannot obtain the documents unless the court compels their disclosure; and
- whether the defendant's attack on the scope of discovery is based on its adversarial, nonobjective position.[100]

The court should also consider the following:

- The defendant bears a heavy burden to justify withholding the documents, which must be substantiated by a proper showing.[101]
- An order permitting discovery is consistent with both the express language of the rules and the numerous cases holding that the rules should be liberally construed.[102]
- An order allowing discovery is consistent with the strong policy favoring full disclosure, and aids in accomplishing the purposes of the discovery rules.[103]
- An order compelling the production of the documents is necessary to offset the defendant's inherent advantages.[104]

---

[98] 8 WRIGHT & MILLER, *supra* note 3, § 2176, at 557.

[99] *See* Kozlowski v. Sears, Roebuck & Co., 73 F.R.D. 73, 75–76 (D. Mass. 1976); King v. Georgia Power Co., 50 F.R.D. 134, 136 (N.D. Ga. 1970).

[100] Stengel v. Kawasaki Heavy Indus., 116 F.R.D. 263, 264 (N.D. Tex. 1987); Sellers v. General Motors Corp., 40 Fed. R. Serv. 2d (Callaghan) 590 (E.D. Pa. 1984); United States v. 30 Jars of "Ahead Hair Restorer for New Hair Growth," 43 F.R.D. 181, 189 (D. Del. 1967); United States v. 216 Bottles of "Sudden Change," 36 F.R.D. 695, 700 (E.D.N.Y. 1965); United Nuclear Corp. v. General Atomic Co., 629 P.2d 231, 287 (N.M. 1980), *cert. denied*, 451 U.S. 901, *reh'g denied*, 452 U.S. 932 (1981); Foster v. Heard, 757 S.W.2d 464, 465–66 (Tex. Ct. App. 1988); Gammon v. Clark Equip. Co., 686 P.2d 1102, 1107 (Wash. Ct. App. 1984),*aff'd en banc*, 707 P.2d 685 (Wash. 1985); *see also* HAYDOCK & HERR, *supra* note 11, § 4.5.2, at 356; 8 WRIGHT & MILLER, *supra* note 3, § 2173, at 544.

[101] See chapter 2, section IV.

[102] See chapter 1, section II.A.

[103] See chapter 1, section I.

[104] *Cf.* Thayer v. Liggett & Myers Tobacco Co., CA No. 5314 (W.D. Mich. Feb. 9, 1970), *quoted in* 8 WRIGHT & MILLER, *supra* note 3, § 2036, at 269 n.32.

- In view of the available alternatives to restricting the scope of discovery, an order compelling disclosure would have little or no harmful effect on the defendant—in contrast to the crippling effect on the plaintiff of an order denying disclosure.

If the documents are truly irrelevant, then the remedy is to prevent their introduction into evidence, a decision best left to the trial judge.[105] Any potential for harm to the defendant can be avoided by entering a protective order limiting dissemination of certain documents, or by shifting the cost incurred in furnishing the documents.[106]

For these reasons, there is very little likelihood that an order permitting discovery will be reversed.[107] There is a much greater likelihood that an order refusing to allow discovery will be reversed, resulting in gross inefficiency and waste of time, effort, and money.

IV. DISCOVERY OF COMPUTERIZED INFORMATION

The scope of discovery properly extends to[108]

- documents or other data in computer format (for example, on disk);[109]
- software necessary to access, search, or manipulate databases (including any instructions or usage manuals);[110] and
- use of an "expert" to assist in accessing, searching, and manipulating the data.

Electronically stored business information is generally discoverable to the same extent as paper documents.[111] Indeed, one eminent jurist has recommended using a responding party's computer capability for the very purpose of improving the efficiency of the discovery process.[112]

---

[105] *See* 8 WRIGHT & MILLER, *supra* note 3, § 2008, at 50–51 n.32.

[106] HAYDOCK & HERR, *supra* note 11, §§ 1.9.2–1.9.3.

[107] *Id.* § 1.4, at 24–25.

[108] This discussion assumes that the information sought is otherwise relevant to the subject matter of the litigation.

[109] Sanders v. Levy, 21 Fed. R. Serv. 2d (Callaghan) 1213, 1218 n.7 (2d Cir. 1976).

[110] As to requiring the responding party to provide software or perform a computer analysis, see *In re* Japanese Elec. Prods. Antitrust Litig. 494 F. Supp. 1257 (E.D. Pa 1980); Fautek v. Montgomery Ward & Co., 96 F.R.D. 141 (N.D. Ill. 1982). For a discussion of closely related topics concerning the criteria that applies when the responding party employs a central repository as a response to discovery requests, see chapter 6, section IV.

[111] Williams v. E.I. DuPont de Nemours & Co., 119 F.R.D. 648 (W.D. Ky. 1987); Colorado *ex rel.* Woodard v. Schmidt-Tiago Constr. Co., 108 F.R.D. 731 (D. Colo. 1985). *See generally* HAYDOCK & HERR, *supra* note 11, § 5.17; DISCOVERY PROCEEDINGS IN FEDERAL COURT, *supra* note 11, § 16.4; 8 WRIGHT & MILLER, *supra* note 3, § 2218.

[112] WILLIAM W. SCHWARZER & LYNN H. PASAHOW, CIVIL DISCOVERY: A GUIDE TO EFFICIENT PRACTICE 16 (1988 & Supp. 1989).

The Federal Rules of Civil Procedure expressly contemplate discovery of computerized data. Rule 26(b)(1) and rule 34(a) include in the scope of discovery "documents or other tangible things." The 1970 amendments redefined "documents" to include "data compilations from which information can be obtained, translated, if necessary, by the respondent through detection devices into reasonably usable form."[113] The 1970 advisory committee's note explains that "[t]he inclusive description of 'documents' is revised to accord with changing technology."[114]

Computerized data discovery may be the only means of obtaining certain information. Computer files may contain information that has never been printed on paper, such as electronic mail—often used for internal memoranda—computer-conducted tests, test results that are analyzed entirely by computers, and compilations of data, including databases. Typically, no hard copy of this type of information is ever generated. Similarly, while paper drafts of documents may be destroyed after the final document is produced, the computer file might still contain an accurate copy of the original document.

Sources of computerized information that are often overlooked include backup tapes, archival tapes, "deleted" information that in fact may be retrievable, and removable hard disks taken home by employees. The only sure way to detect whether a thorough search has been made for electronic data is to gain on-premises access to the computer files (or access by modem) under rule 34.

There is a clear distinction between the discoverability of computerized business information and that of computerized litigation support systems.[115] The former should certainly be discoverable to the same extent as business records stored in a file cabinet; the latter may be subject to work-product protection.[116] However, even where the litigation support system is deemed work product, the facts contained therein are not privileged.

Business records do not acquire work-product protection merely because they have been organized with the assistance of counsel or in anticipation of litigation, though attributes of the file organization may have such protection.[117] For instance, a ruling that counsel's annotated computerized catalog of other injury claims relating to the same product constitutes work product would not prevent discovery by interrogatory of information regarding those claims. The discovery rules require interrogatory answers based on all information available to a party. Thus, even if the database is not

---

[113] FED. R. CIV. P. 34(a); see Adams v. Dan River Mills, Inc., 15 Fed. R. Serv. 2d (Callaghan) 1275, 1276 (W.D. Va. 1972).

[114] FED. R. CIV. P. 34(a) 1970 advisory committee's note.

[115] See appendix 1, section 18.

[116] See id. section 18.3.

[117] See Hoffman v. United Telecommunications, Inc. 117 F.R.D. 436, 439 (D. Kan. 1987). This topic is discussed at length in chapter 5, section IX. The responding party's election of the business records option (e.g., central repository) may result in the waiver of work-product protection to such materials. See chapter 6, section IV.

discoverable, the discovery respondent may be required to use the database to assemble and provide discoverable information.

V. CONCLUSION

The right of every litigant to relevant evidence is a remarkable element of our democracy. It offers those without great wealth and power, such as consumers injured by dangerous products, an opportunity to assert claims. It helps level the playing field between the "haves" and the "have nots," giving the latter reason to hope that their legal challenges against the former will be resolved based on truth. As explored in part two of this book, it is this democratizing element that some manufacturers attempt to thwart through stonewalling.

CHAPTER TWO

PROPER DISCOVERY RESPONSE

This chapter addresses the most important principles governing discovery responses that are frequently violated by the stonewalling party. For the sake of convenience, the party responding to discovery is referred to throughout this book as the defendant, and the party seeking discovery is referred to as the plaintiff. Obviously, the rules are the same no matter which party is seeking discovery.[1]

I. GENERAL RULES GOVERNING THE RESPONSE

As discussed in chapter 1, the rules expressly direct that the parties voluntarily make full and complete disclosure of all relevant information unless a specific, persuasive reason permitted by the rules can be given for withholding certain information. The discovery rules provide explicit guidance with respect to each form of written discovery response:

Interrogatories.[2]

Each interrogatory shall be answered *separately and fully* in writing under oath, unless it is objected to, in which event the objecting party shall state the reasons for objection and shall answer to the extent the interrogatory is not objectionable.[3]

Production of Documents and Things.[4]

The response shall state, *with respect to each item or category,* that inspection and

---

[1] A select bibliography of scholarly materials dealing with discovery generally appears in the Bibliography to this book.

[2] *See generally* AMERICAN LAW OF PRODUCTS LIABILITY 3D § 53:60 (1987 & Supp. 1992); DISCOVERY PROCEEDINGS IN FEDERAL COURT §§ 6.14, 6.16–6.19 (Shepard's eds., 2d ed. 1991 & Supp. 1992); ROGER S. HAYDOCK & DAVID F. HERR, DISCOVERY PRACTICE §§ 4.6.5–4.6.8 (2d ed. 1988 & Supp. 1992); 4A JAMES W. MOORE ET AL., MOORE'S FEDERAL PRACTICE ¶33.25[1] (2d ed. 1991 & Supp. 1992); 8 CHARLES ALAN WRIGHT & ARTHUR R. MILLER, FEDERAL PRACTICE AND PROCEDURE § 2177 (1970 & Supp. 1992).

[3] FED. R. CIV. P. 33(b)(1) (emphasis added).

[4] *See generally* AMERICAN LAW OF PRODUCTS LIABILITY 3D, *supra* note 2, § 53:67.8; DISCOVERY PROCEEDINGS IN FEDERAL COURT, *supra* note 2, §7.13; HAYDOCK & HERR, *supra* note 2, § 5.11; 8 WRIGHT & MILLER, *supra* note 2, § 2213.

related activities will be permitted as requested, unless the request is objected to, in which event *the reasons for objection shall be stated. If objection is made to part of an item or category, the part shall be specified and inspection permitted of the remaining parts.*[5]

Requests for Admission.[6]

If objection is made, the reasons therefore shall be stated. The answer shall *specifically deny the matter or set forth in detail the reasons* why the answering party cannot truthfully admit or deny the matter. A denial shall fairly meet the substance of the requested admission, and when good faith requires that a party qualify an answer or deny only a part of the matter of which an admission is requested, the party shall specify so much of it as is true and qualify or deny the remainder. An answering party may not give lack of information or knowledge as a reason for failure to admit or deny unless that party states that the party has made reasonable inquiry and that the information known or readily obtainable by the party is insufficient to enable the party to admit or deny. A party who considers that a matter of which an admission has been requested presents a genuine issue for trial may not, on that ground alone, object to the request; the party may, subject to the provisions of Rule 37(c), deny the matter or set forth reasons why the party cannot admit or deny it.
. . . *Unless* the court determines that an objection is justified, it *shall* order that an answer be served.[7]

Other provisions impose additional obligations on the respondent.[8]

Generally, a party's response must be full and complete. All responsive known and available information must be disclosed—whether helpful, neutral, or harmful.[9] The failure of the defendant to provide a full and complete response may result in a waiver of the right to later object to the request.[10] The defendant may object to part—but not all—of an individual discovery request but must specify the particular part of the request to which the objection is addressed.[11] The 1993 amendment to rules 33 and

---

[5] FED. R. CIV. P. 34(b) (emphasis added).

[6] *See generally* DISCOVERY PROCEEDINGS IN FEDERAL COURT, *supra* note 2, §§ 9.7, 9.9.8; HAYDOCK & HERR, *supra* note 2, §§ 7.6–7.8; 4A MOORE ET AL., *supra* note 2, ¶ 36.05[4]; 8 WRIGHT & MILLER, *supra* note 2, §2259.

[7] FED. R. CIV. P. 36(a) (emphasis added).

[8] For a more detailed discussion of the control of discovery abuse through the federal rules, see chapter 3.

[9] *See* HAYDOCK & HERR, *supra* note 2, § 4.6.7, at 365; 8 WRIGHT & MILLER, *supra* note 2, § 2177, at 559–60. For discussion of the scope of discovery, see chapter 1, section II.

[10] *See, e.g.*, Slauenwhite v. Bekum Maschinenfabriken, GmbH, 35 Fed. R. Serv. 2d (Callaghan) 975 (D. Mass. 1983); Antico v. Honda of Camden, 85 F.R.D. 34, 35–36 (E.D. Pa. 1979); Clark v. General Motors Corp., 20 Fed. R. Serv. 2d (Callaghan) 679, 685 (D. Mass. 1975). *See generally* HAYDOCK & HERR, *supra* note 2, § 4.5; 8 WRIGHT & MILLER, *supra* note 2, § 2173, at 544 n.68.

[11] *See* 8 WRIGHT & MILLER, *supra* note 2, § 2213, at 641 n.18.

34 clarifies the duty of the responding party to provide a full answer to the extent an interrogatory is not objectionable.[12]

The rules specifically provide that "an evasive or incomplete disclosure, answer, or response is to be treated as a failure to disclose, answer, or respond."[13] What is required is a "candid statement of the information sought or of the fact that objection is made to furnishing the information."[14] "A partial answer by a party reserving an undisclosed objection . . . is not candid."[15]

If the defendant is unable to give a complete answer at the time the answer is due, it should furnish any available relevant information.[16] Further, the defendant's response should set forth (1) a statement (with supporting facts) to the effect that it has conducted a reasonable inquiry to obtain the requested information[17] and (2) the reasons why the requested information is not available. The defendant should supplement its response at a later date when the requested information becomes available.[18]

II. DUTY OF INQUIRY

In an effort to prevent the discovery of its internal documents, a corporate defendant may answer that it does not have the requested document. A variation of this approach occurs when the corporate agent assigned to handle the plaintiff's discovery request states that he or she has "no personal knowledge" of the requested information. Both responses are improper under the rules.[19]

The express wording of the discovery rules makes clear that the defendant has an affirmative duty to conduct an inquiry to get the information necessary to make full disclosure in response to a discovery request. Rule 33(a) requires that a party

---

[12] FED. R. CIV. P. 33(b)(1), 34(b) 1993 advisory committee's note.

[13] FED. R. CIV. P. 37(a)(3). *See generally* 8 WRIGHT & MILLER, *supra* note 2, § 2177, at 568.

[14] Dollar v. Long Mfg., 561 F.2d 613, 616 (5th Cir. 1977), *cert. denied*, 435 U.S. 996 (1978).

[15] *See* 561 F.2d at 617; Casson Constr. Co. v. Armco Steel Corp., 91 F.R.D. 376, 378–80 (D. Kan. 1980).

[16] *See generally* 8 WRIGHT & MILLER, *supra* note 2, § 2181, at 576 n.68.

[17] For a discussion of a party's duty to conduct an inquiry in order to respond to discovery, see section II, *infra*.

[18] Rogers v. Tri-State Materials Corp., 51 F.R.D. 234, 246 (N.D. W. Va. 1970); *see also* 8 WRIGHT & MILLER, *supra* note 2, § 2174, at 556 n.2, § 2177, at 563 n.25, § 2262, at 734 n.39. For discussion of a party's duty to supplement its response, see section III, *infra*. *See generally* 8 WRIGHT & MILLER, *supra* note 2, §§ 2048–49.

[19] *See* General Dynamics Corp. v. Selb Mfg. Co., 481 F.2d 1204, 1210–11 (8th Cir. 1973), *cert. denied*, 414 U.S. 1162 (1974); International Ass'n of Machinists, Dist. 169 v. Amana Refrigeration, Inc., 90 F.R.D. 1, 2 (E.D. Tenn. 1978). *See generally* DISCOVERY PROCEEDINGS IN FEDERAL COURT, *supra* note 2, § 6.11, § 6.19, at 358; *Developments in the Law—Discovery*, 74 HARV. L. REV. 940, 1026–27 (1961).

answering interrogatories must furnish such information as is *"available* to the party."[20] Rule 34(a)(1) requires a party to produce documents and things which are in the party's "possession, *custody or control."*[21] Under rule 36(a),

> an answering party may not give lack of information or knowledge as a reason for failure to admit or deny unless the party states that the party has made *reasonable inquiry* and that the information known or *readily obtainable* by the party is insufficient to enable the party to admit or deny.[22]

In addition, rule 26(g) imposes on the *attorney* an affirmative duty to make a "reasonable inquiry" that a disclosure, request, response, or objection is "complete and correct" at the time it is made.[23]

The response contemplated by the rules does not ordinarily require "independent" research outside the company.[24] In a complex products liability case, however, a fair and adequate response may well require a substantial commitment of time and effort from the defendant.[25] The fact that the preparation a case requires may unavoidably involve the location and production of a significant amount of information does not alone pretermit discovery.[26]

---

[20] *See* 23 AM. JUR. 2D *Depositions and Discovery* § 212, § 219, at 536 (1983 & Supp. 1992) (emphasis added) [hereinafter 23 AM. JUR.]; DISCOVERY PROCEEDINGS IN FEDERAL COURT, *supra* note 2, §§ 6.17, 6.19; HAYDOCK & HERR, *supra* note 2, §§ 4.6.1–4.6.3; 4A MOORE ET AL., *supra* note 2, ¶ 33.26; 8 WRIGHT & MILLER, *supra* note 2, § 2174, at 550–56.

[21] *See* 23 AM. JUR., *supra* note 20, § 249, at 536 (emphasis added); 27 C.J.S. *Discovery* § 71(4) (1959 & Supp. 1992); DISCOVERY PROCEEDINGS IN FEDERAL COURT, *supra* note 2, § 7.6; HAYDOCK & HERR, *supra* note 2, § 5.6; 4A MOORE ET AL., *supra* note 2, ¶ 34.17; 8 WRIGHT & MILLER, *supra* note 2, § 2210; R.M. Garcia, Annotation, *Who Has Possession, Custody, or Control of Corporate Books or Records for Purposes of Order to Produce*, 47 A.L.R. 3d 676 (1973 & Supp. 1992).

[22] 4A MOORE ET AL., *supra* note 2, ¶ 36.04[5], at 36–41; 8 WRIGHT & MILLER, *supra* note 2, § 2261, at 731 n.25; *see* 23 AM. JUR., *supra* note 20, § 342, at 629; *Discovery*, *supra* note 21, § 92; DISCOVERY PROCEEDINGS IN FEDERAL COURT, *supra* note 2, § 9.11; HAYDOCK & HERR, *supra* note 2, § 7.8; J.P. Ludington, Annotation, *Party's Duty Under Federal Rule of Civil Procedure 36(a) and Similar State Statutes and Rules, to Respond to Requests for Admission of Facts Not Within His Personal Knowledge*, 20 A.L.R. 3D 456 (1968 & Supp. 1992).

[23] *See* GREGORY P. JOSEPH, SANCTIONS: THE FEDERAL LAW OF LITIGATION ABUSE § 42 (1989 & Supp. 1991); James A. George et al., *Rule 26(g)—The "Undiscovered Rule,"* Trial, Aug. 1988, at 33; Maurice Rosenberg, *Discovery Abuse*, LITIG., Spring 1981, at 8, 9; *see also* National Ass'n of Radiation Survivors v. Turnage, 115 F.R.D. 543, 555 (N.D. Cal. 1987).

[24] *See* authorities cited in 8 WRIGHT & MILLER, *supra* note 2, §2174, at 550–54; *see also* 23 AM. JUR., *supra* note 20, § 212, at 232; TERRENCE F. KIELY, PREPARING PRODUCTS LIABILITY CASES § 7.6 (1986 & Supp. 1989).

[25] *See* DISCOVERY PROCEEDINGS IN FEDERAL COURT, *supra* note 2, § 6.27, at 390 n.161; *see also* KIELY, *supra* note 24, § 7.6, at 205; 4A MOORE ET AL., *supra* note 2, ¶ 33.20; 8 WRIGHT & MILLER, *supra* note 2, § 2174.

[26] For discussion of the burden objection, see section V.B., *infra*.

A contrary rule would simply foreclose the plaintiff from maintaining a complicated case that necessarily involves extensive discovery. The obvious injustice of such a rule is particularly evident in cases where most of the relevant information is exclusively in the possession of the defendant and available for examination and use by the defendant's employees and experts and can only be obtained by the plaintiff through discovery.

A corporate defendant's duty to respond to a discovery request has been held to require the company to conduct rather extensive research, which may include an investigation[27] or consultation with a third party,[28] including an expert.[29] Situations in which the court might require the defendant to conduct rather extensive research to respond to the plaintiff's request include the following:

- The defendant will have to do roughly the same work to prepare its own case.[30]
- The defendant has produced similar documents in other similar cases.[31]
- The requested information relates to an issue that the defendant itself has raised.[32]
- The defendant is required by law to compile the information for other purposes (such as a notice of proposed adoption of a regulatory standard or a defect investigation by a regulatory agency).[33]

---

[27] *See* Cada v. Costa Line, Inc., 95 F.R.D. 346 (N.D. Ill. 1982); Roesberg v. Johns-Manville Corp., 85 F.R.D. 292 (E.D. Pa. 1980); Flour Mills of Am., Inc. v. Pace, 75 F.R.D. 676, 680–82 (E.D. Okla. 1977); Morgan Smith Automotive Prods., Inc. v. General Motors Corp., 54 F.R.D. 19, 20 (E.D. Pa. 1971); 9H Realty Corp. v. Zurich Ins. Co., 452 N.Y.S.2d 245, 246 (App. Div. 1982). *See generally* 23 AM. JUR., *supra* note 20, §§ 212, 219, 232, 342; DISCOVERY PROCEEDINGS IN FEDERAL COURT, *supra* note 2, § 6.27; 8 WRIGHT & MILLER, *supra* note 2, § 2174, at 554 n.97.

[28] Al-Jundi v. Rockefeller, 91 F.R.D. 590, 593–94 (W.D.N.Y. 1981).

[29] Fautek v. Montgomery Ward & Co., 96 F.R.D. 141, 145–46 (N.D. Ill. 1982) (consultation with computer experts).

[30] Pascale v. G.D. Searle & Co., 90 F.R.D. 55, 59 (D.R.I. 1981); *In re* Folding Carton Antitrust Litig., 83 F.R.D. 256, 259 (N.D. Ill. 1979); Flour Mills of Am., Inc. v. Pace, 75 F.R.D. 676, 680 (E.D. Okla. 1977). *See generally* DISCOVERY PROCEEDINGS IN FEDERAL COURT, *supra* note 2, § 6.27, at 391 n.163; MARK A. DOMBROFF, DISCOVERY § 5.10, at 251 n.19 (1986 & Supp. 1990); 4A MOORE ET AL., *supra* note 2, ¶ 33.20, at 33–110; 8 WRIGHT & MILLER, *supra* note 2, § 2174, at 555 n.1.

[31] *See* Kozlowski v. Sears, Roebuck & Co., 73 F.R.D. 73, 76 (D. Mass. 1976).

[32] *In re* Folding Carton Antitrust Litig., 83 F.R.D. 256, 259 (N.D. Ill. 1979); Flour Mills of Am., Inc. v. Pace, 75 F.R.D. 676, 680 (E.D. Okla. 1977); Bowles v. McMinnville Mfg., 7 F.R.D. 64, 65 (E.D. Tenn. 1946).

[33] *Cf.* Burns v. Thiokol Chem. Corp., 483 F.2d 300, 307 (5th Cir. 1973).

The burden is on the defendant to show that the information is not readily obtainable[34] and to support its position with evidence that the company has made a reasonable inquiry.[35]

> If the answering party lacks information necessary to make a full, fair, and specific answer to an interrogatory, it should so state under oath and set forth in detail the efforts made to obtain the information.[36]

The corporate defendant must produce relevant materials over which it has a right of "control."[37] The requisite control exists where the company has a legal right to obtain the document[38] or where it would ordinarily have access to the document in the usual course of business.[39] Legal ownership of the documents is not required.[40]

The meaning and breadth of "control" should be construed broadly.[41] A "hyper-technical" construction would undermine the policy favoring liberal pretrial discovery.[42] Courts have held that a corporation has a duty to consult with "other relevant sources,"[43] to "make inquiry of every possible source,"[44] and to furnish information "regardless of when or from whom [the information] was acquired."[45]

Courts have specifically construed the duty of inquiry as requiring a party to seek information from its agents or other persons who have acted on its behalf,[46]

---

[34] *See* 8 WRIGHT & MILLER, *supra* note 2, § 2174, at 556 n.2.

[35] Han v. Food & Nutrition Serv., U.S. Dep't of Agric., 580 F. Supp. 1564 (D.N.J. 1984); Budget Rent-A-Car, Inc. v. Hertz Corp., 55 F.R.D. 354, 357 (W.D. Mo. 1972). *See generally* 23 AM. JUR., *supra* note 20, § 213, at 532 nn.50–51, § 342, at 629 n.99.

[36] DISCOVERY PROCEEDINGS IN FEDERAL COURT, *supra* note 2, § 6.17, at 353.

[37] FED. R. CIV. P. 34(a); *see* Haseotes v. Abacab Int'l Computers, Inc., 120 F.R.D. 12, 15 (D. Mass. 1988); *Ex parte* Dorsey Trailers, Inc., 397 So. 2d 98, 104 (Ala. 1981).

[38] Gerling Int'l Ins. Co. v. Commissioner, 839 F.2d 131, 140 (3d Cir. 1988); Searock v. Stripling, 736 F.2d 650, 653 (11th Cir. 1984); Scott v. Arex, Inc., 124 F.R.D. 39, 41 (D. Conn. 1989). *See generally* 23 AM. JUR., *supra* note 20, §§ 212, 219, 249; HAYDOCK & HERR, *supra* note 2, § 5.6; 8 WRIGHT & MILLER, *supra* note 2, § 2210, at 621–22; Garcia, *supra* note 21.

[39] Simon v. G.D. Searle & Co., 119 F.R.D. 680, 681 (D. Minn. 1987); Cooper Indus. v. British Aerospace, Inc., 102 F.R.D. 918, 919–20 (S.D.N.Y. 1984).

[40] *See* DISCOVERY PROCEEDINGS IN FEDERAL COURT, *supra* note 2, § 7.6, at 422 n.29.

[41] Scott v. Arex, Inc., 124 F.R.D. 39, 41 (D. Conn. 1989).

[42] *See* Hart v. Wolff, 489 P.2d 114, 117 (Alaska 1971).

[43] United States v. 58.16 Acres of Land, 66 F.R.D. 570, 572 (E.D. Ill. 1975).

[44] Wallace v. Shade Tobacco Growers Agric. Ass'n, Inc., 21 Fed. R. Serv. 2d (Callaghan) 1130, 1132 (D. Mass. 1975).

[45] Riley v. United Air Lines, Inc., 32 F.R.D. 230, 233 (S.D.N.Y. 1962).

[46] National Ass'n of Radiation Survivors v. Turnage, 115 F.R.D. 543, 556 (N.D. Cal. 1987); Kozlowski v. Sears, Roebuck & Co., 73 F.R.D. 73, 76 (D. Mass. 1976).

including present and former employees.[47] It has been held that a party has "control" of documents that have been turned over to attorneys[48] or to federal agencies.[49] Parties have been found to have similar control over documents maintained by experts,[50] insurers,[51] or investigators employed on the parties' behalf.[52]

A corporation may also be required to furnish information or produce documents in the possession of the following:[53]

- a district office,[54]
- a corporate subsidiary,[55]

---

[47] Stengel v. Kawasaki Heavy Indus., 116 F.R.D. 263, 266 (N.D. Tex. 1987); see DISCOVERY PROCEEDINGS IN FEDERAL COURT, supra note 2, § 7.6, at 423 nn.34–35.

[48] Ex parte Dorsey Trailers, Inc., 397 So. 2d 98, 105 (Ala. 1981); see also 23 AM. JUR., supra note 20, § 212, at 531 nn.40–41, § 249, at 559 n.26; DISCOVERY PROCEEDINGS IN FEDERAL COURT, supra note 2, § 7.6, at 422 n.32; 8 WRIGHT & MILLER, supra note 2, § 2177, at 562 n.23, § 2210, at 621 n.58.

[49] Bowman v. Consolidated Rail Corp., 110 F.R.D. 525, 527 (N.D. Ind. 1986); Karlsson v. Wolfson, 18 F.R.D. 474, 476–77 (D. Minn. 1956).

[50] Simon v. G.D. Searle & Co., 119 F.R.D. 680, 682 (D. Minn. 1987); Hockley v. Zent, Inc., 89 F.R.D. 26, 30–31 (M.D. Pa. 1980); Quadrini v. Sikorsky Aircraft Div., United Aircraft Corp., 74 F.R.D. 594, 594–95 (D. Conn. 1977).

[51] Parrett v. Ford Motor Co., 47 F.R.D. 22, 24 (W.D. Mo. 1968); Bingle v. Liggett Drug Co., 11 F.R.D. 593, 594 (D. Mass. 1951); Biehler v. White Metal Rolling & Stamping Corp., 333 N.E.2d 716, 721 (Ill. App. Ct. 1975). See generally 23 AM. JUR., supra note 20, § 249, at 560 n.30; DISCOVERY PROCEEDINGS IN FEDERAL COURT, supra note 2, § 7.6, at 423 n.33; 8 WRIGHT & MILLER, supra note 2, § 2210, at 622 n.59.

[52] Roberson v. Ryder Truck Lines, Inc., 41 F.R.D. 166, 166–67 (N.D. Miss. 1966).

[53] See generally D.E. Ytreberg, Annotation, Discovery and Inspection: Compelling Party to Disclose Information in Hands of Affiliated or Subsidiary Corporation, or Independent Contractor, Not Made Party to Suit, 19 A.L.R. 3D 1134 (1968 & Supp. 1992).

[54] Parry v. Pyramid Crossgates Co., 551 N.Y.S.2d 77, 78 (App. Div. 1990).

[55] Gerling Int'l Ins. Co. v. Commissioner, 839 F.2d 131, 140–41 (3d Cir. 1988); Transcontinental Fertilizer Co. v. Samsung Co., 108 F.R.D. 650, 652–53 (E.D. Pa. 1985); Brunswick Corp. v. Suzuki Motor Co., 96 F.R.D. 684, 686 (E.D. Wis. 1983); In re Uranium Antitrust Litig., 480 F. Supp. 1138, 1144–45 (N.D. Ill. 1979); Hubbard v. Rubbermaid, Inc., 78 F.R.D. 631, 636 (D. Md. 1978); Sol S. Turnoff Drug Distribs., Inc. v. N.V. Nederlandsche Combinatie Voor Chemische Industrie, 55 F.R.D. 347, 349 (E.D. Pa. 1972); George Hantscho Co. v. Miehle-Goss-Dexter, Inc., 33 F.R.D. 332, 334–35 (S.D.N.Y. 1963); Standard Ins. Co. v. Pittsburgh Elec. Insulation, Inc., 29 F.R.D. 185, 188 (W.D. Pa. 1961); Erone Corp. v. Skouras Theaters Corp., 22 F.R.D. 494, 498 (S.D.N.Y. 1958); American Honda Motor Co. v. Votour, 435 So. 2d 368 (Fla. Dist. Ct. App. 1983), order on remand, No. 79-4686 (Fla. Cir. Ct.Sept. 7, 1983). See generally 23 Am. Jur., supra note 20, §§ 220, 250; PHILLIP I. BLUMBERG, THE LAW OF CORPORATE GROUPS §§ 10.01–10.12 (1983 & Supp. 1992); 4A MOORE ET AL., supra note 2, ¶ 33.26, at 33–152; 8 WRIGHT & MILLER, supra note 2, § 2210, at 623 n.60; Ytreberg, supra note 53.

- a sister corporation (i.e., another subsidiary of a common parent corporation),[56]
- foreign branches,[57]
- the corporate parent,[58]
- a successor corporation,[59] and
- a company with which the defendant has an indemnity agreement.[60]

Production may be ordered even if the documents themselves are beyond the jurisdiction of the court[61] and, under certain circumstances, even if the penal laws of

---

[56] Perini Am., Inc. v. Paper Converting Mach. Co., 559 F. Supp. 552, 552–53 (E.D. Wis. 1983); West v. Johnson & Johnson Prods., Inc., 220 Cal. Rptr. 437, 463–64 (Ct. App. 1985), cert. denied, 479 U.S. 824 (1986). *But see* Pennault Corp. v. Plough, Inc. 85 F.R.D. 257, 263 (D. Del. 1979).

[57] United States v. Bank of Nova Scotia (II), 740 F.2d 817 (11th Cir. 1984), cert. denied, 469 U.S. 1106 (1985); United States v. Bank of Nova Scotia(I), 691 F.2d 1384, 1391 (11th Cir. 1982), cert. denied, 462 U.S. 1119 (1983); First Nat'l City Bank v. IRS, 271 F.2d 616, 619 (2d Cir. 1959), cert. denied, 361 U.S. 948, reh'g denied, 362 U.S. 906 (1960); *In re* Equitable Plan Co., 185 F. Supp. 57, 59–60 (S.D.N.Y.), modified sub nom. Ings v. Ferguson, 282 F.2d 149 (2d Cir. 1960); United Nuclear Corp. v. General Atomic Co., 629 P.2d 231 (N.M. 1980), cert. denied, 451 U.S. 901, reh'g denied, 452 U.S. 932 (1981); *see also* General Atomic Co. v. Exxon Nuclear Co., 90 F.R.D. 290 (S.D. Cal. 1981) (finding that the defendant demonstrated "willfulness and bad faith" in housing its document in Canada in an attempt to rely on the Ontario Act as a "legal impediment"). *See generally* BLUMBERG, *supra* note 55, §§ 10.04–10.12; DOMBROFF, *supra* note 30, § 5.11, at 254; 4A MOORE ET AL., *supra* note 2, § 34.16; 8 WRIGHT & MILLER, *supra* note 2, § 2210, at 623 n.62. *But see In re* Sealed Case, 825 F.2d 494 (D.C. Cir. 1987).

[58] Gerling Int'l Ins. Co. v. Commissioner, 839 F.2d 131, 140–41 (3d Cir. 1988); Snowden v. Connaught Lab., Inc., 137 F.R.D. 336, 340 (D. Kan.), appeal denied, 136 F.R.D. 694 (D. Kan. 1991); Camden Iron & Metal v. Marubeni Am. Corp., 138 F.R.D. 438, 441–42 (D.N.J. 1991); Afros S.P.A. v. Krauss-Maffei Corp., 113 F.R.D. 127, 130 (D. Del. 1986); M.L.C., Inc. v. North Am. Philips Corp., 109 F.R.D. 134, 136–37 (S.D.N.Y. 1986); Ferber v. Sharp Elecs. Corp., 40 Fed. R. Serv. 2d (Callaghan) 950 (S.D.N.Y. 1984); United States v. Toyota Motor Corp., 569 F. Supp. 1158, 1162–63 (C.D. Cal. 1983); *see also* Paseman v. Yamaha Motor Corp., U.S., CA No. 577141 (Cal. Super. Ct. May 5, 1989). *But see* Westinghouse Credit Corp. v. Mountain States Mining & Milling Co., 37 F.R.D. 348 (D. Colo. 1965). *See generally* 23 AM. JUR., *supra* note 20, § 250; BLUMBERG, *supra* note 55, § 10.03; Ytreberg, *supra* note 53.

[59] Anderson v. Cryovac, Inc., 862 F.2d 910, 928–29, 931 (1st Cir. 1988); Pesaplastic, C.A. v. Cincinnati Milacron Co., 799 F.2d 1510, 1520–21 (11th Cir. 1986); Anderson v. Beatrice Foods Co., 127 F.R.D. 1 (D. Mass. 1989); *In re* Richardson-Merrell, Inc., 97 F.R.D. 481, 483–84 (S.D. Ohio 1983). The duty of inquiry may not extend to a former subdivision over which the successor corporation has no control. *See In re* Richardson-Merrell, Inc., *supra*.

[60] Kozlowski v. Sears, Roebuck & Co., 73 F.R.D. 73, 76 (D. Mass. 1976).

[61] Cooper Indus. v. British Aerospace, Inc., 102 F.R.D. 918 (S.D.N.Y. 1984); *In re* Uranium Antitrust Litig., 480 F. Supp. 1138, 1144–45 (N.D. Ill. 1979); United States v. Standard Oil Co., 23 F.R.D. 1, 3–4 (S.D.N.Y. 1958); *see* 4A MOORE ET AL., *supra* note 2, ¶ 34.16; 8 WRIGHT & MILLER, *supra* note 2, § 2210, at 624 n.66.

the country where the document is located forbid disclosure.[62]

A party may also be required to produce documents that are under a sealing order,[63] or that have been seized by a search warrant in a criminal proceeding.[64]

III. DUTY TO SUPPLEMENT RESPONSES

Rule 26(e) imposes a continuing duty to supplement responses to discovery requests—but only in specific situations. The rule provides the exclusive authority for the duty to supplement. The former, pre-1993 amendment rule began with a negative:

> A party who has responded to a request for discovery with a response that was complete when made is under *no* duty to supplement the response to include information thereafter acquired, except as follows . . . .[65]

The former rule provided for seven situations in which a party must supplement its response to a discovery request,[66] as follows:

- with respect to any question directly addressed to "the identity and location of persons having knowledge of discoverable matters;"[67]

- with regard to expert witnesses, any additional data concerning the identity of each expert expected to be called as an expert witness and concerning the subject matter of the expert's testimony;[68]

---

[62] Societe Internationale Pour Participations Industrielles et Commerciales, S.A. v. Rogers, 357 U.S. 197, 211–12 (1958); Cooper Indus. v. British Aerospace, Inc., 102 F.R.D. 918, 920 (S.D.N.Y. 1984); Petruska v. Johns-Manville, 83 F.R.D. 32, 36 (E.D. Pa. 1979); *see also* General Atomic Co. v. Exxon Nuclear Co., 90 F.R.D. 290, 296–99, 307 (S.D. Cal. 1981). *See generally* 23 AM. JUR., supra note 20, § 251; 8 WRIGHT & MILLER, *supra* note 2, §2210, at 624 n.67. *But see In re* Sealed Case, 825 F.2d 494 (D.C. Cir. 1987).

[63] Wauchop v. Domino's Pizza, Inc., 138 F.R.D. 539, 544, 549 (N.D. Ind. 1991); LeBlanc v. Broyhill, 123 F.R.D. 527, 531 (W.D.N.C. 1988); Carter-Wallace, Inc. v. Hartz Mountain Indus., 92 F.R.D. 67, 69–70 (S.D.N.Y. 1981); *see also* DeFord v. Schmid Prods. Co., 120 F.R.D. 648, 654–55 (D. Md. 1987).

[64] United States *ex rel.* Woodard v. Tynan, 776 F.2d 250, 251–52 (10th Cir. 1985).

[65] Former FED. R. CIV. P. 26(e) (emphasis added).

[66] Regarding the duty to supplement generally, see 23 AM. JUR., *supra* note 20, §§ 12–14; DISCOVERY PROCEEDINGS IN FEDERAL COURT, *supra* note 2, §§ 2.15–2.21; HAYDOCK & HERR, *supra* note 2, § 1.8, at 59; 4A MOORE ET AL., *supra* note 2, ¶ 33.25[2]; 8 WRIGHT & MILLER, *supra* note 2, §§ 2048–2050, 2179.

[67] Former FED. R. CIV. P. 26(e)(1)(A); *see* Foster v. Cunningham, 825 S.W.2d 806 (Tex. Ct. App. 1992) (where defense attorney did not show good cause for failing to disclose witness's address, discovered five days before trial, admission of witness's testimony was reversible error).

[68] Former FED. R. CIV. P. 26(e)(1)(B); *see* Jenkins v. Whittaker Corp., 785 F.2d 720, 728 (9th Cir.), *cert. denied*, 479 U.S. 918 (1986); Sharp v. Broadway Nat'l Bank, 784 S.W.2d 669 (Tex. 1990).

- when either a party or its attorney obtains information on the basis of which it knows that the original response was incorrect at the time it was made;[69]
- when either a party or its attorney obtains information upon the basis of which it knows that the response, though correct when made, is no longer true, and the circumstances are such that a failure to amend the response is in substance a knowing concealment[70] (supplementation has been required, for example, where the defendant initially denies the existence of a requested document or other evidence but later learns that such evidence exists and is in the company's possession or control);[71]
- when a duty to supplement responses is imposed by order of the court;[72]
- when a duty to supplement responses is imposed by agreement of the parties;[73] and
- when a duty to supplement responses is imposed by the filing of new requests for supplementation of prior responses.[74]

The new rule 26(e) requires supplementation of required disclosures as well as discovery responses under specific circumstances, as follows:

> (e) Supplementation of Disclosures and Responses. A party who has made a disclosure under subdivision (a) or responded to a request for discovery with a disclosure or response is under a duty to supplement or correct the disclosure or response to include information thereafter acquired if ordered by the court or in the following circumstances:

---

[69] Former FED. R. CIV. P. 26(e)(2)(A); *see* Rozier v. Ford Motor Co., 573 F.2d 1332, 1341–42 (5th Cir. 1978); Bollard v. Volkswagen of Am., Inc., 56 F.R.D. 569, 575–78 (W.D. Mo. 1971); Buehler v. Whalen, 355 N.E.2d 99 (Ill. Ct. App. 1976), *aff'd*, 374 N.E.2d 460 (Ill. 1977).

[70] Former FED. R. CIV. P. 26(e)(2)(B).

[71] *See, e.g.*, Perkinson v. Gilbert/Robinson, Inc., 821 F.2d 686 (D.C. Cir. 1987); Rexrode v. American Laundry Press Co., 674 F.2d 826, 828–29 (10th Cir.), *cert. denied*, 459 U.S. 862 (1982); Dudley v. South Jersey Metal, Inc., 555 F.2d 96, 98 (3d Cir. 1977); Cook v. Calavar Corp., No. 82C 7708 (N.D. Ill. Mar. 21, 1986); Litton Sys. v. AT&T Co., 90 F.R.D. 410, 417 (S.D.N.Y. 1981); King v. American Food Equip. Co., 513 N.E.2d 958, 967 (Ill. App. Ct.), *appeal denied*, 517 N.E.2d 1087 (Ill. 1987); Haumersen v. Ford Motor Co., 257 N.W.2d 7 (Iowa 1977); Rock Island Bank & Trust Co. v. Ford Motor Co., 220 N.W.2d 799 (Mich. Ct. App. 1974); Owen v. F.A. Buttrey Co., 627 P.2d 1233 (Mont. 1981); Berry v. Coleman Sys. Co., 596 P.2d 1365, 1367–68 (Wash. Ct. App.) (ordering new trial where defendant disclosed no prior complaints or legal actions in response to interrogatories but where further investigation revealed 31 similar complaints and 13 legal actions), *review denied*, 92 Wash. 2d 1026 (1979). *See generally* RICHARD H. UNDERWOOD & WILLIAM H. FORTUNE, TRIAL ETHICS § 6.5.3, at 247–48 (1988 & Supp. 1993).

[72] Former FED. R. CIV. P. 26(e)(3); *see* Parrett v. Ford Motor Co., 52 F.R.D. 120, 121 (W.D. Mo. 1969).

[73] Former FED. R. CIV. P. 26(e)(3).

[74] Former FED. R. CIV. P. 26(e)(3).

(1) A party is under a duty to supplement at appropriate intervals its disclosures under subdivision (a) if the party learns that in some material respect the information disclosed is incomplete or incorrect and if the additional or corrective information has not otherwise been made known to the other parties during the discovery process or in writing. With respect to testimony of an expert from whom a report is required under subdivision (a)(2)(B) the duty extends both to information contained in the report and to information provided through a deposition of the expert, and any additions or other changes to this information shall be disclosed by the time the party's disclosures under Rule 26(a)(3) are due.

(2) A party is under a duty seasonably to amend a prior response to an interrogatory, request for production, or request for admission if the party learns that the response is in some material respect incomplete or incorrect and if the additional or corrective information has not otherwise been made known to the other parties during the discovery process or in writing.

The duty to supplement under rule 26(e) extends to all forms of discovery, including interrogatories, depositions,[75] requests for production, and requests for admissions.

"The purpose of the duty to supplement is to prevent unfair surprise and to narrow and define the issues prior to trial so that the trial's progress may be efficient and orderly."[76] The requirement that a party amend a response that, though correct when made, is no longer true is intended to avoid, in the words of the former rule, a "knowing concealment."[77] A "knowing concealment" occurs when a party has new information and knows that the new information is inconsistent with a prior response, yet does not amend the original response.[78]

Considering the potentially fatal effect on the plaintiff's case of suppressing post-response information, it is not surprising that the courts have imposed severe sanctions for violations of this rule. Sanctions have included default judgment, dismissal, exclusion of the subject evidence,[79] and the grant of a new trial.[80]

---

[75] *See, e.g.*, Perkinson v. Gilbert/Robinson, Inc., 821 F.2d 686, 687, 689 (D.C. Cir. 1987); Voegeli v. Lewis, 568 F.2d 89, 96 (8th Cir. 1977); Barnes v. St. Francis Hosp. & Sch. of Nursing, Inc., 507 P.2d 288, 294 (Kan. 1973); Foster v. Cunningham, 825 S.W.2d 806, 808 (Tex. Ct. App. 1992).

[76] Williams v. Washington Hosp. Ctr., 601 A.2d 28, 34 (D.C. 1991); Weiner v. Kneller, 557 A.2d 1306, 1309 (D.C. 1989).

[77] Former FED. R. CIV. P. 26(e)(2)(B).

[78] *See* Petroleum Ins. Agency v. Hartford Accident & Indem. Co., 106 F.R.D. 59, 67–68 (D. Mass. 1985); 8 WRIGHT & MILLER, *supra* note 2, § 2049, at 323.

[79] Bradley v. United States, 866 F.2d 120, 127 (5th Cir. 1989); E.J. Stewart, Inc. v. Aitken Prods., Inc., 607 F. Supp. 883, 846 (E.D. Pa.), *aff'd per curiam*, 779 F.2d 42 (3d Cir. 1985); Weiner v. Kneller, 557 A.2d 1306, 1309 (D.C. 1989); Bell v. Jones, 523 A.2d 982, 990 n.11 (D.C. 1986); Corley v. BP Oil Corp., 402 A.2d 1258, 1261 (D.C. 1979); *see also* Weiss v. Chrysler Motors Corp., 515 F.2d 449 (2d Cir. 1975).

[80] Bradley v. United States, 866 F.2d 120, 127 (5th Cir. 1989); Voegeli v. Lewis, 568 F.2d 89, 96 (8th Cir. 1977); Williams v. Washington Hosp. Ctr., 601 A.2d 28, 34 (D.C. 1991).

Lawyers as well as parties have a strict duty to honor the continuing obligation imposed by rule 26(e). This duty arises out of the relationship among rule 26(e), rule 26(g), rule 11, and rule 37. Both rule 26(g) and rule 11 were amended in 1983 as a part of an overall effort to curb discovery abuse by expressly requiring sanctions. The amendments substituted an objective standard of reasonable care for the former subjective good-faith standard.[81] Rule 26(g) requires a litigant or his attorney to sign every request for, response to, or objection to discovery. Under the rule, this signature certifies that the signer has read the response or objection and, to the best of his or her knowledge, information, and belief, after reasonable inquiry, it is not interposed for any improper purpose, such as to harass or cause unnecessary delay or needless increase in the cost of litigation.

Although the attorney's signature does not certify the truthfulness of the client's response, it does certify that the attorney has made an effort to ensure that the client provided all available information so that the response is as complete as possible and complies with the spirit of the discovery rules.[82] Clearly rule 26(g) is intended to counter delay, evasion, suppression, and other abuses by requiring the attorney to "stop and think about the legitimacy" of a discovery response or objection.[83]

One group of commentators described the connection between rule 26(g) and the duty to supplement discovery responses as follows:

> [It] must be read in conjunction with rule 26(e), which imposes a continuing obligation on attorneys to amend a response if the response is subsequently rendered or discovered to be inaccurate.
>
> * * *
>
> Thus, rule 26(e) read together with rule 26(g) indicates that an attorney who fails to supplement responses is subject to 26(g) sanctions. Considering the nature of discovery and the long-standing obligation of attorneys to supplement responses, 26(g) is logically extended to those continuing obligations.
>
> * * *
>
> Although rule 11 has recently received the most literary and judicial attention, rule 26(g) may emerge as the greater deterrent. Moreover, rule 26(e) appears to be expanding the scope of rules 11 and 26(g). In the wake of the 1983 amendments, courts appear to be imposing not only a more stringent duty to use discovery properly, but a continuing duty to do so.[84]

In at least two situations typical of defective products litigation, the rule 26(e) obligation requires the defendant to supplement its original responses.

---

[81] See chapter 3, section II.C.

[82] FED. R. CIV. P. 26(g) 1983 advisory committee's note.

[83] George et al., *supra* note 23, at 33.

[84] *In re* Yagman, 796 F.2d 1165, 1187 (9th Cir. 1986).

- After making its initial discovery response, the defendant conducts a comprehensive, company-wide search to acquire and index all relevant documents pertaining to the defect involved. It is increasingly common for the company's legal counsel to participate in the corporate sweep for relevant documents.

- After making its initial discovery response, the defendant engages in such activities as tests, additional studies, or simply a reanalysis of extant data that produces relevant information pertaining to the defect.[85] Corporate counsel, again, are more likely than in the past to participate in conducting such activities.

At the very least, a party's continuing obligation to supplement its discovery responses should have the effect of suspending the company's so-called "document retention" program to save from destruction any document potentially relevant to the pending litigation.[86]

Three cases clearly illustrate that the courts will indeed give rule 26(e) an expansive interpretation when applied to post-response tests which are inconsistent with facts previously asserted in discovery responses. In *Board of Directors, Water's Edge, Condominium Unit Owners' Ass'n v. Anden Group*,[87] the court held that even supplementing prior responses might not be adequate when a party is faced with adverse test results: The party might also be required to admit a previously disputed fact.

That action involved a claim for defective plywood used in the construction of a roof. The seller employed experts to test the plywood and determine the safety of the roof. The expert's report indicated that the roof had deteriorated to the point that it was unsafe. The seller supplemented its answers to reflect the adverse test results but failed to admit that the roof needed to be replaced. In imposing rule 37 sanctions, the court rejected the seller's contention that its supplemental answer was the legal equivalent of an admission.

The plaintiffs in *Chemical Engineering v. Essef Industries*[88] charged that the defendant had infringed the plaintiff's patent. The question of Essef's infringement turned on whether the defendant's water purifier, like the plaintiff's device, raised the pH of treated water. The plaintiff failed to supplement its discovery responses after its own tests demonstrated that the defendant's device did not raise the pH. The appellate court held that the plaintiff's failure to supplement its answer justified the sanction of awarding the defendant fees and expenses. The court noted that the "notion that [the plaintiff] was free to refuse to admit the truth because the truth might have defeated

---

[85] Concerning the duty to disclose adverse results of litigation testing both in the present and future litigation involving the same or similar defects, see appendix 1.

[86] See chapter 7, section II.B.

[87] 136 F.R.D. 100, 109 (E.D. Va. 1991).

[88] 795 F.2d 1565 (Fed. Cir. 1986).

its lawsuit is contrary to the duty of candor owed to the court."[89] The court observed that "the presence of a legal dispute does not obviate a party's responsibility to admit the truth of the matter which the party knows to be true in order to avoid forcing the other party to prove the truth of the matter."[90]

Loctite Corp. v. Fel-Pro Inc.[91] also involved a patent infringement claim. The plaintiff's laboratory supervisor reanalyzed his data and concluded that the defendant had probably not infringed the company's patent. The court held that under these circumstances the company had a duty under rule 26(e) to provide the defendant with the newly acquired information. The court's decision to award rule 37 sanctions was based in part on the plaintiff's failure to supplement its discovery responses.

These three cases are consistent with the judicial recognition that rule 26(e) implies a continuing obligation to supplement responses if "in retrospect there exists other information relevant" to the issues raised in the discovery request.[92]

Post-accident testing conducted in conjunction with the adoption of a subsequent remedial measure in particular should fall under rule 26(e). Not only are such tests normally discoverable,[93] the majority of courts have held that they are indeed admissible in evidence.[94]

The language of the recently amended rule 26(e)[95] strengthens the view that the adverse results of post-response tests or studies must be disclosed. Rule 26(e) requires a party to supplement any disclosure or response that the party learns "is

---

[89] *Id.* at 1575 n.11.

[90] *Id.* at 1575.

[91] 94 F.R.D. 1 (N.D. Ill. 1980), *aff'd in part, remanded in part,* 667 F.2d 577 (7th Cir. 1981).

[92] *See* Chubb Integrated Sys. v. National Bank, 103 F.R.D. 52, 61 (D.D.C. 1984).

[93] Lindberger v. General Motors Corp., 56 F.R.D. 433, 434 (W.D. Wis. 1972); Baker v. Procter & Gamble Co., 17 Fed. R. Serv. (Callaghan) 460, 461 (S.D.N.Y. 1952); Harmon v. Ford Motor Co., 453 N.Y.S.2d 475, 476 (App. Div. 1982); *see* AMERICAN LAW OF PRODUCTS LIABILITY 3D, *supra* note 2, §§ 53:37–53:39.

[94] Rocky Mountain Helicopters, Inc. v. Bell Helicopters Textron, 805 F.2d 907, 918 (10th Cir. 1986) ("It would strain the spirit of the remedial measure prohibition of Rule 407 to extend its shield to evidence contained in post-event tests or reports." Court distinguishes "tests" conducted to discover what might have gone wrong from "remedial measures" taken to remedy flaws or failures indicated by the tests); Rozier v. Ford Motor Co., 573 F.2d 1332, 1343 (5th Cir. 1978); Fasanaro v. Mooney Aircraft Corp., 687 F. Supp. 482, 486–87 (N.D. Cal. 1988); Westmoreland v. CBS Inc., 601 F. Supp. 66, 67–68 (S.D.N.Y. 1984) (analogizing to use of internal and governmental accident investigation reports, court found post-accident test reports "one of the best and most accurate sources of evidence and information"); *cf.* Benitez-Allende v. Alcan Aluminio Do Brasil, S.A., 857 F.2d 26, 33 (1st Cir. 1988), *cert. denied,* 489 U.S. 1018 (1989).

[95] The recent amendments are discussed in chapter 3, section III.

incomplete or incorrect." Further, amended rule 37(c)(1) provides that if a party unjustifiably fails to disclose information required by rules 26(a) or 26(e)(1), it may not—unless the failure is harmless—be permitted to use as evidence any witness or information not disclosed.

The rule 26(e) supplementation requirement does not permit a party to change a response merely to submit a more favorable answer. The discovery rules do not provide the parties with any authority to unilaterally amend a previous answer; rather, the discovery rules "seem to require a party to obtain a court order permitting such amendment, which then would require the party to present convincing reasons to the judge."[96]

IV. BURDEN ON PARTY RESISTING DISCOVERY

The rules contemplate voluntary, full disclosure of requested information. Thus, the party resisting discovery has the burden to show why a discovery request is improper.[97] This has been described as a "heavy burden."[98] Whether the objection is heard in the context of the plaintiff's motion to compel or the defendant's motion for a protective order under rule 26(c),[99] the defendant must justify its objection.[100]

The rules specifically demand that the party resisting discovery state its reasons for each objection.[101] This has been interpreted as requiring a specific objection; the defendant must show specifically how each objection applies to the discovery

---

[96] HAYDOCK & HERR, supra note 2, § 4.6.9, at 371.

[97] See DISCOVERY PROCEEDINGS IN FEDERAL COURT, supra note 2, § 6.24, § 7.17, at 441 n.107; HAYDOCK & HERR, supra note 2, § 4.5.3, at 357 n.34, § 5.12; 4A MOORE ET AL., supra note 2, ¶ 33.27, at 33–165, ¶34.05[3], at 34–37 n.3; 8 WRIGHT & MILLER, supra note 2, § 2173, at 542–43 n.64, § 2214, at 644 n.34, § 2263, at 737 n.57.

[98] Blankenship v. Hearst Corp., 519 F.2d 418, 429 (9th Cir. 1975).

[99] 8 WRIGHT & MILLER, supra note 2, § 2214, at 644 n.34; see also 8 WRIGHT & MILLER, supra note 2, § 2176, at 557–58 n.7.

[100] *Interrogatories*: DISCOVERY PROCEEDINGS IN FEDERAL COURT, supra note 2, § 6.24; HAYDOCK & HERR, supra note 2, § 4.5.3; 8 WRIGHT & MILLER, supra note 2, § 2173, at 542–44 nn.64–65. *Requests for Production*: AMERICAN LAW OF PRODUCTS LIABILITY 3D, supra note 2, §53:64; DISCOVERY PROCEEDINGS IN FEDERAL COURT, supra note 2, § 7.15; 4A MOORE ET AL., supra note 2, ¶ 34.05[2]; 8 WRIGHT & MILLER, supra note 2, § 2214, at 644 n.34. *Requests for Admission*: HAYDOCK & HERR, supra note 2, § 7.10, at 464–65; 4A MOORE ET AL., supra note 2, ¶¶36.03[7], 36.06; 8 WRIGHT & MILLER, supra note 2, § 2263, at 737 n.57.

[101] *Interrogatories:* "unless it is objected to, in which event the reasons for objection shall be stated" FED. R. CIV. P. 33(a). *Requests for Production*: "unless the request is objected to, in which event the reasons for objection shall be stated" FED. R. CIV. P. 34(b). *Requests for Admission*: "set forth in detail the reasons why the answering party cannot truthfully admit or deny the matter. . . . Unless the court determines that an objection is justified, it shall order that an answer be served." FED. R. CIV. P. 36(a).

request.[102] The defendant's burden embraces the duty to show specific facts or persuasive legal argument to sustain the validity of the objection.[103] Broadly stated objections using language too general to warrant protection[104] may result in a waiver of the defendant's right to object on any ground.[105]

The 1993 amendment to rule 33 expressly provides "All grounds for an objection to an interrogatory *shall be stated with specificity*" and further that "*any ground not stated in a timely objection is waived* unless the failure to object is excused by the court for good cause shown."[106]

V. SPECIFIC OBJECTIONS

A. Relevance Objection

Relevance—or more precisely, the lack of relevance—is usually the basis of a defendant's challenge to the scope of discovery. The defendant's primary tactic is to attempt to restrict the scope of relevance, but courts and legal scholars alike have uniformly rejected the notion that the responding party can restrict the scope of relevance to its own subjective view of the facts or its own adversarial theory of the case.[107] The

---

[102] Wauchop v. Domino's Pizza, Inc., 138 F.R.D. 539, 543–44 (N.D. Ind. 1991); Schaap v. Executive Indus., 130 F.R.D. 384, 386 (N.D. Ill. 1990); Roesberg v. Johns-Manville Corp., 85 F.R.D. 292, 296–97 (E.D. Pa. 1980); Rupp v. Vock & Weiderhold, Inc., 52 F.R.D. 111, 112 (N.D. Ohio 1971). *See generally Interrogatories*: DISCOVERY PROCEEDINGS IN FEDERAL COURT, *supra* note 2, § 6.20; HAYDOCK & HERR, *supra* note 2, §§ 4.5.1–4.5.3; 4A MOORE ET AL., *supra* note 2, ¶33.27, at 33–160 to –169; 8 WRIGHT & MILLER, *supra* note 2, § 2173, at 542 n.63. *Requests for Production*: DISCOVERY PROCEEDINGS IN FEDERAL COURT, *supra* note 2, § 7.15 HAYDOCK & HERR, *supra* note 2, § 5.12; 8 WRIGHT & MILLER, *supra* note 2, § 2213, at 641 n.18. *Requests for Admission*, DISCOVERY PROCEEDINGS IN FEDERAL COURT, *supra* note 2, § 9.12; HAYDOCK & HERR, *supra* note 2, § 7.9; 8 WRIGHT & MILLER, *supra* note 2, § 2263, at 737 n.57.

[103] *See* HAYDOCK & HERR, *supra* note 2, § 4.5.3, at 357 n.27.

[104] McLeod, Alexander, Powel & Apffel, P.C. v. Quarles, 894 F.2d 1482, 1485 (5th Cir. 1990); Wauchop v. Domino's Pizza, Inc., 138 F.R.D. 538, 544 (N.D. Ind. 1991); Roesberg v. Johns-Manville Corp., 85 F.R.D. 292, 296–97 (E.D. Pa. 1980); White v. Beloginis, 53 F.R.D. 480, 481 (S.D.N.Y. 1971); *see* 4A MOORE ET AL., *supra* note 2, ¶ 33.27, at 33–161 to –165.

[105] Josephs v. Harris Corp., 677 F.2d 985, 992 (3d Cir. 1982); Casson Constr. Co. v. Armco Steel Corp., 91 F.R.D. 376, 379 (D. Kan. 1980); *In re* Folding Carton Antitrust Litig., 83 F.R.D. 260, 264 (N.D. Ill. 1979).

[106] FED. R. CIV. P. 33(b)(4), 1993 amendment (emphasis added). *See* advisory committee's note to the 1993 amendment.

[107] Adolph Coors Co. v. Movement Against Racism, 777 F.2d 1538, 1543 (11th Cir. 1985) (noting that appellant "made clear that they would divulge only that information they deemed discoverable and no more"); Baine v. General Motors Corp., 141 F.R.D. 328, 330 (M.D. Ala. 1991) (noting that General Motors had unilaterally limited its response to a particular year and model automobile, and holding that "[t]his court cannot allow General Motors to define the parameters and content of discovery in this case"); Smith v. Logansport Community Sch.

determination of relevance in a products liability case is properly based on an objective analysis of the defect involved.[108]

With regard to interrogatories, "[i]t is inappropriate for a party to decide for himself that an interrogatory is improper. It is his responsibility either to answer the interrogatory or to object."[109] As for document requests, a response that "all relevant documents responsive to the request have been produced" is likewise improper.

As with other objections, the defendant must provide the court with specific factual allegations supporting its relevance objection.[110] The party resisting discovery on the grounds of relevance has the burden of showing that the information sought is "clearly irrelevant"[111] or "has no possible bearing upon the subject matter."[112]

B. Burden Objection

The issue of relevance bears directly on the question of whether a discovery request is burdensome.[113] Indeed, the burden ruling is ordinarily made after the court's determination of the scope of relevance.[114]

Rule 26(b)(1) was amended in 1983 and again in 1993 to encourage judges to be more aggressive in identifying and discouraging truly burdensome discovery

---

Corp., 139 F.R.D. 637, 648 (N.D. Ind. 1991) (responding party may object to or seek protective order regarding request deemed overly broad, but may not withhold requested documents based on *ex parte* determination of relevance); Stengel v. Kawasaki Heavy Indus., 116 F.R.D. 263, 264 (N.D. Tex. 1987); Sellon v. Smith, 112 F.R.D. 9, 13 (D. Del. 1986); Sellers v. General Motors Corp., 40 Fed. R. Serv. 2d (Callaghan) 590 (E.D. Pa. 1984); Bowman v. General Motor Corp., 64 F.R.D. 62, 68 (E.D. Pa. 1974) ("[t]o exclude such discovery would be to permit the defendant alone to determine whether such information is relevant"); United States v. 30 Jars of "Ahead Hair Restorer for New Hair Growth," 43 F.R.D. 181, 189 (D. Del. 1967); United States v. 216 Bottles of "Sudden Change," 36 F.R.D. 695, 700 (E.D.N.Y. 1965); United Nuclear Corp. v. General Atomic Co., 629 P.2d 231, 287 (N.M. 1980), *cert. denied*, 451 U.S. 901, *reh'g denied*, 452 U.S. 932 (1981); Gammon v. Clark Equip. Co., 686 P.2d 1102, 1107 (Wash. Ct. App. 1984), *aff'd en banc*, 707 P.2d 685 (Wash. 1985); *see also* HAYDOCK & HERR, *supra* note 2, §4.5.2, at 356 n.18; 8 WRIGHT & MILLER, *supra* note 2, § 2173, at 544.

[108] See chapter 1, section II.B.1.

[109] 8 WRIGHT & MILLER, *supra* note 2, § 2173, at 544. This duty has been clarified and strengthened by the 1993 amendments to rule 33(d)(1) and 34(b). Amendments to the Federal Rules of Civil Procedure and Forms, approved by the United States Supreme Court (Apr. 22, 1993), *reprinted in* 146 F.R.D. 401 (1994).

[110] *See, e.g.*, Roesberg v. Johns-Manville Corp., 85 F.R.D. 292, 296–97 (E.D. Pa. 1980).

[111] Independent Prods. Corp. v. Loew's, Inc., 22 F.R.D. 266, 271 (S.D.N.Y. 1958).

[112] La Chemise LaCoste v. Alligator Co., Inc., 60 F.R.D. 164, 171 (D. Del. 1973); *see* 8 WRIGHT & MILLER, *supra* note 2, § 2008, at 46 n.22; see chapter 1, section II.B.

[113] *See, e.g.*, Pilling v. General Motors Corp., 45 F.R.D. 366, 369 (D. Utah 1968).

[114] 4 MOORE ET AL., *supra* note 2, ¶ 26.26, at 26–107 n.39, ¶26.69, at 26–431.

requests. The amendment provided that the extent of discovery shall be limited if the court determines the following:

> (i) the discovery sought is unreasonably cumulative or duplicative, or is obtainable from some other source that is more convenient, less burdensome, or less expensive;[115] (ii) the party seeking discovery has had ample opportunity by discovery in the action to obtain the information sought;[116] or (iii) the burden or expense of the proposed discovery outweighs its likely benefit, taking into account the needs of the case, the amount in controversy, the parties' resources, the importance of the issues at stake in the litigation, and the importance of the proposed discovery in resolving the issues.[117]

A simple general statement that the request is "burdensome," however, is neither an answer nor an objection and may constitute a waiver of the objection.[118] The party resisting discovery on this ground must aver specific facts in support of every objection.[119]

Standing alone, the fact that the defendant will be put to some trouble and expense in the process of responding to a discovery request is not sufficient to support a burden objection.[120] Only an effort that would be "*unduly* burdensome and oppres-

---

[115] The "other sources" contemplated by the 1983 amendment include "public records, government or industry publications, reference works, Freedom of Information Act requests for government records, or informal interviews of knowledgeable persons." WILLIAM W. SCHWARZER & LYNN H. PASAHOW, CIVIL DISCOVERY: A GUIDE TO EFFICIENT PRACTICE 8 (1988 & Supp. 1989).

[116] One principal objective of this language is to discourage attorneys from propounding interrogatories seeking information that they have already obtained in a deposition. Other than this application the "ample opportunity" for discovery language must, in a defective products case, be construed in the context of (1) the fact that the defendant has exclusive possession of critical information and (2) the adequacy of the defendant's response to the plaintiff's discovery request.

[117] The grounds specifically enumerated in this language reflect the practice that existed in many courts prior to the adoption of the 1983 amendment. *See* FED. R. CIV. P. 26(b)(1) 1983 advisory committee's note; chapter 3, sections II.C, III.

[118] *See, e.g.*, Josephs v. Harris Corp., 677 F.2d 985, 992 (3d Cir. 1982); Altech Indus. v. Al Tech Specialty Steel Corp., 528 F. Supp. 521, 523–24 (D. Del. 1981); *In re* Folding Carton Antitrust Litig., 83 F.R.D. 260, 264 (N.D. Ill. 1979). *See generally* 23 AM. JUR., *supra* note 20, §§ 231, 259; 4 MOORE ET AL., *supra* note 2, ¶ 26.56[1], at 26–108, ¶ 26.69, at 26–447.

[119] *See, e.g.*, Martin v. Easton Publishing Co., 85 F.R.D. 312, 316 (E.D. Pa. 1980); Sherman Park Community Ass'n v. Wauwatusa Realty Co., 486 F. Supp. 838, 845 (E.D. Wis. 1980); Flood v. Margis, 64 F.R.D. 59, 61 (E.D. Wis. 1974); Anderson v. United Air Lines, Inc., 49 F.R.D. 144, 147 (S.D.N.Y. 1969). *See generally* DISCOVERY PROCEEDINGS IN FEDERAL COURT, *supra* note 2, § 6.25.

[120] *See* DISCOVERY PROCEEDINGS IN FEDERAL COURT, *supra* note 2, § 6.25, at 388 n.150.

sive"[121] or "*egregiously* burdensome or oppressive"[122] would justify limiting discovery.

> The mere fact that compliance with an inspection order will cause great labor and expense or even considerable hardship and possibility of injury to the business of the party from whom discovery is sought does not of itself require denial of the motion.[123]

Thus, the defendant should be required to respond unless it can persuade the court that the hardship is unreasonable when balanced against the plaintiff's need for the information being sought.[124]

Since 1970, rule 33 has provided the "business records option" of responding to discovery;[125] accordingly, courts have tended to reject undue burden objections in cases where the responding party can produce its business records. This option shifts some of the burden of finding information in company records to the party seeking discovery.[126]

C. Vagueness Objection

In keeping with the general rule of liberal interpretation, the courts have held that considerable latitude, rather than exactness of definition, is to be permitted in the form of inquiry. With regard to interrogatories, rather general language has been permitted so long as the interrogatory gives the other party a reasonably clear indication of the information to be included in its answer.[127]

Similarly, with respect to requests for production:

---

[121] *See* Wirtz v. Capitol Air Serv., Inc., 42 F.R.D. 641, 643 (D. Kan. 1967) (emphasis added). *See generally* 8 WRIGHT & MILLER, *supra* note 2, § 2214, at 647–48 nn.43–44.

[122] Roesberg v. Johns-Manville Corp., 85 F.R.D. 292, 297 (E.D. Pa. 1980) (emphasis added).

[123] 8 WRIGHT & MILLER, *supra* note 2, § 2214, at 647.

[124] *See* Josephs v. Harris Corp., 677 F.2d 985 (3d Cir. 1982); Rich v. Martin Marietta Corp., 522 F.2d 333, 343 (10th Cir. 1975); Hoffman v. United Telecommunications, Inc., 117 F.R.D. 436, 438 (D. Kan. 1987); Federal Deposit Ins. Corp. v. Mercantile Nat'l Bank, 84 F.R.D. 345, 348 (N.D. Ill. 1979); King v. Georgia Power Co., 50 F.R.D. 134, 136–37 (N.D. Ga. 1970); Struthers Scientific & Int'l Corp. v. General Foods Corp., 45 F.R.D. 375, 379 (S.D. Tex. 1968); Trabon Eng'g Corp. v. Eaton Mfg. Co., 37 F.R.D. 51, 59 (N.D. Ohio 1964); Zatko v. Rogers Mfg. Co., 37 F.R.D. 29, 31–32 (N.D. Ohio 1964). *See generally* 23 AM. JUR., *supra* note 20, §§ 231–233, 259; KIELY, *supra* note 24, § 7.5; 8 WRIGHT & MILLER, *supra* note 2, § 2174, at 548.

[125] See chapter 6, section II.

[126] *See* Burns v. Thiokol Chem. Corp., 483 F.2d 300, 307 (5th Cir. 1973); *In re* Folding Carton Antitrust Litig., 83 F.R.D. 260, 265–66 (N.D. Ill. 1979); Concept Indus. v. Carpet Factory, Inc., 59 F.R.D. 546, 548–49 (E.D. Wis. 1973).

[127] 8 WRIGHT & MILLER, *supra* note 2, § 2168, at 515; *see also* AMERICAN LAW OF PRODUCTS LIABILITY 3D, *supra* note 2, §§ 53:58–53:59; DISCOVERY PROCEEDINGS IN FEDERAL COURT, *supra* note 2, § 6.7; HAYDOCK & HERR, *supra* note 2, § 4.4.1; 4A MOORE ET AL., *supra* note 2, ¶ 33.08.

> Even a generalized designation should be sufficient when the party seeking discovery cannot give a more particular description and the party from whom discovery is sought will have no difficulty in understanding what is wanted.
>
> * * *
>
> The goal is that the designation be sufficient to apprise a man of ordinary intelligence what documents are required and that the court be able to ascertain whether the requested documents have been produced.[128]

Finally, with regard to requests for admission, "[e]ach request for an admission should be phrased simply and directly so that it can be admitted or denied without explanation."[129]

Defendants in products liability cases frequently object on the ground that the language of the request is vague and ambiguous even when the company officials or counsel have (or should have) a perfectly clear understanding of what the plaintiff is seeking. As a matter of law, the vagueness objection is not available where the defendant truly understands the meaning of the plaintiff's request:[130] "If a party from whom discovery is requested in fact knows what documents and things are sought, he will be hard put to respond to the request by saying that the designation is insufficient."[131] In any event, the defendant should be required to specify precisely which language it claims is vague, and to either seek further definition or apply an everyday layman's definition.[132]

A carefully drafted *Table of Definitions* may be effective in overcoming this objection. The judicious use of instructions may also be advisable.[133] Defining and clarifying the various terms contained in the actual request for information may be helpful and, more importantly, may eliminate the trap that lies between language that is either too precise (and subject to overly narrow interpretation) or too broad. Where terms are defined, any objection that the request is vague becomes less credible. This

---

[128] 8 WRIGHT & MILLER, *supra* note 2, § 2211, at 629, 631; *see also* AMERICAN LAW OF PRODUCTS LIABILITY 3D, *supra* note 2, § 53:65; DISCOVERY PROCEEDINGS IN FEDERAL COURT, *supra* note 2, §§ 7.11–7.12; HAYDOCK & HERR, *supra* note 2, § 5.8; 4A MOORE ET AL., *supra* note 2, ¶34.07.

[129] 8 WRIGHT & MILLER, *supra* note 2, § 2258, at 721–22. *See generally* DISCOVERY PROCEEDINGS IN FEDERAL COURT, *supra* note 2, § 9.4; HAYDOCK & HERR, *supra* note 2, § 7.3; 4A MOORE ET AL., *supra* note 2, ¶¶ 36.03[4], 36.05[2].

[130] Evtush v. Hudson Bus Transp. Co., 81 A.2d 6, 8–9 (N.J. 1951).

[131] 8 WRIGHT & MILLER, *supra* note 2, § 2211, at 634.

[132] Roesberg v. Johns-Manville Corp., 85 F.R.D. 292, 298, 302 (E.D. Pa. 1980); Mallinckrodt Chem. Works v. Goldman, Sachs & Co., 58 F.R.D. 348, 354 (S.D.N.Y. 1973). *See generally* 23 AM. JUR., *supra* note 20, § 234; DISCOVERY PROCEEDINGS IN FEDERAL COURT, *supra* note 2, § 6.30; HAYDOCK & HERR, *supra* note 2, § 5.12, at 397 n.15; KIELY, *supra* note 24, § 7.11.

[133] *See* DOMBROFF, *supra* note 30, § 5.05; HAYDOCK & HERR, *supra* note 2, § 4.3.2, § 5.9, at 391–92; EDWARD J. IMWINKELRIED & THEODORE Y. BLUMOFF, PRETRIAL DISCOVERY: STRATEGY & TACTICS §§ 7:07–7:08 (1986 & Supp. 1992); KIELY, *supra* note 24, §§ 5.9, 5.13–5.14.

procedure has the added benefit of avoiding needless repetition within the body of the formal request.[134]

VI. CONCLUSION

The legal standards for discovery responses have been set high by the courts and the rule framers. It can be said that our system, despite its adversary character, requires the discovery respondent to help the requesting party make its case. More accurately, it holds both parties responsible for emergence of the truth.

---

[134] *See, e.g.,* Harlem River Consumers Coop. v. Associated Grocers, Inc., 64 F.R.D. 459, 465 (S.D.N.Y. 1974); Diversified Prods. Corp. v. Sports Ctr. Co., 42 F.R.D. 3 (E.D. Md. 1967). *See generally* SCOTT BALDWIN ET AL., THE PREPARATION OF A PRODUCT LIABILITY CASE § 7.6 (2d ed. 1993); DOMBROFF, *supra* note 30, § 5.05; HAYDOCK & HERR, *supra* note 2, § 4.3.3; IMWINKELRIED & BLUMOFF, *supra* note 133, § 7.09; 8 WRIGHT & MILLER, *supra* note 2, § 2168, at 516.

CHAPTER THREE

POLICY CHOICES REPRESENTED BY THE FEDERAL RULES

At the 1982 National Conference on Discovery Reform,[1] Professor John Reed of the University of Michigan School of Law compared discovery abusers with dinosaurs, which he described as "enormous, powerful lizards that had no match, no need to fear any other form of life."[2] Professor Reed pointed out that the dinosaurs became extinct despite the lack of a mortal adversary. "Nobody killed the dinosaurs," he said. "The climate changed and they all died."[3]

Indeed abusive discovery behavior can take on a monstrous life of its own. For reasons traceable perhaps to our law schools, our law firms, the economics of law practice, or simple adversary zeal, civil litigation has long since ceased to be characterized by civility.[4] Nearly every commentator on discovery abuse has looked to the litigation climate established by the Federal Rules of Civil Procedure to identify potential solutions. The difficult task facing rule reformers is to change the climate so as to eradicate pernicious species of discovery conduct and encourage conduct positively directed toward seeking truth and justice.

Adjusting the rules in a manner that adversely impacts only undesirable con-

---

[1] The conference was sponsored by the American Bar Association's Section of Litigation as a forum to discuss the work of its Special Committee for the Study of Discovery Abuse. The proceedings are reported in the Winter 1982 issue of *The Review of Litigation* published by the University of Texas School of Law.

[2] John W. Reed, *Light-Hearted Thoughts About Discovery Reform*, 3 REV. LITIG. 215, 220–21 (1982).

[3] *Id.* at 221.

[4] The decline of professional courtesy among civil litigation adversaries, and the institutional causes for erosion of a professional ethic, are addressed in recent articles by a United States District Court Judge, Marvin E. Aspen, *From the Bench: Doing Something About Civility in Litigation*, LITIG., Winter 1992, at 3, and by the Chair of the American Bar Association's Section of Litigation, Paul J. Bschorr, *Beyond the Bottom Line*, LITIG., Fall 1990, at 1.

duct is not an easy task. Rules intended to promote one worthy objective frequently adversely affect another. For instance, rule 11, requiring attorney certification of pleadings, has been lauded by some as a powerful weapon against litigation abuse,[5] yet it has also been condemned by others because of its potential for misuse by judges who would deny worthy plaintiffs access to justice.[6]

The federal rules governing discovery conduct reflect policy choices between conflicting values. Rules governing discovery procedure can be used to emphasize certain policies over other important, yet conflicting, policies. Section I of this chapter describes six classic areas of conflict. Section II examines the history of rule changes prior to 1993, and section III analyzes the 1993 amendments to the Federal Rules of Civil Procedure in light of these conflicting policies.

I. USE OF THE RULES TO BALANCE CONFLICTING VALUES

As adopted in 1937, the federal discovery rules made some distinct choices in favor of certain policies. These policy choices can be described in terms of areas of conflicting values or viewpoints, as presented in this section. In the years since 1937, while the policies have been debated, rule reformers have resisted making dramatic shifts away from the initial policy choices.

A. Utility of Discovery: Full Disclosure vs. Cost Savings

The most basic debate in fashioning discovery rules involves weighing the value of discovery against its costs. The discovery procedures authorized by the rules represent a clear endorsement of the utility of discovery despite its added burdens. Certainly, greater openness and broader disclosure facilitate the search for truth. Discovery procedures "make a trial less a game of blindman's buff and more a fair contest with the basic issues and facts disclosed to the fullest practicable extent."[7] Many rule reformers in the 1970s and 1980s, however, emphasized the conflicting concern that devoting too much time and effort to the disclosure process was inefficient and costly. They argued that discovery practice was being used tactically by the discovering party to increase costs and delay or to obtain information for commercial

---

[5] *See, e.g.*, Judith L. Maute, *Sporting Theory of Justice: Taming Adversary Zeal with a Logical Sanctions Doctrine*, 20 CONN. L. REV. 7, 23 (1987) ("The 1983 amendments [to rule 11] are a serious effort to reform the adversary culture, taming excessive adversary zeal that secures illegal advantage from an opponent and that threatens institutional values in efficient and acceptable outcomes.") *Id.* at 28. Rule 11 is discussed in section III, *infra*.

[6] *See, e.g.*, Arthur B. LaFrance, *Federal Rule 11 and Public Interest Litigation*, 22 VAL. U. L. REV. 331, 339–43 (1988) ("Rule 11 is antithetical to public interest litigation. The principles advanced by public interest litigation invite lawyers to right wrongs and change the world. Rule 11, to oversimplify, commands that we do so as reasonable people, without disturbing the *status quo ante*.") *Id.* at 333. Rule 11 has been modified by the 1993 amendments to the Federal Rules of Civil Procedure, as discussed later in this chapter.

[7] United States v. Procter & Gamble Co., 356 U.S. 677, 682–83 (1958). For discussion of the history of discovery under the federal rules, see section II, *infra*.

purposes rather than to serve the overriding goal of "the just, speedy, and inexpensive determination of every action."[8] While overuse and misuse of discovery requests may be serious problems in some types of litigation, in other types, including products liability, many litigators, judges, and commentators believe that the goal of full access to relevant information has not yet been achieved. The rules as applied by some courts perpetuate an atmosphere that allows parties to evade discovery and prevent critical information from surfacing.

As observed recently by Magistrate Judge Paul Greene in his assessment of the 1993 amendments to rule 26 of the Federal Rules of Civil Procedure, "[t]he zenith of the extensive latitude of discovery was reached in 1970 when requests for production of documents under rule 34 were authorized as a matter of normal practice rather than upon a demonstration of good cause which had previously been required."[9] The 1983 amendments tend to push the pendulum in the opposite direction, restricting the exchange of information, with the stated goal of reducing costs. The twofold danger of this trend is that it will undermine the search for truth and that, in practice, it will not result in significant cost savings. The 1993 amendments seem to cut both ways, requiring broad initial disclosures but limiting follow-up discovery.

B. Concern with Discovery Overuse vs. Concern with Evasion

A second, closely related area of conflict characterizing discovery reform involves the two types of discovery abuse: (1) overuse or misuse in requests and (2) evasion in responses.[10] Those most concerned by overuse are troubled by discovery rules that liberalize discovery, while those most concerned with evasion are concerned by rules that constrict discovery. To some degree, where you stand on these concerns depends on where you sit.

In products liability cases, manufacturer defendants seek to limit access to information, so manufacturing concerns can be expected to support rule changes that limit discovery requests. Plaintiffs, naturally, are more likely to be concerned with evasion because their prospects of winning depend on access to information in the manufacturer's exclusive possession.

This policy conflict is closely related to the full disclosure versus cost savings issue. Rule shifts intended to advance the policy of full disclosure include provisions to counter evasion. In contrast, cost containment efforts historically have focused on curtailing overuse and misuse. This focus on limiting overuse to limit costs oversimplifies the problem. Excess costs are not only to be imputed to overly broad discovery. Delay and evasion can also dramatically increase the costs of litigation, for example, if the party trying to obtain discovery is forced to seek court intervention or to seek

---

[8] FED. R. CIV. P. 1.

[9] Paul W. Greene, *Reassessment of the Lawyers' Discovery Responsibilities: The Early Disclosure Provisions of the Proposed Amendments to Rule 26, Federal Rules of Civil Procedure*, 53 ALA. LAW. 278, 279 (1992); see section II.B of this chapter.

[10] Overuse and avoidance are compared in chapter 4, section II.

needed information from other sources. Moreover, full information exchange early in litigation encourages just and equitable settlements. When discovery evasion frustrates prompt and fair settlements, both inefficiency and injustice result.

C. Counsel as Advocate vs. Counsel as Officer of the Court

Historically, changes in discovery procedures have attempted to reconcile and balance the attorney's dual roles as client advocate and officer of the court. The 1937 adoption of a discovery scheme based on voluntary compliance presupposed that parties and their lawyers would execute their responsibilities to the justice system in good faith. Thus, the discovery rules represented a significant and conscious shift away from the "sporting theory of justice" criticized by Roscoe Pound in his 1906 address, "The Causes of Popular Dissatisfaction with the Administration of Justice."[11] Pound condemned "our American exaggerations of the common law contentious procedure" and its effects on all aspects of litigation:

> It leads the most conscientious judge to feel that he is merely to decide the contest, as counsel present it, according to the rules of the game, not to search independently for truth and justice. It leads counsel to forget that they are officers of the court and to deal with the rules of law and procedure exactly as the professional football coach with the rules of the sport. It leads to exertion to "get error into the record" rather than to dispose of the controversy finally and upon its merits. It turns witnesses, and especially expert witnesses, into partisans pure and simple. It leads to sensational cross-examinations "to affect credit," which have made the witness stand "the slaughter house of reputations." It prevents the trial court from restraining the bullying of witnesses and creates a general dislike, if not fear, of the witness function which impairs the administration of justice. . . . The inquiry is not, What do substantive law and justice require? Instead, the inquiry is, Have the rules of the game been carried out strictly? If any material infraction is discovered, just as the football rules put back the offending team five or ten or fifteen yards, as the case may be, our sporting theory of justice awards new trials, or reverses judgments, or sustains demurrers in the interest of regular play.[12]

While broadened discovery was intended to facilitate the ascension of facts over adversarial tactics, discovery itself provided a new playing field for competitive maneuvering. Critics charge that the adversarial nature of the discovery process actually undermines the search for truth rather than facilitating it. Legal scholars have continued and extended the sports analogy[13] but have disagreed as to whether reform should focus on rewriting the rules of the game or on calling off the competition alto-

---

[11] Roscoe Pound, *The Causes of Popular Dissatisfaction with the Administration of Justice*, 29 REP. A.B.A. 395, 404–06 (1906), reprinted in 35 F.R.D. 273, 281–82 (1964), and in 40 AM. L. REV. 729, 738–39 (1906).

[12] *Id.* (citations omitted).

[13] *See, e.g.*, Marvin E. Frankel, *The Search for Truth: An Umpireal View*, 123 U. PA. L. REV. 1031 (1975); Bradley W. Foster, Comment, *Playing Hardball in Federal Court: Judicial Attempts to Referee Unsportsmanlike Conduct*, 55 J. AIR L. & COM. 223 (1989).

gether. Some commentators would accept the competitive, adversarial approach to discovery but control it through procedural rules and judicial umpires. Others would reject the competitive model during discovery in favor of a less adversarial system, where litigators are motivated at least as much by their responsibilities as officers of the court and by rules of ethical conduct as they are by their zeal to protect their clients' interests.

A good example of the first approach is reflected in University of Oklahoma law professor Judith Maute's 1987 article, *Sporting Theory of Justice: Taming Adversary Zeal with a Logical Sanctions Doctrine*, which applies the social science tool of *game theory* to litigation abuse.[14] Examining the 1983 amendments to the federal rules, Maute concludes that the rules of the game are sufficiently strict to encourage disclosure. Maute contends that with prompt, rational, consistent, predictable, and reasonably final judicial enforcement, sanctions can be brought to bear to "tame excessive zeal."[15]

U.S. District Court Judge William Schwarzer, director of the Federal Judicial Center, favors a less adversarial, more cooperative approach to discovery. He proposes a voluntary disclosure system, where parties are required to automatically identify relevant documents and witnesses and where further discovery is permitted only upon court order.[16] Schwarzer's approach "depends on the attorneys' good faith, and also exposes them to the risk of sanctions."[17] This proposal is partially reflected in the 1993 amendments to the federal rules, discussed below.

The 1993 amendments also partially reflect the views expressed by magistrate judge and former law professor Wayne Brazil.[18] Brazil advocates complete rejection of the sporting approach to discovery, "shifting counsel's principal obligation during the investigation and discovery stage away from partisan pursuit of clients' interests and toward the court."[19] He favors new rules of professional responsibility and civil procedure and a narrowing of the privilege doctrine, so that all counsel are engaged in

---

[14] 20 CONN. L. REV. 7 (1987). Game theory is a mathematical tool used in the social sciences to evaluate logical strategies that optimize a "player's" utility preferences. *See* authorities cited in Maute, *supra* note 5, at 10 n.3, 30–33 nn.92–101. Game theory is also applied to discovery abuse in Note, *Discovery Abuse Under the Federal Rules: Causes and Cures*, 92 YALE L.J. 352 (1982).

[15] Maute, *supra* note 5, at 10.

[16] William W Schwarzer, *Slaying the Monsters of Costs and Delay: Would Disclosure Be More Effective Than Discovery?*, 74 Judicature 178, 180–81 (1991) [hereinafter Schwarzer, *Slaying the Monsters*]; William W Schwarzer, *The Federal Rules, the Adversary Process, and Discovery Reform*, 50 U. PITT. L. REV. 703, 721–23 (1989).

[17] Schwarzer, *Slaying the Monsters*, *supra* note 16, at 181.

[18] *See* Wayne D. Brazil, *The Adversary Character of Civil Discovery: A Critique and Proposals for Change*, 31 VAND. L. REV. 1295 (1978).

[19] *Id.* at 1349.

the mutual development of facts before trial.[20] Counsel would then shift to an adversarial role during trial. Brazil argues that this approach would have the advantages of the adversarial system without the disadvantages:

> The greatest benefits of adversary litigation derive not from competitive efforts to limit and manipulate the flow of information but from dialectical evaluation of the relevant evidence.... [D]ialectics and Darwinism are not identical, and ... the Darwinian character of trial preparation jeopardizes the attainment of dialectical truth at trial.[21]

The *regulated competition* approach is more realistic than the utopian vision advanced by Brazil and Schwarzer.[22] Discovery abuse and misconduct are best controlled by encouraging and enforcing fair play, rather than by attempting to place the parties on the same team. First, where trial will still be a horse race, it is inconceivable that advocates will not "jockey" for position before trial. Second, it is unrealistic to expect attorneys to be impartial in the discovery aspect of pretrial conduct while engaged in highly competitive motions, which frequently turn on the state of the evidence developed by investigation and discovery. Third, the vast majority of cases settle prior to trial, and counsel and parties are well aware that most cases are won or lost at the negotiation table, based on the evidence that surfaces during discovery.

Finally, the adversarial process, despite its limitations, does achieve benefits in the fact-development phase of litigation: A party's advocate can be expected to take a broader and more creative view than its adversary of what is relevant. The advocate's hunches, based on knowledge and experience and pursued through investigation and discovery, frequently lead to the most important evidence of liability.

Litigation incentives should be used to achieve desired discovery practices, much as economic incentives are used to achieve desired behavior in the marketplace. Governments do not enhance economies by urging individuals to make financial decisions based on the public good. While governments insist on lawful conduct, individuals and businesses are expected to act in accordance with their own interests. Thus, the rules of the game are structured so that self-interested actions will promote public policy objectives.[23] In litigation, professionalism and civility will prevail to the extent they are rewarded. Cooperation and fair play will not be the norm where the advantage goes to those who do not play fairly.

---

[20] *See also* Robert E. Sarazen, *An Ethical Approach to Discovery Abuse*, 4 GEO. J. LEGAL ETHICS 459, 473 (1990).

[21] Brazil, *supra* note 18, at 1360.

[22] In fairness, both Brazil and Schwarzer recognize the value of incentives for cooperative discovery behavior and disincentives for abuse. *See* Brazil, *supra* note 18; Schwarzer, *Slaying the Monsters, supra* note 16. Both of their approaches, however, rely on attorneys and parties accepting that their duty to the public good overrides their self-interest during discovery.

[23] For discussion of the purposes of sanctions, see chapter 10, section I.

D. Judicial Intervention vs. Judicial Laissez-Faire

As explained in *Kramer v. Boeing Co.*,[24] the spirit embodied by the rules "is that discovery be self-effectuating, without need to resort to the court."[25] The intent of the rules that discovery be self-effectuating is no longer understood to mean that courts should avoid stepping in to counter discovery avoidance. Rather, as illustrated by *Kramer*, where a manufacturer acts contrary to the spirit of rule 26 so that the plaintiff is required to resort to the court's aid in obtaining information, "it would be unjust to deny plaintiff's motion for sanctions. Such an order would amount to judicial tolerance of grossly unacceptable discovery practices."[26]

The amendments of 1970, 1980, 1983, and 1993 brought more active supervision of the discovery process by the courts.[27] Since 1980 the judiciary, led by the U.S. Supreme Court,[28] has moved away from the *minimal intrusion* model of participation in discovery and has displayed a willingness to intervene in discovery disputes and to sanction parties, as well as their attorneys, for improper discovery conduct.[29]

Commentators disagree as to whether increased judicial intervention does more to deter abuse or to increase contentiousness and adversity.[30] Some of them warn that "sanctions practice" creates unnecessary satellite litigation and additional waste of judicial resources.[31] Maute noted a "virtual explosion" of reported litigation abuse

---

[24] 126 F.R.D. 690, 692 (D. Minn. 1989).

[25] *Id.* (discussing FED. R. CIV. P. 26(a)) (citations omitted).

[26] *Id.* at 697.

[27] *See* Arthur R. Miller, *Confidentiality, Protective Orders, and Public Access to the Courts*, 105 HARV. L. REV. 427, 450–63 (1991).

[28] In National Hockey League v. Metropolitan Hockey Club, Inc., the Supreme Court approved the trial court's dismissal of an action for failure to provide discovery. The Court observed that sanctions serve both a punitive and a deterrent function. 427 U.S. 639, 643, *reh'g denied*, 429 U.S. 874 (1976); *see also* Roadway Express, Inc. v. Piper, 447 U.S. 752, 763 (1980) (recognizing various sanction authorities and their importance).

[29] *Cf.* Charles R. Richey, *Rule 16 Revisited: Reflections for the Benefit of Bench and Bar*, 139 F.R.D. 525 (1992). *See generally* GREGORY P. JOSEPH, SANCTIONS: THE FEDERAL LAW OF LITIGATION ABUSE (1989 & Supp. 1991).

[30] *See, e.g.*, William W. Kilgarlin, *Sanctions for Discovery Abuse: Is the Cure Worse Than the Disease?*, 54 TEX. B.J. 658 (1991); Charles B. Renfrew, *Discovery Sanctions: A Judicial Perspective*, 2 REV. LITIG. 71, 80–87 (1981); William W Schwarzer, *The Federal Rules, the Adversary Process, and Discovery Reform*, 50 U. PITT. L. REV. 703, 711 (1989).

[31] The Advisory Committee on the Civil Rules observed in 1990 that the rule 11 pleadings provision has been used by the courts much more frequently than the rule 26(g) discovery provision. Judicial Conference of the United States Advisory Committee on the Civil Rules, *Call for Written Comments on Rule 11 of the Federal Rules of Civil Procedure and Related Rules, as Amended in 1983*, 131 F.R.D. 344, 345 (1990). One commentator, however, believes "[r]ule 26(g) is a litigation explosion waiting to be triggered." JOSEPH, *supra* note 29, § 40(A), at 467.

cases[32] but suggested that "[i]n time, the higher standards of reasonableness and good faith enforced by court rules, like other areas of law, will be largely self-executing."[33]

E. Prefiling Proof of Liability vs. Proof Obtained by Discovery

The rules also balance the conflicting goals of preventing frivolous lawsuits and of permitting access to justice to plaintiffs who cannot prove their cases without information in the exclusive possession of defendants. As Professor Arthur LaFrance of Lewis and Clark Law School described the situation, "[t]he fact is that lawsuits are often brought on scanty facts for the simple reason that the facts are in the hands of the adverse party."[34]

As initially promulgated, the discovery rules permitted broad discovery to facilitate a lawsuit grounded in good faith but lacking sufficient evidence. The 1983 amendment of rule 11 to strengthen judicial sanction authority represented a shift toward limiting access to the courthouse by litigants lacking sufficient evidence of liability at the time the suit is filed.[35] Rule 11, which authorizes sanctions against counsel who file suit without sufficient evidence of liability, does not directly discuss discovery. It is, however, integrally connected with the role discovery is designed to play under the rules. The more lawsuits that may have merit that are deterred by rule 11, the further we regress toward the days of pleadings practice and field codes in which a party's case had to be made without the benefit of discovery. Empirical evidence reveals that rule 11 has in fact had a chilling effect on meritorious litigation. Ten percent of attorney respondents in a 1992 study indicated that rule 11 had caused them to decline a case or to advise a client not to pursue a lawsuit that they thought had merit.[36]

Some courts have imposed draconian sanctions against plaintiffs and their counsel for bringing innovative claims against wealthy and powerful entities.[37] Such sanc-

---

[32] Maute, *supra* note 5, at 27.

[33] *Id.* at 27–28.

[34] Arthur B. LaFrance, *Federal Rule 11 and Public Interest Litigation*, 22 VAL. U. L. REV. 331, 341 (1988).

[35] *See generally* Arthur R. Miller, *The Adversary System: Dinosaur or Phoenix*, 69 MINN. L. REV. 1, 19 (1984); Melissa L. Nelken, *Sanctions Under Amended Federal Rule 11—Some "Chilling" Problems in the Struggle Between Compensation and Punishment*, 74 GEO. L.J. 1313, 1338–52 (1986); W. David Snead, Note, *Preventing Frivolous Tort Claims and Defenses: The Need for Flexibility*, 4 GEO. J. LEGAL ETHICS 477, 485–88 (1990).

[36] Herbert Kritzer et al., *Rule 11: Moving Beyond the Cosmic Anecdote*, 75 JUDICATURE 269, 271 (1992).

[37] *See, e.g.,* Avirgan v. Hull, 932 F.2d 1572 (11th Cir. 1991), *cert. denied*, 113 S. Ct. 405 (1992); *cf.* Kamen v. AT&T Co., 791 F.2d 1006 (2d Cir. 1986) (reversing sanction award); *cf. also* Gary Taylor, *Texas Lawyers Hit with Record Sanctions*, NAT'L L.J., June 1, 1992, at 2 (ordering nearly $1 million sanction against counsel and client alleging prominent attorney, medical school, and others "conspired to influence his [prior] divorce case with unsubstantiated allegations of child abuse").

tions can deter the bringing of suits that push the edges of the law. They also can create a dilemma for plaintiffs whose actions must be filed before they are able, through discovery, to fully develop factual support for their claims.

As explained by one commentator,

> The very structure of . . . Rule 11, is designed to intimidate and constrain the bringing of lawsuits. It is always plaintiffs who initiate lawsuits. It is the aggrieved who bring lawsuits. It is victims who bring lawsuits. People who bring lawsuits are, in the large, people who seek to rectify injustices. It is hardly an accident that almost 80% of all Rule 11 sanctions are imposed upon the plaintiff.[38]

Thus, the strengthening of rule 11 represents a decidedly anti-plaintiff policy choice—a choice to limit the role of the discovery process as a legitimate means of acquiring factual support for positions for which a plaintiff has a good-faith basis to believe are true but lacks sufficient proof prior to filing the complaint.

F. Who Pays: Discovering Party vs. Disclosing Party

The discovery rules also reflect choices as to which party should bear the burden and costs of developing information.[39] As previously discussed, the recipient of a discovery request has a responsibility to make a sometimes extensive inquiry before responding.[40]

This in effect requires a litigant to expend time and resources assisting its adversary's investigation and trial preparation. The business records option introduced in the 1970 amendments to the federal rules permits a discovery respondent to shift some of the costs back to the requesting party.[41] These provisions allow the discovery respondent to save the expense of answering interrogatories by merely identifying and producing its business records from which the response can be derived.

The 1980 amendments to the rules put a check on the use of the business records option, readjusting the balance of costs between the discovering and responding parties.

Cost-shifting is also accomplished by sanction provisions that authorize or require awards of expenses and attorney fees. These provisions have been aptly described as an exception to the American Rule that each party bears its own litigation costs.[42]

---

[38] Leonard W. Schroeter, The Politics of Sanctions 2 (Dec. 1991) (unpublished manuscript, on file with the authors).

[39] *See generally* Edward F. Sherman & Stephen O. Kinnard, *Federal Court Discovery in the 80's— Making the Rules Work*, 2 REV. LITIG. 9, 12–38, 65–69 (1981).

[40] See chapter 2, section II.

[41] See chapter 6, section II.

[42] Chambers v. Nasco, Inc., 111 S. Ct. 2123, 2133, *reh'g denied*, 112 S. Ct. 12 (1991).

II. HISTORY OF THE RULES GOVERNING DISCOVERY CONDUCT—1937 THROUGH 1983[43]

The original Federal Rules of Civil Procedure adopted the objective of full and fair disclosure through discovery, and this basic tenet remains largely unchallenged. The history of reform since that time is characterized by efforts to tweak the controls, but there does not appear to have been any definitive overall shift in policy emphasis.

A. Adoption of the Federal Rules of Civil Procedure

The Federal Rules of Civil Procedure were adopted in 1937 and became effective in 1938. While statutory provisions allowing depositions in federal court existed before 1938, depositions were intended for preservation of evidence. Any resulting discovery was purely incidental. Equity rule 58, which provided for some limited discovery, was cumbersome and restrictive.[44] Thus, opportunities for discovery were very limited. Pretrial procedure focused on independent investigation.[45] Legal scholars looked to pretrial disclosure procedures as a way to shift the focus of litigation from gamesmanship to truth-finding. Federal rules 26 through 37 were drafted in an attempt to adopt the best of what were then modern English and state discovery practices.[46]

In 1933 Edson Sunderland, who would later draft the discovery components of the 1938 federal rules,[47] wrote:

> Lawyers who constantly employ [discovery] in their practice find it an exceedingly valuable aid in promoting justice. Discovery procedure serves much the same function in the field of law as the X-Ray in the field of medicine and surgery; and if its use can be sufficiently extended and its methods simplified, litigation will largely cease to be a game of chance.[48]

Reflecting on the rules after their adoption, Sunderland viewed the new discovery provisions as

> mark[ing] the highest point so far reached in the English speaking world in the elimination of secrecy in the preparation for trial. Each party may in effect be called upon by his adversary or by the judge to lay all his cards upon the table, the important con-

---

[43] An excellent history of the rules governing discovery prior to 1980 is found in Brazil, *supra* note 18. This discussion draws heavily from Magistrate Judge Brazil's account and from the sources he cites.

[44] 8 CHARLES ALAN WRIGHT & ARTHUR R. MILLER, FEDERAL PRACTICE AND PROCEDURE § 2002, at 21 (1970 & Supp. 1992). *See generally* Edson R. Sunderland, *The New Federal Rules*, 45 W. VA. L.Q. 5, 19–22 (1938).

[45] GEORGE RAGLAND, JR., DISCOVERY BEFORE TRIAL (1932); Edson R. Sunderland, *The Theory and Practice of Pre-Trial Procedure*, 36 MICH. L. REV. 215 (1937).

[46] 8 WRIGHT & MILLER, *supra* note 44, § 2002, at 21.

[47] WILLIAM A. GLASER, PRETRIAL DISCOVERY AND THE ADVERSARY SYSTEM 11 (1968).

[48] Edson R. Sunderland, *Improving the Administration of Justice*, 167 ANNALS 60, 76 (1933), *quoted in* Brazil, *supra* note 18, at 1299.

sideration being who has the stronger hand, not who can play the cleverer game.[49]

Other commentators were equally enthusiastic about the new procedures. James William Moore and Joseph Friedman, who authored the first major treatise on the new rules, predicted the discovery provisions would be of "great assistance in ascertaining the truth," as well as provide "safeguards against surprise at the trial," and facilitate detection of "false, fraudulent, and sham claims and defenses."[50]

Alexander Holtzhoff, a special assistant to the Attorney General of the United States charged with monitoring federal decisions applying the new rules, lauded their aim "to fulfill[] that concept of litigation which conceives a lawsuit as a means for ascertaining the truth, irrespective of who may be temporarily in possession of the pertinent facts."[51]

The courts likewise praised the new practice.[52] The Supreme Court succinctly described the changes in discovery procedures and their purpose:

> The various instruments of discovery now serve (1) as a device, along with the pretrial hearing under rule 16, to narrow and clarify the basic issues between the parties, and (2) as a device for ascertaining the facts, or information as to the existence or whereabouts of facts, relative to those issues. Thus civil trials in the federal courts no longer need be carried on in the dark. The way is now clear, consistent with recognized privileges, for the parties to obtain the fullest possible knowledge of the issues and facts before trial.[53]

B. 1970 Amendments

The 1970 amendments to the federal discovery rules reflected 32 years of what was widely considered a generally positive experience with rules 26 through 37. The original concept of lawyer control over discovery appeared to be working well, and fears of badgering witnesses, undue expense, and other harassment had not been realized.[54] While numerous suggestions for improvement were advanced and imple-

---

[49] Edson R. Sunderland, *Discovery Before Trial Under the New Federal Rules*, 15 TENN. L. REV. 737, 739 (1939).

[50] 2 JAMES W. MOORE & JOSEPH FRIEDMAN, MOORE'S FEDERAL PRACTICE UNDER THE NEW FEDERAL RULES § 26.01, at 2443–44 (1938), *quoted in* Brazil, *supra* note 18, at 1300.

[51] ALEXANDER HOLTZHOFF, NEW FEDERAL PROCEDURE AND THE COURTS 7 (1940).

[52] *See* Brazil, *supra* note 18, at 1301.

[53] Hickman v. Taylor, 329 U.S. 495, 500 (1947) (citing RAGLAND, *supra* note 45; James A. Pike, *The New Federal Deposition-Discovery Procedure and the Rules of Evidence*, 34 ILL. L. REV. 1 (1939); James A. Pike & John W. Willis, *The New Federal Deposition-Discovery Procedure* (pts. 1–2), 38 COL. L. REV. 1179, 1436 (1938); Sunderland, *supra* note 45)); *see also* United States v. Procter & Gamble Co., 356 U.S. 677, 682–83 (1958) (discovery makes "trial less a game of blindman's buff and more a fair contest with the basic issues and facts disclosed to the fullest practicable extent").

[54] *See* WILLIAM A. GLASER, PRETRIAL DISCOVERY AND THE ADVERSARY SYSTEM (1968), *discussed in* Schwarzer, *supra* note 30, at 704, *and in* 8 WRIGHT & MILLER, *supra* note 44, § 2002, at 22.

mented,[55] these first amendments did not move decidedly in any one philosophical direction.

The 1970 amendments revised the discovery rules in several ways:

Rule 26: This became an introductory provision, applying to all discovery, rather than only to depositions.

Rule 37: Willfulness was removed as a prerequisite to sanctions, thereby strengthening the court's ability to intervene with sanctions.

Rule 34: Court involvement was minimized by deleting the requirement that a party seeking production of documents first show good cause.

Rule 33: Interrogatories were expanded to allow a party to properly seek opinions or contentions related to facts or the application of law to fact, thus expressly broadening the scope of inquiry. However, the interrogatory respondent was also given the option of shifting part of the burden of response to the discovering party by responding to an interrogatory through the business records option.

C. 1980 and 1983 Amendments

Broader discontent with discovery emerged in the mid-1970s. Reform efforts were spurred on by criticisms of the civil justice system, particularly the problems of discovery misuse and overuse, leveled at the 1976 National Conference on the Causes of Popular Dissatisfaction with the Administration of Justice, commonly known as the Pound Conference, sponsored by the American Bar Association and the Judicial Conference of the United States.[56] The ABA also appointed a Special Committee for the Study of Discovery Abuse, which by 1977 had developed recommendations for rule changes[57] that were accepted in large measure by the Advisory Committee on Civil Rules of the Judicial Conference of the United States in its initial report for public comment.[58] These recommendations were made in the midst of intense study, analysis, and public debate of discovery reform in the legal literature.[59]

---

[55] *See* 8 WRIGHT & MILLER, *supra* note 44, § 2003, at 22–24; Brazil, *supra* note 18, at 1339–42.

[56] *See generally* Frank F. Flegal, *Introduction* to *Discovery Abuse: Causes, Effects, and Reform*, 3 REV. LITIG. 1 (1982). The Winter 1982 volume of The Review of Litigation summarizes the proceedings of a national conference on discovery reform sponsored by the American Bar Association's Section of Litigation in cooperation with the University of Texas School of Law. The volume, including Professor Flegal's lead article, and the discovery abuse symposium volume published a year earlier contain interesting reflections on the sources of discontent and the reform efforts which gave rise to the 1980 and 1983 amendments to the discovery rules. *See* 2 REV. LITIG. 1–91 (1981).

[57] American Bar Association Section of Litigation, *Report of the Special Committee for the Study of Discovery Abuse 2 (1977)*, *reprinted in* 92 F.R.D. 149, 152 (1982).

[58] 77 F.R.D. 613 (1978); *see* Flegal, *supra* note 56, at 2.

[59] Flegal, *supra* note 56, at 2–3; *see* DANIEL SEGAL, SURVEY OF LITERATURE ON DISCOVERY FROM 1970 TO THE PRESENT: EXPRESSED DISSATISFACTIONS AND PROPOSED REFORMS 68 (Federal Judicial Ctr. ed., 1978).

The advisory committee revised its recommendations in 1979, concluding that "abuse of discovery, while very serious in certain cases, is not so general as to require . . . basic changes in the rules that govern discovery in all cases."[60] The committee rejected certain recommendations that would have limited the scope of discovery and the number of interrogatories that may have been propounded without leave of the court.[61] The amendments became effective after the U.S. Supreme Court transmitted them to Congress over the dissent of three Justices who felt the reforms did not go far enough to address discovery abuse.[62]

Continued study, analysis, and reform efforts pushed forward the momentum for change,[63] and additional amendments were adopted in 1983. Despite the focus in the literature on discovery misuse and overuse rather than stonewalling, the 1980 and 1983 amendments were a mixed bag, addressing both sorts of abuse.

Rule 26(f): authorized a discovery conference and facilitated greater judicial involvement in discovery.

Rule 37: strengthened judicial intervention by providing sanctions for failure to obey an order issued pursuant to a rule 26(f) discovery conference or to participate in good faith in discovery planning.[64]

Rules 33 and 34: countered the growing use of stonewalling by use of the dump truck and shuffled deck tactics.[65]

The 1983 advisory committee's note expressly recognized both types of discovery abuse—"[e]xcessive discovery and evasion of or resistance to reasonable discovery requests."[66] Amendments included two significant changes directed at overuse.

Rule 26(a)(1): The deletion of the provision that discovery procedures could be limited in frequency only by protective orders cleared the way for use limitations to be imposed pursuant to a rule 26(f) discovery conference.

Rule 26(b)(1): Frequency limitations were also authorized in a new paragraph added to rule 26(b)(1).

Rule 26(g): A new signature requirement applied a rule 11-type certification requirement to discovery requests, responses, and objections.

---

[60] Committee on Rules of Practice and Procedure, *Revised Preliminary Draft of Proposed Amendments to the Federal Rules of Civil Procedure*, 80 F.R.D. 323, 332 (1979); *see also* FED. R. CIV. P. 26(f) 1980 advisory committee's note.

[61] *See* Flegal, *supra* note 56, at 4–5.

[62] 446 U.S. 996, 997–98 (1980) (Powell, J., dissenting).

[63] *See, e.g.*, American Bar Association Section of Litigation, *Second Report of the Special Committee for the Study of Discovery Abuse*, 92 F.R.D. 137 (1982). *See generally* Flegal, *supra* note 56, at 6–7.

[64] FED R. CIV. P. 37(b)(2), 37(g) 1980 advisory committee's note.

[65] *See* FED. R. CIV. P. 33(c), 34(b) 1980 advisory committee's note. These tactics are discussed in chapter 6.

[66] FED. R. CIV. P. 26 1983 advisory committee's note.

III. 1993 RULE AMENDMENTS—FROM DISCOVERY TO DISCLOSURE

The 1993 amendments to the Federal Rules of Civil Procedure[67] represent the most significant change in the approach to information exchange in civil litigation since the adoption of the federal rules gave rise to modern discovery practice. The amendments essentially adopt much of the approach advanced by U.S. District Court Judge William Schwarzer, director of the Federal Judicial Center, and Magistrate Judge Wayne Brazil, that the exchange of relevant information can best be accomplished through voluntary and automatic disclosure.[68] The new rules require automatic disclosure of all witnesses and physical evidence relevant to disputed facts specifically alleged in the pleadings—whether favoring that party or its opponent—shortly after the outset of each case and supplemented as each party's investigation proceeds.[69] Because this information theoretically is to be exchanged voluntarily and without the need for a request, limits are placed on the number of interrogatories each side may pose and on the number and length of depositions.[70]

The stated purposes of the amendments include expediting the sharing of all relevant information and discouraging contentiousness and delay. The advisory committee's note explains that a "major purpose of the revision is to accelerate the exchange of basic information about the case and to eliminate the paper work involved in requesting such information."[71] Moreover, it is the advisory committee's intent that "[t]he litigants should not indulge in gamesmanship with respect to the disclosure obligations."[72] In pursuit of these purposes, the amendments make definite choices among the conflicting policies identified earlier in this chapter. Whether the amended rules meet the objectives stated by their drafters is another question.[73]

A. Requirements of the Amended Rules

The amendments to the Federal Rules of Civil Procedure feature new requirements that promise to dramatically alter the way in which information is exchanged. The practical effect of these new requirements in accomplishing their stated objectives

---

[67] Amendments to the Federal Rules of Civil Procedure and Forms, approved by the United States Supreme Court (Apr. 22, 1993), *reprinted in* 146 F.R.D. 401 (1993) [hereinafter 1993 Amendments]. Sources regarding the 1993 amendments appear in the Bibliography.

[68] 1993 Amendments, *supra* note 67, FED. R. CIV. P. 26(a) advisory committee's note. Brazil and Schwarzer's views are discussed in section I.C of this chapter, *supra*.

[69] 1993 Amendments, *supra* note 67, FED. R. CIV. P. 26(a).

[70] 1993 Amendments, *supra* note 67, FED. R. CIV. P. 30(a)(2)(A), 30(d), 31(a)(2)(A), 33(a).

[71] 1993 Amendments, *supra* note 67, FED. R. CIV. P. 26(a) advisory committee's note.

[72] *Id.*

[73] *See generally* Laurence M. Frankel, *Disclosure in the Federal Courts: A Cure for Discovery Ills?*, 25 ARIZ. ST. L.J. 249 (1993); Thomas M. Mengler, *Eliminating Abusive Discovery Through Disclosure: Is It Again Time for Reform?*, 138 F.R.D. 155 (1992); Paul R. Sugarman & Marc G. Perlin, *Proposed Changes to Discovery Rules in Aid of "Tort Reform": Has the Case Been Made?*, 42 AMER.

will depend largely on how they are interpreted and applied by the courts.

1. Automatic Disclosures

Under the amended rules, certain automatic disclosures are mandated, while additional discovery is limited. The automatic disclosure requirements found in amended rule 26 have been likened to interrogatories of the court.[74]

Four sections have been added to rule 26(a), outlining the parties' disclosure obligations at various stages of the litigation. The first of these subsections mandates initial disclosures of witnesses and physical evidence by each party shortly after commencement of the action without the need for a discovery request. The second subsection requires disclosure of expert information to be made somewhat later. Disclosures required shortly before trial are addressed in the third subsection. The fourth section requires that the disclosures "be made in writing, signed, served, and promptly filed."

The first phase of disclosures is described in amended rule 26(a)(1). Except as otherwise stipulated, ordered, or directed by local rule, each party is required, without awaiting a discovery request, to provide the other parties with four categories of information, based on "information then reasonably available":[75]

> (A) the name and, if known, the address and telephone number of each individual likely to have discoverable information relevant to disputed facts alleged with particularity in the pleadings, identifying the subjects of the information;
>
> (B) a copy of, or a description by category and location of, all documents, data compilations, and tangible things in the possession, custody, or control of the party that are relevant to disputed facts alleged with particularity in the pleadings;
>
> (C) a computation of any category of damages claimed by the disclosing party, making available for inspection and copying as under Rule 34 the documents or other evidentiary material, not privileged or protected from disclosure, on which such computation is based, including materials bearing on the nature and extent of injuries suffered; and
>
> (D) for inspection and copying as under Rule 34 any insurance agreement under which any person carrying on an insurance business may be liable to satisfy part or all of a judgment which may be entered in the action or to indemnify or reimburse for payments made to satisfy the judgment.[76]

These disclosures would generally be made within four months of filing the complaint. A party would not be excused from making these disclosures by claiming that its investigation is not complete or that it believes another party's disclosures are insufficient.[77]

U. L. REV. 1465 (1993). For a critique of the amendments from a defense perspective, see Griffin B. Bell et al., *Automatic Disclosure in Discovery—The Rush to Reform*, 27 GA. L. REV. 1 (1992) (paid for by the Product Liability Advisory Council Foundation).

[74] 1993 Amendments, *supra* note 67, FED. R. CIV. P. 26(a)(1) advisory committee's note.

[75] 1993 Amendments, *supra* note 67, FED. R. CIV. P. 26(a)(1).

[76] *Id.*

[77] *Id.*

An earlier draft of the 1993 amendments required disclosure of witnesses "likely to have information that bears significantly on any claim or defense."[78] In the final draft, however, these requirements were narrowed to provide for disclosures of witnesses and documents "relevant to disputed facts alleged with particularity in the pleadings." The advisory committee's note states that

> [b]road, vague, and conclusory allegations sometimes tolerated in notice pleading—for example, the assertion that a product with many component parts is defective in some unspecified manner—should not impose upon responding parties the obligation at that point to search for and identify all persons possibly involved in, or all documents affecting, the design, manufacture, and assembly of the product.[79]

Thus, the disclosure obligation extends only to specific facts of which the plaintiff is already aware.

This change could have a dramatic effect on pleadings practice. Plaintiffs would be wise to draft future complaints with greater particularity, using industry terms of art to trigger disclosure of relevant information. For example, a complaint filed under the former rules alleging that an automobile's restraint system design was defective might have included the conclusory assertion that the manufacturer knew or should have known of the defect. Under the revised rules, when alleging that the manufacturer knew or should have known the limitations of and dangers posed by the restraint system, plaintiffs' counsel may wish to add details supporting the allegation, such as the manufacturer's design specifications, drawings, and graphics; communications with other manufacturers and contractors; research, literature reviews, tests, and other studies; and incident reports, meeting minutes, and internal memoranda. Specific types of forms or files known to be maintained by the specific manufacturer and reasonably believed to contain relevant information regarding the allegation can be identified by name (for example, "CPIR reports" or "1241 forms" for complaints against General Motors).

This will require plaintiffs' counsel to conduct comprehensive prefiling case preparation, including in products cases a basic education in the relevant technology and a strong understanding of the engineering aspects of the allegedly defective design and safer design alternatives.

The second phase of disclosures, regarding testifying experts, is addressed in amended rule 26(a)(2). "[A]ny person who may be used at trial to present evidence under Rules 702, 703, or 705" must be identified. Those who are either "retained or specially employed to provide expert testimony in the case or whose duties as an employee of the party regularly involve giving expert testimony" have to provide a written report containing the following information:

---

[78] *See* Committee on Rules of Practice and Procedure of the Judicial Conference of the United States, Preliminary Draft of Proposed Amendments to the Federal Rules of Civil Procedure and the Federal Rules of Evidence, *reprinted in* 137 F.R.D. 53, 87–88 (1991).

[79] 1993 Amendments, *supra* note 67, FED. R. CIV. P. 26(a) advisory committee's note.

[A] complete statement of all opinions to be expressed and the basis and reasons therefor; the data or other information considered by the witness in forming the opinions; any exhibits to be used as a summary of or support for the opinions; the qualifications of the witness, including a list of all publications authored by the witness within the preceding ten years; the compensation to be paid for the study and testimony; and a listing of any other cases in which the witness has testified as an expert at trial or by deposition within the preceding four years.

The report requirement can be expected to affect litigation in a number of ways. First, it may require earlier, more thorough case preparation, because any failure to include information in the report will likely lead to exclusion of the information at trial. Second, it will increase the plaintiff's initial cost of obtaining expert testimony, though those costs may be recouped later if the exchange of reports eliminates or shortens expert depositions. Third, it may change the common practice of each side's agreeing to bear the cost of making its expert available for deposition since some parties may not want to take expert depositions. For instance, if the plaintiff is satisfied with the defense expert's report and if, as is common in products liability cases, the expert has already been deposed numerous times in other cases, the plaintiff may choose to forego the expert's deposition. If the defendant chooses to take the deposition of the plaintiff's expert, the defendant may be required to pay the expert's fees and costs pursuant to rule 26(b)(4)(C). Fourth, the report provides an expeditious means for learning what information an expert witness considered in forming opinions, what the expert will be paid, and what prior testimony the expert has given. Fifth, the substance of the experts' reports can be expected to be used by the court in determining the scope of discovery relevance. Accordingly, the plaintiff's expert's report should spell out the kind of information that is important to the expert's analysis, thereby giving the court an understanding of why certain discovery materials are needed.

Expert witnesses are not always good writers. Some experts may have gained their knowledge through practical experience rather than academia and may not be facile with formal written language. While the rule requires that the report be prepared and signed by the witness, the advisory committee's note observes that the rule does not preclude counsel's assistance.

Reports are required only for experts retained for the litigation or for in-house experts testifying for their employers. Eyewitness experts that the plaintiff intends to present, including treating physicians and the defendant's employees or former employees, apparently need not prepare a report. These witnesses must still be identified by the party that offers their testimony, and information regarding these witnesses may be obtained through discovery.

Depositions of testifying experts are expressly allowed, but if a report is required from such an expert, the deposition cannot be taken until after the report is provided. Timing of expert disclosure is within the discretion of the court. In the absence of stipulation or direction from the court, written disclosures must be made at least 90 days before the trial date (except in the case of expert rebuttal evidence, which must be identified within 30 days after the disclosure made by the other party).

Pretrial disclosures, the third phase of information exchanges, are made closer to trial and include identification of the witnesses each party expects to call, as well as "those whom the party may call if the need arises." Trial exhibits and deposition testimony must also be designated at this time. Objections, except those under Federal Rules of Evidence 402 (relevance) and 403 (probative value vs. prejudice), are waived if not made before trial.

2. Presumptive Limits on Discovery

Each *side* in the case (all plaintiffs, all defendants, all third-party defendants) is limited to 10 depositions,[80] either oral or through written questions, and 25 interrogatories.[81] The court is authorized to alter these limits—or the parties may stipulate to do so—and to limit the length of depositions and the number of admission requests by order or by local rule.[82] The list of criteria in rule 26(b) for the exercise of the court's authority to limit discovery has been amended to require that "the burden or expense of the proposed discovery outweighs its likely benefit."

3. Discovery Planning and Scheduling

Amended rule 26(f) mandates a meeting of the parties to plan for discovery. The parties are to meet to discuss their claims and defenses and the possibility of settlement, to make arrangements for required disclosures, and to develop a proposed discovery plan. The plan must indicate the parties' views and proposals concerning the required disclosures, subjects for further discovery, changes in the discovery limits, and any other issues the court should address at a pretrial conference. This meeting is to be held at least 14 days before a rule 16 scheduling conference is held or a rule 16 scheduling order is due. The parties must submit their proposed discovery plan to the court within 10 days after the meeting.

Amended rule 16 (pretrial conferences) expressly includes in its scope consideration of the control and scheduling of discovery, including automatic disclosure and discovery limits. A pretrial order is required "within 90 days after the appearance of a defendant and within 120 days after the complaint has been served on a defendant."[83]

4. Sanctions for Deposition Conduct

The amendments to rule 30 allow sanctions to be imposed immediately, without a finding that a court order has been violated, for conduct that impedes, delays, or otherwise frustrates the fair examination of the deponent.[84] The amendments also codify existing case law regarding two types of discovery misconduct (1) by requiring that an "objection to evidence during a deposition shall be stated concisely and in a nonargumentative and nonsuggestive manner" and (2) by permitting an instruction

---

[80] 1993 Amendments, *supra* note 67, FED. R. CIV. P. 30(a)(2)(A), 31(a).

[81] 1993 Amendments, *supra* note 67, FED. R. CIV. P. 33(a).

[82] 1993 Amendments, *supra* note 67, FED. R. CIV. P. 26(b)(2).

[83] 1993 Amendments, *supra* note 67, FED. R. CIV. P. 16(b)(6).

[84] 1993 Amendments, *supra* note 67, FED. R. CIV. P. 30(d)(2).

to "a deponent not to answer only when necessary to preserve a privilege, to enforce a limitation on evidence directed by the court, or to present a motion" to terminate or limit the deposition.[85]

Video or audio taping of the deposition by any party is permitted unless the court orders otherwise.[86] As discussed in chapter 9, videotape has proven effective in documenting discovery abuses.

B. Policy Choices Reflected in the New Amendments

As discussed above, the original discovery rules and subsequent amendments have reflected choices between conflicting viewpoints on policy issues. The 1993 amendments reflect some significant adjustments in those policy choices. On the surface, the amendments seem to move in a direction that advances full and fair disclosure of relevant evidence. What makes the 1993 amendments difficult to analyze, however, is the danger that the theory and objectives underlying these reforms will be undercut in practice.

1. Utility of Discovery

In theory and intent, the revised rules do not change the scope of discovery. The definition of discovery relevance remains unaltered. Only the mechanism for effectuating the exchange is changed, so that the exchange of relevant evidence is less dependent on the requesting party's ability to frame its requests in terms that will uncover the relevant information. The revised rules demand that the party possessing relevant information bring that information forward at the outset. To the extent that this works, it favors the original discovery objective of elevating substance over form, facts over artful drafting. Thus, while the new rules seek economy by placing numerical limits on certain kinds of discovery (interrogatories and depositions), they do not seek to restrict the scope of the information exchanged.

Unfortunately, under the new disclosure system, the party possessing the information gains even greater control over the exchange. Given the prevalence of stonewalling, there is every reason to fear that some parties will not make full, good-faith disclosure. It seems unreasonable to expect that a party willing to stonewall under the former system will be more forthcoming under a voluntary disclosure system. Manufacturers can be expected to utilize their own adversarial and subjective scope of relevance, a problem described several times previously in this text. If the new system's initial disclosures result in no more disclosure than that which typically occurred in response to "first wave" interrogatories under the old rules, the discovery limits may prevent emergence of the facts, since follow-up discovery is subject to tight presumptive limits. Thus, as under the pre-1993 rules, full disclosure will depend on a combination of the attorney's and the party's inclination to comply with discovery obligations in good faith and the court's inclination to insist on good-faith compliance.

---

[85] 1993 Amendments, *supra* note 67, FED. R. CIV. P. 30(d)(1).

[86] 1993 Amendments, *supra* note 67, FED. R. CIV. P. 30(b)(2).

2. Adversarial Character of Discovery

The rule changes are expressly intended to minimize adversarial conduct in discovery. The advisory committee's note declares that attorneys for the parties are to carry out their discovery duties principally as officers of the court, presumably suspending temporarily their roles as partisan advocates. Such a shift of loyalty by attorneys—and their clients, for that matter—from the party to the process is the linchpin of the amended rules: The benefits to be derived from the amendments are based largely on the presumption that this shift in loyalties will somehow occur. However, no provisions have been made for accomplishing this transformation. It is unrealistic to expect parties in a complex adversarial process not to behave as adversaries from the outset.

There is a historical irony in the motivation underlying the 1993 reforms that should not be overlooked. The reform movement of the 1930s was a response to dissatisfaction with certain effects of adversarial litigation conduct. The current reforms purport to be, like the 1938 reforms, a response to the adversarial nature of litigation. The current reformers may misperceive the former rules as a failed attempt to replace adversarial behavior with a cooperative, inquisitorial approach to development of the facts. The rules are better viewed, however, not as an attempt to *eliminate* adversarial behavior but as a means to *subjugate* it to the facts. When the facts are allowed to emerge, adversarial conduct becomes less important than the facts themselves in determining the outcome of litigation.

3. Overuse vs. Stonewalling

Again, under the 1993 amendments theory and practice may be at odds. The reforms are ostensibly addressed at both discovery overuse and stonewalling. Overuse is directly controlled by numerical limits on depositions and interrogatories. Stonewalling is targeted by disclosure obligations. In practice, however, the objective limits will be much easier to enforce than the disclosure requirements. The opposing party and the court will know if the plaintiff serves more deposition notices than permitted by the rules. However, stonewalling by a party may not be apparent to the other party or the court.

4. Utility of Judicial Intervention

The amendments increase judicial involvement in discovery by expanding the scope of the rule 16 pretrial conference as well as expanding rule 26(b) to encourage judicial limitations on discovery. More importantly, in all but the least complex cases, the judge will be asked to modify discovery limits to permit additional interrogatories and depositions.

5. Prefiling Proof of Liability

The rules' most significant impact in practice may turn out to be their effect on cases where the plaintiff needs discovery from the manufacturer to establish a prima facie case. This is frequently the situation in products liability cases, particularly when a specific defect is litigated for the first time or when the plaintiff is prevented by protective orders from obtaining documents produced by the manufacturer in other cases.

Under the amended rules, the plaintiff must make early disclosure of its supporting evidence, simultaneously with the defendant's voluntary disclosures. As a result the defendant could stonewall its initial disclosures and seek summary judgment on the ground that the evidence disclosed by both sides is insufficient to support the plaintiff's case.[87] If summary judgment is not granted, and if the defendant's failure to make full disclosure is later discovered, the manufacturer could simply blame either the incomplete state of its own investigation at the time of the initial disclosures or the vague wording of the new disclosure requirement.

The rule amendments were never intended to make it more difficult for plaintiffs to bring cases that they can win only with evidence possessed by the defendant. In fact, the new amendments to rule 11 are intended to reduce the deterrents to such suits. Portions of earlier drafts of the 1993 amendments that would have encouraged summary judgments against plaintiffs in such cases were deleted before the amendments were adopted. Still, the courts will need to guard against the scenario described in the previous paragraph to prevent elimination of claims following initial disclosures but before sufficient discovery occurs.

6. Cost-Shifting

The allocation of discovery costs is changed only somewhat by the amendments. Under either discovery or disclosure, the party possessing information bears costs in providing it to its adversary. However, new discovery limitations will have the effect of limiting the costs that a requesting party can impose on the party possessing the information. Cost to the responding party has been added as a factor for courts to consider when they are asked to limit discovery under rule 26(b).

C. Effects of the 1993 Amendments

It is hard to predict what impact, if any, the rule revisions will have on the stonewalling behavior described in this book. Viewed with optimism, the new rules should lead to quicker, more complete disclosure. Viewed with skepticism, or perhaps realism, there is reason to fear that the rules will become one more weapon in the stonewaller's arsenal. If the bulk of relevant information is indeed disclosed early on without the need for discovery requests, greater efficiency and justice obviously will be achieved. It is all too possible, however, that the new provisions will instead lead to the overproduction of unimportant information and the continued suppression of vital information. The new rules' effectiveness in achieving their framers' desired effect of more efficient exchange of all relevant information depends entirely on their application by the courts and on the behavior of parties and counsel.

Unfortunately, it is unclear what new provisions, if any, will bring about the desired change in the behavior of parties, counsel, or the courts. The incentives to stonewall remain. The party with the information monopoly still has every incentive to keep it. The inherent adversarial nature of litigation and the competitive nature of legal practice will still tend to keep counsel functioning as an advocate for the client rather than as a neutral officer of the court when preparing discovery responses. In

---

[87] *See infra* notes 88–92 and accompanying text.

fact, rather than providing recognizable disincentives to discovery misconduct, the new rules may actually increase the incentives to stonewall.

As pointed out by Professor Thomas Mengler in his critique of the proposed rules,

> [u]nder Judge Schwarzer's proposal, because the opportunities for employing an arsenal of discovery weapons are greatly limited and only upon court order, the incentive to conceal should be greater. He all but admits as much by acknowledging that in shifting the burden of persuasion from the party objecting to discovery to the party seeking it, less will be discovered. With a voluntary disclosure philosophy that presumptively cuts against later use of formal discovery, one might be concerned that litigants will be encouraged to appear to be forthcoming at the disclosure stage and thereby minimize the likelihood of formal discovery that might later uncover some concealed secret.[88]

Professor Mengler concludes that this sort of discovery scheme "might well lead to a substantial decrease in the amount of pertinent information disclosed, which might for no ostensibly good reason disparately affect the class of plaintiffs.[89]" His rationale applies particularly to products liability and other litigation characterized by a gross imbalance in initial access to information:

> On the whole, plaintiffs have a greater need for formal discovery than defendants both because plaintiffs typically bear the burden of proof in a case, and, hence, have a greater need for evidentiary support, and because, in certain kinds of cases, the critical information is largely under defendant's possession or control. A discovery reform that encourages district judges to restrict the scope of discovery at an early stage will disparately affect plaintiffs.[90]

Because voluntary disclosure is required only of information "relevant to disputed facts alleged with particularity in the pleadings,"[91] the defendant's disclosure obligation might be read to extend no further than the information already known to the plaintiff. As Professor Mengler points out, early disclosure could result in a narrowing of discovery by the court based on what the plaintiff already knows, and could lead to summary resolution before all relevant facts surface.[92]

By tying disclosure to facts alleged with specificity in the initial pleadings, the amended rules could swing the pendulum back toward the bad old days when form prevailed over fact.

---

[88] Mengler, *supra* note 73, at 163.

[89] *Id.*

[90] *Id.* at 159 (citations omitted).

[91] 1993 Amendments, *supra* note 67, FED. R. CIV. P. 26(a).

[92] Mengler, *supra* note 73, at 159–60 n.24. At the time the Mengler article was written, the proposed amendments also included changes to rule 56 which would promote summary resolution of claims and issues. That proposal was rejected by the Judicial Conference before the proposed amendments were forwarded to the Supreme Court in September 1992. *See* Judicial Conference of the United States, Preliminary Report, Judicial Conference Actions 8 (Sept. 22, 1992).

Even as critical information is withheld, volumes of unneeded documents are likely to be identified pursuant to the automatic disclosure requirements. During consideration of the 1993 amendments, comments from groups representing both the plaintiffs and the defense bar reflected the concern that the mandatory voluntary disclosure requirement will result in overproduction of unimportant documents.[93] It is ironic that the amendments seek to avoid the inefficiencies of broad discovery requests by propounding what amounts to broad standing interrogatories in the form of disclosure requirements.

The dump truck and shuffled deck stonewalling tactics, discussed in chapter 6, that produce volumes of disorganized documents and mix important information with unimportant filler, might actually be encouraged under the amended rules. Currently, under rules 33 and 34, documents produced in response to interrogatories must be identified as containing specific information responsive to specific interrogatories, and documents produced in response to a request for production must either be segregated in accordance with the request or produced as kept in the ordinary course of business.[94] Under the new disclosure requirement, because documents would be identified in bulk rather than in response to specific interrogatories or production requests, they are unlikely to be sorted in a manner that would advance the discovering party's investigative or trial preparation objectives.

Because initial disclosure under the amended rules is subject to each party's subjective, adversarial view of relevance,[95] full disclosure of documents damaging to the disclosing party, yet critical to the discovering party, is unlikely to occur. These types of documents include test results, similar reported incidents, design and evaluation data concerning models other than the precise product model and year at issue, and other information the discovery of which manufacturers routinely object to on relevance grounds. Nor would any objection be required to alert the plaintiff and the court that certain information has been withheld.

The reform approach may have tackled the wrong problem. Stonewalling, and overuse for that matter, result from parties' and counsel's failures to comply with discovery obligations and from the courts' inability or lack of inclination to compel compliance. Changing the obligations does not automatically change the likelihood of compliance. Thus, unless the litigation climate is altered through substantive changes to the incentives affecting discovery practice, rather than just expressions of intent, stonewallers will not become extinct but will merely adapt to the new rules. As discussed elsewhere in this book,[96] the surest way to change incentives is for courts to

---

[93] *See* comments on proposed amendments, August 1991 draft, submitted to the Advisory Committee on the Civil Rules by the Standing Committee on Rules of Practice and Procedure, Judicial Conference of the United States.

[94] See chapter 6.

[95] See chapter 2, section V.A and chapter 5, section IV.

[96] See chapter 10, section V.

impose costs on stonewalling sufficient to deter it.

The civil justice system legitimately can and should insist that litigants comport themselves with civility, legality, and honesty. When litigants know with reasonable certainty what discovery conduct will be tolerated and know that conduct that does not measure up to those objective standards will be met with stringent sanctions, abusive discovery behavior will be effectively curtailed.

If the rule changes are accompanied by greater court awareness of the problem of stonewalling and greater court commitment to stopping it—as sanctioning trends suggest is occurring[97]—the rules offer promise. If courts insist on meaningful and complete disclosure early in the case without the need for discovery requests, the search for truth will clearly be expedited. For this to occur, courts will need to be willing to impose sanctions where they learn that relevant information required to be disclosed under rule 26 has not been disclosed, even if the recalcitrant party argues under a narrow, subjective view of relevance that its nondisclosure is justified. Courts must also be willing to adjust the limits on interrogatories and depositions in complex cases to permit the discovering party to test the sufficiency of its opponent's initial disclosures.

Discovery conduct is at its best when the parties know that the judge does not expect to be bothered with every minor discovery dispute, but that when a serious abuse is brought to the court's attention, the abuse will receive the attention it deserves. When all judges take seriously the obligation of parties to conduct discovery in good faith and the court's responsibility to respond swiftly and effectively to obstructions of discovery, abuses will decline sharply. Proof of this proposition may be anecdotal, but experienced practitioners will agree that their discovery behavior and that of other litigators is affected dramatically by their assessment of what the judge in a particular case will tolerate.

Discovery conduct also improves when the litigants know the judge will not view sympathetically the protestations of the movant in a discovery dispute when that party has itself abused discovery through overly broad requests or evasive responses. In the proper climate, discovery is conducted in good faith not because the parties and their attorneys view cooperation as their moral imperative as officers of the court, but because they view that conduct as being in their best interest.

Rule 1, which is virtually unchanged since it was adopted in 1937, exhorts that the rules "be construed to secure the just, speedy, and inexpensive determination of every action." The rules are not, of course, self-effectuating. They are applied, or not applied, by attorneys for litigants each day. They are enforced, or not enforced, by the courts. Part two of this book describes how far we have fallen from the ideals underlying the discovery rules. It describes how defendants' stonewalling—and the culture of the bar and bench that perpetuates it—lead despite rule 1 to avoidable expense, delay, and injustice.

---

[97] *Id.*

PART TWO:

STONEWALLING

CHAPTER FOUR

STONEWALLING IN PRODUCTS LIABILITY LITIGATION

I. STONEWALLING DENIES PLAINTIFFS ACCESS TO JUSTICE

The increase in the importance of pretrial discovery in the past few decades has radically changed trial practice. Modern trial lawyers spend much more time and effort implementing pretrial discovery procedures than their predecessors. In cases such as products liability actions, where the subject matter is complex, discovery practice is necessarily complex as well. Because the fair determination of a claim turns on the facts, justice turns first on full and fair discovery.

The procedural changes in trial practice during the twentieth century brought about by the advent and rise in modern discovery were accompanied by equally dramatic changes in substantive law, particularly the ascendance of consumer protection and public safety doctrines. Imbalances in the tort system were removed by repudiation of the privity requirement in negligence actions,[1] the emergence of comparative negligence to replace the rule barring a plaintiff's recovery for even slight contributory negligence,[2] and changes in the calculation of damages.[3] Perhaps the most far-reaching single development was the recognition of strict liability in tort for harm caused by defective products.[4]

---

[1] *See* MacPherson v. Buick Motor Co., 111 N.E. 1050, 1053 (1916) (finding auto assembler owes duty of reasonable care to ultimate consumer despite lack of privity). *See generally* William L. Prosser, *The Fall of the Citadel (Strict Liability to the Consumer)*, 50 MINN. L. REV. 791, 793–800 (1966).

[2] *See generally* G. Edward White, *Tort Reform in the Twentieth Century: An Historical Perspective*, 32 VILL. L. REV. 1265, 1284–88 (1987).

[3] *See generally* Joseph A. Page, *Deforming Tort Reform*, 78 GEO. L.J. 649, 651–54 (1990) (reviewing PETER W. HUBER, LIABILITY: THE LEGAL REVOLUTION AND ITS CONSEQUENCES (1988)).

[4] *Id.* at 653; *see, e.g.*, Greenman v. Yuba Power Prods., Inc., 377 P.2d 897, 900–01 (Cal. 1963).

Procedural reforms permitting broad discovery and the emergence of expanded products liability doctrines are not unrelated. The battle of the injured individual against the corporate manufacturer is inherently quixotic, marked by a dramatic imbalance in both resources and access to information. A consumer could not meaningfully challenge a corporation on the safety characteristics of its product if the authority of the courts could not be brought to bear to loosen the corporate monopoly on information about the product, its design, testing and safety characteristics, the basis for decision making on safety features, and other highly relevant information. The ultimate outcome of a products case is dramatically affected by the outcome of the plaintiff's battle for discovery. Unless the court applies the rules so as to achieve their intended purpose, there is little chance that the products liability plaintiff will obtain a result based on the truth.

Two characteristics common to products liability cases give rise to special discovery problems that plaintiff's counsel must overcome. No equivalent obstacles impede the discovery efforts of the defendant.

First, products liability cases almost always involve factually and technically complex issues. A defective products case typically entails several distinct areas of technology in which counsel must become thoroughly knowledgeable in order to understand and properly assess the significance of the physical facts regarding the case. Indeed, merely determining the applicable legal standard often requires a mastery of the relevant technology.

The defendant and its counsel initially enjoy a significant advantage over plaintiff's counsel with respect to technical complexity in at least five areas:

- full knowledge of each of the disciplines of technology involved;
- possession of all of the relevant technical documents . . . concerning the design;
- employment of or access to qualified expert witnesses;
- access to a collaborative mechanism to assist local counsel in case preparation; and
- superior economic resources.

Effective discovery offers the plaintiff the only real hope of overcoming this inherent inequality of resources favoring the defendant.[5]

Second, the defendant has exclusive possession of virtually all of the information relevant to its liability. The pivotal documents relating to the product's safety are the manufacturer's "internal corporate documentation,"[6] which contain information that

---

[5] SCOTT BALDWIN ET AL., THE PREPARATION OF A PRODUCT LIABILITY CASE § 7A.1.2, at 553 (2d ed. 1993); *see also* TERRENCE F. KIELY, PREPARING PRODUCTS LIABILITY CASES §§ 1.4, 1.19, 3.1–3.5 (1986 & Supp. 1989).

[6] KIELY, *supra* note 5, § 3.5, at 81; *see* BALDWIN ET AL., *supra* note 5, § 7.1.1.

the company acquires or generates in the regular course of its business in connection with the design, development, manufacture, and distribution of the product. These documents contain the best evidence—in many instances, the *only* evidence—concerning the principal issues in controversy. As one court has aptly noted, "[c]ases of this nature must rest basically on the records of the manufacturer and what was known to him."[7]

Because these vital documents are exclusively in the defendant manufacturer's possession,[8] the plaintiff in a products case has exceptional discovery needs that are utterly different from those in a "who ran the red light" case, where both sides have equal access to the relevant information. The plaintiff cannot acquire these documents from an impartial source, but must, of necessity, attempt to obtain these documents by requesting their production from the very party sued. Effective use of the discovery process affords the plaintiff the only real hope of acquiring these critical documents.[9]

Indeed, one of the reasons the courts adopted strict products liability was to relieve plaintiffs of the difficulty they faced in obtaining information necessary to prove negligence, evidence generally controlled by manufacturers. Unfortunately, proving a defect frequently requires the same type of evidence as proving negligence. As explained by the California Supreme Court:

> [O]ne of the principal purposes behind the strict product liability doctrine is to relieve an injured plaintiff of many of the onerous evidentiary burdens inherent in a negligence cause of action.... [M]ost of the evidentiary matters which may be relevant to the determination of the adequacy of a product's design under the "risk-benefit" standard—e.g., the feasibility and cost of alternative designs—are similar to issues typically presented in a negligent design case and involve technical matters peculiarly within the knowledge of the manufacturer....[10]

---

[7] Hess v. Pittsburgh Steel Foundry & Mach. Co., 49 F.R.D. 271, 273 (W.D. Pa. 1970); *see also* Computer Assocs. Int'l, Inc. v. America Fundware, Inc., 133 F.R.D. 166, 170 (D. Colo. 1990); Honda Motor Co. v. Salzman, 751 P.2d 489, 493 (Alaska) ("without the design defect documents which Honda withheld, Salzman cannot be expected to prove *either* the existence of a defect *or* causation"), *cert. dismissed*, 487 U.S. 1260 (1988).

[8] *See, e.g.*, Kozlowski v. Sears, Roebuck & Co., 73 F.R.D. 73, 76 (D. Mass. 1976). *See generally* Francis H. Hare, Jr. & James L. Gilbert, *Discovery in Products Liability Cases: The Plaintiff's Plea for Judicial Understanding*, 12 AM. J. TRIAL ADVOC. 413 (1989).

[9] *Cf.* Thomas M. Mengler, *Eliminating Abusive Discovery Through Disclosure: Is It Time Again for Reform?*, 138 F.R.D. 155, 159 n.21 (1992) ("On the whole, plaintiffs have a greater need for formal discovery than defendants both because plaintiffs typically bear the burden of proof in a case and, hence, have a greater need for evidentiary support, and because, in certain kinds of cases, the critical information is largely under defendant's possession or control."); William W Schwarzer, *Slaying the Monsters of Cost and Delay: Would Disclosure Be More Effective Than Discovery?*, 74 JUDICATURE 178, 182 (1991) (acknowledging that in certain types of cases including personal injury actions, the critical information is largely in the defendant's exclusive possession).

[10] Barker v. Lull Eng'g Co., 573 P.2d 443, 455 (Cal. 1978), *quoted in* Rahmig v. Mosley Mach. Co., 412 N.W.2d 56, 78 (Neb. 1987). To relieve this evidentiary burden, the Barker court held that a

The defendant obviously has a powerful economic motive to resist the plaintiff's discovery efforts.[11] Indeed, the more damaging and critical the document, the greater is the defendant's motivation to resist its disclosure. By virtue of the fact that discovery under the rules is intended to take place voluntarily, the initial decision of which documents should be furnished in response to a discovery request is made privately by employees of the defendant. It is inevitable that the subjective nature of this decision will be affected by the defendant's adversarial view of the case.[12]

Thus, the defendant holds an overwhelming informational advantage at the outset of litigation, and it has every economic incentive to maintain that advantage: Not only is the likelihood of winning at trial greatly increased if the contents of these documents are withheld from the jurors' consideration, without these critical documents, the plaintiff may be forced to settle the claim for less than its fair value. It is therefore not surprising that with such a compelling incentive, many defendants respond to the plaintiff's discovery efforts with uncompromising recalcitrance.[13]

---

plaintiff proceeding under the risk-benefit test of design defect need only prove that the product's design proximately caused injury, and the burden then shifts to the defendant to show that on balance the benefits of the challenged design outweigh the risk of danger inherent in such design. *See* Caterpillar Tractor Co. v. Beck, 593 P.2d 871 (Alaska 1979); *see also* Ontai v. Straub Clinic & Hosp., Inc., 659 P.2d 734 (Haw. 1983); Toliver v. General Motors Corp., 482 So. 2d 213 (Miss. 1985); John W. Wade, *On the Nature of Strict Tort Liability for Products*, 44 MISS. L.J. 825, 826 (1973).

[11] The cause and effect relationship between economic incentives and discovery responses is discussed in Wayne D. Brazil, *The Adversary Character of Civil Discovery: A Critique and Proposals for Change*, 31 VAND. L. REV. 1295 (1978). *See also* Earl C. Dudley, Jr., *Discovery Abuse Revisited: Some Specific Proposals to Amend the Federal Rules of Civil Procedure*, 26 U.S.F. L. REV. 189, 220–21 (1992) (noting that the motivation to suppress information is more powerful in large, complex cases); David L. Shapiro, *Some Problems of Discovery in an Adversary System*, 63 MINN. L. REV. 1055 (1979).

[12] *See* Stengel v. Kawasaki Heavy Indus., 116 F.R.D. 263, 264 (N.D. Tex. 1987); Sellers v. General Motors Corp., 40 Fed. R. Serv. 2d (Callaghan) 590 (E.D. Pa. 1984); Bowman v. General Motors Corp., 64 F.R.D. 62, 68 (E.D. Pa. 1974); United States v. 30 Jars of "Ahead Hair Restorer for New Hair Growth," 43 F.R.D. 181, 189 (D. Del. 1967); United States v. 216 Bottles of "Sudden Change," 36 F.R.D. 695, 700 (E.D.N.Y. 1965); United Nuclear Corp. v. General Atomic Co., 629 P.2d 231, 287 (N.M. 1980), *cert. denied*, 451 U.S. 901, *reh'g denied*, 452 U.S. 932 (1981); Foster v. Heard, 757 S.W.2d 464 (Tex. Ct. App. 1988); Gammon v. Clark Equip. Co., 686 P.2d 1102, 1107 (Wash. Ct. App. 1984), *aff'd en banc*, 707 P.2d 685 (Wash. 1985); *see also* ROGER S. HAYDOCK & DAVID F. HERR, DISCOVERY PRACTICE § 4.5.2, at 356 (2d ed. 1988 & Supp. 1992); 8 CHARLES ALAN WRIGHT & ARTHUR R. MILLER, FEDERAL PRACTICE AND PROCEDURE § 2173, at 544 (1970 & Supp. 1992).

[13] The significance of the fact that the responding party has exclusive possession of critical information has been noted in, e.g., Petz v. Ethan Allen, Inc., 113 F.R.D. 494, 496 (D. Conn. 1985); Kozlowski v. Sears, Roebuck & Co., 73 F.R.D. 73, 76 (D. Mass. 1976); King v. Georgia Power Co., 50 F.R.D. 134 (N.D. Ga. 1970); Hess v. Pittsburgh Steel Foundry & Mach. Co., 49 F.R.D. 271, 273 (W.D. Pa. 1970); United Nuclear Corp. v. General Atomic Co., 629 P.2d 231, 254–55 (N.M. 1980), *cert. denied*, 451 U.S. 901, *reh'g denied*, 452 U.S. 932 (1981). *See generally* JAMES L. UNDERWOOD, A GUIDE TO FEDERAL DISCOVERY RULES 99–100 (2d ed. 1985).

II. THE ABUSIVE REQUEST VS. THE STONEWALLING RESPONSE

The term discovery abuse has been used to describe two very different forms of unacceptable litigation behavior. The first is the excessive use or the misuse of discovery *requests*, often for purposes other than obtaining information for litigation. Such overuse or misuse results in inefficiency, expense, and delay. The bulk of academic writing and rule reform efforts of the past two decades have focused on the problems of "overuse" and "misuse," and have sought to curtail the discovery inquiry. A close examination of discovery abuse literature discloses that the most serious and frequently occurring problem with "overuse" centers around commercial litigation between corporations in which "brigades of lawyers employ the rules of discovery like weapons in a Punic War."[14]

This focus on overuse is ironic since the dangers of the second type of discovery abuse—avoidance, or *stonewalling*—can have a much more serious impact on the justice system, particularly in products liability.

Avoidance arises in the discovery response and affects not only the efficiency of the litigation, but worse, the correctness of the result. Avoidance allows defendants a lock on the facts, denying them to the plaintiff and the court. Thus, if unchecked, stonewalling is fatal to the truth.

In products liability litigation, stonewalling of discovery by the defendant can be a great deal more harmful than overuse of discovery by the plaintiff, as the following comparison illustrates. The two forms of abuse are compared from three perspectives: their causes, the difficulty of their detection and prevention, and their consequences.

This comparison presupposes the existence of critical documents in the defendant's possession that can be obtained by the plaintiff only through a discovery request—precisely the situation that exists in the great majority of defective products cases. The analysis also applies to other types of cases, such as professional negligence, employment discrimination, toxic torts, or any other type of action in which the defendant has exclusive possession of vital information.

A. Causes

Institutional factors create built-in disincentives for plaintiffs in products liability litigation to overuse discovery.[15] First, law firms that represent personal injury plaintiffs typically lack the larger law firms' characteristics that often contribute to overuse of discovery.[16] Unlike counsel for defendants and corporate plaintiffs, per-

---

[14] BALDWIN ET AL., *supra* note 5, § 7A.1.3, at 552; *see, e.g.*, Martin I. Kaminsky, *Proposed Federal Discovery Rules for Complex Civil Litigation*, 48 FORDHAM L. REV. 907, 909 (1980); Francis R. Kirkham, *Complex Civil Litigation—Have Good Intentions Gone Awry?*, 70 F.R.D. 199, 203 (1976). For a detailed discussion of this point, see Hare & Gilbert, *supra* note 8, at 417–19.

[15] *See generally* Elizabeth G. Thornburg, *Interlocutory Review of Discovery Orders: An Idea Whose Time Has Come*, 44 SW. L.J. 1045, 1064–65 (1990) (reviewing literature and studies indicating that defendants have greater incentive than plaintiffs to engage in discovery abuse).

[16] *See* Paul J. Bschorr, *Beyond the Bottom Line*, LITIG., Fall 1990, at 1; *see also* Frank F. Flegal, *Introduction to Discovery Abuse: Causes, Effects, and Reform*, 3 REV. LITIG. 1, 29–30 (1982).

sonal injury attorneys generally work on a contingent fee, rather than on an hourly fee, basis. Thus, while overuse of discovery can be used for revenue enhancement by hourly fee lawyers, it is a revenue drain for counsel whose fee does not increase with time billed. At a 1990 American Bar Association annual meeting, discovery abuse and excessive and unnecessary discovery were described as

> primarily a problem of large defense firms. For lawyers who work on a contingency fee basis, discovery is overhead. For corporate firms, however, it is a profit center. Both judges and lawyers accuse some attorneys of "meter running," engaging in protracted discovery simply to generate larger fees. The more fundamental problem, however, is simply that there is too great an economic incentive, and little disincentive, to overuse discovery. Discovery lawyers are content to leave no stone unturned because they are paid by the stone.[17]

Nor is overuse in the best interest of the injured party, for whom delay means continuation of the status quo. Overuse often occurs in commercial litigation where a wealthy party sees an opportunity to exert pressure by draining its opponent's resources. Personal injury plaintiffs must bear their own litigation costs, frequently while faced with large medical bills and loss of income. The disparity of resources clearly favors the manufacturer. While a manufacturer might be tempted to overuse discovery—for instance, by conducting numerous and lengthy depositions—to put pressure on the plaintiff, only a foolish plaintiff would seek to "wear down" General Motors or Ford. Moreover, overly extensive requests by the plaintiff would certainly elicit a response in kind from the defendant, leaving the plaintiff in no position to ask the court for relief.

Finally, while commercial litigants sometimes seek discovery from their adversaries to learn more about their competitors, injured parties use discovery information only to prove their claims. This is not to say that the products liability plaintiff's discovery is always narrowly drawn. The point is that broadly framed discovery requests are generally intended to obtain necessary information for making a case, rather than for other, improper purposes. The history of manufacturer recalcitrance in products liability and other cases puts the plaintiff in a difficult dilemma: If plaintiff's counsel limits written discovery to a few precisely tailored discovery requests, the defendant may give the language an unreasonably narrow interpretation to avoid disclosure. On the other hand, if the request is phrased broadly, the defendant can be expected to object on the grounds that the request is vague and burdensome.[18]

The decision to stonewall discovery may be no more than an extension of the initial corporate decision to market the product despite the existence of a known defect. A manufacturer whose ethics permit a deliberate cost-benefit decision to maximize profits by risking the health or safety of its customers can be expected to stonewall discovery

---

[17] Philip H. Corboy, *Discovery Wars and the Trial Lawyer*, in THE DISCOVERY DILEMMA: ADVANCING JUSTICE OR HINDERING IT? 11 (American Bar Ass'n eds., 1990); *see also* Thornburg, *supra* note 15, at 1065.

[18] Unfortunately this skepticism is supported by the numerous instances documented in reported cases. See chapter 2, section V, and chapter 5, section II.

to avoid having to pay damages that could frustrate its initial cost-benefit balancing.

Although refusing to produce relevant information to escape legal responsibility is unjustified and reprehensible, in recent years it has become standard operating procedure for some corporate defendants in defective product litigation. The history of such products as asbestos, Thalidomide, MER-29, and the Ford Pinto exemplify this approach to defending products liability actions.

B. Means of Detection and Prevention

Compared to stonewalling, overuse of discovery is more easily detected, prevented, and corrected. The overuse of discovery is apparent by its very nature; it may be prevented and corrected with protective orders, perhaps accompanied by appropriate (usually monetary) sanctions. In sharp contrast, stonewalling is always difficult and often impossible to detect and therefore to prevent or correct.

C. Consequences

The consequences of overuse, while significant, are not as debilitating to the justice system as the consequences of stonewalling. The adverse effects of overuse are limited to time and money. These are not insignificant effects, but at least they can be rectified—they do not lead to a failure of justice. Unlike commercial litigation or litigation between private parties, a single plaintiff's overuse of discovery, to the extent not checked by the court, is unlikely to be so onerous to the manufacturer-defendant as to force its capitulation. As noted, no sensible personal injury plaintiff's lawyer would wage a war of resources with a major corporation—a war the plaintiff would be bound to lose.

The adverse impact of stonewalling, on the other hand, reaches the very substance of the case and undermines the ability of the legal system to give all parties a fair trial. Stonewalling deprives not only the plaintiff but also the court and the jury of vital evidence. It therefore diminishes the prospect of a fair trial on the true merits.

III. NEED FOR DETERRENCE

Although no form of discovery abuse should be tolerated, the courts must take decisive and forceful action to correct, punish, and deter stonewalling by corporate defendants whenever they withhold vital information in their possession. Because stonewalling has reached epidemic proportions, and because it may utterly foreclose the substantive rights of the injured person—indeed, that is precisely what the stonewaller intends—a nominally punitive sanction is not calculated to and will not be effective in preventing the practice. The motivation to stonewall is so great that offenders will not comply with discovery requests unless they know *in advance of litigation* that the cost of stonewalling will be greater than the benefits.[19]

Only severe sanctions for stonewalling will offset the powerful economic motivation. The courts must apply disincentives in the forum where the cost decisions are made, the corporate boardroom, by making stonewalling prohibitively expensive.

---

[19] *See* Note, *The Emerging Deterrence Orientation in the Imposition of Discovery Sanctions*, 91 HARV. L. REV. 1033 (1978); see also chapter 10.

CHAPTER FIVE

COMMON TACTICS FOR EVADING DISCLOSURE

I. OVERVIEW: PATTERNS OF DECEPTION

The plaintiff's efforts to obtain information exclusively in the defendant's possession will frequently be met by a wall of unyielding opposition. Although the practice of stonewalling has been with us for as long as discovery has been allowed, in recent years corporate defendants in complex litigation have raised the practice to a new art form.

Various tactics that manufacturers employ to stonewall discovery are cataloged separately here and in the following three chapters solely for the purpose of analysis. These categories overlap. Not all forms of improper discovery responses will fit into any one category described. Unfortunately, the means by which to deceive are as limitless as the human imagination. In practice a manufacturer frequently uses an array of these tactics. Many courts have observed that a defendant's various discovery responses, when viewed collectively, reveal a plan or pattern to subvert meaningful discovery.[1]

---

[1] *See, e.g.*, Malautea v. Suzuki Motor Co., No. CV 490-322 (S.D. Ga. Dec. 30, 1991) (finding pattern of stonewalling, including delay, unreasonably narrow semantical reading of discovery requests, and unilateral limitations on responses was based on subjective, narrow view of relevance, and deliberate cover-up of damaging evidence), *aff'd*, 987 F.2d 1536 (11th Cir.), *cert. denied*, 114 S. Ct. 181 (1993); Hathcock v. Navistar Int'l Transp. Corp., No. 6:92-3190-3 (D.S.C. Oct. 7, 1993) (entering default judgment for pattern of discovery abuses by defendant intended to "confuse, delay and ultimately frustrate meaningful discovery," including willful violations of court orders; Navistar is seeking appellate review); Kobatake v. E.I. DuPont de Nemours & Co., No. 92-132-COL (M.D. Ga. June 8, 1993) (noting that "defendant continues to take every means possible to obstruct discovery to which the plaintiffs are entitled," the court imposes $1 million contingent sanction); National Ass'n of Radiation Survivors v. Turnage, 115 F.R.D. 543, 546 n.1 (N.D.Cal. 1987) (sanctioning United States for pattern of abuses including document destruction and concealment); Kozlowski v. Sears, Roebuck & Co., 71 F.R.D. 594, 597 (D. Mass.) (entering default for "pattern of continuous, flagrant, and willful disregard by the defendant of the letter and spirit of the rules of discovery"), *motion denied*, 73 F.R.D. 73 (D. Mass. 1976); Cooper v. American Honda Motor Co., CA No. 47-35-13,

For instance, in *Kramer v. Boeing Co.*[2] the court imposed sanctions on aircraft manufacturer Pratt & Whitney for its pattern of "grossly unacceptable discovery practices,"[3] observing that, while tactics such as patently misleading objections may not be as serious as intentional document destruction, they can be as effective in concealing highly relevant, properly requested discovery materials. The court imposed rule 37 sanctions after finding that Pratt & Whitney had "intentionally, recklessly, or negligently misled [its] adversaries and the court," thereby failing to fulfill its obligation to provide full, informative, and truthful discovery responses.[4]

Chapters 5 through 8 describe various techniques frequently used to undermine the full and fair exchange of information that the Federal Rules of Civil Procedure are meant to facilitate. The abuses identified here illustrate the pervasiveness of stonewalling in American civil litigation. We hope that the information provided will assist the reader in recognizing and countering stonewalling tactics in whatever form they take.[5]

Referee's Report No. 6A (San Diego County, Cal. Super. Ct. Feb. 11, 1988) (taking judicial notice of decisions of other courts illustrating a "pattern of conduct by Honda" found by courts to have "thwarted the expeditious and effective prosecution of those actions"); King v. American Food Equip. Co., 513 N.E.2d 958, 965-68 (Ill. App. Ct.) (upholding dismissal of manufacturer's third-party action as sanction for "pattern of deliberate and blatant disregard of discovery rules"), *appeal denied*, 512 N.E.2d 1087 (Ill. 1987); Chemical Exch. Indus. v. Vasquez, 709 S.W.2d 257, 259-60 (Tex. Ct. App.) (affirming default judgment on liability as sanction for repeated abuses of discovery process), *rev'd in part*, 721 S.W.2d 284 (Tex. 1986); *see also* Perkinson v. Gilbert/Robinson, Inc., 821 F.2d 686, 691 (D.C. Cir. 1987); Floyd v. Bic Corp., No. 1:89-cv-401-RLV (N.D. Ga. Aug. 31, 1992) (recounting Bic history in case of going to great lengths to avoid discovery regarding allegedly defective lighter), *vacated following settlement*; Fjelstad v. American Honda Motor Co., No. CV 81-227-BLG-JFB (D. Mont. May 23, 1986), *on remand from* 762 F.2d 1334 (9th Cir. 1985); Green v. Shepherd Constr. Co., No. 11740 (N.D. Ga. 1969) (outlining the many instances of discovery abuse by Ford and stating, "It seems to the court that there is a pattern of evasion and lack of candor running through Ford's response to discovery."); Honda Motor Co. v. Salzman, 751 P.2d 489, 493 (Alaska), *cert. dismissed*, 487 U.S. 1260 (1988); Braun v. American Honda Motor Co., No. CV 86-337-BLG-JFB (Mont. Dist. Ct. Sept. 4, 1987) (awarding attorney fees and costs for Honda's unwarranted objections and delay in responding to discovery requests, finding objections and responses "lack merit and were propounded in an effort to mislead or to waste time," *id*. at 3). Significantly, the court in *Braun* took into account the pattern of Honda's discovery abuse in other cases before the court. *Id*. at 4; *cf*. Heathman v. Owens-Corning Fiberglass Corp., No. 87-C-1934, Master's Report (Brazoria County, Tex. Dist. Ct. Dec. 20, 1990) and Searls v. Owens-Corning Fiberglas Corp., No. 88-C-0615, Master's Report (Brazoria County, Tex. Dist. Ct. Dec. 20, 1990) (master's report spelling out in detail various tactics employed by defendant as part of a grand design to resist meaningful discovery).

[2] 126 F.R.D. 690 (D. Minn. 1989).

[3] *Id*. at 697.

[4] *Id*. at 697–98 (citations omitted).

[5] A listing of select authorities dealing with discovery abuse appears in the Bibliography.

II. BOILERPLATE OBJECTIONS

This tactic involves the use of a generalized objection in lieu of an individualized response to a written discovery request, such as "objection is made to the interrogatory as being vague, ambiguous, and not reasonably calculated to lead to the discovery of admissible evidence." Many courts have criticized the use of a litany of unsupported objections.[6] For instance, in *Roesberg v. Johns-Manville Corp.*,[7] the court overruled the defendant's objections, repeated for virtually every other interrogatory, as "overly broad, burdensome, oppressive and irrelevant."[8]

> To voice a successful objection to an interrogatory, [defendant] cannot simply intone this familiar litany. Rather, [defendant] must show specifically how, despite the broad and liberal construction afforded the federal discovery rules, each interrogatory is not relevant or how each question is overly broad, burdensome, or oppressive. . . .[9]

Broad objections based on unsupported generalizations are thus insufficient, and may result in a waiver of the right to object on any ground.[10]

The defendant's response frequently includes a laundry list of insufficiently specific "form" objections.[11] The most common ones are quoted below, along with authorities rejecting their improper invocation.

- *The discovery request is vague and ambiguous and/or the defendant does not understand the meaning or the object of the discovery request.* Vagueness objections are often asserted even when the plaintiff has supplied the defendant with a table of specific definitions.[12]

- *A response to the discovery request would be unduly burdensome and/or oppressive.*[13]

---

[6] *See, e.g.*, Kramer v. Boeing Co., 126 F.R.D. 690, 698 (D. Minn. 1989); Roesberg v. Johns-Manville Corp., 85 F.R.D. 292, 296–97 (E.D. Pa. 1980); *In re* Folding Carton Antitrust Litig., 83 F.R.D. 260, 264 (N.D. Ill. 1979). For discussion of the manufacturer's duty to make specific objections based on stated grounds, see chapter 2, section V.

[7] 85 F.R.D. 292 (E.D. Pa. 1980).

[8] *Id.* at 296.

[9] *Id.*

[10] *See, e.g.*, Dollar v. Long Mfg., N.C., Inc., 561 F.2d 613, 617 (5th Cir. 1977), *cert. denied*, 435 U.S. 996 (1978); Casson Constr. Co. v. Armco Steel Corp., 91 F.R.D. 376, 378–79 (D. Kan. 1980).

[11] *See generally* SCOTT BALDWIN ET AL., THE PREPARATION OF A PRODUCT LIABILITY CASE § 7.4 (2d ed. 1993); RICHARD H. UNDERWOOD & WILLIAM H. FORTUNE, TRIAL ETHICS § 6.5.2, at 244–45 (1988 & Supp. 1993); Roger S. Haydock & David F. Herr, *Interrogatories: Questions and Answers*, 1 Rev. Litig. 263, 288 (1981).

[12] See chapter 2, section V.C.

[13] See chapter 2, section V.B; *see, e.g.*, Roesberg v. Johns-Manville Corp., 85 F.R.D. 292, 296 (E.D. Pa. 1980).

- *The discovery request is overly broad and/or too general and/or too inclusive.*[14]
- *The discovery request seeks irrelevant information and/or information that is beyond the scope of discovery.* The defendant may not limit the broad scope of relevance based on its own subjective and very restrictive views.[15]
- *The information sought is already in the plaintiff's possession.*[16]
- *The information sought is equally available to the plaintiff.*[17]
- *The information sought may be found in the deposition of Witness X and/or in the defendant's pleadings.* The defendant may generally refer to other sources, as well. An interrogatory response which merely references such other sources is insufficient and improper.[18]
- *The answer to the discovery request would be inadmissible at trial.* At any rate, admissibility is no standard for discoverability.[19]
- *The defendant does not possess the requested information.* This response typically does not describe what efforts, if any, the company has made to locate and obtain the requested information.[20]
- *The defendant has located certain documents which contain information pertinent to this discovery request. Copies of these documents are located at the offices of defense counsel. They will be furnished to the plaintiff on request.* This response may be

---

[14] 85 F.R.D. at 296.

[15] *See, e.g.*, Roesberg v. Johns-Manville Corp., 85 F.R.D. 292, 296 (E.D. Pa. 1980); Gammon v. Clark Equip. Co., 686 P.2d 1102, 1107 (Wash. Ct. App. 1984), *aff'd en banc*, 707 P.2d 685 (Wash. 1985); *cf.* Stengel v. Kawasaki Heavy Indus., 116 F.R.D. 263, 264 (N.D. Tex. 1987); Sellers v. General Motors Corp., 40 Fed. R. Serv. 2d (Callaghan) 590, 592–93 (E.D. Pa. 1984) (manufacturer's restrictive view of relevance). The impropriety of a defendant's attempting to limit the scope of discovery is discussed in section IV of this chapter.

[16] *See, e.g.*, Weiss v. Chrysler Motors Co., 515 F.2d 449, 456 (2d Cir. 1975); Broadway & Ninety-Sixth St. Realty Co. v. Loew's Inc., 21 F.R.D. 347, 356–57 (S.D.N.Y. 1958); *see also* 4 JAMES W. MOORE ET AL., MOORE'S FEDERAL PRACTICE ¶ 26.59 (2d ed. 1991 & Supp. 1992).

[17] *See* 4 MOORE ET AL., *supra* note 16, ¶ 26.59.

[18] Continental Ill. Nat'l Bank & Trust Co. v. Caton, 136 F.R.D. 682, 686 (D. Kan. 1991); Atlanta Coca-Cola Bottling Co. v. Transamerica Ins. Co., 61 F.R.D. 115, 116–17, 119–20 (N.D. Ga. 1972); Pilling v. General Motors Corp., 45 F.R.D. 366, 369 (D. Utah 1968); Zatko v. Rogers Mfg. Co., 37 F.R.D. 29, 33 (N.D. Ohio 1964); J.J. Delaney Carpet Co. v. Forrest Mills, Inc., 34 F.R.D. 152 (S.D.N.Y. 1963); Grimmett v. Atchison, Topeka & Sante Fe Ry., 11 F.R.D. 335, 336 (N.D. Ohio 1951); United Nuclear Corp. v. General Atomic Co., 629 P.2d 231, 299 (N.M. 1980) *appeal dismissed*, 451 U.S. 901, *reh'g denied*, 452 U.S. 932 (1981).

[19] See chapter 1 for a discussion of the broad scope of discovery relevance.

[20] See chapter 2, section II, discussing the manufacturer's duty to conduct an inquiry in order to respond to plaintiff's discovery requests, and chapter 2, section III, concerning the manufacturer's duty to supplement its response to discovery requests.

accompanied by a statement to the effect that the defendant will continue its investigation in an effort to identify other relevant information.[21] Such a response should be construed as an agreement to supplement the party's response under 26(e).[22] Indeed, the court should enter an order requiring the party to supplement its response when the documents are found.[23]

- *Not applicable and/or do not recall.*[24]
- *The discovery request seeks an admission of fact.*[25]
- *The discovery request seeks factual opinions or conclusions or legal contentions related to the facts.*[26]
- *The discovery request seeks information protected by the work-product and/or the attorney-client privilege.* This objection is often unaccompanied by any statement of the factual basis or legal justification for the claimed privilege(s).[27]

III. USE OF SEMANTICS

The defendant in a defective-product case often employs an unreasonably narrow interpretation of the plaintiff's discovery request in order to avoid disclosure. When General Motors did so in *Sellon v. Smith*,[28] the trial court upheld a magistrate judge's determination that the corporation "had adopted an unreasonably narrow construction of Plaintiffs' document requests and, therefore, failed to respond properly to the request." The court approved a broad production order, designed to ensure that GM would not continue to unreasonably withhold documents.[29] Similarly, in *Rozier v. Ford Motor Co.*,[30] a new trial was ordered when documents unreasonably withheld by Ford Motor Company were discovered by plaintiff's counsel following a

---

[21] See discussion of the "unfulfilled promise" delay in section V of this chapter.

[22] *See* A.O. Smith Corp. v. Viking Corp., 79 F.R.D. 91, 94 (E.D. Wis. 1978).

[23] *See* Phil Crowley Steel Corp. v. Macomber, Inc., 601 F.2d 342 (8th Cir. 1979); United States v. IBM Corp., 83 F.R.D. 92, 96 (S.D.N.Y. 1979). The manufacturer's duty to supplement its response to discovery requests is discussed in chapter 2, section III.

[24] *See* Philadelphia Hous. Auth. v. American Radiator & Standard Sanitary Corp., 50 F.R.D. 13, 18 (E.D. Pa. 1970) ("Discovery procedures cannot be frustrated by such transparent sham."), *aff'd sub nom.* Mangano v. American Radiator & Standard Sanitary Corp., 438 F.2d 1187 (3d Cir. 1971).

[25] *See* 4A MOORE ET AL., *supra* note 16, ¶ 33.17; FED. R. CIV. P. 33(b).

[26] *See* 4A MOORE ET AL., *supra* note 16, ¶ 33.17; FED. R. CIV. P. 33(b).

[27] *See* Dean v. A.H. Robins Co., 101 F.R.D. 21 (D. Minn. 1984); chapter 1, section III.

[28] 112 F.R.D. 9, 11 (D. Del. 1986).

[29] *Id.*

[30] 573 F.2d 1332, 1341 (5th Cir.), *reh'g denied*, 578 F.2d 871 (5th Cir. 1978).

verdict for Ford. The court also criticized the defendant for its unreasonably narrow reading of a discovery request and court order.[31]

Another example of this tactic occurred in *Malautea v. Suzuki Motor Co.*,[32] where the auto manufacturer objected to terms such as "tests, research, or other investigation," "risk of rollover," "change, alteration, or modification," "risk of personal injury," "substantially similar," "other sport utility vehicle," and "engineer" as being ambiguous. "The Defendants and their lawyers . . . have managed to inject ambiguity into these ordinary words," the trial court commented, comparing defense counsel's explanation of its contorted reading of these terms with Humpty Dumpty's remark in Lewis Carroll's *Through the Looking Glass*: "'When I use a word,' Humpty Dumpty said in rather a scornful tone, 'it means just what I choose it to mean—neither more nor less.'"[33]

The court recognized that "[t]he Defendants' complaints about ambiguity are part of their overall plan to obstruct the Plaintiff's discovery attempts," and that "[t]o the Court's disdain, these tactics are characteristic of the Defendants' actions in this case."[34]

Plaintiffs drafting discovery inquiries are always faced with a dilemma when deciding how specific to be in wording their requests. Precisely worded requests are too easily subjected to unreasonably narrow interpretations, while broader requests are routinely challenged as vague. Providing a table of definitions with interrogatories and requests for production can help resolve this problem, as well as make the actual interrogatories or requests less cumbersome and repetitious.

IV. UNILATERALLY AND SUBJECTIVELY LIMITING THE SCOPE OF RELEVANCE

For a defendant to succeed in preventing the disclosure of its damaging documents, it must somehow overcome the broad scope of discovery. Manufacturers frequently attempt to accomplish this objective by persuading the court to restrict the ambit of relevance to their own subjective view of the facts or adversarial theory of the

---

[31] *Id.*; Emerick v. Fenick Indus., 539 F.2d 1379 (5th Cir. 1976) (striking pleadings and entering judgment for opponent of party who disregarded court order to produce "ledgers and journals" by unreasonably and narrowly construing the term to exclude computerized information); *see also* Floyd v. Bic Corp., No. 1:89-cv-401-RLV (N.D. Ga. Aug. 31, 1992). In *Floyd*, Bic drew a distinction between "proceeding" versus "inquiry" and "correspondence" versus "document" to justify its failure to produce relevant documents. In Berkey Photo's famous antitrust suit against Eastman Kodak, defense counsel employed the tenuous distinction between "correspondence" and "reports" to justify withholding an important letter/report prepared by Kodak's principal expert. *See* Walter Kiechel III, *The Strange Case of Kodak's Lawyers*, FORTUNE, May 8, 1978, at 188, 190.

[32] No. CV 490-322 (S.D. Ga. Dec. 30, 1991), *aff'd*, 987 F.2d 1536 (11th Cir.), *cert. denied*, 114 S. Ct. 181 (1993).

[33] No. CV 490-322, slip op. at 9.

[34] *Id.* at 10.

case. Manufacturers will use this tactic to attempt to shield from disclosure entire categories of information, including product tests, studies, design criteria, design drawings, performance criteria, reports of other similar incidents, and subsequent remedial measures taken. Three arguments are routinely advanced to avoid disclosure of such information:[35]

- Discovery should be limited to information concerning the *particular model type* that caused the plaintiff's injury.[36]
- Discovery should be limited to the *particular year* the product causing the injury was manufactured.[37]
- Discovery should be limited based on the defendant's narrow view of the *circumstances of the particular incident.*

Courts have repeatedly rejected defendants' attempts to so restrict discovery.[38] In its motion to compel, the plaintiff should point out that the defendant's contentions are in direct conflict with the broad objectives as well as specific provisions of the federal discovery rules.[39]

Under rule 26, relevance is determined by the subject matter in dispute. In a products liability case, this means information relating to the plaintiff's claim that the defendant's product poses an unreasonable risk of harm. Any information that has any bearing on the truth of this claim should be discoverable. Thus, courts have liberally permitted discovery of different models, different years, and even significantly different types of equipment than that which caused the plaintiff's injury. They have done so where discovery might improve understanding of engineering principles utilized in the subject product or shed light on the safety of its design.[40]

Under this approach, discovery has been permitted concerning later year automobiles made by the same manufacturer,[41] a surveillance camera using a motor of significantly greater voltage than that alleged to have caused a fire,[42] other types of tools

---

[35] *See generally* TERRENCE F. KIELY, PREPARING PRODUCTS LIABILITY CASES §§ 5.2, 5.3, 7.3 (1986 & Supp. 1989).

[36] *See, e.g.,* Malautea v. Suzuki Motor Co., No. CV 490-322 (S.D. Ga. Dec. 30, 1991) (imposing default sanction for abuses including limiting responses based on defendant manufacturer's subjective, unilateral determination of relevance), *aff'd,* 987 F.2d 1536 (11th Cir.), *cert. denied,* 114 S. Ct. 181 (1993).

[37] 987 F.2d at 1540.

[38] See chapter 2, section V.A.

[39] See chapter 1, section II for a discussion of the proper scope of relevance in discovery and citations to numerous authorities.

[40] *See* Kramer v. Boeing Co., 126 F.R.D. 690, 692–95 (D. Minn. 1989).

[41] Bowman v. General Motors Corp., 64 F.R.D. 62, 68 (E.D. Pa. 1974).

[42] Fireman's Fund Ins. Co. v. ECM Motor Co., 132 F.R.D. 39, 40–41 (W.D. Pa. 1990).

using a method of discharging projectiles similar to that used in the tool at issue,[43] and a different model vehicle with stability characteristics similar to those of the accident vehicle.[44]

The manufacturer's assertions of irrelevance are usually inconsistent with the technical concepts of relevance employed by its own engineers in the development, design, manufacture, and distribution of the product. The plaintiff should have access to the same information that the defendant's technical personnel and corporate managers actually had and considered while developing the product, and which will be made available to the defendant's litigation experts.[45] The purpose of the discovery rules would be defeated if the plaintiff were denied access to this information.

Although responses inevitably represent, either expressly or implicitly, that the documents furnished are all that exist, the manufacturer's capacity for limiting the information it makes available to plaintiffs is well documented. What the plaintiff does not know, and often cannot find out, is to what extent the scope of discovery has been unilaterally restricted to the defendant's subjective and adversarial view of relevance. One critical solution is to assure plaintiffs in similar cases the opportunity to compare discovery as a means to verify the accuracy and completeness of discovery responses.[46]

V. EVASIVE, MISLEADING, OR FALSE RESPONSES

Discovery respondents who are determined to thwart the discovery goal of full and fair information exchange without getting caught may look for ways to appear to answer discovery inquiries without actually revealing any information. This may be accomplished through clever wordsmithing, truthful but incomplete responses, insincere promises to supply the information at a later date, confusing or misleading answers, or plain old lies.

Practitioners report that the practice of evasion is widespread,[47] and that tactics are varied and imaginative. Evasion may begin with delay, discussed in the next section,[48] or with groundless objections, as in *Kramer v. Boeing Co.*, discussed at the outset of this chapter.[49] Defendants often answer with an objection along with a response

---

[43] Lohr v. Stanley-Bostitch, Inc., 135 F.R.D. 162, 164–65 (W.D. Mich. 1991).

[44] Valet v. American Motors Inc., 481 N.Y.S.2d 364 (App. Div. 1984); see chapter 1, section II.B.1.

[45] *See* Kramer v. Boeing Co., 126 F.R.D. 690, 692–95 (D. Minn. 1989).

[46] See chapter 8, section II.

[47] *See, e.g.*, Wayne D. Brazil, *Civil Discovery: Lawyers' View of Its Effectiveness, Its Principal Problems and Abuses*, 1980 AM. B. FOUND. RES. J. 787, 828–29.

[48] *See, e.g.*, Bates v. Firestone Tire & Rubber Co., 83 F.R.D. 535 (D.S.C. 1979); Cooper v. American Honda Motor Co., No. 47 35 13, Referee's Report No. 1 (San Diego County, Cal. Super. Ct. Apr. 18, 1986) (finding Honda's willful and persistent evasive responses and continual obstructive maneuvers were for the purpose of evasion and delay).

[49] 126 F.R.D. 690 (D. Minn. 1989); see notes 2 through 4 of this chapter and accompanying text.

and a statement that the objection is not waived by providing the response. The plaintiff may not challenge the objection because a response has been given; however, the manufacturer may actually be using the objection to conceal the incomplete nature of its response instead of directly stating that its response is incomplete.[50]

In *Bagwell v. Nissan Motor Co.*[51] plaintiff's counsel asked the defendant to identify the employees with knowledge of the design of the component involved. Nissan responded that it was searching its records for this information and would answer when the information was found. More than two years later, Nissan had failed to provide any additional response.[52]

Honda unsuccessfully employed the unfulfilled promise strategy in *Votour v. American Honda Motor Co.*[53] Seven months after the plaintiff had requested certain crash test results, and following two court orders compelling their production, two hearings in which sanctions were imposed, and one unsuccessful attempt at appellate review, Honda continued to respond that the documents would be made "available as soon as possible." When Honda failed to produce any records, the court struck its pleadings and entered a default judgment.

Another popular evasion technique is simply to ignore the content of the request, either answering a more narrow question than was asked or referring the plaintiff to a few benign documents furnished as if they constituted full compliance, or both.[54]

Evasion is also practiced by employing a record system that conceals rather than reveals. The manufacturer may attempt to delay or suppress discovery by maintaining a record system that conceals or even destroys relevant information.[55]

Some manufacturers also attempt to evade disclosure by conducting product tests after the discovery cutoff date set by the court—or even during trial. In this situation, because the discovery phase has ended, unfavorable test results are not disclosed. Favorable test results are sprung on the plaintiffs at trial without warning or

---

[50] *See, e.g.*, Gammon v. Clark Equip. Co., 686 P.2d 1102, 1107 (Wash. Ct. App. 1984), *aff'd en banc*, 707 P.2d 685 (Wash. 1985), *discussed infra* notes 61–65 and accompanying text.

[51] No. 7:90-753-20 (S.C. Dist. Ct. filed Sept. 14, 1992).

[52] *Id.*, Plaintiff's Motion for Sanctions at 3. The case was settled before the district court ruled on the motion for sanctions.

[53] No. 79 4686 CA (L) 01 B (Palm Beach County, Fla. Cir. Ct. Sept. 7, 1983), *on remand from* 435 So. 2d 368 (Fla. Dist. Ct. App. 1983).

[54] *See* Babb v. Ford Motor Co., 535 N.E.2d 676 (Ohio Ct. App. 1987).

[55] *See, e.g.*, Baine v. General Motors Corp., 141 F.R.D. 328, 331 (M.D. Ala. 1991); *In re* Richardson-Merrell, Inc., 97 F.R.D. 481, 483 (S.D. Ohio 1983); Baxter Travenol Lab., Inc. v. LeMay, 93 F.R.D. 379, 383 (S.D. Ohio 1981); *In re* "Agent Orange" Prod. Liab. Litig., 506 F. Supp. 750, 751 (E.D.N.Y. 1980); Kozlowski v. Sears, Roebuck & Co., 73 F.R.D. 73, 76 (D. Mass. 1976); Shatzkamer v. Eskind, 528 N.Y.S.2d 968, 972 (Cir. Ct. 1988); *see also* Stengel v. Kawasaki Heavy Indus., 116 F.R.D. 263, 265–66 (N.D. Tex. 1987); Alliance to End Repression v. Rochford, 75 F.R.D. 441, 447 (N.D. Ill. 1977). Record retention and destruction policies are discussed in greater detail in chapter 7, section II.B.

any opportunity to independently evaluate testing procedures and conclusions. Courts have excluded evidence or have ordered new trials to remedy this type of discovery abuse.[56]

Discovery respondents frequently assert that no records contain the information sought[57] or that specified corporate officers lack responsive knowledge.[58] Because such answers do not address the complete knowledge of the discovery respondent, they should be treated as evasive or incomplete responses—even in the absence of a court order—pursuant to rule 37(a)(3).[59] A response that merely cites to deposition testimony or other documents likewise is nonresponsive.[60]

Evasive, misleading, incomplete, or deceitful discovery responses can be even worse than other forms of stonewalling if they leave the plaintiff with the false impression that the information sought has in fact been fully provided.

This is what occurred in *Gammon v. Clark Equipment Co.*, a products liability action involving a Bobcat loader that tipped and killed the plaintiff's husband.[61] Two years before trial, the plaintiff submitted interrogatories requesting information regarding any personal injuries arising out of the use of "any similar or substantially similar products." Clark answered by objecting to the scope of the interrogatory, but it produced five accident reports. Two years later, just weeks before trial, the plaintiff learned during depositions of the manufacturer's design and safety engineers that five accidents *per year* had been reported to Clark. The court therefore granted the plaintiff's motion to compel and ordered Clark to produce "*all* accident reports and reports of accidents involving a tip over of *any* Bobcat machine ever produced by [Clark]."[62] About 50 more accident reports were produced. After jury selection began, plaintiff's counsel fortuitously learned of even more tip-over accidents for which reports had not been produced. Clark's counsel did not deny that additional reports existed but told the court they were not relevant because those accidents involved different equipment and different circumstances. Further court-ordered discovery on

---

[56] *See* Weiss v. Chrysler Motors Corp., 515 F.2d 449, 457 (2d Cir. 1975) (ordering new trial); Collins v. Interroyal Corp., 466 N.E.2d 1191, 1198 (Ill. App. Ct. 1984) (excluding manufacturer's expert testimony); *cf.* Foster v. Gillette Co., 161 Cal. Rptr. 134, 139–40 (Ct. App. 1979) (late testing by both plaintiff and manufacturer).

[57] *See* Alliance to End Repression v. Rochford, 75 F.R.D. 438, 440 (N.D. Ill. 1976).

[58] *Cf.* Pilling v. General Motors Corp., 45 F.R.D. 366, 369 (D. Utah 1968) (applying rule to individual plaintiff's discovery response).

[59] *See generally* 23 AM. JUR. 2D *Depositions and Discovery* § 219, at 536 (1983 & Supp. 1992) [hereinafter 23 AM. JUR.]; ROGER S. HAYDOCK & DAVID F. HERR, DISCOVERY PRACTICE § 4.6 (2d ed. 1988 & Supp. 1992).

[60] *See* United Nuclear Corp. v. General Atomic Co., 629 P.2d 231, 299 (N.M. 1980), *cert. denied*, 451 U.S. 901, *reh'g denied*, 452 U.S. 932 (1981).

[61] 686 P.2d 1102 (Wash. Ct. App. 1984), *aff'd en banc*, 707 P.2d 685 (Wash. 1985).

[62] *Id.* at 1105.

the extent of Clark's compliance with the court's earlier production order revealed two more boxes of accident reports, which were not turned over until the trial was underway.

Following a jury verdict for Clark, the trial court denied the plaintiff's motion for a new trial, instead awarding $2,500 in sanctions against Clark.[63] The Washington Court of Appeals reversed and ordered a new trial, explaining,

> An award of $2,500 is cheap at twice the price in the context of a $4.5 million wrongful death case. Approval of such a *de minimis* sanction in a case such as this would plainly undermine the purpose of discovery. Far from ensuring that a wrongdoer not profit from his wrong, minimal terms would simply encourage litigants to embrace tactics of evasion and delay.[64]

The appeals court had no difficulty granting a new trial even in the absence of a showing that timely production of the reports would have made a difference at trial, thereby refusing to grant the benefit of the doubt to the party that engaged in misconduct. Nor was a new trial precluded by the fact that plaintiff's counsel did not seek a continuance when the reports ultimately surfaced, since requiring the plaintiff to disrupt her trial presentation would reward the manufacturer's noncompliance.[65]

Another heavy equipment manufacturer was alleged to have fraudulently concealed evidence in *Ostendorf v. International Harvester Co.*[66] As in *Clark*, the plaintiff proceeded to trial assuming that complete responses to discovery had been provided. The plaintiff had been burned "when the fuel tank filler cap of an International Harvester tractor allegedly 'blew off' under pressure." Through interrogatories, the plaintiff requested any tests conducted on the fuel system for that tractor model, and asked whether any officer or employee or other person or company had ever expressed an opinion to management recommending against that type of gas tank. The manufacturer responded that detailed records concerning "specific" tests were no longer available, and that no such recommendation had ever been made "to our knowledge."[67] The jury found for the manufacturer. Nearly four years later, the plaintiff petitioned to set aside the prior judgment for International Harvester on the ground that test reports and other International Harvester documents obtained during the plaintiff's attorney's representation of a different party in another matter showed that International Harvester had not responded fairly to the plaintiff's discovery requests. The court held that the plaintiff was entitled to a hearing on the petition, despite the length of time that had passed since trial. Assuming the truth of the plaintiffs' allegations for purposes of the petition, the court observed,

---

[63] *Id.*

[64] *Id.* at 1107.

[65] *Id.*

[66] 433 N.E.2d 253 (Ill. 1982).

[67] *Id.* at 256.

The existence of these reports, which are clearly material embraced by the interrogatories, demonstrates International Harvester's failure to comply with the requirements of full and frank disclosure imposed by our discovery rules. In light of these documents, International Harvester's responses were, if not outright falsehoods, half-truths . . . [which] *have the effect of affirmative concealment*, since they imply that there is no information or evidence to be sought. They inevitably tend to mislead opposing counsel into the belief that further inquiry is not needed.[68]

In both *Clark* and *Ostendorf* the manufacturer's evasion was discovered fortuitously. While the Washington and Illinois Supreme Courts used strong language in their opinions and took decisive action to restore justice in those particular cases, in neither case were the sanctions imposed likely to serve as a deterrent to similar future behavior. Evasive, misleading, and false discovery responses are difficult to detect and confer a significant advantage. So long as the judicial response is limited to preventing prejudice in the individual case under review, this type of abuse will remain profitable to many manufacturers: their analysis of costs and benefits will continue to favor evasion. Types of abuse that are difficult to detect must be punished by sanctions that are sufficiently severe to deter similar behavior in future.[69]

This is not to say that severe sanctions are never imposed. Many courts have imposed default and dismissal for abuses including evasive or false responses.[70]

For instance, in *Votour v. American Honda Motor Co.*[71] the plaintiff tried unsuc-

---

[68] *Id.* at 257 (emphasis added); *see also* Malautea v. Suzuki Motor Corp., No. CV 490-322, slip op. at 33 (S.D. Ga. Dec. 30, 1991) ("Regardless of how tricky the Defendants have been in avoiding an overt lie, their actions have had the same result as an outright lie would have had."), *aff'd*, 987 F.2d 1536 (11th Cir.), *cert. denied*, 114 S. Ct. 181 (1993).

[69] *See* Charles R. Nesson, *Incentives to Spoliate Evidence in Civil Litigation: The Need for Vigorous Judicial Action*, 13 CARDOZO L. REV. 793 (1991); see also chapter 10, section V.

[70] *See, e.g.,* Malautea v. Suzuki Motor Co., No. CV 490-322 (S.D. Ga. Dec. 30, 1991) (imposing default sanction for abuses including cover-up of damaging evidence), *aff'd*, 987 F.2d 1536 (11th Cir.), *cert. denied*, 114 S. Ct. 181 (1993); Altschuler v. Samsonite Corp., 109 F.R.D. 353, 356–58 (E.D.N.Y. 1986) (entering default judgment against defendant for gross negligence in failing to produce documents); Casson Constr. Co. v. Armco Steel Corp., 91 F.R.D. 376, 385 (D. Kan. 1980) (approving default judgment as sanction for bad faith refusal to disclose relevant information); Penthouse Int'l, Ltd. v. Playboy Enters., 86 F.R.D. 396 (S.D.N.Y. 1980) (dismissing plaintiff's claims for failure to comply with discovery order), *aff'd*, 663 F.2d 371 (2d Cir. 1981); Bollard v. Volkswagen of Am., Inc., 56 F.R.D 569 (W.D. Mo. 1971) (entering default for obstructive discovery conduct and misinformation); Ultracashmere House, Ltd. v. Meyer, 407 So. 2d 125, 129 (Ala. 1981) (affirming default judgment for failure to comply with discovery orders); Hawes Firearms Co. v. Edwards, 634 P.2d 377 (Alaska 1981) (striking gun manufacturer's defenses as sanction for noncompliance with order compelling discovery); Morgan v. Southern Cal. Rapid Transit Dist., 237 Cal. Rptr. 756, 761–62 (Ct. App. 1987) (affirming propriety of sanction striking answer for willful failure to provide correct spelling of name of physician who examined defendant's employee bus driver before wreck, but reversing on procedural grounds), *overruled in part on other grounds*, Schwab v. Rondel Homes, Inc., 808 P. 2d 226 (Cal. 1991); Greenleaf v. Massachusetts Bay Transp. Auth., 494 N.E.2d 402, 404–05 (Mass.

cessfully for two years to get the defendant manufacturer's crash tests. Finally the court struck the defendant's pleadings and entered a default judgment holding that the defendant had been "deceptive and deliberately evasive" in its response and had adopted an approach "designed to obfuscate" the discovery rules.[72] But this type of sanction, together with monetary sanctions that go beyond reimbursement of costs, must be used regularly and predictably if stonewalling is to be effectively deterred.[73]

Other types of sanctions have included remedies closely tied to the particular abuse at issue, such as excluding evidence, deeming facts admitted, or striking particular defenses.[74] For instance, in *Caterpillar Tractor Co. v. Donahue*,[75] as a sanction for Caterpillar's failure to comply with a discovery order, the court refused to admit a film of an experiment supporting the manufacturer's contention that its tractor was not negligently designed. In *Manko v. United States*[76] in response to the government's refusal, despite a court order, to produce documents regarding the swine flu vaccine, the court deemed certain facts established that resulted in proof of causation.[77]

As a sanction for repeated discovery misconduct by Honda in *Fjelstad v. Ameri-*

App. Ct. 1986) (affirming default judgment for defendant railroad's persistent failure or refusal to furnish reports of other similar incidents, as ordered); United Nuclear Corp. v. General Atomic Co., 629 P.2d 231 (N.M. 1980) (entering default against General Atomic Co., a partnership of Gulf Oil Co. and a subsidiary of Dutch-Shell Oil Co., for stonewalling discovery), *appeal dismissed*, 451 U.S. 901, *reh'g denied*, 452 U.S. 932 (1981); Moraes Arantes v. Gotham Taxi Corp., 497 N.Y.S.2d 682, 683 (App. Div. 1986) (affirming default judgment as sanction for defendant's failure to produce documents as ordered).

[71] No. 79 4686 CA (L) 01 B (Palm Beach County, Fla. Cir. Ct. Sept. 7, 1983), *on remand from* 435 So. 2d 368 (Fla. Dist. Ct. App. 1983).

[72] No. 79 4686 CA (L) 01 B, slip op. at 2; *see also* Salzman v. Honda Motor Co., No. 4FA-85-1325 (Alaska Super. Ct. Dec. 4, 1986) (granting default judgment as sanction for willful suppression of documents stating "I cannot believe Honda's behavior in this case. I have never seen a party who has been so willing to violate court orders, never in my entire career."), *aff'd*, 751 P.2d 489 (Alaska), *cert. dismissed*, 487 U.S. 1260 (1988); Brandt v. R.L. Atwood, Inc., No. 85-6366-H (Nueces County, Tex. Dist. Ct. Mar. 30, 1987) (entering default judgment after finding that Honda "willfully failed and . . . refused to comply with the Court's orders on discovery motions").

[73] *See* Judith L. Maute, *Sporting Theory of Justice: Taming Adversary Zeal with a Logical Sanctions Doctrine*, 20 CONN. L. REV. 7 (1987); Nesson, *supra* note 69.

[74] *See, e.g.*, Dyess v. Uniroyal Tire Co., C.A. No. 86-2366-CA-A (Marion County, Fla. Cir. Ct. Sept. 3, 1987) (excluding defendant's expert evidence as a sanction for its failure to disclose existence of other similar incidents).

[75] 674 P.2d 1276, 1284–85 (Wyo. 1983).

[76] 636 F. Supp. 1419 (W.D. Mo. 1986), *aff'd in part*, 830 F.2d 831 (8th Cir. 1987).

[77] 636 F. Supp. at 1437–38.

can Honda Motor Co.,[78] a motorcycle design defect case, the trial court precluded the manufacturer from presenting any causation evidence or late-identified witnesses, precluded consideration of the issue of the plaintiff's fault, and limited Honda's proof and contentions at trial to those included in pleadings and discovery responses before discovery sanctions were first imposed.

In *West v. Johnson & Johnson Products, Inc.*,[79] a case involving toxic shock syndrome allegedly caused by tampons manufactured by the defendant, the court responded to the manufacturer's evasion of discovery of its test reports with an adverse inference instruction to the jury. The jury found for the plaintiff, and a California appellate court approved the use of the instruction as a sanction.[80]

In *Carey Canada, Inc. v. Hinely*,[81] an asbestos case, the court of appeals upheld retroactive and prospective fines for withholding documents under false pretenses. The appellate court also upheld most of the evidentiary sanctions imposed, including deeming as established the manufacturer's sale of asbestos, the plaintiff's exposure, the manufacturer's failure to warn of the product's dangerous characteristics, the manufacturer's negligence, and the manufacturer's knowing suppression and cover-up of the product's dangers, which were intended "to maximize corporate profits in complete and utter disregard of the adverse health effects."[82]

VI. DELAY

Plaintiffs' attorneys in *Moseley v. General Motors Corp.*, which resulted in a large jury verdict against General Motors based on pickup truck fuel tanks located outside the side frame rails, observed that "in obstructing discovery the defendant acts with one eye on the clock and the other on the court."[83] This aptly describes manufacturers who employ the strategy of delay. Defendants who do not resort to evidence destruction or suppression, either because of ethical considerations or fear of being caught, will frequently turn to delay as a means of accomplishing the same objectives. Because delay can be nearly as effective in concealing the facts, it likewise should be sanctioned both harshly and consistently.

Delay, with its inevitable consequence of increased expense, is the most common form of discovery abuse.

---

[78] No. CV 81-227-BLG-JFB (D. Mont. May 23, 1986), *on remand from* 762 F.2d 1334 (9th Cir. 1985).

[79] 220 Cal. Rptr. 437 (Ct. App. 1985), *cert. denied*, 478 U.S. 824 (1986).

[80] *Id.* at 440, 462–64.

[81] 352 S.E.2d 398 (Ga. Ct. App. 1986), *rev'd in part*, 356 S.E.2d 202 (Ga.) (reducing fine pursuant to statutory limitation), *cert. denied*, 484 U.S. 898 (1987), *vacated in part en banc*, 366 S.E.2d 242 (Ga. Ct. App. 1988) (vacating excess fine pursuant to Georgia Supreme Court's order).

[82] *Id.* at 401–02.

[83] Plaintiffs' Motion for Sanctions Against Defendant General Motors Corporation for Violating the Court's Discovery Orders, Moseley v. General Motors Corp., No. 90-V-6276 (Fulton County Ct., Ga. Apr. 13, 1992) (submitted by James E. Butler, Robert D. Cheeley, Patrick A. Dawson, and Gerald Davidson).

The defendant may employ a variety of maneuvers to protract the discovery process and suppress the disclosure of relevant information. Such maneuvers may include the following:

- seeking extensions of time for response,
- voluntarily providing little or no meaningful information and objecting on a variety of grounds to the plaintiff's discovery requests,
- forcing the plaintiff to file motions to compel discovery and then requesting evidentiary hearings,
- denying the existence of documents,
- asserting that documents are privileged and requesting in camera inspection,
- filing motions for reconsideration of orders compelling production of particular documents,
- filing motions for recusal of a referee or special master,
- seeking appellate review of discovery orders,
- dumping undifferentiated masses of documents on the plaintiff shortly before trial or providing access to a central depository in which documents are mislabeled and out of sequence and for which no adequate index is provided, and
- insisting on a protective order forbidding plaintiff's counsel from discussing the contents of discovery materials with any other lawyer or expert representing plaintiffs in other similar cases against the same defendants. A rejection of the defendant's motion for a restrictive protective order is likely to be followed by another round of motions for reconsideration and efforts to seek appellate review.

A special master presiding over sanctions hearings in a 1990 asbestos case in Texas found that both the corporate defendant and its counsel had resorted to virtually all these maneuvers in what the master described as "a grand design for handling discovery" in all the asbestos cases the defendant faced.[84]

---

[84] Heathman v. Owens-Corning Fiberglas Corp., No. 87-C-1934, Master's Report (Brazoria County, Tex. Dist. Ct. Dec. 20, 1990) and Searls v. Owens-Corning Fiberglas Corp., No. 88-C-0615, Master's Report (Brazoria County, Tex. Dist. Ct. Dec. 20, 1990). The special master recommended payment of plaintiff's attorney fees and the imposition of substantial monetary fines against both the corporate defendant and defense counsel. The defendants sought mandamus to review the trial court's adoption of the master's recommendation. The Texas Court of Appeals affirmed the award of attorney fees but reversed the imposition of monetary sanctions holding that Texas law provided trial courts with no authority to order monetary fines for discovery abuse. Owens-Corning Fiberglas Corp. v. Caldwell, 807 S.W.2d 413 (Tex. Ct. App. 1991). Subsequently the Texas Supreme Court in *Braden v. Downey*, 811 S.W.2d 922 (Tex. 1991), upheld the trial court's authority to impose monetary sanctions in accordance with certain criteria. Following the decision in *Braden*, the trial court reinstated the monetary sanctions initially imposed against the defendant and its counsel in the principal action.

Delay can be used not only to distort the truth-finding function of discovery to the advantage of the manufacturer—and to the detriment of the injured party and the justice system—but also to distort settlements. Some manufacturers will withhold the most damaging documents, hoping to settle the case based on an inaccurate assessment of the merits by the plaintiff. Assuming that severe sanctions can be avoided by ultimately turning over documents if needed, the manufacturer meanwhile gains an enormous advantage in settlement discussions by maintaining its monopoly on information. The plaintiff may settle the case for less than its true value if discovery responses have failed to reveal prior complaints, internal memoranda, or other internal documents that would strengthen the plaintiff's hand at trial and thus strengthen its settlement position.

Manufacturers also use delay to exacerbate the imbalance of resources in their favor:[85] Delay costs money. The plaintiff is put to additional expense in obtaining documents[86] as well as in developing expert opinions based on incomplete information. Some manufacturers make a practice of delaying their production of documents needed for depositions. After the deposition is completed, they produce additional documents, which they claim have just come to the attorney's attention. At best, resources are wasted in retaking the deposition. At worst, the plaintiff does not have the resources to take another deposition. Manufacturers know that by running the meter, they increase pressure for settlement and are likely to get a better deal.

Delay also affects development of the facts. Until the defendant is completely forthcoming, the plaintiff's independent investigation is based on incomplete information. By then, resource or time constraints may prohibit repeating the investigation. Thus, the plaintiff's entire theory of the case, as well as its approach to depositions and to other aspects of discovery, is distorted. Furthermore, expert and lay witnesses may give testimony on the record based on an incomplete view of the truth. These distortions cannot always be set straight once the information is made available. In *Wierbinski v. Volkswagen of America, Inc.*,[87] the defendant failed to produce an accident reconstruction computer program and program extension to support its position as expressed by its expert until the middle of trial. Because this information was needed

---

[85] "For example, a party may make heavy demands or delay his responses in order to draw out the litigation and increase his adversary's costs. Such dilatory tactics obviously work to the advantage of wealthier parties and hence compound inefficiency with inequity." Note, *The Emerging Deterrence Orientation in the Imposition of Discovery Sanctions*, 91 HARV. L. REV. 1033, 1036 n.23 (1978).

[86] *See* Armentrout v. FMC Corp., No. 85-CV-2344 (Boulder County, Colo. Dist. Ct. May 1, 1987) (imposing sanctions for manufacturer's inaccurate discovery responses and false denials that information exists include paying all costs for future discovery necessitated by the "plaintiff's need to retrace discovery").

[87] No. 784330 (Cal. Super. Ct. Feb. 19, 1987), *aff'd*, No. A038364 (Cal. Ct. App. Dec. 30, 1988), *reprinted in* 11444–47 Automotive Litig. Rep. (Jan. 17, 1989).

for effective rebuttal of the defense expert's reconstruction,[88] a new trial was ordered.[89]

At a minimum, courts must shift the costs of delay back to the party responsible for the delay, and they should be willing to adjust time schedules to avoid prejudice to the extent possible. Punitive, deterrent sanctions are needed as well, because not all prejudice can be cured by shifting costs or moving trial dates.

An effective approach to sanctions begins with the recognition that delay itself causes harm. Manufacturers have frequently argued against imposition of sanctions when information is ultimately provided. Courts have recognized, however, that sanctions can and should be imposed despite ultimate compliance.[90] Thus, courts have properly imposed sanctions where information is disclosed on the eve of trial.[91] One court, in imposing sanctions against counsel and precluding admission of evidence revealed on the eve of trial, aptly analogized that the responsible attorney, "for improper purposes, threw a grenade into plaintiff's trial camp the night before trial began."[92] The court admonished that "[l]itigation, however, is not war. To the con-

---

[88] *See also* Lopez v. Foremost Paving, Inc., 796 S.W.2d 473, 477 (Tex. Ct. App. 1990) (where defendant failed to timely produce videotape simulation of defendant's version of the accident, admission of the exhibit in evidence constituted reversible error); Owens v. Yamaha Motor Co., No. 88-0244-R (E.D. Va. Dec. 16, 1988) (after defense verdict, ordering new trial where "defendants deliberately withheld information from the plaintiffs, and in effect, endeavored to try this lawsuit by ambush").

[89] The sanctions for causing delay are discussed in chapter 10.

[90] *See, e.g.*, Mutual Fed. Sav. & Loan Ass'n v. Richards & Assocs., 872 F.2d 88 (4th Cir. 1989); United States v. Di Mucci, 879 F.2d 1488, 1494 (7th Cir. 1989); Fautek v. Montgomery Ward & Co., 96 F.R.D. 141, 145 (N.D. Ill. 1982); *In re* Air Crash Disaster Near Chicago, Ill., 90 F.R.D. 613 (N.D. Ill. 1981); Perez v. Hartmann, 543 N.E.2d 1023, 1025–27 (Ill. App. Ct. 1989); Wach v. Martin Varnish Co., 422 N.E.2d 172, 174–75 (Ill. App. Ct.1981); *see also* Factory Air Conditioning Corp. v. Westside Toyota, Inc., 579 F.2d 334 (5th Cir. 1978) (where defendant failed to answer 69 interrogatories, filed blanket objections, and still failed to answer for two weeks after ordered to do so, default judgment entered despite defendant's new counsel's subsequent untimely filing of answers); Hammond v. Honda Motor Co., No. 8:88-3435-17 (D.S.C. Feb. 14, 1990) (assessing Honda $1,200 for tardy responses and awarding plaintiff $2,000 in attorney fees), *reported in* Prod. Safety & Liab. Rep. (BNA) 1359 (Dec. 7, 1990); City of Houston v. Arney, 680 S.W.2d 867, 872 (Tex. Ct. App. 1984) (upholding default judgment against defendant for failure to timely answer plaintiff's interrogatories even though answers were filed on day of sanctions hearing); Samples v. R.L. Atwood, Inc., No. 84-6496-H (Nueces County, Tex. Dist. Ct. Feb. 5, 1987) (imposing severe monetary sanctions despite ultimate compliance).

[91] West v. Johnson & Johnson Prods., Inc., 220 Cal. Rptr. 437, 463–64 (Ct. App. 1985), *cert. denied*, 479 U.S. 824 (1986); Foster v. Gillette Co., 161 Cal. Rptr. 134, 139 (Ct. App. 1979); Stancil v. K.S.B. Inv. & Management Co., 577 N.E.2d 452, 456–57 (Ohio Ct. App. 1991) (finding that trial court committed reversible error in admitting documents submitted by the defendant for the first time in the middle of defense case at trial).

[92] Royalty Petroleum Co. v. Arkla, Inc., 129 F.R.D. 674, 680 (W.D. Okla. 1990).

trary, it is supposed to be a quiet, dignified search for the truth."[93]

Courts have also refused to recognize untimely objections, in accordance with the rule requiring that discovery requests be responded to or objected to within 30 days, unless an extension is sought and obtained. Thus, the manufacturer who delays its production or response to an interrogatory cannot later make an objection.[94] Rule 33(b)(4) now expressly provides that any ground not stated in a timely objection to an interrogatory is waived unless the party's failure to object is excused by the court for good cause shown.

A manufacturer's motivations for delay—and tactics frequently used in achieving delay—were examined by a federal district court in *Dean v. A.H. Robins Co.*,[95] one of many cases documenting this manufacturer's discovery abuses in products cases involving IUD contraceptive devices.[96] The court recounted how depositions of Robins's officers

> progressed at an exceedingly slow pace, primarily because of the deponents' difficulties in answering even the most basic of questions due to lack of recollection.... Plaintiffs' attorneys informed the court that the deposition of board chairman E. C. Robins, Sr. was stalled by his inability to recall any conversations with top company officers concerning the Dalkon Shield. Robins, Sr. did state that his recollection would be refreshed by minutes of the company's board of directors meetings; the company, however, refused to provide those minutes.[97]

When the court ordered production of the minutes for in camera inspection, it learned that Robins, Sr. and his son, chief executive officer of the corporation, had attended nearly every board meeting in question and demonstrated a detailed knowledge of corporate affairs. These were considered "crucial revelations, given the fact that both of these officers claimed lack of knowledge due to both poor recollection of events and limited participation in the concerns of the company."[98]

Discovery delays continued. Deposition delays were so long that the judge began attending depositions. He observed signaling between the corporate deponents

---

[93] *Id.*

[94] *See* Demary v. Yamaha Motor Corp., 125 F.R.D. 20 (D. Mass. 1989); Antico v. Honda of Camden, 85 F.R.D. 34 (E.D. Pa. 1979).

[95] 101 F.R.D. 21 (D. Minn. 1984).

[96] *See also* Craig v. A.H. Robins Co., 790 F.2d 1 (1st Cir. 1986); Harre v. A.H. Robins Co., 750 F.2d 1501 (11th Cir. 1985), *vacated in part*, 866 F.2d 1303 (11th Cir. 1989); Gardiner v. A.H. Robins Co., 747 F.2d 1180 (8th Cir. 1984); *In re* A.H. Robins Co., 107 F.R.D. 2 (D. Kan. 1985); A.H. Robins Co. v. Devereaux, 415 So. 2d 30 (Fla. Dist. Ct. App. 1982), *review denied*, 426 So. 2d 25 (Fla. 1983). The story of the tragic Dalkon shield litigation, emphasizing the use of bankruptcy procedures to insulate A.H. Robins's corporate officers, directors, and shareholders, is related in RICHARD B. SOBOL, BENDING THE LAW (1991).

[97] 101 F.R.D. at 22.

[98] *Id.*

and their attorneys.[99] Document discovery was likewise delayed, prompting repeated efforts by the plaintiff to obtain documents to refresh the recollection of deponents and impeach previous testimony. In its decision, the court indicated its frustration with the defendant's behavior:

> The court has gone over the matter time and time again. The pattern is the same: the defendant either appears to accept the court's orders without objection and then fails to abide by them, or recoils at the slightest hint of a new directive and asks for additional time to prepare its response. This lends much credence to the plaintiffs' claim that the company's nationwide strategy in defending the thousands of Dalkon Shield cases against it is to wage a "war of attrition": prolonging and protracting the litigation so as to wear down its opponents without giving them a fair opportunity to have their suits heard.[100]

Another tactic used by Robins was to use shell game tactics with its attorneys, each of whom disavowed responsibility for positions taken. "[W]hat is absolutely unacceptable is the defendant's practice of obscuring the responsibility of its attorneys so that it is impossible to determine at any given moment who is accountable for representations made to the court."[101] Another delay tactic criticized by the court was Robins's practice of insisting on in camera review of documents for privilege when its own attorneys had never reviewed the materials for nonprivileged information.[102]

Sanctions for delay frequently include reimbursement of costs, including attorney fees, incurred by the party seeking discovery.[103] To determine who should pay

---

[99] *Id.* at 23.

[100] *Id.*

[101] *Id.*; *see also* Fjelstad v. American Honda Motor Co., No. CV 81-227-BLG-JFB (D. Mont. May 23, 1986), *on remand from* 762 F.2d 1334 (9th Cir. 1985); A.H. Robins Co. v. Devereaux, 415 So. 2d 30 (Fla. Dist. Ct. App. 1982), *review denied*, 426 So. 2d 25 (Fla. 1983).

[102] 101 F.R.D. at 24–25. Defense counsel in the asbestos litigation also raised questions of privilege concerning documents they had never seen or read. Some of the documents they claimed were privileged were blank pages. Heathman v. Owens-Corning Fiberglas Corp., No. 87-C-1934, Master's Report (Brazoria County, Tex. Dist. Ct. Dec. 20, 1990) and Searls v. Owens-Corning Fiberglas Corp., No. 88-C-0615, Master's Report (Brazoria County, Tex. Dist. Ct. Dec. 20, 1990).

[103] *See, e.g.*, Lindsey v. United States, 693 F. Supp. 1012, 1026–27 (W.D. Okla. 1988) (assessing costs for rule 16 discovery order violation); Fautek v. Montgomery Ward & Co., 96 F.R.D. 141, 146 (N.D. Ill. 1982); J.M. Cleminshaw Co. v. City of Norwich, 93 F.R.D. 338 (D. Conn. 1981) (noting that award of fees and expenses is the mildest of sanctions authorized by rule 37); Parrett v. Ford Motor Co., 52 F.R.D. 120 (W.D. Mo. 1969); *see also* Simmons v. American Honda Motor Co., No. 1:91-CV-0079-RCF (N.D. Ga. June 1, 1992) (awarding attorney fees and costs as sanction for defendant's repeated disregard of the rules of discovery at the expense of plaintiffs and their case); Shaddix v. Syntex Lab., No. CV 89-L-0659-S (N.D. Ala. Apr. 30, 1990) (imposing monetary sanctions for delay, noting "pervasive and systematic nature of defendants' discovery abuse"); Babb v. Ford Motor Co., 535 N.E.2d 676, 683–84 (Ohio Ct. App. 1987) ("In this case, the circumstances strongly suggest that the manufacturer provided

these costs, the court may attempt to ascertain whether delay was caused by the party[104] or its counsel.[105]

Courts sometimes impose evidentiary sanctions tailored to the specific circumstances or consequences of delay. For instance, in *Hammond v. Coastal Rental & Equipment Co.*[106] the plaintiffs sought the defendant's payroll records, which were available to the defendant when the plaintiff's discovery request was made and when the responses were due. When the defendant delayed production of the records, the plaintiff sought and obtained a court order compelling production. The defendant continued to delay, and the documents were later destroyed by fire. Consequently, the court ordered that an audit prepared by the plaintiffs would be taken as true.[107]

In *Perez v. Hartmann*[108] the court precluded medical negligence defendants from introducing an EKG strip sought by plaintiffs well before trial because it had not been produced until a month before trial. *In Stanton v. Iver Johnson's Arms, Inc.*,[109] as a sanc-

---

unreasonably evasive and incomplete answers. . . . They further suggest that the manufacturer had no good justification for its obdurate resistance to discovery."); Weathers v. Honda Motor Co., No. 8:89-1371-17 (D.S.C. Feb. 14, 1990) (finding that "the inordinate and unexplained delay of more than six months in providing any responses to the discovery request of the plaintiff is unacceptable," the court ordered the defendant to pay attorney fees and expenses for producing requested records); Hammond v. Honda Motor Co., No. 8:88-3435-17 (D.S.C. Feb. 14, 1990) (assessing defendants $1,200 for tardy responses and awarding plaintiff $2,000 in attorney fees); Tellez v. Ford Motor Co., No. 13273 (Kleberg County, Tex. Dist. Ct. Sept. 9, 1987) (ordering defendant to pay plaintiff's attorney fees in part for its failure to timely produce requested documents); Wilson v. General Motors Corp., No. 85-CI-01868 (Bexar County, Tex. Dist. Ct. Sept. 25, 1985) (imposing monetary sanctions for manufacturer's failure to produce court-ordered documents).

[104] *See, e.g.*, Fautek v. Montgomery Ward & Co., 96 F.R.D. 141, 145 (N.D. Ill. 1982) (assessing costs, including expert and attorney fees, against defendant that supplied misinformation to counsel, which was then communicated to plaintiff); Parrett v. Ford Motor Co., 52 F.R.D. 120, 122 (W.D. Mo. 1969) (imposing sanctions against automaker defendant for discovery delay; court found that firm representing Ford had never before failed to perform discovery obligations fully and promptly).

[105] Royalty Petroleum Co. v. Arkla, Inc., 129 F.R.D. 674, 684–85 (W.D. Okla. 1990) (sanctioning defense counsel when defense served supplemental responses to interrogatories containing new allegations, neither signed by counsel nor stated under oath, on eve of trial); J.M. Cleminshaw Co. v. City of Norwich, 93 F.R.D. 338, 354 (D. Conn. 1981) (invoking inherent authority to require defense counsel to pay monetary sanction to court where defense counsel was responsible for serious delays and plaintiff's resulting costs were relatively low).

[106] 95 F.R.D. 74 (S.D. Tex. 1982).

[107] *Id.* at 78.

[108] 543 N.E.2d 1023 (Ill. App. Ct. 1989); *see also* Royalty Petroleum Co. v. Arkla, Inc., 129 F.R.D. 674 (W.D. Okla. 1990), *discussed supra* notes 92–93 and accompanying text.

[109] 88 F.R.D. 290 (D. Mont. 1980).

tion for the manufacturer's persistent failure to timely respond to discovery requests, the court designated certain facts supporting the plaintiff's claim to be taken as true.[110]

Delay in responding to a request for admissions carries its own sanction: pursuant to rule 36(a), a request for admission is deemed admitted if not responded to within 30 days, unless additional time is granted by the court.

While courts sometimes appear to miss the significance of delay,[111] most judges recognize the corrupting effect delay has on the truth-finding process. The ultimate sanctions of default or striking the defendant's answer have frequently been imposed in response to stonewalling conduct that included delay tactics.[112]

For example, in *Bollard v. Volkswagen of America, Inc.*[113] the manufacturer managed discovery through in-house counsel and limited the authority given to trial counsel, in efforts the court found "obviously . . . calculated to delay and obstruct the completion of discovery."[114] The manufacturer slowly trickled information—and frequently misinformation—to the plaintiff in violation of discovery deadlines. The court penalized Volkswagen's discovery conduct by entering a default judgment, noting the

> frustration of the judicial process which results when a defendant corporation refuses to give trial counsel the authority [to control discovery] required by the local rules and attempts to handle matters through house counsel who are either not acquainted with the pretrial rules or not predisposed to obeying them.[115]

VII. SHELL GAME

Manufacturers sometimes attempt to avoid disclosure by contending that they do not physically possess documents or information requested by the plaintiff. Rule 34, however, requires production of documents in the "possession, custody or con-

---

[110] *Id.* at 292.

[111] *See* Robinson v. Audi NSU Auto Union Aktiengesellschaft, 739 F.2d 1481, 1483–84 (10th Cir. 1984) (concluding trial court did not abuse its discretion in refusing to exclude manufacturer's expert testimony where expert's deposition was delayed until 12 days into trial despite court order).

[112] *See, e.g.*, Marquis Theatre Corp. v. Condado Mini Cinema, 846 F.2d 86, 90 (1st Cir. 1988) (striking answer); Carlucci v. Piper Aircraft Corp., 102 F.R.D. 472, 477, 485–89 (S.D. Fla. 1984) (default), *aff'd in part, rev'd in part*, 775 F.2d 1440 (11th Cir. 1985); Ultracashmere House, Ltd. v. Meyer, 407 So. 2d 125, 129 (Ala. 1981) (default); A.H. Robins Co. v. Devereaux, 415 So. 2d 30, 32 (Fla. Dist. Ct. App. 1982) (striking defenses), *review denied*, 426 So. 2d 25 (Fla. 1983); Binyon v. Nesseth, 646 P.2d 1043, 1046 (Kan. 1982) (default); Van Wert v. Green-Pepper, 542 N.Y.S.2d 815, 816–17 (App. Div. 1989) (striking answer); Allright, Inc. v. W.L. Van Scoyoc, 784 S.W.2d 942, 944 (Tex. Ct. App. 1990) (default).

[113] 56 F.R.D. 569 (W.D. Mo. 1971).

[114] *Id.* at 578.

[115] *Id.* at 583.

trol" of the party.[116] Thus, where documents are *obtainable* by the manufacturer, the fact that the requested documents are not located on the manufacturer's premises does not excuse it from producing them.[117]

A manufacturer may, for example, store documents at its foreign offices, affiliates, or subsidiaries.[118] As one court pointed out, "When a party places documents outside this country with the expectation that production of those documents will be frustrated in litigation here, the strong policy in favor of broad discovery dictates that that party bear the consequences of the dilemma created by the realization of its expectations."[119] In ordering production of documents held by defendant manufacturer's nonparty foreign subsidiaries, another court noted,

> By refusing to conduct foreign searches for documents, [defendant] provides for itself a means of shielding otherwise discoverable information. A discoveree cannot avoid a proper discovery request by utilizing record keeping which conceals rather than discloses.[120]

Another court ordering production of documents in the possession of a defendant manufacturer's foreign affiliate observed,

> Defendant cannot be allowed to shield crucial documents from discovery by parties with whom it has dealt in the United States merely by storing them with its affiliate abroad. Nor can it shield documents by destroying its own copies and relying on customary access to copies maintained by its affiliate abroad. *If defendant could so easily evade discovery, every United States company would have a foreign affiliate for storing sensitive documents.*[121]

---

[116] FED. R. CIV. P. 34(a). For discussion of the extent of a party's duty of inquiry, see chapter 2, section II.

[117] See chapter 2, section II.

[118] *See, e.g.*, Cooper Indus. v. British Aerospace, Inc., 102 F.R.D. 918 (S.D.N.Y. 1984); General Atomic Co. v. Exxon Nuclear Co., 90 F.R.D. 290 (S.D. Cal. 1981); Carey Canada, Inc. v. Hinely, 352 S.E.2d 398, 401–03 (Ga. Ct. App. 1986), *rev'd in part*, 356 S.E.2d 202 (Ga.), *cert. denied*, 484 U.S. 898 (1987), *vacated in part en banc*, 366 S.E.2d 242 (Ga. Ct. App. 1988); United Nuclear Corp. v. General Atomic Co., 629 P.2d 231, 308–09 (N.M. 1980) (upholding default sanction for numerous stonewalling practices), *appeal dismissed*, 451 U.S. 901, *reh'g denied*, 452 U.S. 932 (1981).

[119] 629 P.2d at 309.

[120] *In re* Richardson-Merrell, Inc., 97 F.R.D. 481, 483 (S.D. Ohio 1983); *see also* Baine v. General Motors Corp., 141 F.R.D. 328, 331 (M.D. Ala. 1991); Baxter Travenol Lab., Inc. v. LeMay, 93 F.R.D. 379, 383 (S.D. Ohio 1981); Alliance to End Repression v. Rochford, 75 F.R.D. 441, 447 (N.D. Ill. 1977); Kozlowski v. Sears, Roebuck & Co., 73 F.R.D. 73, 76 (D. Mass. 1976).

[121] Cooper Indus. v. British Aerospace, Inc., 102 F.R.D. 918, 920 (S.D.N.Y. 1984) (emphasis added); *see also* Hubbard v. Rubbermaid, Inc., 78 F.R.D. 631 (D. Md. 1978) (ordering corporate respondent to furnish subsidiary's records).

Similarly, a manufacturer cannot avoid production by turning the requested documents over to a third party. In *Biehler v. White Metal Rolling & Stamping Corp.*,[122] the court ordered a new trial as a result of the defendants' stonewalling. The court expressed particular concern that one defendant "had sought to evade production of information and documents" by turning over certain documents to its insurance company:

> Neither a litigant nor *the insurer of a litigant* can frustrate discovery procedures by fragmenting its knowledge among different agents or attorneys. . . . We believe . . . that these defendants have fragmented their knowledge of relevant evidence among three corporate entities [defendants and insurer] with the result of frustrating discovery procedures.[123]

VIII. STONEWALLING IN DEPOSITIONS

Once considered an effective means for learning information, depositions are now described by some as "theaters for posturing and maneuvering rather than efficient vehicles for the discovery of relevant facts or the perpetuation of testimony."[124] The following are tactics commonly used to diminish the value of a deposition.

Failing to attend a properly noticed deposition:[125] Where no protective order has been sought, a party's failure to attend a deposition, like the failure to provide a response to a proper discovery request, is immediately sanctionable.[126]

Failing to produce a knowledgeable deponent in response to a rule 30(b)(6) deposition notice:[127] Sometimes a professional witness is designated who artfully avoids disclos-

---

[122] 333 N.E.2d 716 (Ill. App. Ct. 1975).

[123] *Id.* at 721 (quoting Drehle v. Fleming, 274 N.E. 2d 53, 55 (Ill. 1971)).

[124] Federal Bar Council Committee on Second Circuit Courts, *A Report on the Conduct of Depositions* (1990), *reprinted in* 131 F.R.D. 613, 613 (1990).

[125] Perkinson v. Gilbert/Robinson, Inc., 821 F.2d 686, 688–89 (D.C. Cir. 1987) (sanctioning defendant for failing to produce an employee to be deposed); Altschuler v. Samsonite Corp., 109 F.R.D. 353, 356 (E.D.N.Y. 1986) (finding defendant refused to submit an employee for a scheduled deposition); Payne v. Coates-Miller, Inc., 386 N.E.2d 398, 400 (Ill. App. Ct. 1979) (finding attorney for defendant in criminal contempt for willfully impeding progress of pretrial discovery by failing to notify defendant's employee of a deposition and failing to comply with a document discovery request); Downer v. Aquamarine Operators, Inc., 701 S.W.2d 238, 243 (Tex. 1985) (striking defendant's answer where president of company failed to appear at an oral deposition), *cert. denied*, 476 U.S. 1159 (1986); McFarland v. Szakalun, 809 S.W.2d 760, 762 (Tex. App. Ct. 1991) (sanctioning attorney for failing to accompany client to deposition).

[126] FED. R. CIV. P. 37(d).

[127] *See* Sieck v. Russo, 869 F.2d 131, 134 (2d Cir. 1989) (entering default judgments against defendants who twice consciously absented themselves from scheduled depositions); Thomas v. Hoffmann-LaRoche, Inc., 126 F.R.D. 522, 525 (N.D. Miss. 1989) (finding defendant failed to produce deponents knowledgeable in the requested categories); Castro v. Alden Leeds, Inc., 535 N.Y.S.2d 73, 75 (App. Div. 1988) (finding defendant company's most knowledgeable employee left court's jurisdiction before being deposed).

ing or who cannot supply any relevant information and instead merely articulates the manufacturer's defenses. Rule 30(b)(6) permits the deposing attorney to designate the subject matter of the inquiry, and the defendant must select and produce one or more persons who are competent to testify on its behalf concerning the designated topics.[128] Sanctions against defense counsel have been imposed under rule 37(d) for failure to attend a properly noticed deposition in cases where deponents without knowledge of the noticed subject matter were produced for a rule 30(b)(6) deposition.[129]

Instructing the deponent not to answer a legitimate inquiry calling for nonprivileged information:[130] A lawyer may not instruct a witness not to answer a question during a deposition unless the question seeks privileged information or information subject to a limitation on evidence directed by the court, unless counsel wishes to adjourn the deposition for the purpose of seeking a protective order from what he or she believes is annoying, embarrassing, oppressive, or bad faith conduct by opposing counsel.[131] Rule 30(c) provides that "evidence objected to [at depositions] shall be taken subject to the objections." A lawyer who instructs a deponent not to answer on grounds other than privilege or trade secret should do so only where "serious harm [is] likely to result from responding to any given question."[132]

---

[128] "[T]he organization so named *shall* designate one or more officers, directors, or managing agents, or other persons who consent to testify on its behalf . . . . The persons so designated *shall* testify as to matters known or reasonably available to the organization." FED. R. CIV. P. 30(b)(6) (emphasis added).

[129] THOMAS V. HOFFMAN-LAROCHE, INC., 126 F.R.D. 522 (N.D. MISS. 1989); SEE ALSO 8 CHARLES ALAN WRIGHT & ARTHUR R. MILLER, FEDERAL PRACTICE & PROCEDURE §§ 2103, 2110 (1970 & Supp. 1992); *cf.* Plevy v. Scully, 89 F.R.D. 665 (W.D.N.Y. 1981).

[130] Castillo v. St. Paul Fire & Marine Ins. Co., 938 F.2d 776, 779 (7th Cir. 1991) (affirming district court's dismissal of plaintiff's action for willful disobedience of court order to respond to questions approved by the court). *See generally* Ralston Purina Co. v. McFarland, 550 F.2d 967, 973 (4th Cir. 1977); International Union of Elec., Radio & Mach. Workers v. Westinghouse Elec. Corp., 91 F.R.D. 277, 279–80 (D.D.C. 1981); HAYDOCK & HERR, *supra* note 59, § 3.7.5.

[131] FED. R. CIV. P. 30(d)(1) and (3). *See* Eggleston v. Chicago Journeymen Plumbers' Local Union No. 130, 657 F.2d 890, 902 (7th Cir. 1981), *cert. denied*, 455 U.S. 1017 (1982); Ralston Purina Co. v. McFarland, 550 F.2d 967, 973 (4th Cir. 1977); First Tenn. Bank v. Federal Deposit Ins. Corp., 108 F.R.D. 640 (E.D. Tenn. 1985); Coates v. Johnson & Johnson, 85 F.R.D. 731, 735 (N.D. Ill. 1980); Shapiro v. Freeman, 38 F.R.D. 308, 311–12 (S.D.N.Y. 1965); Smith v. Gardy, 569 So. 2d 504, 507 (Fla. Dist. Ct. App. 1990), *review denied*, 581 So. 2d 1310 (Fla. 1991). *But see* Eckert v. Hurley Chicago Co., 638 F. Supp. 699, 705 (N.D. Ill. 1986) (finding instruction to deponent not to answer badgering questions proper); LaPenna v. Upjohn Co., 110 F.R.D. 15, 19 (E.D. Pa. 1986) (finding deponent need not answer broad, time-wasting questions). *See generally* HAYDOCK & HERR, *supra* note 59, § 3.7.5; UNDERWOOD & FORTUNE, *supra* note 11, § 6.5.1; Steven J. Helmers, *Depositions: Objections, Instructions and Sanctions*, 33 S.D. L. REV. 272, 276–80 (1988).

[132] Nutmeg Ins. Co. v. Atwell, Vogel & Sterling, 120 F.R.D. 504, 508 (W.D. La. 1988).

Making disruptive objections or using objections or signals to coach the witness:[133] The use of a steady stream of objections, either to deprive the examiner of the right to a fair opportunity to make discovery or as a vehicle to coach the witness, justifies the imposition of sanctions.[134] Such conduct has been criticized by one court as "unprofessional and insulting."[135]

The 1993 amendments to rule 30 were adopted for the specific purpose of preventing abusive deposition tactics.[136] They require concise statement of objections in a nonargumentative and nonsuggestive manner. These amendments and the misconduct they are designed to prevent are discussed in a seminal opinion by Judge Robert Gawthrop III.[137] Broad adoption and enforcement of the guidelines set forth in Judge Gawthrop's order would prevent the abusive tactics that have become commonplace in oral depositions.

Changing an answer after the deposition is concluded:[138] Although rule 30(e) provides a mechanism for the witness to make changes to the deposition transcript,[139] the rule does not contemplate either wholesale changes or altering the original so that it is unreadable.[140] Moreover, if further cross-examination is necessitated by the changes, the court may permit the *reopening of the deposition*[141] or *suppress it altogether.*[142]

---

[133] Langston Corp. v. Standard Register Co., 95 F.R.D. 386, 390 (N.D. Ga. 1982). *See generally* UNDERWOOD & FORTUNE, *supra* note 11, § 6.5.1, at 241.

[134] Ralston Purina Co. v. McFarland, 550 F.2d 967, 973–74 (4th Cir. 1977); Unique Concepts, Inc. v. Brown, 115 F.R.D. 292, 294 (S.D.N.Y. 1987); Kelly v. GAF Corp., 115 F.R.D. 257, 258 (E.D. Pa. 1987); Shapiro v. Freeman, 38 F.R.D. 308, 311–12 (S.D.N.Y. 1965). *See generally* Frank F. Flegal, *Introduction* to *Discovery Abuse: Causes, Effects, and Reform*, 3 REV. LITIG. 1, 20, 43–44 (1982); William W Schwarzer & Lynn H. Pasahow, *Efficient Discovery: Advice for Counsel Taking Depositions*, INSIDE LITIG., July 1988, at 20 ("elaborating on the merits of an objection unless requested to do so by the examining attorney is improper, especially when the argument, whether intentionally or inadvertently, suggests the answer to the witness").

[135] *See* Stengel v. Kawasaki Heavy Indus., 116 F.R.D. 263, 268 (N.D. Tex. 1987).

[136] Amendments to the Federal Rules of Civil Procedure and Forms, approved by the United States Supreme Court (Apr. 22, 1993), *reprinted in* 146 F.R.D. 401 (1994), FED. R. CIV. P. 30(d)(1), 30(d)(2) advisory committee's note.

[137] Hall v. Clifton Precision, 150 F.R.D. 525 (E.D. Pa. 1993).

[138] *See generally* 23 AM. JUR., *supra* note 59, § 162; HAYDOCK & HERR, *supra* note 59, §§ 3.8.4–3.8.5; UNDERWOOD & FORTUNE, *supra* note 11, § 6.5.1, at 241–42; 8 WRIGHT & MILLER, *supra* note 129, § 2118.

[139] Note that the rule expressly requires the deponent to state the reasons for making any changes. FED. R. CIV. P. 30(e).

[140] Allen & Co. v. Occidental Petroleum Corp., 49 F.R.D. 337, 340 (S.D.N.Y. 1970).

[141] Colin v. Thompson, 16 F.R.D. 194, 195 (W.D. Mo. 1954); De Seversky v. Republic Aviation Corp., 2 F.R.D. 113, 115 (E.D.N.Y. 1941).

[142] UNDERWOOD & FORTUNE, *supra* note 11, § 6.5.1, at 242.

These tactics have become so commonplace that some district courts have adopted local rules specifically providing sanctions for abusive deposition conduct.[143]

IX. STONEWALLING CONCERNING EXPERT WITNESSES[144]

Because pivotal liability issues such as defect and causation typically turn on expert testimony, it is not surprising that defendants in products cases frequently stonewall discovery of their experts' opinions. Manufacturers have been sanctioned for withholding such information in an astonishing number of cases. Defendants frequently use one or more of the following tactics to stonewall the discovery of expert opinion testimony.

Failure to properly disclose the expert's identity: Courts generally exclude the testimony of expert witnesses whose identity was not properly disclosed to the opponent during discovery.[145]

Late or untimely disclosure: The defendant may also attempt to avoid disclosing the identity or the opinions of an expert witness by simply delaying the formal employment of the expert until after the discovery cutoff date or by waiting until the eve of trial or even until trial has commenced to make the disclosure.[146]

---

[143] *See, e.g.*, D. COLO. LOC. R. 30.1C.

[144] See also chapter 1, section III.B and appendix 1.

[145] Yukon Equip., Inc. v. Gordon, 660 P.2d 428, 431–32 (Alaska 1983) (properly excluding testimony where expert not identified in witness list as required by pretrial order), *overruled in part on other grounds*, Williford v. L.J. Carr Indus., Inc., 783 P.2d 235 (Alaska 1989); Stafford v. Sears, Roebuck & Co., 413 A.2d 1238 (Del. 1980) (ruling trial court erred in permitting the defendant's expert witness to testify since he was not identified in interrogatories inquiring about the defendant's expert witnesses); Tacke v. Vermeer Mfg. Co., 713 P.2d 527, 533 (Mont. 1986) (finding grounds for reversal where undisclosed and unqualified expert testimony admitted); Williams v. Union Carbide Corp., 734 S.W.2d 699, 700–02 (Tex. Ct. App. 1987) (finding admission of testimony of undisclosed expert witness constituted grounds for reversal); Texas Employers' Ins. Ass'n v. Meyer, 620 S.W.2d 179, 180 (Tex. Civ. App. 1981) (properly excluding testimony where expert not identified in interrogatory responses); *see also* Sequoia Mfg. Co. v. Halec Constr. Co., 570 P.2d 782, 789–90 (Ariz. Ct. App. 1977); *cf.* Sharp v. Broadway Nat'l Bank, 784 S.W.2d 669, 671–72 (Tex. 1990) (modifying judgment to exclude attorney fees awarded entirely on testimony given by expert whose identity was not disclosed in discovery). *See generally* John D. Hodson, Annotation, *Propriety of Allowing State Court Civil Litigant to Call Expert Witness Whose Name or Address Was Not Disclosed During Pretrial Discovery Proceedings*, 58 A.L.R. 4TH 653 (1987 & Supp. 1992).

[146] Bradley v. United States, 866 F.2d 120 (5th Cir. 1989) (finding trial court erred in admitting testimony of expert witnesses designated by defendant after discovery deadline expired); Daniels v. Rapco Foam, Inc., 762 P.2d 717 (Colo. Ct. App. 1988) (ruling trial court abused its discretion in allowing expert testimony where expert was designated less than 25 days before trial, unaccompanied by either a summary of qualifications or a detailed statement of opinions); Mulrooney v. Wambolt, 575 A.2d 996 (Conn. 1990) (affirming trial court's exclusion

Inadequate or partial disclosure of expert opinion testimony: There are two variations on the partial disclosure ploy: (1) providing some limited information in discovery but withholding important materials relied on by the expert and (2) attempting to present expert testimony on a topic different from that disclosed in discovery. In both circumstances, courts have barred or limited the expert opinion testimony.[147]

Appellate courts frequently have reversed trial courts for failing to exclude the testimony of undisclosed experts or experts about whom full disclosure was not made.[148]

---

of expert testimony where defense first informed plaintiff on day of trial of intent to call doctor as a witness); Jarmon v. Jinks, 520 N.E.2d 783, 787–88 (Ill. App. Ct. 1987) (finding trial court did not err in barring testimony of medical expert not timely disclosed), *appeal denied*, 522 N.E.2d 1245 (Ill. 1988); Vazirzadeh v. Kaminski, 510 N.E.2d 1096, 1101–02 (Ill. App. Ct.) (reversing defense verdict where defendant's expert witness not timely disclosed and his testimony was prejudicial), *appeal denied*, 515 N.E.2d 128 (Ill. 1987); McClanahan v. Deere & Co., 648 S.W.2d 222, 229–30 (Mo. Ct. App. 1983); Jackson v. Booth Memorial Hosp., 547 N.E.2d 1203, 1205–06 (Ohio Ct. App. 1988) (finding three experts' testimony should have been excluded where based on newly discovered theory of defense not disclosed to the plaintiffs prior to trial); Thompson v. Kawasaki Motors Corp., 824 S.W.2d 212, 215–17 (Tex. Ct. App. 1991) (excluding expert testimony as sanction for manufacturer's failure to supplement interrogatory responses), *writ granted*, 37 Tex. Sup. Ct. J. 438 (1994); Builder's Equip. Co. v. Onion, 713 S.W.2d 786 (Tex. Ct. App. 1986) (finding trial court did not abuse its discretion in suppressing testimony of expert witnesses not timely identified).

[147] Weiss v. Chrysler Motors Corp., 515 F.2d 449, 454–57 (2d Cir. 1975) (ruling plaintiffs entitled to new trial where defendant manufacturer's testimony allowed despite lack of full disclosure of topics or basis on which its expert would testify); Daniels v. Rapco Foam, Inc., 762 P.2d 717 (Colo. Ct. App. 1988) (finding trial court abused its discretion in allowing expert testimony where expert designated less than 25 days before trial, unaccompanied by either a summary of qualifications or a detailed statement of opinions); Perry v. Hospital of St. Raphael, 550 A.2d 645, 647 (Conn. App. Ct. 1988) (affirming exclusion of expert testimony where name of expert was disclosed, but subject matter and basis of proposed testimony not disclosed until two weeks before trial); Pipkin v. Hamer, 501 So. 2d 1365 (Fla. Dist. Ct. App.) (limiting testimony of defendant's expert to reports previously furnished plaintiff), *review denied*, 513 So. 2d 1062 (Fla. 1987); Huelsmann v. Berkowitz, 568 N.E.2d 1373, 1376–77 (Ill. App. Ct. 1991) (properly barring defendant's expert from testifying as a sanction for inadequate interrogatory response); Parsons v. City of New York, 573 N.Y.S.2d 677 (App. Div. 1991) (ordering new trial where summary of expert's opinion provided only five days before trial did not accurately reflect trial testimony); Binder v. Jones & Laughlin Steel Corp., 520 A.2d 863, 869 (Pa. Super. Ct.) (excluding expert testimony for failure to file required report), *appeal denied*, 533 A.2d 90 (Pa. 1987); *see also* Collins v. Interroyal Corp., 466 N.E.2d 1191 (Ill. App. Ct. 1984) (precluding defendant's expert from testifying about analysis prepared after trial began); LeBarron v. Haverhill Coop. Sch. Dist., 127 F.R.D. 38 (D.N.H. 1989) (affirming exclusion of expert testimony where plaintiff failed to disclose substance of or grounds upon which teaching was based).

[148] Weiss v. Chrysler Motors Corp., 515 F.2d 449, 454–57 (2d Cir. 1975) (ruling plaintiffs entitled to new trial where defendant manufacturer's testimony allowed despite lacking full disclosure of topics and basis on which its expert would testify); Daniels v. Rapco Foam, Inc., 762 P.2d 717 (Colo. Ct. App. 1988) (finding trial court abused its discretion in allowing expert testimony where expert designated less than 25 days before trial, unaccompanied by either a

Because plaintiff's counsel cannot assume that the trial court will disallow the testimony of an undisclosed expert witness,[149] plaintiff's counsel would be well advised to serve the manufacturer with an additional set of interrogatories one or two months before trial, specifically requesting the manufacturer to supplement its prior responses concerning the identity of all witnesses it expects to examine at trial.[150]

Under the 1993 amendment to rule 26(a)(3),[151] expert discovery includes detailed reports and depositions as of right. The new rule might well be compatible with the use of rule 45 document subpoenas to obtain reports and other information in the possession of adverse experts. Indeed, one court has already upheld the use of a

---

summary of qualifications or a detailed statement of opinions); Stafford v. Sears, Roebuck & Co., 413 A.2d 1238 (Del. 1980) (ruling trial court erred in permitting defendant's expert witness to testify where expert not identified in interrogatory responses); Vazirzadeh v. Kaminski, 510 N.E.2d 1096, 1101–03 (Ill. App. Ct.) (reversing defense verdict where defendant's expert not disclosed as a witness and his testimony was prejudicial), *appeal denied*, 515 N.E.2d 128 (Ill. 1987); Tacke v. Vermeer Mfg. Co., 713 P.2d 527, 533 (Mont. 1986) (finding admission of testimony by undisclosed and unqualified expert constituted grounds for reversal); Jackson v. Booth Memorial Hosp., 547 N.E.2d 1203 (Ohio Ct. App. 1988) (finding three experts' testimony should have been excluded where based on newly discovered theory of defense not disclosed to the plaintiffs prior to trial); Sharp v. Broadway Nat'l Bank, 784 S.W.2d 669, 671–72 (Tex. 1990) (modifying judgment to exclude attorney fees awarded based entirely on testimony given by expert whose identity was not disclosed in discovery); Williams v. Union Carbide Corp, 734 S.W.2d 699, 700–02 (Tex. Ct. App. 1987) (ruling admission of testimony of undisclosed expert witness constituted grounds for reversal); *see also* Bradley v. United States, 866 F.2d 120 (5th Cir. 1989) (ruling trial court erred in admitting testimony of two expert witnesses designated by the defendant after the discovery deadline had expired); Miranti v. Orms, 833 P.2d 164 (Mont. 1992). Obviously the rule works both ways. *See* Radmer v. Ford Motor Co., 813 P.2d 897 (Idaho 1991) (finding reversible error where trial court failed to exclude testimony of *plaintiff's* expert witness when plaintiff failed to supplement discovery responses prior to trial to disclose the expert's new theory of liability). *See generally* Hodson, *supra* note 145.

[149] Patterson v. F.W. Woolworth Co., 786 F.2d 874, 879–80 (8th Cir. 1986); DeMarines v. KLM Royal Dutch Airlines, 580 F.2d 1193, 1201–02 (3d Cir. 1978); Eisbach v. Jo-Carroll Elec. Coop., Inc., 440 F.2d 1171, 1173 (7th Cir. 1971); Dychalo v. Copperloy Corp., 78 F.R.D. 146 (E.D. Pa.), *aff'd per curiam*, 588 F.2d 820 (3d Cir. 1978); Foster v. Gillette Co., 161 Cal. Rptr. 134, 138–40 (Ct. App. 1979); Scott v. E.I. DuPont de Nemours & Co., 783 P.2d 938, 941 (Mont. 1989); *see also* Dabney v. Montgomery Ward & Co., 692 F.2d 49, 52–53 (8th Cir. 1982), *cert. denied*, 461 U.S. 957 (1983); *cf.* Robinson v. Audi NSU Auto Union Aktiengesellschaft, 739 F.2d 1481 (10th Cir. 1984) (finding defendant disclosed expert's identity but did not allow opposing counsel to depose the expert until 12 days before trial). *See generally* 8 WRIGHT & MILLER, *supra* note 129, § 2050, at 327 n.6.

[150] For discussion of the duty to supplement responses to discovery requests, see chapter 2, section III. *See generally* DISCOVERY PROCEEDINGS IN FEDERAL COURT §§ 2.20, 12.27 (Shepard's eds., 2d ed. 1991 & Supp. 1992).

[151] The recent amendments to the federal rules are discussed in chapter 3, section III.

rule 45 subpoena requiring an expert to disclose categories of documents mentioned in his or her deposition.[152]

X. PROBING PLAINTIFF'S KNOWLEDGE OF MANUFACTURER'S DOCUMENTS TO FACILITATE STONEWALLING

The value of plaintiffs' information exchange groups has not gone unnoticed by the courts[153] or by manufacturer defendants. Among the other benefits of collaboration,[154] information sharing allows plaintiffs to ferret out stonewalling by comparing discovery responses to see if the manufacturer has withheld information in one or more cases.[155] As a result, products liability defendants frequently seek to learn what plaintiffs already know about their internal documents before responding to discovery requests. Once armed with this information, the manufacturer can tailor its discovery responses to avoid revealing any new information to the plaintiff.

In recent years some manufacturers have gone to great lengths to eliminate the possibility that a plaintiff will acquire internal documents that the defendant does not choose to disclose. For existing products that are or may be the subject of litigation, the defendant's in-house counsel will perform a sweep of all potentially relevant internal documents and prepare a comprehensive index.[156] For new products, counsel will monitor every activity at every stage in the development of the product, collecting and indexing all documents.[157] In both situations, the resulting index is intended to represent the universe of the manufacturer's relevant internal documents. The manufacturer will then attempt to compel the plaintiff to list all the internal documents that are available to the plaintiff's counsel through, for example, a litigation support group. By comparing this list to its index, the defendant can withhold documents not on the plaintiff's list without fear of detection. Furnishing the manufacturer with a complete list of all documents known to all plaintiffs handling similar cases

---

[152] Quaile v. Carol Cable Co., No. 90-7415 (E.D. Pa. Oct. 5, 1992).

[153] *See, e.g.*, Kraszewski v. State Farm Gen. Ins. Co., 139 F.R.D. 156, 160 (N.D. Cal. 1991); Baker v. Liggett Group, Inc., 132 F.R.D. 123, 125–29 (D. Mass. 1990); Ward v. Ford Motor Co., 93 F.R.D. 579, 580 (D. Colo. 1982).

[154] For discussion of the many benefits of information sharing and how defendants use restrictive confidentiality orders to stop collaboration among plaintiffs, see chapter 8.

[155] See chapter 8, section II; *see, e.g.*, Stengel v. Kawasaki Heavy Indus., 116 F.R.D. 263, 268 (N.D. Tex. 1987); Buehler v. Whalen, 374 N.E.2d 460, 467 (Ill. 1978); Gammon v. Clark Equip. Co., 686 P.2d 1102, 1106 (Wash. Ct. App. 1984), *aff'd en banc*, 707 P.2d 685 (Wash. 1985).

[156] *See* Scott M. Kline, *Advising Clients on the Destruction of Documents Prepared and Used to Formulate Discovery Responses: Perils and Pitfalls*, 11 REV. LITIG. 47 (1991).

[157] An article in the *Wall Street Journal* describes in detail the role Ford Motor Company's house counsel played in gathering documents relating to the design of the Bronco II. *See* Milo Geyelin & Neal Templin, *Ford Attorneys Played Unusually Large Role in Bronco II's Launch*, WALL ST. J., Jan. 5, 1993, at A1, A6.

necessarily puts the manufacturer in a position to evaluate the likelihood that the suppression of any "new" documents will be detected.

Manufacturers began using this tactic in the late 1980s after a decade of getting caught withholding critical documents and after having failed in their initial attempts to prevent information sharing.[158] Viewed in the context of the overall development of stonewalling tactics in products liability cases, it is clear that the defendant's real purpose in seeking to compel the plaintiff to identify the corporate manufacturer's own records is to facilitate the suppression of previously undisclosed and relevant material.

The manufacturer may ask directly for identification of all its documents that the plaintiff obtained from other sources. Another approach is to seek discovery of all of the plaintiff's contacts with other plaintiffs' attorneys.[159] Regardless of how it is worded, such discovery is improper.[160]

There are at least four reasons why courts should not compel plaintiffs to furnish defendant manufacturers with this type of information: (1) the defendant's request is beyond the permissible scope of discovery, (2) the information sought is available from another source, (3) the information sought is entitled to protection from discovery as attorney work product, and (4) allowing this "discovery" discourages cooperative efforts among plaintiffs and facilitates stonewalling.

A. Request Exceeds the Scope of Discovery

In a request of this type, the documents sought were originally created by the defendant and have always been in its possession and control. Although the documents were created by the defendant's employees in the ordinary course of the business of designing, testing, manufacturing, and marketing the subject product and are therefore relevant, the defendant is not actually seeking to acquire these documents; it already has them. Rather, the defendant seeks plaintiff counsel's *knowledge* of these documents, which is simply not relevant to the defendant's case,[161] and is not "reasonably calculated to lead to the discovery of admissible evidence."[162]

---

[158] See chapter 8, section I.

[159] The form of the defendant's request may look something like the following:

> Plaintiff is requested to produce a list (or copies) of any and all internal documents which the plaintiff or his or her attorney have in their possession or control or have access to by virtue of their relationship with the Attorneys Information Exchange Group (AIEG) or any other association, organization or group of attorneys, or any individual lawyer, regarding any litigation of information relating to the XYZ product manufactured, tested, studied, assembled, or distributed by the defendant.

[160] *See* Smith v. Florida Power & Light Co., 19 FLA. L. WEEKLY D462 (Fla. Dist. Ct. App. 1994).

[161] *Cf.* Smith v. Bic Corp., 121 F.R.D. 235, 244–45 (E.D. Pa. 1988) (holding that information about which manufacturer's documents are in the hands of third parties, and how they may have been acquired, is not relevant), *aff'd in part, rev'd in part*, 869 F.2d 194 (3d Cir. 1989).

[162] FED. R. CIV. P. 26(b)(1).

Although the knowledge of a *party* may occasionally be relevant to a disputed issue, what an *attorney* has learned in preparing the case is totally outside the scope and objectives of legitimate discovery; the defendant cannot assert that it needs the requested information to prepare its case for trial. While the plaintiff is typically required by court rule or order to disclose all anticipated trial exhibits at some point well in advance of trial, this information cannot be obtained in discovery.[163]

The defendant may contend that an order compelling a response to its request is supported by the liberal construction traditionally accorded the discovery rules. Nothing could be further from the truth. The cardinal objective of the discovery rules is the emergence of the facts.[164] This information is sought—and frequently used—by defendants to *defeat* rather than advance the full disclosure objective of the discovery rules by facilitating stonewalling. Plaintiff's counsel may point out to the court the irony of the defendant's position; this is likely to be the *only* area in which the manufacturer seeks liberal construction of discovery relevance.

The plaintiff may also cite authority that, although rarely used, supports the proposition that the court should require the requesting party to make a threshold showing of relevance when the court has serious doubts concerning the relevance of the requested information.[165] A manufacturer would be hard pressed to make such a showing when seeking its own documents from the plaintiff.

B. Information Available from Another, More Convenient Source

Another argument that can be used to counter a defendant's request for its own documents can be found in the language of rule 26. Since 1983, the rule has provided that "[t]he frequency or extent of use of the discovery methods . . . shall be limited by the court if it determines that: (i) the discovery sought is . . . obtainable from some other source that is more convenient, less burdensome, or less expensive."[166] The manufacturer's own documents are obviously conveniently available to it.

C. Information Protected by Work-Product Doctrine

A third argument available to plaintiffs in this situation is the work-product doctrine, recognized by the Supreme Court in its seminal decision in *Hickman v. Taylor*[167] and codified in federal rule 26(b)(3). The rule states in part:

---

[163] *See, e.g.*, Aktiebolaget Vargos v. Clark, 8 F.R.D. 635, 636 (D.D.C. 1949). *See generally* MARK A. DOMBROFF, DISCOVERY § 12.48 (1986 & Supp. 1990); 8 WRIGHT & MILLER, *supra* note 129, § 2012, at 98 n.96.

[164] See generally chapter 1.

[165] *See In re* Remington Arms Co., 952 F.2d 1029 (8th Cir. 1991) (request for claimed trade secret documents); Fine v. Facet Aerospace Prods. Co., 133 F.R.D. 439, 443 (S.D.N.Y. 1990); Payne v. Howard, 75 F.R.D. 465, 469 (D.D.C. 1977).

[166] FED. R. CIV. P. 26(b)(2). *See* FED. R. CIV. P. 26(b)(1)(i) 1983 advisory committee's note.

[167] 329 U.S. 495 (1947).

> Subject to the provisions of subdivision (b)(4) of this rule, a party may obtain discovery of documents and tangible things otherwise discoverable under subdivision (b)(1) of this rule and prepared in anticipation of litigation or for trial by or for another party or by or for that other party's representative (including the other party's attorney, consultant, surety, indemnitor, insurer, or agent) only upon a showing that the party seeking discovery has substantial need of the materials in the preparation of the party's case and that the party is unable without undue hardship to obtain the substantial equivalent of the materials by other means. In ordering discovery of such materials when the required showing has been made, the court shall protect against disclosure of the mental impressions, conclusions, opinions, or legal theories of an attorney or other representative of a party concerning the litigation.

The Supreme Court explained in *Hickman* the policy basis of the work-product doctrine:

> Historically, a lawyer is an officer of the court and is bound to work for the advancement of justice while faithfully protecting the rightful interests of his clients. In performing his various duties, however, it is essential that a lawyer work with a certain degree of privacy, free from unnecessary intrusion by opposing parties and their counsel. Proper preparation of a client's case demands that he assemble information, sift what he considers to be the relevant from the irrelevant facts, prepare his legal theories and plan his strategy without undue and needless interference. That is the historical and the necessary way in which lawyers act within the framework of our system of jurisprudence to promote justice and to protect their clients' interests.[168]

A discovery request seeking plaintiff counsel's knowledge of the defendant's own documents obtained to prepare the client's case for trial clearly "falls outside the arena of discovery and contravenes the public policy underlying the orderly prosecution . . . of legal claims. Not even the most liberal of discovery theories can justify unwarranted inquiries into the files and the mental impressions of an attorney."[169]

Some cases hold that a party must make a threshold showing supporting its asserted entitlement to work-product protection.[170] The burden then shifts to the party seeking discovery to overcome the protection from discovery afforded by the doctrine.[171] The weight of the burden depends on whether the court finds that the requested information is ordinary or opinion work product. A plaintiff counsel's acquisition of documents in anticipation of litigation or for trial is clearly entitled to ordinary work-product protection under rule 26(b)(3). Furthermore, the great major-

---

[168] Hickman v. Taylor, 329 U.S. at 510–11.

[169] Hickman, 329 U.S. at 510. A succinct statement of the policy basis of the work-product doctrine is contained in the advisory committee's note to the 1970 Amendment to FED. R. CIV. P. 26. *See generally* DISCOVERY PROCEEDINGS IN FEDERAL COURT, *supra* note 150, §§ 16.11–16.18; 8 WRIGHT & MILLER, *supra* note 129, §§ 2021–2028.

[170] *See* Toledo Edison Co. v. G.A. Technologies, Inc., 847 F.2d 335, 339 (6th Cir. 1988). *See generally* 8 WRIGHT & MILLER, *supra* note 129, § 2024.

[171] *See* 8 WRIGHT & MILLER, *supra* note 129, § 2025; DISCOVERY PROCEEDINGS IN FEDERAL COURT, *supra* note 150, §§ 16.15, 16.17.

ity of cases have held that an attorney's selection and compilation of documents is entitled to special protection as opinion work product.[172]

The distinction in the two categories of work product should make no difference, however, in the difficulty of overcoming the work-product protection if for no other reason than that the defendant already possesses the documents and therefore has full and complete knowledge of the contents of the requested information.[173]

The fact that several lawyers participating in a litigation support group have coordinated their efforts to select and compile the documents does not waive the work-product protection. Collaborative efforts of parties sharing a common litigation interest are entitled to work-product protection.[174]

The fact that the documents may have been selected and compiled in connection with an earlier lawsuit likewise does not result in loss of work-product protection. The courts have held that work-product materials retain their protection in subsequent related litigation.[175] As for computerized litigation support systems, the few

---

[172] See Shelton v. American Motors Corp., 805 F.2d 1323, 1329 (8th Cir. 1986); Sporck v. Peil, 759 F.2d 312, 315–16 (3d Cir.), cert. denied, 474 U.S. 903 (1985); In re Grand Jury Subpoena Dated Nov. 8, 1979, 622 F.2d 933, 935 (6th Cir. 1980); Smith v. Florida Power & Light Co., 19 FLA. L. WEEKLY D462 (Fla. Dist. Ct. App. 1994); Smith v. Bic Corp., 121 F.R.D. 235, 244–45 (E.D. Pa.1988), aff'd in part, rev'd in part, 869 F.2d 194, 201–202 (3d Cir. 1989); Omaha Pub. Power Dist. v. Foster Wheeler Corp., 109 F.R.D. 615, 616 (D. Neb. 1986); James Julian, Inc. v. Raytheon Co., 93 F.R.D. 138, 144 (D. Del. 1982); In re LTV Sec. Litig., 89 F.R.D. 595, 612 (N.D. Tex. 1981); In re Antitrust Grand Jury Investigation, 500 F. Supp. 68, 71 (E.D. Va. 1980); Berkey Photo, Inc. v. Eastman Kodak Co., 74 F.R.D. 613, 616 (S.D.N.Y. 1977).

[173] See Smith v. Florida Power & Light Co., 19 FLA. L. WEEKLY D462 (Fla. Dist. Ct. App. 1994). In addition to "substantial need" (clearly not present) Fed. R. Civ. P. 26(b)(3) requires the manufacturer to show that it could not obtain the "substantial equivalent" of the requested information from an alternate source "without undue hardship." This should be literally impossible to establish.

[174] United States v. Gulf Oil Corp., 760 F.2d 292, 295–96 (Temp. Emer. Ct. App. 1985); Castle v. Sangamo Weston, Inc., 744 F.2d 1464, 1466–67 (11th Cir. 1984); United States v. McPartlin, 595 F.2d 1321, 1336–37 (7th Cir.), cert. denied, 444 U.S. 833 (1979); Continental Oil Co. v. United States, 330 F.2d 347 (9th Cir. 1964); Schachar v. American Academy of Ophthalmology, Inc., 106 F.R.D. 187, 191–92 (N.D. Ill. 1985); Transmirra Prods. Corp. v. Monsanto Chem. Co., 26 F.R.D. 572, 578–79 (S.D.N.Y. 1960); Western Fuels Ass'n v. Burlington No. R.R., 102 F.R.D. 201 (D. Wyo. 1984); see HAYDOCK & HERR, supra note 59, § 2.5.12, at 171–72 (citing Castle v. Sangamo Weston, Inc., 744 F.2d 1464 (11th Cir. 1986)).

[175] Federal Trade Comm'n v. Grolier Inc., 462 U.S. 19, 26 (1983); In re Murphy, 560 F.2d 326 (8th Cir. 1977); United States v. Leggett & Platt, Inc., 542 F.2d 655, 660 (6th Cir. 1976), cert. denied, 430 U.S. 945 (1977); Duplan Corp. v. Moulinage et Retorderie de Chavanoz, 509 F.2d 730 (4th Cir. 1974), cert. denied, 420 U.S. 997 (1975); United States v. O.K. Tire & Rubber Co., 71 F.R.D. 465, 467 (D. Idaho 1976). See generally D. Christopher Wells, *The Attorney Work Product Doctrine and Carry-Over Immunity: An Assessment of Their Justifications*, 47 U. PITT. L. REV. 675 (1986); Neal E. Tackabery, Note, *Discovery of an Attorney's Work Product in Subsequent Litigation*, 1974 DUKE L.J. 799.

courts that have considered the issue have generally held that these enjoy near absolute protection from discovery as opinion work product.[176]

Defendants frequently cite *Bohannon v. Honda Motor Co.*[177] as authority supporting a request for identification of the defendant's own documents. To our knowledge, *Bohannon* is the only authority to do so, contrary to the majority of cases that have considered the issue.[178] A number of other district courts have declined to follow *Bohannon*, rejecting defendants' attempts to compel plaintiffs to supply a list of the defendant's own internal documents that the plaintiff has obtained from other sources.[179] In any event, the finding in *Bohannon* does not apply to a request by a defendant to obtain the documents (or a list thereof) selected by plaintiff's attorneys for inclusion in a case-specific document banking system because that court repeatedly stated that the plaintiff had failed to establish that the documents sought by the defendant's request had been subjected to an attorney selection process or that disclosure would reveal counsel's work product.[180]

D. Allowing Beneficial Collaboration vs. Enabling Evasion[181]

The court considering such a request should be made aware that allowing the manufacturer to use this tactic would have a chilling effect on collaboration by plaintiffs. As a practical matter, plaintiffs are not likely to share their work product if it may fall into the hands of their opponents. As a legal matter, any order compelling disclosure would place the plaintiff's attorney in a quandary, since access to information in the possession of plaintiffs' litigation groups typically is subject to stringent restrictions that impose a contractual obligation not to disclose the information to others. Ownership issues arise because litigation groups typically do not own documents—they bank them for individual members who retain ownership. A court order requiring either plaintiff's counsel or a litigation group to breach contractual obligations may have far-reaching adverse implications. Courts are justifiably loath to compel disclosure where to do so would be in violation of a valid confidentiality agreement.[182]

---

[176] *See* United States v. AT&T Co., 642 F.2d 1285, 1296–1301 (D.C. Cir. 1980); Santiago v. Miles, 121 F.R.D. 636, 640 (W.D.N.Y. 1988); *In re* IBM Peripherals, 5 Computer L. Serv. Rep. (Callaghan) 878 (N.D. Cal. 1975); see also chapter 1, section IV and appendix 1.

[177] 127 F.R.D. 536 (D. Kan. 1989).

[178] *See generally* authorities cited *supra* note 172.

[179] McInerney v. Suzuki Motor Co., CA No. 90-0475-CIV-KING (S.D. Fla. June 4, 1990); Steen v. Chrysler Motors Corp., CA No. C4-91-601951 (St. Louis County, Minn. Feb. 21, 1993); Eimers v. Honda Motor Co., CA No. 90-25 (W.D. Pa. Dec. 12, 1991); Young v. J.I. Case Co., CA No. 3:90 CV 00630 (E.D. Va. Mar. 26, 1991).

[180] Bohannon v. Honda Motor Co., 127 F.R.D. 536, 539–40 (D. Kan. 1989).

[181] See generally chapter 8.

[182] *See* Snowden v. Connaught Lab., Inc., 137 F.R.D. 336, 346 (D. Kan.), *appeal denied*, 136 F.R.D. 694 (D. Kan. 1991).

Stonewalling is facilitated if such requests are permitted in two ways. First, collaboration, including verification (as discussed in chapter 8), would be chilled. Second, the defendant would be able to craft its responses to the plaintiff's discovery requests to avoid disclosing information not already known by that plaintiff.

A simple balancing of the interests involved should impel the court to deny the manufacturer's request. On the one hand, the defendant has no legitimate need to discover the identity of documents already in its possession. Because the court will inevitably require both parties to exchange a complete list of all documents expected to be used at trial, an order denying the request will result in no prejudice to the defendant. On the other hand, an order directing the plaintiff's counsel to reveal the full extent not only of his or her knowledge, but also the knowledge of all other counsel participating in a cooperative effort, would result in severe and irreparable prejudice to all present and potential plaintiffs with similar claims against that manufacturer.

Should the court grant the defendant's request, the plaintiff is advised to take steps to require the manufacturer to produce every document it has produced in all other similar cases, as well as a list of particular documents selected by defense counsel for use in other cases. To paraphrase the old adage, what's full disclosure for the goose should be full disclosure for the gander. Unless the court also requires the defendant to disclose at the same time the products of its own collaborative mechanism, defense counsel will be granted a tremendous and unjust advantage over the plaintiff in every individual case.

In no event should the court require the plaintiff to answer the defendant's request until *after* the defendant has fully responded to the plaintiff's initial discovery request.[183] This timing is necessary to avoid suppression of relevant information.

XI. CONCLUSION

In affirming default judgment against Suzuki Motor Company for its ongoing stonewalling in a recent automotive crashworthiness case, Judge Fay of the Eleventh Circuit closed his opinion with the following observations. These prescient comments make a fitting conclusion for this chapter as well:

> Having examined the misconduct in this case and affirmed the sanctions imposed, we feel compelled to remark on the disturbing regularity with which discovery abuses occur in our courts today. The Federal Rules of Civil Procedure were adopted in 1937 in the hope of securing "the just, speedy, and inexpensive determination of every action." Fed. R. Civ. P. 1. Today, fifty-six years later, the drafters of these rules certainly would be disappointed to see how far from that ideal we remain. The discovery rules in particular were intended to promote the search for truth that is the heart of our judicial system. However, the success with which the rules are applied toward this search for truth greatly depends on the professionalism and integrity of the attorneys involved. Therefore, it is appalling that attorneys,

---

[183] Dodson v. Persell, 390 So. 2d 704, 708 (Fla. 1980); DiMichel v. South Buffalo Ry. Co., 604 N.E.2d 63, 68 (N.Y. 1992); Altesman v. Eli Lilly & Co., 559 N.Y.S.2d 563, 565 (App. Div. 1990); Wind v. Eli Lilly & Co., 559 N.Y.S.2d 561, 563 (App. Div. 1990).

like defense counsel in this case, routinely twist the discovery rules into some of "the most powerful weapons in the arsenal of those who abuse the adversary system for the sole benefit of their clients."

All attorneys, as "officers of the court," owe duties of complete candor and primary loyalty to the court before which they practice. An attorney's duty to a client can never outweigh his or her responsibility to see that our system of justice functions smoothly. This concept is as old as common law jurisprudence itself. In England, the first licensed practitioners were called "Servants at law of our lord, the King" and were absolutely forbidden to "deceive or beguile the Court." In the United States, the first Code of Ethics, in 1887, included one canon providing that "the attorney's office does not destroy . . . accountability to the Creator," and another entitled "Client is not the Keeper of the Attorney's Conscience."

Unfortunately, the American Bar Association's current Model Rules of Professional Conduct underscore the duty to advocate zealously while neglecting the corresponding duty to advocate within the bounds of the law. As a result, too many attorneys have forgotten the exhortations of these century-old canons. Too many attorneys, like defense counsel in this case, have allowed the objectives of the client to override their ancient duties as officers of the court. In short, they have sold out to the client.

We must return to the original principle that, as officers of the court, attorneys are servants of the law rather than servants of the highest bidder. We must rediscover the old values of our profession. The integrity of our justice system depends on it.[184]

---

[184] *Malautea v. Suzuki Motor Co., Ltd.*, 987 F.2d 1536, 1546–47 (11th Cir.), *cert. denied*, 114 S. Ct. 181 (1993) (citations omitted).

CHAPTER SIX

DUMP TRUCK DISCOVERY

I. OVERVIEW: DUMP TRUCKS, SHUFFLED DECKS, AND NEEDLES IN HAYSTACKS

In the motion picture *Class Action*,[1] the lawyers for the fictional Argo Motors discover—and must deal with—the "smoking gun" memo showing that the corporation had knowledge of the avoidable and tragic defect in a particular model car long before the first car was sold. When one defense attorney balks at destroying the document, the defense team decides instead to bury it among boxloads of irrelevant documents delivered to their opponent's small firm in a moving van. To make matters worse, the documents are randomly shuffled before being loaded into the boxes. A voluminous index containing no information of real value is provided to the plaintiff's counsel in a purported showing of good faith. The scene in which Gene Hackman and his bright young assistants shift futilely through the mass of papers searching for a needle in the haystack would be comical if it did not so accurately reflect the pernicious practice of *dump truck discovery*.

The prevalence of attempts to subvert meaningful discovery by responding to specific inquiries with volumes of documents—undifferentiated as to subject matter and with no meaningful index—has been well documented.[2] Manufacturers employ

---

[1] Twentieth Century Fox 1991.

[2] *See* Scripps Clinic & Research Found. v. Baxter Travenol Lab., Inc., No. 87-140-CMW, 1988 U.S. Dist. LEXIS 7495 (D. Del. June 21, 1988) (finding Baxter produced 45,000 unindexed documents; Scripps made general reference to boxes containing 6,700 documents); Derson Group, Ltd. v. Right Management Consultants, Inc., 119 F.R.D. 396 (N.D. Ill. 1988) (ruling interrogatory response was improper by general reference to 33,000 documents already produced); Holben v. Coopervision, Inc., 120 F.R.D. 32, 33–34 (E.D. Pa. 1988) (finding defendant contact lens manufacturer's response to interrogatory seeking information concerning test results was improper where defendant unloaded volumes of unspecified information in bulk on plaintiff); Sabel v. Mead Johnson & Co., 110 F.R.D. 553 (D. Mass.) (finding reference to 154,000 page new drug application, with inadequate index, was improper response to interrogatories), *later proceedings*, 112 F.R.D. 211 (D. Mass. 1986); American Rockwool, Inc. v.

dump truck tactics with equal vigor in response to both interrogatories and requests for production.

As in *Class Action*, the "shuffled deck" is often employed concurrently with the dump truck response: The manufacturer not only delivers the documents in an unorganized mass, it also buries important information among innocuous papers.[3] As poetically described by one commentator,

> [T]he responding party attempts to drown its adversary in the sea of documents, scrambled together in an unmapped mass, or to bury key documents in the pile by "shuffling the deck" rather than producing documents in their original form or in an otherwise orderly state.[4]

The superficial attraction for a stonewaller is that this technique gives the impression of a forthcoming response while successfully hiding critical documents. When the plaintiff moves to compel specific answers to its specific questions, the defendant invariably protests that it has opened its files, producing thousands of documents at great effort and expense.

Owens-Corning Fiberglas Corp., 109 F.R.D. 263, 266 (E.D.N.C. 1985) (finding discovery response directing plaintiff to warehouse where more than one million unsorted documents were stored constituted abuse of discovery procedures); Kozlowski v. Sears, Roebuck & Co., 73 F.R.D. 73, 76–77 (D. Mass. 1976); *see also* Rainbow Pioneer #44-18-04A v. Hawaii-Nevada Inv. Corp., 711 F.2d 902 (9th Cir. 1983); T.N. Taube Corp. v. Marine Midland Mortgage Corp., 136 F.R.D. 449 (W.D.N.C. 1991); Compagnie Francaise d'Assurance Pour le Commerce Exterieur v. Phillips Petroleum Co., 105 F.R.D. 16, 44 (S.D.N.Y. 1984); Flour Mills of Am., Inc. v. Pace, 75 F.R.D. 676, 682 (E.D. Okla. 1977); Clark v. General Motors Corp., 20 Fed. R. Serv. 2d (Callaghan) 679, 682 (D. Mass. 1975); Thomason v. Leiter, 52 F.R.D. 290, 290–91 (M.D. Ala. 1971); *In re* Master Key Antitrust Litig., 53 F.R.D. 87 (D. Conn. 1971). *See generally* MARK A. DOMBROFF, DOMBROFF ON UNFAIR TACTICS § 1.19, at 35 (1984 & Supp. 1988); RICHARD H. UNDERWOOD & WILLIAM H. FORTUNE, TRIAL ETHICS § 6.5.4 (1988 & Supp. 1993). Section III of this chapter discusses use of these tactics in connection with several variants of the business records option including a central document repository.

[3] *See, e.g.*, LaPeire v. Volkswagen, A.G., No. 88-2979, 1989 U.S. Dist. LEXIS 5371 (E.D. Pa. May 15, 1989) (finding entire NHTSA investigation file on unintended acceleration incidents was broader than request to identify complaints); ITT Life Ins. Co. v. Thomas Nastoff, Inc., 108 F.R.D. 664, 666 (N.D. Ind. 1985). *See generally* MARK A. DOMBROFF, DISCOVERY § 5.02 (1986 & Supp. 1990); UNDERWOOD & FORTUNE, *supra* note 2, § 6.5.4; Wayne D. Brazil, *The Adversary Character of Civil Discovery: A Critique and Proposals for Change*, 31 VAND. L. REV. 1295, 1323–25 (1978); Philip H. Corboy, *Discovery Wars and the Trial Lawyer*, 1990 A.B.A. ANN. CONVENTION 5; Frank F. Flegal, *Introduction to Discovery Abuse: Causes, Effects, and Reform*, 3 REV. LITIG. 1, 23 (1982); Edward F. Sherman & Stephen D. Kinnard, *Federal Court Discovery in the 80's—Making the Rules Work*, 95 F.R.D. 245, 250 (1983).

[4] Martin I. Kaminsky, *Proposed Federal Discovery Rules for Complex Civil Litigation*, 48 FORDHAM L. REV. 907, 974 (1980); *see also* THE AMERICAN BAR ASSOCIATION SECTION OF LITIGATION, REPORT OF THE SPECIAL COMMITTEE FOR THE STUDY OF DISCOVERY ABUSE 22 (1977).

There are several variations of the dump truck response.[5] Regardless of which variant is used, the abusive effect on the discovery process is the same: Information is delivered in a form that is not readily usable by the opposing party. Further, the dump truck tactic may be used as a device to cloak the suppression of critical evidence. The abusive effect of this tactic is the same whether employed in response to interrogatories or requests for production.

All forms of the dump truck response should be considered as an election to use the business records option as an alternative to the method of response contemplated by the discovery rules. The business records option rules, as amended, were drafted specifically to allow courts to identify and correct the abusive effect of the various forms of the dump truck tactic.[6] Courts should insist that central document repositories, reading rooms, and all other such forms of the business records response comply with the criteria inherent in the business records option.[7] These criteria were incorporated in the business records option for this very reason.

II. INTENDED USE OF THE BUSINESS RECORDS OPTION

Although courts in individual cases had long allowed the practice of responding to discovery by producing business records, specific language describing the business records option was first included in the federal rules in 1970.[8] The business records option is contained in rules 33(d),[9] 34(b),[10] and 45(d).[11]

The traditional objectives of discovery remain the same whether or not the responding party chooses to employ the business records option. The business records option is intended to aid the discovery process. A careful reading of the pertinent authorities clearly indicates that the authors of the federal rules had no intention of permitting the option to be used as a vehicle for discovery misconduct. Indeed,

---

[5] The variant forms of the dump truck response include delivery of individual records to the office of plaintiff's counsel in an individual case, establishment of central document repositories (including the so-called "reading rooms") for use in all cases involving the same product, and the on-site inspection of business records in their natural habitat. Computers may be used to replicate all of the variant forms of the dump truck response.

[6] See section II.A, *infra*.

[7] See section II.B, *infra*.

[8] Concerning the business records option to answering interrogatories, see generally DISCOVERY PROCEEDINGS IN FEDERAL COURT §§ 6.33–6.35 (Shepard's eds., 2d ed. 1991 & Supp. 1992); 4A MOORE ET AL., MOORE'S FEDERAL PRACTICE (2d ed. 1991 & Supp. 1992) ¶33.25[5]; 8 CHARLES ALAN WRIGHT & ARTHUR R. MILLER, FEDERAL PRACTICE AND PROCEDURE § 2178 (1970 & Supp. 1992). Concerning response to request for production, see DISCOVERY PROCEEDINGS IN FEDERAL COURT, *supra*, § 7.16; 4A MOORE ET AL., *supra*, ¶ 34.05[1]; 8 WRIGHT & MILLER, *supra*, (Supp. 1993).

[9] FED. R. CIV. P. 33(d). This was rule 33(c) until 1993.

[10] FED. R. CIV. P. 34(b).

[11] FED. R. CIV. P. 45(d)(1).

rules 33(d) and 34(b) were twice amended with an aim toward preventing the dump truck response.[12] The advisory committee's note to the 1970[13] and 1980[14] amendments makes clear the specific intent to prevent the dump truck response.[15] The language of the 1970 and 1980 amendments essentially establishes three criteria that must be met as prerequisites to a party's use of the business records option.[16] By scrutinizing a party's response according to these three criteria, the court can ensure that a proffered use of the business records option does indeed achieve the traditional objectives of discovery: full disclosure of all relevant information in a usable form.

A. Objectives of the Business Records Option

The language of both the rules and the advisory committee's note makes clear that the business records option is not intended as a generic substitute for the standard or traditional response to a discovery request. Because of the enormous potential for its abuse, the business records option is limited to situations where a proper response (1) would require an analysis or compilation of raw data and (2) would require the responding party to engage in excessively burdensome or expensive research into its own business records.[17] As its title implies, the option to produce business records is available only with respect to records that qualify as "business records."[18]

In these limited circumstances, the rule alters the method of response by shifting[19] part of the burden of finding the answer from the responding party to the requesting party—if, indeed, the burden of deriving or ascertaining the answer is substantially the same for the requesting party as it would be for the responding party.

---

[12] *See generally* 4A MOORE ET AL., *supra* note 8, ¶¶ 33.25[5.–5], 34.01[8–9].

[13] FED R. CIV. P. 33(c), 34(b) 1970 advisory committee's notes.

[14] FED. R. CIV. P. 33(c), 34(b) 1980 advisory committee's notes.

[15] *See* Holben v. Coopervision, Inc., 120 F.R.D. 32, 34 (E.D. Pa. 1988). *See generally* 4A MOORE ET AL., *supra* note 8, ¶ 33.25[5.–5], at 33–143.

[16] See section II.B, *infra*.

[17] *See* 4A MOORE ET AL., *supra* note 8, ¶ 33.25[5.–1], at 33–132 (paraphrasing FED. R. CIV. P. 33 1970 advisory committee's note).

[18] Davis v. Fendler, 650 F.2d 1154, 1158 n.3 (9th Cir. 1981); Hoffman v. United Telecommunications, Inc., 117 F.R.D. 436, 438 (D. Kan. 1987); EEOC v. Anchor Continental, Inc., 74 F.R.D. 523, 525–26 (D.S.C. 1977). *See generally* DISCOVERY PROCEEDINGS IN FEDERAL COURT, *supra* note 8, § 6.33, at 408–09; 4A MOORE ET AL., *supra* note 8, ¶ 33.25[5.–3], at 33–139. Documents produced under the business records option are implicitly certified to be the party's own records kept in the ordinary course of business, and thus, qualify for admission into evidence by the opponent under the business record exception to the hearsay rule, FED. R. EVID. 803(6), without further authentication. *In re* Japanese Elec. Prods. Antitrust Litig., 723 F.2d 238, 287–88 (3d Cir. 1983).

[19] *See* FED. R. CIV. P. 33(c) 1970 advisory committee's note; Avramidis v. Atlantic Richfield Co., 120 F.R.D. 450, 452 (D. Mass. 1988).

"The idea behind the rule is that when the burden of deriving information from documents is equal between the parties, the interrogating party should bear the burden of compiling the information."[20]

The business records option is not intended to and does not change the underlying scope or objectives of the discovery rules. Courts have noted that the following general principles of discovery apply even where the responding party has elected to use the business records option method of response:

The Scope of Discovery: "This provision [rule 33(d)], *without undermining the liberal scope of interrogatory discovery,* places the burden of discovery upon its potential benefitee. . . ."[21]

Full Disclosure: "It would be antipathetic to the spirit of the discovery rules to assume that the newly added rule 33(c) [now 33(d)] was intended to diminish the duty of the parties to provide all information requested."[22]

Full, Complete, and Nonevasive Responses: "Rule 33(c) [now 33(d)] allows parties to opt to produce business records to aid in answering the interrogatories, not to avoid answering them."[23]

Duty of Inquiry: Corporations still have a duty to conduct an inquiry to locate information under their control that may be needed in making a proper response to a discovery request.[24] Indeed, unless and until the company conducts an inquiry of its records, it will not be in a position to provide the necessary factual support for its election to employ the business records option.[25]

---

[20] Compagnie Francaise d'Assurance Pour le Commerce Exterieur v. Phillips Petroleum Co., 105 F.R.D. 16, 44 (S.D.N.Y. 1984). *See generally* DISCOVERY PROCEEDINGS IN FEDERAL COURT, *supra* note 8, § 6.34; 4A MOORE ET AL., *supra* note 8, ¶ 33.25[5.–2].

[21] FED. R. CIV. P. 33 1970 advisory committee's note (emphasis added) (citing LOUISELL, MODERN CALIFORNIA DISCOVERY 124–25 (1963)).

[22] *In re* Master Key Antitrust Litig., 53 F.R.D. 87, 90 (D. Conn. 1971); *see also* Trane Co. v. Klutznick, 87 F.R.D. 473, 476 (W.D. Wis. 1980); Budget Rent-A-Car, Inc. v. Hertz Corp., 55 F.R.D. 354, 357 (W.D. Mo. 1972).

[23] Scripps Clinic & Research Found. v. Baxter Travenol Lab., Inc., No. 87-140-CMW, 1988 U.S. Dist. LEXIS 7495, at 2 (D. Del. June 21, 1988); Sabel v. Mead Johnson & Co., 110 F.R.D. 553, 555 (D. Mass.), *later proceedings*, 112 F.R.D. 211 (D. Mass 1986); *see also* Chubb Integrated Sys., Ltd. v. National Bank, 103 F.R.D. 52, 61 (D.D.C. 1984) (ruling parties "have a duty to provide true, explicit, responsive, complete and candid answers"); Miller v. Doctor's Gen. Hosp., 76 F.R.D. 136 (W.D. Okla. 1977) (stating "answers to interrogatories must be responsive, full, complete and unevasive").

[24] *See, e.g.,* American Rockwool, Inc. v. Owens-Corning Fiberglas Corp., 109 F.R.D. 263, 266 (E.D.N.C. 1985) (holding rule 33(c) responding party is charged with knowledge of the party's agents and has a duty to reasonably inquire whether agents possess the information in a more convenient form). Concerning the duty of inquiry generally, see chapter 2, section II.

[25] Manville Sales Corp. v. Paramount Sys., Inc., No. 86-4157, 1987 U.S. Dist. LEXIS 9688 (E.D. Pa. Oct. 27, 1987). *See generally* 4A MOORE ET AL., *supra* note 8, ¶ 33.26 (stating the answer should set forth in detail the efforts made to obtain the information).

Duty to Supplement Responses: The defendant's duty to supplement its responses to discovery remains unchanged.[26]

B. Prerequisites to Invoking the Business Records Option

Three conditions must be met for a party to invoke the business records option. These three conditions, described below, are inherent in the 1970 and 1980 amendments to the rules authorizing use of the business records option. Since the amendments to rules 33 and 34 were adopted for the same reason, it seems clear that the prerequisites for the use of the option are the same whether it is employed as a response to an interrogatory or a request for production.[27] According to the advisory committee's note to the 1970 amendment to rule 34(b), "The procedure provided in rule 34 is essentially the same as that in rule 33, as amended, and the discussion in the note appended to that rule is relevant to rule 34 as well."[28]

The three prerequisites for invoking the business records option may serve as criteria for the court's determination of the acceptability of the defendant's response or as a standard for identifying and correcting an abusive response.

1. Burden of Response

The business records option may only be invoked if there is a bona fide burden involved in compiling or extracting the answer, above and beyond simply referring to the records, *and* the burden is substantially the same for both parties.

Burden of Extracting Information: Virtually every interrogatory requires some kind of burden to answer; however, to invoke the business records option, the defendant must show that the burden of responding exceeds the effort that would be required in making a traditional narrative answer.[29] The option can be used only where a proper answer to a particular question requires some kind of interpretation or compilation of the defendant's business records.[30] The discovery respondent bears the burden of

---

[26] Friction Div. Prods., Inc. v. E.I. DuPont de Nemours & Co., 658 F. Supp. 998, 1003–04 (D. Del. 1987); Brennan v. Glens Falls Nat'l Bank & Trust Co., 19 Fed. R. Serv. 2d (Callaghan) 721 (N.D.N.Y. 1974). The duty to supplement generally is discussed in chapter 2, section III.

[27] See section II.C, *infra*.

[28] FED. R. CIV. P. 34(b) 1970 advisory committee's note.

[29] FED. R. CIV. P. 33(c) 1970 advisory committee's note, *quoted in* Pascale v. G.D. Searle & Co., 90 F.R.D. 55, 60 (D.R.I. 1981); T.N. Taube Corp. v. Marine Midland Mortgage Corp., 136 F.R.D. 449, 453 (W.D.N.C. 1991); Blake Assocs., Inc. v. Omni Spectra, Inc., 118 F.R.D. 283, 289 (D. Mass. 1988); Sabel v. Mead Johnson & Co., 110 F.R.D. 553, 556 (D. Mass.), *later proceedings*, 112 F.R.D. 211 (D. Mass. 1986). In commenting on the addition of the business record option to rule 33, the advisory committee noted that "[t]his is a new subdivision . . . relating *especially* to interrogatories which require a party to engage in *burdensome or expensive research into* his own business records in order to give an answer."

[30] FED. R. CIV. P. 33(c) states that the option may be employed when the answer may be "derived or ascertained" from business records. *See, e.g.*, T.N. Taube Corp. v. Marine Midland Mortgage Corp., 136 F.R.D. 449, 451 (W.D.N.C. 1991); Thomason v. Leiter, 52 F.R.D. 290 (M.D. Ala. 1971); *see also* FED. R. CIV. P. 33(c) 1970 advisory committee's note.

demonstrating why the proper response would be exceedingly burdensome and why the business records option is justified.[31]

This basic prerequisite is sometimes overlooked by counsel. As noted by one court,

> It seems to me that both parties have failed to address a critical threshold issue. Before determining whether the burden of deriving information from business records is substantially the same for both parties, the first question under rule 33(c) [now 33(d)] is whether there exists a "burden" at all within the meaning of the rule. An interrogated party can rely on rule 33(c) only if there is some burden involved in compiling or extracting the requested information, above and beyond the simple task of referring to the records in order to answer the interrogatories.... Answering interrogatories often requires the interrogated party to refer to written documents, particularly where the party is a corporate entity. If a party could invoke rule 33(c) in every such case, by claiming that the "burden" of "deriving" the information from the records is substantially the same for both parties, discovery would be thwarted at every turn.[32]

Thus, the option has not been allowed for responding to questions that merely call for the identification of persons[33], documents,[34] or things,[35] or where a narrative

---

[31] Lacey v. Superior Dental Lab., Inc., 21 Fed. R. Serv. 2d (Callaghan) 1375, 1377 (E.D. Pa. 1974). *See generally* 4A MOORE ET AL., *supra* note 8, ¶ 33.25[5.–2], at 33–134.

[32] Pascale v. G.D. Searle & Co., 90 F.R.D. 55, 60 (D.R.I. 1981). For other authorities dealing with the nature of this threshold burden, see Puerto Rico Aqueduct & Sewer Auth. v. Clow Corp., 108 F.R.D. 304, 307–08 (D.P.R. 1985); Budget Rent-A-Car, Inc. v. Hertz Corp., 55 F.R.D. 354 (W.D. Mo. 1972).

[33] Davis v. Fendler, 650 F.2d 1154, 1157 n.1, 1158 n.3 (9th Cir. 1981) (ordering party to name officers, directors and stockholders, and dates and locations of directors' meetings); Penza v. Drexel Burnham Lambert, Inc., No. 88-6809, 1989 U.S. Dist. LEXIS 10193 (E.D. Pa. Aug. 28, 1989) (managers, authors, employees working on account); Garcia v. Victoria Indep. Sch. Dist., 17 Empl. Prac. Dec. (CCH) ¶ 8544 (S.D. Tex. 1978) (ordering party to identify expert even though name appears somewhere in records).

[34] Blake Assocs., Inc. v. Omni Spectra, Inc., 118 F.R.D. 283, 288–89 (D. Mass. 1988) (finding rule 33(d) response improper where question asks respondent to identify certain documents); Thomason v. Leiter, 52 F.R.D. 290 (M.D. Ala. 1971) (same); Friction Div. Prods. v. E.I. DuPont de Nemours & Co., 658 F. Supp. 998, 1003–04 (D. Del. 1987) (ordering party to identify documents showing existence of prior art); SCM Corp. v. Xerox Corp., 21 Fed. R. Serv. 2d (Callaghan) 1377 (D. Conn. 1975) (compelling party to identify documents identifying license agreements); Harlem River Consumers Coop., Inc. v. Associated Grocers, Inc., 64 F.R.D. 459, 463 (S.D.N.Y. 1974) (ordering party to identify documents showing conspiracy); Atlanta Coca-Cola Bottling Co. v. Transamerica Ins. Co., 61 F.R.D. 115 (N.D. Ga. 1972) (ordering party to identify documents constituting contract); Budget Rent-A-Car, Inc. v. Hertz Corp., 55 F.R.D. 354, 357 (W.D. Mo. 1972) (finding response improper where question asks respondent to identify certain documents).

[35] United States v. Chevron U.S., Inc., No. 88-6681, 1989 U.S. Dist. LEXIS 10236 (E.D. Pa. Aug. 30, 1989) (compelling party to identify refinery equipment).

answer could be prepared simply by reference to existing materials.[36]

Burden Substantially the Same for Both Parties: Rule 33(d) expressly provides that the business records option may be invoked only where "the burden of deriving or ascertaining the answer is substantially the same for the party serving the interrogatory as for the party served." Thus, if the burden on the plaintiff of deriving the answer is greater than it would be for the defendant, the court should order the defendant to supply a full narrative answer.[37]

The parties' relative familiarity with the business records in question is an important factor in assessing whether the burden is substantially similar.[38] The Third Circuit Court of Appeals, addressing this point, observed the following:

> Evidence in the records supports the district court's finding that the burden of extracting the information from the business records would be greater on the party serving the interrogatory than on the party served. Many of the records were hand written, and apparently difficult to read. The district court further observed that each party served with interrogatories was more familiar with his bookkeeping methods and records than was the defendant. This evidence amply supports the finding that the burdens were not substantially the same. Therefore, the rule 33(c) [now 33(d)] ruling shall be upheld.[39]

Although an important factor, familiarity with one's own records is not conclusive proof that the burden of analyzing the subject records is unequal.[40]

The question of whether the burden of deriving an answer is substantially the same for the plaintiff as it would be for the defendant also depends on how fully the defendant has discharged its duty to provide the plaintiff with a specific desig-

---

[36] Diaflon, Inc. v. Allied Chem. Corp., 534 F.2d 221, 225–26 (10th Cir.), *cert. denied*, 429 U.S. 886 (1976); Pascale v. G.D. Searle & Co., 90 F.R.D. 55, 60 (D.R.I. 1981); Thomason v. Leiter, 52 F.R.D. 290, 291 (M.D. Ala. 1971).

[37] Pascale v. G.D. Searle & Co., 90 F.R.D. 55, 61 (D.R.I. 1981). *See generally* DISCOVERY PROCEEDINGS IN FEDERAL COURT, *supra* note 8, § 6.34; 4A MOORE ET AL., *supra* note 8, ¶ 33.25[5.–2].

[38] Puerto Rico Aqueduct & Sewer Auth. v. Clow Corp., 108 F.R.D. 304, 308–09 (D.P.R. 1985) (rejecting plaintiff's effort to invoke option based on parties' disparate familiarity with subject records); EEOC v. Anchor Continental, Inc., 74 F.R.D. 523, 525 (D.S.C. 1977) ("When one of the parties is the Federal government and government records are involved, it is difficult to imagine circumstances when the burden of deriving an answer would be the same."); Chrapliwy v. Uniroyal, Inc., 17 Fed. R. Serv. 2d (Callaghan) 719, 722 (N.D. Ind. 1973) (rejecting option because of defendant's familiarity with computerized business records); *see also* Foster v. Boise-Cascade, Inc., 20 Fed. R. Serv. 2d (Callaghan) 466, 470 (S.D. Tex. 1975).

[39] Al Barnett & Son, Inc. v. Outboard Marine Corp., 611 F.2d 32, 35 (3d Cir. 1979).

[40] *See* Sabel v. Mead Johnson & Co., 110 F.R.D. 553, 556 (D. Mass.), *later proceedings*, 112 F.R.D. 211 (D. Mass. 1986) (noting principle but ruling that defendant failed to carry burden of showing effort was substantially similar); Compagnie Francaise d'Assurance Pour le Commerce Exterieur v. Phillips Petroleum Co., 105 F.R.D 16, 44 (S.D.N.Y. 1984); Saddler v. Musicland-Pickwick Int'l, Inc., 31 Fed. R. Serv. 2d (Callaghan) 760, 761 (E.D. Tex. 1980).

nation of particular documents. This issue is addressed in the discussion of the third prerequisite below.

2. Information Contained in the Records

As noted earlier, the business records option merely alters the *form* of the response—it is not intended as a device to frustrate the full disclosure objective of the discovery rules.[41] The option cannot be invoked unless the proffered records in fact contain all the requested information. The requesting party, by examining the proffered records, should be able to derive an answer that corresponds in every respect with the standards for a complete discovery response. The option may not be invoked by a response that says in effect that the information sought may or may not be found in certain records.[42] "The option device of Rule 33(c) [now 33(d)] may be used only if the party to whom the interrogatory was directed is prepared to say that the answer *will be found* in the designated records."[43]

Of course, if the rule 33(d) option is elected, the referenced documents must actually be produced. A party may not invoke rule 33(d) in lieu of providing a narrative response to the interrogatory and then withhold the specified documents by claiming privilege.[44]

3. Duty to Specify

A response under the business records option must specify the responsive documents "in sufficient detail to permit the interrogating party to locate and to identify, as readily as can the interrogating party, the records from which the answer may be ascertained."[45] In applying this criterion, the courts often speak of the

---

[41] See section II.A, *supra*.

[42] Diaflon, Inc. v. Allied Chem. Corp., 534 F.2d 221, 226 (10th Cir.), *cert. denied*, 429 U.S. 886 (1976); Sabel v. Mead Johnson & Co., 110 F.R.D. 553, 555–56 (D. Mass.), *later proceedings*, 112 F.R.D. 211 (D. Mass 1986); ITT Life Ins. Co. v. Thomas Nastoff, Inc., 108 F.R.D. 664, 666 (N.D. Ind. 1985); Lacey v. Superior Dental Lab., Inc., 21 Fed. R. Serv. 2d (Callaghan) 1375, 1376 (E.D. Pa. 1974); In re Master Key Antitrust Litig., 53 F.R.D. 87, 90 (D. Conn. 1971). *See generally* DISCOVERY PROCEEDINGS IN FEDERAL COURT, *supra* note 8, § 6.35, at 411; 8 WRIGHT & MILLER, *supra* note 8, § 2178 (Supp. 1993).

[43] 8 WRIGHT & MILLER, *supra* note 8, § 2178, at 301 (Supp. 1993) (emphasis added).

[44] Blake Assocs., Inc. v. Omni Spectra, Inc., 118 F.R.D. 283, 290 (D. Mass. 1988). *See also* note 56, *infra*, and accompanying text.

[45] FED. R. CIV. P. 33(d). *See generally* DISCOVERY PROCEEDINGS IN FEDERAL COURT, *supra* note 8, § 6.35 ("The responding party cannot merely offer his business records for inspection, but has a 'duty to specify, by category and location' the records from which *he knows* the answers to the interrogatories can be found."); 4A MOORE ET AL., *supra* note 8, ¶ 33.25[5.–5], at 33–144 (emphasis added); 8 WRIGHT & MILLER, *supra* note 8, § 2178 (Supp. 1993).

respondent's "duty to specify" its records.[46] This requirement was expressly added to the rule in 1980, as explained by the advisory committee, "to make it clear that a responding party has the duty to specify, by category and location, the records from which answers to interrogatories can be derived."[47]

The specification requirement is designed to ensure that a party electing to employ the option will produce documents in their most convenient and usable form.[48] Courts have strictly enforced the requirement to avoid the dump truck abuse of the business records option.[49]

The specification requirement applies to both the contents of the proffered records and the method by which the records are organized. Thus, the court may require the party invoking the option to (1) provide a knowledgeable employee to locate or decipher the records[50], (2) provide codes or software to extract information from computerized records,[51] (3) translate documents written in a foreign lan-

---

[46] T.N. Taube Corp. v. Marine Midland Mortgage Corp., 136 F.R.D. 449, 455 (W.D.N.C. 1991); Scripps Clinic & Research Found. v. Baxter Travenol Lab., Inc., No. 87-140-CMW, 1988 U.S. Dist. LEXIS 7495, at 1 (D. Del. June 21, 1988); Holben v. Coopervision, Inc., 120 F.R.D. 32, 34 (E.D. Pa. 1988).

[47] FED. R. CIV. P. 33(c) 1980 advisory committee's note.

[48] Diaflon, Inc. v. Allied Chem. Corp., 534 F.2d 221, 226 (10th Cir.), *cert. denied*, 429 U.S. 886 (1976); ITT Life Ins. Co. v. Thomas Nastoff, Inc., 108 F.R.D. 664, 666 (N.D. Ind. 1985); Texaco, Inc. v. Dominguez, 812 S.W.2d 451, 458 (Tex. Ct. App. 1991). *See generally* 4A MOORE ET AL., *supra* note 8, ¶ 33.25[5.1], at 33–133; 8 WRIGHT & MILLER, *supra* note 8, § 22.13; Edward F. Sherman & Stephen D. Kinnard, *Federal Court Discovery in the 80's—Making the Rules Work*, 95 F.R.D. 245, 253 (1983).

[49] *See, e.g.*, Rainbow Pioneer # 44-18-04A v. Hawaii-Nevada Inv. Corp., 711 F.2d 902, 906 (9th Cir. 1983); United States v. Chevron U.S., Inc., No. 88-6681, 1989 U.S. Dist. LEXIS 10236 (E.D. Pa. Aug. 30, 1989); Penza v. Drexel Burnham Lambert, Inc., No. 88-6809, 1989 U.S. Dist. LEXIS 10193 (E.D. Pa. Aug. 28, 1989); Avramidis v. Atlantic Richfield Co., 120 F.R.D. 450, 452 (D. Mass. 1988); Blake Assocs., Inc. v. Omni Spectra, Inc., 118 F.R.D. 283, 288–90 (D. Mass. 1988); Sabel v. Mead Johnson & Co., 112 F.R.D. 211 (D. Mass. 1986); American Rockwool, Inc. v. Owens-Corning Fiberglas Corp., 109 F.R.D. 263, 266 (E.D.N.C. 1985); Compagnie Francaise d'Assurance Pour le Commerce Exterieur v. Phillips Petroleum Co., 105 F.R.D. 16, 44 (S.D.N.Y. 1984); Clark v. General Motors Corp., 20 Fed. R. Serv. 2d (Callaghan) 679, 682 (D. Mass. 1975); Budget Rent-A-Car, Inc. v. Hertz Corp., 55 F.R.D. 354, 357 (W.D. Mo. 1972). *See generally* DISCOVERY PROCEEDINGS IN FEDERAL COURT, *supra* note 8, § 6.35.

[50] Robinson v. Lehman, 33 Fair Empl. Prac. Cas. (BNA) 710, 711 (E.D. Pa. 1983) (requiring defendant to provide assistance in locating documents in answering specific questions); Saddler v. Musicland-Pickwick Int'l, Inc., 31 Fed. R. Serv. 2d (Callaghan) 760, 762 (E.D. Tex. 1980); Technitrol, Inc. v. Digital Equip. Corp., 62 F.R.D. 91, 93 (N.D. Ill. 1973) (making filing system available to plaintiff).

[51] American Rockwool, Inc. v. Owens-Corning Fiberglas Corp., 109 F.R.D. 263, 264–65 (E.D.N.C. 1985) (parties agreeing to hire computer expert and split cost); Fautek v. Montgomery Ward

guage,[52] (4) furnish existing indices, lists, tables, or other aids for identifying relevant information,[53] or (5) furnish existing compilations of raw data.[54] Such compilations may be required to be produced even when they are work product.[55] One author has

---

& Co., 96 F.R.D. 141, 144–45 (N.D. Ill. 1982); *In re* Japanese Elec. Prods. Antitrust Litig., 494 F. Supp. 1257, 1261–62 (E.D. Pa. 1980); Bell v. Automobile Club, 80 F.R.D. 228, 233 (E.D. Mich. 1978), *appeal dismissed per curiam*, 601 F.2d 587 (6th Cir.), *cert. denied*, 442 U.S. 918 (1979); Chrapliwy v. Uniroyal, Inc., 17 Fed. R. Serv. 2d (Callaghan) 719, 722 (N.D. Ind. 1973) (rejecting option for failure to provide code to computerized records); Adams v. Dan River Mills, Inc. 54 F.R.D. 220 (W.D. Va. 1972); see chapter 1, section IV, for further discussion of discovery of computerized information.

[52] Societe Nationale Industrielle Aerospatiale v. United States Dist. Court, 482 U.S. 522, 546 n.80 (1987); Stapleton v. Kawasaki Heavy Indus., 69 F.R.D. 489 (N.D. Ga. 1975). *But see In re* Puerto Rico Elec. Power Auth., 687 F.2d 501, 504–10 (1st Cir. 1982); Rosado v. Mercedes-Benz of N. Am., Inc., 480 N.Y.S.2d 124 (App. Div. 1984). *See generally* ROGER S. HAYDOCK & DAVID F. HERR, DISCOVERY PRACTICE § 5.13 (2d ed. 1988 & Supp. 1992).

[53] LaPeire v. Volkswagen, A.G., No. 88-2979, 1989 U.S. Dist. LEXIS 5371 (E.D. Pa. May 15, 1989) (defendant offered plaintiff indexed compilation of all similar incidents prepared for NHTSA; court noted that if more specific compilation existed, including computerized information that is directly responsive to plaintiff's inquiry, it should be furnished); Scripps Clinic & Research Found. v. Baxter Travenol Lab., Inc., No. 87-140-CMW, 1988 U.S. Dist. LEXIS 7495 (D. Del. June 21, 1988) (compelling both parties to produce an index each company had prepared of its business records); Sabel v. Mead Johnson & Co., 110 F.R.D. 553, 556–57 (D. Mass.) (court initially finding that index provided by the defendant was inadequate and instructing defendant to provide narrative answer; on further proceeding, the court required the defendant to correlate specific questions to specific documents and page numbers internal to each document), *further proceedings*, 112 F.R.D. 211, 212–13 (D. Mass. 1986); American Rockwool, Inc. v. Owens-Corning Fiberglas Corp., 109 F.R.D. 263, 266 (E.D.N.Y. 1985) (instructing defendant to furnish index which the company had prepared of its own records); Marshall v. Great Lakes Recreation Co., 85 Lab. Cas. (CCH) ¶ 33,756 (E.D. Mich. 1979) (instructing defendant to furnish correlation of certain records); Federal Prescription Serv., Inc. v. American Pharmaceutical Ass'n, 1978-2 Trade Cas. (CCH) ¶ 62,195 (D.D.C. 1978) (instructing defendant to provide indices and tabs to relevant records to guide requesting party; defendant agreed and offered to provide additional assistance); United States v. Rust Eng'g Co., 72 F.R.D. 195, 196 (W.D. Pa. 1976) (defendant agreeing to prepare index with accompanying description of relevant files); *see also* Rainbow Pioneer # 49-18-04A v. Hawaii-Nevada Inv. Corp., 711 F.2d 902, 906 (9th Cir. 1983).

[54] Rich v. Martin Marietta Corp., 522 F.2d 333, 345 (10th Cir. 1975) (instructing defendant to furnish compilation of statistical information which either existed or would be developed in preparation of the defendant's own case); *see also* Hoffman v. United Telecommunications, Inc., 117 F.R.D. 436, 438 (D. Kan. 1987); Pascale v. G.D. Searle & Co., 90 F.R.D. 55, 61 (D.R.I. 1981).

[55] Rich v. Martin Marietta Corp., 522 F.2d 333, 345 (10th Cir. 1975); LaPeire v. Volkswagen, A.G., No. 88-2979, 1989 U.S. Dist. LEXIS 5371 (E.D. Pa. May 15, 1989) (ruling if defendant possesses more specific index of similar incidents, it should be furnished to plaintiff); Scripps Clinic &

stated that "if the rule 33(c) [now 33(d)] option is selected, abstracts or compilations prepared by counsel in anticipation of litigation may not be entitled to work-product protection."[56]

C. Application of the Business Records Option to Rules 34(b) and 45(d)

The final paragraph of rule 34(b) provides that "[a] party who produces documents for inspection shall produce them as they are kept in the usual course of business or shall organize and label them to correspond with the categories in the request." The question that arises is whether the defendant has an absolute option to choose the first alternative and thereby avoid producing the documents in a manner that is much more meaningful and useful to the plaintiff.

Because this provision of rule 34(b) was adopted for the very purpose of preventing such abuses as the deliberate mixing of "critical documents with others in the hope of obscuring significance,"[57] it seems unlikely that courts would perpetuate such an abuse by allowing an absolute option. Indeed, most cases that have considered the question have held that despite the rule's ambiguity, it should not be read as giving the party from whom the discovery is sought an absolute option to produce records as kept in the usual course of business. The responding party "should be required to produce [the documents] in a form that will make reasonable use of them possible."[58]

Courts have uniformly rejected the notion that corporate defendants can escape their primary discovery obligations by maintaining an inadequate filing and storage

---

Research Found. v. Baxter Travenol Lab., Inc., No. 87-140-CMW, 1988 U.S. Dist. LEXIS 7495 (D. Del. June 21, 1988) (existing work-product index of documents must be produced); ITT Life Ins. Co. v. Thomas Nastoff, Inc., 108 F.R.D. 664 (N.D. Ind. 1985) (finding no objection that some work-product research is required); American Rockwool, Inc. v. Owens-Corning Fiberglas Corp., 109 F.R.D. 263, 266 (E.D.N.C. 1985) (ordering defendant to produce index of customer records company had prepared); Saddler v. Musicland-Pickwick Int'l, Inc., 31 Fed. R. Serv. 2d (Callaghan) 760, 761 (E.D. Tex. 1980) (ruling any compilation that exists must be produced); Federal Prescription Serv., Inc. v. American Pharmaceutical Ass'n, 1978-2 Trade Cas. (CCH) ¶ 62,195 (D.D.C. 1978) (ordering that files produced must be accompanied by indices and designated by tabs to guide requesting party); Flour Mills of Am., Inc. v. Pace, 75 F.R.D. 676, 680–81 (E.D. Okla. 1977) (ruling respondent may have to research own records and give summary if it would do so for trial); *see also* note 45 and associated text, *supra*.

[56] Michael Jacobs, *Using the Production of Business Records Option for Answering Interrogatories Under Fed. R. Civ. P. 33(c)*, NEWSL. RULES & PROC. COMMITTEE (TIPS SECTION, AMERICAN BAR ASS'N), Winter 1989, at 29.

[57] FED. R. CIV. P. 34(b) 1980 advisory committee's note.

[58] 8 WRIGHT & MILLER, *supra* note 8, § 2213, at 319 (Supp. 1993) (emphasis added); *see* Board of Educ. v. Admiral Heating & Ventilating, Inc., 104 F.R.D. 23, 36 n.20 (N.D. Ill. 1984); *In re* Dayco Corp. Derivative Sec. Litig., 99 F.R.D. 616, 624 n.8 (S.D. Ohio 1983) (holding rule 34(b) "does not grant an absolute option to the producer of documents"); Texaco, Inc. v. Dominguez, 812 S.W.2d 451, 457–58 (Tex. Ct. App. 1991) (ruling the option contained in rule 34(b) as to how to produce the records does not belong exclusively to the producing party).

system.[59] It follows, then, that they certainly should not allow defendants to achieve the same objective by producing documents in a disorganized form. One article discussing use of the rules to avoid discovery abuse properly concludes that

> [t]he discovered party should have to show that producing the documents as kept in the usual course of business will not appreciably interfere with the ability of the discovering party to find the documents relevant to those categories [of its request]. If the filing system is not adequate for finding the relevant documents without undue delay and expense, then the discovered party shall not be allowed to produce documents as kept unless it provides additional resources to aid the discovering party.[60]

Several courts have held that the plaintiff may insist that the defendants segregate documents produced under rule 34(b) so as to correspond with the categories in the plaintiff's request.[61]

On the other hand, *Steenbergen v. Ford Motor Co.*[62] includes dicta supporting a very questionable and dangerous interpretation of rule 34(b). The court in *Steenbergen* held that the trial court did not err in allowing the defendant automaker to refer a plaintiff generally to documents "collected in the reading room *in the usual course of its business* of defending itself in passive restraint litigation."[63] The court's analysis was based on the highly questionable premise that the "usual course of business" language of the Texas equivalent of rule 34(b) is satisfied by any manner in which a corporate defendant's litigation department chooses to organize its documents when responding to discovery, as opposed to the manner in which the company maintains the documents in the usual course of its principal business.

The holding of the *Steenbergen* court is in conflict with the principle that the defendants should not restrict disclosure based on the defendant's own subjective, adversarial, and therefore very limited view of the nature of the subject matter in dispute.[64] Furthermore, the court's reading of rule 34(b) is neither logical nor in accor-

---

[59] *See* Baine v. General Motors Corp., 141 F.R.D. 328, 331 (M.D. Ala. 1991); Baxter Travenol Lab., Inc. v. LeMay, 93 F.R.D. 379, 383 (S.D. Ohio 1981); Alliance to End Repression v. Rochford, 75 F.R.D. 441, 447 (N.D. Ill. 1977); Kozlowski v. Sears, Roebuck & Co., 73 F.R.D. 73, 76 (D. Mass. 1976).

[60] Sherman & Kinnard, *supra* note 3, at 258.

[61] *See* T.N. Taube Corp. v. Marine Midland Mortgage Corp., 136 F.R.D. 449, 456 (W.D.N.C. 1991) (ordering documents produced "in a manner clearly indicating which of these documents respond to plaintiff's specific request for production"); Board of Educ. v. Admiral Heating & Ventilating, Inc., 104 F.R.D. 23, 36 (N.D. Ill. 1984); *In re* Dayco Corp. Derivative Sec. Litig., 99 F.R.D. 616, 624 (S.D. Ohio 1983) (compelling party to produce a list, "keyed as much as possible, to the specific document requests"); Texaco, Inc. v. Dominguez, 812 S.W.2d 451, 458 (Tex. Ct. App. 1991) (ruling trial court properly ordered party producing documents "to identify which documents satisfy which request").

[62] 814 S.W.2d 755 (Tex. Ct. App. 1991).

[63] *Id.* at 759.

[64] See chapter 5, section IV.

dance with the history of the requirement, and its reasoning is patently circular in nature. Disorganization cannot be excused by a showing that it is a party's "usual business practice" to produce documents requested in litigation in a disorganized fashion.[65] The *Steenbergen* construction of rule 34(b) is merely dicta, as the court's holding relied on the principle of waiver.[66] Its acceptance by other courts would have the unfortunate effect of judicially endorsing a classic stonewalling tactic.

When the federal rules were amended in 1991, a provision was included in rule 45 to provide the business records option to a person responding to a subpoena. The provision reads, "A person responding to a subpoena to produce documents shall produce them as they are kept in the usual course of business or shall organize and label them to correspond with the categories of the demand."[67] The amended rule extends to nonparties the same duties imposed on parties by the last paragraph of rule 34(b).

III. ABUSE OF THE BUSINESS RECORDS OPTION IN RECENT PRACTICE

Until recently, the dump truck response was most frequently used in individual cases in which the defendants simply delivered a mass of undifferentiated records to the office of plaintiff's counsel. Most of the reported cases discussing this form of discovery misconduct involved this situation.[68] Other practices involving abuse of the business records option to engage in dump truck discovery have emerged in recent years and have become common in complex tort cases. These are described below.

A. Central Document Repositories Operated by Defendants

There seems to be a growing tendency by defendant manufacturers to simply refer all plaintiffs in similar cases to a central document repository rather than responding to specific requests in individual cases. Some sort of centralized document production may be a practical necessity in some situations where numerous plaintiffs seek access to the same voluminous collection of documents.[69] Unfortunately, this device for improving efficiency frequently has been used as a tool to frustrate discovery and to introduce dramatic inefficiencies into the discovery process. The central document repository has been used as a stationary dump truck, with all the adverse effects of traditional dump truck discovery. The repository can add further disadvan-

---

[65] *See* authorities cited in note 61, *supra*.

[66] After initially accepting Ford's response, the plaintiff requested and received over 16,000 documents—without limitation on the right to request additional materials. The lower court ruled that having found Ford's response satisfactory for over two years, the plaintiff could not be heard to complain for the first time at trial. This is the ruling the appellate court affirmed. 814 S.W.2d at 759.

[67] FED. R. CIV. P. 45(d)(1).

[68] *See* notes 2 and 3, *supra*.

[69] See sections IV.A and IV.B, *infra*.

tage: the plaintiff may have to examine the mountains of produced documents in an inhospitable environment.

The various forms that central document repositories may take are a function of one or more of the following variables:[70]

Location: The repository may be physically located on the defendant's premises (on-site) or set up at an off-site address.

Contents: The repository may include or purport to include all requested documents, or, as is the case in repositories sometimes known as "reading rooms," the repository may include only those documents deemed relevant by the defendant.

Organization of records: The documents in the repository may be maintained in the order in which they are kept in the usual course of the defendant's business, or the defendant might attempt to organize them by subject—perhaps to correspond with the categories of the plaintiff's requests—or the defendant might adopt an arbitrary method of organization.

A response that refers one or more plaintiffs to a collection of documents should be treated as a business records option response. The court should not approve such a response until it is satisfied that the defendant's document repository meets the three prerequisites for the business records option described in section II. The abusive use of the central document repository arises from a failure to comply with one or more of these three essential prerequisites. For instance, repositories frequently fail to meet the prerequisite that the burden of deriving information sought be specified with particularity. The repository often results in a disproportionate burden on the plaintiff to derive the answer or locate the documents. This may result either from the defendant's failure to adequately specify the location or contents of documents in the repository, or from the use of logistical obstacles to impede the effective use of the repository. Repositories also often fail to comply with the prerequisite that the documents produced contain all of the information sought. Repositories are often used to camouflage suppression of relevant information.

The problems created by central document repositories are illustrated in the following examples.

1. Honda's ATV Repository

Honda Motor Company[71] routinely responds to plaintiffs' discovery requests in all-terrain vehicle (ATV) litigation by referring plaintiffs' counsel to its document repository in Torrence, California—home to an estimated 1.4 million documents. Plaintiffs' lawyers involved in ATV litigation are critical of Honda's document repository for the following reasons:[72]

---

[70] Central document repositories that are accessible by a computer may take any of the forms discussed *infra*.

[71] Various Honda entities typically are named as defendants in the ATV litigation, including Honda Motor Co. and American Honda Motor Co.

[72] These criticisms are set forth in detail in the affidavits of various plaintiffs' counsel submitted in Lee v. Honda Motor Co., CA No. 9103-01752 (Or. Cir. Ct. Feb. 4, 1992).

- The repository does not include all the documents relevant to the ATV litigation. Indeed, many of the critical documents are *not* included in Honda's repository. The overwhelming majority of the documents in the repository are totally irrelevant to the principal issues in dispute in the ATV litigation.
- Honda does not provide an adequate index to the materials in its repository. Plaintiffs' attorneys have found the index Honda provides to be incomplete and absolutely useless for locating documents in the repository. At least one court has agreed that this index is inadequate. In *Lee v. Honda Motor Co.*,[73] the court ordered the defendant to make available to the plaintiff the defendant's own more detailed version of the index.[74] The court did, however, permit Honda to redact and withhold certain information that was clearly work product.
- Visiting Honda's repository is difficult, time-consuming, and expensive for most plaintiffs' lawyers.
- Honda makes on-site access to the documents difficult through its cumbersome procedures for document review.

Honda's approach exemplifies all that is wrong with the use of document repositories. The primary problem is that Honda continues to control the documents and the means of accessing them; it has never "produced" the documents in the traditional sense of providing them to plaintiffs. Its practices of not allowing attorneys to browse through the documents in the stacks, not allowing them to review more than one box of documents at a time, not providing a copying machine, not allowing side-by-side comparison of documents not contained in the same box, and most importantly, not providing a meaningful index, have resulted in document production that impedes, rather than facilitates, full and fair disclosure of information. The shortcomings of the Honda repository are particularly apparent when compared with plaintiff-controlled repositories such as the one used in the L-Tryptophan multidistrict litigation.[75]

2. Reading Rooms

A reading room is one variation of a central document repository, in which the party making production acknowledges that the repository only contains those documents that its own litigation department has selected. Almost by definition, the documents in a reading room are limited to those that satisfy the defendant's adversarial and narrow view of relevance.[76] While a visit to the reading room may be of some assistance early in the proceedings as the parties informally confer and refine the scope of discovery, the plaintiff should make clear to the defendant and the court that

---

[73] *Id.*

[74] *Id.*, Findings of Fact, Conclusions of Law, and Order (Feb. 4, 1992).

[75] For a discussion of this particular document repository, which was court-authorized, see INSIDE LITIG. Nov. 1991, at 1. Repositories operated by plaintiffs are discussed generally later in this chapter.

[76] See chapter 5, section IV.

by accepting the defendant's invitation to visit the facility for on-site inspection, the plaintiff does not waive normal discovery procedures.

B. Abusive Use of Computers

Documents originally created in hardcover format may be converted to a variety of computer-readable formats (imaging, CD-ROMs, microfiche, etc.). With increasing frequency in recent years, critical information may be initially generated in a computer-readable format. In either event, the defendant may proffer the plaintiff a central document repository in computer format that possesses some or all of the abuses previously discussed.

This is not to say that any use of computer technology in discovery is abusive. To the contrary, production of material in electronic format can be an efficient way to convey information.[77] In the federal multidistrict breast implant litigation, for instance, computer technology has been used to disseminate millions of pages of documents produced by the manufacturers to attorneys representing thousands of plaintiffs, and to facilitate indexing of those documents. Compact disks containing scanned images of the documents are available at a modest price. Essentially, the repository goes to the lawyers instead of the other way around. The danger posed by this technology is that because production of large numbers of documents can be accomplished so quickly and inexpensively, overproduction of unimportant, nonresponsive documents may be encouraged.

IV. PREVENTING ABUSES OF THE CENTRAL DOCUMENT REPOSITORY

A. Proper Procedures for Business Records Option

While central document repositories offer the potential for cost savings, they also unfortunately offer even greater potential for abuse. Therefore the court should only approve central repositories that satisfy the three prerequisites for the business records option. In addition, the following procedural safeguards should be employed.

1. Prior Court Approval

The discovery rules clearly contemplate that a party wishing to invoke the business records option should seek a protective order.[78] Some manufacturers simply establish a central document repository without prior court approval, without the plaintiff's advice or consent, and without making any attempt to satisfy the criteria for the business records option. Use of a central document repository should be the exception, not the rule, in producing documents to another party in litigation. Rule 34 permits the party requesting production to "specify a reasonable time, place, and manner" for production.[79] The party on whom the request is served must either per-

---

[77] See discussion of discovery of computerized information in chapter 1, section IV.

[78] *See, e.g.,* Colony Cadillac & Oldsmobile, Inc. v. Yerdon, 558 A.2d 364, 366 (Me. 1989).

[79] FED. R. CIV. P. 34(b).

mit production as requested or object with specificity.[80] To protect the legitimate interests of both plaintiffs and defendants, the manufacturer seeking to utilize a central document repository should be required to file a motion for protective order, under rule 26(c)(2) or (3), "that the discovery may be had only on specified terms and conditions, including a designation of the time or place" or "that the discovery may be had only by a method of discovery other than that selected by the party seeking discovery."[81] In ruling on such a motion, the court could take steps to ensure that the procedures proposed satisfy the criteria for proper discovery including the prerequisites and requirements of the business records option.

2. Assurance of Full Disclosure

The court should require the manufacturer to furnish the plaintiff with an inventory of all the documents contained in its repository and to certify that the repository does constitute full disclosure of all requested information. To verify the accuracy of the defendant's representations, counsel for the plaintiff should consider taking depositions to identify what business records the manufacturer has, how they are stored and indexed in the usual course of the defendant's business, and how they have been assembled for access by plaintiffs.[82]

3. Assistance in Obtaining Answers or Locating Requested Documents

This requirement is a function of the first and third prerequisites for the business records option. The courts should require the manufacturer to furnish the plaintiff an index that allows the plaintiff to locate pertinent documents and ascertain answers with substantially the same effort as the defendant would have exerted. The defendant's failure to provide an adequate index (or the equivalent) is one of the most common shortcomings of central document repositories.[83]

4. Logistics of Access and Use

The logistics of access are a function of the first prerequisite for the business records option. The court should consider such factors as ease of access to the chosen location, hours the repository is open, provisions for the plaintiff to examine documents without supervision or interruption, procedures for copying documents, and the cost incurred in traveling to and using the facility.

---

[80] *Id.*

[81] FED. R. CIV. P. 26(c)(2), 26(c)(3).

[82] *See* Marker v. Union Fidelity Life Ins. Co., 125 F.R.D. 121, 125–27 (M.D.N.C. 1989). In the federal multidistrict breast implant litigation, in order to test the validity of one defendant's contention that it could not locate pertinent records, United States District Court Judge Sam Pointer entered an order permitting plaintiffs' counsel to depose corporate record custodians and to conduct an on-site examination of the company's record-keeping system. Record at 113, *In re* Silicone Gel Breast Implant Prod. Liab. Litig., MDL-926 (N.D. Ala. Dec. 3, 1992).

[83] The details of the defendant's duty to specify are discussed in section II.B.3, *supra.*

B. Examples of Proper Use of the Business Records Center

Centralized production procedures that have worked well in some instances are described below.

1. On-Site Inspection

An on-site inspection of the defendant's documents may indeed be conducted in a fashion that complies with the requirements for the business records option. As one court observed,

> [T]here is some authority for the proposition that, when the volume of material sought would make copying and shipment difficult and oppressive for the party in possession, or when the distance between the parties is great, the court may demur from ordering production and may instead order inspection in a manner convenient to the party in possession.[84]

On-site inspection of documents may reduce discovery costs while the issues are narrowed and the scope of relevance is refined. In a products liability case involving the drug Halcion, the defendant Upjohn offered to allow the plaintiff to inspect at its corporate offices its 400,000-page collection of documents contained in Upjohn's new drug application. Commenting on this offer, the court stated that "[w]hile this may not provide all the information that plaintiffs require, it is perhaps the best place to narrow the search for other documents specifically identified."[85]

Similarly, in *Federal Deposit Insurance Corp. v. Blackburn*,[86] the FDIC established a central document repository in its Knoxville offices for the voluminous records that it had assembled, indexed, and summarized. The FDIC first filed a motion for a protective order seeking the court's approval of the repository as an acceptable response to both interrogatories and requests for production. While the court approved the FDIC's use of the depository as a convenient means of production, it held that the repository would not relieve the FDIC of the obligation to provide specific responses to discovery requests in the traditional manner required by rules 33(a) and 34(b).[87]

In recent years, most major corporations have acquired the ability to search their business records by computer.[88] Using computers to locate relevant documents may ultimately replace the conventional form of the business records option response: Courts may eventually compel the parties to collaborate in conducting a computer

---

[84] Baine v. General Motors Corp., 141 F.R.D. 328, 331 (M.D. Ala. 1991) (citing 4A MOORE ET AL., *supra* note 8, ¶ 34.19 and Compagnie des Bauxites de Guinee v. Insurance Co. of N. Am., 651 F.2d 877, 883 (3d Cir. 1981)).

[85] Upjohn Co. v. Missouri Court of St. Charles County, CA No. 60725 (Mo. Ct. App. Apr. 28, 1992).

[86] 109 F.R.D. 66 (E.D. Tenn. 1985).

[87] *Id.* at 70.

[88] The defendant's obligation to provide the plaintiff with the software and codes necessary to identify relevant records is discussed in chapter 1, section IV.

search of the defendant's business records rather than attempt to determine whether the contents and organization of a production meet the criteria for the business records option.

2. Court-Operated Repository

The concept of a central document repository is endorsed in the *Manual for Complex Litigation (Second)*, as follows:

> Central document depositories may be of great value in the efficient, economical management of voluminous documents. By depositing documents at one or more convenient locations, counsel may reduce substantially the expensive, burdensome, time-consuming, and wasteful efforts that otherwise may result when many parties attempt to review documents located in widely separated places. Use of a depository also facilitates a determination as to what documents have been produced and what information is in them, avoiding the disputes about those matters that sometimes occur.[89]

Court-supervised central document repositories have been established in two recent instances involving complex products liability litigation. The court supervising the multidistrict silicone breast implant litigation set up a national depository in Cincinnati for use by all federal and state litigants.[90] Working with the court, the parties developed a detailed protocol to govern the operation of the facility. The expenses are shared among the parties. In the federal asbestos class action litigation, the Manville Personal Injury Settlement Trust established a central document repository in Denver to provide access to Johns-Manville's corporate records. The trust bears the entire cost of operating the facility, and a full-time staff assists users in locating records.[91]

Authority of the court to establish a document repository can be found in rule 5(d), which requires that all papers required to be served on a party shall be filed with the court unless the court orders otherwise. In most jurisdictions the court orders otherwise, frequently by local rule. Nonetheless, rule 5(d) apparently permits the court to require that all discovery materials in any individual action be kept on file in the clerk's office, subject to whatever conditions and provisions concerning access the court deems fit to impose.[92]

---

[89] MANUAL FOR COMPLEX LITIGATION (SECOND) § 21.442 (1985). For a discussion of the early use of a central document depository to facilitate discovery in hundreds of related antitrust lawsuits in federal courts across the country, see CHARLES A. BANE, THE ELECTRICAL EQUIPMENT CONSPIRACIES—THE TREBLE DAMAGE ACTIONS 135 (1973); Phil C. Neal & Perry Goldberg, *The Electrical Equipment Antitrust Cases: Novel Judicial Administration*, 50 A.B.A. J. 621 (1964).

[90] *In re* Silicone Gel Breast Implant Prod. Liab. Litig., MDL-926, Case Management Order 5 (N.D. Ala. Sept. 15, 1992).

[91] Based on personal conversations between Frances H. Hare, Jr. and David Austern, Chief Legal Officer for the Manville Personal Injury Settlement Trust.

[92] *Cf. In re* "Agent Orange" Prod. Liab. Litig., 821 F.2d 139, 146–47 (2d Cir.), *cert. denied*, 484 U.S. 953 (1987).

Rule 5(d) recognizes that discovery materials can be of interest to individuals and entities who may not otherwise have access to them, "such as members of a class, litigants similarly situated, or the public generally."[93] This authority has been used by courts to establish a document repository to provide public access to information of public import. For example, in *In re "Agent Orange" Product Liability Litigation*,[94] the Second Circuit approved the trial court's reliance on rule 5(d) to require filing of all discovery materials because the toxicity of the defoliant to which many American service personnel (and others) were exposed during the Vietnam war[95] was considered to be information of public import.

In *Graham v. Wyeth Laboratories*,[96] the court observed that tremendous time and effort had gone into the discovery and development of evidence regarding the DPT vaccine at issue, and that similar litigation was likely in the future. Without citing any particular authority, the court directed that discovery documents be retained and stored by the Clerk of the Court, to be made available to any attorney engaged in similar litigation in any federal or state court, if authorized by a trial judge in those cases.[97] The court explained its rationale in establishing the library:

> Given cooperation and time, I remain convinced this directive puts in place an entirely workable and productive facility, which can and will be of interest to all litigants, both sides, as pertains to this most provocative and complex subject, and hopefully will serve to substantially reduce costs and expenses otherwise expended in the preparation and trial of such a case.[98]

Moreover, the judge recognized that individuals other than lawyers would be interested in the assembled materials:

> Additionally, because the trial record of this case probably will be of interest to researchers, academics, institutions, consumer groups, members of the medical profession or associations, private or governmental, legal associations such as the ATLA and/or Defense Research Institute, and even law students, all in the interest of stimulating scientific and/or public discourse or learning regarding whooping cough vaccinations and their ramifications, they are all welcomed here.[99]

In an admirable attempt to improve the utility and efficiency of the central document library, the court intended to add to the facility

> additional material supplied from time to time by other litigants, lawyers, judges, or associations following the trial of successive cases, and such additions will be

---

[93] FED. R. CIV. P. 5(d) 1980 advisory committee's notes.

[94] 821 F.2d 139 (2d Cir.), *cert. denied*, 484 U.S. 953 (1987).

[95] *Id.* at 146–47.

[96] 118 F.R.D. 511 (D. Kan.), *vacated sub nom.* Wyeth Lab. v. United States Dist. Court, 851 F.2d 321 (10th Cir. 1988).

[97] 118 F.R.D. at 514.

[98] *Id.*

[99] *Id.*

welcome. If space constraints become a problem here, this facility can and will be moved to a more convenient place such as the Wichita Bar Association Law Library, The Wichita State University, or Washburn or Kansas University Schools of Law, or elsewhere.[100]

Despite its good intentions and reasonable approach, the trial court's broad directive was vacated by the Tenth Circuit. The appellate court concluded that the judiciary had not been granted authority by Congress to establish a "library" of the type envisioned by the trial court, regardless of the obvious benefits.[101] As the Tenth Circuit recognized, however, the trial court had acted within its authority insofar as its order applied to materials filed with the court in the course of that litigation.[102]

With their limited resources, the courts may not be in the best position to manage access to a document repository. Insufficient experience exists to assess the workability of this sort of arrangement.

3. Plaintiff-Operated Central Document Repository

One of the biggest problems with the use of central document repositories is that, in some instances, the documents are not produced to the plaintiff at all, and instead, remain in the hands of the defendant. The Honda repository, described earlier in this chapter, illustrates how defense control of a document repository can undercut the objectives of discovery. This problem was avoided in the L-Tryptophan litigation,[103] where the court permitted counsel for the plaintiffs to operate the central document depository containing the defendant's discovery materials. Plaintiffs in other cases could access the materials by paying a fee to cover the expenses of the repository; plaintiff's counsel overseeing the repository receive no fees or compensation for those services.

Courts in two other major products cases have entered orders allowing a plaintiffs' litigation support group to operate a central depository. In litigation involving the Ford Bronco II[104] and Honda ATVs,[105] courts have appointed the Attorneys Information Exchange Group (AIEG)[106] to serve as a clearinghouse for the defendant's discovery materials.

---

[100] *Id.*

[101] Wyeth Lab. v. United States Dist. Court, 851 F.2d 321, 324 (10th Cir. 1988).

[102] 851 F.2d at 324 n.3.

[103] The L-Tryptophan MDL document repository, authorized by the court, is described in INSIDE LITIG., Nov. 1991, at 1.

[104] Nelson v. Ford Motor Co., CA No. 91-698-2 (Saline County, Ark. Cir. Ct. Feb. 19, 1992).

[105] Oberg v. Honda Motor Co., CA No. A-8709-05897 (Multnomah County, Or. Cir. Ct. Feb. 17, 1990).

[106] AIEG is a nonprofit organization organized to assist plaintiffs in handling certain types of defective-product cases.

Allowing a plaintiffs' litigation support group to manage discovery materials more closely resembles the normal discovery procedures established by the rules than does a defense-operated repository. Management of repositories by plaintiffs acting under court-approved safeguards can accommodate the manufacturer's legitimate interests in efficiency while avoiding the abuses that have historically been associated with defense-managed repositories.

Quality of access is of great importance, and it is the principal distinction favoring management by plaintiffs rather than by defendants. When plaintiffs operate their own facility, they frequently can provide access at virtually any time and on any day with little or no advance notice. Access to a defendant-operated facility is usually given only by appointment, requiring advance arrangements that accommodate the schedule and convenience of defense counsel or its personnel. Typically plaintiffs impose no time limitation on examining documents. The contrary is typically true in defense-managed repositories. Finally, there is a tremendous difference in the work environments: In a plaintiff-operated facility, counsel can inspect documents without being monitored or interrupted and can openly discuss the technical and strategic significance of the documents without disclosing their work product to the opponent.

The expense of operating a central document repository for products litigation involving many parties and thousands, or even millions, of documents can be enormous. Allowing a plaintiff's litigation group to manage the facility avoids a potentially acrimonious debate over who pays for the costs of a defense-operated facility because the members of the litigation group expect to share all costs.

A court can safely approve a plaintiff-managed central document repository without adversely affecting the manufacturer's legitimate interests: The manufacturer retains the cost benefits of a single collective disclosure of relevant documents and is typically not expected to share in the expense of operating the facility. Furthermore, if the circumstances justify limiting disclosure, the court can forbid the disclosure of certain documents to the defendant's competitors or to the public at large.

Next to the outright suppression of information, the dump truck response is probably the most prevalent and most harmful abuse of discovery in current litigation. Indeed, the two tactics often go hand in hand, particularly in complex litigation involving voluminous documents and multiple plaintiffs. In these circumstances, the defendant is subject to a great if not irresistible temptation to use a central document repository that obfuscates its suppression of critical documents. Only by the stringent application of the three prerequisites for the business records option can the court prevent this discovery misconduct and ensure that the objectives of discovery are met.

CHAPTER SEVEN

DOCUMENT DESTRUCTION AND OTHER SPOLIATION OF EVIDENCE[1]

I. MAGNITUDE OF THE PROBLEM

Judging from the sheer number of reported cases, the destruction, alteration, and other spoliation[2] of evidence by a party or prospective party to litigation have become widespread in the past decade.[3] Another possible explanation for the growth of these cases is that evidence spoliation is being detected with greater frequency. According to Lawrence Solum, Professor of Law, Loyola Law School, and Stephen Marzen, an Assistant United States Solicitor General, "more than 80 percent of the cases involving discovery sanctions for evidence destruction have been reported since 1980."[4] This information may be stale news to those who regularly litigate against large corporations; nevertheless, it is a sad commentary on the state of our discovery system.[5]

A recent trial court opinion describes evidence of egregious acts of document destruction by General Motors and its lawyers.[6] The opinion indicates that the depo-

---

[1] This chapter includes material originally published in Richard L. Whitworth & James L. Gilbert, *Punishing Evidence Destruction*, TRIAL, Nov. 1992, at 66.

[2] *Spoliation* has been defined as "failure to preserve property for another's use as evidence in pending or future litigation," County of Solano v. Delancy, 216 Cal. App.3d 207, 264 Cal. Rptr. 721 (Cal. App. 1 Dist. 1989), County of Solano v. Delancy, 264 Cal. Rptr. 721, 724 n.4 (Ct. App. 1989), *review denied and ordered not published officially,* 1990 Cal. LEXIS 488 (Cal. Feb. 1, 1990) and "rendering discoverable matter permanently unavailable to the court and the opposing party." JAMIE S. GORELICK ET AL., DESTRUCTION OF EVIDENCE (1989 & Supp. 1991).

[3] An extensive list of cases in which courts have imposed sanctions for the destruction of evidence appears in GORELICK ET AL., *supra* note 2, § 3.1, at 66 n.3.

[4] GORELICK ET AL., *supra* note 2, at 11–12.

[5] Defendants are not the only ones who receive sanctions for evidence destruction. *See, e.g., In re* Estate of Soderholm, 469 N.E.2d 410, 418 (Ill. App. Ct. 1984) (finding plaintiffs destroyed diaries and created counterfeits after production order was entered).

[6] Cameron v. General Motors Corp., No. 6:93-1278-3 (D.S.C. Feb. 28, 1994), *stricken in relevant part, In re* General Motors Corp., No. 94-1011 (4th Cir. Mar. 23, 1994).

sition of one General Motors's engineer describes General Motors's lawyers "shredding" and "carting" away to be shredded documents from the engineer's files.[7] The judge concludes that a review of the documents submitted to him

> reveals a substantial likelihood that perhaps perjury and the systematic destruction of documents involving gross misconduct by General Motors' regional counsel occurred. . . . There i s clearly evidence having a sufficient foundation in fact to establish a *prima facie* case that the documents for which an attorney-client privilege is asserted are subject to the crime-fraud exception.[8]

Unfortunately, the judge's findings were stricken by the Fourth Circuit at General Motors's request.[9] The Fourth Circuit held that the findings were improper because the trial judge recused himself from the case. Even though the Fourth Circuit opinion states that the stricken language should not be cited as authority, the trial court's viewpoint seems to be informative regarding General Motors's conduct in handling documents and in conducting litigation.

Document spoliation is the most permanent means of undermining the truth-finding function of the civil justice system. It has been aptly described as "the most egregious variant of nonproduction"[10] and as "inflict[ing] the ultimate prejudice upon the opposing party."[11]

As used here, *evidence* means any item or information that appears reasonably likely to lead to the discovery of admissible evidence.[12] The term is not limited to evidence that would be admissible at trial; rather it includes all materials within the broad scope of discovery set forth in the civil rules.[13] *Spoliation* includes any attempt to permanently deprive the other party and the court of evidence.

The most common form of spoliation is the destruction of documents to avoid accountability.[14] Spoliation may also involve defacing a document, or "doctoring" it

---

[7] *Id.* at 37.

[8] *Id.* at 48. At the end of the scathing 59-page opinion the judge grants General Motors' motion to recuse, removing himself from the case to prevent the possibility of an appearance of impartiality based on his appearance on the same legal education programs as plaintiff's counsel. *Id.* at 58–59.

[9] *In re* General Motors Corp., No. 94-1011 (4th Cir. Mar. 23, 1994).

[10] National Ass'n of Radiation Survivors v. Turnage, 115 F.R.D. 543, 558 n.4 (N.D. Cal. 1987).

[11] Computer Assocs. Int'l, Inc. v. American Fundware, Inc., 133 F.R.D. 166, 170 (D. Colo. 1990); *see also* Honda Motor Co. v. Salzman, 751 P.2d 489, 493 (Alaska), *cert. dismissed*, 487 U.S. 1260 (1988).

[12] *See* FED. R. CIV. P. 26(b).

[13] *See, e.g.*, Wm. T. Thompson Co. v. General Nutrition Corp., 593 F. Supp. 1443, 1445 (C.D. Cal. 1984). *See generally* GORELICK ET AL., *supra* note 2, at 91–93 and cases cited therein.

[14] *See, e.g.*, Capellupo v. FMC Corp., 126 F.R.D. 545 (D. Minn. 1989); Telectron, Inc. v. Overhead Door Corp., 116 F.R.D. 107 (S.D. Fla. 1987) (entering default judgment where defendant cor-

to change its contents.[15] Spoliation of other physical evidence, including the allegedly defective product, is not uncommon.[16] In two reported cases, key evidence was sold.[17]

Whatever its form, the spoliation of evidence takes a heavy—if not fatal—toll on truth-finding, completely undermining the objective of the civil justice system.

> Our adversarial system of civil justice rests upon access of all parties to all evidence bearing on the controversy between them, including that in the control of adverse parties. This, of course, requires the absolute honesty of each party in answering discovery requests and complying with discovery orders. Destruction or concealment by a party of relevant documents in its files threatens the viability and public acceptance of the system.[18]

---

poration's legal counsel ordered destruction of documents the day he was served with the plaintiff's complaint); *In re* "Agent Orange" Prod. Liab. Litig., 98 F.R.D. 558 (E.D.N.Y. 1983) (permitting discovery regarding circumstances surrounding destruction of documents); *In re* Air Crash Disaster Near Chicago, Ill.*, 90 F.R.D. 613, 620–21 (N.D. Ill. 1981) (sanctioning defendant airliner for destruction of report concerning the cause of the crash); Roberti v. F. Ronci Co., 486 A.2d 1087, 1089 (R.I. 1985) (entering default judgment for destruction of relevant documents).

[15] *See* Carlucci v. Piper Aircraft Corp., 102 F.R.D. 472, 482 (S.D. Fla. 1984) (alteration of flight test data), *aff'd in part, rev'd in part*, 775 F.2d 1440 (11th Cir. 1985); Petersen v. Wellington Puritan Mills, No. 874032 (S.F. County, Cal. Super. Ct. July 26, 1990), *discussed in* INSIDE LITIG., Sept. 1990, at 7–9 (alteration of rope-strength test data); *cf.* Pope v. Federal Express Corp., 138 F.R.D. 675, 683 (W.D. Mo. 1990) (fabrication of false evidence).

[16] *See, e.g.*, DePuy, Inc. v. Eckes, 427 So. 2d 306 (Fla. Dist. Ct. App. 1983) (affirming default judgment where plaintiff turned over failed hip prosthesis to defendant for examination pursuant to an agreed order not to destroy the fracture site, and defendant subsequently lost the part); Wong v. City of Honolulu, 665 P.2d 157, 160–61 (Haw. 1983) (deeming negligence as sanction for defendant's destruction of traffic signal control box); Corona v. A-B-C Packaging Mach. Corp., 514 N.Y.S.2d 756 (App. Div. 1987) (affirming sanction striking answer of manufacturer for destruction of allegedly defective box-making machine); Ferraro v. Koncal Assocs., 467 N.Y.S.2d 284 (App. Div. 1983) (affirming order precluding manufacturer from offering any evidence at trial in support of its defense as sanction for disposing of allegedly defective clothes rack after receiving request for inspection); Southern Pac. Transp. Co. v. Evans, 590 S.W.2d 515, 518–19 (Tex. Civ. App. 1979) (affirming default judgment where defendant dismantled allegedly defective vehicle), *cert. denied*, 449 U.S. 994 (1980); *see also* Graves v. Daley, 526 N.E.2d 679 (Ill. App. Ct. 1988) (affirming dismissal of plaintiff's complaint for destruction of allegedly defective furnace prior to filing complaint).

[17] *See, e.g.*, Valenstein v. Bayonne Bolt Corp., 6 F.R.D. 363, 364–65 (E.D.N.Y. 1946) (striking relevant portion of complaint as sanction where plaintiff sold bolts alleged in contract action to be defective); Hyosung (Am.), Inc. v. Woodcrest Fabrics, Inc., 483 N.Y.S.2d 226, 227 (App. Div. 1984) (striking answer as sanction where defendant in contract action sold fabric it alleged to be defective to third party), *appeal dismissed*, 488 N.Y.S.2d 649 (Ct. App. 1985).

[18] Litton Sys., Inc. v. AT&T Co., 91 F.R.D. 574, 576 (S.D.N.Y. 1981), *aff'd*, 700 F.2d 785 (2d Cir. 1983).

II. DUTY TO PRESERVE EVIDENCE

Destruction or other spoliation of evidence can be viewed as a breach of the duty to preserve evidence. An understanding of the breach requires first an analysis of the nature and scope of the underlying duty.

A. Nature and Scope of the Duty

As explained by one federal district court judge,

> Sanctions may be imposed against a litigant who is on notice that documents and information in its possession are relevant to litigation, or potential litigation, or are reasonably calculated to lead to the discovery of admissible evidence, and destroys such documents and information. While a litigant is under no duty to keep or retain every document in its possession once a complaint is filed, it is under a duty to preserve what it knows, or reasonably should know, is relevant in the action, is reasonably calculated to lead to the discovery of admissible evidence, is reasonably likely to be requested during discovery, and/or is the subject of a pending discovery request.[19]

In sanctions cases such as this one, and in cases recognizing tort liability for evidence spoliation, discussed later in this chapter, the courts have recognized the duty to preserve evidence, broadly construed as any discoverable material in present or potential litigation.[20]

This duty extends beyond documents that have actually been requested in pending litigation[21] to potentially discoverable documents relevant to pending litigation that have not yet been requested. The duty is breached even if those documents are destroyed or altered as a matter of business routine, not to avoid liability.[22]

Moreover, a party's spoliation of evidence is not excused merely because it occurs before the complaint is filed. Numerous courts have imposed sanctions against parties for destroying documents before a lawsuit was actually filed, where the party knew or reasonably should have foreseen that the subject litigation would be commenced, or where the party engaged in document spoliation primarily to suppress potentially unfavorable evidence.[23]

---

[19] Wm. T. Thompson Co. v. General Nutrition Corp., 593 F. Supp. 1443, 1455 (C.D. Cal. 1984) (citations omitted).

[20] *See, e.g.,* Telectron, Inc. v. Overhead Door Corp., 116 F.R.D. 107, 127 (S.D. Fla. 1987); *In re* "Agent Orange" Prod. Liab. Litig., 506 F. Supp. 750, 751 (E.D.N.Y. 1980); Bowmar Instrument Corp. v. Texas Instruments, Inc., 25 Fed. R. Serv. 2d (Callaghan) 423, 427 (N.D. Ind. 1977).

[21] *See, e.g.,* Perkinson v. Houlihan's/D.C., Inc., 4 Fed. R. Serv. 3d (Callaghan) 219 (D.D.C. 1985); Ricco v. Deepdale Gardens Apartments Corp., 493 N.Y.S.2d 498, 500 (App. Div. 1985).

[22] National Ass'n of Radiation Survivors v. Turnage, 115 F.R.D. 543, 554 (N.D. Cal. 1987).

[23] *See, e.g.,* Capellupo v. FMC Corp., 126 F.R.D. 545, 550–53 (D. Minn. 1989) (finding defendant systematically embarked on intentional destruction of evidence in anticipation of class action litigation); National Ass'n of Radiation Survivors v. Turnage, 115 F.R.D. 543, 556–57 (N.D.

This far-reaching approach is necessary because, as courts have recognized, a pattern of stonewalling can begin well before discovery, and before filing, when defendants try to purge their files of inculpatory evidence to prevent the truth from ever surfacing.[24] One outrageous example of this practice is described in *Craig v. A.H. Robins Co.*[25] The *Craig* case is one of many documenting Robins's stonewalling of discovery in cases involving its tragically defective intrauterine contraceptive device.[26] In *Craig* the plaintiff was permitted to present evidence that, after punitive damages had been awarded in an earlier lawsuit, the company's general counsel ordered the destruction of numerous internal documents relating to the device.[27]

Apart from the common law duty to preserve documents or physical evidence that may constitute discoverable material in pending or future litigation, federal and state laws impose myriad record-keeping requirements, which may give rise to a duty to preserve documents.[28] Where these requirements have been violated, an adverse inference instruction or sanction may be appropriate. In addition, where a legally recognized duty to preserve documents has been violated, a separate cause of action for spoliation may lie, as discussed later in this chapter.

Cal. 1987) (ruling defendant "knew or should have known" that destroyed documents were elevant and discoverable); Wm. T. Thompson Co. v. General Nutrition Corp., 593 F. Supp. 1443, 1455 (C.D. Cal. 1984) (finding defendant was on notice that documents in its possession were relevant to "potential litigation"); United States v. ACB Sales & Serv., Inc., 95 F.R.D. 316, 318 (D. Ariz. 1982) (finding litigation was "reasonably" foreseeable and defendant's document destruction program was motivated by an attempt to suppress evidence); Alliance to End Repression v. Rochford, 75 F.R.D. 438, 440–41 (N.D. Ill. 1976) (finding defendant destroyed documents after notice that suit was about to be filed); *see also* Valenstein v. Bayonne Bolt Corp., 6 F.R.D. 363, 364–65 (E.D.N.Y. 1946); Prudential Ins. Co. v. Lawnsdail, 15 N.W.2d 880, 883 (Iowa 1944); Farulla v. Ralph A. Freundlich, Inc., 279 N.Y.S. 228, 245–48 (Sup. Ct. 1935); *cf.* Bowmar Instruments Corp. v. Texas Instruments, Inc., 25 Fed. R. Serv. 2d (Callaghan) 423, 427 (N.D. Ind. 1977) (finding plaintiff failed to demonstrate defendant knew that lawsuit would be filed when documents were destroyed).

[24] *See, e.g.,* Capellupo v. FMC Corp., 126 F.R.D. 545 (D. Minn. 1989); Alliance to End Repression v. Rochford, 75 F.R.D. 438, 440 (N.D. Ill. 1976).

[25] 790 F.2d 1 (1st Cir. 1986).

[26] *See also* Harre v. A.H. Robins Co., 750 F.2d 1501 (11th Cir. 1985), *vacated in part,* 866 F.2d 1303 (11th Cir. 1989); Gardiner v. A.H. Robins Co., 747 F.2d 1180 (8th Cir. 1984); In re A.H. Robins Co., 107 F.R.D. 2 (D. Kan. 1985); Dean v. A.H. Robins Co., 101 F.R.D. 21 (D. Minn.), *mandamus denied,* 732 F.2d 161 (8th Cir. 1984); A.H. Robins Co. v. Devereaux, 415 So. 2d 30 (Fla. Dist. Ct. App. 1982), *petition denied,* 426 So. 2d 25 (Fla. 1983).

[27] 790 F.2d 1, 3–4 (1st Cir. 1986).

[28] *See generally* DONALD S. SKUPSKY, RECORDKEEPING REQUIREMENTS: THE FIRST PRACTICAL GUIDE TO HELP YOU CONTROL YOUR RECORDS (1989); John M. Fedders & Lauryn H. Guttenplan, *Document Retention and Destruction: Practical, Legal and Ethical Considerations,* 56 NOTRE DAME LAW. 5 (1980).

Other potential sources of an enforceable duty to preserve evidence may include contracts explicitly or implicitly requiring preservation,[29] written or oral representations to the opposing party that evidence will be preserved,[30] the provisions of the party's own document retention policy,[31] more aptly called a document destruction policy, or its actions to preserve the evidence.[32]

Counsel for prospective plaintiffs may consider notifying the prospective defendants of the claim under investigation to demand that documents potentially relevant to the action be preserved.[33]

B. Document Retention Policies

Most large business organizations, as well as a growing number of smaller organizations, have institutionalized policies regarding the retention and destruction of documents. While such policies can certainly serve legitimate business purposes such as saving space and money, they have been used by some organizations as an excuse to destroy unfavorable evidence in anticipation of litigation.[34] As explained by Professor Dale A. Oesterle in his 1983 article on document destruction,

> Businesses routinely destroy documents in order to keep the documents out of the hands of opponents in future legal proceedings. An amusing set of euphemisms has grown up around the practice: programs of "preventive maintenance" or "law compliance" include a "document retention" schedule to eliminate "misleading," "improvident," or "erroneous" documents for the purpose of "optimizing the position" of the corporation in the event of litigation. The naked truth is that many corporations purposefully operate programs to destroy evidence. Where corporations once destroyed

---

[29] *See* Miller v. Allstate Ins. Co., 573 So. 2d 24, 27 (Fla. Dist. Ct. App. 1990), *review denied*, 581 So. 2d 1307 (Fla. 1991), *discussed infra* notes 87–88 and accompanying text.

[30] *See* Jones v. Goodyear Tire & Rubber Co., 137 F.R.D. 657, 663 (C.D. Ill. 1991) (finding where defendant, in stipulated protective order, agreed to preserve and maintain evidence provided to it for inspection, loss of that evidence properly resulted in directed verdict for plaintiff despite lack of showing that loss was willful or deliberate), *aff'd sub nom.* Marrocco v. General Motors Corp., 966 F.2d 220, 224 (7th Cir. 1992); *cf.* Lewis v. Darce Towing Co., 94 F.R.D. 262, 266 (W.D. La. 1982) (excluding evidence derived from autopsy where plaintiff failed to amend discovery response to inform defendant of intention to perform autopsy).

[31] Document retention and destruction policies are discussed in the following section of this chapter.

[32] *Cf.* discussion of destructive testing in section II.C, *infra*.

[33] *See, e.g.*, Wm. T. Thompson Co. v. General Nutrition Corp., 593 F. Supp. 1443, 1446 (C.D. Cal. 1984); *In re* Grand Jury Investigation (Gen. Motors Corp.), 31 F.R.D. 1 (S.D.N.Y. 1962) (finding letter put GM on notice).

[34] *See, e.g., In re* Comair Air crash Litig., CA No. 79-104, slip op. at 2 (E.D. Ky. Dec. 8, 1986); Carlucci v. Piper Aircraft Corp., 102 F.R.D. 472, 481, 485–86 (S.D. Fla. 1984) (finding purpose of ongoing document destruction program was to purge files of records that might be detrimental in a lawsuit), *aff'd in part, rev'd in part*, 775 F.2d 1440 (11th Cir. 1985).

documents primarily because they were costly to store, index, and retrieve, now many corporations destroy documents primarily to reduce litigation "exposure."[35]

Industry literature actually recommends that companies destroy their internal records to minimize their potential liability. For instance, one book on safety engineering contains this advice:

> In the event there is an accident that might result in a liability suit, four basic things will help your company defend the case. These are: . . . 3. Get rid of non-essential office memos—especially those pertaining to opinions or asking questions involving hazards and safety.[36]

In an extensive discussion of legal and ethical aspects of document retention policies, another article observed that one objective of companies using document retention programs is "a substantial reduction of legal risks flowing from documents."[37]

A 1990 *National Law Journal* article on document retention and destruction observed that in the management of documents, "[in addition to saving money on storage and retrieval,] fewer documents also means fewer opportunities for exposure to legal liabilities, for both the lawyer and the client, based on evidence from the defendant's own files."[38] The article even recommends ways to best destroy potential evidence. "Paper would be shredded, pulverized or turned into formless pulp. Microfilm would be burned or chemically cleaned of its image and computer disks would be magnetically erased, if not physically destroyed."[39] Merely throwing the documents in the trash can is specifically warned against because the documents "may be found by investigators and pieced into a sensible case . . . [o]r extra copies of documents in unknown locations may later be discovered, after complete destruction was believed to have been performed and so represented in discovery proceedings."[40] Courts have sanctioned corporate defendants for adopting a record retention or destruction policy primarily for the purpose of destroying incriminating evidence rather than for a legitimate purpose, such as saving space.[41]

---

[35] Dale A. Oesterle, *A Private Litigant's Remedies for an Opponent's Inappropriate Destruction of Relevant Documents*, 61 TEX. L. REV. 1185, 1185–86 (1983) (footnotes omitted).

[36] WILLIAM P. ROGERS, *Systems Safety Engineering and Product Liability*, in INTRODUCTION TO SYSTEM SAFETY ENGINEERING 81 (1971).

[37] Fedders & Guttenplan, *supra* note 28, at 13; *see also* PRACTICING LAW INSTITUTE, PREVENTION AND DEFENSE OF MANUFACTURERS' PRODUCTS LIABILITY 758–61 (1970).

[38] Steven Lenkowsky, *Destroying Retained Documents—Goal Is to Safeguard Confidentiality*, NAT'L L.J., May 14, 1990, at 23.

[39] *Id.*

[40] *Id.; see also* Stacy Shapiro, *Needless Papers May Haunt Manufacturers*, BUS. INS., Apr. 17, 1989, at 48.

[41] *See, e.g.*, Lewy v. Remington Arms Co., 836 F.2d 1104, 1111–12 (8th Cir. 1988); *In re* Comair Aircrash Litig., CA No. 79-104 (E.D. Ky. Dec. 8, 1986); Carlucci v. Piper Aircraft Corp., 102 F.R.D. 472, 481, 485 (S.D. Fla. 1984), *aff'd in part, rev'd in part,* 775 F.2d 1440 (11th Cir. 1985); United States v. ACB Sales & Serv., Inc., 95 F.R.D. 316, 318 (D. Ariz. 1982). Record retention/destruction policies are discussed in greater detail in section II.B of this chapter.

In *Lewy v. Remington Arms Co.*[42] the Eighth Circuit Court of Appeals considered the effect of a document retention program on the destruction of relevant evidence. Specifically at issue was a jury instruction that "[i]f a party fails to produce evidence which is under his control and reasonably available to him and not reasonably available to the adverse party, then you may infer that the evidence is unfavorable to the party who could have produced it and did not."[43] The manufacturer argued on appeal that this instruction should not have been given. It asserted that since the subject documents had been destroyed pursuant to its routine procedures, an adverse inference was not warranted. The Eighth Circuit remanded for consideration of the following factors:

> First, the court should determine whether Remington's record retention policy is reasonable considering the facts and circumstances surrounding the relevant documents. For example, the court should determine whether a three year retention policy is reasonable given the particular document. A three year retention policy may be sufficient for documents such as appointment books or telephone messages, but inadequate for documents such as customer complaints. Second, in making this determination the court may also consider whether lawsuits concerning the complaint or related complaints have been filed, the frequency of such complaints, and the magnitude of the complaints.
>
> Finally, the court should determine whether the document retention policy was instituted in bad faith. In cases where a document retention policy is instituted in order to limit damaging evidence available to potential plaintiffs, it may be proper to give an instruction similar to the one requested by the Lewys. Similarly, even if the court finds the policy to be reasonable given the nature of the documents subject to the policy, the court may find that under the particular circumstances certain documents should have been retained notwithstanding the policy. For example, if the corporation knew or should have known that the documents would become material at some point in the future then such documents should have been preserved. Thus, a corporation cannot blindly destroy documents and expect to be shielded by a seemingly innocuous document retention policy.[44]

One document destruction policy that was found not to pass muster was described in *Carlucci v. Piper Aircraft Corp.*[45] The stated purpose was the elimination of documents that might be detrimental to Piper in a lawsuit.[46] As a result, sanctions

---

[42] 836 F.2d 1104 (8th Cir. 1988).

[43] *Id.* at 1111.

[44] *Id.* at 1112 (citing Gumbs v. International Harvester, Inc., 718 F.2d 88, 96 (3d Cir. 1983); Boyd v. Ozark Air Lines, Inc., 568 F.2d 50, 53 (8th Cir. 1977)).

[45] 102 F.R.D. 472, 481–86 (S.D. Fla. 1984), *aff'd in part, rev'd in part*, 775 F.2d 1440 (11th Cir. 1985); *see also In re* Comair Aircrash Litig., CA No. 79-104, slip op. at 2 (E.D. Ky. Dec. 8, 1986) (finding Piper's document retention policy "a sham for a program to destroy unfavorable design and test data in anticipation of litigation and even after the inception of litigation").

[46] 102 F.R.D. at 481.

were imposed against Piper, including default.[47]

Even where an organization's document destruction policy may be considered legitimate, it must be suspended once the organization is on notice that documents may be relevant to litigation. In *National Association of Radiation Survivors v. Turnage*[48] the U.S. Veterans Administration was sanctioned for the destruction of documents that was done purportedly in accordance with a routine destruction policy. The court found that the government has an affirmative obligation to retain discoverable materials, and that this obligation "requires that the agency or corporate officers having notice of discovery obligations communicate those obligations to employees in possession of discoverable materials."[49]

C. Destructive Testing

It is critical that plaintiffs' counsel be aware that there will be disastrous consequences if the plaintiffs, their attorneys, or their experts alter or destroy evidence either before or after a suit is filed. In *Nally v. Volkswagen of America, Inc.* the plaintiffs suffered a summary judgment because their expert allegedly did destructive testing and lost parts from the car involved in the crash. The appellate court remanded the issue to the trial court for an evidentiary hearing on whether the expert had in fact altered the vehicle or lost important parts.[50] This is not to say destructive testing may never be done. However, application should be made to the court for leave to undertake the testing. The court can then set appropriate conditions, which typically include allowing the opposing party to participate in the testing and to conduct an inspection before alteration of the evidence.[51]

Three other recent cases underscore the need to preserve evidence and refrain from destructive testing in the absence of a court order or the opponent's permission or presence.[52] Defense counsel are keenly aware of opportunities to call for sanctions

---

[47] The series of discovery abuses perpetrated by Piper in this case, and the court's response, are described in Kay Latona & A. Hinda Klein, *Discovery Abuse: Making Piper Pay*, TRIAL, Feb. 1987, at 69.

[48] 115 F.R.D. 543 (N.D. Cal. 1987).

[49] *Id.* at 558.

[50] 539 N.E.2d 1017, 1021–22 (Mass. 1989).

[51] *See* Cameron v. District Court, 565 P.2d 925 (Colo. 1977) (en banc); *cf.* Sarver v. Barrett Ace Hardware, Inc., 349 N.E.2d 28 (Ill. 1976).

[52] *See* Marrocco v. General Motors Corp., 966 F.2d 220 (7th Cir. 1992) (affirming dismissal where loss of evidence resulting from plaintiff's inspection of vehicle made it impossible for GM to support its case); American Family Ins. Co. v. Village Pontiac GMC, 585 N.E.2d 1115 (Ill. App. Ct. 1992) (finding destruction of car after inspection by plaintiffs' expert warranted barring of evidence of car's condition, leading to summary judgment); *see also* Ralston v. Casanova, 473 N.E.2d 444 (Ill. App. Ct. 1984) (finding plaintiff's expert's disassembly and testing of seat belt in violation of protective orders preserving seat belt in present condition and prohibiting

against plaintiffs for evidence spoliation.[53] Of course, improper destructive testing by defendants also occurs, and is also sanctionable.[54]

III. REMEDIES FOR EVIDENCE DESTRUCTION OR SPOLIATION

Various penalties and remedies have long been available in response to evidence destruction, including discovery sanctions, the adverse inference rule, criminal penalties, professional discipline, and recovery under traditional negligence principles in cases where the spoliator had a duty to the plaintiff to preserve the evidence. In addition, new remedies have emerged to address the shortcomings of traditionally available remedies.

A. Traditionally Available Penalties and Remedies

1. Discovery Sanctions[55]

Federal and state rules of procedure authorize the court to impose discovery sanctions ranging from awarding attorney fees and costs to default judgment.[56] Although default is a severe sanction, courts have found it an appropriate remedy for spoliation.[57] Evidentiary sanctions closely tied to the nature of the evidence destroyed or spoliated have also been imposed.[58] In one case, a plaintiff whose expert conducted destructive testing on the allegedly defective seat belt was prohibited from offering

---

destructive testing without authorization from court warranted exclusion of evidence regarding seat-belt condition, resulting in summary judgment for defendants); *cf.* Lewis v. Darce Towing Co., 94 F.R.D. 262 (W.D. La. 1982) (excluding evidence derived from autopsy where plaintiff failed to amend discovery response to inform defendant of intention to perform autopsy).

[53] *See, e.g.*, Saverio LaManna, *Spoliation of Evidence in Products Litigation*, FOR DEF., Oct. 1991, at 9.

[54] *See, e.g.*, Rockwell Int'l Corp. v. Menzies, 561 So. 2d 677 (Fla. Dist. Ct. App. 1990); *cf.* cases cited *supra* note 15.

[55] Discovery sanctions are discussed in detail in chapter 10.

[56] *See* FED. R. CIV. P. 37(b).

[57] *See, e.g.*, Computer Assocs. Int'l, Inc. v. American Fundware, Inc., 133 F.R.D. 166, 168 (D. Colo. 1990); Telectron, Inc. v. Overhead Door Corp., 116 F.R.D. 107 (S.D. Fla. 1987); Carlucci v. Piper Aircraft Corp., 102 F.R.D. 472, 485–86 (S.D. Fla. 1984), *aff'd in part, rev'd in part*, 775 F.2d 1440, 1449–54 (11th Cir. 1985); Roberti v. F. Ronci Co., 486 A.2d 1087 (R.I. 1985); Southern Pac. Transp. Co. v. Evans, 590 S.W.2d 515, 518–19 (Tex. Civ. App. 1979), *cert. denied*, 449 U.S. 994 (1980); *see also* Marrocco v. General Motors Corp., 966 F.2d 220 (7th Cir. 1992); Capellupo v. FMC Corp., 126 F.R.D. 545, 552 (D. Minn. 1989); Wm. T. Thompson Co. v. General Nutrition Corp., 593 F. Supp. 1443, 1455–56 (C.D. Cal. 1984).

[58] Hammond v. Coastal Rental & Equip. Co., 95 F.R.D. 74 (S.D. Tex. 1982) (taking plaintiff's audit as true where defendant's payroll records destroyed by fire during period of unwarranted delay in producing them); Pompa v. Hojancki, 281 A.2d 886 (Pa. 1971) (excluding evidence where bottle fragments not retained).

any testimony on the condition of the belt at the time of the accident. Without that evidence, the court granted summary judgment for the defendants.[59] In another case, a Florida Court of Appeals upheld the use of evidence of document destruction, engaged in to avoid detection of a serious aircraft defect, to justify imposing punitive damages.[60]

Sanctions are appropriate wherever evidence has been destroyed or altered, regardless of whether the spoliation is intentional, negligent, or inadvertent.[61] This makes sense for two reasons. First, one purpose of sanctions is to counter prejudice to the party whose case has been undermined by less than full disclosure. Even where the spoliation was inadvertent, it makes sense for the responsible party, rather than the innocent party, to bear the adverse consequences. Second, because it is very difficult to prove intent, if sanctions are to have a deterrent effect, they must be imposed regardless of lack of proof of intent.

2. Unfavorable Inference

Intentional spoliation may justify an instruction that the jury can infer that the now-unavailable evidence would have been unfavorable to the destroyer.[62] Where the spoliation was unintentional, some courts have refused to instruct that an adverse inference may be drawn.[63] Other courts, however, recognizing that the burden of the loss of evidence must be borne by one party or the other, have placed that burden on

---

[59] Ralston v. Casanova, 473 N.E.2d 444 (Ill. App. Ct. 1984).

[60] Piper Aircraft Corp. v. Coulter, 426 So. 2d 1108 (Fla. Dist. Ct. App.), *review denied*, 436 So. 2d 100 (Fla. 1983).

[61] *See, e.g.*, Welsh v. United States, 844 F.2d 1239 (6th Cir. 1988) (ruling negligent destruction of evidence in medical malpractice action warrants rebuttable presumption of negligence and proximate causation); Jones v. Goodyear Tire & Rubber Co., 137 F.R.D. 657, 664 (C.D. Ill. 1991) (finding where defendant, in stipulated protective order, agreed to preserve and maintain evidence provided to it for inspection, loss of that evidence properly resulted in directed verdict for plaintiff despite lack of showing that loss was willful or deliberate), *aff'd sub nom* Marrocco v. General Motors Corp., 966 F.2d 220, 224 (7th Cir. 1992); Hammond v. Coastal Rental & Equip. Co., 95 F.R.D. 74 (S.D. Tex. 1982) (taking plaintiff's audit as true where defendant's documents destroyed by fire during period of unwarranted delay in production); Pompa v. Hojancki, 281 A.2d 886 (Pa. 1971) (finding plaintiff's loss of bottle fragments in products liability action alleging bottle defect warrants exclusion of evidence regarding the fragments).

[62] *See, e.g.*, Brown & Williamson Tobacco Corp. v. Jacobson, 827 F.2d 1119, 1135 (7th Cir. 1987) ("jury was allowed to infer that the destroyed documents would have seriously damaged the defendants' case"), *cert. denied*, 485 U.S. 943 (1988); Nation-Wide Check Corp. v. Forest Hills Distribs., Inc., 692 F.2d 214 (1st Cir. 1982) (finding adverse inference properly drawn regardless of whether bad faith shown); Miller v. Montgomery County, 494 A.2d 761, 768 (Md. Ct. Spec. App.) (allowing inference that destroyed traffic signal component was defective), *cert. denied*, 498 A.2d 1185 (Md. 1985). *See generally* Fedders & Guttenplan, *supra* note 28, at 53–55.

[63] *See* Friends For All Children, Inc. v. Lockheed Aircraft Corp., 587 F. Supp. 180, 208 (D.D.C.), *aff'd*, 746 F.2d 816 (D.C. Cir. 1984).

the party responsible for the destruction, even absent a showing of intent.[64] This approach is warranted not only by the severe prejudice to the other party's case, but also by the difficulty of proving that evidence spoliation was intentional. While the adverse inference is sometimes helpful, it is an inadequate deterrent because the spoliator may prefer taking its chances with an adverse inference to letting the jury see the damaging evidence.

3. Criminal Penalties

Where the spoliation of evidence violates a penal law, criminal sanctions may be available.[65] Criminal penalties, of course, do not compensate the injured party.

4. Professional Discipline

If an attorney is involved in the improper spoliation of evidence, disciplinary measures prescribed by law for violation of rules governing attorney ethics and conduct may be taken.[66]

5. Traditional Negligence Claims

The spoliation or loss of evidence can give rise to a negligence claim against the spoliator where a legal duty to preserve the evidence can be shown and the other elements of common law negligence are present. For instance, in *Wilson v. Beloit Corp.* summary judgment against an injured employee was reversed to determine if the employer, who had lost parts of the injury-causing machine, had a statutory or other

---

[64] *See, e.g.*, DeLaughter v. Lawrence County Hosp., 601 So. 2d 818, 821–22 (Miss. 1992) (finding where portion of patient chart inadvertently lost by hospital, inference arises that information was adverse to the hospital); *cf.* Battocchi v. Washington Hosp. Ctr., 581 A.2d 759, 767 (D.C. 1990) (presumption requires conduct constituting gross indifference or reckless disregard). In *Williams v. Washington Hosp. Ctr.*, 601 A.2d 28, 32 (D.C. 1991), the defendant hospital in a malpractice action lost a foreign object which had been removed from the patient's eye. Finding the defendants guilty of willful and reckless disregard for the preservation of relevant evidence within its exclusive control, the court held that the plaintiff was entitled to an adverse inference instruction and that a new trial should have been granted for the hospital's failure to supplement its discovery response before the last day of trial.

[65] *See* United States v. Berkowitz, 927 F.2d 1376 (7th Cir.) (holding theft and destruction of government records constitutes obstruction of justice), *cert. denied*, 112 S. Ct. 141 (1991); United States v. Simmons, 444 F. Supp. 500 (E.D. Pa. 1978) (finding that after grand jury subpoena was served, employees were told to destroy documents by flushing them down the toilet), *aff'd*, 591 F.2d 206 (3d Cir. 1979). *See generally* Fedders & Guttenplan, *supra* note 28.

[66] *In re* Bear, 578 S.W.2d 928 (Mo. 1979) (en banc); *see also* Document Destruction in Business Litigation from a Practitioner's Point-of-View: The Ethical Rules vs. Practical Realities, 2 ST. MARY'S L.J. 637 (1989), Ricardo G. Cedillo & David Lopez, *Document Destruction in Business Litigation from a Practitioner's Point-of-View: The Ethical Rules v. Practical Realities*, 20 ST. MARY'S L.J. 637, 641 (1989); Robert E. Sarazen, Note, *An Ethical Approach to Discovery Abuse*, 4 GEO. J. LEGAL ETHICS 459 (1990).

duty to preserve the parts.[67] In *Fox v. Cohen*, a medical negligence case, the court held that a valid claim could be stated against a hospital and named employees for the negligent loss or destruction of medical records that state statute and administrative regulations required hospitals to keep.[68] The claim was dismissed, however, since the underlying malpractice claim was still pending and no damage had been suffered yet due to the loss of the records.[69]

B. Evolving Remedies

In the mid-1980s, to counter the inequities and inadequacies of the remedies described above, some courts began to recognize spoliation of evidence as a tort that can be remedied under the following causes of action:[70]

1. Intentional Spoliation

The elements of intentional spoliation have been defined by one court as follows:

(1) Pending or probable litigation involving the plaintiff; (2) knowledge by the defendant of the existence or likelihood of the litigation; (3) intentional "acts of spoliation" on the part of the defendant designed to disrupt the plaintiff's case; (4) disruption of the plaintiff's case; and (5) damages proximately caused by the acts of the defendant.[71]

In *Smith v. Superior Court*[72] California recognized the tort of intentional spoliation of evidence. The plaintiff allegedly was severely injured when a wheel part flew off an oncoming van and struck her windshield. The van was towed to the dealer who had installed the presumably defective wheels. Two weeks later the dealer agreed with the plaintiff's lawyer to maintain the van parts, but subsequently allegedly "lost, destroyed or otherwise disposed of the physical evidence which [it] had promised to maintain for Plaintiffs."[73] The loss of the evidence was alleged to have significantly prejudiced the plaintiff's chance to obtain compensation for her injuries.

In adopting the new tort, the court commented, "While intentional spoliation of evidence has not been recognized as a tort heretofore, we conclude that a prospective civil action in a product liability case is a valuable 'probable expectancy' that the court must protect from the kind of interference alleged herein."[74]

---

[67] 869 F.2d 1162 (8th Cir. 1989), *aff'd*, 921 F.2d 765 (8th Cir. 1990).

[68] 406 N.E.2d 178 (Ill. App. Ct. 1980).

[69] *Id.*

[70] *See generally* WARREN FREEDMAN, THE TORT OF DISCOVERY ABUSE (1989).

[71] County of Solano v. Delancy, 264 Cal. Rptr. 721, 729 (Ct. App. 1989) (footnote omitted), *review denied and ordered not published officially,* 1990 Cal. LEXIS 488 (Cal. Feb. 1, 1990).

[72] 198 Cal. Rptr. 829 (Ct. App. 1984).

[73] *Id.* at 832.

[74] *Id.* at 837.

In *Hazen v. Municipality of Anchorage* an undercover police officer secretly recorded his conversation with the owner of a massage parlor.[75] After the owner's arrest for prostitution, her attorneys listened to the tape and concluded that it contained clear evidence that the client had not offered sexual acts. During a dismissal hearing on the criminal charge, after the defense attorney asked that the surveillance tape recording be preserved for use in a contemplated civil suit, the court tape recorder picked up the voice of someone from the prosecution table whispering, "Wait till you hear what is on the tape now."

After filing a civil suit for false arrest, defamation, malicious prosecution, and civil rights violations, the plaintiff and her attorney discovered that the police tape had been altered and had become inaudible. A tort claim for intentional spoliation was then added to the other claims. In reversing the trial court's dismissal of the intentional spoliation claim, the appellate court held that: "Hazen's prospective false arrest and malicious prosecution actions were valuable probable expectancies. If the arrest tape was intentionally altered, this was an unreasonable interference with these expectancies that can be remedied in tort."[76]

2. Negligent Spoliation

Soon after *Smith*, Florida recognized a new tort of negligent spoliation of evidence. In *Bondu v. Gurvich*[77] a widow claimed that the loss of anesthesiology records prevented her from winning a medical negligence case against the anesthesiologist and the hospital for her husband's death during heart surgery. The court reasoned that because a state statute and administrative regulations imposed a duty on the hospital to make and maintain records, the plaintiff had stated a valid claim for breach of that duty and for damages proximately caused by the breach.[78]

In another Florida case, *Continental Insurance Co. v. Herman*,[79] the court identified the elements of proof of negligent spoliation of evidence as

> (1) existence of a potential civil action, (2) a legal or contractual duty to preserve evidence which is relevant to the potential civil action, (3) destruction of that evidence, (4) significant impairment in the ability to prove the lawsuit, (5) a causal relationship between the evidence destruction and the inability to prove the lawsuit, and (6) damages.[80]

---

[75] 718 P.2d 456, 458 (Alaska 1986).

[76] *Id.* at 464; *see also* Pau v. Yosemite Park & Curry Co., 928 F.2d 880, 886 (9th Cir. 1991) (applying California law) (recognizing tort, but holding that intent to destroy evidence not proved where bicycle involved in accident was confused with another bicycle).

[77] 473 So. 2d 1307 (Fla. Dist. Ct. App. 1984), *review denied*, 484 So. 2d 7 (Fla. 1986).

[78] *Id.* at 1312–13.

[79] 576 So. 2d 313 (Fla. Dist. Ct. App. 1990).

[80] *Id.* at 315.

Several other courts have adopted this tort,[81] although some have rejected these theories based on policy considerations[82] or because existing remedies were deemed adequate.[83]

3. Fraudulent Concealment of Evidence

In *Viviano v. CBS, Inc.*[84] New Jersey recognized a new cause of action for fraudulent concealment of evidence, the elements of which are very similar to the tort of intentional spoliation. The plaintiff was an employee who was injured in a work-related incident. She sued her employer and supervisor for fraudulently concealing information relevant to her products liability claims against the manufacturer of the machine that caused her injury. In upholding a jury verdict awarding the employee compensatory and punitive damages, the New Jersey appellate court outlined the following elements of a cause of action for fraudulent concealment of evidence: (1) the defendant was legally obligated to disclose the subject evidence; (2) the evidence was material to the plaintiff's underlying personal injury case; (3) the plaintiff could not readily have learned of the evidence without the defendant disclosing it; (4) the defendant intentionally failed to disclose the evidence to the plaintiff; and (5) the plaintiff was harmed by relying on the nondisclosure.[85]

In recognizing this cause of action, the court observed

> This state's system of civil litigation is founded in large part on a litigant's ability under the authority of the Supreme Court rules, to investigate and uncover evidence after filing suit. Destruction of evidence known to be relevant to pending litigation violates the spirit of liberal discovery. Intentional destruction of evidence manifests a shocking disregard for orderly judicial procedures and offends tradi-

---

[81] *See, e.g.*, De Vera v. Long Beach Pub. Transp. Co., 225 Cal. Rptr. 789, 795 (Ct. App. 1986) (finding bus driver had duty to obtain information from other driver in collision for use by injured bus passengers in future tort litigation); Velasco v. Commercial Bldg. Maintenance Co., 215 Cal. Rptr. 504, 506 (Ct. App. 1985) (finding custodian discarded brown paper bag, found on attorney's desk, containing bottle fragments intended for use in possible products case).

[82] Koplin v. Rosel Well Perforators, Inc., 734 P.2d 1177 (Kan. 1987) (employer lost injury-causing machine); Panich v. Iron Wood Prods. Corp., 445 N.W.2d 795 (Mich. Ct. App. 1989) (employer disposed of electrical box), *appeal denied*, 434 Mich. 891 (1990); *see also* Murphy v. Target Prods., 580 N.E.2d 687 (Ind. Ct. App. 1991) (rejecting claim based on employer's failure to preserve allegedly defective power saw for use in suit against third party absent agreement to preserve).

[83] La Raia v. Superior Court, 722 P.2d 286, 290 (Ariz. 1986) (landlord destroyed container of toxic chemical spray that injured tenant) (en banc); Miller v. Montgomery County, 494 A.2d 761, 768 (Md. Ct. Spec. App.) (county lost part of defective traffic signal), *cert. denied*, 498 A.2d 1185 (Md. 1985); Pharr v. Cortese, 559 N.Y.S.2d 780 (Sup. Ct. 1990) (alteration of medical records).

[84] 597 A.2d 543 (N.J. Super. Ct. App. Div. 1991), *cert. denied*, 606 A.2d 375 (N.J. 1992).

[85] *Id.* at 548.

tional notions of fair play. Consequently, recognizing the defendants' liability for willfully concealing [subject evidence] is not inconsistent with either the letter or the rationale of New Jersey's policy of affording immunity to testimony given during the course of judicial proceedings.[86]

4. Contract Actions for Spoliation

Florida has also recognized a contract remedy for evidence spoliation. In *Miller v. Allstate Insurance Co.* the plaintiff's attorney agreed to relinquish a wrecked automobile to the plaintiff's insurer, Allstate, so it could prepare its defense to a possible claim by a passenger.[87] In exchange, Allstate agreed to preserve the car and make it available for inspection by the plaintiff's experts, but the company later sold the car to a salvage yard where it was disposed of. Although Allstate acknowledged that Florida recognized the tort of negligent spoliation, the company claimed that the plaintiff's choice of a contract action was fatal. The court disagreed, holding that "[w]here the parties have a contract, and the same act or transaction constitutes both a breach of the agreement, express or implied, and a tort, the tort may be waived and the injured party may sue on the contract."[88]

IV. CONCLUSION

The courts have recognized the duty to preserve evidence potentially discoverable in pending or foreseeable litigation. They have begun to recognize new means of dealing with the breach of that duty. The trend is toward imposing severe consequences for evidence spoliation, whether intentional or not. Given the difficulty of detecting spoliation and the need to deter it, we can only hope that this trend continues.

---

[86] *Id.* at 550.

[87] 573 So. 2d 24, 25–26 (Fla. Dist. Ct. App. 1990), *review denied*, 581 So. 2d 1307 (Fla. 1991).

[88] *Id.* at 27.

CHAPTER EIGHT

CONFIDENTIALITY ORDERS— THE STONEWALLER'S SHIELD[1]

I. ISOLATING PLAINTIFFS

Plaintiffs have learned that, through collaborative efforts, they can better detect stonewalling by comparing manufacturers' disclosures. In many documented instances, the manufacturer's failure to make full disclosure would have gone unnoticed and litigation would have been resolved on the basis of less than the whole truth, had not counsel for different plaintiffs compared notes on their investigations and discovery.[2] Collaboration among plaintiffs in similar cases also serves other worthy ends, including efficiency in discovery and trial preparation, as discussed later in this chapter.[3] In sum, by promoting full and fair access by all parties to relevant information, collaboration advances the policies underlying modern discovery.

Unfortunately, many defendant manufacturers in products liability cases attempt to deprive plaintiffs of the benefits of collaboration, including the ability to detect stonewalling, by seeking restrictive confidentiality orders. Manufacturers typically seek protective orders that prevent the disclosure of discovery materials to anyone other than the plaintiff in the instant case, plaintiff's counsel, and plaintiff's experts. Of course, such an order implicates not only the need for information sharing among plaintiffs in similar cases, but also precludes the public's access to information that may be important to assessing the safety of consumer goods. Because this book is

---

[1] For an in-depth treatment of this topic, *see* FRANCIS H. HARE, JR., JAMES L. GILBERT, WILLIAM M. REMINE III, CONFIDENTIALITY ORDERS (1988). An extensive bibliography of this topic, prepared by the Association of Trial Lawyers of America, is included in the Bibliography. For the defense perspective on confidentiality orders, *see* Alfred W. Cortese, Jr., *ATLA's Protective Order Campaign: Undermining Confidence in the Courts*, 18 Prod. Safety & Liab. Rep. (BNA) 465 (1991); Lawyers for Civil Justice Task Force, *Court Approved Confidentiality Orders: Why They Are Needed*, 57 DEF. COUNS. J. 89 (1990).

[2] See *infra* section II.

[3] See *infra* section II.B.

about the effects of stonewalling on plaintiffs, most of this chapter focuses on the need for sharing of information among plaintiffs handling similar cases, rather than on the related but distinct issues associated with public access to information.[4] The public's right of access to discovery materials is discussed later in this chapter. For purposes of this chapter, the term "restrictive confidentiality order" refers to a protective order governing the confidentiality of information made available through discovery that fails to allow sharing of discovery materials among litigants in similar cases.

A. Purported Grounds for Confidentiality

Rule 26(c) permits a party or other discovery respondent to seek a protective order "to protect a party or person from annoyance, embarrassment, oppression, or undue burden or expense," including orders that preclude or restrict the dissemination of discovery materials that constitute "a trade secret or other confidential research, development, or commercial information."[5] Certainly there are situations in which confidentiality should legitimately be assured by a protective order, particularly in commercial litigation. But unlike commercial litigation,[6] the documents typically in dispute in products liability cases rarely contain information that satisfies the legal criteria for trade secret protection.[7]

In early cases where manufacturers sought restrictive confidentiality orders, some frankly acknowledged that their reason for seeking the order was to prevent information sharing. For instance, Ford Motor Company expressly justified its motion in one case as follows:

> The information, if traded with other law firms engaged in similar litigation with Ford, would allow these attorneys to pool their information pertaining to this corporate giant, more adequately prepare their case for trial, simplify the discovery process, confirm Ford's candor in responding to discovery requests, and, accordingly, potentially result in verdicts against Ford Motor Company.[8]

In *Earl v. Gulf & Western Manufacturing*[9] the court denied the defendant's motion for a restrictive confidentiality order because "[t]he only reason advanced by Gulf & Western for the order is its fear that the Earls might pass the information along to other plaintiffs involved in litigation against Gulf & Western."[10] In fact, the vast

---

[4] The public's right of access to discovery materials is discussed at section IV, *infra*.

[5] FED. R. CIV. P. 26(c)(7).

[6] *Cf.* Farnsworth v. Procter & Gamble Co., 758 F.2d 1545 (11th Cir. 1985) (upholding protective order to prevent discovery from third party, Centers for Disease Control, of names and addresses of participants in toxic shock syndrome study).

[7] See *infra* section III.C.1.

[8] Affidavit of Rudolph J. Persico, attached in support of the Defendant's Motion for Protective Order, Green v. Ford Motor Co., No. 403572 (San Diego County, Cal. Super. Ct. Apr. 16, 1971).

[9] 366 N.W.2d 160 (Wis. Ct. App. 1985).

[10] *Id.* at 164–65.

majority of courts and legal scholars examining such arguments have rejected them, recognizing the benefits of information sharing by plaintiffs.[11]

Only after numerous courts had rejected this ground for relief did defendants in products cases begin to assert new grounds for restrictive confidentiality orders. At first, manufacturers contended that their crash tests or other product safety evaluations, internal memoranda about safety concerns, records of other injuries allegedly caused by the product, and the like were entitled to protection as trade secret information under rule 26(c)(7). Plaintiffs' lawyers were initially able to counter this new strategy by demonstrating that the defendant's motion, though based on a different ground, applied to the same documents involved in earlier cases for which no trade secret claim had been made.

As discussed later in this chapter, the courts have narrowly interpreted the term *trade secret* and have not hesitated to deny confidentiality protection to documents not falling within that narrow scope. The overwhelming majority of opinions reject the trade secret ground as a justification for limiting the dissemination of discovery materials in products cases.[12] With virtual uniformity, courts have continued to permit information sharing among plaintiffs with similar cases, even when finding that certain documents are entitled to protection as trade secrets.[13] As a result, manufacturers are now seeking the same old remedy on new-found grounds, asserting a corporate right to privacy,[14] constitutional protection against "taking" private property without compensation or due process,[15] and even copyright protection.[16]

B. Defendants' True Motivation

While manufacturers are certainly justified in seeking to prevent disclosure of legitimate trade secrets to competitors, in the overwhelming majority of products liability cases, the manufacturer's true purpose for seeking a restrictive confidentiality order is to forbid plaintiff's counsel the benefits of sharing information with other plaintiffs' lawyers handling similar cases.[17] In these cases, manufacturers routinely seek restrictive confidentiality orders not to protect industrial trade secrets from their competitors but rather to isolate each individual plaintiff's counsel handling a similar case. They attempt to create an obstacle that would uniquely impede the plaintiff's efforts to prepare for trial, while leaving undisturbed the defendant's right to participate in an information-sharing, collaborative mechanism.

---

[11] See section II of this chapter and appendix 2.

[12] *See* HARE, GILBERT & REMINE, *supra* note 1, § 7.8.

[13] *Id.* at 195.

[14] *See* Arthur R. Miller, *Confidentiality, Protective Orders, and Public Access to the Courts*, 105 HARV. L. REV. 428 (1991).

[15] *Id.*

[16] Grundberg v. Upjohn Co., 137 F.R.D. 372, 388 (D. Utah 1991).

[17] *See* HARE, GILBERT & REMINE, *supra* note 1, § 7.6.

The view that the manufacturer's real purpose in seeking a restrictive confidentiality order is to prevent information sharing among plaintiffs is not just plaintiff's counsel's paranoia: It is supported by the history and nature of manufacturers' efforts to prevent information sharing among plaintiffs, by articles written by the defense bar, and by the observations of many courts and legal scholars.

Other aspects of defendant manufacturers' behavior strongly suggest a motivation other than protection of the value of truly sensitive, proprietary information. First, restrictive confidentiality orders are sought in virtually every products liability case for *all* information disclosed in discovery rather than actual trade secret information. This shotgun approach points to a motive broader than simply protecting true trade secrets from falling into the hands of competitors.

Second, manufacturers are typically unwilling to agree to orders that protect the confidentiality of information by restricting disclosure of discovery documents to plaintiffs with similar cases who agree to be bound by the terms of the order. This type of order protects against disclosures to competitors without frustrating the legitimate objectives of information sharing among plaintiffs.[18]

One article written for defense lawyers recommends that manufacturers "adopt a uniform stance regarding discovery in product liability cases"[19] that includes routinely seeking restrictive orders "even where defense counsel can make no special claim of confidentiality."[20] One defense firm's promotional newsletter, *Products Liability Update*, makes the following observations and recommendations:

> The recent increase in breast implant lawsuits presents a compelling discovery issue: the "borrowing" by plaintiffs of information already produced in related implant litigation. Substantial information in the form of documents and depositions was produced by implant manufacturers in the breast implant cases already filed and concluded through trial or settlement prior to the recent explosion of implant litigation. *Plaintiffs in the recently filed cases will certainly seek access to discovery already produced by implant defendants and will "share" discovery as an efficient and inexpensive way to circumvent the burdens of conducting their own original discovery. Implant defendants should vigorously oppose the borrowing and sharing of discovery by plaintiffs.*[21]

---

[18] Such confidentiality orders may present other problems, such as limiting public access to important safety information, particularly if too broadly drawn. See section IV of this chapter.

[19] Kerry A. Kearney & Tracey G. Benson, *Preventing Non-Party Access to Discovery Materials in Products Liability Actions: A Defendant's Primer*, 1987 CURRENT ISSUES L. & MED. 36.

[20] *Id.* at 40–41.

[21] *Shielding Discovery in Related Litigation, in Breast Implant Litigation—The Defense Perspective*, PRODUCTS LIABILITY UPDATE (Rivkin, Radler & Kremer, N.Y., Ill. and Cal.), May 1992, at 5 (emphasis added). While the newsletter does make passing reference to "confidential business information," *id.* at 7, it is clear in context that the purpose of the position urged is to keep plaintiffs in the dark and deny them "efficient and inexpensive" access to relevant information. Admirably, the newsletter does advise that "management and the business staff must understand that old copies of documents concerning the product which were saved despite company retention policies cannot be discarded once litigation has begun."

A number of legal scholars have recognized that the true motive of the defendant in seeking a restrictive confidentiality order is to deny plaintiffs the benefit of coordinating their discovery efforts. As described by one leading authority on discovery,

> Defense attorneys often attempt to use protective orders in order to discourage discovery and prevent formal and informal plaintiffs' attorneys' groups from coordinating discovery among themselves. Discovery in complex drug or products liability cases, often against major corporations, can be virtually impossible. In order to extract the relevant information from the defendants, plaintiffs must often go through numerous sets of interrogatories, and countless costly motions to compel. If the defense is successful in instituting a protective order, depending on its scope, the plaintiff's attorney could be completely isolated from these coordinating groups and forced to incur considerable expense in order to gain otherwise readily available information.[22]

As another scholar observed, "Frivolous claims of confidentiality have been asserted to cause delay and disruption, to drive up discovery expenses and to make it difficult for opposing counsel to assimilate and understand the information being sought."[23]

Many in the judiciary have also come to recognize the defendant's real objective in seeking a restrictive confidentiality order. In one federal products liability case, this motivation did not become apparent until trial, when the true significance of the protective order surfaced:

> Defendant in this case enjoyed all the advantages that wealth naturally produces. . . . It sought, in addition, to restrict plaintiff's own flexibility in trial preparation. The success of this effort magnified the existing inequalities of these parties.
>
> * * *
>
> As the total picture developed during the trial, it appeared that the protective order was serving defendant well in areas unrelated to the protection of its trade secrets or legitimate procedural rights. . . . First, while defendant may properly be protected from disclosure of its trade secrets, the order it sought and obtained was much broader. It required that "material and information made available in discovery proceedings not be divulged or made available to any other person, directly or indirectly, including by copy or summary thereof, or by giving information pertaining thereto, except to the extent introduced as evidence at trial. . . ." Plaintiff's attor-

---

Breast Implant Litigation: How to Control the Documents, in Breast Implant Litigation—The Defense Perspective, PRODUCTS LIABILITY UPDATE (Rivkin, Radler & Kremer, N.Y., Ill. and Cal.), May 1992, at 1.

[22] MARK A. DOMBROFF, DISCOVERY § 1.20, at 47–48 (1986 & Supp. 1990).

[23] Martin I. Kaminsky, *Proposed Federal Discovery Rules for Complex Civil Litigation*, 48 FORDHAM L. REV. 907, 929 (1980); *see also* TERRENCE F. KIELY, PREPARING PRODUCTS LIABILITY CASES § 7.21, at 225 n.15 (1986 & Supp. 1989); Michael Dore, *Confidentiality Orders—The Proper Role of the Courts in Providing Confidential Treatment for Information Disclosed Through the Pre-Trial Discovery Process*, 14 NEW ENG. L. REV. 1, 7 n.39 (1978).

neys were prohibited from disclosing, discussing or referring to, with any other person, any material, privileged or not, which was furnished by defendant. Fruitful consultation between plaintiff's attorneys with similar cases in other areas was thus effectively throttled. Counsel could not refer to or discuss any matters pertaining to facts revealed by [defendant] Liggett & Myers. Without discussing particulars, any consultation would be largely fruitless. Defendant thus succeeded, to a very significant degree, in isolating plaintiff from outside assistance and advice.

* * *

In over-all effect, [the restrictive confidentiality order] magnifies the burden any plaintiff will face in the trial of a similar lawsuit. It is calculated to do so. It has already been used for this purpose.[24]

Another court made the general observation

District courts are today being bombarded by an ever increasing number of requests for protective orders. Some of the increase may be attributed to legitimate attempts by litigants to stem the increasing use of abusive discovery tactics. Much of the increase, though, must be attributed to a practice among some attorneys to automatically seek protective orders in every case where any potential for embarrassment or harm, no matter how slight, exists.[25]

II. VALUE OF INFORMATION SHARING

The value of information sharing among plaintiffs in similar cases has been broadly recognized in a growing body of case law in state and federal courts and in the legal literature.[26] A review of the authorities makes clear that a consensus of legal opinion, from a wide variety of perspectives, strongly advocates the practice. Judges and scholars agree that sharing of discovery among plaintiffs is necessary to promote full, fair, and efficient access to information, to deter and detect stonewalling, and to advance the truth-finding function of the judicial system. A restrictive confidentiality order that precludes information sharing among counsel with similar cases is therefore in conflict with the purposes of the Federal Rules of Civil Procedure.[27]

---

[24] Thayer v. Liggett & Myers Tobacco Co., CA No. 5314 (W.D. Mich. Feb. 19, 1970), *reprinted in* HARE, GILBERT & REMINE, *supra* note 1, app. A-1; see also appendix 2.

[25] Ericson v. Ford Motor Co., 107 F.R.D. 92, 94 (E.D. Ark. 1985); *see also* Wilson v. American Motors Corp., 759 F.2d 1568, 1571 (11th Cir. 1985); Earl v. Gulf & W. Mfg. Co., 366 N.W.2d 160, 164–65 (Wis. Ct. App. 1985).

[26] Appendix 2 contains a broad collection of authorities approving collaboration among plaintiffs.

[27] *See, e.g.*, Wilson v. American Motors Corp., 759 F.2d 1568 (11th Cir. 1985); Deford v. Schmid Prods. Co., 120 F.R.D. 648, 654 (D. Md. 1987); Ward v. Ford Motor Co., 93 F.R.D. 579, 580 (D. Colo. 1982); Parsons v. General Motors Corp., 85 F.R.D. 724, 726 (N.D. Ga. 1980); Johnson Foils, Inc. v. Huyck Corp., 61 F.R.D. 405, 409 (N.D.N.Y. 1973). A proposed amendment to rule 26(c) would require courts to consider the value of information sharing in ruling on motions to modify protective orders. *See* 26(c)(3)(C), Proposed Amendments to Rules of Civil Procedure, *reprinted in* 150 F.R.D. 383, 387 (1993).

A. Leveling the Playing Field

In every products case, local defense counsel benefit from a sophisticated and very effective collaborative mechanism for investigation, case preparation, and discovery. In addition to its inherent advantages of superior knowledge and resources, the corporate defendant saves time and money by coordinating its defenses in numerous lawsuits. These advantages enable the company to research and organize volumes of factual material for the immediate use of its attorneys in similar cases, a nationwide effort managed by in-house counsel or an outside firm.

The defendant manufacturer undertakes this type of defense to achieve five goals: (1) to use its financial resources most efficiently, (2) to coordinate research and discovery, (3) to understand the idiosyncracies of local practice in each jurisdiction, (4) to maintain consistency among each of its local counsel, and (5) to develop discovery and trial strategies that further disadvantage each plaintiff.[28]

It is, of course, perfectly legitimate for the manufacturer to have the benefit of such coordinated efforts. Indeed, without a coordinated defense, it would be difficult for each of the defendant's local counsel to adequately prepare the company's case.[29]

In cases where there are multiple defendants, the defendants may join together to achieve the same objectives. Articles in some defense counsel publications have recommended that defendants enter into an agreement among themselves to coordinate their defenses.[30] These agreements generally require some defendants to waive claims or cross-claims against other defendants and to refrain from developing aspects of the case that would not be in the interests of other defendants, and they may provide that all defendants will share the cost of any judgments against one or more of them.[31] The existence and terms of these agreements typically are not revealed to the plaintiff's counsel or the court.

Some competing manufacturers have begun to coordinate their efforts by sharing legal briefs, depositions, and interrogatories, and instituting other collaborative efforts.[32] These defense litigation support groups include the Defense Research

---

[28] Al Parnell, *The Coordinated Group Defense*, FOR DEF., Nov. 1980, at 16.

[29] Ward v. Ford Motor Co., 93 F.R.D. 579, 580 (D. Colo. 1983) (defendant, Ford, "admitted that it, quite properly, coordinates its defenses in the cases filed against it throughout the United States").

[30] *See, e.g.*, Sheridan & McGraw, *A Strategy for Defending Multidefendant Lawsuits*, FOR DEF., Aug. 1983, at 18, 19.

[31] *Id.* at 21. Multiple defendant cooperation agreements that provide for judgment sharing are particularly useful in jurisdictions that do not recognize a right of contribution among joint tortfeasors.

[32] Foy Devine, *Litigation Support Groups*, 11 LEADER'S PRODUCT LIABILITY NEWSL., May 1985, at 1; David Ranii, *For the Other Side: Defense Lawyer Group Gaining New Vitality*, NAT'L L.J., Sept. 13, 1982, at 1; *see also* HARE, GILBERT & REMINE, *supra* note 1, §§ 3.1, 7.3.

Institute[33] and the Industrial Defense Library.[34] Automotive manufacturers have formed the Product Liability Advisory Council for the purpose of submitting amicus curiae briefs in products liability actions involving automotive products.[35]

As discussed earlier,[36] the plaintiff in a nonconsolidated products liability action has an even greater need than the defendant to share discovery materials with other plaintiffs involved in similar cases. In part because of the complexity of modern products liability litigation, it is difficult, if not impossible, for a plaintiff's counsel to adequately prepare the client's case single-handedly, particularly when faced with a well-prepared opponent.[37] This problem is not limited to solo practitioners or small firms: Even large plaintiffs' firms lack the resources to develop the expertise necessary to handle more than one or two complex products cases at a time alone, without help from other plaintiffs' counsel. Allowing defendants but not plaintiffs access to information sharing only exacerbates the imbalance of resources that favors defendants from the outset.

The trend toward class actions, multidistrict litigation procedures, and partial or full consolidation of cases in single jurisdictions has resulted from the growing awareness of the utility and efficiency of information sharing among parties with similar causes of action. These procedures have been used extensively in products liability litigation but are often not available where the claims present different causation and damages issues.

Until the advent of plaintiffs' litigation support groups, plaintiffs (and plaintiffs' counsel) in individual unconsolidated cases were the only players involved in complex products liability litigation with no access to formal information-sharing mechanisms. In products liability cases brought as class actions or consolidated in state or federal courts, (for instance, through multidistrict litigation procedures) all parties have access to all discovery materials. As discussed above, each local defense counsel in an individual unconsolidated products case has access to collaborative mechanisms coordinated by the defendant manufacturer or consortiums of industries or defendants. Thus, only plaintiffs in individual actions were left to discover and process relevant information alone to the extent their resources and knowledge, in isolation, permitted.

In the mid-1980s, recognizing the need to level the playing field and to make discovery and case preparation affordable and effective for the individual plaintiff, plaintiffs' lawyers formed litigation support groups.[38] These groups provided a forum for

---

[33] Ranii, *supra* note 32, at 1; *see* Devine, *supra* note 32, at 1.

[34] Devine, *supra* note 32, at 1.

[35] *Id.*

[36] See generally chapter 4.

[37] The significance of this point is presented in detail in Francis H. Hare, Jr. & James L. Gilbert, *Discovery in Products Liability Cases: The Plaintiff's Plea for Judicial Understanding*, 12 AM. J. TRIAL ADVOC. 413 (1989).

[38] *See* authorities and discussion in HARE, GILBERT & REMINE, *supra* note 1, §§ 3.3, 7.4.

previously isolated plaintiffs to compare notes and to put together the true story of a product's design, testing, and use. For the first time, individual plaintiffs had access to many of the benefits and efficiencies of class actions and consolidated cases. An equally important benefit of collaboration among plaintiffs was the new ability to uncover incomplete disclosure by manufacturers, and to bring this stonewalling to the attention of the courts.

B. Benefits of Information Sharing by Plaintiffs

Collaboration among plaintiffs to share information in similar cases can be justified, first, by the three objectives of the Federal Rules of Civil Procedure specified in rule 1: "the just, speedy, and inexpensive determination of every action."[39]

1. Justice

Contemporary products litigation typically involves a large number of highly technical documents. When a number of experts and skilled trial lawyers work as a team to select, analyze, and summarize the technological significance and strategic implications of the relevant documents, they will produce a more thorough and comprehensive work product than will one firm with little or no previous experience with the product handling a single case. The effect is to raise the case preparation status of an individual plaintiff to the level of the leading practitioners in the field. A more truthful and accurate picture of the facts emerges and surprises at trial are minimized. Given the access to collaborative mechanisms enjoyed by each local defense counsel, information sharing among plaintiffs is needed to avoid skewed and unjust results in individual cases.

2. Efficiency

The cooperative effort of plaintiffs handling similar cases enhances the discovery process in at least three ways. First, and most obvious, information sharing can avoid duplication of discovery work. Second, by working together, plaintiffs' counsel can refine the language of discovery requests, achieving greater accuracy and specificity. Third, over time, coordinated discovery can narrow the scope of discovery to documents of particular significance, saving time and money.

3. Reduced Expense

Unlike defense counsel who are paid by the hour, plaintiffs' counsel have no economic incentive to conduct lengthy or unnecessary discovery. Information sharing among plaintiffs with similar cases produces many cost savings by avoiding duplication of discovery procedures in the following ways:

- narrower discovery requests,
- joint participation in discovery depositions,

---

[39] FED. R. CIV. P. 1.

- pooling common documents (including deposition and trial transcripts) in a central depository available at reduced costs,
- summaries of key internal documents,
- shared research,
- availability of top experts,
- model briefs addressed to common legal issues, and
- joint funding of research and litigation tests concerning the product's defect.

These efficiencies spare plaintiffs—and in some instances, defendants as well—unnecessary costs, lowering an often insurmountable barrier to access to the justice system.

C. Verification of Full Disclosure

In addition to the benefits discussed above, information sharing also provides plaintiffs the opportunity to verify the completeness and accuracy of a defendant manufacturer's response to discovery requests.

The principal obstacle to plaintiffs' discovery in a defective product case arises from the fact that the corporate defendant initially has exclusive possession of all of the company's tests and studies concerning the safety of the product.

The manufacturer's internal documents constitute the single most important source of information in a products liability case. If the plaintiff's counsel is to properly prepare the case, he or she must have a fair knowledge and understanding of these tests, studies, and other internal documents relating to the safety of the product.[40] Discovery requests that reflect the collective experience of a number of attorneys handling similar cases are much more likely to produce the relevant information than the shot-in-the-dark efforts of a lawyer handling a single case. Plaintiffs' lawyers who specialize in defective product litigation strongly agree that sharing information accumulated over time by many plaintiffs is the only way to achieve the full-disclosure objective of the discovery rules.

The powerful motive of self-preservation impels the defendant to withhold the production of its relevant internal documents. Indeed, the hotter the "smoking gun," the tighter the defendant's grip. In a single, isolated case, this powerful motive operates on the defendant with full force. Information sharing among plaintiffs' counsel handling similar cases provides a necessary counterforce. When they can compare a defendant's responses to discovery in several cases, plaintiffs' lawyers have a means to verify the accuracy of the defendant's response in an individual case.

Unjustified withholding of requested and relevant information may subject the defendant to a number of adverse consequences, including—but by no means limited to—the imposition of judicial sanctions.[41] To cite a few of the many cases where col-

---

[40] See chapter 1, section II.

[41] See generally chapter 10.

laboration revealed discovery misconduct by defendants, in *Sellers v. General Motors Corp.*[42] a new trial was ordered after such a collaboration uncovered critical evidence withheld by manufacturer defendants. New trials were also ordered in both *Gammon v. Clark Equipment Co.*[43] and *Ostendorf v. International Harvester Co.*[44] when plaintiffs' counsel discovered through post-trial discussions with other counsel proof of similar claims and lawsuits the existence of which the defendants had denied. In *Stengel v. Kawasaki Heavy Industries*[45] the court imposed discovery sanctions for "the sporadic-episodic production of . . . test results coupled with the undisputed fact the final set of test results were only produced because counsel for the Plaintiff knew these tapes had been produced in another case."[46]

Discovery sharing, however, is by no means a foolproof method of detecting evidence suppression: If the defendant uniformly suppresses the same material in all similar cases, the existence of important documents and information may never be detected. Nevertheless, experience has shown that information sharing through plaintiffs' litigation support groups has frequently uncovered suppression of critical information. When manufacturers know that plaintiffs have access to a large pool of investigative and discovery information, their apprehension of the consequences of being caught withholding relevant information may overcome their motivation to conceal damaging facts.[47]

III. COMBATING A MOTION FOR A RESTRICTIVE CONFIDENTIALITY ORDER

Plaintiffs' counsel can and must oppose efforts to isolate them from their colleagues with similar cases. Fortunately, as described in the following discussion, effective means are available to do so.

A. Voluntary Agreement Trap

The manufacturer defendant often promises to produce all the relevant documents the plaintiff needs to prepare his or her case if plaintiff's counsel will simply agree to the restrictive confidentiality order. Plaintiffs' counsel who have taken this bait and stipulated to an order have suffered the consequences.[48] The manufacturer's

---

[42] 40 Fed. R. Serv. 2d (Callaghan) 590 (E.D. Pa. 1984).

[43] 686 P.2d 1102 (Wash. Ct. App. 1984), *aff'd en banc*, 707 P.2d 685 (Wash. 1985).

[44] 433 N.E.2d 253 (Ill. 1982).

[45] 116 F.R.D. 263 (N.D. Tex. 1987).

[46] *Id.* at 268; *see also* Rozier v. Ford Motor Co., 573 F.2d 1332 (5th Cir.) (ordering new trial when information withheld was discovered by plaintiff's counsel post-trial), *reh'g denied*, 578 F.2d 871 (5th Cir. 1978); Bollard v. Volkswagen of Am., Inc., 56 F.R.D. 569 (W.D. Mo. 1971); Rock Island Bank & Trust Co. v. Ford Motor Co., 220 N.W.2d 799 (Mich. Ct. App. 1974) (same).

[47] For numerous authorities discussing the "verification" principle and its effect as a deterrent on the manufacturer's consideration of the cost and benefits of suppressing its internal documents in defective product litigation, see generally Introduction and chapter 1.

[48] *See* Tom Riley & Mary K. Hoefer, *Protective Orders: Machiavelli Would Be Pleased*, Trial, Nov. 1984, at 30. Numerous "horror stories" are reported in Hare, Gilbert & ReMine, *supra* note 1, §§ 4.14–4.20.

duty to produce relevant documents exists whether or not a confidentiality order has been entered,[49] and the manufacturer will resist the plaintiff's discovery efforts with equal vigor[50] with or without a restrictive confidentiality order: The defendant's suggestion that a restrictive confidentiality order will enhance the discovery process should be viewed with great skepticism. In fact, just the opposite is true: Discovery is suppressed by such orders and enhanced by information sharing.[51]

In short, the plaintiff in a defective product case must never voluntarily agree to a restrictive confidentiality order for the following reasons:

- The plaintiff must have access to a cooperative mechanism to be able to fairly and adequately prepare its case.
- Such an order isolates the plaintiff but not the defendant. This situation guarantees the defendant a huge—and unfair—advantage.
- Such an order denies the plaintiff an opportunity to verify the accuracy or completeness of the defendant's discovery response.
- Such an order will not expedite or enhance the quality of discovery because the manufacturer will stonewall discovery in any event. An order will simply make it much more difficult for the plaintiff to detect the stonewalling.
- Such an order will greatly increase the cost of discovery by denying access to information obtained by other plaintiffs and by increasing the time spent on obtaining and understanding the manufacturer's documents.
- Implementing the order may require the plaintiff to disclose the identity of consulting experts who are given information produced during discovery and/or to disclose counsel's work product reflecting information the defendant claims is confidential.
- A restrictive confidentiality order inevitably leads to the injection of divisive collateral issues unrelated to the preparation or resolution of the case on the merits.

Defendants often argue that stipulated protective orders are routinely employed in complex litigation. Although parties in *commercial* litigation often agree to protective orders, businesses usually have a strong, mutual interest in maintaining confidentiality of trade secrets and financial information.[52] In a products case, on the other hand, the plaintiff has everything to lose and nothing to gain by agreeing to an order that isolates his or her counsel from other counsel handling similar cases. In stark

---

[49] *See* HARE, GILBERT & REMINE, *supra* note 1, § 7.11, at 213–14.

[50] *See* Brandimarti v. Caterpillar, Inc., No. GD 83-12468 (Allegheny County, Pa. Ct. C.P. Oct. 11, 1985), *reprinted in* HARE, GILBERT & REMINE, *supra* note 1, app. A-2.

[51] *See* authorities cited in HARE, GILBERT & REMINE, *supra* note 1, § 7.11, at 215; section II.B, *supra*.

[52] *See* authorities cited and quoted in Hare & Gilbert, *supra* note 37, at 423 and HARE, GILBERT & REMINE, *supra* note 1, § 7.13, at 226–30.

contrast, the defendant manufacturer, who has exclusive possession of most, if not all, of the information the plaintiff needs, has everything to gain and nothing to lose from such an order.

B. Defendant's Legal Burden of Proof

Counsel should not presume that the court has a full understanding of either the nature or the weight of the manufacturer's burden of proof. Judicial understanding of this issue is increasing as manufacturers persist in routinely seeking restrictive confidentiality orders. However, in the absence of some specific exposure to the topic, the court may well underestimate the requirements of the good cause showing that must be made by the defendant before the court is justified in exercising its power under rule 26(c)(7) to restrict the discovery process. The plaintiff's brief on this topic should include the following points:[53]

1. Manufacturer's Heavy Burden of Proof [54]

As a general proposition, the federal rules contemplate that discovery proceedings will take place in the open unless compelling reasons exist for imposing restrictions.[55] The presumption is that no order is necessary; therefore, the movant must show a positive reason justifying entry of any restrictive order. A mere argument that no reason exists not to enter an order does not suffice.[56]

2. Standard of Particularized Proof

To sustain its burden, the manufacturer must make "a particular and specific demonstration of fact, as distinguished from stereotype and conclusory statements."[57] The standard of particularized proof applies in two ways. First, it requires the identification of the specific discovery materials the disclosure of which the movant seeks to restrict.[58] Ordinarily, the manufacturer should be required to specify the particular

---

[53] For a detailed discussion of the manufacturer's burden of proof, see HARE, GILBERT & REMINE, *supra* note 1, §§ 6.7, 7.8.

[54] United States v. United Fruit Co., 410 F.2d 553, 557 (5th Cir.), *cert. denied*, 396 U.S. 820 (1969).

[55] *See, e.g.*, Public Citizen v. Liggett Group, Inc., 858 F.2d 775, 789 (1st Cir. 1988), *cert. denied*, 488 U.S. 1030 (1989); In re "Agent Orange" Prod. Liab. Litig., 821 F.2d 139, 145–46 (2d Cir.), *cert. denied*, 484 U.S. 953 (1987); Kraszewski v. State Farm Gen. Ins. Co., 139 F.R.D. 156, 159 (N.D. Cal. 1991).

[56] Earl v. Gulf & W. Mfg. Co., 366 N.W.2d 160, 165 (Wis. Ct. App. 1985).

[57] *See, e.g.*, General Dynamics Corp. v. Selb Mfg. Corp., 481 F.2d 1204, 1212 (8th Cir. 1973), *cert. denied*, 414 U.S. 1162 (1974).

[58] *See, e.g.*, Koster v. Chase Manhattan Bank, 93 F.R.D. 471, 481 (S.D.N.Y. 1982). For a discussion of the showing required in numerous cases, see Jacqueline S. Guénégo, Note, *Trends in Protective Orders Under Federal Rule of Civil Procedure 26(c): Why Some Cases Fumble While Others Score*, 60 FORDHAM L. REV. 541 (1991). There are occasions where a manufacturer has been permitted to identify documents by "category." *See, e.g.*, Culligan v. Yamaha Motor Corp., 110 F.R.D. 122, 124 (S.D.N.Y. 1986).

documents that it seeks to protect. Second, the movant must also identify the particular circumstances in which disclosure of those materials would inflict competitive harm.[59] In short, the standard requires oral testimony or affidavits identifying specific harm that would result from the disclosure of particular documents.

Requiring the manufacturer to specify particular documents to be protected is important because of the requirement that the *court*, not the defendant, must ultimately decide whether a particular document is entitled to judicial protection. If the defendant were allowed to identify groups of documents rather than specific documents, it would become a "self-appointed censor."[60]

3. Probability and Quality of Alleged Harm

The mere suggestion of some vague possibility of harm to the defendant manufacturer is not sufficient to justify the restriction of discovery materials. The manufacturer must demonstrate that disclosure will work a "clearly defined and very serious injury."[61] Both the likelihood and the severity of the perceived harm must be significant.

4. Character of Alleged Harm

Courts have made it abundantly clear that the judicial power to restrict the dissemination of material claimed to be trade secrets extends only to documents that possess a "competitive use" value.[62] Manufacturers often gloss over or ignore this aspect of their burden of proof.

5. Weighing Countervailing Interests

In determining both (1) whether to enter an order and (2) the scope of an order under consideration, the court must consider the effect that an order limiting the use of discovery materials would have on countervailing interests.[63] This involves a balancing of competing needs and interests,[64] including the plaintiff's need for information sharing and the effect an order will have on the court and the judicial system in general.[65]

C. Requirements for Trade Secret Protection

In order to justify judicial restriction of the use of discovery materials under rule

---

[59] *See, e.g.*, United States v. Hooker Chems. & Plastics Corp., 90 F.R.D. 421, 425 (W.D.N.Y. 1981); Johnson Foils, Inc. v. Huyck Corp., 61 F.R.D. 405, 409 (N.D.N.Y. 1973).

[60] United States v. IBM Corp., 82 F.R.D. 183, 184 (S.D.N.Y. 1979).

[61] *See, e.g.*, Waelde v. Merck, Sharp & Dohme, 94 F.R.D. 27, 28 (E.D. Mich. 1981); Zenith Radio Corp. v. Matsushita Elec. Indus. Co., 529 F. Supp. 866, 890–91 (E.D. Pa. 1981).

[62] The *competitive use* characteristic is addressed in greater detail in section III.C.1, *infra*.

[63] *See, e.g.*, General Dynamics Corp. v. Self Mfg. Co., 481 F.2d 1204, 1212 (8th Cir. 1973), *cert. denied*, 414 U.S. 1162 (1974); Koster v. Chase Manhattan Bank, 93 F.R.D. 471, 479 (S.D.N.Y. 1982); United States v. Hooker Chems. & Plastics Corp., 90 F.R.D. 421, 425 (W.D.N.Y. 1981); *see* HARE, GILBERT & REMINE, *supra* note 1, §§ 6.5–6.7.

[64] *See, e.g.*, Garcia v. Peeples, 734 S.W.2d 343, 347–48 (Tex. 1987).

[65] *See* HARE, GILBERT & REMINE, *supra* note 1, §§ 4.14–4.20, 6.5–6.7, 7.17.

26(c)(7), the manufacturer must satisfy the court that the contents constitute trade secrets.[66] With regard to discovery materials, courts consider secrecy to be the exception, not the rule.[67] The type of documents typically involved in defective product cases (as opposed to commercial litigation) rarely meet the rigorous "trade secrets" test.

In evaluating trade secret claims, a number of courts have adopted the Restatement of Torts's criteria:

- the extent to which the information is known outside of the company,
- the extent to which the information is known by employees and by independent contractors involved with the company,
- the extent of the measures taken by the company to guard the secrecy of the information,
- the value of the information to the company and to its competitors,
- the amount of effort or money expended in developing the information, and
- the ease or difficulty with which the information could be properly acquired or duplicated by others.[68]

The movant must show that the six factors relate to each specified document or to each distinguishable category of documents for which rule 26(c)(7) protection is sought.[69]

One federal court of appeals held that, in a federal case based on diversity jurisdiction, what constitutes a trade secret for purposes of rule 26(c)(7) protection should be determined based on state law, which in that state meant applying the Restatement of Torts' criteria identified above.[70]

Following are points of law bearing on whether particular information constitutes a trade secret.

1. Competitive Use

A manufacturer is not entitled to an order restricting the use of discovery materi-

---

[66] The term "confidential research, development, or commercial information" in rule 26(c)(7) does not implicate a separate and independent ground for a protective order involving a different burden of proof or a different criteria than is applicable to a "trade secret." *See* HARE, GILBERT & REMINE, *supra* note 1, § 7.8, at 177–80.

[67] Citicorp v. Interbank Card Ass'n, 478 F. Supp. 756, 765 (S.D.N.Y. 1979).

[68] RESTATEMENT (SECOND) OF TORTS § 757 cmt. b (1939), *applied in* Smith v. Bic Corp., 869 F.2d 194, 200 (3d Cir. 1989); Deford v. Schmid Prods. Co., 120 F.R.D. 648, 653 (D. Md. 1987); Waelde v. Merck, Sharp & Dohme, 94 F.R.D. 27, 28–29 (E.D. Mich. 1981); *see also* Cuno Inc. v. Pall Corp., 117 F.R.D. 506, 508 (E.D.N.Y. 1987) (five of the factors used).

[69] Waelde v. Merck, Sharp & Dohme, 94 F.R.D. 27, 28–29 (E.D. Mich. 1981); Reliance Ins. Co. v. Barron's, 428 F. Supp. 200, 202–03 (S.D.N.Y. 1977); Farnum v. G.D. Searle & Co., 339 N.W.2d 384, 389 (Iowa 1983).

[70] Smith v. Bic Corp., 869 F.2d 194, 200 (3d Cir. 1989).

als on a showing that the company internally regards the document as confidential. The unique value of a trade secret lies in its *competitive use* value—that is, the competitive advantage the information gives its owner over competitors.[71]

Both conceptually and historically, the rule 26(c)(7) justification for judicial intervention was developed for commercial litigation.[72] The classic categories of trade secrets include secret formulas, customer lists, and business records reflecting cost and pricing or sources of supply.[73] A plaintiff's counsel should call the court's attention to the fact that all (or the great majority) of the cases cited in the defendant's brief are commercial law disputes involving these classic trade secret categories. The conceptual applicability of these categories to the engineering and technical documents involved in a products case is tenuous at best.[74]

Many of the relevant documents in a products case deal directly with the product's safety. Manufacturers often collaborate in their efforts to develop safer products. Although one company may adopt an alternative approach, rarely would the difference satisfy the test for a trade secret. Furthermore, many of the relevant documents describe defects and product failures, information that has little or no competitive use value.

Courts have held that documents reflecting the following types of information do not warrant protection as trade secrets: the hazardous nature of a product[75] or matters affecting the public health,[76] bad management,[77] and broad allegations of embarrassment or the threat of injury to a corporation's reputation.[78]

2. Matters of General Knowledge

Trade secret protection does not extend to information that is general knowledge in the industry. For example, in a case involving a defective motor vehicle, the manu-

---

[71] Ruckelshaus v. Monsanto Co., 467 U.S. 986, 1012 (1984); Waelde v. Merck, Sharp & Dohme, 94 F.R.D. 27, 29–30 (E.D. Mich. 1981).

[72] *See* HARE, GILBERT & REMINE, *supra* note 1, § 7.8, at 182–83.

[73] *See* 12 ROGER M. MILGRIM, MILGRIM ON TRADE SECRETS § 2.09 (1993).

[74] *See* HARE, GILBERT & REMINE, *supra* note 1, § 7.8, at 182–83.

[75] *In re* Upjohn Co. Antibiotic Cleocin Prods. Liab. Litig., 81 F.R.D. 482, 484–85 (E.D. Mich. 1979).

[76] Garcia v. Peeples, 734 S.W.2d 343, 348 n.4 (Tex. 1987).

[77] Brown & Williamson Tobacco Corp. v. Federal Trade Comm'n, 710 F.2d 1165, 1180 (6th Cir. 1983), *cert. denied*, 465 U.S. 1100 (1984).

[78] Cipollone v. Liggett Group, Inc., 785 F.2d 1108, 1121 (3d Cir. 1986); Joy v. North, 692 F.2d 880, 894 (2d Cir. 1982), *cert. denied*, 460 U.S. 1051 (1983); Hawley v. Hall, 131 F.R.D. 578, 584–85 (D. Nev. 1990); Vassiliades v. Israely, 714 F. Supp. 604, 606 (D. Conn. 1989); Turick v. Yamaha Motor Corp. U.S., 121 F.R.D. 32, 35 (S.D.N.Y. 1988); Smith v. Bic Corp., 121 F.R.D. 235, 239, 241 (E.D. Pa. 1988), *aff'd in part, rev'd in part*, 869 F.2d 194 (3d Cir. 1989); United States v. General Motors Corp., 99 F.R.D. 610, 612 (D.D.C. 1983); United States v. Hooker Chems. & Plastics Corp., 90 F.R.D. 421, 426 (W.D.N.Y. 1981). *See generally* HARE, GILBERT & REMINE, *supra* note 1, § 7.8, at 176–77.

facturer's documents typically relate to matters of basic physics and fundamental engineering principles that are common knowledge for automotive engineers.[79] Plaintiff's counsel should provide the court with a bibliography of published articles containing references to the same type of technical information as is contained in the manufacturer's internal documents, along with a supporting affidavit from an expert.

The plaintiff can also frequently show that the allegedly secret information is too stale to warrant protection. Although age is not conclusive, outdated information rarely satisfies either the secrecy or the competitive use requirement for a trade secret.[80]

3. Matters in the Public Domain

Information that has been shared with the defendant's competitors or is in the public domain cannot, as a matter of law, constitute a trade secret.[81] Proof that the information contained in the manufacturer's documents is, in fact, in the public domain may include the following: the exchange of information between companies in the industry,[82] public disclosure to the state or federal government (such as information required by federal regulatory agencies),[83] and a patent application (also available from the federal government).[84] The information is also in the public domain if it has been produced in other cases without a confidentiality order or introduced in evidence during trial without a sealing order.[85]

4. Sale of a Product

The sale of a product constitutes a public disclosure that defeats a claim of confidentiality where the nature of the trade secret is ascertainable by reverse engineer-

---

[79] *See, e.g.*, Midland-Ross Corp. v. Sunbeam Equip. Corp., 316 F. Supp. 171, 177–78 (W.D. Pa.), *aff'd*, 435 F.2d 159 (3d Cir. 1970); *cf.* Smith v. Bic Corp., 869 F.2d 194, 199–201 (3d Cir. 1989).

[80] *See, e.g.*, Deford v. Schmid Prods. Co., 120 F.R.D. 648, 653 (D. Md. 1987); Parsons v. General Motors Corp., 85 F.R.D. 724, 726 (N.D. Ga. 1980); United States v. IBM Corp., 67 F.R.D. 40, 49 (S.D.N.Y. 1975).

[81] *See* RESTATEMENT (SECOND) OF TORTS § 757 cmt. b (1939), *applied in* Smith v. Bic Corp., 809 F.2d 194, 200 (3d Cir. 1989); *see also* Nestle Foods Corp. v. Aetna Casualty & Sur. Co., 129 F.R.D. 483, 484–85 (D.N.J. 1990); United States v. IBM Corp., 67 F.R.D. 40, 46 n.9 (S.D.N.Y. 1975).

[82] *See* Nestle Foods Corp. v. Aetna Casualty & Sur. Co., 129 F.R.D. 483, 484–85 (D.N.J. 1990) (finding claims of loss of competitive advantage if files disclosed to plaintiff without protective order "disingenuous" where insurance company shared files with competitors as part of collaborative litigation defense efforts); HARE, GILBERT & REMINE, *supra* note 1, § 7.8, at 185–86.

[83] *See* HARE, GILBERT & REMINE, *supra* note 1, § 7.8, at 186.

[84] 55 AM. JUR. 2D *Monopolies, Restraints of Trade, and Unfair Trade Practices* § 706 (1983 & Supp. 1992); *see* Midland-Ross Corp. v. Sunbeam Equip. Corp., 316 F. Supp. 171, 177–78 (W.D. Pa.) *aff'd*, 435 F.2d 159 (3d Cir. 1970).

[85] *See* HARE, GILBERT & REMINE, *supra* note 1, § 7.8, at 186–87.

ing—i.e., testing or examination by an expert.[86]

D. Documents Obtained Outside of Discovery

The court's power to enter a protective order under rule 26(c) does not extend to documents not obtained through discovery in the instant case.[87] Because manufacturers have exclusive possession of their internal documents, it is frequently impossible to obtain critical documents outside of discovery in the first few cases involving a particular product. However, as more cases develop, plaintiff's counsel may learn that the documents requested in the present case have been produced or introduced into evidence in other cases without a restrictive confidentiality order. The best sources for this information are groups such as the Association of Trial Lawyers of America,[88] the Attorneys Information Exchange Group,[89] Trial Lawyers for Public Justice,[90] and the Center for Auto Safety.[91] Such groups work to acquire technical information not subject to a restrictive confidentiality order that would be of assistance to consumers and plaintiffs' counsel in the preparation and presentation of a defective product case.

As mentioned above, plaintiffs' counsel should also check with regulatory agencies to determine if useful information has been furnished to the agency in the course of a product approval proceeding, a defect investigation, or other agency activity.[92]

E. Identical Discovery Requests

Counsel representing plaintiffs in similar cases against the same manufacturer may wish to file identical discovery requests. A comparison of the manufacturer's responses may disclose significant, unjustifiable differences.[93] Disclosing that fact to

---

[86] Midland Ross Corp. v. Sunbeam Equip. Corp., 316 F. Supp. 171, 177–78 (W.D. Pa.), aff'd, 435 F.2d 159 (3d Cir. 1970); cf. Smith v. Bic Corp., 869 F.2d 194, 199–201 (3d Cir. 1989) ("information that is in the public domain or which has been 'reverse engineered,'—i.e., garnered by beginning with the finished product and determining the process used to manufacture it—cannot be protected as trade secrets"). In Smith the court held that despite sale and distribution of the butane lighter in question, certain information which could not be ascertained by reverse engineering, such as specifications and tolerances of components, could constitute trade secrets.

[87] See Seattle Times Co. v. Rhinehart, 467 U.S. 20, 34 (1984); In re Rafferty, 864 F.2d 151, 155 (D.C. Cir. 1988).

[88] The Exchange, ATLA, 1050 31st Street, N.W., Washington, D.C. 20007-4499; (800) 344-3023 or (202) 965-3500; FAX (202) 337-0977.

[89] AIEG, 651 Beacon Parkway West, Suite 115, Birmingham, Ala. 35209, (205) 945-4860.

[90] TLPJ, Project ACCESS, 1625 Massachusetts Ave., N.W., Suite 100, Washington, D.C. 20036, (202) 797-8600.

[91] Center for Auto Safety, 2001 S Street, N.W., Washington, D.C. 20009, (202) 328-7700.

[92] See generally FEDERAL YELLOW BOOK (1986 & Supp. 1994).

[93] See examples cited in Hare & Gilbert, supra note 37, at 424–36.

the court should strongly support the plaintiff's need for information sharing to verify the completeness and accuracy of the defendant's response to discovery requests.

F. Interrogatories to Identify Disputed Documents

The manufacturer often refuses to produce its internal documents until the confidentiality order issue is resolved. This puts both the plaintiff and the court in a difficult position: Without having seen the documents, it is impossible for the plaintiff to meaningfully respond to the manufacturer's confidentiality claims or for the court to make an informed ruling.[94] Interrogatories requesting the manufacturer to identify its internal documents may provide some insight. If the defendant objects to even listing relevant documents, this evidence of the defendant's recalcitrance toward discovery should support the plaintiff's request for the court's assistance. If the defendant answers the interrogatories, identifying documents it claims are confidential, the list of documents may shed light on the nature and content of the manufacturer's documents that will be helpful to the court in assessing, and plaintiff's counsel in addressing, the merits of the confidentiality claim. Moreover, counsel may use the list to learn whether it includes important documents produced in other similar cases. Even if documents produced in other cases are covered by a restrictive confidentiality order, counsel with access to those documents may nonetheless confirm whether additional relevant documents exist. Any stonewalling uncovered by this means can be brought to the court's attention.

G. Deposing the Manufacturer's Affiants

The manufacturer may file one or more affidavits to provide factual support for its motion for a restrictive confidentiality order. In that case, plaintiff's counsel should consider orally examining each affiant to inquire into the factual basis for the assertions contained in the affidavit. Questioning the witness on each of the six trade secret criteria frequently demonstrates that the asserted scope of the trade secret claim is unreasonably broad. Manufacturers often file virtually the same affidavit in case after case, regardless of the product model type or age. Plaintiff's counsel may show the witness several such affidavits and ask why the company's opinion never varies. Counsel should also require the witness to identify specific documents and to state precisely the factual basis for the claim that disclosure of those documents will result in a *clearly defined and very serious harm* to the competitive use of the information. If the witness participates in the manufacturer's litigation support for local counsel, this fact should also be elicited.

H. Counter Affidavits

Plaintiff's counsel should furnish the court with affidavits setting forth facts in opposition to the manufacturer's motion. An affidavit from a qualified expert should explain why the information contained in the manufacturer's documents is not com-

---

[94] The court can, of course, insist on reviewing the documents in camera.

mercially sensitive and why its disclosure would not result in a *clearly defined and very serious harm*. An attorney with experience handling similar cases can attest in a second affidavit that (1) the same or similar defect is at issue in other cases, (2) relevant documents are the same in similar cases, (3) access to those documents is critical, (4) local defense counsel have the benefit of a collaborative mechanism, (5) plaintiff's counsel needs access to a similar mechanism, and (6) entry of a restrictive confidentiality order will frustrate, not advance, the discovery process. Another attorney affidavit can address any significant disparities in the manufacturer's responses to discovery in similar cases.

I. Proposed Alternative Order

In opposition to a motion for a confidentiality order, plaintiff's counsel should first insist that the manufacturer has failed to make the required showing, discussed above. In the event that the court concludes that some of the manufacturer's documents contain information that meets the trade secret criteria, plaintiff's counsel should propose an order that protects against disclosure to the defendant's competitors or to the public in general but permits disclosure to experts and lawyers representing plaintiffs in similar cases. Such an order reflects a balanced solution between the manufacturer's need to protect any true trade secrets and the plaintiff's compelling need for information sharing.[95] Of course, such an order fails to achieve the benefits of public access, as discussed in the following section. An order permitting some sharing of information is nonetheless preferable to a protective order permitting no disclosure to other plaintiffs.

IV. PUBLIC ACCESS TO DISCOVERY INFORMATION

The public debate over court secrecy has intensified in recent years as more courts recognize the need to protect public access to information uncovered in litigation. Numerous commentators have explored the dangers and inherently undemocratic nature of court secrecy,[96] making a strong ethical case for public disclosure. A

---

[95] *See* authorities cited in HARE, GILBERT & REMINE, *supra* note 1, § 7.17. The defendant manufacturer cannot make the necessary showing merely by suggesting the possibility of a leak to a competitor. Waelde v. Merck, Sharp & Dohme, 94 F.R.D. 27, 29–30 (E.D. Mich. 1981); Garcia v. Peeples, 734 S.W.2d 343, 348 (Tex. 1987). See other authorities cited in Francis H. Hare, Jr. et al., *Confidentiality Orders in Products Liability Cases*, 13 AM. J. TRIAL ADVOC. 597, 608 (1989).

[96] *See, e.g.*, Joan Claybrook, *Going Public About Defective Products*, TRIAL, Nov. 1989, at 34; Lloyd Doggett & Michael J. Mucchetti, *Public Access to Public Courts: Discouraging Secrecy in the Public Interest*, 69 TEX. L. REV. 643 (1991); Hare & Gilbert, *supra* note 37; Hare et al., *supra* note 95; Riley & Hoefer, *supra* note 48; Georgia Sargeant, *Secrecy Orders Veiling Heart Valve Defects Are Assailed*, TRIAL, May 1990, at 12; Nicole Schultheis & Arthur Bryant, *Unnecessary Secrecy in Civil Litigation: Combatting the Threat to Effective Self-Governance*, 3 MD. J. CONTEMP. LEGAL ISSUES 49 (1991). The entire Fall 1991 issue of the *Maryland Journal of Contemporary Legal Issues* (Vol. 3) is devoted to examining record sealing from various perspectives. Leading articles arguing that reforms are not needed to counter court secrecy include Richard L. Marcus, *The Discovery Confidentiality Controversy*, 1991 U. ILL. L. REV. 457; Miller, *supra* note 14.

1991 note in the *Georgetown Journal of Legal Ethics* examined the defense attorney's predicament on learning of a potentially dangerous product still on the market, and explored "the tension between the ethical duty of the lawyer as a partisan advocate on behalf of her client and her responsibility as a citizen in the context of a products liability lawsuit."[97]

Florida litigator Dianne Jay Weaver[98] recently placed this problem in historical context:

> Secrecy practices arose along with the development of expanded and simplified access to redress for injuries caused by negligence and by defects in consumer goods. As the rights of the injured were improved, inevitable attempts were made to insulate potential defendants from liability. In many cases, to the lasting credit of American industry, the response was to make products and services safer. In other cases, regrettably, the response was to frustrate government efforts at regulation and to isolate consumers and deny them an understanding of the dangers they face in everyday life. As a result, in many situations the individual now has no way at all to obtain information that can determine health, financial well-being, and life itself.[99]

Weaver describes, by example, the secrecy surrounding the dangerously defective Bjork-Shiley artificial heart valve, even as valves were being placed in more patients.[100]

A. Constitutional Basis for Public Disclosure

Two separate rights grounded in the First Amendment to the U.S. Constitution are implicated by restrictive confidentiality orders: the free speech right of the discovering party to disclose discovered information free of prior restraint and the right of public access to court proceedings.

Limits on the constitutional right to public disclosure of discovery documents were upheld by the Supreme Court in *Seattle Times Co. v. Rinehart*.[101] In this case a unanimous Court recognized that the First Amendment right to disseminate information gained through discovery was implicated by a protective order prohibiting publication of discovered information but upheld the order against a constitutional challenge.[102] Noting that the right to discovery arises strictly from legislative entitle-

---

[97] Elizabeth Torphy-Donzella, Note, *Products Liability Litigation and Third-Party Harm: The Ethics of Nondisclosure*, 5 GEO. J. LEGAL ETHICS 435, 435–36 (1991).

[98] Co-chair (1990–1994), Discovery Abuse Committee, Association of Trial Lawyers of America.

[99] Dianne Jay Weaver, *Secrets That Can Kill Have No Place in Our Courts*, 18 Prod. Safety & Liab. Rep. (BNA) 701, 703 (1991).

[100] *Id.* at 703 (citing *Hearings Before the Senate Subcomm. on Courts and Administrative Practice, Comm. on the Judiciary*, 101st Cong., 2d Sess. 7 (May 17, 1990)).

[101] 467 U.S. 20 (1984). For a more in-depth discussion of this case and of First Amendment ramifications of confidentiality orders generally, see HARE, GILBERT & REMINE, *supra* note 1, § 6.10, at 139–44; Schultheis & Bryant, *supra* note 96, at 73–79.

[102] Seattle Times Co. v. Rinehart, 467 U.S. 20, 37 (1984).

ment, the Court upheld rule 26(c) restrictions on dissemination. The Court subjected the protective order to First Amendment scrutiny but reasoned that the protective order issued under this rule survived that scrutiny because it furthered a substantial government interest unrelated to the suppression of expression, with no greater limitation of speech rights than necessary.[103]

The showing made in support of the protective order at issue in *Seattle Times* was extremely strong. The case involved a libel suit by a religious sect against the newspaper. The trial court allowed the newspaper to obtain membership and donor lists through discovery, but it prohibited publication of that information after the plaintiff showed that disclosure would negatively affect its fund-raising and would likely subject identified individuals to physical harm. The protective order application related a history of harassment, threats, and assaults on the sect's membership.[104]

On review, the Supreme Court distinguished the essentially private nature of discovery from the public nature of other court proceedings.[105] Since *Seattle Times*, two courts have recognized a presumptive public right, under rule 26(c), of access to discovery materials, but they did not clearly identify whether this right is a constitutional one.[106] When documents are introduced as evidence or appended to pleadings, however, the First Amendment right to public access clearly attaches.[107]

B. Legislation and Court Rules

Since *Seattle Times* a number of jurisdictions have addressed, legislatively or through rule making, the public's interest in access to discovery documents.[108] For instance, Texas Rule of Civil Procedure 76(a) creates a presumption of openness for court records, including unfiled discovery that concerns "matters that have a probable adverse effect upon the general public health or safety, or the administration of public office, or the operation of government." A stringent showing is required before secrecy may be imposed, and a public hearing is required before a court may enter a

---

[103] *Id.* at 34–37.

[104] *Id.* at 37.

[105] *Id.* at 33.

[106] Public Citizen v. Liggett Group, Inc., 858 F.2d 775, 789 (1st Cir. 1988), *cert. denied*, 488 U.S. 1030 (1989); *In re* "Agent Orange" Prod. Liab. Litig., 821 F.2d 139, 145–46 (2d Cir.), *cert. denied*, 484 U.S. 953 (1987).

[107] Republic of Phil. v. Westinghouse Elec. Corp., 139 F.R.D. 50, 56–62 (D.N.J.), *motion for stay denied*, 949 F.2d 653 (3d Cir. 1991) (challenge to unsealing of documents unlikely to succeed on the merits).

[108] *See* SAN DIEGO COUNTY, CAL. SUPER. CT. R. DIV. II, GEN. CIV. LITIG. § 6.9 (1990); DEL. SUPER. CT. CIV. R. 5(g) (Michie 1991); DEL. CT. CH. R. 5(g) (Michie 1991); FLA. STAT. ANN. § 69.081 (West Supp. 1993) (Sunshine in Litigation Act prohibits court from entering any order with purpose or effect of concealing a public hazard; any agreement or contract with such pur-

confidentiality order or an order sealing documents. The motivation for this rule was explained by Texas Supreme Court Justice Lloyd Doggett, a proponent of the rule, and Texas Supreme Court Briefing Attorney Michael Mucchetti:

> Courts . . . flourish when bathed in the cleansing, edifying illumination of public inspection. Concealing information when its release would enhance government accountability or avert danger to health and safety sacrifices the public interest and jeopardizes confidence in the judicial system. Unfortunately, sealing orders, protective orders, and confidentiality agreements are increasingly employed to stifle public scrutiny.[109]

C. Privacy and Property Rights as a Bar to Public Disclosure

Manufacturers are now asserting a constitutional right to protective orders either barring discovery of trade secrets and other confidential information or severely curtailing disclosure. In addition to asserting a purported corporate right to privacy, manufacturers invoke the Fifth Amendment prohibition against the taking of private property without just compensation, which applies to the states through the Fourteenth Amendment. This position was briefed by drug manufacturer Eli Lilly & Co. and its amicus curiae, the Product Liability Advisory Council, in a recent mandamus proceeding before the Supreme Court of Texas. The court granted the writ of mandamus, allowing discovery but limiting its dissemination.[110] The court's one-page order did not address the constitutional issues raised.

The Product Liability Advisory Council describes itself as a nonprofit corporation of 92 manufacturers representing every major industry in the United States.[111] Its arguments as amicus curiae in *Eli Lilly & Co.* are supported by Professor Arthur Miller

---

pose or affect is void and unenforceable); GA. UNIFORM SUPER. CT. R. 21.2 (1991) (no order limiting access may be granted "except upon a finding that the harm otherwise resulting to the privacy of the person . . . clearly outweighs the public interest"); N.Y. COMP. CODES R. & REGS. tit. 22, § 216.1 (1991) (no sealing of court record, definition of which excludes documents not filed with court, absent showing of good cause and consideration of interests of the public as well as the parties); N.C. GEN. STAT. § 132 (Supp. 1991); TEX. GOV'T CODE ANN. § 22.010 (West Supp. 1993) (directing Texas Supreme Court to issue rules regarding the seal of court records); TEX. R. CIV. P. ANN. r. 76(a), 166b(5)(c) (West Supp. 1993) (court records presumed open to public; sealing prohibited except on stringent showing and after public hearing); VA. CODE ANN. § 8.01–420.01 (Michie 1992) (no discovery protective order in a personal injury or wrongful death action shall prohibit attorney from obtaining leave of court to share information with other attorney in similar action who agrees to be bound by order). *See generally* Marcus, *supra* note 96, at 463–67; Miller, *supra* note 14, at 441–45.

[109] Doggett & Mucchetti, *supra* note 96, at 644.

[110] Eli Lilly & Co. v. Marshall, No. D-1827 (Tex. Dec. 4, 1991).

[111] Brief of amici curiae in Eli Lilly & Co. v. Marshall, No. D-1827 (Mar. 5, 1992); *see also* Brief of amicus curiae Product Liability Advisory Council in Armentrout v. FMC Corp., No. 91SC312 (Colo. Feb. 18, 1992).

of Harvard University in his recent article defending the use of protective orders, based in part on constitutional privacy and property rights.[112] As Professor Miller acknowledged, his article was assisted by a research grant from the Product Liability Advisory Council Foundation.[113]

A critique of these arguments is beyond the scope of this book. However, claiming a right to privacy for corporations and attacking legitimate discovery as a *taking* for Fifth Amendment purposes requires a considerable stretch of those constitutional concepts beyond their currently recognized limits. Regardless of the merits of these novel new grounds for the same old protective order, an order that permits discovery but limits dissemination to litigants involved in similar cases does not compromise the interests that critics of "unfettered public disclosure" have addressed.[114]

The arguments that manufacturers make to justify a protective order in a defective product case are often pretenses and rarely (if ever) justify precluding cooperation among litigants in similar cases. Courts, scholars, and legislators have recognized that provision for information sharing accommodates plaintiffs' compelling needs and causes manufacturers little or no harm.

---

[112] Miller, *supra* note 14, at 463–77; *see also* Note, *Trade Secrets in Discovery: From First Amendment Disclosure to Fifth Amendment Protection*, 104 HARV. L. REV. 1330, 1336–45 (1991).

[113] Miller, *supra* note 14, at 428.

[114] *See* Miller, *supra* note 14. The court in one recent case specifically called attention to the pivotal distinction between information sharing and the general publication of information. *See* Kraszewski v. State Farm Gen. Ins. Co., 139 F.R.D. 156, 160 (N.D. Cal. 1991).

CHAPTER NINE

TURNING THE TABLES ON STONEWALLERS[1]

Litigators are used to dealing with bad facts. Facts adverse to the client's position are part of what makes litigating difficult, but they are even more a part of what keeps the litigator's task interesting. If all our cases were "no contest" winners on the facts, they could be litigated and won by any marginally competent attorney. Any litigator's first objective when dealing with bad facts is to try to minimize their negative impact; however, creative litigators often go beyond that basic and obvious function and attempt to find a silver lining that will allow them to use a bad fact to make some point that is actually helpful to their client's case.

This approach applies not only to bad facts found in the evidence but can also be used to deal with some of the bad facts of life in litigation. Stonewalling by manufacturers is one such fact of life, one that is unlikely to go away given the tremendous incentives for manufacturers to evade discovery through one means or another.[2] This harsh reality should be dealt with in the same way as other case negatives. First, it must be uncovered. Second, its negative impact must be mitigated. Third, the litigator must look for ways to turn stonewalling to the plaintiff's advantage by making the manufacturer bear the costs of its discovery abuse.

The purpose of this chapter is to identify means by which discovery procedures themselves can be used to uncover stonewalling, and to recommend ways to make the stonewaller bear the consequences of its misconduct—tactics that may also help to deter future stonewalling.

I. USING DISCOVERY TO FLUSH OUT EVIDENCE DESTRUCTION

Like a detective, plaintiff's counsel must follow every lead. Counsel's discovery plan should include a strategy for uncovering both deliberate and inadvertent suppression or destruction of evidence. Clearly the question of whether the manufacturer has, in fact, suppressed relevant documents—including inquiry concerning the

---

[1] This chapter includes some material originally published in Richard L. Whitworth & James L. Gilbert, *Punishing Evidence Destruction*, TRIAL, Nov. 1992, at 66.

[2] See generally chapter 4.

company's document retention program—is a legitimate topic of discovery by the plaintiff.[3]

A. Interrogatories and Requests for Production

Proof that evidence exists or once existed must be secured at the earliest possible stage in the lawsuit. If asked the right questions, an opponent may disclose the existence of a document before realizing its importance. This is not likely to happen, of course, where a corporate defendant has been sued many times for the same product defect. But even this type of defendant may be somewhat more vulnerable to harmful disclosure early in the lawsuit. The postfiling search for evidence[4] should include well-planned interrogatories and requests for production of documents. At a minimum, this discovery should seek the following:

Description of corporate activities: This information must include each activity relevant to the product, such as research, design, testing, manufacturing, and marketing for all material time periods.

Description of corporate procedures: This information should give the plaintiff an understanding of at least the basic types of documents that the corporation should have generated for each activity, together with information about document distribution.

Identification of people with responsibility: This information must include the persons with overall responsibility for each activity and procedure. These people should be knowledgeable about the specific types of documents generated for each activity, the path of document distribution, and the policies for document retention as written and as actually practiced. Former employees are often an excellent source of information. These people may sometimes be identified and located through depositions of current employees or by securing employee directories, corporate organizational charts, and internal memoranda.

Identification of documents: This information should include documents generated for each relevant activity as well as the minutes of meetings of the board of directors or other groups. These minutes may refer to studies, tests, reports, or other docu-

---

[3] *See* Anderson v. Cryovac, Inc., 862 F.2d 910, 930 (1st Cir. 1988); Craig v. A.H. Robins Co., 790 F.2d 1, 3 (1st Cir. 1986); Telectron, Inc. v. Overhead Door Corp., 116 F.R.D. 107, 118–26 (S.D. Fla. 1987); Alexander v. National Farmers' Org., 614 F. Supp. 745, 755 (W.D. Mo. 1985); Wm. T. Thompson Co. v. General Nutrition Corp., 593 F. Supp. 1443, 1446, 1454 (C.D. Cal. 1984); Carlucci v. Piper Aircraft Corp., 102 F.R.D. 472, 481–82 (S.D. Fla. 1984), *aff'd in part, rev'd in part*, 775 F.2d 1440 (11th Cir. 1985); *In re* "Agent Orange" Prod. Liab. Litig., 98 F.R.D. 558, 559–60 (E.D.N.Y. 1983); Penthouse Int'l, Ltd. v. Playboy Enters., 86 F.R.D. 396, 398–99, 403 (S.D.N.Y. 1980), *aff'd*, 663 F.2d 371 (2d Cir. 1981).

[4] It is assumed that an appropriate prefiling investigation and search for evidence have been completed, including contacting sources like the ATLA Exchange, the Attorneys Information Exchange Group (AIEG) and any appropriate litigation support groups. This type of information sharing is encouraged by the courts. *See* Ward v. Ford Motor Co., 93 F.R.D. 579 (D. Colo. 1982) (automobile products case); Waelde v. Merck, Sharp & Dohme, 94 F.R.D. 27, 30 (E.D. Mich. 1981) (drug products case).

ments which later may be destroyed or withheld.

When requesting documents, insist on seeing the originals. With a photocopy, counsel may be unable to detect erasures, white-outs, differences in ink colors, write-overs or strikeovers, and other alterations. Documents obtained from sources such as other plaintiffs' attorneys, plaintiffs' document repositories, court files, government agencies, and consumer safety groups should be compared with documents produced by the defendant. This comparison may reveal that the defendant has withheld or altered documents.

Customer complaints, claims, and lawsuits over similar incidents: This information will yield names of other plaintiffs' attorneys handling similar cases. It may take a court order compelling discovery to convince the defendant that the request for this "similar incident" information is properly worded and that the information sought is relevant and not privileged.

Corporate organizational charts: These documents will provide several types of useful information: the chain of command; relationships among the various departments, divisions, and groups; possible paths of document distribution; and (in some cases) the names of people who may be knowledgeable about documents. Many defendants, in a magnificent display of zealous stonewalling, will oppose production of their organizational charts. Their objections may include lack of relevance, confidentiality, burdensomeness, overbreadth, and many other imaginative but baseless claims. When these objections fail, the corporation may assert that after diligent search, it has found that organizational charts for relevant periods no longer exist.

Document retention plans: These documents provide information as to types of documents generated, retention periods, statements of policy, and provisions for exceptions and suspension.

Counsel should scrutinize document retention plans carefully for possible inconsistencies—for example, shorter retention periods for important documents than for insignificant documents. In a 1988 case involving document destruction, the Eighth Circuit ruled that a corporation cannot destroy documents that it knows (or should know) may become material at some future point, expecting to be shielded by a document retention policy:[5] "[W]here a document retention policy is instituted in order to limit damaging evidence available to potential plaintiffs, it may be proper to give an [adverse inference] instruction."[6]

Be sure to obtain all documents associated with the retention policy, including forms and charts, as well as all documents modifying, suspending, or interpreting the plan. Finally, obtain records of documents destroyed, which may reveal telling examples of deviation from the plan.

Responses to initial interrogatories and requests for production must be carefully reviewed. This review may reveal an obvious gap in the documents produced, based on the activities and procedures that the corporation has acknowledged having conducted.

---

[5] Lewy v. Remington Arms Co., 836 F.2d 1104, 1112 (8th Cir. 1988); see also chapter 7, section II.

[6] 836 F.2d at 1112.

If counsel has not already done so, it is important at this time to obtain from any other available sources the following documents: correspondence between the defendant and any relevant government agency, together with submissions and reports to the agency; the defendant's written responses to requests for production and interrogatories in similar litigation; and transcripts of pertinent depositions of the defendant's officers, employees, and experts in similar litigation. These documents may refer to other important documents that the defendant has failed to produce.

B. Depositions

Counsel should notice corporate depositions as soon as possible. The discovery rules require corporations and certain other entities to designate people to testify "as to matters known or reasonably available" to them that are set forth with "reasonable particularity" in the deposition notice.[7]

The notice for the initial round of depositions should require the corporation to designate people to testify on the subjects of the written discovery, including corporate organization; types and names of documents generated; document retention policies; documents destroyed; and customer complaints, claims, and lawsuits relating to similar incidents.

Early depositions may disclose the existence of documents that the corporation will later decide to destroy;[8] fortunately, not all corporate employees are willing to cover up improper document destruction.[9]

All employee witnesses should be asked to identify the type of documents generated by their departments and to describe how those documents are distributed to other employees and departments. Where are the documents kept? How are they filed or indexed? What is the witness's understanding of how the document retention policy is supposed to work and how it actually works? Since the date that written discovery was served, has anyone in the corporation asked the witness if he or she knows of the existence or whereabouts of documents or other information on any subject? A response to the last question should give some indication of how diligently the corporation is looking for information necessary to respond to the written discovery.

C. Finding Proof of Suppression or Spoliation

Once the first round of discovery is complete, what can be done if it appears that a document has been withheld, lost, destroyed, or altered? As a starting point, counsel should locate other plaintiffs' counsel or any other person who has actually seen the unaltered document and obtain an affidavit confirming this fact, together with the

---

[7] FED. R. CIV. P. 30(b)(6).

[8] *See, e.g.,* Penthouse Int'l, Ltd. v. Playboy Enters., 86 F.R.D. 396, 398–99 (S.D.N.Y. 1980), *aff'd,* 663 F.2d 371 (2d Cir. 1981).

[9] *Cf.* Telectron v. Overhead Door Corp., 116 F.R.D. 107, 118–26 (S.D. Fla. 1987) (finding corporate counsel ordered immediate destruction of documents on day complaint and request for production were served).

affiant's best recollection of the content of the document. If counsel has managed to obtain a copy of an internal document from another source that the defendant cannot or will not produce (or produces with alterations), immediate steps should be taken to authenticate the copy. For example, an affidavit from the attorney who obtained the document from the defendant in another case should be secured. At this point, depending on the rules of evidence and procedure in counsel's jurisdiction, one strategy would be simply to take no immediate action and instead confront the defendant with the document for the first time at trial. An alternative strategy would be to file an appropriate motion or action with the court.

II. EMBRACING YOUR OPPONENT'S DISCOVERY MISCONDUCT

Of course, we as consumers would all be better off if stonewalling by manufacturers were to disappear from the face of the earth, because stonewalling results in massive injustices. Where detected, however, stonewalling also presents some opportunities. These should not be viewed as opportunities to take unfair advantage of a situation; rather, they are merely opportunities to make the manufacturer bear the costs of its own improper conduct.

The most basic way to shift the costs of an opponent's discovery misconduct is to seek and obtain sanctions that are more advantageous to the plaintiff's case than the withheld evidence would have been. For example, an adverse inference instruction to the jury may, in some instances, be more effective than the unavailable document would have been in attempting to prove a point. Courts may be inclined or convinced to take other measures designed to more than compensate for the adverse impact of stonewalling when it is discovered.

Indeed, to achieve the intended punitive and deterrent effects of sanctions, courts should impose a sanction greater than that calculated to counter the minimal provable prejudice created by the misconduct. After all, the party being sanctioned should not be entitled to the benefit of the doubt as to what the unavailable evidence would have shown. Moreover, given the difficulty of detecting stonewalling, sanctions must do more than simply negate the adverse impact of a particular instance of stonewalling if the sanctions are to serve as a deterrent.[10] The court should be encouraged to impose stringent sanctions such as striking segments of pleadings, precluding certain evidence, precluding evidence supporting particular defenses, or even entering default—even when the plaintiff cannot prove that such a sanction is minimally necessary to counter the effects of the stonewalling.

Plaintiff's counsel should also examine whether the stonewalling conduct gives rise to a separate cause of action, such as a breach of contract or tort action for spoliation of evidence.[11]

---

[10] Charles R. Nesson, *Incentives to Spoliate Evidence in Civil Litigation: The Need for Vigorous Judicial Action*, 13 CARDOZO L. REV. 793 (1991).

[11] See chapter 7, section III; *see also* Campbell v. Amerada Hess Corp., No. H87-0057(R) (S.D. Miss. May 24, 1988) and No. 1-88-2310 (Forrest County, Miss. Cir. Ct. May 24, 1988), *discussed in* 31 ATLA L. REP. 456 (1988) (to support claims for compensatory and punitive damages for negligence and intentional misconduct resulting in oil pipeline worker's injury, action alleged conspiracy to conceal facts proving liability, false discovery response filing, and perjured testimony).

Discovery misconduct can also provide an opportunity to educate the judge about some aspect of the case or the defendant's character or its assertions in the litigation. A protective order hearing or a hearing on the discoverability of other incidents involving similar products can provide an opportunity to familiarize the judge with the relevant technology, which will be helpful to the court both in understanding the immediate dispute and in presiding over the trial.

A hearing can also be used to give the judge advance warning of an anticipated defense tactic. In a recent case, for example, two of the authors represented an individual injured in a gasoline truck explosion that resulted from the design of the trailer tank's vapor recovery system. The defendants included one of the world's largest oil companies, which had provided design specifications for the truck. In discovery it became clear that the oil company intended to minimize the extent of its involvement in the truck's design: It denied virtually all knowledge of vapor recovery systems and claimed that it could not find in its records information regarding the relevant technology. In support of a motion to compel discovery, the plaintiff submitted a lengthy list identifying the dozens of interrogatories, requests for production, and admission requests to which the oil company had responded "don't know," "can't find," or both. The judge, apparently as skeptical as we were of the truth of these answers, gave the oil company 24 hours to supplement its responses, after which a sanctions request would be entertained if we still believed the response to be lacking. Volumes of additional information were produced within days. More importantly, the judge's comments made clear that the court would be wary of any claims of ignorance by this defendant at trial. The case was resolved shortly after the discovery hearing.

Attempts at stonewalling can also provide opportunities to educate the jury. For example, automakers routinely seek to prevent discovery of crash tests and other safety data, and when required to produce such information, they seek protective orders. In support of a motion for a protective order, they present affidavits asserting the proprietary and confidential nature of safety data. They also present documentation of procedures in place to keep that information out of the public domain. At trial they invariably argue that the plaintiff fully knew the dangers involved in driving the vehicle, yet assumed that risk. It is certainly fair for plaintiff's counsel to present evidence of the lengths to which the automaker has gone to keep hazard information a secret: The jury can be told that the defendant has data about the safety characteristics and hazards of its product that it intentionally keeps from the public, and that the plaintiff could not possibly have known about prior to the accident.

Where stonewalling suggests dishonesty, proof of the dishonesty can be used to undermine the credibility of the stonewaller. This was done in the trial of an antitrust action against Eastman Kodak Company.[12] Kodak's defense relied heavily on its expert economist's testimony. During cross-examination, the economist mentioned documents he had prepared that had never been turned over to the plaintiff during

---

[12] Berkey Photo, Inc. v. Eastman Kodak Co., 457 F. Supp. 404 (S.D.N.Y. 1978), *aff'd in part, rev'd in part,* 603 F.2d 263 (2d Cir. 1979), *cert. denied,* 444 U.S. 1093 (1980).

discovery despite proper requests. Kodak's lead attorney revealed that another member of the litigation team had these documents in his closet. The judge ruled that the plaintiff could use the fact of the suppression of these documents to impeach the economist's testimony. Even though the information in the withheld documents was of limited value, the jury apparently reacted strongly to the revelation, awarding the plaintiff $37 million, to be trebled under the antitrust laws. Although the amount of damages was reduced by the trial court and reversed in part by the appellate court, this case certainly illustrates the potentially dramatic impact a party's unfair dealings during discovery can have on a jury.[13]

Frequently, a little mystery is better than the bare facts. If the evidence is alleged by the defendant to have disappeared under bizarre circumstances that are too much for you to believe, chances are they will also be difficult for the jury to believe. Even if the loss or unavailability of a particular piece of evidence does not point the jury to any particular conclusion, it may at least lead jurors to view skeptically the defendant's version of events.

Videotape is a wonderful tool for capturing, memorializing, and turning the tables on stonewalling conduct. The harsh realism of video can convey information lost in a cold transcript. Thus, important witness statements and depositions should be videotaped. The mere presence of the camera may deter misconduct in the deposition. Video excerpts of objections made by defense counsel to cue the witness can make a strong impression on the judge at a discovery hearing.

Jurors are generally perceptive and good judges of character. When shown videotape of a deposition or excerpts from an interrogatory in which the defendant's officials, including its chief of safety engineering, assert that they do not know what the plaintiff means by the terms "safety" or "test," jurors will recognize exactly what the plaintiff's counsel recognizes: that this defendant has something to hide. Other characteristics of witnesses, such as arrogance, disdain, dishonesty, embarrassment, or shame, may escape the written transcript but are captured vividly on videotape.

Experienced litigators have all encountered the witness who knows nothing during a deposition but has a remarkable recovery of memory at trial. The witness who was obstinate and evasive when the plaintiff was attempting to learn the facts in discovery becomes amiable and forthcoming when presented to the jury as a defense witness. Where this occurs, video excerpts of the witness's deposition provide excellent impeachment evidence. Video not only casts doubt directly on the credibility of a newly remembered response, it also informs the jury of this witness's willingness to change his or her story and "adapt" the facts to the purpose at hand.

There is one important prerequisite to the use of any of these tactics for making the defendant bear the consequences of its misconduct—the plaintiff's own discovery conduct must be beyond reproach. The video excerpt of the obstinate deposition witness will not be persuasive when defense counsel counters with excerpts of harass-

---

[13] Walter Kiechel III, *The Strange Case of Kodak's Lawyers*, FORTUNE, May 8, 1978, at 188; Nesson, *supra* note 10, at 797.

ment or unfair questions by the plaintiff's counsel. Allegations of stonewalling by a plaintiff who has not been forthcoming with disclosures will not be well received either. Nor will plaintiff's complaints be heard sympathetically when the plaintiff's overly broad request is met with an overly narrow response.[14]

Techniques for turning the tables on stonewallers share two characteristics. First, they seek to take the impact of the misconduct beyond the confines of the private interactions between plaintiff and defendant and bring it to the attention of the judge and jury. While discovery is meant to be conducted largely between the parties without court intervention, it is impossible to shift the consequences of stonewalling without first moving the conflict from a private to a broader forum. The second characteristic of table-turning techniques is that they seek merely to impose on the stonewaller the natural and logical consequences of its own behavior. If the defendant seeks to be duplicitous in discovery, let its duplicitous character be known to the trier of fact. If its counsel's goal is obfuscation, let the judge know that counsel cannot be relied on to bring clarity to the facts. If the manufacturer values secrecy over disclosure, let its subsequent claims of openness be viewed with skepticism.

While this analogy may be a bit of a stretch, it is interesting to observe that for the past two decades, much of the literature on child-rearing has directed parents to modify children's behavior by exposing them to the natural consequences of their actions[15] rather than simply punishing them. Perhaps the approach that has helped shape the behavior of a new generation can help modify the behavior of litigators and parties who believe the consequences of their cheating in discovery will be borne solely by their opponents.

---

[14] For discussion of the plaintiff's dilemma when deciding how specifically or generally to word discovery requests, see chapter 5, section III.

[15] *See, e.g.*, RUDOLF DREIKURS, CHILDREN: THE CHALLENGE 76–85 (1964).

CHAPTER TEN

SANCTIONS

I. PURPOSES OF SANCTIONS

Courts have long exercised their inherent power to enforce "submission to their lawful mandates."[1] This inherent authority has been supplemented with statutes and rules authorizing imposition of sanctions. Whatever the source of authority, sanctions imposed for improper discovery conduct address some or all of the same objectives. The following purposes have been identified, ranging from narrow, case-specific objectives to more general, institutional goals.

Compelling discovery: The most basic purpose of a discovery sanction is to compel a particular action in a particular case.[2] As stated in one treatise, "[w]ithout adequate sanctions the procedure for discovery would be ineffectual."[3] Sanctions imposed for this purpose might take the form of coercive contempt, daily monetary penalties imposed pursuant to rule 37 for failure to comply with a court order, or contingent future sanctions for failure to meet deadlines established pursuant to a rule 26(f) discovery conference.

Punishment: Sanctions may properly be used for punishing or exacting retribution for unacceptable litigation behavior.[4]

Compensation: Sanctions can serve the purpose of compensating the court and

---

[1] Chambers v. NASCO, Inc. 111 S. Ct. 2123, 2132, *reh'g denied*, 112 S. Ct. 12 (1991).

[2] *Id.* at 2132–33; Carlucci v. Piper Aircraft Corp., 775 F.2d 1440, 1453 (11th Cir. 1985); Southern Pac. Transp. Co. v. Evans, 590 S.W.2d 515, 518–19 (Tex. Civ. App. 1979), *cert. denied*, 449 U.S. 994 (1980); *see* Maurice Rosenberg, *Sanctions to Effectuate Pretrial Discovery*, 58 COLUM. L. REV. 480, 482 (1958) ("In the federal system, the main objective of a set of rules punishing evasion of pretrial discovery procedures is to promote free and full disclosure of relevant, non-privileged information and evidence.").

[3] 8 CHARLES ALAN WRIGHT & ARTHUR R. MILLER, FEDERAL PRACTICE AND PROCEDURE § 2281, at 753 (1970 & Supp. 1992).

[4] National Hockey League v. Metropolitan Hockey Club, Inc., 427 U.S. 639, 642–43, *reh'g denied*, 429 U.S. 874 (1976); Carlucci v. Piper Aircraft Corp., 775 F.2d 1440, 1453 (11th Cir. 1985).

other parties for additional expense caused by one party's abusive conduct.[5] This compensatory purpose has not been viewed as contrary to the so-called American Rule, which prohibits fee-shifting based on the merits. Rather, this sanction has been characterized as falling within an exception to the rule for either the willful disobedience of a court order or conduct undertaken "in bad faith, vexatiously, wantonly, or for oppressive reasons."[6]

Thus, where appropriately applied, a cost-shifting sanction is not used to compensate for a good-faith claim that does not prevail. Unfortunately, the compensatory purpose of sanctions can be improperly used by courts to negate the American Rule, especially when sanctions are imposed under rule 11 for claims determined to be unfounded. Where actual misconduct is not involved, or where the line between bringing a claim that does not succeed on the merits and bringing a frivolous claim is unclear, the use of sanctions can have an adverse impact on the justice system by discouraging legitimate claims, including litigation that pushes the frontiers of current jurisprudence.[7] The 1993 amendments to rule 11 mitigate this danger.[8]

Vindication of judicial authority: Regardless of whether disobedience to the court's mandate results in any practical prejudice, a sanction may be appropriate to vindicate and reassert the court's authority.[9]

Special deterrence: Sanctions are frequently used by trial courts for the purpose of deterring further misconduct by the same party in the same case.

General deterrence: Another important purpose of sanctions is to deter others from engaging in similar misconduct.[10] This function was specifically endorsed by the U.S. Supreme Court in *National Hockey League v. Metropolitan Hockey Club, Inc.*[11]

II. SANCTION AUTHORITIES

Discovery sanctions are specifically authorized by rule 16(f) (discovery confer-

---

[5] 775 F.2d at 1453.

[6] Chambers v. NASCO, Inc., 111 S. Ct. 2123, 2133, *reh'g denied*, 112 S. Ct. 12 (1991).

[7] *See, e.g.*, Arthur B. LaFrance, *Federal Rule 11 and Public Interest Litigation*, 22 VAL. U. L. REV. 331, 333–34 (1988); Melissa L. Nelken, *Sanctions Under Amended Federal Rule 11 — Some "Chilling" Problems in the Struggle Between Compensation and Punishment*, 74 GEO. L.J. 1313 (1986). The dangers of rule 11 are discussed briefly in chapter 3, section I.E.

[8] *See* FED. R. CIV. P. 11 1993 advisory committee's note, Amendments to the Federal Rules of Civil Procedure and Forms, approved by the United States Supreme Court (Apr. 22, 1993), *reprinted in* 146 F.R.D. 401 (1993) [hereinafter 1993 Amendments].

[9] 111 S. Ct., at 2132–33.

[10] Carlucci v. Piper Aircraft Corp., 775 F.2d 1440, 1453 (11th Cir. 1985). *See generally* Judith L. Maute, *Sporting Theory of Justice: Taming Adversary Zeal with a Logical Sanctions Doctrine*, 20 CONN. L. REV. 7 (1987); Note, *The Emerging Deterrence Orientation in the Imposition of Discovery Sanctions*, 91 HARV. L. REV. 1033 (1978).

[11] 427 U.S. 639, 643, *reh'g denied*, 429 U.S. 874 (1976); *see also* Southern Pac. Transp. Co. v. Evans, 590 S.W.2d 515, 518–19 (Tex. Civ. App. 1979), *cert. denied*, 449 U.S. 994 (1980).

ences and ensuing orders), rule 26(g) (abuses relating to signed discovery papers), rule 30(d)(2) (obstruction of deposition), and rule 37 (violation of discovery orders and other specified abuses).[12] The courts may also call on various other bases of authority for imposing sanctions, including statutory authority to sanction certain abusive litigation tactics and the court's inherent authority over proceedings.[13]

A. Fed. R. Civ. P. 37

Rule 37 is the only provision in the federal rules devoted expressly to combating stonewalling. Most of the case law addressing stonewalling revolves around rule 37 motions to compel discovery or rule 37 orders imposing sanctions. Rule 37 is last in order of the discovery rules, but perhaps first in importance, as it establishes mechanisms by which the other rules can be made effective.[14] As summarized in the advisory committee's note accompanying the extensive 1970 amendments strengthening this provision, "Rule 37 provides generally for sanctions against parties or persons unjustifiably resisting discovery." The rule permits immediate sanctions for failure to provide certain types of discovery and allows imposition of sanctions for any conduct contrary to a discovery order. The rule's nonexclusive list of permissible sanctions ranges from awards of costs and fees to the so-called death penalty sanctions of dismissal or default.

1. Sanctionable Conduct

Rule 37 authorizes discretionary sanctions for four types of discovery misconduct:

(1) failure to comply with a discovery order (rule 37(b));

(2) unwarranted failure to admit in response to a rule 36 request for admission (rule 37(c));

(3) failure of a party to attend its own deposition, to answer interrogatories, or to respond to a request for inspection (rule 37(d)); and

(4) failure to participate in the framing of a rule 26(f) discovery plan (rule 37(g)).

The specific conduct sanctionable under the provisions of rule 37, as applied by the courts, is discussed in greater detail below.

---

[12] FED. R. CIV. P. 11 has also been used to sanction discovery abuse.

[13] *See generally* AMERICAN BAR ASSOCIATION SECTION OF LITIGATION, SANCTIONS: RULE 11 & OTHER POWERS (Melissa L. Nelken ed., 3d ed. 1992); DISCOVERY PROCEEDINGS IN FEDERAL COURT (Shepard's eds., 2d ed. 1991 & Supp. 1992); GREGORY P. JOSEPH, SANCTIONS: THE FEDERAL LAW OF LITIGATION ABUSE (1989 & Supp. 1991). Sanction authorities and their applicability are summarized in the table at appendix 3.

[14] *See* Fisher v. Marubeni Cotton Corp., 526 F.2d 1338 (8th Cir. 1985) (citing 8 WRIGHT & MILLER, *supra* note 3, § 2281, at 753.

2. Sanctionable Entity

Rule 37 provides express authority for the court to impose sanctions on the party, the attorney, or both.

3. Authorized Sanctions

The rule provides for a wide range of discretionary sanctions, depending on the type of discovery misconduct at issue.[15]

The court has broad discretion under rule 37 to "make such orders . . . as are just."[16] Permissible sanctions include, but are not limited to, the following:

> (A) An order that the matters regarding which the order was made or any other designated facts shall be taken to be established for the purposes of the action in accordance with the claim of the party obtaining the order;
>
> (B) An order refusing to allow the disobedient party to support or oppose designated claims or defenses, or prohibiting that party from introducing designated matters in evidence;
>
> (C) An order striking out pleadings or parts thereof, or staying further proceedings until the order is obeyed, or dismissing the action or proceeding or any part thereof, or rendering a judgment by default against the disobedient party;
>
> (D) In lieu of any of the foregoing orders or in addition thereto, an order treating as a contempt of court the failure to obey any orders except an order to submit to a physical or mental examination. . . .

Rule 37 also contains several cost- and fee-shifting provisions.

Some courts have awarded interest on monetary sanctions,[17] while others have held that prejudgment interest is not authorized by rule 37.[18]

4. Procedures

Some misconduct is immediately sanctionable under rule 37, such as a party's failure to attend its own deposition, failure to serve answers to interrogatories or respond to requests for inspection, or failure to participate in framing a discovery plan. For other types of stonewalling, seeking sanctions includes a two-step procedure. When faced with an inadequate response, the party seeking discovery must first move pursuant to rule 37(a) for an order compelling discovery: It is the violation of a discovery *order* that is sanctionable under rule 37(b). Note that failure to obey a dis-

---

[15] Specific sanctions are discussed in section III, *infra*.

[16] FED. R. CIV. P. 37(b)(2); *see, e.g.*, National Hockey League v. Metropolitan Hockey Club, 427 U.S. 639, 642–43, *reh'g denied*, 429 U.S. 874 (1976); Perkinson v. Gilbert/Robinson, Inc., 821 F.2d 686, 689–90 (D.C. Cir. 1987); Gates v. United States, 752 F.2d 516, 517 (10th Cir. 1985); Fonseca v. Regan, 734 F.2d 944, 947–48 (2d Cir.), *cert. denied*, 469 U.S. 882 (1984); Tamari v. Bache & Co. (Leb.), S.A.L., 729 F.2d 469, 472 (7th Cir. 1984). *But see* Pesaplastic, C.A. v. Cincinnati Milacron Co., 799 F.2d 1510, 1519 (11th Cir. 1986) (discretion not unbridled).

[17] *See* Wm. T. Thompson Co. v. General Nutrition Corp., 104 F.R.D. 119, 123 (C.D. Cal. 1985).

[18] Remington Prods., Inc. v. North Am. Philips Corp., 763 F. Supp. 683, 686 (D. Conn. 1991).

covery order entered pursuant to rule 26(f) (discovery conference) is sanctionable under rule 37(b) without the need for a motion to compel.

Some discovery responses have been considered so inadequate as to be treated as no response at all, subjecting the party to sanctions without the need for a motion and order compelling discovery. Thus, while the "failure to appear" requirement has generally been strictly construed to apply only where the deponent "literally fails to show up for a deposition,"[19] one court has imposed rule 37(d) sanctions against defense counsel where deponents without knowledge of the subject matter noticed were produced for a rule 30(b)(6) deposition.[20] Similarly, while sanctions for the failure to answer or object to interrogatories and the failure to respond to a production or inspection request are sometimes held to apply only to a total failure to respond rather than an inadequate response,[21] evasive, false, or misleading responses have sometimes resulted in sanctions without the need for an order compelling discovery.[22]

While a party is entitled to some notice and opportunity for hearing on the record before sanctions are imposed,[23] notice and an opportunity for written briefing may suffice. A courtroom hearing is generally not required where there is no material, factual dispute, particularly where briefing has been permitted.[24] Some appellate courts have stated that the trial court should articulate its reasons for imposing a particular sanction in sufficient detail to permit appellate review.[25] If the sanction is in the nature of criminal contempt, additional procedures, including notice and hearing, may be required.[26] Severe sanctions such as default and dismissal carry elevated due process requirements.[27]

---

[19] *See* Salahuddin v. Harris, 782 F.2d 1127, 1131 (2d Cir. 1986).

[20] Thomas v. Hoffman-LaRoche, Inc., 126 F.R.D. 522, 525 (N.D. Miss. 1989); *cf.* Plevy v. Scully, 89 F.R.D. 665 (W.D.N.Y. 1981).

[21] Minnesota Mining & Mfg. Co. v. Eco Chem, Inc., 757 F.2d 1256, 1260 (Fed. Cir. 1985); Laclede Gas Co. v. G.W. Warnecke Corp., 604 F.2d 561, 565 (8th Cir. 1979); Fox v. Studebaker-Worthington, Inc., 516 F.2d 989, 995 (8th Cir. 1975).

[22] EEOC v. Sears, Roebuck & Co., 114 F.R.D. 615, 626 (N.D. Ill. 1987), *further proceedings*, 138 F.R.D. 523 (N.D. Ill. 1991); Fautek v. Montgomery Ward & Co., 96 F.R.D. 141, 145 n.5 (N.D. Ill. 1982); *cf.* Badalamenti v. Dunham's, Inc., 896 F.2d 1359 (Fed. Cir.), *cert. denied*, 498 U.S. 851 (1990).

[23] Roadway Express, Inc. v. Piper, 447 U.S. 752 (1980); Pesaplastic, C.A. v. Cincinnati Milacron Co., 799 F.2d 1510, 1522 (11th Cir. 1986).

[24] *See, e.g.,* Thomas E. Hoar, Inc. v. Sara Lee Corp., 882 F.2d 682, 688 (2d Cir. 1989), *aff'd*, 900 F.2d 522 (2d Cir. 1990); Kraszewski v. State Farm Gen. Ins. Co., 130 F.R.D. 111, 114–15 (N.D. Cal. 1984). *See generally* DISCOVERY PROCEEDINGS IN FEDERAL COURT, *supra* note 13, § 12.11.

[25] *See* Black Ass'n v. City of New Orleans, 911 F.2d 1063, 1066 (5th Cir. 1990); Insurance Benefit Adm'rs, Inc. v. Martin, 871 F.2d 1354, 1361–63 (7th Cir. 1989).

[26] *See* FED. R. CRIM. P. 42(b); section III.G, *infra*.

[27] Due process is discussed in section III.F, *infra*.

B. Fed. R. Civ. P. 26(g)

Rule 26(g) creates an accountability requirement applicable to discovery papers. The requirement is similar to that of the more frequently utilized rule 11, except that rule 26(g) applies specifically to discovery materials.

1. Sanctionable Conduct

The 1983 addition of rule 26(g) was *potentially* the most far-reaching of the amendments directed toward curbing discovery abuse. The rule "imposes an affirmative duty to engage in pretrial discovery in a responsible manner."[28] It imposes a signature and certification requirement paralleling that of rule 11.[29] Whereas rule 11 governs pleadings and motions, including motions relating to discovery, rule 26(g) applies to discovery requests, responses, and objections, as well as automatic disclosures made pursuant to the 1993 amendments to rule 26. The Advisory Committee on Civil Rules recently observed that the rule 11 pleadings provision has been used by the courts much more frequently than the rule 26(g) discovery provision.[30] One commentator, however, believes rule 26(g) is a "litigation explosion waiting to be triggered."[31]

Rule 26(g) requires that every discovery request, response, or objection be signed by an attorney, or if a party is not represented, by the party. The signature constitutes certification that the signer has read the document and that, "to the best of the signer's knowledge, information, and belief, formed after a reasonable inquiry," the document is

> (1) consistent with these rules and warranted by existing law or a good faith argument for the extension, modification, or reversal of existing law;
> (2) not interposed for any improper purpose, such as to harass or to cause unnecessary delay or needless increase in the cost of litigation; and
> (3) not unreasonable or unduly burdensome or expensive, given the needs of the case, the discovery already had in the case, the amount in controversy, and the importance of the issues at stake in the litigation.[32]

Disclosures made pursuant to 26(a)(1) (initial disclosures) and 26(a)(3) (pretrial disclosures) must also be signed by the attorney or unrepresented party, certifying that "to the best of the signer's knowledge, information, and belief, formed after a reasonable inquiry, the disclosure is complete and correct as of the time it is made."[33]

Sanctions are authorized if certification is made in violation of the rule without

---

[28] *See* FED. R. CIV. P. 26(g) 1983 advisory committee's note.

[29] *See* Apex Oil Co. v. Belcher Co., 855 F.2d 1009, 1015 (2d Cir. 1988) (finding rule 11 case precedent persuasive in interpreting rule 26(g)).

[30] Judicial Conference of the United States Advisory Committee on the Civil Rules, *Call for Written Comments on Rule 11 of the Federal Rules of Civil Procedure and Related Rules, as Amended in 1983*, 131 F.R.D. 344, 345 (1990).

[31] JOSEPH, *supra* note 13, § 40, at 467.

[32] FED. R. CIV. P. 26(g)(2).

[33] FED. R. CIV. P. 26(g)(1).

substantial justification.[34] The only penalty provided in the rule for failure to sign a document is that the filing will be stricken unless it is signed promptly after the omission is called to the attention of the party, and a party is not obligated to take any action with respect to the filing until it is signed.[35] One court, however, after finding that a discovery response filed without signature was filed for improper purposes and would have justified rule 26(g) sanctions if signed, used its inherent authority to impose sanctions.[36]

The rule

> does not require the signing attorney to certify the truthfulness of the client's factual responses to a discovery request. Rather, the signature certifies that the lawyer has made a reasonable effort to assure that the client has provided all the information and documents available to him that are responsive to the discovery demand.[37]

Gregory P. Joseph, in his book, *Sanctions: The Federal Law of Litigation Abuse*, identifies the following conduct found by courts to constitute "inadequate or unreasonable inquiry into the factual basis of discovery papers":[38]

- failing to produce responsive documents,[39]
- responding wrongly to a document request,[40]
- failing to know the location of responsive documents,[41]
- answering an interrogatory incorrectly,[42]
- furnishing incomplete or evasive answers to interrogatories,[43]
- providing nonsensical answers to interrogatories,[44] and

---

[34] FED. R. CIV. P. 26(g)(3); *see, e.g.*, National Ass'n of Radiation Survivors v. Turnage, 115 F.R.D. 543, 555–56 (N.D. Cal. 1987); Itel Containers Int'l Corp. v. Puerto Rico Marine Management, Inc., 108 F.R.D. 96, 102–03 (D.N.J. 1985).

[35] FED. R. CIV. P. 26(g)(2).

[36] Royalty Petroleum Co. v. Arkla, Inc., 129 F.R.D. 674 (W.D. Okla. 1990). The court's inherent authority to impose sanctions is discussed in section II.G, *infra*.

[37] *See* FED. R. CIV. P. 26(g) 1983 advisory committee's note.

[38] JOSEPH, *supra* note 13, § 42(B)(1), at 485–86, Supp. at 159.

[39] National Ass'n of Radiation Survivors v. Turnage, 115 F.R.D. 543, 554 (N.D. Cal. 1987).

[40] Fretz v. Keltner, 109 F.R.D. 303, 309–10 (D. Kan. 1985).

[41] Tise v. Kule, 37 Fed. R. Serv. 2d (Callaghan) 846, 849 (S.D.N.Y. 1983).

[42] Smith v. Flaminaire, S.A., No. 87-0795 (E.D. Pa. July 1, 1988); Thornton-Trump v. United States, 12 Cl. Ct. 262 (1987).

[43] Chapman & Cole v. Itel Container Int'l B.V., 116 F.R.D. 550, 560 (S.D. Tex. 1987), *aff'd*, 865 F.2d 676 (5th Cir.), *cert. denied*, 493 U.S. 872 (1989).

[44] Hopei Garments (H.K.) Ltd. v. Oslo Trading Co., No. 87 Civ. 0932 (MBM) (S.D.N.Y. Mar. 8, 1988).

- failure to admit a concededly true fact requested in a rule 36(a) request for admission.[45]

2. Sanctionable Entity

Sanctions are expressly authorized against "the person who made the certification, the party on whose behalf the request, response, or objection is made, or both."[46]

3. Authorized Sanctions

Rule 26(g) authorizes "an appropriate sanction," which may include reasonable expenses and attorney fees. According to the 1983 advisory committee's note, "The nature of the sanction is a matter of judicial discretion to be exercised in light of the particular circumstances." Costs, including fees, are frequently imposed, sometimes in a significant amount.[47]

4. Procedures

As with rule 37, some opportunity for notice and hearing is required before rule 26(g) sanctions are imposed. The 1983 advisory committee's note to the rule observes that "in most cases the court will be aware of the circumstances and only a brief hearing should be necessary."

C. Fed. R. Civ. P. 16(f)

Rule 16 gives the court authority to hold a pretrial conference and to enter scheduling orders.

1. Sanctionable Conduct

Rule 16(f) authorizes sanctions for the failure to attend a pretrial conference, to prepare for the conference, to participate in good faith, or to obey a scheduling or pretrial order. Delay in responding to discovery requests or in producing requested documents can be sanctionable as a violation of a rule 16 schedule order.[48]

2. Sanctionable Entity

Sanctions may be imposed on either the party or its attorney. The court should make a specific finding to determine who is at fault.[49]

---

[45] Apex Oil Co. v. Belcher Co., 855 F.2d 1009, 1015 (2d Cir. 1988).

[46] FED. R. CIV. P. 26(g).

[47] *See* National Ass'n of Radiation Survivors v. Turnage, 115 F.R.D. 543, 559 (N.D. Cal. 1987); Itel Containers Int'l Corp. v. Puerto Rico Marine Management, Inc., 108 F.R.D. 96, 107 (D.N.J. 1985).

[48] *See* Royalty Petroleum Co. v. Arkla, Inc., 129 F.R.D. 674, 680–81 (W.D. Okla. 1990); Lindsey v. United States, 693 F. Supp. 1012, 1025–28 (W.D. Okla. 1988); Olga's Kitchen, Inc. v. Papo, 108 F.R.D. 695, 708–09 (E.D. Mich. 1985), *aff'd in part, rev'd in part per curiam,* 815 F.2d 79 (6th Cir. 1987).

[49] *See* M.E.N. Co. v. Control Fluidics, Inc., 834 F.2d 869, 873–74 (10th Cir. 1987).

3. Authorized Sanctions

As with rule 37, the court is authorized to make such orders "as are just," including those identified in rule 37(b)(2)(B)–(D), and cost shifting.

4. Procedures

As with other sanction provisions, the sanctioned party must be given notice and an opportunity to be heard.[50]

D. Fed. R. Civ. P. 30(d)(2)

Added by the 1993 amendments, this rule "explicitly authorizes the court to impose the cost resulting from obstructive tactics that unreasonably prolong a deposition on the person engaged in such obstruction."[51]

1. Sanctionable Conduct

Sanctions are authorized where a deponent or another party impedes or delays the examination during a deposition or where "other conduct . . . has frustrated the fair examination of the deponent."[52]

2. Sanctionable Entity

Sanctions may be imposed on "the persons responsible,"[53] including a party, attorney, or nonparty witness.[54]

3. Authorized Sanctions

The rule authorizes "an appropriate sanction, including the reasonable costs and attorney fees incurred by any parties as a result thereof."[55]

4. Procedures

No special procedures are specified.

E. Fed. R. Civ. P. 30(g)

This rule shifts the costs incurred when a party noticing a deposition fails to attend the deposition or to properly subpoena the witness.

---

[50] *See* Newton v. AC&S, Inc., 918 F.2d 1121, 1127 (3d Cir. 1990); Ford v. Alfaro, 785 F.2d 835, 840 (9th Cir. 1986); *see also* GJB & Assocs. v. Singleton, 913 F.2d 824, 831–32 (10th Cir. 1990) (deeming subsequent hearing adequate for relatively minor sanction).

[51] 1993 Amendments, *supra* note 8, FED. R. CIV. P. 30(d)(2) advisory committee's note.

[52] 1993 Amendments, *supra* note 8, FED. R. CIV. P. 30(d)(2).

[53] *Id.*

[54] 1993 Amendments, *supra* note 8, FED. R. CIV. P. 30(d)(2) advisory committee's notes.

[55] 1993 Amendments, *supra* note 8, FED. R. CIV. P. 30(d)(2).

1. Sanctionable Conduct

The rule applies where the party giving notice of a deposition fails to attend or proceed with the deposition or where the witness does not attend because he or she was not subpoenaed.

2. Sanctionable Entity

Rule 30(g) specifies only the party giving notice of the deposition as a sanctionable entity.

3. Authorized Sanctions

The court may order reimbursement of reasonable expenses, including attorney fees, incurred by parties attending the deposition and their attorneys.

4. Procedures

No special procedures are specified.

F. 28 U.S.C. § 1927

Though narrow in scope, § 1927 has been used to sanction abusive discovery that cannot be properly redressed by the sanctions provisions of the federal rules.

1. Sanctionable Conduct

Pursuant to § 1927, counsel can be assessed costs and fees for multiplying litigation "unreasonably and vexatiously."[56] This statutory authority has been used to punish many kinds of discovery misconduct,[57] including needlessly prolonging depositions through repetitive questions, improper objections and instructions to clients not to answer, and other disruptive behavior.[58]

In *Itel Containers International Corp. v. Puerto Rico Marine Management, Inc.*[59] the defendant knew but concealed from the court and plaintiff that no basis existed for diversity jurisdiction because the defendant was, like the plaintiff, a Delaware corporation. The defendant deliberately and in bad faith drafted an unresponsive interroga-

---

[56] The full statutory provision reads as follows:

Any attorney or other person admitted to conduct cases in any court of the United States or any Territory thereof who so multiplies the proceedings in any case unreasonably and vexatiously may be required by the court to satisfy personally the excess costs, expenses, and attorney's fees reasonably incurred because of such conduct.

[57] *See, e.g.*, Carlucci v. Piper Aircraft Corp., 775 F.2d 1440 (11th Cir. 1985); *see* Howard B. Prossnitz, Fines Against the Trial Lawyer, LITIG., Fall 1983, at 36–38.

[58] *See* Brignoli v. Balch, Hardy & Scheinman, Inc., 126 F.R.D. 462, 466 (S.D.N.Y. 1989); *see also* American Directory Serv. Agency, Inc. v. Beam, 131 F.R.D. 15, 17–18 (D.D.C. 1990); Thomas v. Hoffman-LaRoche, Inc., 126 F.R.D. 522, 524–25 (N.D. Miss. 1989); Unique Concepts, Inc. v. Brown, 115 F.R.D. 292, 293 (S.D.N.Y. 1987).

[59] 108 F.R.D. 96 (D.N.J. 1985).

tory answer to conceal the lack of diversity, attempting to stall until the statute of limitations ran on at least some of the claims. Pursuant to § 1927, the defendant was held responsible for the plaintiff's excess costs due to the deception.[60] The court also cited the certification requirements of rules 7, 11, and 26(g) in imposing sanctions.

Section 1927 has also been used to sanction a pattern of discovery misconduct—such as failing to produce documents and refusing to answer deposition questions—for purposes of delay or increasing costs.[61] In *Apex Oil Co. v. Belcher Co.*[62] § 1927 sanctions were imposed because defense counsel had unreasonably and vexatiously complicated the proceedings by repeatedly refusing to make discovery and refusing to attempt to resolve the disputes with opposing counsel as required by local rule; the defendant complied with the discovery requests only after the plaintiff's counsel had moved to compel responses.

2. Sanctionable Entity

Section 1927, by its terms, authorizes sanctions only against attorneys.[63] Despite the "satisfy personally" language in the statute, in at least one case § 1927 sanctions have been imposed on a law firm as well as on an individual attorney.[64]

3. Authorized Sanctions

The statute authorizes an award of "excess costs, expenses, and attorney's fees reasonably incurred" because of the misconduct. Thus, § 1927 is essentially a cost-shifting provision. The statute was amended in 1980 to add "expenses, and attorney's fees reasonably incurred because of such conduct" as recoverable costs.[65] Before that amendment, the statutory phrase "excess costs" had been interpreted very narrowly.[66]

4. Procedures

As with other sanctions provisions, minimum due process requires notice and some opportunity to be heard.[67]

G. Inherent Power of the Court

Courts have the inherent power to manage their own proceedings and to control the conduct of those who appear before them.[68] The court may exercise this inherent

---

[60] *Id.* at 105–06.

[61] *In re* Yagman, 796 F.2d 1165, 1187 (9th Cir.), *reh'g denied*, 803 F.2d 1085 (9th Cir. 1986).

[62] 855 F.2d 1009, 1020 (2d Cir. 1988).

[63] *See* Smith Int'l, Inc. v. Texas Commerce Bank, 844 F.2d 1193, 1197 (5th Cir. 1988).

[64] Brignoli v. Balch, Hardy & Scheinman, Inc., 735 F. Supp. 100, 102 (S.D.N.Y. 1990).

[65] Antitrust Procedural Improvements Act of 1980, Pub. L. No. 96-349, § 3, 94 Stat. 1156 (1980) (codified as amended at 28 U.S.C. § 1927 (1988)).

[66] Roadway Express, Inc. v. Piper, 447 U.S. 752, 761–63 (1980).

[67] *See id.* at 767.

[68] Chambers v. NASCO, Inc., 111 S. Ct. 2123, 1232, *reh'g denied*, 112 S. Ct. 12 (1991).

power to impose sanctions for discovery misconduct undertaken in bad faith.[69]

1. Sanctionable Conduct

Like 28 U.S.C. § 1927, inherent powers have been invoked to sanction the purposeful impairment of discovery where rules 26(g) and 37 do not strictly apply. Where one of the federal rules regulating discovery directly applies, however, resorting to inherent powers may be neither warranted nor permissible.[70]

The court's inherent authority to impose sanctions has been invoked for the destruction of evidence by a party with notice of a claim, even though the evidence was not subject to an outstanding discovery request.[71] Inherent powers have also been used to redress the fabrication of false evidence,[72] misconduct in a deposition,[73] and evasion[74] and delay[75] in discovery.

2. Sanctionable Entity

Inherent authority can be used to impose sanctions on parties,[76] counsel,[77] or pro se litigants[78] where warranted by the individual's bad faith conduct in the litigation.

3. Authorized Sanctions

Courts have used broad discretion in imposing a variety of sanctions under their

---

[69] *See generally* JOSEPH, *supra* note 13, § 25, at 371; Prossnitz, *supra* note 57, at 38.

[70] *See* 111 S. Ct. at 2135 n.14; Societe Internationale Pour Participations Industrielles et Commerciales, S.A. v. Rogers, 357 U.S. 197, 207 (1958). *But see In re* Sealed Case, 825 F.2d 494 (D.C. Cir. 1987); North Am. Watch Corp. v. Princess Ermine Jewels, 786 F.2d 1447, 1451 (9th Cir. 1986) (inherent powers and rule 37 both allow sanction of dismissal for willful violation of discovery orders).

[71] Capellupo v. FMC Corp., 126 F.R.D. 545, 550–51 (D. Minn. 1989) (finding destruction of evidence prior to commencement of case but after claim made known to defendant); National Ass'n of Radiation Survivors v. Turnage, 115 F.R.D. 543, 554 (N.D. Cal. 1987) ("sanctions for the destruction of potentially discoverable documents, regardless of whether they were specifically responsive to outstanding discovery requests, are an authorized exercise of the court's inherent power to preserve and protect its jurisdiction and the integrity of proceedings before it"); Wm. T. Thompson Co. v. General Nutrition Corp., 104 F.R.D. 119, 122 (C.D. Cal. 1985); Wm. T. Thompson Co. v. General Nutrition Corp., 593 F. Supp. 1443, 1455 (C.D. Cal. 1984).

[72] Pope v. Federal Express Corp., 138 F.R.D. 675, 683 (W.D. Mo. 1990).

[73] Thomas v. Hoffman-LaRoche, Inc., 126 F.R.D. 522, 525 (N.D. Miss. 1989) (obstruction of deposition); Unique Concepts, Inc. v. Brown, 115 F.R.D. 292, 293–94 (S.D.N.Y. 1987).

[74] *See* Schmidt v. Ford Motor Co., 112 F.R.D. 216, 220–21 (D. Colo. 1986).

[75] Lipsig v. National Student Mktg. Corp., 663 F.2d 178, 181–82 (D.C. Cir. 1980).

[76] Alyeska Pipeline Serv. Co. v. Wilderness Soc'y, 421 U.S. 240, 258–59 (1975).

[77] Roadway Express, Inc. v. Piper, 447 U.S. 752, 766 (1980).

[78] Van Sickle v. Holloway, 791 F.2d 1431, 1437 (10th Cir. 1986).

inherent authority.[79] Sanctions for discovery misconduct have included an award of costs including (sometimes enormous) attorney fees,[80] a fine paid to the court,[81] double costs,[82] allowing the fact-finder to draw adverse inferences from document destruction,[83] and default.[84]

4. Procedures

As with other sanction authorities, certain minimal due process must be provided to support the imposition of inherent power sanctions. Thus, notice and some opportunity to be heard are required, both in determining whether the requisite bad faith existed and in assessing fees.[85]

III. TYPES OF SANCTIONS

Rules 11 and 26(g) authorize "an appropriate sanction," which may include expenses and attorney fees incurred because of the violation. Similarly, rule 37(b)(2) allows the court in which the action is pending to make "such orders in regard to the failure which are just."[86] For violations of these rules, the nature of the sanction is left to the discretion of the court,[87] as with sanctions imposed pursuant to the court's inherent authority.[88] Section 1927, as discussed above, specifies the nature of the sanction (costs and fees) rather than leaving it to the court's discretion.

---

[79] *See generally* Capellupo v. FMC Corp., 126 F.R.D. 545, 551–53 (D. Minn. 1989); JOSEPH, *supra* note 13, § 27.

[80] *See, e.g.*, Chambers v. NASCO, Inc., 111 S. Ct. 2123, 2130–31, (nearly one million dollars), *reh'g denied*, 112 S. Ct. 12 (1991); 126 F.R.D. at 553; National Ass'n of Radiation Survivors v. Turnage, 115 F.R.D. 543, 559 (N.D. Cal. 1987); J.M. Cleminshaw Co. v. City of Norwich, 93 F.R.D. 338, 352–54 (D. Conn. 1981).

[81] 115 F.R.D. at 559; 93 F.R.D. at 360.

[82] 126 F.R.D. at 553.

[83] *Id.* at 552 (citing Alexander v. National Farmers' Org., 687 F.2d 1173, 1205–06 (8th Cir. 1982), *cert. denied*, 461 U.S. 937 (1983)); 115 F.R.D. at 557.

[84] Wm. T. Thompson Co. v. General Nutrition Corp., 593 F. Supp. 1443, 1455–56 (C.D. Cal. 1984).

[85] Chambers v. NASCO, Inc., 111 S. Ct. 2123, 2136, 2139, *reh'g denied* 112 S. Ct. 12 (1991); Roadway Express, Inc. v. Piper, 447 U.S. 752, 767 n.14 (1980).

[86] *See* Fonseca v. Regan, 734 F.2d 944, 947–48 (2d Cir.) (broad discretion of trial court), *cert. denied*, 469 U.S. 882 (1984); Tamari v. Bache & Co. (Leb.) S.A.L., 729 F.2d 469, 472 (7th Cir. 1984). *But see* Pesaplastic, C.A. v. Cincinnati Milacron Co., 799 F.2d 1510, 1519 (11th Cir. 1986) (discretion not unbridled); Professional Seminar Consultants, Inc. v. Sino Am. Technology Exch. Council, Inc. 727 F.2d 1470, 1474 (9th Cir. 1984) (holding sanction must be just and specifically related to the particular claim regarding the discovery order violated).

[87] *See* FED. R. CIV. P. 1983 (26)(g) advisory committee's note ("nature of the sanction is a matter of judicial discretion to be exercised in light of the particular circumstances"); Albright v. Upjohn Co., 788 F.2d 1217, 1222 (6th Cir. 1986).

[88] McCandless v. Great At. & Pac. Tea Co., 697 F.2d 198, 201–02 (7th Cir. 1983).

The following types of sanctions have been imposed pursuant to the various sanction authorities discussed in the preceding section.[89]

A. Awarding Attorney Fees and Costs[90]

This sort of fee shifting is a narrow exception to the American Rule, which prohibits fee shifting in most cases.[91] The use of this sanction in response to improper litigation conduct serves the "dual purpose of 'vindicat[ing] judicial authority without resort to the more drastic sanctions available for contempt of court and mak[ing] the prevailing party whole for expenses caused by his opponent's obstinacy.'"[92]

Expenses and fees are expressly authorized by 28 U.S.C. § 1927, suggested as options under rules 11 and 26, and mandated by rule 37—except for failure to participate in good faith in the framing of a discovery plan and unjustified failure to admit, where cost shifting is authorized rather than required. Where rule 37 provides that the court "shall" award costs including attorney fees, the court should not utilize discretion to deny reasonable expenses absent substantial justification or circumstances making such an award unjust. Substantial justification is found when reasonable people could disagree as to whether the requested discovery was required.[93] If expenses are not awarded, specific findings may be required.[94]

Expenses can also be assessed pursuant to the inherent powers of the court.[95]

Cost shifting is authorized by rule 37(c) to sanction the unjustified failure to admit, in response to a request for admission, the genuineness of any document, or the truth of any matter ultimately proven. The rule requires the court to award "the reasonable expenses incurred in making that proof, including reasonable attorney's fees," unless it finds that (1) the request was held objectional, (2) the admission was of no substantial importance, (3) the party had reasonable grounds to believe it might prevail on the matter, or (4) other good reason.

Frequently the court will make a determination of whether to impose the sanction of costs and fees before conducting fact finding on the actual costs incurred.

---

[89] For citations to cases in various jurisdictions applying particular sanctions, see DISCOVERY PROCEEDINGS IN FEDERAL COURT, *supra* note 13, §§ 12.12–12.31.

[90] *See generally* DISCOVERY PROCEEDINGS IN FEDERAL COURT, *supra* note 13, §§ 12.29–12.31.

[91] Chambers v. NASCO, Inc., 111 S. Ct. 2123, 2133, *reh'g denied*, 112 S. Ct. 12 (1991).

[92] *Id.* at 2133 (quoting Hutto v. Finney, 437 U.S. 678, 689 n.14 (1978)).

[93] *In re* Akros Installations, Inc., 834 F.2d 1526, 1530 (9th Cir. 1987); *see also* Midland-Ross Corp. v. Ztel, Inc., 113 F.R.D. 664, 666 (D. Mass. 1987). *But see* FED. R. CIV. P. 37(a)(4) 1970 advisory committee's note ("The amendment does not significantly narrow the discretion of the court, but rather presses the court to address itself to abusive practices").

[94] Metrocorps, Inc. v. Eastern Mass. Junior Drum & Bugle Corps Ass'n, 912 F.2d 1, 2 (1st Cir. 1990).

[95] *See* Ryan v. Hatfield, 578 F.2d 275, 277 (10th Cir. 1978) (citing equitable authority); *see also* Hall v. Cole, 412 U.S. 1, 4–5 (1973).

When fact finding is addressed, the party seeking fees should support its claim with an affidavit and other documentation.

B. Imposing Fines

Occasionally, courts wishing to impose monetary sanctions have found reimbursement of costs inadequate for vindicating the misuse of the judicial process or for deterring future misconduct. These courts have imposed an additional assessment on the stonewalling party, payable either to the party seeking discovery,[96] and/or to the court.[97]

C. Precluding Issues or Evidence

Rule 37(b)(2)(B) specifically authorizes orders precluding designated issues and evidence from being addressed or introduced by disobedient parties. This authority has frequently been used to exclude expert testimony where no disclosure—or incomplete disclosure—has been made regarding the expert's identity or expected testimony.[98] Preclusion of testimony has also been ordered where a party fails to allow a witness's deposition to be taken[99] or where a witness refuses to produce documents as ordered.[100] Where a party has evaded discovery regarding certain claims or defenses, an order precluding or opposing that claim or defense may be imposed.[101] One court used a five-factor test to determine whether preclusion was an appropriate sanction:

- whether the other party in the case had been prejudiced;
- whether the prejudice could be cured;
- the practical importance of the evidence or the issue;
- the recalcitrant party's good or bad faith; and
- the potential for abuse if the evidence or the issue was not precluded.[102]

---

[96] *See* Capellupo v. FMC Corp., 126 F.R.D. 545, 553 (D. Minn. 1989) (double costs payable to plaintiff).

[97] Malautea v. Suzuki Motor Co., No. CV 490-322 (S.D. Ga. Dec. 30, 1991), *aff'd*, 987 F.2d 1536 (11th Cir.), *cert. denied*, 114 S. Ct. 181 (1993); 126 F.R.D. at 552; National Ass'n of Radiation Survivors v. Turnage, 115 F.R.D. 543, 559 (N.D. Cal. 1987); Huber v. Henley, 669 F. Supp. 1474, 1477 (S.D. Ind. 1987); J.M. Cleminshaw Co. v. City of Norwich, 93 F.R.D. 338, 360 (D. Conn. 1981); *see also* Hammond v. Honda Motor Co., No. 8:88-3435-17 (D.S.C. Feb. 14, 1990).

[98] See chapter 5, section IX.

[99] Western Reserve Oil & Gas Co. v. Key Oil, Inc., 626 F. Supp. 948, 949–50 (S.D. W. Va. 1986).

[100] Wilson v. Johns-Manville Sales Corp., 810 F.2d 1358, 1362–63 (5th Cir.), *cert. denied*, 484 U.S. 828 (1987).

[101] Smith v. Schlesinger, 513 F.2d 462, 467 n.10 (D.C. Cir. 1975); Beau Prods., Inc. v. Permagrain Prods., Inc., 97 F.R.D. 50, 55 (M.D. Pa. 1983); Kuhns v. State, 10 Cal. Rptr. 2d 773, 777 (Ct. App. 1992).

[102] Lewis v. Darce Towing Co., 94 F.R.D. 262, 266–67 (W.D. La. 1982).

D. Deeming Facts Established

Rule 37(b)(2)(A) specifically authorizes the court to designate facts to be taken as established for purposes of the action. This sanction is appropriate where the ability of the discovering party to prosecute or defend the action was impaired by stonewalling conduct.[103] For instance, the U.S. Supreme Court approved the establishment of personal jurisdiction over a foreign defendant that refused to submit to discovery of jurisdictional facts.[104] Because establishment of facts can be practically dispositive of liability, the court's discretion to impose this sanction may be narrower than for other sanctions.[105]

E. Striking Pleadings

Rule 37(b)(2)(C) authorizes the court to strike pleadings in whole or in part. This, too, is considered an extreme sanction since it may result in dismissal or default.[106] This sanction was imposed in one case where the defendant exhibited bad faith and callous disregard of its discovery obligations by conduct that included twice failing to appear for depositions and failing to produce documents.[107]

F. Ordering Default or Dismissal

A default judgment against a defendant or a dismissal of a plaintiff's complaint may be available as a sanction against repeated conduct in violation of a court order.[108] Where a willful failure to comply with a discovery order significantly hampers the opposing party's trial preparation, a dismissal or default judgment is properly entered.[109] Even deliberate *partial* compliance with a discovery order may justify striking a party's pleadings and entering a dismissal or default judgment.[110]

Because this is an extreme sanction, the court's discretion to impose it is nar-

---

[103] *See* Rogers v. Chicago Park Dist., 89 F.R.D. 716, 718–19 (N.D. Ill. 1981).

[104] Insurance Corp. of Ir., Ltd. v. Compagnie des Bauxites de Guinee, 456 U.S. 694, 707–09 (1982); *see* Stephen F.J. Martin, Note, *Federal Rules of Civil Procedure—Discovery Sanctions*, 27 Vill. L. Rev. 744 (1981–1982); *cf.* English v. 21st Phoenix Corp., 590 F.2d 723, 728 (8th Cir.), *cert. denied*, 444 U.S. 832 (1979).

[105] *See* DISCOVERY PROCEEDINGS IN FEDERAL COURT, *supra* note 13, §12.13 and cases cited therein. The greater procedural requirements for imposing dispositive sanctions are discussed in section III.F, *infra*.

[106] *See* DISCOVERY PROCEEDINGS IN FEDERAL COURT, *supra* note 13, §12.13 and cases cited therein.

[107] Eastway Gen. Hosp., Ltd. v. Eastway Women's Clinic, Inc., 737 F.2d 503 (5th Cir. 1984), *cert. denied*, 470 U.S. 1052 (1985).

[108] *See, e.g.*, Hicks v. Feeney, 850 F.2d 152, 154–55 (3d Cir. 1988) (finding repeated, willful failure of party to give deposition testimony), *cert. denied*, 488 U.S. 1005 (1989).

[109] Hindmon v. National-Ben Franklin Life Ins. Corp., 677 F.2d 617, 621–22 (7th Cir. 1982) (citing numerous cases from other jurisdictions in accord); Barta v. Long, 670 F.2d 907 (10th Cir. 1982).

[110] Emerick v. Fenick Indus., 539 F.2d 1379 (5th Cir. 1976).

rower than for other sanctions.[111] Nonetheless, in appropriate circumstances, these sanctions are warranted and should be imposed.[112]

Courts have recognized that "[b]ecause of the harshness of dismissal, considerations of due process require that violation of the discovery rules is a sufficient ground only when it is a result of 'willfulness, bad faith, or [some] fault of petitioner's rather than inability to comply.'"[113] A willful failure to comply has been described as intentional noncompliance, as distinguished from involuntary noncompliance.[114] But as the numerous cases imposing the sanction of dismissal illustrate, this sanction does not require a finding of actual intent or bad faith as long as there is some fault.

The sort of fault that has led courts to impose ultimate sanctions includes, of course, intentional, willful, or deliberate efforts to frustrate the full disclosure of information, or any other actions that constitute evidence of classic bad faith.[115] For instance, in *Votour v. American Honda Motor Co.*[116] the plaintiff tried unsuccessfully for two years to obtain the defendant manufacturer's crash tests. Finally, the court struck the defendant's pleadings and entered a default judgment, holding that the defendant had been "deceptive and deliberately evasive" in its response and had adopted an approach "designed to obfuscate the discovery rules."[117]

In *Gates v. United States*[118] the plaintiff's complaint was dismissed because of his repeated failure to appear for depositions, even after a court order was issued. In *Affanato v. Merrill Bros.*[119] a default judgment was entered against a defendant for failure

---

[111] *See* Mutual Fed. Sav. & Loan Ass'n v. Richards & Assocs., Inc., 872 F.2d 88, 92 (4th Cir. 1989).

[112] *See* DISCOVERY PROCEEDINGS IN FEDERAL COURT, *supra* note 13, §§12.19–12.25 and cases cited therein.

[113] Toma v. City of Weatherford, 846 F.2d 58, 60 (10th Cir. 1988) (citing National Hockey League v. Metropolitan Hockey Club, Inc., 427 U.S. 639, 640 (1976)); M.E.N. Co. v. Control Fluidics, Inc., 834 F.2d 869, 872 (10th Cir. 1987); *see also* Societe Internationale Pour Participations Industrielles et Commerciales, S.A. v. Rogers, 357 U.S. 197, 212 (1958); Tennant Co. v. Hako Minuteman, Inc., 878 F.2d 1413, 1416–17 (Fed. Cir. 1989); Beavers v. American Cast Iron Pipe Co., 852 F.2d 527, 530–31 (11th Cir. 1988).

[114] Toma v. City of Weatherford, 846 F.2d 58, 60 (10th Cir. 1988); (citing M.E.N. Co. v. Control Fluidics, Inc., 834 F.2d 869, 872–73 (10th Cir. 1987)).

[115] *See, e.g.*, Malautea v. Suzuki Motor Co., No. CV 490-322 (S.D. Ga. Dec. 30, 1991), *aff'd*, 987 F.2d 1536 (11th Cir.), *cert. denied*, 114 S. Ct. 181 (1993).

[116] No. 79 4686 CA (L) 01 B (Palm Beach County, Fla. Cir. Ct. Sept. 7, 1983).

[117] *Id.*; *see also* Salzman v. Honda Motor Co., No. 4FA-85-1325 (Alaska Super. Ct. Dec. 4, 1986) (granting default judgment as sanction for willful suppression of documents stating, "I cannot believe Honda's behavior in this case. I have never seen a party who has been so willing to violate court orders, never in my entire career."), *aff'd*, 751 P.2d 489 (Alaska), *cert. dismissed*, 487 U.S. 1260 (1988); Brandt v. R.L. Atwood, Inc., No. 85-6366-H (Nueces County, Tex. Dist. Ct. Mar. 30, 1987) (entering default judgment after finding that Honda "willfully failed and . . . refused to comply with the Court's orders on discovery motions").

[118] 752 F.2d 516 (10th Cir. 1975).

[119] 547 F.2d 138 (1st Cir. 1977).

to respond to interrogatories or to produce documents after repeated requests and an order of the court.

Even absent overt or provable bad faith, courts have been willing to impose severe sanctions where a party either knew or should have known that its conduct would impede full and fair disclosure. For example, reliance on a document retention policy to justify the destruction of evidence before a complaint is filed is not sufficient to avoid dispositive sanctions where it was reasonably foreseeable that the documents destroyed would be subject to discovery in pending or future litigation.[120]

Finally, even where an act of evidence destruction is inadvertent, courts have been willing to impose dispositive sanctions where the party responsible for the destruction had a legal duty to preserve the evidence or where allowing the party to proceed despite its destruction of the evidence would be unfair to the opposing party.[121]

Stricter procedural requirements may attach to afford due process to a party faced with a dispositive sanction, and specific findings of fact and conclusions of law must be made.[122] Factors to be considered by the court in determining whether a dispositive sanction is appropriate include the prejudice caused to the party seeking discovery, the appropriateness of a lesser sanction, and the personal involvement of the party in the misconduct.[123]

Lesser sanctions may not be appropriate where they have failed to deter discovery misconduct in the past, or where the discovery abuser has acted in flagrant disregard of the court and the discovery process.[124] For instance, in entering default judgment against Chrysler Motors, one Texas court observed:

> The Court has considered for almost three and one-half months the availability of less stringent sanctions and whether less stringent sanctions would fully promote compliance by Chrysler with this Court's discovery order; the Court had initially declined to strike Chrysler's pleadings and has been seeking to determine less stringent sanctions which could be expected to obtain proper compliance by Chrysler with this Court's orders and with the discovery rules; the Court notes that substantial monetary sanctions previously imposed herein on Chrysler had not successfully promoted full compliance with this Court's orders and that the pattern of misconduct has continued; the Court, reluctantly, finds that no sanction less stringent than those ordered herein will secure compliance with the Court's orders and applicable rules. . . .[125]

---

[120] For discussion of the duty to preserve evidence and the use of a document retention policy to attempt to justify spoliation, see chapter 7, section II.

[121] See chapter 7, section III.

[122] *See* Patton v. Aerojet Ordnance Co., 765 F.2d 604, 608 (6th Cir. 1985); *In re* MacMeekin, 722 F.2d 32, 34–35 (3d Cir. 1983); Kwik Way Stores, Inc. v. Caldwell, 745 P.2d 672, 678 (Colo. 1987) (en banc).

[123] DISCOVERY PROCEEDINGS IN FEDERAL COURT, *supra* note 13, §§12.19–12.25 and cases cited therein.

[124] *Id.* at § 12.24.

[125] Garcia v. Chrysler Motors, No. 88-2682-B, slip op. at 4 (Nueces County, Tex. Dist. Ct. Aug. 8, 1991).

Similarly, a Florida court entered default judgment against Honda Motor Company after observing that "[w]arnings have been given and sanction orders have been issued, and even now, on the eve of trial, the Defendants have wilfully disregarded the Courts [sic] Orders and continue their 'stone-wall' activities with regards to discovery efforts."[126] The court found that Honda had been "evasive and deceptive" and that its discovery conduct had been "wilful . . . deliberate and . . . in bad faith and [its] actions have been merely calculated to delay, obfuscate and avoid legitimate disclosures and to turn the process for discovery in these courts into an endurance contest, and a total waste of judicial time and effort."[127]

G. Charging Contempt

Rule 37(b)(2)(D) permits a court to treat a failure to comply with a discovery order as a contempt of court. Contempt sanctions are used to accomplish two functions: either to compel compliance with a court order (coercive contempt) or to punish an affront to the court's authority (penal contempt).[128] Reviewing courts will look to the purpose and nature of the sanction to determine whether it is remedial—and therefore civil in nature—or punitive—and therefore criminal in nature. Unlike criminal contempt, a civil contempt order may be upheld in the absence of proof of willfulness.[129] Where the sanction constitutes both civil and criminal contempt, it should be considered criminal for purposes of determining its validity.[130]

Civil contempt can be used to enforce compliance with a discovery order,[131] for example, by imposing a fine for each day that the recalcitrant party is not in compliance.[132] Civil contempt can also be used to compensate the discovering party for harm suffered as a result of the discovered party's violation of a discovery order.[133]

Criminal contempt is used to punish noncompliance with a court order and to deter noncompliance by others.[134] Unless a violation of a court order occurs in the

---

[126] Votour v. American Honda Motor Co., No. 79 4686 CA (L) 01 B, slip op. at 1 (Palm Beach County, Fla. Cir. Ct. Sept. 7, 1983).

[127] *Id.* at 3.

[128] *See generally* DISCOVERY PROCEEDINGS IN FEDERAL COURT, *supra* note 13, §§ 12.26–12.28.

[129] *Cf.* McComb v. Jacksonville Paper Co., 336 U.S. 187, 191 (1949); *In re* Elias, 98 B.R. 332, 337 (Bankr. N.D. Ill. 1989). *But see In re* Johnson, 148 B.R. 532, 538 (Bankr. N.D. Ill. 1992).

[130] Falstaff Brewing Corp. v. Miller Brewing Co., 702 F.2d 770, 778–79 (9th Cir. 1983); *see also* Carey Canada, Inc. v. Hinely, 356 S.E.2d 202 (Ga.) (reversing as to fine that trial court imposed as civil contempt sanction and adopting reasoning of dissenting and concurring opinion below, 352 S.E.2d 398, 406–07 (Ga. Ct. App. 1986), finding that fine constituted criminal contempt), *cert. denied*, 484 U.S. 898 (1987).

[131] *See, e.g.*, United States v. Westinghouse Elec. Corp., 648 F.2d 642, 651 (9th Cir. 1981).

[132] *See, e.g., In re* Howe, 800 F.2d 1251 (4th Cir. 1986); New York v. Shore Realty Corp., 763 F.2d 49, 54 (2d Cir. 1985).

[133] Taylor v. Home Ins. Co., 646 F. Supp. 923, 931 (W.D.N.C. 1986).

[134] *See, e.g.*, Blake Assocs., Inc. v. Omni Spectra, Inc., 118 F.R.D. 283, 293–94 (D. Mass. 1988).

presence of the court, a criminal contempt order may be entered only after notice and hearing and only upon a finding beyond a reasonable doubt of a willful violation.[135]

The sanction of contempt may be imposed on a party, a lawyer, or even a non-party. Rule 37(b)(1) specifically authorizes a court to consider as contempt the failure of a deponent to be sworn or to answer questions after being directed to do so by the court; however, the contempt sanction is not available against a witness for refusing to answer particular questions at a deposition because the subpoena orders attendance and testimony but not answers to particular questions.[136] On the other hand, a non-party who violates a court order requiring production of documents may be held in contempt,[137] as may an expert witness who violates a protective order.[138]

H. Removing Counsel

While discovery sanctions are most frequently chosen from the list in rule 37(b)(2), the court's broad discretion has been used to impose creative sanctions. For instance, in *Lelsz v. Kavanagh*,[139] a class action challenging the care and treatment provided to mentally retarded citizens by a state agency, the court removed the state's lead counsel from participation in the case as a sanction for litigation abuses including discovery misconduct.[140]

In *Wilson v. Volkswagen of America*[141] the court initially granted default judgment and held a trial only on the amount of damages, which the jury assessed in excess of $1 million. In response to Volkswagen's motion for a new trial, the court held firm to its belief that the defendant had willfully failed to disclose discoverable information. The court further expressed its conviction that Volkswagen's counsel "adopted non-disclosure as a means of defense in product liability defense claims against Volkswagen."[142] The court granted the motion conditionally, however, granting Volkswagen a new trial on liability only if it would agree to use different counsel.[143] The original default order was subsequently reversed by the Fourth Circuit Court of Appeals.[144]

---

[135] For a discussion of when an evidentiary hearing is required, see ROGER S. HAYDOCK & DAVID F. HERR, DISCOVERY PRACTICE §8.5.3, at 485 n.12 (2d ed. 1988 & Supp. 1992).

[136] Fremont Energy Corp. v. Seattle Post Intelligencer, 688 F.2d 1285, 1286–87 (9th Cir. 1982).

[137] United States Catholic Conference v. Abortion Rights Mobilization, Inc., 487 U.S. 72 (1988).

[138] Quinter v. Volkswagen of Am., 676 F.2d 969, 972 (3d Cir. 1982).

[139] 137 F.R.D. 646 (N.D. Tex. 1991).

[140] *Id.* at 655.

[141] Nos. 75-0163-R and 75-0164-R (E.D. Va. June 21, 1976).

[142] *Id.* at 1.

[143] *Id.* at 3.

[144] Wilson v. Volkswagen of Am., Inc., 561 F.2d 494 (4th Cir. 1977), *cert. denied*, 434 U.S. 1020 (1978).

IV. APPELLATE REVIEW

In the federal courts, many discovery matters are heard in the first instance by a magistrate, pursuant to 28 U.S.C. §636(b). Failure to appeal to the district court from a magistrate's order may constitute a waiver of any arguments relating to the correctness of the magistrate's ruling.[145]

A. Reviewability

Discovery orders imposing sanctions on parties are generally interlocutory in nature[146] and immediately appealable only by certification under 28 U.S.C. § 1292(b). To justify certification, the movant must show "that there is a controlling question of law on which there is substantial ground for difference of opinion and that an immediate interlocutory appeal would materially advance the ultimate determination of th[e] case."[147]

On the other hand, an order imposing dismissal or default judgment as a sanction is appealable as soon as the judgment is entered.[148] Denial of an injunction as a discovery sanction is also immediately appealable.[149] An order imposing dismissal or default as a conditional sanction to be imposed at a future date if discovery is not made does not ripen into an appealable order until the threatened judgment is actually entered.

Civil contempt is not immediately appealable, in contrast to criminal contempt, which is appealable because it punishes a violation of law and is itself a final judgment.[150] An order imposing sanctions against an attorney or other nonparty has been held to be immediately appealable,[151] though some courts have not permitted an appeal of discovery sanctions against an attorney until the conclusion of the case.[152]

---

[145] Merritt v. International Bhd. of Boilermakers, 649 F.2d 1013, 1019 (5th Cir. 1981).

[146] *See, e.g.*, Robinson v. Tanner, 798 F.2d 1378, 1380–81 (11th Cir. 1986) (rule 37 sanction), *cert. denied*, 481 U.S. 1039 (1987); *cf.* Cipollone v. Liggett Group, Inc., 785 F.2d 1108, 1116 (3d Cir. 1986) (holding denial of protective order is not reviewable), *cert. denied*, 484 U.S. 976 (1987).

[147] *In re* A.H. Robins Co., 107 F.R.D. 2 (D. Kan. 1985); *cf.* Black Ass'n v. City of New Orleans, 911 F.2d 1063, 1065 (5th Cir. 1990) (ruling discovery sanction not final judgment absent a certification under rule 54(b), since it does not dispose of a separate substantive claim).

[148] Aurora Bancshares Corp. v. Weston, 777 F.2d 385, 386 (7th Cir. 1985).

[149] *Id.*

[150] IBM Corp. v. United States, 493 F.2d 112, 114–15 (2d Cir. 1973), *cert. denied*, 416 U.S. 995 (1974); *see* Hodgson v. Mahoney, 460 F.2d 326 (1st Cir.), *cert. denied*, 409 U.S. 1039 (1972).

[151] Cheng v. GAF Corp., 713 F.2d 886, 888–90 (2d Cir. 1983); *see also* Ford v. Temple Hosp., 790 F.2d 342, 347 (3d Cir. 1986) (holding 28 U.S.C. § 1927 sanctions are immediately appealable).

[152] G.J.B. & Assocs., Inc. v. Singleton, 913 F.2d 824 (10th Cir. 1990); *In re* Licht & Semonoff, 796 F.2d 564 (1st Cir. 1986); Eastern Maico Distribs., Inc., v. Maico-Fahrzeugfabrik, GmbH, 658 F.2d 944, 947–51 (3d Cir. 1981) (holding rule 37 sanction against attorney not immediately appealable).

Where an immediate appeal is available, the attorney must appeal when the order is entered rather than wait until the conclusion of the case.[153]

In a 1990 article, Professor Elizabeth Thornburg of Southern Methodist University reviewed empirical data regarding the experience of courts and litigants in various jurisdictions that differed in their approaches to interlocutory review of discovery orders.[154] She looked particularly at Texas state cases in which, unlike cases in federal court or most other state jurisdictions, interlocutory review of discovery orders is more liberally available through mandamus.[155] Professor Thornburg concluded that greater availability of interlocutory review of discovery orders would promote fairness without significantly decreasing efficiency.[156]

B. Standard of Review

The standard of review for discovery sanction orders is whether the trial court abused its discretion.[157] An abuse of discretion occurs when the trial court bases its decision on an erroneous conclusion of law or where there is no rational basis for the ruling. Thus, the party challenging the sanction is not entitled to the benefit of the doubt,[158] but rather "bears a heavy burden of demonstrating that the trial judge was clearly not justified" in imposing the sanction.[159]

C. Review of Magistrate's Determination

Where a discovery matter is referred by a federal district court judge to a magistrate for resolution, the judge may reconsider the magistrate's order only where the order is shown to be clearly erroneous or contrary to law.[160] "The clearly erroneous standard requires that the court affirm the decision of the magistrate unless 'on the entire evidence [it] is left with the definite and firm conviction that a mistake has been

---

[153] Mesirow v. Pepperidge Farm, Inc., 703 F.2d 339, 345 (9th Cir.), cert. denied, 464 U.S. 820 (1983).

[154] Elizabeth G. Thornburg, *Interlocutory Review of Discovery Orders: An Idea Whose Time Has Come*, 44 Sw. L.J. 1045 (1990).

[155] *Id.* at 1049–55. Mandamus review may be available in other jurisdictions as well on a proper showing.

[156] *Id.* at 1047, 1085–86.

[157] *See, e.g.,* Chambers v. NASCO, Inc., 111 S. Ct. 2123, 2138, *reh'g denied,* 112 S. Ct. 12 (1991); National Hockey League v. Metropolitan Hockey Club, Inc., 427 U.S. 639, 642, *reh'g denied,* 429 U.S. 874 (1976); Perkinson v. Gilbert/Robinson, Inc., 821 F.2d 686, 689 (D.C. Cir. 1987); Gates v. United States, 752 F.2d 516, 517 (10th Cir. 1985).

[158] Profile Gear Corp. v. Foundry Allied Indus., 937 F.2d 351, 353 (7th Cir. 1991).

[159] Fashion House, Inc. v. K Mart Corp., 892 F.2d 1076, 1081 (1st Cir. 1989) (quoting Spiller v. U.S.V. Lab., Inc., 842 F.2d 535, 537 (1st Cir. 1988)).

[160] 28 U.S.C. § 636(b)(1)(A) (1988); Fed. R. Civ. P. 72(a); Cipollone v. Liggett Group, Inc., 785 F.2d 1108, 1120 (3d Cir. 1986), *cert. denied,* 484 U.S. 976 (1987).

committed.'"[161] However, orders dispositive of a claim or defense are reversible de novo.[162] Alternatively, the court can designate a magistrate not to resolve a matter but to conduct hearings and submit proposed findings of fact and recommendations for resolution, subject to the judge's de novo review of challenged portions.[163]

V. ROLE OF SANCTIONS IN COUNTERING STONEWALLING

Illinois Supreme Court Justice Dooley was right in observing that "[o]ur discovery procedures are meaningless unless a violation entails a penalty proportionate to the gravity of the violation. Discovery for all parties will not be effective unless trial courts do not countenance violations, and unhesitatingly impose sanctions proportionate to the circumstances."[164] Unfortunately, the sanctions imposed by courts to date frequently have not been proportionate to the harm done to the discovering party and cannot begin to deter stonewalling. Steep, punitive sanctions, even if assessed to the court rather than the plaintiff, are needed to change the corporate calculus—that is, to make the cost of stonewalling outweigh the benefits—so that discovery crimes do not pay.

In an insightful 1991 article, Professor Charles Nesson of Harvard Law School questioned the degree to which current sanctions practice actually deters evidence spoliation or suppression.[165] Nesson's views arise in part from the failure of both the trial and appellate courts to appropriately sanction stonewalling in a toxic tort suit in which he participated as an attorney.[166] As Nesson pointed out, sanctions decisions are frequently long on powerful, critical rhetoric but short on action that truly achieves deterrence.[167] His analysis of deterrence uses Justice Holmes's admonition to view the law "from the vantage of a 'bad man' who cares only for the material consequences of his actions."[168] Nesson outlined the powerful incentives to spoliate evidence and observed that spoliation is detected only in the most fortuitous of circumstances. Given the great potential of gain by suppressing evidence and the small risk of detection and punishment, Nesson concluded that the prevailing judicial

---

[161] Snowden v. Connaught Lab., Inc., 136 F.R.D. 694, 697 (D. Kan. 1991) (quoting United States v. United States Gypsum Co., 333 U.S. 364, 395 (1948); Ocelot Oil Corp. v. Sparrow Indus., 847 F.2d 1458, 1464 (10th Cir. 1988)).

[162] 28 U.S.C. § 636(b)(1) (1988); FED. R. CIV. P. 72(b).

[163] 28 U.S.C. § 636(b)(1)(B) (1988).

[164] Buehler v. Whalen, 374 N.E.2d 460, 467 (Ill. 1978).

[165] Charles R. Nesson, *Incentives to Spoliate Evidence in Civil Litigation: The Need for Vigorous Judicial Action*, 13 CARDOZO L. REV. 793 (1991).

[166] *Id.* at 793–94 (discussing Anderson v. Cryovac, Inc., 862 F.2d 910 (1st Cir. 1988), *aff'd sub nom.* Anderson v. Beatrice Foods Co., 900 F.2d 388 (1st Cir.), *cert. denied*, 498 U.S. 891 (1990)).

[167] *Id.* at 800–05.

[168] *Id.* at 795 (citing Oliver Wendell Holmes, Jr., *The Path of the Law*, 10 HARV. L. REV. 457, 459 (1897)).

calculus as to what type of sanction will deter stonewalling conduct is inaccurate:

> Judges have imposed truly painful sanctions only in cases where the spoliators demonstrated subjective bad faith in flagrantly destroying evidence which was essential to their opponents' case. In such cases courts sometimes characterize their sanctions as punitive, but in fact even in these cases the typical sanction is merely compensatory; the sanctions seem severe only because the effects of the spoliation have been extensive. Courts' mistaken impression that they are imposing punitive sanctions is epitomized by the common description of default and dismissal as the "ultimate sanction." Thus courts have maintained that defaulting a defendant or dismissing a plaintiff deters future spoliation. This is sophistry. There is nothing punitive in imposing default or dismissal in a case the spoliator would have lost anyway. Default merely follows from the reasonable inference that if a party willfully and repeatedly destroyed irreplaceable evidence which is essential to his opponent's case, that evidence would have proved devastating. Dismissing a spoliating plaintiff means that the plaintiff loses, as he should have. Defaulting a spoliating defendant still leaves damages to be assessed. In such cases even default may not fully compensate the plaintiff; the defendant may have profited to the extent that he spoliated evidence which would have aroused the jury's ire and resulted in inflated and possibly punitive damages for the underlying tort.[169]

Professor Nesson's review of cases where evidence was altered or destroyed led him to conclude that "the precedents are devoid of a single example of a court imposing a punitive sanction on a spoliator designed to offset the powerful incentive of the bad man's cost-benefit analysis."[170]

Sanctions imposed by many courts over the years have not been severe enough to change manufacturers' discovery behavior. This is demonstrated by the long history of documented discovery abuse by Ford Motor Company. Of course, these documented instances likely represent just the tip of the iceberg. Because of the difficulty of detecting this type of abuse, it can reasonably be assumed that Ford successfully cheated in discovery many times for every time it was caught. Moreover, published opinions result from only a small percentage of the cases in which stonewalling is detected: Most such cases are handled without published order, especially in the state court systems, and most do not surface on appeal.[171] While Ford's conduct has been severely criticized in published opinions,[172] the sanctions imposed have not made it worth Ford's while to change its discovery behavior.

---

[169] Nesson, *supra* note 165, at 801–02 (footnotes omitted).

[170] *Id.* at 803 (footnote omitted).

[171] *See* Colonial Times, Inc. v. Gasch, 509 F.2d 517, 526 (D.C. Cir. 1975) (noting that "discovery issues ... while important to the general course of litigation, are often collateral ... and thus lost to appellate review in fact if not in theory").

[172] In addition to reported cases, *see* Green v. Shepherd Constr. Co., No. 11740 (N.D. Ga. Oct. 21, 1969), *cited in* Bollard v. Volkswagen of Am., Inc., 56 F.R.D. 569, 582 n.3 (W.D. Mo. 1971); Cooke v. Ford Motor Co., No. 89-551 (Van Zandt County, Tex. Dist. Ct. Nov. 20, 1990). The numerous stonewalling techniques employed by Ford in the Pinto litigation are set forth in great detail

In 1969 a federal district court levied the relatively nominal sanction of $500 in costs and attorney fees against Ford after finding its interrogatory answers false, or evasive and obstructive of the discovery rules, or both.[173] In 1974 the Michigan Court of Appeals ordered a new trial when the plaintiff's counsel discovered after a defense verdict in the original trial that Ford had test reports that it had insisted before trial did not exist.[174]

Despite—or perhaps because of—the limited sanctions in these cases, Ford apparently continued to believe that hiding automotive testing information in violation of discovery rules and orders was in its best interest. In 1977 the Iowa Supreme Court upheld a jury verdict and judgment against Ford for the death of a child when a Ford vehicle suddenly accelerated rapidly and struck her.[175] Despite proper discovery requests, Ford had failed to reveal before trial relevant information concerning test procedures, and it had affirmatively denied the ability to identify any such tests. Ford's expert had testified at deposition that Ford did not have access to a vehicle similar to that involved in the accident, but at trial, Ford sought to introduce test films as well as an exemplar vehicle. Its expert testified in an offer of proof that he had, in fact, conducted specific, relevant tests. The Iowa Supreme Court upheld the trial court's decision to exclude the test films and the exemplar vehicle as a discovery sanction.[176]

The following year, Ford's stonewalling was sanctioned in two reported cases, *Rozier v. Ford Motor Co.*[177] and *Buehler v. Whalen*.[178] In *Rozier* the plaintiff's husband had been fatally burned in a fire resulting from a rear-end collision and an allegedly faulty gas tank. After a verdict for the defense, the plaintiff's counsel fortuitously learned of a document responsive to its discovery request that had not been produced by Ford despite a court order. In holding that the plaintiff was entitled to a new trial, the Fifth Circuit found

> Through its misconduct in this case, Ford completely sabotaged the federal trial machinery, precluding the "fair contest" which Federal Rules of Civil Procedure are intended to assure. Instead of serving as a vehicle for ascertainment of the truth, the trial in this case accomplished little more than the adjudication of a hypothetical fact situation imposed by Ford's selective disclosure of information.[179]

---

in JOSEPH KELNER & FRANCIS MCGOVERN, SUCCESSFUL LITIGATION TECHNIQUES—STUDENT EDITION (1981). *Cf.* Jarecki v. Ford Motor Co., 237 N.W.2d 191, 193–94 (Mich. Ct. App. 1975) (finding evidence that Ford gave misinformation to police investigating accident was properly admitted on issue of whether Ford attempted to avoid fair adjudication of liability).

[173] Parrett v. Ford Motor Co., 52 F.R.D. 120 (W.D. Mo. 1969).

[174] Rock Island Bank & Trust Co. v. Ford Motor Co., 220 N.W.2d 799 (Mich. Ct. App. 1974).

[175] Haumersen v. Ford Motor Co., 257 N.W.2d 7 (Iowa 1977).

[176] *Id.* at 14.

[177] 573 F.2d 1332 (5th Cir.), *reh'g denied*, 578 F.2d 871 (5th Cir. 1978).

[178] 374 N.E.2d 460 (Ill. 1978).

[179] 573 F.2d at 1346.

In *Buehler v. Whalen*, Ford again failed to disclose testing despite a proper discovery request. The plaintiff's counsel obtained test records that had been produced in other litigation,[180] proving that Ford had falsely answered interrogatories by disavowing knowledge of certain tests. Ford's in-house expert reiterated that denial at trial but was confronted with the test documents in cross-examination. The trial court denied the plaintiff's motion to strike Ford's pleadings and enter default judgment, however, and instead instructed the jury that unfavorable inferences could be drawn from Ford's failure to produce the documents. The jury returned a verdict for the plaintiff. The state supreme court not only upheld the trial court's decision to give the adverse inference instruction, but also stated that "under the circumstances, the trial court would have been justified in striking the answer of this defendant and submitting to the jury only the issue of damages."[181]

Despite this experience, Ford's abuses continued. In a 1987 reported opinion, Ford's violation of discovery orders was again sanctioned—but not severely or dispositively.[182] Then in 1990, a Texas trial court found that Ford had refused to comply with the court's discovery orders, noted that Ford had been repeatedly cited for discovery misconduct, and found the company "guilty of the same pattern and practice of discovery abuse as that for which Ford previously has been sanctioned." The court ordered Ford to fully comply with discovery orders.[183]

In each of these cases Ford's subterfuge was eventually discovered. However, as observed by the *Buehler* court: "the opposing party may well have been forced to trial without truth, and truth is the heart of all discovery. . . . Disclosure is the object of all our discovery procedures. It is the opinion of this court that trial courts should make disclosure a reality."[184]

Even though in each of these cases the court recognized that Ford's discovery conduct was evasive at best and dishonest at worst, in no case was Ford appreciably worse off than it would have been had it honestly complied with the requirements of the discovery rules. The sanctions went some distance, in some of the reported cases, toward correcting the prejudice to the plaintiff (though not the terrible prejudice resulting from justice delayed, including the financial and emotional costs of continued litigation), but despite its documented pattern of stonewalling, in no case was Ford severely punished.

From Ford's standpoint, stonewalling has probably been profitable. Because most deception is discovered only by chance, Ford and other stonewalling defendants

---

[180] 374 N.E.2d at 466–68. This well illustrates the need for the sharing of discovery among counsel for different plaintiffs in similar actions. Manufacturers routinely seek to prohibit such sharing through protective orders, as discussed in chapter 8.

[181] 374 N.E.2d at 467.

[182] Babb v. Ford Motor Co., 535 N.E.2d 676, 680 (Ohio Ct. App. 1987).

[183] Cooke v. Ford Motor Co., No. 89-551, slip op. at 2 (Van Zandt County, Tex. Dist. Ct. Nov. 20, 1990).

[184] 374 N.E.2d at 467.

are probably caught in only a fraction of the cases in which they cheat in discovery. Therefore, if the sanctions merely level the playing field in those cases, the manufacturer comes out ahead[185] and will conduct discovery the same way in future cases.

Ford should not be singled out. Its abuses, while outrageous, are not exceptional.[186] Because too few courts have taken seriously the U.S. Supreme Court's

---

[185] Ford's deceptions are not limited to litigation, and extend to administrative investigations as well. For example, in September 1977, during the National Highway Transportation Safety Administration's (NHTSA) investigation of reports that certain vehicles spontaneously shifted from park to reverse, NHTSA requested information from Ford concerning other injuries and damages alleged to have resulted from transmission failure or malfunction. The Director of NHTSA's Office of Defects Investigation later testified under oath that "I thereafter learned that that information was substantially incomplete, and that Ford was then aware of many more such incidents." Affidavit of Lynn L. Bradford, Reed v. Ford Motor Co., No. IP86-134C (S.D. Ind. filed Dec. 22, 1987).

[186] *See, e.g.*, Erskine v. Consolidated Rail Corp., 814 F.2d 266 (6th Cir. 1987) (ordering new trial where railroad suppressed report of internal investigation); Rexrode v. American Laundry Press Co., 674 F.2d 826 (10th Cir.) (finding that though manufacturer initially denied knowing of any other similar claims, three supplemental responses identified 14 other claims, and defendant's answers to interrogatories in another case identified 15 additional claims), *cert. denied*, 459 U.S. 862 (1982); Greenville County Sch. Dist. v. U.S. Gypsum Co., CA No. 82-3142-14 (D.S.C. Feb. 28, 1986) (imposing $25,000 sanction for asbestos manufacturer's failure to produce requested documents); Brown v. United States Elevator Corp., 102 F.R.D. 526, 531 (D.D.C. 1984) (sanctioning manufacturer for failing to comply with discovery order without justification); Sellers v. General Motors Corp., 40 Fed. R. Serv. 2d (Callaghan) 590 (E.D. Pa. 1984) (granting new trial where defendant prior to first trial denied existence of newly discovered evidence of other similar claims); Fautek v. Montgomery Ward & Co., Inc., 96 F.R.D. 141, 144–46 (N.D. Ill. 1982) (sanctioning defendant for providing misinformation in discovery); United States v. Reserve Mining Co., 412 F. Supp. 705, 710–13 (D. Minn.) (fining defendant $200,000 litigation costs for withholding production of documents in violation of plaintiff's discovery requests and a court order), *aff'd*, 543 F.2d 1210 (8th Cir. 1976); Avalos v. Clark Equip. Co., CA No. EAC 60984 (L.A. County, Cal. Super. Ct. Apr. 12, 1989) (ordering manufacturer to pay plaintiff's fee for unwarranted refusal to produce requested documents); Biehler v. White Metal Rolling & Stamping Corp., 333 N.E.2d 716 (Ill. App. Ct. 1975) (ordering new trial in part for defendant's failure to disclose existence of other similar incidents); Taylor v. Cessna Aircraft Co., 696 P.2d 28, 31–33 (Wash. Ct. App.) (ordering new trial for defendant's failure to produce relevant tests), *review denied*, 103 Wash. 2d 1040 (1985); *see also* Stengel v. Kawasaki Heavy Indus., 116 F.R.D. 263, 268 (N.D. Tex. 1987) (imposing sanctions against all-terrain vehicle manufacturer for incomplete production of test results discovered by plaintiff's counsel through a comparison with documents produced in other case); Hense v. G.D. Searle & Co., 452 N.W.2d 440, 445–46 (Iowa 1990) (sanctioning IUD manufacturer for failure to disclose existence of document index); Berry v. Coleman Sys. Co., 596 P.2d 1365, 1368 (Wash. Ct. App.) (affirming new trial order based on failure to disclose other claims of injury due to product), *review denied*, 92 Wash. 2d 1026 (1979). In Berkey Photo's antitrust action against Eastman Kodak, Kodak's counsel filed a sworn affidavit that a suitcase full of documents which an expert had identified in deposition as having been delivered to the defendant's law firm had been discarded and destroyed. This affidavit was

admonition to use discovery sanctions to deter stonewalling,[187] widespread abuses continue because they are profitable. It is disturbing that civil litigators interviewed in one survey reported that actual dishonesty or bad faith had impeded discovery in 14 percent of all cases and in a remarkable 18 percent of large cases.[188] Both for punitive and deterrent effect, such conduct should be met with severe sanctions.

Sanctions must be imposed promptly, consistently, and with the expectation of finality.[189] Without the expectation of finality, the effectiveness of sanctions as a deterrent can be lost. Appellate decisions minimizing discovery misconduct and vacating sanctions imposed as a result of that misconduct do not help in assuring the effectiveness of sanctions as a deterrent.[190]

VI. CONCLUSION

In some circles, discovery has gotten a bad name. It has been pilloried as a waste of time and resources. It has been tainted by the bad behavior of those who seek to subvert it. It is loathed and feared by those whose wrongs toward others make them vulnerable to justice. After all, it allows the poorest, least-informed plaintiff to compel the greatest economic enterprise to share what it knows about whatever has injured the plaintiff. We should not forget that discovery is a great equalizer. It is an American, democratic institution of which we should be proud. Does it need improvement? Surely. Has it outlived its usefulness? Not a chance, so long as truth and justice remain the objectives of our court system.

Changes in discovery behavior are badly needed. Volumes have been written about the problems of overuse and misuse of discovery requests. Much less attention has been focused on the other side of discovery misconduct: discovery avoidance. Both problems need to be addressed. However, reform efforts must be directed selectively toward those elements of the system that do not work. Caution is needed to avoid eliminating discovery's important benefits in the name of increasing efficiency. Specifically, reforms in rules or their application that attempt to quash the use of discovery to prevent its misuse are too simplistic, and end up throwing the baby out with the bath water.

Suffolk University law professors Paul Sugarman and Marc Perlin discuss this problem in their recent critique of the discovery reforms proposed by former Vice President Dan Quayle's Council on Competitiveness.[191] The Council's proposals

---

false. The subject documents were in defense counsel's office at the time—a fact that counsel later admitted. Walter Kiechel III, *The Strange Case of Kodak's Lawyers*, FORTUNE, May 8, 1978, at 188, 190.

[187] *See* National Hockey League v. Metropolitan Hockey Club, Inc., 427 U.S. 639, 643, *reh'g denied*, 429 U.S. 874 (1976). *See generally* Nesson, *supra* note 165.

[188] Wayne D. Brazil, *Civil Discovery: Lawyers' View of Its Effectiveness, Its Principal Problems and Abuses*, 1980 AM. B. FOUND. RES. J. 833, 838.

[189] *See* Maute, *supra* note 10.

[190] *Id.*

[191] *See* Paul R. Sugarman & Marc G. Perlin, *Proposed Changes to Discovery Rules in Aid of "Tort Reform": Has the Case Been Made?*, 42 AMER. U. L. REV. 1465 (1993).

would have narrowed the scope of discovery in the name of unburdening American enterprise. Sugarman and Perlin recall that the discovery rules were adopted to shift the focus of litigation to the merits rather than the "technical niceties of pleadings."[192] They remind us that discovery serves no less important a purpose than "assuring that right and justice shall have the most favorable opportunity of prevailing."[193] In products liability cases, they observe, the consumer alleging injury due to a product defect needs information that is commonly available only from the defendant's own files.[194]

> A consumer litigant alleging injury from a defective product and having the burden of proof needs information concerning that product. Without that information, little can be accomplished. "Modern products liability claims, toxic tort claims and environmental litigation would be simply inconceivable without the combination of liberal pleading, liberal joinder, and liberal discovery. The total effect of this development has redounded to the benefit of 'have nots' relative to 'haves.'"[195]

The article points out the real agenda of the Council's proposals to curtail the scope of discovery:

> The common thread running through the Council's proposals and former Vice President Quayle's related article is an interest in improving the lot of product manufacturers by reducing the adverse impact of consumer litigation. To accomplish this purpose, they seek to change the rules of discovery, the result of which is likely to be less information available to plaintiffs who bear the burden of proof. The formulation of changes that will be applicable to all civil litigation in the federal courts with the goal of promoting the interests of a class of civil litigants—product manufacturers—and on the basis of assertions unsupported by empirical data runs a real risk of making the wrong change for the wrong reason.[196]

Sugarman and Perlin conclude that "[g]ranting one class of litigant an advantage over another is not an adequate reason for credible change."[197]

Stonewalling is not likely to be solved with rule changes. The incentives to suppress highly relevant information damaging to the party possessing it are great, no matter what procedural means are used to uncover that evidence. Stonewalling can only be controlled by changing the nature of these incentives. Since the incentive to suppress is strong, the disincentive must be stronger.

Deterrence is dependent on two factors: the likelihood of detection and the

---

[192] *Id.* at 1494.

[193] *Id.* at 1497 (quoting Justice William J. Brennan, Jr., Address at the Round Table in Administration of Justice, San Juan, Puerto Rico (Feb. 5, 1962), *quoted in* G. Joseph Tauro, *Improving the Quality of Justice in Massachusetts*, 49 MASS. L.Q. 7, 19 (1964)).

[194] Sugarman & Perlin, *supra* note 191, at 1497.

[195] *Id.* at 1497 (citing Stephen N. Subrin, *Fireworks on the 50th Anniversary of the Federal Rules of Civil Procedure*, 73 JUDICATURE 4, 6 (1989), quoting Professor Geoffrey Hazard, Address at the 50th Anniversary of Federal Rules Conference (Oct. 7–8, 1988)).

[196] Sugarman & Perlin, *supra* note 191, at 1495.

[197] *Id.* at 1494.

severity of the penalty imposed. Much of the responsibility with respect to both of these factors lies with the courts. The likelihood of detection can be improved if courts refrain from granting restrictive protective orders that prevent plaintiffs in similar cases from sharing information. Federal courts should also be willing, under the new federal rules, to permit the depositions and interrogatories that are often needed to fully probe the sufficiency of disclosures. With respect to penalties, trial judges need to impose stringent sanctions for stonewalling conduct, rather than light sanctions that the stonewaller will gladly absorb as a cost of doing business. Sanctions must be imposed consistently, predictably, and with finality, and they must be upheld by appellate courts where justified by the offending party's behavior.

The courts cannot, however, be asked to shoulder the entire burden of curtailing discovery misconduct. Attorneys, individually and through their associations, must take a large measure of responsibility for reform. Our litigation "culture" needs adjustment. The economic structures of practice that create incentives for lawyers to encourage stonewalling must be reevaluated. Attorneys must examine their motives and learn to take pride not just in winning, but in winning fairly. Attorneys must renew their commitment to ideals of integrity: Neither plaintiffs' counsel nor defense counsel should tolerate cheating by clients, and in law firms a young associate's lack of regard for honesty and fair play should be scorned, not rewarded. Lawyers entering the profession must bring their ideals with them and refuse to compromise those ideals for professional advancement or pecuniary gain.

All that is at stake is truth and justice.

APPENDIX 1

DISCOVERY OF PARTICULAR TOPICS

This appendix is divided into sections. Each section consists of up to six parts: Commentary, Rules, Secondary Sources, Case Law, *See also,* and *Contra*. Not every section includes all six parts. For instance, § 1 covers Jurisdiction; because no rules specifically address that topic, there is no "Rules" heading in that section. Some sections don't list any case law. For those sections, the authors were unable to locate any relevant cases, and they encourage readers to share information with them.

§ 1 JURISDICTION

Commentary
A court has the power to permit discovery of facts concerning the basis of the court's jurisdiction.

Secondary Sources
AMERICAN LAW OF PRODUCTS LIABILITY 3D § 53:47 (1987 & Supp. 1992).

4 MOORE ET AL., MOORE'S FEDERAL PRACTICE ¶ 26 (2d ed. 1991 & Supp. 1992).

4A MOORE ET AL., MOORE'S FEDERAL PRACTICE ¶ 33.16 (2d ed. 1991 & Supp. 1992).

8 WRIGHT & MILLER, FEDERAL PRACTICE AND PROCEDURE § 2009, at 52 n.34 (1970 & Supp. 1992).

Case Law
Filus v. Lot Polish Airlines, 907 F.2d 1328 (2d Cir. 1990) (holding that until a reasonable basis for jurisdiction was established under Foreign Sovereign Immunities Act, plaintiff was allowed only limited discovery on issue of jurisdiction).

Majd-pour v. Georgiana Community Hosp., 724 F.2d 901, 903 (11th Cir. 1984) (holding that dismissal was premature without affording party opportunity to proceed with reasonable discovery to demonstrate jurisdiction).

Eaton v. Dorchester Dev., Inc., 692 F.2d 727, 729–30 (11th Cir. 1982) (holding that a federal court had power to allow discovery on jurisdiction and that dismissal for lack of subject-matter jurisdiction was premature until such discovery is completed).

See also

Oppenheimer Fund, Inc. v. Sanders, 437 U.S. 340 (1978).

McKesson Corp. v. Islamic Republic of Iran, 138 F.R.D. 1 (D.D.C. 1991).

Goldstein v. Compudyne Corp., 262 F. Supp. 524 (S.D.N.Y. 1966).

Gleneagle Ship Management v. Leondakos, 581 So. 2d 222 (Fla. Dist. Ct. App. 1991), *review granted*, 602 So. 2d 1282 (Fla. 1992).

Smith v. Johns-Manville Corp., 489 A.2d 336 (R.I. 1985).

Peterson v. Spartan Indus., 310 N.E.2d 513 (N.Y. 1974).

§ 2 FACT/LAW DISTINCTION

Commentary

Courts have permitted interrogatories that call for mixed conclusions of fact and law. Also permissible are legal conclusions that require the applications of law to fact. Only one kind of interrogatory is objectionable on the ground that it seeks a legal conclusion: one that seeks an answer to an abstract legal issue unrelated to the facts of the case.

Rules

FED. R. CIV. P. 26(b)(1), 33(b).

Secondary Sources

DISCOVERY PROCEEDINGS IN FEDERAL COURT § 16.6 (Shepard's eds., 2d ed. 1991 & Supp. 1992).

4 MOORE ET AL., *supra* § 1, ¶ 26.56[3].

4A MOORE ET AL., *supra* § 1, ¶ 33.12.

8 WRIGHT & MILLER, *supra* § 1, § 2167.

Case Law

Schaap v. Executive Indus., 130 F.R.D. 384, 388 (N.D. Ill. 1990) (holding that interrogatories into factual basis of defendant's contention that mobile home was merchantable and fit for a particular purpose were not objectionable).

B. & S. Drilling Co. v. Halliburton Oil Well Cementing Co., 24 F.R.D. 1, 3 (S.D. Tex. 1959) (holding that "Interrogatories may inquire into the factual or evidentiary basis of a party's allegations.").

See also

Donovan v. Porter, 584 F. Supp. 202 (D. Md. 1984).

Roesberg v. Johns-Manville Corp., 85 F.R.D. 292, 298 (E.D. Pa. 1980).

Hayes v. Xerox Corp., 718 P.2d 929 (Alaska 1986).

§ 3 OPINIONS/CONCLUSIONS

Commentary

Courts have permitted interrogatories that elicit opinions or conclusions that are incidental to the facts, noting that the line between fact and conclusion is frequently uncertain and illogical.

Rules

FED. R. CIV. P. 26(b)(1), 33(b).

Secondary Sources

DISCOVERY PROCEEDINGS IN FEDERAL COURT, *supra* § 2, § 16.6.

DOMBROFF, DISCOVERY §§ 2.15–2.25, 12.36–12.37, 12.56 (1986).

HAYDOCK & HERR, DISCOVERY PRACTICE § 4.2.3 (2d ed. 1988 & Supp. 1992).

4 MOORE ET AL., *supra* § 1, ¶ 26.56[3].

4A MOORE ET AL., *supra* § 1, ¶ 33.17.

8 WRIGHT & MILLER, *supra* § 1, § 2167.

Case Law

Baise v. Alewel's, Inc., 99 F.R.D. 95, 96–97 (W.D. Mo. 1983) (products case; summer sausage) (holding that a party's knowledge of the literature regarding a product's hazard was an appropriate subject for a request for an admission).

Roesberg v. Johns-Manville Corp., 85 F.R.D. 292, 298 (E.D. Pa. 1980).

Union Carbide Corp. v. Travelers Indem. Co., 61 F.R.D. 411 (W.D. Pa. 1973).

Ballard v. Allegheny Airlines, Inc., 54 F.R.D. 67, 69 (E.D. Pa. 1972).

Anderson v. United Air Lines, Inc., 49 F.R.D. 144, 147–49 (S.D.N.Y. 1969) (products case; hydraulic fluid on aircraft flight control system) (allowing request for admission seeking expert's opinion of stated facts; while technical conclusions generally were presented in the form of expert's opinion, they were opinions of fact upon which the trier of fact relied).

Diversified Prods. Corp. v. Sports Ctr. Co., 42 F.R.D. 3, 4–5 (D. Md. 1967) (patent proceeding) ("An interrogatory is not objectionable merely because it involves an opinion contention or legal conclusion.").

§ 4 CONTENTIONS

Commentary

The majority of courts have allowed contention interrogatories concerning a claim or defense involved in the action, holding that they serve a useful purpose in narrowing the issues.

Rules

FED. R. CIV. P. 26(b)(1), 33(b).

Secondary Sources

23 AM. JUR. 2D *Depositions and Discovery* §§ 204, 236 (1983 & Supp. 1992).

DISCOVERY PROCEEDINGS IN FEDERAL COURT, *supra* § 2, § 16.2.

DOMBROFF, *supra* § 3, § 12.56.

HAYDOCK & HERR, *supra* § 3, § 4.2.3.

4 MOORE ET AL., *supra* § 1, ¶ 26.56[2].

8 WRIGHT & MILLER, *supra* § 1, §§ 2167–2168, at 2255–2256.

Case Law

Schaap v. Executive Indus., 130 F.R.D. 384, 388 (N.D. Ill. 1990).

Roesberg v. Johns-Manville Corp., 85 F.R.D. 292, 297–98 (E.D. Pa. 1980).

Green v. Shepherd Constr. Co., CA No. 11740 (N.D. Ga. Oct. 21, 1969) (products case; spring shackle) (ordering Ford to answer plaintiff's contention interrogatories).

Pressley v. Boehlke, 33 F.R.D. 316, 317 (W.D.N.C. 1963).

United States v. Renault, Inc., 27 F.R.D. 23, 29 (S.D.N.Y. 1960).

B. & S. Drilling Co. v. Halliburton Oil Well Cementing Co., 24 F.R.D. 1, 2–3 (S.D. Tex. 1959) (negligence action by employee against employer) (finding an interrogatory proper where it sought plaintiff's contentions and names of witnesses from whom plaintiff obtained information).

Chenault v. Nebraska Farm Prods., Inc., 9 F.R.D. 529 (D. Neb. 1949).

Ex parte Dorsey Trailers, Inc., 397 So. 2d 98, 105 (Ala. 1981).

Richmond v. American Honda Motor Co., 571 So. 2d 491 (Fla. Dist. Ct. App. 1990) (products case; motorcycle) (requiring plaintiff to answer interrogatory requesting her to admit substantive testimony that her expert witness had given in previous case).

§ 5 IMPEACHMENT

§ 5.1 GENERALLY

(See also § 5.2)

Commentary

Impeachment evidence is generally discoverable. The court may impose conditions to protect the impeachment value of the information.

Secondary Sources

DISCOVERY PROCEEDINGS IN FEDERAL COURT, *supra* § 2, § 16.7.

HAYDOCK & HERR, *supra* § 3, § 1.4, at 22.

Martyn, Annotation, *Discovery, in Civil Case, of Material Which Is or May Be Designed for Use in Impeachment*, 18 A.L.R. 3D 922 (1968).

8 WRIGHT & MILLER, *supra* § 1, § 2015.

Case Law

Davidson Pipe Co. v. Laventhol & Horwath, 120 F.R.D. 455 (S.D.N.Y. 1988).

Bockweg v. Anderson, 117 F.R.D. 563, 565–66 (M.D.N.C. 1987) (medical negligence action) (reading rules 26(b)(1) and 26(b)(4)(A) as complimentary and supportive of "liberal discovery of expert witnesses, including information relevant only for impeachment," court held that plaintiff's expert witnesses must answer questions relating to their involvement in other professional negligence actions).

Westhemeco Ltd. v. New Hampshire Ins. Co., 82 F.R.D. 702 (S.D.N.Y. 1979).

Powell v. Merrimack Mut. Fire Ins. Co., 80 F.R.D. 431, 433 (N.D. Ga. 1978).

Novak v. Good Will Grange No. 127, Patrons of Husbandry, Inc., 28 F.R.D. 394, 396 (D. Conn. 1961) (negligence action against building owner) (finding that discovery of insurance information was relevant to an action for negligence in the maintenance of a building).

Plitt v. Griggs, 585 So. 2d 1317, 1322 (Ala. 1991) (medical negligence action) (holding that a medical expert could be required to disclose identity of person who prepared his tax return, as that information might lead to discovery of amount of money expert earned from testifying for plaintiff in other professional negligence actions).

Williams v. Dixie Elec. Power Ass'n, 514 So. 2d 332, 336–37 (Miss. 1987) (en banc).

McAdoo v. Odgen, 573 So. 2d 1084 (Fla. Dist. Ct. App. 1991) (personal injury; automobile accident) (finding that plaintiff was entitled to production of bills that defendant's expert had submitted to companies for whom he had acted as an expert; information might serve to demonstrate expert's bias).

Richmond v. American Honda Motor Co., 571 So. 2d 491 (Fla. Dist. Ct. App. 1990) (products case; motorcycle) (requiring plaintiff to answer interrogatory requesting her to admit substantive testimony that her expert witness had given in previous case).

Lopez v. Foremost Paving, Inc., 796 S.W.2d 473 (Tex. Ct. App. 1990) (wrongful death and personal injury action; vehicular accident) (finding that defendant failed to produce videotape simulation of defendant's version of accident; introduction in evidence at trial held reversible error).

Wierbinski v. Volkswagen A.G., CA No. A038364 (Cal. Ct. App. Dec. 30, 1988) (products case; suspension system) (ordering automaker to produce accident reconstruction computer program and software which defendant failed to do until middle of trial; trial court's order affirmed, granting plaintiff new trial following verdict for defendant), *reprinted in* Automotive Litig. Rep. 11444-47 (Jan. 17, 1989).

§ 5.2 SURVEILLANCE FILMS

(See also § 5.1)

Commentary

Surveillance films are a form of impeachment evidence and as such are usually discoverable. A rather large number of courts have required the production of surveillance films (and "out takes") only after the plaintiff has given his or her deposition.

Secondary Sources

Casper, *Looking Fraudulent Surveillance in the Eye*, TRIAL, Jan. 1993, at 137.

Siemens, Comment, *The Discoverability of Personal Injury Surveillance and Missouri's Work Product Doctrine*, 57 MO. L. REV. 871 (1992).

Wakefield, Annotation, *Photographs of Civil Litigant Realized by Opponent's Surveillance as Subject to Pretrial Discovery*, 19 A.L.R. 4TH 1236 (1983).

Case Law

Romero v. Chiles Offshore Corp., 140 F.R.D. 336 (W.D. La. 1992).

Forbes v. Hawaiian Tug & Barge Corp., 125 F.R.D. 505, 507–08 (D. Haw. 1989) (personal injury action in admiralty) (allowing discovery of surveillance movies, provided that impeaching character of the movies was preserved).

Daniels v. National R.R. Passenger Corp., 110 F.R.D. 160 (S.D.N.Y. 1986).

Martin v. Long Island R.R., 63 F.R.D. 53 (E.D.N.Y. 1974).

Blyther v. Northern Lines, Inc., 61 F.R.D. 610 (E.D. Pa. 1973).

Snead v. American Export-Isbrandtsen Lines, Inc., 59 F.R.D. 148, 151 (E.D. Pa. 1973) (personal injury) (permitting discovery of surveillance film).

DiMichel v. South Buffalo Ry., 604 N.E.2d 63 (N.Y. 1992) (personal injury action against employer) (defendant's surveillance films (and any "out takes") of an injured person were held discoverable; the court noted that if the defense did not use the films at trial, the plaintiff could not encourage the jury to speculate about them. The court stated that withholding the films until after the plaintiff's deposition would ameliorate the concern that pretrial disclosure would allow plaintiff to tailor his or her testimony to the film.).

Cabral v. Arruda, 556 A.2d 47, 49 (R.I. 1989) (negligence action; automobile accident) (holding that "where a plaintiff learns that surveillance material is to be introduced at trial, its nondisclosure constitutes a showing of undue hardship," rendering such material discoverable).

Dodson v. Persell, 390 So. 2d 704, 706–07 (Fla. 1980).

Boldt v. Sanders, 111 N.W.2d 225, 227 (Minn. 1961) (personal injury; automobile accident) (allowing discovery of plaintiff's medical history).

Kane v. Her-Pet Refrigeration, Inc., 587 N.Y.S.2d 339 (App. Div. 1992) (personal injury; automobile accident) (holding that surveillance was discoverable).

Guillot v. Miller, 580 So. 2d 1104, 1106–07 (La. Ct. App. 1991).

Shenk v. Berger, 587 A.2d 551, 555–56 (Md. Ct. Spec. App. 1991) (personal injury; automobile accident) (finding that surveillance films were discoverable).

Ranft v. Lyons, 471 N.W.2d 254, 261–62 (Wis. Ct. App. 1991).

Davis v. Daddona, CA No. CV89-0102503 (Conn. Super. Ct. Apr. 2, 1990).

§ 6 IDENTIFICATION OF PERSONS PARTICIPATING IN RESPONSE

Commentary

Most courts have held that discovery requests seeking identities of persons who participated in discovery responses are objectionable on the grounds of work-product immunity.

In view of the fact that the trial court's pretrial order ordinarily requires disclosure of anticipated witnesses and exhibits (*see Wirtz v. Hooper-Holmes Bureau, Inc.*, 327 F.2d 939, 943 (5th Cir. 1964)), the great majority of federal courts that have addressed the issue have held that pretrial disclosure of a party's anticipated trial witnesses and exhibits cannot be obtained by discovery.

Rule

1993 Amendments, FED. R. CIV. P. 26(a)(3)(A).

Secondary Sources

DISCOVERY PROCEEDINGS IN FEDERAL COURT, *supra* § 2, § 6.10, at 346.

DOMBROFF, *supra* § 3, § 12.49.

8 WRIGHT & MILLER, *supra* § 1, § 2172 at 538.

Case Law

Maritime Cinema Serv. Corp. v. Movies En Route, Inc., 60 F.R.D. 587, 591 (S.D.N.Y. 1973).

Evans v. International Bhd. of Elec. Workers, Local Union 2127, 313 F. Supp. 1354, 1360 (N.D. Ga. 1969).

United States v. National Steel Corp., 26 F.R.D. 599, 600 (S.D. Tex. 1960).

Hopkinson Theatre, Inc. v. RKO Radio Pictures, Inc., 18 F.R.D. 379, 383 (S.D.N.Y. 1956).

Maple Drive-In Theatre Corp. v. Radio-Keith-Orpheum Corp., 153 F. Supp. 240, 244 (S.D.N.Y. 1956).

Contra

Bagwell v. Nissan Motor Co., No. 7:90–753, 1991 U.S. Dist. LEXIS 171225 (D.S.C. Jan. 30, 1991) (holding that the identities of those who helped the manufacturer answer plaintiff's interrogatories were not protected as attorney work product).

Casson Constr. Co. v. Armco Steel Corp., 91 F.R.D. 376, 376, 385 (D. Kan. 1980) (antitrust action) (characterizing as the "last straw" an interrogatory requesting identity of those preparing responses.

Lloyd v. Cessna Aircraft Co., 434 F. Supp. 4, 8 (E.D. Tenn. 1976).

Rogers v. Tri-State Materials Corp., 51 F.R.D. 234, 247 (N.D. W. Va. 1970).

§ 7 INSURANCE/INDEMNITY INFORMATION

Commentary

Fed. R. Civ. P. 26(b)(2) states:

> A party may obtain discovery of the existence and contents of any insurance agreement under which any person carrying on an insurance business may be liable to satisfy part or all of a judgment which may be entered in the action or to indemnify or reimburse for payments made to satisfy the judgment.

The extent of discovery permitted under this rule, however, is not limited to the policy's monetary stake. Indemnity agreements, secondary insurance, and other information not specifically provided for in FED. R. CIV. P. 26(b)(2) may be discoverable.

Rule

FED. R. CIV. P. 26(b)(2).

Secondary Sources

DISCOVERY PROCEEDINGS IN FEDERAL COURT, *supra* § 2, § 16.9.

DOMBROFF, *supra* § 3, § 12.41.

HAYDOCK & HERR, *supra* § 3, § 1.5.

Jhong, Annotation, *Pretrial Examination or Discovery to Ascertain from Defendant in Action or Injury, Death, or Damages, Existence and Amount of Liability Insurance and Insurer's Identity*, 13 A.L.R. 3D 822 (1967).

4 MOORE ET AL., *supra* § 1, ¶ 26.62[2].

8 WRIGHT & MILLER, *supra* § 1, § 2009, at 68 n.47, § 2010.

Case Law

Henderson v. Zurn Indus., 131 F.R.D. 560, 562–63 (S.D. Ind. 1990) (personal injury) (holding that plaintiff was entitled to discover defendant's indemnity policy—not limited to policy limits).

§ 8 TAX RETURNS

Commentary

Although the statutory statement of privilege for tax returns is not absolute, there is a valid public policy against their disclosure, and courts should not order the disclosure of income tax returns where the information sought is readily obtainable by other means or from other sources. *See, e.g., Biliske v. American Live Stock Ins. Co.*, 73 F.R.D. 124, 126 n.2 (D. Okla. 1977); *Federal Sav. & Loan Ins. Corp. v. Krueger*, 55 F.R.D. 512, 514 (N.D.

Ill. 1972). One court forbade the discovery of tax returns where all possible relevant information could be obtained from W-2 wage and tax statements already made available to defendants. *Maldonado v. St. Croix Discount, Inc.,* 77 F.R.D. 501, 503 (D.V.I. 1978).

Rules

26 U.S.C. §§ 6103(a), 7213(a) (1988).

26 C.F.R. § 301.6103 (1993).

Secondary Sources

AMERICAN LAW OF PRODUCTS LIABILITY 3D, *supra* § 1, § 53.85.

Cross, Annotation, *Discovery and Inspection of Income Tax Returns in Actions Between Private Individuals,* 70 A.L.R. 2D 240 (1960).

DISCOVERY PROCEEDINGS IN FEDERAL COURT, *supra* § 2, § 16.10.

Smith, Annotation, *Validity, Construction, and Effect of State Laws Requiring Public Officials to Protect Confidentiality of Income Tax Returns or Information,* 1 A.L.R. 4TH 959 (1980).

8 WRIGHT & MILLER, *supra* § 1, § 2019, at 162–64.

Case Law

Premium Serv. Corp. v. Sperry & Hutchinson Co., 511 F.2d 225, 229 (9th Cir. 1975).

Mitsui & Co. v. Puerto Rico Water Resources Auth., 79 F.R.D. 72 (D.P.R. 1978).

Stark v. Photo Researchers, Inc., 77 F.R.D. 18, 21 (S.D.N.Y. 1977).

Shaver v. Yacht Outward Bound, 71 F.R.D. 561, 563 (N.D. Ill. 1976).

Hunt v. Windon, 604 So. 2d 395, 397–98 (Ala. 1992) (citizen suit) (holding that it was not an abuse of discretion to require defendant to produce income-tax records under an appropriate protective order).

§ 9 MEDICAL RECORDS

§ 9.1 GENERALLY

Commentary

The discoverability of medical records may arise in either of two situations. First, either party may seek information concerning the opposing party's mental or physical condition for reasons that pertain to the case in chief. Second, either party may want to know what medical information is already known to the opposing party; e.g., what knowledge the defendant has of the plaintiff's medical history or present condition.

Rules

FED. R. CIV. P. 26(b)(3), 26(b)(4), 35.

FED. R. EVID. 501.

Secondary Sources

AMERICAN LAW OF PRODUCTS LIABILITY 3D, *supra* § 1, §§ 53:9, 53:51.

Cramer, *Discovery of Medical and Hospital Records*, 58 FLA. B.J. 149 (1984).

DISCOVERY PROCEEDINGS IN FEDERAL COURT, *supra* § 2, § 15.43.

Frantz, Annotation, *Discovery of Hospital's Internal Records or Communications as to Qualifications or Evaluations of Individual Physician*, 81 A.L.R. 3D 944 (1977).

Garrity, *Discovery of an Insurer's Files: Now You See It, Now You Don't*, 20 FORUM 20 (1984).

Jennings, *Litigating Medical Device Product Liability Claims*, 20 FORUM 141 (1984).

Johns, Annotation, *Pretrial Testimony or Disclosure on Discovery by Party to Personal Injury Action as to Nature of Injuries or Treatment as Waiver of Physician-Patient Privilege*, 25 A.L.R. 3D 1401 (1969).

Marvel, Annotation, *Commencing Action Involving Physical Condition of Plaintiff or Decedent as Waiving Physician-Patient Privilege as to Discovery Proceedings*, 21 A.L.R. 3D 912 (1968).

4 MOORE ET AL., *supra* § 1, ¶ 26.56[5].

4A MOORE ET AL., *supra* § 1, ¶¶ 33.18, 34.13.

Reisler & Samworth, *Production of Medical Records*, 6 ADVOC. Q. 257 (1985).

Case Law

Vincent v. Connaught Lab., Inc., 131 F.R.D. 156 (E.D. Mo. 1990).

Brown v. Eli Lilly & Co., 131 F.R.D. 176 (D. Neb. 1990).

Bohrer v. Merrill-Dow Pharmaceuticals, Inc., 22 F.R.D. 217 (D.N.D. 1987).

Schuler v. United States, 113 F.R.D. 518 (W.D. Mich. 1986).

Marte v. W.O. Hickok Mfg. Co., 552 N.Y.S.2d 297, 298 (App. Div. 1990) (products case; machinery) (recognizing plaintiff's right to discover contents of his own personnel file maintained by his employer, a third-party defendant).

Renucci v. Mercy Hosp., 508 N.Y.S.2d 518, 519 (App. Div. 1986).

Contra

8 WRIGHT & MILLER, *supra* § 1, § 2015, at 118 n.46.

§ 9.2 PLAINTIFF'S MEDICAL RECORDS

Commentary

A party's medical history may be relevant to the subject matter of a claim or defense in a pending action. In that event, the party's prior medical records dealing with the pertinent condition may be discoverable. Discovery should not extend to medical conditions which are not directly related to a specific claim or defense. A court may restrict the discovery of all or portions of a party's medical records out of respect for the party's right of privacy.

Secondary Sources

DISCOVERY PROCEEDINGS IN FEDERAL COURT, *supra* § 2, § 15.43.

Marvel, Annotation, *Commencing Action Involving Physical Condition of Plaintiff or Decedent as Waiving Physician-Patient Privilege as to Discovery Proceedings*, 21 A.L.R. 3D 912 (1968).

Wakefield, Annotation, *Physician-Patient Privilege as Extending to Patient's Medical or Hospital Records*, 10 A.L.R. 4TH 552 (1981).

Case Law

Boldt v. Sanders, 111 N.W.2d 225 (Minn. 1961) (personal injury; automobile accident) (allowing discovery of plaintiff's medical history).

§ 9.3 DEFENDANT'S MEDICAL RECORDS

Commentary

A party's medical history may be relevant to the subject matter of a claim or defense in a pending action. In that event, the party's prior medical records dealing with the pertinent condition may be discoverable. Discovery should not extend to medical conditions which are not directly related to a specific claim or defense. A court may restrict the discovery of all or portions of a party's medical records out of respect for the party's right of privacy.

§ 9.4 COURT-APPOINTED PHYSICIAN OR OTHER EXPERT

Commentary

A party who has been compelled to submit to a physical or mental examination under rule 35 should be entitled to orally depose the examining physician.

Rule

FED. R. CIV. P. 35.

Secondary Sources

HAYDOCK & HERR, *supra* § 3, § 6.11.

8 WRIGHT & MILLER, *supra* § 1, § 2237.

Case Law

Crowe v. Nivison, 145 F.R.D. 657 (D. Md. 1993) (holding that rule 35 allows examined party's taking of deposition of examining physician for use at trial).

Smith v. Oelenschlager, No. 86-7161 1987 U.S. Dist. LEXIS 3123 (E.D. Pa. Apr. 22, 1987) (personal injury; negligence action) (allowing plaintiff to depose court-appointed examining doctor after defendant chose not to call the doctor as a witness at trial).

Contra

Brown v. Ringstad, 142 F.R.D. 461, 463 (S.D. Iowa 1992) (holding that where the defendant decided not to call the court-appointed examining medical expert as a witness, the plaintiff may depose the expert only upon a showing of exceptional circumstances).

§ 9.5 PLAINTIFF'S MEDICAL RECORDS IN POSSESSION OF DEFENDANT

Commentary

Defendants frequently obtain copies of the plaintiff's medical records without the knowledge or consent of the plaintiff or counsel for the plaintiff. The defendant's insurance company may acquire the plaintiff's records from medical databases available to insurance carriers. Although the practice is the subject of considerable controversy, defense counsel may make direct ex parte contact with the plaintiff's physician or hospital. However the plaintiff's medical records are acquired by the defendant, the plaintiff should be entitled to obtain through discovery copies of any of his or her own medical records in the defendant's possession.

§ 10 IDENTIFICATION OF PARTIES

Commentary

Information disclosing the correct legal designation of an entity named as a party defendant is clearly discoverable. Information concerning the relationship between multiple defendants named in an action may be relevant and therefore discoverable for any one of several reasons, including (1) the identification of the proper party, (2) the identification of sources of discoverable information, and (3) the disclosure of the interest or bias of witnesses. The latter reason is particularly applicable in cases in which a joint defense agreement exists among various defendants.

Rule

FED. R. CIV. P. 26(b)(1).

Secondary Sources

8 WRIGHT & MILLER, *supra* § 1, § 2009, at 75 n.49, § 2013.

Case Law

In re Dayco Corp. Derivative Sec. Litig., 99 F.R.D. 616 (S.D. Ohio 1983), *motion overruled, motion sustained*, 102 F.R.D. 468 (S.D. Ohio 1984).

Ex parte Dorsey Trailers, Inc., 397 So. 2d 98, 106–07 (Ala. 1981).

City of Long Beach v. Superior Court, 134 Cal. Rptr. 468 (Ct. App. 1976).

§ 11 DEFENDANT'S ORGANIZATIONAL STRUCTURE

Commentary

The justification for permitting discovery of a defendant's organizational structure is that such information may lead to disclosure of the identity of potential witnesses and relevant documents as contemplated by Fed. R. Civ. P. 26(b)(1).

Secondary Sources
Kiely, Preparing Products Liability Cases §§ 1.18, 3.50–3.55 (1986 & Supp. 1989).

Case Law
Marker v. Union Fidelity Life Ins. Co., 125 F.R.D. 121, 126–27 (M.D.N.C. 1989) (insurance contract action) (compelling defendant to produce employee familiar with retrieval of computerized data for rule 30(b)(6) deposition).

Carter-Wallace, Inc. v. Hartz Mountain Indus., 92 F.R.D. 67, 70 (S.D.N.Y. 1981) (antitrust action) (holding that information concerning defendant's organizational structure was discoverable).

Clark v. General Motors Corp., 20 Fed. R. Serv. 2d (Callaghan) 679, 682–83 (D. Mass. 1975) (products case; stove) (holding that name of person presently in charge of design was discoverable).

Blackner v. Clark Equip. Co., CA No. 2860 (Philadelphia, Pa. Ct. C.P. Nov. 7, 1983) (products case; forklift rollover).

§ 12 MEMBERSHIP IN TRADE ORGANIZATIONS

Commentary
The defendant's membership in a trade organization might well lead to discovery of such relevant information as (1) the state of the art, (2) applicable industry or in-house standards, (3) relevant research and development, (4) identity of lay or expert witnesses, (5) interest or bias of opposing witnesses, and (6) identity of potential defendants. Such information would be of particular value if the corporate manufacturer raised the defense that the product complied with the state of the art, industry custom, industry standard, or a governmental regulation.

Secondary Sources
Kiely, *supra* § 11, § 1.17.

Case Law
Roesberg v. Johns-Manville Corp., 85 F.R.D. 292, 300–01 (E.D. Pa. 1980) (products case; asbestos) (holding that request for defendant to identify all trade organizations, associations, or other entities to which it has belonged should be answered).

Kelleher v. Omark Indus., 20 Fed. R. Serv. 2d (Callaghan) 199, 201–02 (D. Mass. 1975) (products case; stud gun) (holding that plaintiff was entitled to discover identity of defendant's employees in independent research responsible for designing and developing the stud gun, including industry standards and state, local, and federal regulations).

Budget Rent-A-Car, Inc. v. Hertz Corp., 55 F.R.D. 354, 358 (W.D. Mo. 1972) (antitrust action) (finding that a reference to membership directory was an insufficient response to a request for names of certain persons involved with car rental association to which defendant belonged).

Blackner v. Clark Equip. Co., CA No. 2860 (Philadelphia, Pa. Ct. C.P. Nov. 7, 1983) (products case; forklift rollover).

§ 13 IDENTITY OF COMPETITORS AND/OR MEMBERS OF THE INDUSTRY

Commentary

The identity of the defendant's competitors or other companies that make up the relevant industry may well lead to discovery such as (1) the state of the art, (2) applicable industry or in-house standards, (3) relevant research and development, (4) identity of lay or expert witnesses, (5) interest or bias of opposing witnesses, and (6) identity of potential defendants. Such information would be of particular value if the corporate manufacturer raised the defense that the product complied with the state of the art, industry custom, industry standard, or a governmental regulation.

Secondary Sources

KIELY, *supra* § 11, § 1.17.

Case Law

Kaplan v. Roux Lab., Inc., 76 N.Y.S.2d 601 (App. Div. 1948).

§ 14 CORPORATE RECORD RETENTION/DESTRUCTION PROGRAM
(See also § 45)

Commentary

Some corporations have adopted programs regarding the retention and destruction of records that come into existence in the ordinary course of the company's business. Because the implementation of such a program might affect the availability of an admittedly relevant document, discovery of the terms and details of the program is well within the scope of permissible discovery. Further, the defendant's intent in using a document retention/destruction program to destroy potentially relevant evidence might well be admissible at trial or relevant in determining whether to impose sanctions.

Secondary Sources

GORELICK ET AL., DESTRUCTION OF EVIDENCE chs. 3, 8, 9, 10 (1989 & Supp. 1991).

Whitworth & Gilbert, *Punishing Evidence Destruction*, TRIAL, Nov. 1992, at 66.

Case Law

In re "Agent Orange" Prod. Liab. Litig., 98 F.R.D. 558, 559 (E.D.N.Y. 1983).

§ 15 IDENTIFICATION OF NONEXPERT WITNESSES

§ 15.1 GENERALLY

Commentary

FED. R. CIV. P. 26(b)(1) states that "the identity and location of persons having knowledge of any discoverable matter is generally discoverable if it is not privileged information." An inquiry that seeks the identity of potential witnesses should be distinguished from a discovery request seeking to compel an opposing party to identify (1) persons who participated in preparation of the responses to previous discovery and (2) witnesses an opposing party expects to call at trial. As to persons participating in discovery responses, see § 6. Most federal courts have held that pretrial discovery of a party's anticipated trial witnesses is not permitted.

Secondary Sources

Connelly, Annotation, *Right to Elicit Expert Testimony from Adverse Party Called as Witness*, 88 A.L.R. 2D 1186 (1963).

Day, *The Ordinary Witness Doctrine: Discovery of the Pre-Retention Knowledge of a Nonwitness Expert Under Federal Rule 26(b)(4)(B)*, 38 ARK. L. REV. 763 (1985).

DISCOVERY PROCEEDINGS IN FEDERAL COURT, *supra* § 2, § 16.5.

Klein, Annotation, *Identity of Witnesses Whom Adverse Party Plans to Call to Testify at Civil Trial, as Subject of Pretrial Discovery*, 19 A.L.R. 3D 1114 (1968).

McDonald, Comment, *The In-House Expert Witness: Discovery Under the Federal Rules of Civil Procedure*, 33 S.D. L. REV. 283 (1988).

Pielemeier, *Discovery of Non-Testifying "In-House" Experts Under Federal Rule of Civil Procedure 26*, 58 IND. L.J. 597 (1982–1983).

Case Law

Marker v. Union Fidelity Life Ins. Co., 125 F.R.D. 121, 126–27 (M.D.N.C. 1989) (insurance contract action) (permitting 30(b)(6) deposition of person knowledgeable about company's general record-keeping storage and retrieval system).

Durham v. Hoffman-LaRoche, CA No. CV 89-L-0075-S (N.D. Ala. order on motion to reconsider, Nov. 8, 1989) (products case; drug Accutane) (requiring manufacturer to produce adverse drug reaction reports that included names of reporting physicians).

Kelleher v. Omark Indus., 20 Fed. R. Serv. 2d (Callaghan) 199, 201–02 (D. Mass. 1975) (products case; stud gun) (while finding that statements taken from witnesses during an investigation in anticipation of litigation were protected, the court held that names and addresses of persons giving them were not protected and allowed plaintiff to discover identity of persons involved in the design of the product).

Clark v. General Motors Corp., 20 Fed. R. Serv. 2d (Callaghan) 679, 682–83 (D. Mass. 1975) (products case; stove) (ordering defendant to provide name of person in defendant's company who was in charge of the design of the product involved in the action).

Green v. Shepherd Constr. Co., CA No. 11740 (N.D. Ga. Oct. 21, 1969) (products case; spring shackle) (ordering Ford to identify present and former employees having information about the design and specifications of the subject product).

Butler v. United States, 226 F. Supp. 341, 343 (W.D. Mo. 1964) (Federal Tort Claims Act case) (holding that work-product privilege did not apply to custodian of documents).

B. & S. Drilling Co. v. Halliburton Oil Well Cementing Co., 24 F.R.D. 1, 3 (S.D. Tex. 1959) (negligence action by employee against employer) (holding that interrogatories may require disclosure of names of persons having knowledge of facts pertaining to the cause of action).

Cohen v. Procter & Gamble Distrib. Co., 18 F.R.D. 301, 301–02 (D. Del. 1955) (products case; detergent) (finding that names and addresses of defendant's employees who have knowledge of communications from the public concerning harmfulness of product were discoverable as were names of persons who had made investigations on behalf of defendant in other similar lawsuits).

Bloomquist v. ConAgra, Inc., 481 N.W.2d 156, 161 (Neb. 1992) (negligence action; personal injury) (finding that the identity of witnesses with knowledge of damaging admissions was discoverable).

Marte v. W.O. Hickok Mfg. Co., 552 N.Y.S.2d 297, 298 (App. Div. 1990) (products case; rotating gears) (recognizing plaintiff's right to discover list of all of third-party defendant's employees who operated a similar machine on or prior to the date of the subject accident).

Wagi v. Silver Ridge Park W., 580 A.2d 1093 (N.J. Super. Ct. Law Div. 1989) (finding that neither attorney-client nor work-product privilege protects from release the names and addresses of witnesses; however, court refused to require production of the witness's statements).

See also

Roesberg v. Johns-Manville Corp., 85 F.R.D. 292, 297–98 (E.D. Pa. 1980).

In re Anthracite Coal Antitrust Litig., 81 F.R.D. 516, 519 (M.D. Pa. 1979).

Newsom v. Breon Lab., Inc., 709 S.W.2d 559 (Tenn. 1986) (allowing plaintiff to discover the names of physicians who submitted drug reaction or drug experience reports to the manufacturer under a protective order that forbade the disclosure of the names in the absence of written permission).

Foster v. Cunningham, 825 S.W.2d 806 (Tex. Ct. App. 1992) (allowing request for identity of potential witnesses during a deposition).

Hunter v. Hawkes Hosp., 574 N.E.2d 1147 (Ohio Ct. App. 1989).

§ 15.2 IDENTIFICATION OF BLOOD DONORS AND OTHER RELATED SITUATIONS

Commentary

The Social Security Administration has issued final regulations to govern the Blood Donor Locator Service, which it will establish and conduct pursuant to the Technical and Miscellaneous Revenue Act of 1988 (Pub. L. No. 100–647, § 8008, 102 Stat. 3783, 3784-87 (1988)). Under these regulations, the agency will furnish to participating states, at their request, the last known personal mailing address of donors whose blood donations indicate that they are or may be HIV-infected.

Secondary Sources

Ellmore, Annotation, *Discovery of Identity of Blood Donor*, 56 A.L.R. 4TH 755 (1987).

Kunin, Note, *Transfusion-Related AIDS Litigation: Permitting Limited Discovery from Blood Donors in Single Donor Cases*, 76 CORNELL L. REV. 927 (1991).

Case Law

Watson v. Lowcountry Red Cross, 974 F.2d 482 (4th Cir. 1992) (AIDS case) (plaintiff sought identity of the donor or the opportunity to examine the donor through a court-appointed intermediary; court held that the discovery of the identity of the donor would not lead to a depletion of the blood supply and that the donor's right of privacy was not violated. The court permitted discovery of the donor where the identity would be known only to the court and the donor's court-appointed lawyer.).

Farnsworth v. Procter & Gamble Co., 758 F.2d 1545, 1547 (11th Cir. 1985) (products case; toxic shock) (allowing both parties to obtain copy of study conducted by Centers for Disease Control; however, court denied access to the names and addresses of study participants).

Doe v. American Nat'l Red Cross, 788 F. Supp. 884, 889 (D.S.C. 1992) (AIDS case) (finding that blood collection agency could not be compelled to disclose donor's identity in actions alleging transfusions of HIV-contaminated blood under South Carolina statute).

Sampson v. American Nat'l Red Cross, 139 F.R.D. 95, 99–100 (N.D. Tex. 1991) (AIDS case) (finding that plaintiff's counsel and experts were entitled to obtain identity of donor, subject to appropriate protective order forbidding disclosure of name).

Borzillieri v. American Nat'l Red Cross, 139 F.R.D. 284 (W.D.N.Y. 1991) (AIDS case) (permitting limited discovery from blood donor whose blood had infected plaintiff's decedent, but to protect donor's identity, interrogatory was delivered to donor through defense counsel).

Stenger v. Lehigh Valley Hosp. Ctr., 609 A.2d 796 (Pa. 1992) (AIDS case) (permitting limited discovery of blood donors in AIDS test results and holding that anonymous discovery would unintrusively safeguard privacy rights and help insure that blood collection centers screen blood responsibly).

Most v. Tulane Medical Ctr., 576 So. 2d 1387 (La. 1991) (HIV case) (permitting plaintiff to discover identity of one donor and conduct limited inquiry concerning blood bank's screening process).

Doe v. Puget Sound Blood Ctr., 819 P.2d 370 (Wash. 1991) (en banc) (AIDS case) (permitting the estate of a man who died from AIDS allegedly caused by tainted blood transfusion to discover the blood donor's identity).

Laburre v. East Jefferson Gen. Hosp., 555 So. 2d 1381 (La. 1990) (hepatitis case) (refusing to permit plaintiff to discover the identities of everyone who had donated blood).

See also

Irwin Memorial Blood Bank v. Superior Court, 279 Cal. Rptr. 911 (Ct. App. 1991).

Howell v. Spokane & Inland Empire Blood Bank, 818 P.2d 1056, 1061 (Wash. 1991).

Snyder v. Mekhjian, 582 A.2d 307, 313–15 (N.J. Super. Ct. App. Div. 1990).

§ 15.3 ANTICIPATED TRIAL WITNESSES

Commentary

In view of the fact that the trial court's pretrial order ordinarily requires disclosure of anticipated witnesses and exhibits (*see Wirtz v. Hooper-Holmes Bureau, Inc.*, 327 F.2d 939, 942 (5th Cir. 1964)), the majority of federal courts that have addressed the issue have held that pretrial disclosure of a party's anticipated trial witnesses and exhibits cannot be obtained by discovery.

Rules

1993 Amendments, FED. R. CIV. P. 26(a)(1), 26(a)(3).

Secondary Sources

DISCOVERY PROCEEDINGS IN FEDERAL COURT, *supra* § 2, § 16.5.

DOMBROFF, *supra* § 3, § 12.48.

8 WRIGHT & MILLER, *supra* § 1, §§ 2012, 2013.

Case Law

Wirtz v. Continental Fin. & Loan Co. of W. End, 326 F.2d 561, 564 (5th Cir. 1964).

Wirtz v. B.A.C. Steel Prods., Inc., 312 F.2d 14, 16 (4th Cir. 1962).

Padovani v. Bruchhausen, 293 F.2d 546, 549–50 (2d Cir. 1961).

Colorado v. Schmidt-Tiago Constr. Co., 108 F.R.D. 731, 735 (D. Colo. 1985) (antitrust action) (holding that names of persons scheduled or likely to be called as witnesses were discoverable).

Uinta Oil Refining Co. v. Continental Oil Co., 226 F. Supp. 495, 505–06 (D. Utah 1964).

Contra

Brennan v. Engineered Prods., Inc., 506 F.2d 299, 303 n.2 (8th Cir. 1974) (Fair Labor Standards Act suit) (holding that the identities of witnesses to be called at trial were not discoverable).

§ 16 EXPERT WITNESSES

§ 16.1 GENERALLY

(See also §§ 9, 22.5, 46)

Commentary

The discovery rules seem to describe three categories of expert witnesses:

1. Trial experts: An expert who is anticipated to be called at trial. Discovery concerning this type of expert is limited. *See* FED. R. CIV. P. 26(b)(4)(A) and § 16.3, *infra*.

2. Consulting experts: An expert with whom counsel has consulted but who does not expect to be called at trial as a witness. Discovery is generally not allowed. *See* FED. R. CIV. P. 26(b)(4)(B) and § 16.2, *infra*.

3. Fact witness: Someone who acquired facts and knowledge (albeit expertise) in the ordinary course of the defendant's business. Discovery from such an "expert" is like any other fact witness. *See* § 15.1 *supra*, § 16.2, *infra*.

Rules

FED. R. CIV. P. 26(b)(1), 26(b)(4)(A), 26(b)(4)(B), 45.

Secondary Sources

AMERICAN LAW OF PRODUCTS LIABILITY 3D, *supra* § 1, §§ 53:14–53:27.

Annotation, *Admissibility of Testimony of Expert, as to Basis of His Opinion, to Matters Otherwise Excludible as Hearsay—State Cases*, 89 A.L.R. 4TH 456 (1991).

Cannon, Note, *Federal Discovery Practices Concerning Expert Witnesses*, 14 OKLA. CITY U. L. REV. 391 (1989).

Chu, *Discovery of Experts*, LITIG., Winter 1982, at 13.

Comment, *Discovery of Expert Information Under the Federal Rules*, 10 U. RICH. L. REV. 706 (1976).

Connelly, Annotation, *Right to Elicit Expert Testimony from Adverse Party Called as Witness*, 88 A.L.R. 2D 1186 (1963).

Connors, *A New Look at an Old Concern—Protecting Expert Information from Discovery Under the Federal Rules*, 18 DUQ. L. REV. 271 (1980).

Crockett, Note, *Discovery of Expert Information*, 47 N.C. L. REV. 401 (1969).

Day & Dixon, *A Judicial Perspective on Expert Discovery Under Federal Rule 26(b)(4): An Empirical Study of Trial Court Judges and a Proposed Amendment*, 20 J. MARSHALL L. REV. 377 (1987).

Diestelmeier, Note, *Business Litigation: Liberal Discovery of Expert Witness Reports or Insulation from Discovery Under the Work Product Doctrine?*, 16 J. CORP. L. 71 (1990).

DISCOVERY PROCEEDINGS IN FEDERAL COURT, *supra* § 2, §§ 3.10–3.11, 16.19–16.24.

DOMBROFF, *supra* § 3, §§ 2.15–2.25, 12.38–12.39, ch. 13.

Epstein, *Deposing Expert Witnesses*, PLI Order No. H4-5042 (Apr. 1, 1988).

Foster, Annotation, *Pretrial Deposition-Discovery of Opinions of Opponent's Expert Witnesses*, 86 A.L.R. 2D 138 (1962).

Graham, *Discovery of Experts Under Rule 26(b)(4) of the Federal Rules of Civil Procedure:*

Part One, An Analytical Study, 1976 U. ILL. L. FORUM 895.

Graham, *Discovery of Experts Under Rule 26(b)(4) of the Federal Rules of Civil Procedure: Part Two, An Empirical Study and a Proposal,* 1977 U. ILL. L. FORUM 169.

HAYDOCK & HERR, *supra* § 3, §§ 1.7, 1.7.2, 1.7.7, 1.7.8.

Hayes & Ryder, *Rule 26(b)(4) of the Federal Rules of Civil Procedure: Discovery of Expert Information,* 42 U. MIAMI L. REV. 1101 (1988).

Joseph, *Current Issues in Discovery,* PLI Order No. HI4-5124 (Feb. 19, 1992).

Leval, *Discovery of Experts Under the Federal Rules,* LITIG., Fall 1976, at 16.

Lewis, Note, *Discovery Under the Federal Rules of Civil Procedure of Attorney Opinion Work Product Provided to an Expert Witness,* 53 FORDHAM L. REV. 1159 (1985).

Marcus, *Discovery Along the Litigation/Science Interface,* 57 BROOK. L. REV. 381 (1991).

McLaughlin, *Discovery and Admissibility of Expert Testimony,* 63 NOTRE DAME L. REV. 760 (1988).

McLaughlin, *Discovery and Admissibility of Expert Testimony,* 33 TRIAL LAW. GUIDE 533 (1989).

4 MOORE ET AL., *supra* § 1, ¶ 26.66[3].

Nelson, Comment, *Discovery of Attorney-Expert Communications: Current State of, and Suggestions for, Federal and Missouri Practice,* 57 MO. L. REV. 247 (1992).

Preuss, *Finding an Achilles Heel: Discovery Techniques for Adverse Experts,* 59 DEF. COUNS. J. 351 (1992).

Riesel, *Discovery and Examination of Scientific Experts,* PRAC. LAW., Sept. 1986, at 59.

Riesel, *Pre-Trial Discovery of Experts, Scientific Proof, and Examination of Experts in Environmental Litigation,* C534 A.L.I.-A.B.A. 485 (1990).

Schatz, *How to Prepare the Expert and Defend His Deposition,* PLI Order No. H4-5042 (Apr. 1, 1988).

Schwab et al., *Scope of Discovery Against Expert Witnesses Under the Federal Rules,* PLI Order No. H4-5042 (Apr. 1, 1988).

Sims, Note, *Treating Experts Like Ordinary Witnesses: Recent Trends in Discovery of Testifying Experts Under Federal Rule of Civil Procedure 26(b)(4),* 66 WASH. U. L.Q. 787 (1988).

Trenkner, Annotation, *Pretrial Discovery of Facts Known and Opinions Held by Opponent's Experts Under Rule 26(b)(4) of Federal Rules of Civil Procedure,* 33 A.L.R. FED. 403 (1977).

Vuckovich, Case Note, Diminskis v. Chicago Transit Authority, *Circumventing the Expert Witness Discovery,* 21 LOY. U. CHI. L.J. 887 (1990).

Wells, Note, *Interaction Between 26(b)(3) and 26(b)(4) of the Federal Rules of Civil Procedure: Conflict and Confusion in the Federal Courts,* 9 AM. J. TRIAL ADVOC. 319 (1985).

Whitehead, *Expert Witnesses in Discovery and Trial,* PLI Order No. H4-5053 (Oct. 1, 1988).

Wildermuth, Note, *Blind Man's Bluff: An Analysis of the Discovery of Expert Witnesses Under Federal Rule of Civil Procedure 26(b)(4) and a Proposed Amendment*, 64 IND. L.J. 925 (1989).

8 WRIGHT & MILLER, *supra* § 1, §§ 2029–2031, 2034.

§ 16.2 FACT WITNESS EXPERTS

(See also § 15.1)

Commentary

This category of "expert" witnesses involves ordinary fact witnesses who just happen to be experts, e.g., employees of the defendant manufacturer who acquire facts and information in the performance of their ordinary job duties for the defendant company.

Rule

FED. R. CIV. P. 26(b)(1).

Secondary Sources

See also references cited in § 16.1, *supra*.

HAYDOCK & HERR, *supra* § 3, §§ 1.7.1, 1.7.4, 1.7.5.

Labaton, Note, *Discovery and Testimony of Unretained Experts: Creating a Clear and Equitable Standard to Govern Compliance with Subpoenas*, 1987 DUKE L.J. 140.

Ladd, *Discovery of Nonwitness Experts*, 36 FED'N INS. & CORP. COUNS. Q. 307 (1986).

McDonald, Comment, *Gimme Shelter? Not if You Are a Non-Witness Expert Under Rule 26(b)(4)(B)*, 56 U. CIN. L. REV. 1027 (1988).

McDonald, Comment, *The In-House Expert Witness: Discovery Under the Federal Rules of Civil Procedure*, 33 S.D. L. REV. 283 (1988).

Pielemeier, *Discovery of Non-Testifying "In-House" Experts Under Federal Rule of Civil Procedure 26*, 58 IND. L.J. 597 (1983).

Case Law

Axelson, Inc. v. McIlhany, 798 S.W.2d 550 (Tex. 1990) (gas well explosion) (defendant sought discovery of witnesses who were active participants in the well's operation and who were later designated consulting experts. Reversing the lower court, court held that the information sought was not shielded by discovery by merely changing the designation of a person with knowledge of relevant facts to a consulting expert. Court further held that persons who gain factual information by virtue of their involvement relating to the incident or transaction giving rise to the litigation did not qualify as consultant experts because the consultation was not the only source of information.).

Neal v. Lu, 530 A.2d 103, 107–08 (Pa. Super. Ct. 1987) (medical negligence action) (defendant doctor during discovery failed to list himself as expert witness; court held that state equivalent of rule 26(b)(4) applied only to discovery of experts retained or specially employed in anticipation of litigation. Rule did not apply to facts and opinions acquired in the usual and ordinary course of business prior to the commencement of litigation: "The Rule simply does not apply to expert opinions of a party when a matter within that party's field of expertise is at issue.").

§ 16.3 TRIAL EXPERTS

Commentary

There are two criteria for a trial expert: A trial expert (1) must have acquired facts and opinions in anticipation of litigation or for trial and (2) is a witness whom the party expects to call at trial.

FED. R. CIV. P. 26(b)(4)(A) sets forth both the method and the scope of discovery unless the court orders otherwise. Initially, discovery of information from trial experts may only be acquired by interrogatories. As to the scope of discovery, the rule specifically states that the experts' names, the subject matter of their opinions, and the substance of the facts and opinions to which they are expected to testify are discoverable. The majority of courts also allow discovery of the qualifications of a trial expert. The courts are divided, though, on whether information concerning the interest or bias of a trial expert is discoverable.

Rule

FED. R. CIV. P. 26(b)(4)(A).

Secondary Sources

See references cited in § 16.1, *supra*.

Case Law

In re American Tobacco Co., 880 F.2d 1520, 1527–28 (2d Cir. 1989) (products case; cigarettes) (holding that expert's privilege did not extend to all existing documentary evidence).

Marino v. Otis Eng'g Corp., 839 F.2d 1404 (10th Cir. 1988).

Bogosian v. Gulf Oil Corp., 738 F.2d 587 (3d Cir. 1984) (antitrust action) (finding that documents reflecting "core work product" of attorney's legal theories were not so significant to expert's testimony as to waive protected status when the documents were shown to the expert).

Shelak v. White Motor Co., 581 F.2d 1155 (5th Cir. 1978).

Hawkins v. South Plains Int'l Trucks, Inc., 139 F.R.D. 679 (D. Colo. 1991) (products case; defective hot oil unit on truck) (defendant sought discovery from plaintiff's testifying expert; court required disclosure of (1) specific documents or scientific writings that expert reviewed for present case and (2) files of prior similar cases with which expert had been involved. The court refused to compel discovery of the expert's tax returns, but required plaintiff to produce other information reflecting the expert's income.).

Hotchkiss v. Sears, Roebuck & Co., 139 F.R.D. 313, 315, 316 (M.D. Pa.1991) (products case; radial arm saw) (refusing to allow defendant to depose plaintiff's trial expert or to compel plaintiff to produce expert's report).

Anker v. G.D. Searle & Co., 126 F.R.D. 515 (M.D.N.C. 1989).

In re Kegg, 116 F.R.D. 643 (N.D. Ohio 1987).

Bockweg v. Anderson, 117 F.R.D. 563, 565–66 (M.D.N.C. 1987) (medical negligence action) (reading rules 26(b)(1) and 26(b)(4)(A) as complimentary and supportive of "liberal discovery of expert witnesses, including information relevant only for impeachment," court held that plaintiff's expert witnesses must answer questions relating to their involvement in other professional negligence actions).

North Carolina Elec. Membership Corp. v. Carolina Power & Light Co., 108 F.R.D. 283, 286 (M.D.N.C. 1985) (holding that opinion work product was privileged and nondiscoverable even when furnished to a testifying trial expert).

Boring v. Keller, 97 F.R.D. 404, 407–08 (D. Colo. 1983) (medical negligence action) (ordering production of attorney work-product documents furnished to a testifying trial expert).

Quadrini v. Sikorsky Aircraft Div., 74 F.R.D. 594, 595 (D. Conn. 1977) (helicopter crash) (allowing discovery of documents prepared for expert to review).

Clark v. General Motors Corp., 20 Fed. R. Serv. 2d (Callaghan) 679, 683 (D. Mass. 1975) (products case; stove) (finding that the identity of expert witnesses to be called at trial must be disclosed upon request).

Breedlove v. Beech Aircraft Corp., 57 F.R.D. 202 (N.D. Miss. 1972).

Luey v. Sterling Drug, Inc., 240 F. Supp. 632, 635–36 (W.D. Mich. 1965) (products case; drug Aralen) (holding that the adverse party may examine the expert witness and his records if necessary for trial preparation and if the information could not be obtained by independent investigation or research).

Plitt v. Griggs, 585 So. 2d 1317, 1321–22 (Ala. 1991) (medical negligence action) (requiring medical expert to disclose identity of person who prepared tax return as that information might lead to discovery of amount of money expert earned from testifying for plaintiff in other professional negligence actions).

Tom L. Scott, Inc. v. McIlhaney, 798 S.W.2d 556 (Tex. 1990).

Ex parte Morris, 530 So. 2d 785, 787–88 (Ala. 1988) (medical negligence action) (holding that it was not an abuse of discretion to refuse to compel an expert witness to produce his income tax records).

Wood v. Tallahassee Memorial Regional Med. Ctr., Inc., 593 So. 2d 1140 (Fla. Dist. Ct. App.) (medical negligence action) (ordering plaintiff's nontreating medical witnesses to produce in camera their tax returns for preceding five years to the extent they reflected income received from activities associated with professional negligence actions), *review denied*, 599 So. 2d 1281 (Fla. 1992).

Keating v. Dominick's Finer Foods, Inc., 587 N.E.2d 57, 60 (Ill. App. Ct. 1992) (negligence action; personal injury) (implicitly recognizing discoverability of information concerning expert's financial interest and bias).

McAdoo v. Ogden, 573 So. 2d 1084 (Fla. Dist. Ct. App. 1991) (personal injury; automobile accident) (holding that plaintiff was entitled to production of bills defendant's expert submitted to other companies for which he had acted as an expert; information might serve to demonstrate expert's bias).

Jasopersaud v. Rho, 572 N.Y.S.2d 700, 703 (App. Div. 1991) (medical negligence action) (finding that qualifications of an expert were subject to discovery).

Richmond v. American Honda Motor Co., 571 So. 2d 491 (Fla. Dist. Ct. App. 1990) (products case; motorcycle) (requiring plaintiff to answer interrogatory requesting her to admit substantive testimony that her expert witness had given in previous case).

Rosario v. General Motors Corp., 543 N.Y.S.2d 974 (App. Div. 1989).

Marinelli v. Volkswagen of Am., Inc., CA No. CV89-3301 (Jefferson County, Ala. Cir. Ct. Apr. 24, 1991, Oct. 22, 1991, Feb. 19, 1992) (products case; vehicle rollover) (defendant's expert witness based his testimony in part on accident reconstruction analysis performed with the aid of a computer. In three separate orders the court instructed the defendant to provide plaintiff's counsel with an exact copy of the computer disk utilized by the defendant's expert witness including the software employed in the computer program.).

§ 16.4 CONSULTING EXPERTS

(See also § 22.5)

Commentary

A consulting expert is one "who has been retained or specially employed by another party in anticipation of litigation or preparation for trial and who is not expected to be called as a witness at trial." FED. R. CIV. P. 26(b)(4)(B). Discovery from a consulting expert is generally not permitted except on a showing of exceptional circumstances.

Rule

FED. R. CIV. P. 26(b)(4)(B).

Secondary Sources

See also references cited in § 16.1, *supra*.

Abraham, *The Use of Nontestifying Experts*, PLI Order No. H4-5042 (Apr. 1, 1988).

AMERICAN LAW OF PRODUCTS LIABILITY 3D, *supra* § 1, §§ 53:25–53:26.

Baron, *Learning of . . . Talking to . . . and Using . . . the Opponent's Consulting Expert Under the Federal Rules*, 31 S. TEX. L. REV. 539 (1990).

Clayton, Note, *In re* Shell Oil Refinery: *Great Expense Alone Is Not Enough to Satisfy the Exceptional Circumstances Standard of Federal Rule of Civil Procedure 26(b)(4)(B)*, 36 S.D. L. REV. 721 (1991).

Crockett, Note, *Civil Procedure—Discovery of Expert Information*, 47 N.C. L. REV. 401 (1969).

Day, *The Ordinary Witness Doctrine: Discovery of the Pre-Retention Knowledge of a Nonwitness Expert Under Federal Rule 26(b)(4)(B)*, 38 ARK. L. REV. 763 (1985).

DISCOVERY PROCEEDINGS IN FEDERAL COURT, *supra* § 2, § 16.23.

Emerick, Note, *Discovery of the Nontestifying Expert Witness' Identity Under the Federal Rules of Civil Procedure: You Can't Tell the Players Without a Program*, 37 HASTINGS L.J. 201 (1985).

HAYDOCK & HERR, *supra* § 3, §§ 1.7–1.7.6.

Hull, *Pre-Trial Discovery of Trial Preparation Materials Prepared, and Non-Testifying Experts Retained, in Anticipation of Prior Litigation*, 21 IND. L. REV. 57 (1988).

Imwinkelried, *The Application of the Attorney-Client Privilege to Non-Testifying Experts: Reestablishing the Boundaries Between the Attorney-Client Privilege and the Work Product Protection*, 68 WASH. U. L.Q. 19 (1990).

Ladd, *Discovery of Nonwitness Experts*, 36 FED'N INS. & CORP. COUNS. Q. 307 (1986).

McDonald, Comment, *Gimme Shelter? Not if You Are a Non-Witness Expert Under Rule 26(b)(4)(B)*, 56 U. CIN. L. REV. 1027 (1988).

McDonald, Comment, *The In-House Expert Witness: Discovery Under the Federal Rules of Civil Procedure*, 33 S.D. L. REV. 283 (1988).

4 MOORE ET AL., *supra* § 1, ¶ 26.66[4].

Note, *Discovery of Retained Nontestifying Experts' Identities Under the Federal Rules of Civil Procedure*, 80 MICH. L. REV. 513 (1982).

Parker, *Pitfalls of Testing Products in Design Defect Actions*, 60 DEF. COUNS. J. 37 (1993).

Pielemeier, *Discovery of Non-Testifying "In-House" Experts Under Federal Rule of Civil Procedure 26*, 58 IND. L.J. 597 (1983).

Platt, Comment, *Discovery of the Nonwitness Expert Under Federal Rule of Civil Procedure 26(b)(4)(B)*, 67 IOWA L. REV. 349 (1982).

Stasney, Recent Development, 22 ST. MARY'S L.J. 1171 (1991).

Stolte, Note, *A Policy Analysis of the Exceptional Circumstances Standard: Is* Coates v. AC & S, Inc. *Simply Another Step Toward the Search for Truth in Expert Discovery?*, 37 S.D. L. REV. 639 (1992).

8 WRIGHT & MILLER, *supra* § 1, §§ 2032–2033.

Case Law

Cox v. Piper, Jaffray & Hopwood, Inc., 848 F.2d 842 (8th Cir. 1988).

Chemical Eng'g Corp. v. Essef Indus., 795 F.2d 1565, 1575 n.11 (Fed. Cir. 1986) (patent infringement) (plaintiff failed to supplement its discovery response after its own in-house testing demonstrated that the defendant's device probably did not violate the suspect patent; court held that the plaintiff's failure to file a supplemental answer warranted sanctions and stated that the "notion that [the plaintiff] was free to refuse to admit the truth because the truth might have defeated its lawsuit is contrary to the duty of candor owed the court.").

Marine Petroleum Co. v. Champlin Petroleum Co., 641 F.2d 984, 994 (D.C. Cir. 1979) (price-fixing case) (court held that defendant's nontestifying independent consultant could not be deposed as to facts or opinions acquired after he began preparing for the litigation; court noted that rule 26(b)(4)(B) did not prevent discovery from a party or another with whom the expert shared the subject information.). *See also Puerto Rico Aqueduct & Sewer Auth. v. Clow Corp.*, 108 F.R.D. 304 (D.P.R. 1985). *Contra Roberts v. Heim*, 130 F.R.D. 424, 428 (N.D. Cal. 1989).

Nevels v. Ford Motor Co., 439 F.2d 251 (5th Cir. 1971).

Board of Directors, Water's Edge, Condominium Unit Owners' Ass'n v. Anden Group, 136 F.R.D. 100, 109 (E.D. Va. 1991) (products case; building material) (sanctioning defendant for failing to supplement its response to discovery requests by disclosing experts' adverse test results obtained subsequent to the institute of litigation).

Coates v. AC & S, Inc., 133 F.R.D. 109 (E.D. La. 1990).

In re Shell Oil Refinery, 132 F.R.D. 437, 441–43 (E.D. La. 1990) (catalytic cracking unit explosion) (court held that cost in the range of $230,000 to $315,000 to duplicate defendant's tests did not satisfy the "exceptional circumstances" requirement; court rejected per se rule barring "in-house experts" from protection under rule 26(b)(4)(B) and listed factors that effect determination. Court also noted that facts and opinions acquired prior to employees' special retention were not protected from discovery.), *clarified*, 134 F.R.D. 148 (E.D. La. 1990). Other cases indicating that rule 26(b)(4)(B) protection could be applied to regular employees include *Marine Petroleum Co. v. Champlin Petroleum Co.*, 641 F.2d 984, 993 (D.C. Cir. 1979); *In re Sinking of Barge "Ranger I,"* 92 F.R.D. 486, 489 n.5 (S.D. Tex. 1981); *Seiffer v. Topsy's Int'l, Inc.*, 69 F.R.D. 69, 72 n.3 (D. Kan. 1975).

Perry v. Jeep Eagle Corp., 126 F.R.D. 542, 544–45 (S.D. Ind. 1989) (products case; automobile) (plaintiff sought to depose consulting expert who had done testing for the defendant; court held that rule 26(b)(4)(D) prohibited discovery of both facts and opinions held by nontestifying experts absent a showing of exceptional circumstances.).

In re Snyder, 115 F.R.D. 211 (D. Ariz. 1987).

Eliasen v. Hamilton, 111 F.R.D. 396, 401 (N.D. Ill. 1986) (securities case) (offering justification for consulting-expert rule).

Kansas-Nebraska Natural Gas Co. v. Marathon Oil Co., 109 F.R.D. 12, 14–16 (D. Neb. 1985) (holding that under the circumstances in-house employees would not qualify as consulting experts).

Delcastor, Inc. v. Vail Assocs., Inc., 108 F.R.D. 405, 409 (D. Colo. 1985) (mudslide) (construing the "exceptional circumstances" language of rule 26(b)(4)(B) to require the moving party to show an inability to discover the equivalent information).

Grindell v. American Motors Corp., 108 F.R.D. 94 (W.D.N.Y. 1985) (products case; automobile) (plaintiff sought to depose consulting expert who had done testing for the defendant; court held that rule 26(b)(4)(B) prevented discovery of both facts and opinions held by nontestifying experts.).

United States v. 22.80 Acres of Land, 107 F.R.D. 20, 21–22, 25 (N.D. Cal. 1985) (finding that an appraisal report by employee of government was discoverable for either of two reasons: (1) employee not "retained or specially employed" and/or (2) report not prepared in anticipation of litigation; work-product privilege waived for portions of report disclosed to supervisors in preparing for deposition).

Wright v. Jeep Corp., 547 F. Supp. 871 (E.D. Mich. 1982).

Roesberg v. Johns-Manville Corp., 85 F.R.D. 292 (E.D. Pa. 1980) (products case; asbestos) ("If an expert who will not testify at trial has been retained by the opposing party, the 'facts known or opinions held' by the expert may be discovered as provided in FED. R. CIV. P. 35(b) or 'upon a showing of exceptional circumstances. . .' .").

Loctite v. Fel-Pro Inc., 94 F.R.D. 1 (N.D. Ill. 1980) (patent infringement) (finding that plaintiff met the burden of demonstrating "exceptional circumstances," justifying discovery from a nontestifying consultant and sanctioning the plaintiff for failing to supplement its discovery responses; the plaintiff failed to provide the defendant with its laboratory supervisor's re-evaluation concluding that the defendant had probably not infringed the plaintiff's patent), *aff'd in part, remanded in part*, 667 F.2d 577 (7th Cir. 1981).

Gentron Corp. v. H.C. Johnson Agencies, Inc., 79 F.R.D. 415, 418–19 (E.D. Wis. 1978) (contract action) (when plaintiff proposed to use consultant expert to analyze discovery materials, defendant proposed protective order that would require disclosure of the identity of consultive expert; court issued protective order requiring plaintiff to indicate to the court, rather than to its adversary, the identity of experts to be used solely for consultation).

Pearl Brewing Co. v. Joseph Schlitz Brewing Co., 415 F. Supp. 1122, 1138–39 (S.D. Tex. 1976) (antitrust action) (holding that the inordinate amount of time, money, or resources that would have to be expended by the party seeking discovery to duplicate the work of the nontestifying expert could be a significant factor in determining whether "exceptional circumstances" exist). *See also In re "Agent Orange" Prod. Liab. Litig.*, 105 F.R.D. 577, 580–81 (E.D.N.Y. 1985).

Virginia Elec. & Power Co. v. Sun Shipbuilding & Dry Dock Co., 68 F.R.D. 397, 406–08 (E.D. Va. 1975) (holding that an employee of party could not qualify as a nontestifying consultant under rule 26(b)(4)(B)).

Inspiration Consol. Copper Co. v. Lumbermens Mut. Casualty Co., 60 F.R.D. 205, 208–10 (S.D.N.Y. 1973).

Spartanics, Ltd. v. Dynetics Eng'g Corp., 54 F.R.D. 524, 527 (N.D. Ill. 1972) (patent infringement) (requiring notice to the adversary of the names of any independent experts to whom confidential materials might be shown).

Axelson, Inc. v. McIlhany, 798 S.W.2d 550, 554 (Tex. 1990) (gas well explosion) (defendant sought discovery of witnesses who were active participants in the well's operation and who were later designated consulting-only experts. Reversing the lower court, the court held that the information sought was "not shielded from discovery by merely changing the designation of a person with knowledge of relevant facts to a 'consulting-only' expert." The court further held that "persons who gain factual information by virtue of their involvement relating to the incident or transaction giving rise to the litigation do not qualify as consulting-only experts because the consultation is not their only source of information.").

Tom L. Scott, Inc. v. McIlhany, 798 S.W.2d 556 (Tex. 1990).

State ex. rel. Burlington N. R.R. v. District Court, 779 P.2d 885, 890 (Mont. 1989) (action by railroad employee) (holding that identification was discoverable only on showing of exceptional circumstances; *but see* dissent at 895–96).

Williamson v. Superior Court, 582 P.2d 126, 132 (Cal. 1978) (products case; tire and tire-changing machine) (first-defendant's expert produced a report that defective design of co-defendant's product caused plaintiff's injury; discovery of report allowed where the two defendants entered into an agreement which provided that the first defendant was to withdraw its expert—to preclude discovery—in return for indemnification against any liability.).

Neuswanger v. Ikegai Am. Corp., 582 N.E.2d 192 (Ill. App. Ct. 1991) (products case; industrial machine) (estate of worker killed in industrial accident sued manufacturer of machine. Anticipating litigation, employer's workers' compensation carrier hired consulting expert who videotaped field inspection of machine. Plaintiff served subpoena seeking production of the videotape. Court held that rule protecting work product of consultant expert applied only to "parties." Further, court held that videotape was discoverable as a "tangible thing"—under Illinois rule which exempts from work-product protection tangible things which do not reveal attorney's or consultant's opinions.).

American Bldgs. Co. v. Kokomo Grain Co., 506 N.E.2d 56 (Ind. Ct. App. 1987) (breach of contract, negligence, fraud, and strict liability case in building collapse) (holding that protection from disclosure created by rule 26(b)(4)(B) did not extend to subsequent litigation since expert did not prepare his report in anticipation of future litigation). *See also Sullivan v. Sturm, Ruger & Co.,* 80 F.R.D. 489 (D. Mont. 1978); *National Steel Prods. Co. v. Superior Court,* 210 Cal. Rptr. 535 (Ct. App. 1985); *Grinnell Corp. v. Hackett,* 70 F.R.D. 326, 333 (D.R.I. 1976). *Contra, In re "Agent Orange" Prod. Liab. Litig.,* 105 F.R.D. 577, 580 (E.D.N.Y. 1985) (based on the fact that the two cases were part of the same multidistrict litigation) and *Hermsdorfer v. American Motors Corp.,* 96 F.R.D. 13 (W.D.N.Y. 1982) (protecting information obtained for the purpose of preparing for the present case and all other similar litigation against the defendants).

§ 17 IDENTIFICATION OF DOCUMENTS

§ 17.1 GENERALLY

(See also §§ 14, 17.4, 18, 22.1, 23, 34, 35, 38, 46, 48)

Commentary

FED. R. CIV. P. 26(b)(1) provides that "[p]arties may obtain discovery regarding any matter, not privileged, which is relevant to the subject matter involved in the pending action." This expressly includes any matter that, though not itself admissible, would reasonably appear to lead to the discovery of admissible evidence.

Concerning the legal duty to conduct a reasonable inquiry in order to respond to a discovery request, see chapter 2, section II of this book.

Rule

FED. R. CIV. P. 26(b)(1).

Secondary Sources

DISCOVERY PROCEEDINGS IN FEDERAL COURT, *supra* § 2, §§ 6.33–6.35.

HAYDOCK & HERR, *supra* § 3, § 1.4, at 22.

KIELY, *supra* § 11, §§ 1.17, 7.26.

4 MOORE ET AL., *supra* § 1, ¶ 26.58.

4A MOORE ET AL., *supra* § 1, ¶¶ 33.20, 33.22, 34.10.

8 WRIGHT & MILLER, *supra* § 1, §§ 2012, 2211.

Case Law

Marker v. Union Fidelity Life Ins. Co., 125 F.R.D. 121, 126–27 (M.D.N.C. 1989) (insurance contract action) (permitting 30(b)(6) deposition of person knowledgeable about company's general record-keeping storage and retrieval system).

Colorado v. Schmidt-Tiago Constr. Co., 108 F.R.D. 731, 735 (D. Colo. 1985) (antitrust action) (holding that an interrogatory to identify specific documents was proper).

Bowman v. General Motors Corp., 64 F.R.D. 62, 64–65 (E.D. Pa. 1974), *later proceedings*, 427 F. Supp. 234 (E.D. Pa. 1977).

Scovill Mfg. Co. v. Sunbeam Corp., 61 F.R.D. 598 (D. Del. 1973).

Roesberg v. Johns-Manville Corp., 85 F.R.D. 292, 301–03 (E.D. Pa. 1980) (products case; asbestos) (holding that mere claim of a privilege did not justify a refusal to identify documents requested by plaintiff).

Hess v. Pittsburgh Steel Foundry & Mach. Co., 49 F.R.D. 271, 272–73 (W.D. Pa. 1970) (products case; grinding wheel) (holding that plaintiff was entitled to intercompany correspondence concerning other companies' complaints and manufacturer's recommendations to correct conditions).

Green v. Shepherd Constr. Co., CA No. 11740 (N.D. Ga. Oct. 21, 1969) (products case; spring shackle) (ordering Ford to identify tests and studies concerning the safety of the subject product).

Butler v. United States, 226 F. Supp. 341 (W.D. Mo. 1964) (Federal Tort Claims Act case) (holding that the work-product privilege did not extend to the custodian of documents).

Lee v. Honda Motor Co., CA No. 9103-01752 (Multnomah County, Or. Cir. Ct. Feb. 4, 1992) (products case; ATV) (ordering defendant manufacturer to produce accurate index of materials contained in defendant's central depository although the index was prepared in anticipation of litigation, because plaintiffs had a substantial need for accurate index and were unable to obtain a substantial equivalent without undue hardship).

§ 17.2 "TRADE SECRETS" AND OTHER CLAIMS OF PRIVILEGE

Commentary

If the defendant satisfies the court that requested information meets the legal criteria for a trade secret, the court may not compel its disclosure unless the plaintiff shows that the need and importance of the information outweigh the threat of harm to the defendant likely to result from permitting discovery. Following this balancing of interests, the court may (1) require disclosure, (2) deny disclosure, or (3) require disclosure and issue a protective order limiting the use and dissemination of the material by the plaintiff. In the large majority of cases, courts adopt the third approach.

Rule

FED. R. CIV. P. 26(c)(7).

Secondary Sources

AMERICAN LAW OF PRODUCTS LIABILITY 3D, *supra* § 1, §§ 53:11, 53:33.

DISCOVERY PROCEEDINGS IN FEDERAL COURT, *supra* § 2, § 10.13.

Gross, Annotation, *What Is Computer "Trade Secret" Under State Law*, 53 A.L.R. 4TH 1046 (1987).

HARE, GILBERT & REMINE, CONFIDENTIALITY ORDERS §§ 6.2–6.7, 7.8 (1988).

HAYDOCK & HERR, *supra* § 3, §§ 1.9.8, 2.5.8.

KIELY, *supra* § 11, § 7.26.

4 MOORE ET AL., *supra* § 1, ¶¶ 26.60[4], 26.75.

Watson, Annotation, *Discovery of Trade Secret in State Court Action*, 75 A.L.R. 4TH 1009 (1990).

8 WRIGHT & MILLER, *supra* § 1, § 2043.

Case Law

Federal Open Mkt. Comm. of Fed. Reserve Sys. v. Merrill, 443 U.S. 340, 362 n.24 (1979) (Freedom of Information Act suit) ("[O]rders forbidding any disclosure of trade secrets or confidential commercial information are rare. More commonly, the trial court will enter a protective order restricting disclosure to counsel, or to the parties.").

Centurion Indus. v. Warren Steurer & Assocs., 665 F.2d 323, 325–26 (10th Cir. 1981) (patent infringement) (holding that trade secrets were discoverable under an appropriate protective order).

Hartman v. Remington Arms Co., CA No. 90-4074-CV-C-5 (W.D. Mo. Apr. 13, 1992) (products case; defective rifle) (overruling manufacturer's contention that requested documents contained "trade secret" information, the court required defendant company to produce research and development on a New Bolt Action Rifle as potentially reflecting feasibility of alternative designs. Court's order included information contained in defendant company's Customer Sales Analysis touching on alternative designs and post-injury research reflecting the priority level and cost consideration of alternative designs.), *modified* Apr. 28, 1992, *further modified* May 5, 1992. See also *In re Remington Arms Co.*, 952 F.2d 1029 (8th Cir. 1991), *on remand*, 143 F.R.D. 673 (D. Mo. 1992).

Snowden v. Connaught Lab., Inc., 137 F.R.D. 336, 346 (D. Kan.) (products case; DPT vaccine) (holding that trade secret research conducted by defendant manufacturer was subject to discovery under protective order limiting further dissemination), *appeal overruled*, 136 F.R.D. 694 (D. Kan.), *reconsideration denied*, 138 F.R.D. 138 (D. Kan. 1991).

Exxon Chem. Patents, Inc. v. Lubrizol Corp., 131 F.R.D. 668, 671 (S.D. Tex. 1990) (patent infringement) (holding that trade secrets were discoverable under an appropriate protective order).

Henson v. Wyeth Lab., Inc., 118 F.R.D. 584, 586 n.2 (W.D. Va. 1987) (holding that trade secrets were discoverable under an appropriate protective order).

Coca-Cola Bottling Co. v. Coca-Cola Co., 107 F.R.D. 288, 290 (D. Del. 1985) (contract, patent infringement, and antitrust action) (holding that the secret formula for Coca-Cola was discoverable under an appropriate protective order), *later proceedings*, 110 F.R.D. 363 (D. Del. 1986).

Triangle Ink & Color Co. v. Sherwin-Williams Co., 61 F.R.D. 634, 636 (N.D. Ill. 1974) (contract action) (holding that trade secrets were discoverable under an appropriate protective order).

Eli Lilly & Co. v. Marshall, 829 S.W.2d 157 (Tex. 1992) (products case; drug Prozac) (trial court ordered defendant to produce FDA documents reflecting defendant's evaluation of drug's safety and effectiveness including clinical studies, chemical analysis, adverse reaction reports, and proposed labels. Texas Supreme Court granted mandamus and ordered trial court to hold hearing and rule on the merits of defendant's motion for a protective order under Texas rule 76a.), *mandamus granted*, 850 S.W.2d 155 (Tex. 1993).

Remington Arms Co. v. Canales, 837 S.W.2d 624 (Tex. 1992) (class action with respect to the safety of the Model 700 Rifle).

Lamitie v. Emerson Elec. Co., 535 N.Y.S.2d 650 (App. Div. 1988) (products case; hot water heater) (holding that communications between manufacturer and consumer product safety commission were not privileged under Consumer Product Safety Act; act applied to public disclosure—not to judicial proceedings; furthermore, manufacturer failed to make sufficient showing that communications were trade secrets and court would not adopt "critical self-analysis privilege" to protect communications), *appeal dismissed per curiam*, 540 N.E.2d 714 (N.Y. 1989).

Hutchison v. Luddy, 606 A.2d 905 (Pa. Super. Ct.) (sexual molestation action) (ordering production of documents relating to defendant priest and reports of alleged contact between other priests and male children; court rejected defendant's argument that documents were protected under church canon law and statutory priest-penitent privilege), *appeal withdrawn*, 611 A.2d 712 (Pa. 1992).

See also

Hotchkiss v. Sears, Roebuck & Co., 139 F.R.D. 313, 315, 316 (M.D. Pa. 1991).

Deas v. Carson Prods. Co., 569 N.Y.S.2d 167 (App. Div. 1991).

§ 17.3 TRANSLATION OF FOREIGN LANGUAGE DOCUMENTS

Commentary

In situations involving parties who are foreign nationals and residents of countries that are signatories of the Hague Evidence Convention, the provisions of this treaty should be consulted. *See* the Convention on the Taking of Evidence Abroad in Civil or Commercial Matters (Hague Evidence Convention), 25 U.S.T. 2555, T.I.A.S. No. 744 (1969); 8 MARTINDALE-HUBBELL LAW DIRECTORY (1988).

Rule

FED. R. CIV. P. 34(a).

Secondary Sources

DISCOVERY PROCEEDINGS IN FEDERAL COURT, *supra* § 2, § 7.16, at 440.

HAYDOCK & HERR, *supra* § 3, § 5.13.

Case Law

Appalachian Ins. Co. v. Control Data Corp., CA No. 3-79-499 (D. Minn. Dec. 11, 1981), *cited and discussed in* HAYDOCK & HERR, *supra* § 3, § 5.13, at 399–400 n.2 (holding that defendant who was ordered to produce existing translations of foreign language documents was not entitled to recoup from the party seeking discovery the cost of having the translations made).

Stapleton v. Kawasaki Heavy Indus., 69 F.R.D. 489 (N.D. Ga. 1975) (property damage claim) (ordering defendant to pay plaintiff's translation cost for documents produced by defendant in Japanese).

Contra

In re Puerto Rico Elec. Power Auth., 687 F.2d 501, 510 (1st Cir. 1982) (breach of contract and tort action) (refusing to require party to translate documents into English on condition that the party reimburse the opposing party for translation expenses already incurred).

§ 17.4 LIST OF DOCUMENTS OR BIBLIOGRAPHY

(See also §§ 18.2, 18.3, 23, 49)

Commentary

Ordinarily it is appropriate to request a list of documents pertinent to the subject matter in dispute; for example, a list of all standards applicable to design, manufacture, and distribution of the subject product. However, a list of documents selected by an attorney for use in the litigation is entitled to work-product protection. See § 49, *infra*, and chapter 5, section X of this book.

Rule

1993 Amendments, FED. R. CIV. P. 26(a)(1)(B).

Case Law

Blackner v. Clark Equip. Co., CA No. 2860 (Philadelphia, Pa. Ct. C.P. Nov. 7, 1983) (products case; forklift rollover).

§ 17.5 INDEX OF DOCUMENTS

Commentary

The court may require the party invoking the option to (1) provide a knowledgeable employee to locate or decipher records, (2) provide codes or software to extract information from computerized records, (3) translate documents written in a foreign language, (4) furnish existing indices, lists, tables, or other aids for identifying relevant information, or (5) furnish existing compilations of raw data. See chapter 6 of this book, section II.B.3, footnotes 50 through 54.

Rules

FED. R. CIV. P. 33(c), 34(b).

Case Law

Baine v. General Motors Corp., 141 F.R.D. 328 (M.D. Ala. 1991) (products case; seat-belt locking mechanism) (defendant attempted to limit scope of discovery to the same year and model type vehicle. Noting that the parameters of discovery should not be limited by the subjective and adversarial view of the manufacturer, the court found that other model vehicles involved the same "defect" and compelled the defendant to produce documents concerning those models. In response to GM's contention that physical location and delivery of the subject documents would be extremely burdensome, the court ordered that the plaintiff be allowed to inspect records at the defendant's facility and required the defendant to furnish plaintiff with a index of the subject records.).

§ 17.6 ABSTRACTS OR SUMMARIES OF DOCUMENTS

Commentary

The advisory committee's note to the 1980 amendment to rule 33(c) provides "[I]f the information sought exists in the form of compilations, abstracts or summaries then available to the responding party, those should be made available to the interrogating party."

Rule

FED. R. CIV. P. 33(c).

§ 17.7 STATISTICS

Commentary

Unless protected by work product, a statistical analysis of some issue relating to the subject matter of a claim or defense should be discovered.

Case Law

Hotchkiss v. Sears, Roebuck & Co., 139 F.R.D. 313, 315–16 (M.D. Pa. 1991) (products case; radial arm saw) (compelling manufacturer to produce report containing compilation of statistics on accidents involving radial arm saws).

Roesberg v. Johns-Manville Corp., 85 F.R.D. 292 (E.D. Pa. 1980).

§ 18 DOCUMENTS IN COMPUTER FORM

§ 18.1 GENERALLY

Commentary

FED. R. CIV. P. 34(a) permits the discovery of any "data compilations from which information can be obtained, translated, if necessary, by the respondent through detection devices into reasonably usable form." The courts typically hold that information stored in computers is discoverable. The fact, standing also, that relevant information was originally generated or subsequently manipulated by use of a computer or subsequently stored in computer format should not affect its discoverability.

The topic under discussion should be carefully distinguished from the use of computers as a litigation support mechanism (*see* § 18.2, *infra*) and the attorney's selection of particular documents for use in a particular case (*see* § 49, *infra*).

Secondary Sources

DISCOVERY PROCEEDINGS IN FEDERAL COURT, *supra* § 2, § 16.4.

Electronic Data Information Enhances Discovery Methods, Civil Trial Manual (BNA), 25 (Feb. 17, 1993).

HAYDOCK & HERR, *supra* § 2, § 5.17.

Howie, *Electronic Media Discovery,* TRIAL, Jan. 1993, at 70.

Meyer, *What Is Your Computer Hiding?*, A.B.A. J., Feb. 1993, at 89.

Morris, *Hospital Computers in Court,* MOD. USES LOGIC L., June 1993, at 61, 64.

8 WRIGHT & MILLER, *supra* § 1, § 2218.

Case Law

Emerick v. Fenick Indus., 539 F.2d 1379 (5th Cir. 1976) (holding that the scope of discovery extended to information in computer format, including computerized summaries).

Farnsworth v. Procter & Gamble Co., 758 F.2d 1545 (11th Cir. 1985) (allowing both parties to obtain copy of a study conducted by Centers for Disease Control; however, court denied access to the names and addresses of the study participants).

Baine v. General Motors Corp., 141 F.R.D. 328 (M.D. Ala. 1991) (holding that the scope of discovery extended to information in computer format, including software programs employed in manipulating and accessing information).

In re Air Crash Disaster at Detroit Metro. Airport, 130 F.R.D. 634, 636 (E.D. Mich. 1989) (requiring manufacturer to produce flight director's simulation run program and data on computer-readable nine-track magnetic tape).

Marker v. Union Fidelity Life Ins. Co., 125 F.R.D. 121, 126–27 (M.D.N.C. 1989) (compelling defendant to produce employee who was familiar with retrieval of computerized data for 30(b)(6) deposition).

Fautek v. Montgomery Ward & Co., 96 F.R.D. 141, 144–45 (N.D. Ill. 1982) (holding that the defendant failed to disclose computer codes necessary to understand system).

In re Japanese Elec. Prods. Antitrust Litig., 494 F. Supp. 1257 (E.D. Pa. 1980) (ordering plaintiff to create a computer tape containing the requested data in a form that could be read by the defendant's computer and ordering the defendant to pay the cost for generating the tape).

Pearl Brewing Co. v. Joseph Schlitz Brewing Co., 415 F. Supp. 1122, 1136 (S.D. Tex. 1976) (containing a comprehensive discussion of the problems presented where a computer market simulation is the object of discovery).

Adams v. Dan River Mills, Inc., 15 Fed. R. Serv. 2d (Callaghan) 1275, 1276 (W.D. Va. 1972) (holding that the responding party must furnish computer data in manner understandable to the requesting party; court required responding party to bear cost and expense of compiling the data and translating it into a readable printout).

American Bankers Ins. Co. v. Caruth, 786 S.W. 2d 427 (Tex. Ct. App. 1990) (entering default judgment against defendant who first failed to produce computer files and then failed to produce them within the time ordered).

Marinelli v. Volkswagen of Am., Inc., CA No. CV89-3301 (Jefferson County, Ala. Cir. Ct. Apr. 24, 1991, Oct. 22, 1991, Feb. 19, 1992) (products case; vehicle rollover) (defendant's expert witness based his testimony in part on accident reconstruction analysis performed with the aid of a computer. In three separate orders the court instructed the defendant to provide plaintiff's counsel with a copy of the computer disk utilized by the defendant's expert witness including the software employed in the computer program.).

Contra

Williams v. Owens-Illinois, Inc., 665 F.2d 918, 933 (9th Cir.) (finding that party need not produce computer tapes where previously produced wage cards included information sought), *cert. denied*, 459 U.S. 971 (1982).

See also

Newton v. General Motors Corp., CA No. 92-638 (W.D. La. Nov. 5, 1993) (ordering defendant to permit plaintiff to observe defendant's search of certain databases and to propose additional search terms, and to provide results of search in computer readable format; court further ordered defendant to permit plaintiff to review entire microfilm records pertaining to certain requests).

Shafer-Kleoppel v. General Motors Corp., CA No. 93-0498-CV-W-8 (W.D. Mo. Sept. 3, 1993) (ordering defendant to permit plaintiff access to corporate databases).

Williams v. General Motors Corp., CA No. CV 392-037-DHB (S.D. Ga. Mar. 2, 1993) (compelling GM to produce various computer databases and to provide plaintiff with the assistance of a knowledgeable operator).

Barron v. General Motors Corp., CA No. H88-0049 (R) (S.D. Miss. Aug. 27, 1992) (ordering defendant to provide plaintiff and an expert of plaintiff's choosing access to certain computer databases to conduct search in accordance with procedure outlined in order).

Holder v. General Motors Corp., CA No. CV 91-019 (Fayette County, Ala. Cir. Ct. Aug. 23, 1993) (ordering defendant to permit plaintiff to search certain computer databases).

La France v. General Motors Corp., CA No. 90-021866 (Harris County, Tex. Dist. Ct. July 6, 1993) (following three separate orders commanding GM to permit plaintiffs access to various databases containing information relevant to plaintiff's discovery requests, court order described procedure for on-site access to databases, conduct of search, and printing of results of search).

Langham v. General Motors Corp., CA No. 30448 (Fannin County, Tex. Dist. Ct. Mar. 11, 1993) (ordering defendant to produce employee for deposition who could describe GM computer databases).

Rossetto v. General Motors Corp., CA No. 2293 (Westmoreland County, Pa. Ct. C.P. Mar. 19, 1993) (permitting plaintiff to search certain computer databases).

Skebo v. Ford Motor Co., CA No. 92VS67182E (Fulton County, Ga. Oct. 22, 1993) (on appeal primarily addressed to procedure for access allowed by trial court's order, rather than the discoverability of relevant not privileged electronic databases).

Svoboda v. Mossy Oldsmobile Inc., CA No. 90-053353 (Harris County, Tex. Dist. Ct. Oct. 9, 1992) (ordering plaintiff access to GM databases).

Wierbinski v. Volkswagen A.G., CA No. A038364 (Cal. Ct. App. Dec. 30, 1988) (ordering automaker to produce accident computer program and software for program when defendant failed to do so until middle of trial; appellate court affirmed trial court's order granting plaintiff new trial following verdict for defendant), *reprinted in* Automotive Litig. Rep. 11444-47 (Jan. 17, 1989).

§ 18.2 FACTS/INFORMATION IN COMPUTER FORMAT

(See also §§ 17, 38)

Commentary

The discoverability of facts and information in an electronic or computer format is discussed in chapter 1, section IV of this book.

Rules

FED. R. CIV. P. 26(b)(1), 34(a), 45.

FED. R. EVID. 803(6), 803(8).

Secondary Sources

AMERICAN LAW OF PRODUCTS LIABILITY 3D, *supra* § 1, § 53:13.

BALDWIN ET AL., THE PREPARATION OF A PRODUCT LIABILITY CASE § 7B.12.10, 696–97 (2d ed. 1993).

Comment, *A Reconsideration of the Admissibility of Computer-Generated Evidence*, 126 U. PA. L. REV. 425 (1977).

DISCOVERY PROCEEDINGS IN FEDERAL COURT, *supra* § 2, § 16.4.

DOMBROFF, *supra* § 3, § 5.08.

HAYDOCK & HERR, *supra* § 3, §§ 5.17, 9.7.4.

Howie, *Electronic Media Discovery, What You Can't See Can Help (or Hurt) You*, TRIAL, Jan. 1993, at 70.

Jenkins, *Computer-Generated Evidence Specially Prepared for Use at Trial*, 52 CHI.-KENT L. REV. 600 (1976).

Long, Comment, *The Discovery and Use of Computerized Information: An Examination of Current Approaches*, 13 PEPPERDINE L. REV. 405 (1986).

Note, *Appropriate Foundation Requirements for Admitting Computer Printouts into Evidence*, 1977 WASH. U. L.Q. 59.

Ortner, *Computer-Based Information as Evidence*, C601 A.L.I.-A.B.A. 127 (May 10, 1991).

SCHWARZER & PASAHOW, CIVIL DISCOVERY: A GUIDE TO EFFICIENT PRACTICE 16 (1988 & Supp. 1989).

SIEMER, TANGIBLE EVIDENCE: HOW TO USE EXHIBITS AT TRIAL (2d ed. 1989).

Sprowl, *Evaluating the Credibility of Computer-Generated Evidence*, 52 CHI.-KENT L. REV. 547 (1976).

Tapper, *Evidence from Computers*, 8 GA. L. REV. 562 (1974).

THE USE OF COMPUTERS IN LITIGATION (John Hardin Young et al. eds., 1979).

White, *Taking the Byte Out of Discovery: Protecting Computer Information from Disclosure*, TRIAL, Mar. 1983, at 44.

8 WRIGHT & MILLER, *supra* § 1, § 2218.

Case Law

Farnsworth v. Procter & Gamble Co., 758 F.2d 1545 (11th Cir. 1985) (products case; toxic shock) (allowing both parties to obtain a copy of a study conducted by Centers for Disease Control; however, court denied access to the names and addresses of study participants).

Sanders v. Levy, 21 Fed. R. Serv. 2d (Callaghan) 1213, 1218 n.7 (2d Cir. 1976).

Baine v. General Motors Corp., 141 F.R.D. 328 (M.D. Ala. 1991) (products case; defective seat-belt locking mechanism) (defendant attempted to limit scope of discovery to the same year and model type vehicle. Noting that the parameters of discovery should not be limited by the subjective and adversarial view of the manufacturer, the court found that other model vehicles involved the same "defect" and compelled the defendant to produce documents concerning those models. In response to GM's contention that physical location and delivery of the subject documents would be extremely burdensome, the court ordered that the plaintiff be allowed to inspect records at the defendant's facility and required the defendant to furnish plaintiff with an index of the subject records.).

Marker v. Union Fidelity Life Ins. Co., 125 F.R.D. 121, 126–27 (M.D.N.C. 1989) (insurance contract action) (compelling defendant to produce an employee familiar with retrieval of computerized data for 30(b)(6) deposition).

In re Air Crash Disaster at Detroit Metro. Airport, 130 F.R.D. 634, 636 (E.D. Mich.) (products case; commercial aircraft) (requiring manufacturer to produce flight director's simulation run program and data on computer-readable nine-track magnetic tape), *later proceedings*, 130 F.R.D. 641 (E.D. Mich. 1989).

Hoffman v. United Telecommunications, Inc., 117 F.R.D. 436, 439 (D. Kan. 1987).

Williams v. E.I. DuPont de Nemours & Co., 119 F.R.D. 648 (W.D. Ky. 1987).

Colorado ex rel. Woodard v. Schmidt-Tiago Constr. Co., 108 F.R.D. 731 (D. Colo. 1985).

Fautek v. Montgomery Ward & Co., 96 F.R.D. 141, 144–46 (N.D. Ill. 1982) (employment discrimination action) (sanctioning defendant for failing to disclose computer codes necessary to understand system).

In re Japanese Elec. Prods. Antitrust Litig., 494 F. Supp. 1257, 1261–62 (E.D. Pa. 1980) (antitrust case) (ordering plaintiff to create a computer tape containing the requested data in a form that could be read by the defendant's computer where the defendant offered to pay the cost for generating the tape).

Pearl Brewing Co. v. Joseph Schlitz Brewing Co., 415 F. Supp. 1122, 1134–36 (S.D. Tex. 1976) (antitrust action) (containing a comprehensive discussion of the problems presented where a computer market simulation was the object of discovery).

Adams v. Dan River Mills, Inc., 15 Fed. R. Serv. 2d (Callaghan) 1275, 1276–77 (W.D. Va. 1972) (employment discrimination action) (responding party must furnish computer data in manner understandable to the requesting party; court required requesting party to bear cost and expense of compiling the data and translating it into a readable printout).

Wierbinski v. Volkswagen A.G., CA No. A038364 (Cal. Ct. App. Dec. 30, 1988) (products case; suspension system) (ordering automaker to produce accident computer program and software for program which defendant failed to do until middle of trial; appellate court affirmed trial court's order granting plaintiff new trial following verdict for defendant), *reprinted in* Automotive Litig. Rep. 11444-47 (Jan. 17, 1989).

Marinelli v. Volkswagen of Am., Inc., CA No. CV89-3301 (Jefferson County, Ala. Cir. Ct. Apr. 24, 1991, Oct. 22, 1991, Feb. 19, 1992) (products case; vehicle rollover) (defendant's expert witness based his testimony in part on accident reconstruction analysis performed with the aid of a computer. In three separate orders the court instructed the defendant to provide plaintiff's counsel with a copy of the computer disk utilized by the defendant's expert witness including the software employed in the computer program.).

Blackner v. Clark Equip. Co., CA No. 2860 (Philadelphia, Pa. Ct. C.P. Nov. 7, 1983) (products case; forklift rollover).

Contra

Williams v. Owens-Illinois, Inc., 665 F.2d 918, 933 (9th Cir.) (employment discrimination action) (refusing to compel party to produce computer tapes where previously produced wage cards included information sought), *cert. denied*, 459 U.S. 971 (1982).

§ 18.3 USE OF COMPUTER IN LITIGATION SUPPORT

(See also §§ 22, 49)

Commentary

Information generated by a computer in preparation for trial is normally protected from discovery by the work-product doctrine. This topic should be distinguished from the subject matter of §18.2, *supra*.

Rule

FED. R. CIV. P. 26(b)(3).

Secondary Sources

Cook & Reed, *Discovery of Computerized Litigation Support Systems*, 33 TRIAL LAW. GUIDE (1989).

Goldenberg, DISCOVERY OF COMPUTERIZED LITIGATION SUPPORT SYSTEMS IN FEDERAL COURT (Monograph prepared for Aspen Systems Corp., Dec. 30, 1987).

Goldenberg, *How to Protect Computerized Files from Discovery*, NAT'L L.J., Mar. 28, 1988, at 22, 28.

Friedman, Note, *Computer Discovery in Federal Litigation: Playing by the Rules*, 69 GEO. L.J. 1465 (1981).

Fromholz, *Discovery, Evidence, Confidentiality, and Security Problems Associated with the Use of Computer-Based Litigation Support Systems*, 1977 WASH. U. L.Q. 445.

HAYDOCK & HERR, *supra* § 3, §§ 5.17, 9.7.4.

Howie, *Electronic Media Discovery, What You Can't See Can Help (or Hurt) You*, TRIAL, Jan. 1993, at 70.

KINNEY, LITIGATION SUPPORT SYSTEMS: AN ATTORNEY'S GUIDE (2d ed. 1992).

Long, Comment, *The Discovery and Use of Computerized Information: An Examination of Current Approaches*, 13 PEPPERDINE L. REV. 405 (1986).

McCrea, Note, *Disclosure of Attorney Work Product Under Federal Rule of Evidence 612: An Abrogation of Work Product Protection?*—Sporck v. Peil, 59 TEMP. L.Q. 1043–69 (1986).

4 MOORE ET AL., *supra* § 1, ¶ 26.64[3].

Packard, Case Note, *Opinion Work Product, Expert Witness Discovery, and the Interaction of Rules 26(b)(3) and 26(b)(4)(A):* Bogosian v. Gulf Oil Corporation, 1985 B.Y.U. L. REV. 573.

Pinkus & Williams, *Discovery of Litigation Support Systems: The Invasion and Protection of the Front Lines*, 3 AM. J. TRIAL ADVOC. 165 (1979).

Poirier et al., *Computer-Based Litigation Support Systems: The Discoverability Issue*, 54 UMKC L. REV. 440 (1986).

Prendergast, *The Use of Data Processing in Litigation*, 17 JURIMETRICS J. 227 (1977).

Sherman & Kinnard, *The Development, Discovery, and Use of Computer Support Systems in Achieving Efficiency in Litigation*, 79 COL. L. REV. 267 (1979).

White, *Taking the Byte Out of Discovery: Protecting Computer Information from Disclosure*, TRIAL, Mar. 1983, at 44.

Williams, *Protection from Discovery of Information Contained in a Litigation Support System*, in THE USE OF COMPUTERS IN LITIGATION 191 (John Hardin Young et al. eds., 1979).

8 WRIGHT & MILLER, *supra* § 1, § 2024.

Case Law

Hoffman v. United Telecommunications, Inc., 43 Empl. Prac. Dec. (CCH) § 37,183 (D. Kan.), *later proceedings*, 117 F.R.D. 440 (D. Kan. 1987).

Grumman Aerospace Corp. v. Titanium Metals Corp. of Am., 91 F.R.D. 84, 89 (E.D.N.Y. 1981).

In re IBM Peripherals, 5 Computer L. Serv. Rep. 878, 879 (N.D. Cal. 1975) (defense counsel had developed a computerized trial support system with summaries and analyses of defendant's documents; court denied plaintiff's discovery of the system because the information sought could not be segregated from the lawyer's mental impressions and theories and permitting discovery "would impinge on the right of [defense] counsel to organize material in the perspective they want to put it in, and to utilize such information in their trial preparation").

Control Data Corp. v. IBM Corp., 1973-1 Trade Cas. (CCH) ¶ 74, 363 (D. Minn. 1973).

§ 19 DEFENDANT'S RELATIONSHIP WITH THE GOVERNMENT

(See also § 48.3)

Commentary

Many activities of a corporate defendant may require interaction with a government agency, e.g., promulgation of safety regulations, compliance with environmental and/or safety regulations, or investigation of potential defects.

Information involving any of these activities may well be relevant to the subject matter of a case, particularly if the defendant raises the defense of preemption or compliance with a governmental standard. Furthermore, the defendant's relationship to a regulatory agency may disclose information bearing on the interest or bias of its employees or of an expert witness.

A distinction must be drawn between this section and § 48.3, *infra*. In this section the defendant is in possession of the requested information, while § 48.3 deals with situations in which the government has the information that is being sought. It should also be noted that in some situations the defendant may have a duty to request and obtain from the government documents in the government's possession.

Secondary Sources

AMERICAN LAW OF PRODUCTS LIABILITY 3D, *supra* § 1, § 53:12.

DISCOVERY PROCEEDINGS IN FEDERAL COURT, *supra* § 2, §§ 15.31–15.40, 15.44–15.45.

HAYDOCK & HERR, *supra* § 3, §§ 2.5.2, 2.5.9.

KIELY, *supra* § 11, §§ 1.16, 1.24, 3.44–3.49.

4 MOORE ET AL., *supra* § 1, ¶ 26.61.

8 WRIGHT & MILLER, *supra* § 1, § 2019.

Case Law

Zuckerbraun v. General Dynamics Corp., 935 F.2d 544 (2d Cir. 1991) (granting the U.S. Navy a "state security privilege" with regard to case against missile contractor).

Anderson v. Cryovac, Inc., 862 F.2d 910 (1st Cir. 1988) (finding that the report prepared by an independent testing company and filed with the EPA was discoverable), *on remand, Anderson v. Beatrice Foods*, 127 F.R.D. 1 (D. Mass. 1989).

Farnsworth v. Procter & Gamble Co., 758 F.2d 1545 (11th Cir. 1985) (products case; toxic shock) (allowing party to obtain a copy of a study conducted by the Centers for Disease Control; however, court denied access to the names and address of study participants).

Black v. Sheraton Corp. of Am., 564 F.2d 550 (D.C. Cir. 1977).

Floyd v. Bic Corp., CA No. 1:89-cv-401-RLV (N.D. Ga. Nov. 2, 1992) (order vacated following settlement) (products case; disposable lighter) (compelling defendant to respond to plaintiff's inquiry concerning any proceedings conducted by the Consumer Product Safety Commission relating to the alleged defect and awarding attorney fees to plaintiff for prosecution of motion to compel as sanction for defendant's failure to produce requested documents based on defendant's distinction between the word "proceeding" and "inquiry").

Williams v. Vulcan-Hart Corp., 136 F.R.D. 457 (W.D. Ky. 1991) (sex discrimination suit) (plaintiff sought to discover portions of affirmative action plan prepared by defendant in compliance with federal guidelines; defendant objected, contending that the documents were privileged as "self-critical analysis"; noting that Kentucky law refused to recognize the privilege, the court granted the plaintiff's discovery request).

Simmons v. American Honda Motor Co., CA No. 1:91-cv-0079-RCF (N.D. Ga. production order Dec. 17, 1991, sanction order June 1, 1992) (products case; sidestand on motorcycle) (court ordered manufacturer to produce (1) customer complaints; (2) reports of other similar incidents; (3) tests and studies of subject and other model motorcycles; (4) blueprints, diagrams, drawings, photographs, etc. of subject and other model motorcycles; and (5) contents of the NHTSA defect investigation file. The district court sanctioned Honda for its repeated disregard of discovery rules and court's order.).

In re "Agent Orange" Prod. Liab. Litig., 97 F.R.D. 427 (E.D.N.Y. 1983).

Firestone Tire & Rubber Co. v. Coleman, 432 F. Supp. 1359 (N.D. Ohio 1976) (holding certain documents exempt from disclosure under Freedom of Information Act: (1) interoffice memoranda, (2) work product, (3) confidential trade secrets, (4) nonfinal thoughts, (5) experiments by defendant, and (6) pending information; documents obtainable under FOIA: federal standards used by the defendant in the subject product).

Bowman v. General Motors Corp., 64 F.R.D. 62, 65, 68 n.6 (E.D. Pa. 1974) (products case; automobile) (holding that the request for information about any dealings that defendant had with any governmental body in regard to the construction, design, and performance of the fuel system was appropriate).

FTC v. Bramman, 54 F.R.D. 364 (W.D. Mo. 1972) (allowing parties discovery from FTC of their own reports to third parties; no absolute executive privilege exists for administrative reports).

Meyer v. G.D. Searle & Co., 41 F.R.D. 290 (E.D.N.Y. 1966) (products case; drug Enovid) (permitting discovery of new drug application).

Luey v. Sterling Drug, Inc., 240 F. Supp. 632 (W.D. Mich. 1965) (products case; drug Aralen) (allowing plaintiff to discover defendant's warnings to profession, dosage determination, and relationship to efficacy and side effects).

Eli Lilly & Co. v. Marshall, 829 S.W.2d 157 (Tex. 1992) (products case; drug Prozac) (trial court ordered defendant to produce FDA documents reflecting defendant's evaluation of drug's safety and effectiveness including clinical studies, chemical analysis, adverse reaction reports, and proposed labels. Texas Supreme Court granted mandamus and ordered trial court to hold hearing and rule on the merits of defendant's motion for a protective order under Texas rule 76a.).

Agrivest Partnership v. Central Iowa Prod. Credit Ass'n, 373 N.W.2d 479 (Iowa 1985) (finding no privilege for the defendant where not asserted by Farm Credit Association).

Light v. State, 547 N.E.2d 1073 (Ind. 1980) (holding that federal statute forbidding disclosure or use of reports in evidence did not bar pretrial discovery of Department of Transportation accident reports for portion of highway at which claimant was involved in accident).

Lamitie v. Emerson Elec. Co., 535 N.Y.S.2d 650 (App. Div. 1988) (products case; hot water heater) (holding that communications between manufacturer and consumer product safety commission were not privileged under Consumer Product Safety Act; act applied to public disclosure—not to judicial proceedings; furthermore, volumes of material provided to FDA by defendants were discoverable but must be examined on-site according to FDA rules).

Snyder v. Parke, Davis & Co., 391 N.Y.S.2d 579 (App. Div. 1977) (finding that manufacturer failed to make sufficient showing that communications were trade secrets; court would not adopt "critical self-analysis privilege" to protect communications), *appeal dismissed per curiam*, 540 N.E.2d 714 (N.Y. 1989).

Dunshie v. General Motors Corp., CA No. A-136,024 (Jefferson County, Tex. Dist. Ct.) (products liability case; "window shade" seat belt), *appeal dismissed*, 822 S.W.2d 345 (Tex. Ct. App. 1992).

§ 20 DEFENDANT'S ASSETS/NET WORTH

Commentary

The majority of courts permit discovery of information concerning the defendant's net worth in connection with a claim for punitive damages. Some courts, however, only allow this discovery upon the plaintiff's prima facie showing of the validity of the claim. If otherwise permissible, discovery of the defendant's assets may include annual reports, balance sheets, profit and loss statements, and other relevant financial reports.

Secondary Sources

AMERICAN LAW OF PRODUCTS LIABILITY 3D, *supra* § 1, § 53:50.

DISCOVERY PROCEEDINGS IN FEDERAL COURT, *supra* § 2, § 16.8.

DOMBROFF, *supra* § 3, § 12.43.

McLoughlin, Annotation, *Necessity of Determination or Showing of Liability for Punitive Damages Before Discovery or Reception of Evidence of Defendant's Wealth*, 32 A.L.R. 4TH 432 (1984).

McMahon, Annotation, *Discovery of Defendant's Sales, Earnings and Profits on Issue of Punitive Damages in Tort Action*, 54 A.L.R. 4TH 998 (1987).

4 MOORE ET AL., *supra* § 1, ¶ 26.56[5].

8 WRIGHT & MILLER, *supra* § 1, § 2009, at 54 n.36.

Case Law

City of Newport v. Fact Concerts, Inc., 453 U.S. 247 (1981) (holding that information concerning defendant's financial condition was relevant and discoverable on a claim of punitive damages).

Roberts v. Jeep Eagle Corp., CA No. 1:89-cv-238-HTW (N.D. Ga. Jan. 4, 1993) (products case; liftgate) (court compelled defendant to produce (1) reports of similar incidents occurring both before and after subject claim (at 3–4); (2) requested photographs, overruling defendant's work-product and attorney-client objections on grounds that photographs do not disclose mental impressions (at 4); (3) documents and testimony produced in other cases (at 2–3, 11); (4) tests concerning similar models (at 11); (5) information concerning profits defendants realized per vehicle during certain years pertinent to the litigation (at 12); (6) information concerning defendant's consideration of an alternative design (at 7,12–13); and (7) information concerning defendant's consideration of a subsequent remedial measure (at 7, 12–13); court allowed plaintiff to depose defendant's vice–president for the reason that he participated in a decision to suppress an internal memorandum concerning the defective condition of the subject liftgate (at 6–7).).

Mid Continent Cabinetry, Inc. v. George Koch Sons, Inc., 130 F.R.D. 149, 151–52 (D. Kan. 1990) (following overwhelming majority of decisions, court held that plaintiff need not make a prima facie showing that it was entitled to punitive damages in order to discover financial information from defendant). *Contra John Does I-VI v. Yogi*, 110 F.R.D. 629 (D.D.C. 1986).

Baker v. CNA Ins. Co., 123 F.R.D. 322, 329–30 (D. Mont. 1988) (holding that information concerning defendant's financial status was discoverable as relevant to plaintiff's claim for punitive damages; court did not require plaintiff to establish a prima facie case as a condition preceding).

Magnaleasing, Inc. v. Staten Island Mall, 76 F.R.D. 559 (S.D.N.Y. 1977) (proceeding in aid of judgment) (holding that judgment creditor was entitled to discover settlement agreement between judgment debtor and third party).

Miller v. Doctor's Gen. Hosp., 76 F.R.D. 136, 140 (W.D. Okla. 1977) (civil rights action) (where punitive damages claimed, holding that defendant's financial condition was a proper subject for discovery).

Delgado v. Kitzman, 793 S.W.2d 332 (Tex. Ct. App. 1990) (holding that plaintiff was allowed discovery of defendant's net worth).

See also

St. Joseph Hosp. v. INA Underwriters Ins. Co., 117 F.R.D. 24 (D. Me. 1987).

Rupe v. Fourman, 532 F. Supp. 344, 350–51 (S.D. Ohio 1981).

In re Folding Carton Antitrust Litig., 76 F.R.D. 420 (N.D. Ill. 1977).

Vollert v. Summa Corp., 389 F. Supp. 1348, 1351–52 (D. Haw. 1975).

§ 21 MINUTES OF CORPORATE MEETINGS

Commentary

The business of companies that manufacture products is routinely conducted by various corporate committees. Where otherwise relevant, the minutes of these meetings should be discoverable. Indeed in product defect cases, the pivotal issues in dispute (e.g., the existence and magnitude of risk, the feasibility and cost/benefits of alternative designs, the adequacy of industry standards or governmental regulations) are almost always the subject of corporate committee meetings.

Secondary Sources

KIELY, *supra* § 11, §§ 3.50–3.55.

8 WRIGHT & MILLER, *supra* § 1, § 2009, at 79 n.50.

Case Law

Bilhorn v. Lipman, 411 N.Y.S.2d 722 (App. Div. 1978) (products case; drug) (allowing plaintiff discovery of a transcript of a meeting since document might be relevant to issue of defendant's knowledge of dangerousness of drug).

Garst v. General Motors Corp., CA No. 90-8857-NP (Wexford County, Mich. Cir. Ct. Sept. 21, 1992) (products case; rear seat, lap belt only) (plaintiff requested reports of tests, studies and investigations and minutes of committee meetings reflecting the basis of GM's decision to equip its vehicle with the rear seat shoulder harness. GM attempted to limit the scope of discovery to (1) its subjective and adversarial view of the facts of the particular accident, (2) the particular model year and model type of vehicle involved, and (3) rear-seat occupants of the same or substantially similar size vehicle as the plaintiff. The court granted plaintiff's motion to compel and ordered GM to produce the requested documents, holding that in view of the nature of the defect involved, the scope of relevant discovery extended to other year model and model types and alternate designs. The court rejected GM's attempt to limit the production of minutes of committee meetings to certain specified committees. The court ordered the production of post- and pre-accident documents, noting that GM had withdrawn its "time limitation" objection.).

§ 22 TRIAL PREPARATION

§ 22.1 GENERALLY

(See also §§ 16.4, 17.5, 18.3, 39, 46, 49)

Commentary

The work-product doctrine was initiated to protect an attorney's private files, preparations for trial, and evaluations of his or her case from scrutiny by opponents. Generally, work product has been divided into two categories: (1) "ordinary" work product, which includes materials prepared in anticipation of litigation, and (2) "opinion" work product, which consists of the legal analysis, mental impressions, etc., of the attorney.

The differences in the two lie in the distinction that the facts underlying "ordinary" work product are still discoverable, and the work product itself is discoverable upon a showing that the requesting party has a "substantial need" for the information, and finding a "substantial equivalent" would create "undue hardship." On the other hand, "opinion" work product is discoverable only under the rarest of circumstances (e.g., waiver by the attorney or the client).

Rule

FED. R. CIV. P. 26(b)(3).

Secondary Sources

DISCOVERY PROCEEDINGS IN FEDERAL COURT, *supra* § 2, §§ 16.11–16.18.

HAYDOCK & HERR, *supra* § 3, § 1.6.

4 MOORE ET AL., *supra* § 1, ¶¶ 26.64–26.65.

8 WRIGHT & MILLER, *supra* § 1, §§ 2021–2028.

Case Law

See following sections dealing with specific trial preparation materials.

§ 22.2 STATEMENTS

Commentary

Rule 26(b)(3) explicitly makes statements by a party or witness discoverable by the person who made the statement. Beyond this, the initial discoverability of a statement is normally determined by whether it was taken in the ordinary course of business or in anticipation of litigation. Even if the court finds that the statement was acquired in anticipation of litigation, the court may require its production on a showing that the party seeking discovery has a substantial need for the statement and, further, is unable without undue hardship to obtain the substantial equivalent of the statement by other means.

If the defendant takes the position that plaintiff's counsel is forbidden to talk to one of its employees, the court should take that into account in determining whether to compel the production of the employee's statement or authorize an interview with the employee. *See, e.g., Morrison v. Brandeis Univ.*, 125 F.R.D. 14 (D. Mass. 1989); *see also* 4 WEINSTEIN & BERGER, WEINSTEIN'S EVIDENCE §801(d)(2)(D)[01] (1992 & Supp. 1993).

Rule

FED. R. CIV. P. 26(b)(3).

Secondary Sources

AMERICAN LAW OF PRODUCTS LIABILITY 3D, *supra* § 1, § 23.21.

Annotation, *Statements of Parties or Witnesses as Subject of Pretrial or Other Disclosure, Production or Inspection*, 73 A.L.R. 2D 12 (1960).

HAYDOCK & HERR, *supra* § 3, § 1.6.2.

4 MOORE ET AL., *supra* § 1, ¶ 26.65.

8 WRIGHT & MILLER, *supra* § 1, §§ 2027, 2028.

Case Law

Hickman v. Taylor, 329 U.S. 495, 504 (1947) (wrongful death action) (holding that witness statements obtained and prepared by counsel after claim had arisen were not discoverable).

Miles v. M/V Miss. Queen, 753 F.2d 1349, 1351 (5th Cir. 1985) (party's statement) (holding that plaintiff had the right to discover from defendant his own statements to third-party insurer).

Phillips v. Dallas Carriers Corp., 133 F.R.D. 475, 480–81 (M.D.N.C. 1990) (holding that a statement taken from defendant truck driver by insurance adjuster on day of accident was not protected by attorney-client privilege; even if statement was work product, motorist was still entitled to discovery, as motorist had no direct memory of collision and defendant driver was unable to recall significant aspects of collision).

McNulty v. Bally's Park Place, Inc., 120 F.R.D. 27, 30 (E.D. Pa. 1988) (although constituting work product, statement of sole eyewitness who was no longer available was discoverable because moving party showed substantial need and unavailability from other sources).

Hirstein v. American Motors Corp., 112 F.R.D. 436 (N.D. Ind. 1986) (nonparty statement) (holding that third party may provide to plaintiff copies of the third party's statements to defendant as work-product protection did not apply).

Shannon v. Hansen, 469 N.W.2d 412 (Iowa 1991) (holding that statements made by witnesses to police officer investigating motor vehicle accident were not protected by public officer's privilege).

State ex rel. Burlington N. R.R. v. District Court, 779 P.2d 885, 890–91 (Mont. 1989) (action under Federal Employers Liability Act) (holding that witness's statements taken by railroad company's claims representative within 24 hours of accident were discoverable).

DeMoss Rexall Drugs v. Dobson, 540 N.E.2d 655, 657 (Ind. Ct. App. 1989) (finding that statement of pharmacy's representatives made to insurer's claims representative were discoverable).

Soltani-Rastegar v. Superior Court, 256 Cal. Rptr. 255, 258 (Ct. App. 1989) (negligence action; automobile accident) (holding that defendant's statements made to insurance company's claim representative were not discoverable).

Wagi v. Silver Ridge Park W., 580 A.2d 1093 (N.J. Super. Ct. Div. 1989) (holding that the attorney-client privilege protected statements but not names of witnesses).

§ 22.3 COURSE OF BUSINESS MATERIALS

(See also §§ 14, 16.2, 17, 18, 19, 21, 23, 38.1)

Commentary

Access to materials prepared in the usual and ordinary course of the defendant's business should not be limited under the work-product doctrine. The work-product doctrine (embodied in rule 26(b)(3)) restricts discovery only as to materials prepared in anticipation of litigation or for trial. Even then the doctrine does not preclude discovery of the underlying facts. Finally, even when applicable, the doctrine does not accord an absolute privilege: The party may still be able to gain access to those materials upon a showing of exceptional circumstances.

Rule

FED. R. CIV. P. 26(b)(3).

Secondary Sources

AMERICAN LAW OF PRODUCTS LIABILITY 3D, *supra* § 1, §§ 53:14–53:21.

DISCOVERY PROCEEDINGS IN FEDERAL COURT, *supra* § 2, §§ 16.11–16.18.

HAYDOCK & HERR, *supra* § 3, § 1.6.

4 MOORE ET AL., *supra* § 1, ¶¶ 26.63–26.64.

Wagner, Annotation, *Protection from Discovery of Attorney's Opinion Work Product Under Rule 26(b)(3) of Federal Rules of Civil Procedure*, 84 A.L.R. FED. 779 (1987).

8 WRIGHT & MILLER, *supra* § 1, §§ 2021–2028.

Case Law

Holmgren v. State Farm Mut. Auto. Ins. Co., 976 F.2d 573 (9th Cir. 1992) (bad-faith claim) (plaintiff sought to obtain correspondence between the insurer and its attorney to establish bad-faith claim; court held that the attorneys' opinion work product was discoverable since the state of mind of the insurer was an essential element of the bad-faith claim sounding in the failure to properly settle plaintiff's personal injury claim.).

Chemical Eng'g Corp. v. Essef Indus., 795 F.2d 1565, 1575 n.11 (Fed. Cir. 1986) (patent infringement) (plaintiff failed to supplement its discovery response after its own in-house testing demonstrated that the defendant's device probably did not violate the subject patent; court held that the plaintiff's failure to file a supplemental answer warranted sanctions and commented that the "notion that [the plaintiff] was free to refuse to admit the truth because the truth might have defeated its lawsuit is contrary to the duty of candor owed the court.").

Blough v. Food Lion, Inc., 142 F.R.D. 622, 624 (E.D. Va. 1992) (personal injury action) (holding that defendant's accident report of subject incident was not prepared in anticipation of litigation and was therefore discoverable).

Harper v. Auto Owners Ins. Co., 138 F.R.D. 655, 663 (S.D. Ind. 1991) (holding that documents developed by insurance company before it notified its insured that its claim was denied were presumptively not prepared in anticipation of litigation).

Fine v. Facet Aerospace Prods. Co., 133 F.R.D. 439 (S.D.N.Y. 1990) (products case; aircraft) (holding that defendant manufacturer's internal report addressing problem of water in fuel systems of its aircraft, testing done, and possible solutions were subject to discovery; court overruled defendant's objection based on attorney-client privilege; report was drafted by manufacturer's engineering department for purpose of risk management).

Airheart v. Chicago & N.W. Transp. Co., 128 F.R.D. 669, 671–72 (D.S.D. 1989) (negligence action against railroad) (holding insurance company's accident investigation report discoverable).

Schmidt v. California State Auto. Ass'n, 127 F.R.D. 182, 184 n.3 (D. Nev. 1989) (finding that the routine processing of material prepared by an attorney functioning primarily as a claims adjuster in ordinary course of business was not immunized from discovery by attorney-client privilege or work product).

State v. Hogan, 588 N.E.2d 560 (Ind. Ct. App. 1992) (holding state's blanket claim of privilege insufficient to preclude discovery of documents showing that state had prior knowledge of unsafe road conditions that caused plaintiff's accident; court required evidentiary hearing with respect to discoverability of particular documents).

Calkins v. Perry, 564 N.Y.S.2d 943 (App. Div. 1990) (holding that accident reports that were prepared by defendants as part of business routine were subject to discovery).

See also

Reedy v. Lull Eng'g Co., 137 F.R.D. 405 (M.D. Fla. 1991).

In re Air Crash Disaster at Sioux City, Iowa, 133 F.R.D. 515 (N.D. Ill. 1990).

Carte Blanche (Sing.) PTE, Ltd. v. Diners Club Int'l, Inc., 130 F.R.D. 28 (S.D.N.Y. 1990).

Bohannon v. Honda Motor Co., 127 F.R.D. 536 (D. Kan. 1989).

Henson v. Wyeth Lab., Inc., 118 F.R.D. 584 (W.D. Va. 1987).

Schuler v. United States, 113 F.R.D. 518 (W.D. Mich. 1986).

Garcia v. Peeples, 734 S.W.2d 343 (Tex. 1987).

Marte v. W.O. Hickok Mfg. Co., 552 N.Y.S.2d 297 (App. Div. 1990).

§ 22.4 INVESTIGATIVE MATERIALS

(See also §§ 22.5, 39, 46, 48)

Commentary

The determining factor concerning the discoverability of investigative materials is whether the materials were prepared in the ordinary course of business (in which event they are discoverable) or in anticipation of litigation (in which event they are not discoverable). Investigative reports fall under the auspice of "ordinary" work product, which allows for the discovery of the underlying facts and the reports themselves with a showing of substantial need and undue hardship in finding a substantial equivalent.

Note also that in many circumstances a defendant's investigative report may have been prepared in the usual course of business. Those cases have been cited in § 22.3, *supra*.

Rule

FED. R. CIV. P. 26(b)(3).

Secondary Sources

AMERICAN LAW OF PRODUCTS LIABILITY 3D, *supra* § 1, §§ 53:14–53:21.

DISCOVERY PROCEEDINGS IN FEDERAL COURT, *supra* § 2, §§ 16.11–16.18.

HAYDOCK & HERR, *supra* § 3, § 1.6.

4 MOORE ET AL., *supra* § 1, ¶¶ 26.63–26.64.

8 WRIGHT & MILLER, *supra* § 1, §§ 2021–2028.

Case Law

Holmgren v. State Farm Mut. Auto. Ins. Co., 976 F.2d 573 (9th Cir. 1992) (bad-faith claim) (plaintiff sought to obtain correspondence between the insurer and its attorney to establish bad-faith claim. The court held that the attorneys' opinion work product was discoverable since the state of mind of the insurer was an essential element of the bad-faith claim sounding in the failure to properly settle plaintiff's personal injury claim.).

Anderson v. Cryovac, Inc., 862 F.2d 910 (1st Cir. 1988) (holding that a report prepared by an independent testing company and filed with the EPA was discoverable), *on remand, Anderson v. Beatrice Foods Co.*, 127 F.R.D. 1 (D. Mass. 1989).

Simon v. G.D. Searle & Co., 816 F.2d 397, 401 (8th Cir. 1987) (holding an internal corporate report discoverable), *cert. denied*, 484 U.S. 917 (1987).

Roberts v. Jeep Eagle Corp., CA No. 1:89-cv-238-HTW (N.D. Ga. Jan. 4, 1993) (products case; liftgate) (court compelled defendant to produce (1) reports of similar incidents occurring both before and after subject claim (at 3–4); (2) requested photographs, overruling defendant's work product and attorney-client objections on grounds that photographs do not disclose mental impressions (at 4); (3) documents and testimony produced in other cases (at 2–3, 11); (4) tests concerning similar models (at 11); (5) information concerning profits defendants realized per vehicle during certain years pertinent to the litigation (at 12); (6) information concerning defendant's consideration of an alternative design (at 7, 12–13); and (7) information concerning defendant's consideration of a subsequent remedial measure (at 7, 12–13); court allowed plaintiff to depose defendant's vice-president for the reason that he participated in a decision to suppress an internal memorandum concerning the defective condition of the subject liftgate (at 6–7).).

Bradley v. Melroe Co., 141 F.R.D. 1 (D.D.C. 1992) (products case; skid loader) (learning of seven other incidents involving the same interlock mechanism alleged to be defective in the present case, plaintiff sought production of the in-house investigative file for each incident; court ordered the production of the factual data contained in each of the in-house investigative files but permitted the defendant to redact all mental impressions, opinions, evaluations, recommendations, and theories).

Hawkins v. South Plains Int'l Trucks, Inc., 139 F.R.D. 682 (D. Colo. 1991) (products case; truck hot-oil unit) (plaintiff's compensation insurance carrier was co-plaintiff to action. Insurance carrier served subpoena on plaintiff's employer, directing employer to produce its accident investigation file. Employer's internal claims attorney had in fact conducted an investigation within days after the incident. Employer objected on the basis that this accident file constituted privileged attorney work product. Court held that rule 26(b)(3) work-product protection does not extend to a nonparty.). *See also* 8 WRIGHT & MILLER, *supra* § 1, § 2024, at 201–02.

Hotchkiss v. Sears, Roebuck & Co., 139 F.R.D. 313, 315–16, 317–18 (M.D. Pa. 1991) (products case; radial arm saw) (defendant compelled to produce (1) records pertaining to research and development of a potential guard for the saw, (2) market studies concerning saws and who used them, (3) three reports reflecting the pattern of injuries associated with the use of radial arm saws, (4) documents regarding hazards associated with the use of the subject guard on radial arm saws including follow-up interviews of purchasers of saws with the guard, (5) reports of testing performed by manufacturer on alternate guards, and (6) records of attempts to develop other types of guards for saw blade. Court found that conditions imposed by confidentiality order would adequately protect defendant's trade secret concerns.).

McFadden v. Norton Co., 118 F.R.D. 625, 629 (D. Neb. 1988) (products case; grinding wheel) (holding manufacturer's accident investigation report discoverable).

Sham v. Hyannis Heritage House Hotel, Inc., 118 F.R.D. 24, 26–27 (D. Mass. 1987) (wrongful death action) (holding an insurance investigator's report discoverable).

Peterson v. Chesapeake & Ohio Ry., 112 F.R.D. 360 (W.D. Mich. 1986) (holding an internal corporate report discoverable).

In re Comair Air Disaster Litig., 100 F.R.D. 350 (E.D. Ky. 1983) (products case; aircraft) (employee of the defendant manufacturer investigated the accident and compiled a report of his findings. That report was turned over to another of the defendant's employees for review in preparation for deposition. The court found that it was necessary in the "interests of justice" to compel production of the report. Using the balancing test, the court placed emphasis on the plaintiff's unequal access to the wreckage.). *See* § 46, *supra*.

Miles v. Bell Helicopter Co., 385 F. Supp. 1029, 1032–33 (N.D. Ga. 1974) (wrongful death action) (holding that defendant's accident investigation report was discoverable).

Carlson v. Chisholm-Moore Hoist Corp., 21 F.R.D. 144 (S.D.N.Y. 1957) (products case; chain hoist) (after plaintiff's injury, the hoist had been returned to defendant for testing and inspection, and certain parts were replaced; reports and memoranda relating to these repairs were held discoverable; plaintiff was also held entitled to production of defendant's correspondence and reports relating to the accident), *aff'd*, 281 F.2d 766 (2d Cir. 1960).

Ex parte McEllen, No. 1911403, 1992 Ala. LEXIS 1192 (Ala. Oct. 16, 1992) (plaintiffs were advised by Prudential-Bache to make certain investments—which failed. Plaintiff sought to prove that a local Pru-Bache department head was guilty of self-dealing. Trial court ordered Pru-Bache to produce two investigative reports relating to the possibilities of department heads self-dealing. The Alabama Supreme Court affirmed, stating that information acquired by an attorney while acting in a nonlegal capacity (e.g., as an investigator) was not protected by the attorney-client privilege. The court further held that conclusory affidavit filed by defendant failed to carry the necessary burden of proof to establish that the report was prepared "in anticipation of litigation."), *withdrawn per curiam*, 629 So. 2d 815 (Ala. 1993).

Waste Management, Inc. v. International Surplus Lines Ins. Co., 579 N.E.2d 322, 329–30 (Ill. 1991) (declaratory judgment action) (in subsequent declaratory judgment action raising coverage question, insurer sought production of defense counsel's file. The court determined that the work-product rule was not intended to bar discovery of defense counsel's mental impressions and case assessment as they related to the underlying litigation, in the subsequent declaratory judgment action. Since the attorney's impression in the underlying action did not necessarily disclose the attorney's impression in the declaratory judgment action, the court ruled that the purpose of the work-product doctrine was not served and thus not available to protect the attorney's file.).

Light v. State, 547 N.E.2d 1073 (Ind. 1989) (holding that federal statute forbidding disclosure or use of reports in evidence did not bar pretrial discovery of Department of Transportation accident reports for portion of highway at which claimant was involved in accident).

Stringer v. Eleventh Court of Appeals, 720 S.W.2d 801, 802 (Tex. 1986) (negligence action against railroad) (holding railroad company investigator's accident report discoverable).

Terry v. Lawrence, 700 S.W.2d 912, 913 (Tex. 1985) (negligence action against automobile owner/driver) (holding that photographs of vehicles and accident scene taken by insurance investigator were discoverable).

Williamson v. Superior Court, 582 P.2d 126 (Cal. 1978) (products case; tire and tire-changing machine) (co-defendant's experts developed a report that defective design of other defendant's product caused plaintiff's injury. The two defendants entered into an agreement which provided that the first defendant would withdraw its expert to preclude discovery of the offending report. In return, the co-defendant would indemnify the first against any liability it might incur. The court required production of first defendant's expert's report.).

State v. Hogan, 588 N.E.2d 560 (Ind. Ct. App. 1992) (holding that state's blanket claim of privilege was insufficient to preclude discovery of documents showing that state had prior knowledge of unsafe road conditions that caused plaintiff's accident; court required evidentiary hearing with respect to discoverability of particular documents).

Texas Dep't of Mental Health & Mental Retardation v. Davis, 775 S.W.2d 467, 471 (Tex. Ct. App. 1989) (wrongful death action) (holding school's investigation report discoverable).

Foster v. Heard, 757 S.W.2d 464 (Tex. Ct. App. 1988) (holding investigative report of incident discoverable).

O'Connell v. Jones, 529 N.Y.S.2d 19, 20–21 (App. Div. 1988) (slip and fall case) (holding that photographs of sidewalk where icy conditions no longer existed were discoverable where moving party had shown substantial need and unavailability from other sources).

Crowe v. Lederle Lab., 510 N.Y.S.2d 228, 229 (App. Div. 1986) (products case; vaccine) (holding that medical services department report was discoverable where report was prepared for dual purposes of preparing for litigation and as part of company's regular course of business).

Lee v. Honda Motor Co., CA No. 9103-01752 (Multnomah County, Or. Cir. Ct. Feb. 4, 1992) (products case; ATV) (ordering defendant manufacturer to produce accurate index of materials contained in central depository created by defendant although the index was prepared in anticipation of litigation; the plaintiffs had a substantial need for an accurate index and were unable without undue hardship to obtain a substantial equivalent).

Cooper v. American Honda Motor Corp., CA No. 473513 (San Diego County, Cal. Super. Ct., Referee Report No. 1, Apr. 18, 1986) (products case; ATV) (ordering Honda to produce entire claims files involving ATV accidents on pavement so as to permit the plaintiff to determine whether there were accidents other than those he had already specified by number to the defendants; court specifically provided that the period coverage should "include all such accidents to date and not merely up to the date of the accident involved in this case").

Contra

Zaban v. McCombs, 568 So. 2d 87 (Fla. Dist. Ct. App. 1990) (holding that the file of an investigator hired by corporate employer to inquire into employee's work-related accident was within work-product privilege).

Smith v. Thornton, 765 S.W.2d 473, 475–77 (Tex. Ct. App. 1988) (negligence action against owner of plant premises) (holding that an accident investigation report for type of accident not normally investigated by company was not discoverable).

§ 22.5 LITIGATION TESTING

(See also §§ 5, 9.5, 16.3, 18.2, 34, 36, 38.1, 39, 40, 45)

Commentary

Litigation testing is conducted for the purpose of portraying the opposing parties' adversarial view of the facts. Litigation testing is performed ex parte. Therefore, neither the accuracy of the factual basis nor the conclusions suggested by a litigation test are subject to independent verification and cross-examination.

This type of evidence is normally discoverable.

It should be noted that in sharp contrast to other forms of demonstrative evidence, the trustworthiness of tests or films portraying one party's adversarial view of disputed facts are highly suspect and are rarely admitted into evidence.

As the cases below indicate, litigation testing conducted for a particular case albeit temporarily protected under rule 26(b)(4)(B) should be subject to discovery in subsequent litigation. The major reason for this is to provide the plaintiff with an opportunity to verify the conditions under which the testing was performed, just as the court ordinarily does in permitting the discovery of surveillance films. *See* § 5.2, *supra*.

Furthermore, the defendant may well have a duty to furnish the plaintiff information disclosed in subsequent testing or independent investigations in obedience to its duty to supplement discovery responses under rules 26(e) and 37(c).

Secondary Sources

AMERICAN LAW OF PRODUCTS LIABILITY 3D, *supra* § 1, §§ 53:71–53:73.

DISCOVERY PROCEEDINGS IN FEDERAL COURT, *supra* § 2, § 7.8.

Case Law

Anderson v. Cryovac, Inc., 862 F.2d 910 (1st Cir. 1988) (holding that a report prepared by an independent testing company and filed with the EPA was discoverable), *on remand, Anderson v. Beatrice Foods Co.*, 127 F.R.D. 1 (D. Mass. 1989).

Chemical Eng'g Corp. v. Essef Indus., 795 F.2d 1565, 1575 n.11 (Fed. Cir. 1986) (patent infringement) (plaintiff failed to supplement its discovery response after its own test demonstrated that the defendant's device probably did not violate the patent; the court held that the plaintiff's failure to file a supplemental answer warranted sanctions and commented that the "notion that the plaintiff was free to refuse to admit the truth because the truth might have defeated its lawsuit is contrary to the duty of candor owed the court.").

Roberts v. Jeep Eagle Corp., CA No. 1:89-cv-238-HTW (N.D. Ga. Jan. 4, 1993) (products case; liftgate) (court compelled defendant to produce (1) reports of similar incidents occurring both before and after subject claim (at 3–4); (2) requested photographs, overruling defendant's work product and attorney-client objections on grounds that photographs do not disclose mental impressions (at 4); (3) documents and testimony produced in other cases (at 2–3, 11); (4) tests concerning similar models (at 11); (5) information concerning profits defendants realized per vehicle during certain years pertinent to the litigation (at 12); (6) information concerning defendant's consideration of an alternative design (at 7, 12-13); and (7) information concerning defendant's consideration of a subsequent remedial measure (at 7, 12–13); court allowed plaintiff to depose defendant's vice-president for the reason that he participated in a decision to suppress an internal memorandum concerning the defective condition of the subject liftgate (at 6–7).).

Board of Directors, Water's Edge, Condominium Unit Owners' Ass'n v. Anden Group, 136 F.R.D. 100, 109 (E.D. Va. 1991) (sanctioning party for failing to supplement its response to discovery requests by disclosing adverse test results acquired by independent experts hired by the defending party subsequent to the institute of litigation).

Hotchkiss v. Sears, Roebuck & Co., 139 F.R.D. 313, 316 (M.D. Pa. 1991) (products case; radial arm saw) (in preparation for trial, plaintiff had made videotapes depicting the operation of the radial arm saw with a guard attached; the court ordered plaintiff to produce copies of whatever tapes they planned to present at trial.).

Reedy v. Lull Eng'g Co., 137 F.R.D. 405 (M.D. Fla. 1991) (allowing defendant to discover videotapes and photographs of accident site made by plaintiff because of exceptional circumstances, but not the audio portion of videotape).

In re Shell Oil Refinery, 132 F.R.D. 437 (E.D. La. 1990) (holding that cost in the range of $230,000 to $315,000 to duplicate defendant's tests did not satisfy the "exceptional circumstances" requirement; court rejected per se rule barring "in-house experts" from protection under rule 26(b)(4)(B) and listed factors that effect determination. The court also noted that facts and opinions acquired prior to employees' special retention were not protected from discovery), *clarified*, 134

F.R.D. 148 (E.D. La. 1990). Other cases indicating that rule 26(b)(4)(B) protection could be applied to regular employees include *Marine Petroleum Co. v. Champlin Petroleum Co.*, 641 F.2d 984 (D.C. Cir. 1979); *In re Sinking of Barge "Ranger I,"* 92 F.R.D. 486, 489 n.5 (S.D. Tex. 1981); *Seiffer v. Topsy's Int'l, Inc.*, 69 F.R.D. 69 (D. Kan. 1975).

Kansas-Nebraska Natural Gas Co. v. Marathon Oil Co., 109 F.R.D. 12 (D. Neb. 1985) (holding that under the circumstances in-house employees would not qualify as consulting experts).

Loctite Corp. v. Fel-Pro Inc., 94 F.R.D. 1, 10–11 (N.D. Ill. 1980) (patent infringement case) (finding that plaintiff met burden of demonstrating "exceptional circumstances," justifying discovery from nontestifying consultant, the court also sanctioned the plaintiff for failing to supplement its discovery responses by providing the defendant with a report of its laboratory supervisors' reevaluation that concluded that the defendant had probably not infringed the plaintiff's patent), *aff'd in part, remanded in part*, 667 F.2d 577 (7th Cir. 1981).

Leding v. United States Rubber Co., 23 F.R.D. 220 (D. Mont. 1959) (products case; defective boot) (holding that the defendant's investigation and testing of boot were not privileged as work product).

Caterpillar Tractor Co. v. Donahue, 674 P.2d 1276 (Wyo. 1983) (wrongful death action against the manufacturer for front-end loader that rolled over) (holding that trial court properly excluded film offered by manufacturer showing a simulated rollover for failure to furnish film to plaintiff in response to discovery request; plaintiff would have been surprised and prejudiced because of the defendant's failure to provide statistical data of the conditions under which the experiment was conducted).

Williamson v. Superior Court, 582 P.2d 126 (Cal. 1978) (products case; tire and tire-changing machine) (one of the co-defendant's experts developed a report that defective design of other co-defendant's product caused plaintiff's injury. The two defendants entered into an agreement which provided that the first defendant would withdraw its expert to preclude discovery of the offending report. In return, the co-defendant would indemnify the first against any liability it might incur. The court compelled production of the report written by the first defendant's expert.).

Neuswanger v. Ikegai Am. Corp., 582 N.E.2d 192 (Ill. App. Ct. 1991) (products case; industrial machine) (estate of employee killed in industrial accident sued manufacturer of machine. Anticipating litigation, plaintiff's employer and workers' compensation carrier hired consulting expert who video taped re-enactment of incident. Plaintiff served subpoena seeking production of the tape. The court held that rule protecting work product of consultant expert applied only to "parties." Further, court held that videotape was discoverable as a "tangible thing" under Illinois rule, which exempts from work-product protection tangible things that do not reveal attorney's or consultant's opinions.).

Lopez v. Foremost Paving, Inc., 796 S.W.2d 473 (Tex. Ct. App. 1990) (where defendant failed to produce videotape simulation of defendant's version of accident until ten days before trial, introduction in evidence at trial held reversible error).

Wierbinski v. Volkswagen A.G., CA No. A038364 (Cal. Ct. App. Dec. 30, 1988) (products case; design of suspension system causing rollover) (ordering automaker to produce accident reconstruction computer program and software for program, which defendant failed to do until middle of trial; appellate court affirmed trial court's order granting plaintiff new trial following verdict for defendant), *reprinted in* Automotive Litig. Rep. 11444-47 (Jan. 17, 1989).

American Bldgs. Co. v. Kokomo Grain Co., 506 N.E.2d 56 (Ind. Ct. App. 1987) (holding that protection from disclosure created by rule 26(b)(4)(B) did not extend to subsequent litigation since expert did not prepare his report in anticipation of future litigation). To the same effect, see *Sullivan v. Sturm, Ruger & Co.*, 80 F.R.D. 489 (D. Mont. 1978); *Grinnell Corp. v. Hackett*, 70 F.R.D. 326, 333 (D.R.I. 1976); *National Steel Prods. Co. v. Superior Court*, 210 Cal. Rptr. 535 (App. Ct. 1985). *Contra In re "Agent Orange" Prod. Liab. Litig.*, 105 F.R.D. 577, 580 (E.D.N.Y. 1985) (based on the fact that the two cases were part of the same multidistrict litigation); *Hermsdorfer v. American Motors Corp.*, 96 F.R.D. 13, 15 (W.D.N.Y. 1982) (protecting information obtained for the purpose of preparing for the present case and all other similar litigation against the defendants).

Marinelli v. Volkswagen of Am., Inc., CA No. CV89-3301 (Jefferson County, Ala. Cir. Ct. Apr. 24, 1991, Oct. 22, 1991, Feb. 19, 1992) (products case; vehicle rollover) (defendant's expert witness based his testimony in part on accident reconstruction analysis performed with the aid of a computer. In three separate orders the court instructed the defendant to provide plaintiff's counsel with a copy of the computer disk utilized by the defendant's expert witness including not only the relevant data but the software employed in the computer program.).

Sherman v. M. Lowenstein & Sons, Inc., 248 N.Y.S.2d 1000 (Sup. Ct. 1964) (products case; pajamas) (ordering plaintiff to produce tested pajamas or test results where other similar pajamas were no longer available for defendant to conduct own tests).

Contra

Abrams v. Vaughan & Bushnell Mfg. Co., 325 N.Y.S.2d 976, 979 (App. Div. 1971) (products case; hammer) (holding that a test conducted after commencement of action was not discoverable).

§ 23 TECHNICAL LITERATURE

§ 23.1 GENERALLY

(See also §§ 17.4, 17.6, 17.7, 18.2, 37–39, 48)

Commentary

Technical literature is intended to refer to published materials and may include any of the following categories of information: authoritative treatises, technical articles or papers, studies or statistics involving the particular defect or failure mode involved, and applicable governmental or industry standards. Any issue in dispute may be the subject matter of some technical literature. This literature is generally discoverable.

Rules

FED. R. EVID. 803(4), 803(6), 803(8), 803(17), 803(18), 803(24).

Secondary Sources

AMERICAN LAW OF PRODUCTS LIABILITY 3D, *supra* § 1, §§ 53:52–53:53.

KIELY, *supra* § 11, ch. 1.

Case Law

Baise v. Alewel's, Inc., 99 F.R.D. 95, 96–97 (W.D. Mo. 1983) (holding that a party's knowledge of the literature regarding a product's hazard was an appropriate subject for a request for an admission).

Blackner v. Clark Equip. Co., CA No. 2860 (Philadelphia, Pa. Ct. C.P. Nov. 7, 1983) (products case; forklift rollover).

§ 23.2 STATUTES AND REGULATIONS

(See also § 17.4)

Commentary

The defendant may contend that the product conforms to some statute or governmental regulation. If so, the court should permit full discovery of the basis of this contention. The defendant's knowledge of any applicable statutes or regulations may well be relevant in a products liability case for a number of reasons.

Secondary Sources

AMERICAN LAW OF PRODUCTS LIABILITY 3D, *supra* § 1, §§ 53:52–53:53.

KIELY, *supra* § 11, §§ 1.16, 1.24, 3.44–3.49.

Case Law

Cipollone v. Liggett Group, Inc., 112 U.S. 2608 (1992) (holding that the Federal Cigarette Labeling and Advertising Act did not preempt state law claims for the failure to warn or for fraudulent concealment of health hazards of cigarettes by manufacturers; this holding should make manufacturer's documents related to hazards of smoking discoverable).

§ 23.3 STANDARDS (GOVERNMENT, INDUSTRY, FOREIGN, IN-HOUSE)

(See also § 17.4)

Commentary

The defendant may contend that the product conforms to some standard. If so, the court should permit full discovery of the basis of this contention. The defendant's knowledge of any applicable standards may well be relevant in a products liability case for a number of reasons.

Secondary Sources

AMERICAN LAW OF PRODUCTS LIABILITY 3D, *supra* § 1, §§ 53:52–53:53.

KIELY, *supra* § 11, §§ 1.16, 1.24, 1.49–1.52, 3.44–3.49.

Case Law

Kramer v. Boeing Co., 126 F.R.D. 690, 695 (D. Minn. 1989) (products case; airplane) (holding that documents related to an ongoing dialogue between the manufacturer and the FAA about safety standards were clearly discoverable).

Kelleher v. Omark Indus., 20 Fed. R. Serv. 2d (Callaghan) 199, 202 (D. Mass. 1975) (products case; stud gun) (compelling defendant to answer interrogatory requesting identity of any trade or industry associations having rules or standards regulating stud guns).

Earl v. Gulf & W. Mfg. Co., 366 N.W.2d 160, 164 (Wis. Ct. App. 1985) (products case; industrial press) (holding that information regarding foreign manufacturing standards was discoverable).

Ribley v. Harsco Corp., 377 N.Y.S.2d 375, 376–77 (Sup. Ct. 1975) (products case; manure spreader) (holding that safety standards published by government agencies or professional or industrial organizations were discoverable; plaintiff entitled to discover information as to changes in design, tests regarding safety, and compliance with safety standards), *aff'd*, 394 N.Y.S.2d 740 (App. Div. 1977).

§ 23.4 PATENTS

(See also § 17.4)

Commentary

Patents are relevant and potentially admissible at trial for any one of the following reasons: (1) as showing the existence and/or feasibility of an alternative design, (2) as bearing on the defendant's knowledge of the hazard, (3) as directly bearing on the issue of "defect," that is, to show that the product was not in a reasonably safe condition or that it failed to meet the reasonable expectations of the ordinary consumer, (4) in direct examination as part of the basis of the expert's opinion testimony, and (5) in cross-examination of the defendant's expert witness.

Secondary Sources

Kessler & Brookman, *Patents in Product Cases—A Useful Source for Attorneys*, TRIAL, Nov. 1985, at 79.

KIELY, *supra* § 11, § 1.48.

McKeown, *Patent Records as a Source of Evidence in Products Liability Suits*, PRAC. LAW., Oct. 1983, 13.

8 WRIGHT & MILLER, *supra* § 1, § 2009, at 69 n.48.

Case Law

Chubb Integrated Sys. Ltd. v. National Bank, 103 F.R.D. 52, 58–59 (D.D.C. 1984).

Xerox Corp. v. IBM Corp., 399 F. Supp. 451 (S.D.N.Y. 1975) (patent infringement) (dealing with public availability of trade secrets).

Struthers Scientific & Int'l Corp. v. General Foods Corp., 45 F.R.D. 375 (S.D. Tex. 1968).

§ 23.5 AUTHORITATIVE PUBLICATIONS

Commentary

Learned treatises and other authoritative publications may be admitted into evidence. The court should consider the defendant's knowledge of the contents of authoritative technical literature as an appropriate inquiry. Indeed, most jurisdictions recognize that the defendant has a duty to stay abreast of technical developments and advances as they attest to the safety of the defendant's product.

Rule

FED. R. EVID. 803(18).

§ 24 CONTRACTUAL PROVISIONS

(See also §§ 19, 48)

Commentary

The defendant's duty may be legally affected by applicable contractual provisions. The quality and the performance of a product may also be the subject matter of a contract between the defendant and some third party. This is true of virtually all products built for use by the government, whether civilian or military.

Secondary Sources

8 WRIGHT & MILLER, *supra* § 1, § 2009, at 64 n.42.

Case Law

In re Hoechst Celanese Corp., 584 N.Y. 2d 805 (App. Div. 1992) (coverage dispute) (overruling appellant's "unduly burdensome" objection, court ordered production of documents relating to the drafting, development, and interpretation of standard-form general liability insurance policy language although appellant was not a party to the underlying action).

§ 25 ENVIRONMENT OF USE

(See also §§ 3, 4, 23, 26, 27, 33, 38–39, 40)

Commentary

The phrase "environment of use" refers to the real world conditions under which a product is actually used. Information concerning a product's environment of use is clearly within the scope of discovery.

Secondary Sources

BALDWIN ET AL., *supra* § 18.2, §§ 1.3.1, 7.3.1, 7.5, 7.9.3, 8.8.

§ 26 HAZARD IDENTIFICATION

(See also §§ 3, 4, 18, 23, 25, 27, 36, 38–39)

Commentary

The phrase "hazard identification" refers to the efforts the defendant makes in the ordinary development of a product to identify hazards likely to be associated with the product in its real world environment of use. Materials in the possession or control of the defendant which relate to hazards associated with the use of the product are clearly discoverable. Indeed, in a general sense, such materials constitute the principal objective of discovery in a defective products case.

Secondary Sources

BALDWIN ET AL., *supra* § 18.2, §§ 1.3.1, 1.3.2, 2.5.3, 7.3.1.

Case Law

Farnsworth v. Procter & Gamble Co., 758 F.2d 1545 (11th Cir. 1985) (products case; toxic shock) (allowing party to obtain a copy of a study conducted by the Centers for Disease Control; however, court denied access to the names and addresses of the women who participated in the study).

Rozier v. Ford Motor Co., 573 F.2d 1332, 1342 (5th Cir.) (products case; fuel system integrity) (affirming district court's granting plaintiff a new trial following verdict for the defendant for Ford's failure to produce cost/benefits study of alternate design configuration), *reh'g denied*, 578 F.2d 871 (5th Cir. 1978).

Fine v. Facet Aerospace Prods. Co., 133 F.R.D. 439, 444 (S.D.N.Y. 1990) (products case; aircraft) (holding that defendant manufacturer's internal report addressing problem of water in fuel systems of its aircraft, testing done, and possible solutions were subject to discovery; court overruled defendant's objection based on attorney-client privilege; report was drafted by manufacturer's engineering department for purpose of risk management).

Roesberg v. Johns-Manville Corp., 85 F.R.D. 292, 300–01, 303–04 (E.D. Pa. 1980) (products case; asbestos) (holding that interrogatories seeking defendant's knowledge of interrelationship between handling asbestos products and asbestos-related diseases should be answered).

§ 27 DESIGN OBJECTIVES

(See also §§ 3, 4, 25, 26, 38, 39)

Commentary

Prior to the actual design of a product, the manufacturer typically defines and describes specific design objectives to be achieved in and by the intended performance of the product. Materials concerning or reflecting the design objectives of a product should be discoverable.

Secondary Sources

BALDWIN ET AL., *supra* § 18.2, §§ 7.3.1, 7.5, 7.9.3, 8.8.

§ 28 SPECIFICATIONS/FORMULAE/INGREDIENTS

(See also § 17.2)

Commentary

The basic specifications or formula for a product are ordinarily discoverable. In the event that this information satisfies the legal criteria for a trade secret, the court can usually provide adequate protection for the defendant's interest by entering a protective order limiting the dissemination of these materials.

Secondary Sources

AMERICAN LAW OF PRODUCTS LIABILITY 3D, *supra* § 1, §§ 53:35, 53:40, 53:46.

Case Law

Simmons v. American Honda Motor Co., CA No. 1:91-cv-0079-RCF (N.D. Ga. production order December 17, 1991; sanction order June 1, 1992) (products case; sidestand on motorcycle) (ordering manufacturer to produce blueprints, diagrams, drawings, photographs, etc. of subject and other model motorcycles; the district court sanctioned Honda for its repeated disregard of discovery rules and court's order).

Smith v. Bic Corp., 121 F.R.D. 235, 239–41 (E.D. Pa. 1988) (products case; disposable lighter) (holding that design specifications were discoverable), *aff'd in part, rev'd in part*, 869 F.2d 194 (3d Cir. 1989).

Clark v. General Motors Corp., 20 Fed. R. Serv. 2d (Callaghan) 679, 682 (D. Mass. 1975) (products case; stove) ("considering the allegations made, nothing could be more relevant" than the dimensions of the stove, materials of which it was composed, its method of operation, etc.).

Bowman v. General Motors Corp., 64 F.R.D. 62, 66, 68 (E.D. Pa. 1974) (products case; automobile) (holding that plaintiff may discover specifications of composition, durability, strength, and fire resistance or nonflammability of the materials used within the automobile in question for the model years of that automobile's date of manufacture to the time of the accident).

Glick v. McKesson & Robbins, Inc., 10 F.R.D. 477, 480 (W.D. Mo. 1950) (products case; suntan lotion) (holding that the gist of plaintiff's claim was that she was injured by the ingredients in the lotion; the ingredients, therefore, were relevant to the factual issues in this case).

Jampole v. Touchy, 673 S.W.2d 569, 574 (Tex. 1984) (products case; automobile) (holding that diagrams and assembly instructions of automobile fuel system were proper aids in determining whether manufacturing defect existed and were therefore discoverable).

Farnum v. Bristol-Myers Co., 219 A.2d 277, 280 (N.H. 1966) (products case; deodorant) (holding that the trial court had authority to order disclosure of ingredients in secret formula in advance of trial if essential or of "urgent necessity").

Bleacher v. Bristol-Myers Co., 163 A.2d 526, 529 (Del. Super. Ct. 1960) (products case; deodorant) (holding that ingredients and quantity thereof contained in formula were discoverable).

Dunshie v. General Motors Corp., CA No.A-136,024 (Jefferson County, Tex. Dist. Ct.) (products case; "window shade" seat belt), *appeal dismissed*, 822 S.W.2d 345 (Tex. Ct. App. 1992).

§ 29 PRODUCTION RECORDS

(See also § 17)

Commentary

Many corporations retain production records to keep track of the numbers, type, and methods used to manufacture a given product. These records are normally kept in the ordinary course of business and therefore are usually discoverable.

§ 30 QUALITY-ASSURANCE RECORDS

(See also § 17)

Commentary

Much like production records, quality-assurance records are designed to ensure that a product is meeting certain standards established by either the government or a manufacturer. Since these records are kept in the ordinary course of business, they are generally discoverable.

§ 31 PACKAGING

Commentary

The significance of a product's packaging is found in two parts: (1) the warnings and/or instructions for use and (2) a defect in the packaging which may cause injury. Information concerning a defendant's choice of packaging may, in an appropriate case, be relevant and discoverable.

Case Law

Wind v. Eli Lilly & Co., 559 N.Y.S.2d 561, 563 (App. Div. 1990) (products case; DES) (compelling defendant to produce information relating to the appearance and packaging of its product for the three years prior to the plaintiff's birth).

§ 32 PATH OF DISTRIBUTION

(See also § 17)

Commentary

The phrase "path of distribution" refers to the movement of the product from the date it was assembled as a finished product to the present time. Information concerning the path of distribution is ordinarily discoverable for any one of a number of reasons: (1) it may disclose the identity of potential witnesses, (2) it may be relevant to the condition of the product at the time of the incident, (3) it may be relevant to the condition of the product at the time it was examined by a testifying expert, (4) it may reflect the character of the typical or ordinary user, and (5) it may reflect the method or type of uses to which the product is exposed.

Secondary Sources

BALDWIN ET AL., *supra* § 18.2, §§ 7.12.2, 7B.12.14.

Case Law

Roesberg v. Johns-Manville Corp., 85 F.R.D. 292, 298 (E.D. Pa. 1980) (products case; asbestos) (finding that an interrogatory seeking to discover "chain of distribution" was not overly vague or ambiguous and should be answered).

Kaplan v. Roux Lab., Inc., 76 N.Y.S.2d 601 (App. Div. 1948) (products case; hair dye).

§ 33 WARNINGS AND/OR INSTRUCTIONS

(See also §§ 17, 23, 31)

Commentary

Information concerning any warnings issued by the manufacturer with respect to the product are generally discoverable whether they were given before or after the date of the alleged injury.

Secondary Sources

AMERICAN LAW OF PRODUCTS LIABILITY 3D, *supra* § 1, §§ 53:48–53.49.

Case Law

Hotchkiss v. Sears, Roebuck & Co., 139 F.R.D. 313, 315–16, 317–18 (M.D. Pa. 1991) (products case; radial arm saw) (ordering defendant to produce owner's manual for the subject radial arm saw and for other saws produced during a nine-year period).

Roesberg v. Johns-Manville Corp., 85 F.R.D. 292, 297–98 (E.D. Pa. 1980) (products case; asbestos) (holding that interrogatory that asked "whether defendant ever advised ultimate product purchasers or users of potential cancers or other diseases possibly contractible by use of or exposure to [their] products" was appropriate).

Clark v. General Motors Corp., 20 Fed. R. Serv. 2d (Callaghan) 679, 683 (D. Mass. 1975) (products case; stove) (holding that warnings issued prior to and after plaintiff's injury were relevant and discoverable).

Luey v. Sterling Drug, Inc., 240 F. Supp. 632, 636 (W.D. Mich. 1965) (drug case; Aralen) (allowing plaintiff to discover defendant's warnings to professionals, dosage determinations, and relationship to efficacy and side effects).

Hindelang v. R.D. Werner Co., 469 N.W.2d 2 (Mich. Ct. App. 1991) (claiming failure to warn of instability of ladder and necessary precautions for safe use).

Brown v. Daisy Mfg. Co., 514 N.Y.S.2d 300, 301 (App. Div. 1987) (products case; gun) (holding that instructions, manuals, and warnings given by manufacturer pertaining to use of gun were discoverable).

Fibron Prods., Inc. v. Hooker Chem. Corp., 206 N.Y.S.2d 659, 665 (Sup. Ct. 1960).

§ 34 MATERIALS PRODUCED IN OTHER CASES

Commentary

Documents produced in other cases, though subject to protective orders, are ordinarily discoverable in the present case.

Secondary Sources

AMERICAN LAW OF PRODUCTS LIABILITY 3D, *supra* § 1, § 53:18.

Case Law

Kirshner v. Uniden Corp. of Am., 842 F.2d 1074, 1079–81 (9th Cir. 1988) (personal injury action) (where plaintiff obtained documents written by defendant from another case, not through discovery, defendant sought a protective order requiring plaintiff to return the documents; lower court granted order; appellate court reversed; district court's power to control discovery did not extend to material discovered in another action).

Roberts v. Jeep Eagle Corp., CA No. 1:89-cv-238-HTW (N.D. Ga. Jan. 4, 1993) (products case; liftgate) (court compelled defendant to produce (1) reports of similar incidents occurring both before and after subject claim (at 3–4); (2) requested photographs, overruling defendant's work product and attorney-client objections on grounds that photographs do not disclose mental impressions (at 4); (3) documents and testimony produced in other cases (at 2–3, 11); (4) tests concerning similar models (at 11); (5) information concerning profits defendants realized per vehicle during certain years pertinent to the litigation (at 12); (6) information concerning defendant's consideration of an alternative design (at 7, 12–13); and (7) information concerning defendant's consideration of a subsequent remedial measure (at 7, 12–13); court allowed plaintiff to depose defendant's vice-president for the reason that he participated in a decision to suppress an internal memorandum concerning the defective condition of the subject liftgate (at 6–7).).

Hutto v. Bic Corp., CA No. 91-644-N (E.D. Va.) and *Floyd v. Bic Corp.*, CA No. 1:89-cv-401-RLV (N.D. Ga. Sept. 2, 1992) (products cases; disposable lighter) (same lawyer represented the plaintiffs in both cases. The defendant produced certain documents in *Hutto* that were not produced in *Floyd* despite the court's order directing the production of the documents. The court in *Hutto* granted the plaintiff's petition to forward the documents produced in *Hutto* to the court in *Floyd*, subject to the same protective order entered in *Hutto*.). [Note: The court's order in *Floyd* was vacated following the settlement.]

Wauchop v. Domino's Pizza, Inc., 138 F.R.D. 539, 544, 549 (N.D. Ind. 1991) (holding that the fact that information sought in present case was sealed under a protective order in another case did not affect its discoverability in present case).

LeBlanc v. Broyhill, 123 F.R.D. 527, 530–31 (W.D.N.C. 1988) (federal fraud action) (requiring defendants to disclose discovery materials generated in connection with related state action).

Deford v. Schmid Prods. Co., 120 F.R.D. 648, 655 (D. Md. 1987) (holding that documents produced in other case were discoverable unless "specifically barr[ed]" by confidentiality order).

Carter-Wallace, Inc. v. Hartz Mountain Indus., 92 F.R.D. 67, 69 (S.D.N.Y. 1981) (holding that documents produced in other case were discoverable although previously subject to a confidentiality order).

See also

In re Upjohn Co. Antibiotic Cleocin Prods. Liab. Litig., 664 F.2d 114 (6th Cir. 1981).

Olympic Ref. Co. v. Carter, 332 F.2d 260, 266 (9th Cir.), *cert. denied*, 379 U.S. 900 (1964).

Contra

Grundberg v. Upjohn Co., 140 F.R.D. 459 (D. Utah 1991) (products case; drug Halcion) (holding that nonparties to dismissed action against manufacturer could not obtain, from court in which dismissed suit had been pending, documents that had been submitted under seal or covered by protective order; strong public policy encouraging settlements would be largely defeated by permitting access to discovery documents by nonparties. The court could not enter affirmative discovery orders forcing dissemination of sealed discovery documents when both parties in closed and dismissed case opposed dissemination.).

§ 35 TRANSCRIPTS OF TESTIMONY IN OTHER CASES

Commentary

In view of the fact that testimony of witnesses taken in another proceeding may indeed be admissible in evidence under certain conditions, (*see* Fed. R. Evid. 801(d)(2)(D), 804(a), 804(b)(1) and FED. R. CIV. P. 32(a)(4)), the majority of courts has allowed discovery of such transcripts.

Rules

FED. R. CIV. P. 32(a).

FED. R. EVID. 613, 801(d)(2)(D), 803, 804(b)(1).

Secondary Sources

Addison, *Authenticating Evidence Obtained from Other Cases*, 55 TEX. B.J. 509 (1992).

AMERICAN LAW OF PRODUCTS LIABILITY 3D, *supra* § 1, § 53:18.

CLEARY, MCCORMICK ON EVIDENCE ch. 25 (3d ed. 1984 & Supp. 1987).

4 WEINSTEIN & BERGER, WEINSTEIN'S EVIDENCE § 804(b)(1)[01–07] (1992 & Supp. 1993).

8 WRIGHT & MILLER, *supra* § 1, § 2150.

Case Law

Roberts v. Jeep Eagle Corp., CA No. 1:89-cv-238-HTW (N.D. Ga. Jan. 4, 1993) (products case; liftgate) (court compelled defendant to produce (1) reports of similar incidents occurring both before and after subject claim (at 3–4); (2) requested photographs, overruling defendant's work product and attorney-client objections on grounds that photographs do not disclose mental impressions (at 4); (3) documents and testimony produced in other cases (at 2–3, 11); (4) tests concerning similar models (at 11); (5) information concerning profits defendants realized per vehicle during certain years pertinent to the litigation (at 12); (6) information concerning defendant's consideration of an alternative design (at 7, 12–13); and (7) information concerning defendant's consideration of a subsequent remedial measure (at 7, 12–13); court allowed plaintiff to depose defendant's vice-president for the reason that he participated in a decision to suppress an internal memorandum concerning the defective condition of the subject liftgate (at 6–7).).

Malautea v. Suzuki Motor Corp., CA No. CV 490-322 (S.D. Ga. Dec. 31, 1991) (court sanction order on appeal to the 11th Cir.) (products case; Samurai rollover) (ordering defendants to produce transcripts of depositions of engineers taken in other cases although appealed under protective order in other case), *aff'd*, 987 F.2d 1536 (11th Cir.), *cert. denied*, 114 S. Ct. 181 (1993).

Valego v. Ortho Pharmaceutical Corp., Prod. Liab. Rep. (CCH) ¶10,348 (D. Mass. 1984) (refusing to require defendant to produce copies of all depositions that had been taken in a similar suit brought against the defendant).

Carter-Wallace, Inc. v. Hartz Mountain Indus., 92 F.R.D. 67, 70 (S.D.N.Y. 1981) (antitrust suit) (holding that plaintiffs were entitled to order compelling defendants to produce transcripts of all depositions in recently settled litigation against them).

Roesberg v. Johns-Manville Corp., 85 F.R.D. 292, 302 (E.D. Pa. 1980) (products case; asbestos) (finding that "testimony from other lawsuits instigated against [defendant] . . . to recover for injuries resulting from use of asbestos . . . could hardly be more relevant").

Richmond v. American Honda Motor Co., 571 So. 2d 491 (Fla. Dist. Ct. App. 1990) (products case) (requiring plaintiff to answer interrogatory requesting her to admit substantive testimony that her expert witness had given in previous case).

Ielovich v. Taylor Mach. Works, Inc., 513 N.Y.S.2d 175, 176 (App. Div. 1987) (products case; top loader) (holding that transcripts of proceedings concerning claims similar in nature to the accident in question were discoverable).

Carson v. Armstrong World Indus., CA No. 86-L-823 (Madison County, Ill. Cir. Ct. July 2, 1990) (products case; asbestos) (imposing severe sanctions in part for defendant's failure to produce depositions taken in another asbestos case, the production of which the court had earlier ordered).

See also

Dykes v. Raymark Indus., 801 F.2d 810 (6th Cir. 1986), *cert. denied*, 481 U.S. 1038 (1987).

Mainland Indus. v. Standal's Patents Ltd., 799 F.2d 746 (Fed. Cir. 1986).

Hendrix v. Raybestos-Manhattan, Inc., 776 F.2d 1492 (11th Cir. 1985).

Dartez v. Fibreboard Corp., 765 F.2d 456 (5th Cir. 1985).

DeLuryea v. Winthrop Lab., 697 F.2d 222 (8th Cir. 1983).

Murray v. Toyota Motor Distrib., Inc., 664 F.2d 1377 (9th Cir.), *cert. denied*, 457 U.S. 1106 (1982).

Allen v. G.D. Searle & Co., 122 F.R.D. 580 (D. Or. 1988).

Deford v. Schmid Prods. Co., 120 F.R.D. 648, 655 (D. Md. 1987).

§ 36 OTHER SIMILAR INCIDENTS (INCLUDING ADVERSE-REACTION REPORTS)

(See also §§ 17, 18, 22.3, 22.4, 25–27, 41, 48.3)

Commentary

Other similar incidents may involve an array of factual situations in which the defect in question has manifested itself on some other occasion. The other incidents may refer to any one of the following categories: (1) the appearance of early signs of incipient failure, (2) complaints by other users, (3) existence of other lawsuits, (4) the occurrence of other individual incidents, or (5) studies of a common failure mode based on a number of other individual incidents.

As indicated by the rather large number of cases cited below, the courts generally permit the discovery of information concerning the occurrence of other similar incidents. These incidents may be admissible at trial for any of the following reasons: (1) to show the existence or relative danger of a defect, (2) to show the defect caused the incident in question, (3) to show the defendant had "notice" of the dangerous condition, and (4) tie in connection with certain collateral issues such as qualifications of expert witnesses or for purposes of impeachment. Hare & Shelly, *The Admissibility of Other Similar Incident Evidence: A Three-Step Approach*, 15 AM. J. TRIAL ADVOC. 541 (1992).

Most courts do not limit discovery to incidents involving the identical product but permit discovery so long as the same or reasonably similar "defect" is involved. Thus, in determining when information is relevant to the existence of a defect, the court should not adopt a legal standard of relevance that is more restrictive than the standard applied by practitioners experienced in the field. *See Jackson v. Firestone Tire & Rubber Co.*, 788 F.2d 1070 (5th Cir. 1986); *Lohr v. Stanley-Bostitch, Inc.*, 135 F.R.D. 162 (W.D. Mich. 1991); *Fireman's Fund Ins. Co. v. ECM Motor Co.*, 132 F.R.D. 39 (W.D. Pa. 1990); *Kozlowski v. Sears, Roebuck & Co.*, 73 F.R.D. 73 (D. Mass. 1976); *Trevizo v. Astec Indus.*, 751 P.2d 980 (Ariz. Ct. App. 1987); *Gowler v. Ferrell-Ross Co.*, 563 N.E.2d. 773 (Ill. App. Ct. 1990), *appeal dismissed per curiam*, 571 N.E.2d 148 (Ill. 1991); *Hindelang v. R.D. Werner Co.*, 469 N.W.2d 2 (Mich. Ct. App. 1991); *Johantgen v. Hobart Mfg. Co.*, 407 N.Y.S.2d 355 (App. Div. 1978). *See generally* AMERICAN LAW OF PRODUCTS LIABILITY 3D, *supra* §1, §§ 53:41–53:43; HAYDOCK & HERR, *supra* § 3, § 1.4, 19–20; KIELY, *supra* § 11, §§ 5.25.6, 7.3.

Secondary Sources

AMERICAN LAW OF PRODUCTS LIABILITY 3D, *supra* § 1, §§ 53:41–53:44.

2A FRUMER & FRIEDMAN, PRODUCTS LIABILITY § 17.02[1] (rev. ed. 1992).

Hare & Shelly, *The Admissibility of Other Similar Incident Evidence: A Three-Step Approach*, 15 AM. J. TRIAL ADVOC. 541 (1992).

Woerner, Annotation, *Pre-trial Discovery to Secure Opposing Party's Private Reports or Records as to Previous Accidents or Incidents Involving the Same Place or Premises*, 74 A.L.R. 2D 876 (1960).

8 WRIGHT & MILLER, *supra* § 1, § 2009, at 75 n.49 & 79 n.50.

Case Law

Melton v. Deere & Co., 887 F.2d 1241, 1245 (5th Cir. 1989) (products case; combine's vertical unloader) (finding that evidence concerning accidents post-dating the present incident may shed important light on the issue of the product's risk or danger).

Weeks v. Remington Arms Co., 733 F.2d 1485, 1491–92 (11th Cir. 1984) (products case; shotgun) (holding that it was an abuse of discretion to refuse to grant the plaintiff's request to produce files concerning other accidents occurring when the defendant's shotgun fired with the safety on; refusal to grant plaintiff's access to the defendant's record denied the plaintiff an opportunity to establish that the other accidents were substantially similar to the case at bar).

Josephs v. Harris Corp., 677 F.2d 985, 991 (3d Cir. 1982) (products case; printing press) (holding that information was discoverable regarding prior accidents involving printing press that injured plaintiff and similar presses of manufacturer; trial court reversed for refusing to allow plaintiff's discovery).

Roberts v. Jeep Eagle Corp., CA No. 1:89-cv-238-HTW (N.D. Ga. Jan. 4, 1993) (products case; liftgate) (court compelled defendant to produce (1) reports of similar incidents occurring both before and after subject claim (at 3–4); (2) requested photographs, overruling defendant's work product and attorney-client objections on grounds that photographs do not disclose mental impressions (at 4); (3) documents and testimony produced in other cases (at 2–3, 11); (4) tests concerning similar models (at 11); (5) information concerning profits defendants realized per vehicle during certain years pertinent to the litigation (at 12); (6) information concerning defendant's consideration of an alternative design (at 7, 12–13); and (7) information concerning defendant's consideration of a subsequent remedial measure (at 7, 12–13); court allowed plaintiff to depose defendant's vice-president for the reason that he participated in a decision to suppress an internal memorandum concerning the defective condition of the subject liftgate (at 6–7).).

Simmons v. American Honda Motor Co., CA No. 1:91-cv-0079-RCF (N.D. Ga. production order Dec. 17, 1991; sanction order June 1, 1992) (products case; sidestand on motorcycle) (ordering manufacturer to produce (1) customer complaints, (2) reports of other similar incidents, and (3) contents of the NHTSA defect investigation file; the district court sanctioned Honda for its repeated disregard of discovery rules and court's order).

Rodgers v. General Motors Corp., CA No. CIV 1-90-89 (E.D. Tenn. Nov. 21, 1991) (products case; rear seat shoulder harness and noncollapsible steering wheel) (requiring production of relevant tests and studies and other complaints involving the same defect irrespective of the make, model, or year of the vehicle involved).

Baine v. General Motors Corp., 141 F.R.D. 328 (M.D. Ala. 1991) (products case; defective seat-belt locking mechanism) (defendant attempted to limit scope of discovery to the same year model and model type vehicle. Noting that the parameters of discovery should not be limited by the subjective and adversarial view of the manufacturer, the court found that many other model vehicles involved the same "defect" and compelled the defendant to produce documents concerning other models possessing the same locking mechanism. In response to GM's contention that physical location and delivery of the subject documents would be extremely burdensome, the court ordered that the plaintiff be allowed to inspect the records at the defendant's facility.).

Hotchkiss v. Sears, Roebuck & Co., 139 F.R.D. 313, 315–16, 317–18 (M.D. Pa. 1991) (products case; radial arm saw) (defendant compelled to produce (1) records pertaining to research and development of a potential guard for the saw, (2) market studies concerning saws and who used them, (3) three reports reflecting the pattern of injuries associated with the use of radial arm saws, (4) documents regarding hazards associated with the use of the subject guard on radial arm saws including follow-up interviews of purchasers of saws with the guard, (5) reports of testing performed by manufacturer on alternate guards, and (6) records of attempts to develop other types of guards for saw blade. The court found that conditions imposed by confidentiality order would adequately protect defendant's trade secret concerns.).

Durham v. Hoffman-LaRoche, Inc., CA No. CV 89-L-0075-S (N.D. Ala. order on motion to reconsider, Nov. 8, 1989) (products case; drug Accutane) (requiring manufacturer to produce adverse drug reaction reports that included names of reporting physicians).

Smith v. Bic Corp., 121 F.R.D. 235, 242, 243–44 (E.D. Pa. 1988) (products case; disposable lighter) (holding that the defendant failed to show good cause why information pertaining to other complaints and accidents should not be disclosed), *aff'd in part, rev'd in part*, 869 F.2d 194 (3d Cir. 1989).

Clark v. General Motors Corp., 20 Fed. R. Serv. 2d (Callaghan) 679, 685–86 (D. Mass. 1975) (products case; stove) (holding that prior and subsequent complaints were relevant within the meaning of rule 26(b)(1)).

Eli Lilly & Co. v. Marshall, 829 S.W.2d 157 (Tex. 1992) (products case; drug Prozac) (after trial court ordered defendant to produce FDA documents reflecting defendant's evaluation of drug's safety and effectiveness including clinical studies, chemical analysis, adverse reaction reports, and proposed labels; Texas Supreme Court granted mandamus and ordered trial court to hold hearing and rule on the merits of defendant's motion for a protective order under Texas rule 76a.).

Chicago Cutlery Co. v. District Court, 568 P.2d 464, 466 (Colo. 1977) (en banc) (products case; knife) (allowing plaintiff limited discovery of defendant's customer lists in order to show similar injuries to other persons was cause of incident rather than personal susceptibility of plaintiff).

Farnum v. Bristol-Myers Co., 219 A.2d 277, 279 (N.H. 1966) (products case; deodorant) (holding that discovery should not be limited to complaints made before date of plaintiff's purchase).

Cooper v. American Honda Motor Co., CA No. 473513 (San Diego County, Cal. Super. Ct. Referee Report No. 1, Apr. 18, 1986) (products case; ATV) (ordering Honda to produce entire claims files involving ATV accidents on pavement so as to permit plaintiff to determine whether other accidents exist than those already specified by number to the defendants; the court specifically provided that the coverage period should "include all such accidents to date and not merely up to the date of the accident involved in this case").

See also

Averbach v. Rival Mfg. Co., 879 F.2d 1196 (3d Cir. 1989), *cert. denied*, 493 U.S. 1023 (1990).

Cook v. Kartridg Pak Co., 840 F.2d 602 (8th Cir. 1988).

Rexrode v. American Laundry Press Co., 674 F.2d 826 (10th Cir.), *cert. denied*, 459 U.S. 862 (1982).

Dollar v. Long Mfg., N.C., Inc., 561 F.2d 613, 617–18 (5th Cir. 1977) (wrongful death action) (holding that trial court abused discretion in denying plaintiff's request for information concerning subsequent accidents; appellate court further noted that defendant's failure to mention two subsequent accidents was evasive), *cert. denied*, 435 U.S. 996 (1978).

Bradley v. Melroe Co., 141 F.R.D. 1 (D.D.C. 1992) (products case; skid loader) (plaintiff sought production of in-house investigative files for seven incidents involving same interlock device alleged to be defective in present case; court ordered production of factual data contained in each file and permitted defendant to redact all mental impressions, opinions, evaluations, recommendations, and theories).

Lohr v Stanley-Bostitch, Inc., 135 F.R.D. 162 (W.D. Mich. 1991).

Fine v. Facet Aerospace Prods. Co., 133 F.R.D. 439, 444 (S.D.N.Y. 1990) (holding that summary of prior claims prepared by in-house counsel was not privileged because "[n]o legal acumen was required" to prepare it).

Kramer v. Boeing Co., 126 F.R.D. 690, 695 (D. Minn. 1989) (products case; airplane) (holding that other similar accidents were discoverable).

Fann v. Giant Food, Inc., 115 F.R.D. 593, 595 (D.D.C. 1987).

Harris v. Upjohn Co., 115 F.R.D. 191 (S.D. Ill. 1987).

Carlucci v. Piper Aircraft Corp., 102 F.R.D. 472 (S.D. Fla. 1984).

Morrison v. Syntex Lab., Inc., 101 F.R.D. 747 (D.D.C. 1984).

Dean v. A.H. Robins Co., 101 F.R.D. 21 (D. Minn. 1984).

Roesberg v. Johns-Manville Corp., 85 F.R.D. 292 (E.D. Pa. 1980).

Bates v. Firestone Tire & Rubber Co., 83 F.R.D. 535 (D.S.C. 1979).

Kozlowski v. Sears, Roebuck & Co., 73 F.R.D. 73, 75 (D. Mass. 1976) (products case; pajamas) (holding that information concerning accidents similar to the one alleged in complaint was "clearly relevant" and a proper subject for pretrial discovery).

Kelleher v. Omark Indus., 20 Fed. R. Serv. 2d (Callaghan) 199, 201 (D. Mass. 1975) (products case; stud gun) (holding that prior and subsequent accidents involving the same or similar products were discoverable).

Uitts v. General Motors Corp., 58 F.R.D. 450, 452 (E.D. Pa. 1972) (products case; automobile) (holding that if prior similar accidents with identical equipment were relevant to causation, subsequent accidents are also relevant and were discoverable).

Hess v. Pittsburgh Steel Foundry & Mach. Co., 49 F.R.D. 271 (W.D. Pa. 1970) (products case; grinding wheel) (permitting plaintiff to discover intercompany correspondence among four competing companies relating to all complaints and recommendations to correct conditions when grinding wheels were used).

Hammill v. Hyster Co., 42 F.R.D. 173 (E.D. Wis. 1967) (products case; crane tip-over) (permitting discovery as to other tipping incidents involving any model of crane manufactured by the defendant, but limited to incidents occurring on or before the date of incident involved in present case).

Bowen v. Whitehall Lab., Inc., 41 F.R.D. 359 (S.D.N.Y. 1966).

Newsom v. Breon Lab., Inc., 709 S.W.2d 559 (Tenn. 1986) (allowing plaintiff to discover names of physicians who submitted drug reaction or drug experience reports to manufacturer under a protective order that forbade the disclosure in the absence of written permission).

Cloroben Chem. Corp. v. Comegys, 464 A.2d 887 (Del. 1983) (products case; drain cleaner) (finding that defendant willfully failed to produce claims file regarding similar incidents; this evidence in part supported award of punitive damages).

Kuiper v. District Court, 632 P.2d 694 (Mont. 1981).

Hindelang v. R.D. Werner Co., 469 N.W.2d 2 (Mich. Ct. App. 1991) (permitting discovery of information concerning other year and model types possessing the same defect as the subject product).

Kramer v. J.I. Case Mfg. Co., 815 P.2d 798 (Wash. Ct. App. 1991).

Mendelowitz v. Xerox Corp., 573 N.Y.S.2d 548, 552 (App. Div. 1991) (products case; asbestos) (permitting discovery of similar incidents involving not only identical product, but other models involving the same defect).

Rogers v. Johnson & Johnson Prods., Inc., 585 A.2d 1004 (Pa. Super. Ct. 1990) (holding that plaintiff was entitled to discover information regarding other incidents even though products were not from same product batch and circumstances surrounding other incidents were not revealed).

Brown v. Daisy Mfg. Co., 514 N.Y.S.2d 300, 301 (App. Div. 1987) (products case; gun) (holding that information about similar subsequent accidents was discoverable).

Lemmo v. State, 232 Cal. Rptr. 420, 424 (Ct. App. 1986) (wrongful death action) (permitting plaintiffs to discover State Department of Transportation Traffic Accident Surveillance Analysis System printouts and accident reports for time and location requested). [Note: this opinion was subsequently withdrawn.]

Earl v. Gulf & W. Mfg. Co., 366 N.W.2d 160, 163 (Wis. Ct. App. 1985) (products case; industrial press) (holding that prior similar accidents were discoverable).

Berry v. Coleman Sys. Co., 596 P.2d 1365 (Wash. Ct. App.) (products case; grinding stone) (holding that failure to disclose prior similar accidents and/or complaints as requested by interrogatories constituted grounds for new trial), *review denied*, 92 Wash. 2d 1026 (1979).

Johantgen v. Hobart Mfg. Co., 407 N.Y.S.2d 355, 356 (App. Div. 1978) (products case; meat grinder) (holding that plaintiff was entitled to disclosure of information regarding claims similar in nature whether prior or subsequent to plaintiff's claim; further, the cases did not require identical products or instruments, rather, they required that other accidents involve same defect or same or similar design).

Carnibucci v. Marlin Firearms Co., 380 N.Y.S.2d 807, 808 (App. Div. 1976) (products case; .22-caliber rifle) (holding that subsequent similar claims were discoverable).

Abrams v. Vaughan & Bushnell Mfg. Co., 325 N.Y.S.2d 976, 979 (App. Div. 1971) (products case; hammer) (holding that plaintiff was entitled to disclosure of information regarding claims similar in nature whether made prior or subsequent to plaintiff's purchase of the hammer).

Carr v. Marty Patino, Domino's Pizza, Inc., CA No CV89-5577 (Wahoe County, Nev. Dist. Ct. Jan. 17, 1991).

Brandimarti v. Caterpillar, Inc., CA No. G.D. 83-12468 (Allegheny County, Pa. Ct. C.P. Oct. 11, 1985) (products case) (allowing plaintiff discovery of other similar incidents).

Blackner v. Clark Equip. Co., CA No. 2860 (Philadelphia, Pa. Ct. C.P. Nov. 7, 1983) (products case; forklift rollover) (compelling defendant to produce accident reports of other similar incidents involving same and similar products).

Van Langen v. Chadwick, 414 A.2d 618 (N.J. Super. Ct. Law Div. 1980) (allowing plaintiff's request for admissions concerning facts about prior accidents at same location).

§ 37 OTHER COMPLAINTS AND/OR LAWSUITS

(See also §§ 17, 18, 22.3, 22.4, 25, 26, 36, 41, 48.3)

Commentary

Other complaints and/or other lawsuits may involve an array of factual situations in which the defect in question has manifested itself on some other occasion. The complaint and/or lawsuit may refer to any one of the following categories: (1) the appearance of early signs of incipient failure, (2) complaints by other users, (3) existence of other lawsuits, (4) the occurrence of other individual incidents, or (5) studies of a common failure mode based on a number of other individual incidents.

As indicated by the rather large number of cases cited below, the courts generally permit the discovery of information concerning the occurrence of other similar incidents. These incidents may be admissible at trial for any of the following reasons: (1) to show the existence or relative danger of a defect, (2) to show the defect caused the incident in question, (3) to show the defendant had "notice" of the dangerous condition, and (4) in connection with certain collateral issues such as qualifications of expert witnesses or for purposes of impeachment. Hare & Shelly, *The Admissibility of Other Similar Incident Evidence: A Three-Step Approach*, 15 AM. J. TRIAL ADVOC. 541 (1992).

Most courts do not limit discovery to incidents involving the identical product, but permit discovery so long as the same or reasonably similar "defect" is involved. Thus, in determining when information is relevant to the existence of a defect, the court should not adopt a legal standard of relevance that is more restrictive than the standard applied by practitioners experienced in the field. *See Jackson v. Firestone Tire & Rubber Co.*, 788 F.2d 1070 (5th Cir. 1986); *Lohr v. Stanley-Bostitch, Inc.*, 135 F.R.D. 162 (W.D. Mich. 1991); *Fireman's Fund Ins. Co. v. ECM Motor Co.*, 132 F.R.D. 39 (W.D. Pa. 1990); *Kozlowski v. Sears, Roebuck & Co.*, 73 F.R.D. 73 (D. Mass. 1976); *Trevizo v. Astec Indus.*, 751 P.2d 980 (Ariz. Ct. App. 1987); *Gowler v. Ferrell-Ross Co.*, 563 N.E.2d 773 (Ill. App. Ct. 1990), *appeal dismissed per curiam*, 571 N.E.2d 148 (Ill. 1991); *Hindelang v. R.D. Werner Co.*, 469 N.W.2d 2 (Mich. Ct. App. 1991); *Johantgen v. Hobart Mfg. Co.*, 407 N.Y.S.2d 355 (App. Div. 1978). *See generally* AMERICAN LAW OF PRODUCTS LIABILITY 3D, *supra* § 1, §§ 53:41–53:43; HAYDOCK & HERR, *supra* § 3, § 1.4, 19–20; KIELY, *supra* § 11, §§ 5.25.6, 7.3.

Secondary Sources

AMERICAN LAW OF PRODUCTS LIABILITY 3D, *supra* § 1, §§ 53:41–53:44.

2A FRUMER & FRIEDMAN, *supra* § 36, § 7.02[1].

8 WRIGHT & MILLER, *supra* § 1, § 2009, at 75 n.49 & 79 n.50.

Case Law

Averbach v. Rival Mfg. Co., 879 F.2d 1196 (3d Cir. 1989) (products case; can opener) (when plaintiff asked defendant to list similar complaints received within five years, defendant filed a misleading response limiting answer to the particular model of can opener that plaintiff had owned), *cert. denied*, 493 U.S. 1023 (1990).

Weeks v. Remington Arms Co., 733 F.2d 1485 (11th Cir. 1984) (products case; shotgun) (holding that it was an abuse of discretion to refuse to grant the plaintiff's request to produce files concerning other accidents occurring when the defendant's shotgun fired with the safety on; refusal to grant plaintiff's access to the defendant's record denied the plaintiff an opportunity to establish that the other accidents were substantially similar to the case at bar).

Josephs v. Harris Corp., 677 F.2d 985, 991 (3d Cir. 1982) (products case; printing press) (reversing district court for refusing to permit plaintiff to discover identity of other persons injured by defendant's product).

Rodgers v. General Motors Corp., CA No. CIV 1-90-89 (E.D. Tenn. Nov. 21, 1991) (products case; rear seat shoulder harness and noncollapsible steering wheel) (requiring production of relevant tests and studies and other complaints involving the same defect irrespective of the make, model, or year of the vehicle involved).

Fine v. Facet Aerospace Prods. Co., 133 F.R.D. 439, 444 (S.D.N.Y. 1990) (holding that summary of prior claims prepared by in-house counsel was not privileged because no legal acumen was required to prepare it).

In re Air Crash Disaster at Detroit Metro. Airport, 130 F.R.D. 641–43 (E.D. Mich. 1989) (products case; commercial airplane) (airline sought production from co-defendant of in-house investigative study conducted by manufacturer in response to a complaint by another customer; the court rejected manufacturer's contention and compelled production of all materials dealing with the requested study prior to the date of the crash in question. However, the court exempted the post-accident portions of the study as work product on grounds of the manufacturer's affidavit that this portion of the study was conducted in anticipation of litigation.).

Smith v. Bic Corp., 121 F.R.D. 235, 242, 243–44 (E.D. Pa. 1988) (products case; disposable lighter) (holding that the defendant failed to show good cause why information pertaining to other complaints and accidents should not be disclosed), *aff'd in part, rev'd in part*, 869 F.2d 194 (3d Cir. 1989).

Tytel v. Richardson-Merrell, Inc., 9 Fed. R. Serv. 2d (Callaghan) 33.321-1 (S.D.N.Y. 1965) (products case; drug MER/29) (overruling defendant's objection to interrogatory requesting specific information as to other claims involving MER/29).

See also

Ericson v. Ford Motor Co., 107 F.R.D. 92 (E.D. Ark. 1985).

Roesberg v. Johns-Manville Corp., 85 F.R.D. 292, 301 (E.D. Pa. 1980) (products case; asbestos) (holding that information from other actions instituted against defendant bore directly on issues of notice and causation).

Cohen v. Procter & Gamble Distrib. Co., 18 F.R.D. 301, 302 (D. Del. 1955) (products case; detergent) (holding that names and addresses of others to whom defendant had made payments because of injuries resulting from use of product were discoverable).

Boudreaux v. Ford Motor Co., 533 So. 2d 1213, 1219 (La. 1988) (redhibition action) (holding that consumer audit records and statistical summaries were not confidential under Louisiana law).

Cloroben Chem. Corp. v. Comegys, 464 A.2d 887 (Del. 1983) (products case; drain cleaner) (finding that the defendant willfully failed to produce claims files regarding similar incidents; this evidence in part supported award of punitive damages).

Chicago Cutlery Co. v. District Court, 568 P.2d 464 (Colo. 1977) (products case; knife) (allowing plaintiff limited discovery of defendant's customer lists in order to show similar injuries to other persons; proof to show that product was cause of incident rather than personal susceptibility of plaintiff).

Farnum v. Bristol-Myers Co., 219 A.2d 277, 279 (N.H. 1966) (products case; deodorant) (holding that discovery should not be limited to complaints made before date of plaintiff's purchase).

State ex rel. Martel v. Gallagher, 797 S.W.2d 730 (Mo. Ct. App. 1990) (tenant suit against landlord for fall on common steps) (holding that plaintiff should have been allowed to discover whether there had been complaints about any steps in apartment within past five years; trial court should not have limited discovery only to complaints concerning subject steps within limited period of two years).

City of Azusa v. Superior Court, 236 Cal. Rptr. 621, 623 (Ct. App. 1987) (civil rights action) (holding that plaintiffs were entitled to names and addresses only of others who complained that police officers had used excessive force).

Berry v. Coleman Sys. Co., 596 P.2d 1365 (Wash. Ct. App.) (products case; grinding stone) (ordering a new trial where defendant answered "no" to interrogatory concerning prior complaints and legal actions; "investigation revealed that [defendant] had received 31 complaints of similar injuries or occurrences and was a party to 13 legal actions involving similar products"), *review denied*, 92 Wash. 2d 1026 (1979).

Peluso v. Rochester Gen. Hosp., 409 N.Y.S.2d 292, 294 (App. Div. 1978) (products case; dialysis machine) (holding that the plaintiff was entitled to disclosure of information as to claims similar in nature to his own).

Abrams v. Vaughan & Bushnell Mfg. Co., 325 N.Y.S.2d 976 (App. Div. 1971) (products case; hammer) (holding that the plaintiff was entitled to disclosure of information regarding claims similar in nature to plaintiff's, whether made prior or subsequent to plaintiff's purchase of the hammer).

Ribley v. Harsco Corp., 377 N.Y.S.2d 375, 376–77 (Sup. Ct. 1975) (products case; manure spreader) (holding that information concerning other claims—before or after subject claim—involving the same or similar drive-shaft were discoverable), *aff'd*, 394 N.Y.S.2d 740 (App. Div. 1977).

Bleacher v. Bristol-Myers Co., 163 A.2d 526, 528 (Del. Super. Ct. 1960) (products case; deodorant) (holding that other complaints and defendant's investigative reports made thereon were discoverable).

§ 38 TESTS/STUDIES

§ 38.1 GENERALLY

(See also §§ 17, 18, 22.5, 23, 39, 40, 48)

Commentary

A test or study on any subject matter relevant to the controversy is ordinarily discoverable.

Secondary Sources

AMERICAN LAW OF PRODUCTS LIABILITY 3D, *supra* § 1, §§ 53:35–53:39.

KIELY, *supra* § 11, §§ 1.17, 1.19, ch. 3.

Soehnel, Annotation, *Products Liability: Personal Injury or Death Allegedly Caused by Defect in Aircraft or Its Parts, Supplies, or Equipment*, 97 A.L.R. 3D 627 (1980).

Case Law

Anderson v. Cryovac, Inc., 862 F.2d 910 (1st Cir. 1988) (holding that a report prepared by independent testing company and filed with the EPA was discoverable), *on remand, Anderson v. Beatrice Foods Co.*, 127 F.R.D. 1 (D. Mass. 1989).

Simmons v. American Honda Motor Co., CA No. 1:91-cv-0079-RCF (N.D. Ga. production order Dec. 17, 1991; sanction order June 1, 1992) (products case; sidestand on motorcycle) (court ordered manufacturer to produce (1) tests and studies of subject and other model motorcycles; (2) blueprints, diagrams, drawings, photographs, etc. of subject and other model motorcycles; and (3) contents of the NHTSA defect investigation file. The district court sanctioned Honda for its repeated disregard of discovery rules and court's order.).

Snowden v. Connaught Lab., Inc., 137 F.R.D. 336, 345–46 (D. Kan.) (products case; vaccine) (holding that pre- and post-sale research was discoverable to determine if manufacturer could have made safer product), *aff'd*, 136 F.R.D. 694 (D. Kan. 1991).

Fine v. Facet Aerospace Prods. Co., 133 F.R.D. 439, 444 (S.D.N.Y. 1990) (products case; aircraft) (holding that the defendant manufacturer's internal report addressing problem of water in fuel systems of its aircraft, testing done, and possible solutions was subject to discovery; court overruled defendant's objection based on attorney-client privilege; report was drafted by manufacturer's engineering department for purpose of risk management).

Sellon v. Smith, 112 F.R.D. 9, 14 (D. Del. 1986) (products case; automobile) (holding that rear-impact tests for any model incorporating similar fuel storage system were discoverable).

Baker v. Procter & Gamble Co., 17 Fed. R. Serv. (Callaghan) 460, 461 (S.D.N.Y. 1952) (products case) (holding that information about product tests made by the defendant was "clearly relevant to the issue of the exercise of due care in the manufacture and preparation of the product").

Eli Lilly & Co. v. Marshall, 829 S.W.2d 157 (Tex. 1992) (products case; drug Prozac) (trial court ordered defendant to produce FDA documents reflecting defendant's evaluation of drug's safety and effectiveness including clinical studies, chemical analysis, adverse reaction reports, and proposed labels. Texas Supreme Court granted mandamus and ordered trial court to hold hearing and rule on the merits of defendant's motion for a protective order under Texas rule 76a.).

Dunshie v. General Motors Corp., CA No. A-136,024 (Jefferson County, Tex. Dist. Ct.) (products case; window shade, seat-belt) (allowing plaintiff discovery of defendant's tests and studies), *appeal dismissed*, 822 S.W.2d 345 (Tex. Ct. App. 1992).

Fibron Prods., Inc. v. Hooker Chem. Corp., 206 N.Y.S.2d 659 (Sup. Ct. 1960) (products liability; liquid resin) (allowing discovery of defendant's tests and studies).

See also

Perry v. Jeep Eagle Corp., 126 F.R.D. 542 (S.D. Ind. 1989).

Kramer v. Boeing Co., 126 F.R.D. 690 (D. Minn. 1989).

Culligan v. Yamaha Motor Corp., 110 F.R.D. 122 (S.D.N.Y. 1986).

Parsons v. General Motors Corp., 85 F.R.D. 724, 726 (N.D. Ga. 1980).

Kelleher v. Omark Indus., 20 Fed. R. Serv. 2d (Callaghan) 199, 202 (D. Mass. 1975) (products case; stud gun) (holding that post-accident test results were discoverable).

Clark v. General Motors Corp., 20 Fed. R. Serv. 2d (Callaghan) 679, 683, 689 (D. Mass. 1975) (allowing discovery of test conducted after witness's deposition).

Bowman v. General Motors Corp., 64 F.R.D. 62, 66–68 (E.D. Pa. 1974) (products case; automobile) (holding that crash test information was discoverable for model years from date of manufacture to date of accident).

Hess v. Pittsburgh Steel Foundry & Mach. Co., 49 F.R.D. 271 (W.D. Pa. 1970) (products case; grinding wheel) (holding that the plaintiff was entitled to discover intercompany correspondence among four competing companies relating to all complaints and recommendations to correct conditions where grinding wheels were used).

Green v. Shepherd Constr. Co., CA No. 11740 (N.D. Ga. Oct. 21, 1969) (products case; spring shackle) (ordering Ford to produce tests and studies concerning the safety of the subject product).

Glick v. McKesson & Robbins, Inc., 10 F.R.D. 477, 480 (W.D. Mo. 1950) (products case; suntan lotion) (holding that discovery of test regarding injurious effects to human skin was not burdensome). *See also Baker v. Procter & Gamble*, 17 Fed. R. Serv. (Callaghan) 460, 461 (S.D.N.Y. 1952).

Hindelang v. R.D. Werner Co., 469 N.W.2d 2 (Mich. Ct. App. 1991).

Lopez v. Foremost Paving, Inc., 796 S.W.2d 473 (Tex. Ct. App. 1990) (personal injury action) (finding that the defendant failed to produce videotape simulation of defendant's version of accident until ten days before trial; introduction in evidence at trial held reversible error).

Tompkins v. Log Sys., 385 S.E.2d 545 (N.C. Ct. App. 1989), *review denied*, 389 S.E.2d 819 (N.C. 1990).

Blackner v. Clark Equip. Co., CA No. 2860 (Philadelphia, Pa. Ct. C.P. Nov. 7, 1983) (products case; forklift rollover) (allowing discovery of defendant's tests and studies of subject product and alternative designs).

Abrams v. Vaughan & Bushnell Mfg. Co., 325 N.Y.S.2d 976, 979 (App. Div. 1971) (products case; hammer) (permitting discovery of chemical metallurgical test results.).

§ 38.2 OTHER YEAR OR MODEL TYPES

(See also §§ 38.3, 38.4)

Commentary

Information concerning studies and tests with respect to other models is generally discoverable so long as the same or reasonably similar defect is involved. Subject to this limitation, it should make no difference whether the test or study is conducted on an earlier or later model.

Secondary Sources

AMERICAN LAW OF PRODUCTS LIABILITY 3D, *supra* § 1, §§ 53:35–53.39.

KIELY, *supra* § 11, §§ 3.11–3.12.

Case Law

Dollar v. Long Mfg., N.C., Inc., 561 F.2d 613 (5th Cir. 1977), *cert. denied*, 435 U.S. 996 (1978).

Hartman v. Remington Arms Co., Inc., CA No. 90-4074-CV-C-5 (W.D. Mo. Apr. 13, 1992) (products case; rifle) (overruling manufacturer's contention that requested documents contain "trade secret" information, the court required defendant company to produce research and development on a New Bolt Action Rifle as potentially reflecting feasibility of alternative designs. The court's order included information contained in defendant company's Customer Sales Analysis touching on alternative designs. The court's order embraced post-injury research reflecting the priority level and cost consideration of alternative designs.), *modified*, Apr. 28, 1992, *further modified*, May 5, 1992. *See In re Remington Arms Co.*, 952 F.2d 1029 (8th Cir. 1991).

Baine v. General Motors Corp., 141 F.R.D. 328 (M.D. Ala. 1991) (products case; defective seat-belt locking mechanism) (defendant attempted to limit scope of discovery to the same year model and model type vehicle. Noting that the parameters of discovery should not be limited by the subjective and adversarial view of the manufacturer, the court found that many other model vehicles involved the same "defect" and compelled the defendant to produce documents concerning other models possessing the same defect. In response to GM's contention that physical location and delivery of the subject documents would be extremely burdensome, the court ordered that the plaintiff be allowed to inspect records at the defendant's facility and required the defendant to furnish plaintiff with an index of the subject records.).

Lohr v. Stanley-Bostitch, Inc., 135 F.R.D. 162, 164–65 (W.D. Mich. 1991) (permitting discovery of information concerning other year and model types possessing the same defect as the subject product).

Rodgers v. General Motors Corp., CA No. CIV 1-90-89 (E.D. Tenn. Nov. 21, 1991) (products case; rear seat shoulder harness and noncollapsible steering wheel) (requiring production of relevant tests and studies and other complaints involving the same defect, irrespective of the make, model, or year of the vehicle involved).

Simmons v. American Honda Motor Co., CA No. 1:91-cv-0079-RCF, N.D. Ga. production order Dec. 17, 1991; sanction order June 1, 1992) (products case; sidestand on motorcycle) (ordering manufacturer to produce tests and studies of subject and other model motorcycles; the district court sanctioned Honda for its repeated disregard of discovery rules and court's order).

Fireman's Fund Ins. Co. v. ECM Motor Co., 132 F.R.D. 39, 40–41 (W.D. Pa. 1990) (products case; electric motor) (holding that the plaintiff was entitled to discover Underwriters Laboratories' file concerning test done on different motor with appropriate protective order to assure confidentiality).

Kramer v. Boeing Co., 126 F.R.D. 690, 693 (D. Minn. 1989) (products case; airplane) (holding that discovery should be allowed to extend beyond the exact component part in dispute).

Perry v. Jeep Eagle Corp., 126 F.R.D. 542 (S.D. Ind. 1989).

In re Air Crash Disaster at Detroit Metro. Airport, 130 F.R.D. 641, 643 (E.D. Mich. 1989) (products case; commercial airplane) (airline sought production from co-defendant of in-house investigative study conducted by manufacturer in response to a complaint of another customer; the court rejected manufacturer's contention and compelled production of all materials dealing with the requested study prior to the date of the occurrence of the crash in question. However, the court exempted the post-accident portions of the study as work product on the grounds that the manufacturer's affidavit that this portion of the study was conducted in anticipation of litigation.).

Culligan v. Yamaha Motor Corp., 110 F.R.D. 122, 126 (S.D.N.Y. 1986) (products case; ATV) (holding that discovery of information concerning similar models was routinely permitted).

Swain v. General Motors Corp., 81 F.R.D. 698, 700 (W.D. Pa. 1979) (products case; motor mount) (holding that information concerning prior motor mounts was clearly relevant).

Clark v. General Motors Corp., 20 Fed. R. Serv. 2d (Callaghan) 679, 686 (D. Mass. 1975) (products case; stove) (holding that information concerning different models or similar products may be reasonably calculated to lead to admissible evidence).

Kelleher v. Omark Indus., 20 Fed. R. Serv. 2d (Callaghan) 199, 200 (D. Mass. 1975) (products case; stud gun) (holding that discovery of information about similar products was permissible).

Bowman v. General Motors Corp., 64 F.R.D. 62, 68 (E.D. Pa. 1974) (products case; automobile) (holding that the design detail and testing information relating to subsequent models of the same type of automobile were discoverable).

Uitts v. General Motors Corp., 58 F.R.D. 450, 452 (E.D. Pa. 1972) (products case; automobile) (holding that discovery should not be limited to model of truck involved in accident).

Hess v. Pittsburgh Steel Foundry & Mach. Co., 49 F.R.D. 271 (W.D. Pa. 1970) (products case; grinding wheel) (holding that plaintiff was entitled to discover intercompany correspondence among four competing companies relating to all complaints and recommendations to correct conditions where grinding wheels were used).

Hammill v. Hyster Co., 42 F.R.D. 173 (E.D. Wis. 1967) (products case; crane tip-over) (holding that discovery was permitted as to other tipping incidents regarding any model of crane manufactured by the defendant but limited to incidents occurring on or before the date of incident involved in the present case).

Remington Arms Co. v. Canales, 837 S.W.2d 624 (Tex. 1992) (class action regarding safety of Model 700 rifle).

Jampole v. Touchy, 673 S.W.2d 569, 573–74 (Tex. 1984) (products case; automobile) (holding that "automobiles need not be identical in order for tests on one to be relevant" to an action involving another).

General Motors Corp. v. Lawrence, 651 S.W.2d 732 (Tex. 1983) (products case; truck) (rejecting defendant's attempt to limit scope of discovery to its subjective and adversarial view of the particular facts of the incident and permitting discovery of information concerning other models over a 23-year time period).

Hindelang v. R.D. Werner Co., 469 N.W.2d 2 (Mich. Ct. App. 1991) (products case; extension ladder) (permitting discovery of information concerning other year and model types possessing the same defect as the subject product).

Mendelowitz v. Xerox Corp., 573 N.Y.S.2d 548, 552 (App. Div. 1991).

Tompkins v. Log Sys., Inc., 385 S.E.2d 545 (N.C. Ct. App. 1989), *review denied*, 389 S.E.2d 819 (N.C. 1990).

Felle v. Gillette Co., 524 N.Y.S.2d 927 (App. Div. 1988) (products case; butane lighter) (permitting discovery concerning earlier models of product).

Dunshie v. General Motors Corp., CA No. A-136,024 (Jefferson County, Tex. Dist. Ct.) (products case; window shade seat-belt) (allowing discovery of tests and studies involving other models possessing same defect), *appeal dismissed*, 822 S.W.2d 345 (Tex. Ct. App. 1992).

Garst v. General Motors Corp., CA No. 90-8857-NP (Wexford County, Mich. Cir. Ct. Sept. 21, 1992) (products case; rear seat, lap belt only) (Plaintiff requested (1) tests and studies reflecting the relative safety/danger to a rear seat occupant restrained by a lap belt only and/or lap/shoulder harness involved in a frontal and front angle collision and (2) reports of tests, studies and investigations, and minutes of committee meetings reflecting the basis of GM's decision to equip its vehicle with the rear seat shoulder harness. GM attempted to limit the scope of discovery to (1) its subjective and adversarial view of the facts of the particular accident, (2) the particular model year and type of vehicle involved, and (3) rear seat occupants of the same or substantially similar size as the plaintiff. The court granted plaintiff's motion to compel and ordered GM to produce the requested documents, holding that in view of the nature of the defect involved, the scope of relevant discovery extended to other year model and model types and alternate designs. The court rejected GM's attempt to limit the production of minutes of committee meetings to certain committees. The court ordered the production of post- as well as pre-accident documents, noting that GM had withdrawn its "time limitation objection." In response to GM's "burdensome objection" the court noted that plaintiff's counsel had expressed his willingness to go, together with his staff, to GM's facility and conduct a detailed examination of the subject documents once the material was brought together.).

§ 38.3 ALTERNATIVE DESIGNS

(See also §§ 38.2, 38.4)

Commentary

Information concerning alternative designs is ordinarily discoverable. Indeed, under some circumstances, the plaintiff may have the burden to produce evidence concerning the existence and/or feasibility of an alternative design.

Secondary Sources

AMERICAN LAW OF PRODUCTS LIABILITY 3D, *supra* § 1, §§ 53:35–53:39.

Annotation, *Burden of Proving Feasibility of Alternative Safe Design in Products Liability Action Based on Defective Design*, 78 A.L.R. 4TH 154 (1990).

KIELY, *supra* § 11, §§ 3.11, 3.12, 3.27.

Case Law

Rozier v. Ford Motor Co., 573 F.2d 1332, 1342 (5th Cir.) (products case; fuel system integrity) (granting plaintiff new trial following verdict for the defendant for Ford's failure to produce cost/benefits study of alternate design configuration), *reh'g denied*, 578 F.2d 871 (5th Cir. 1978). *See also Rock Island Bank & Trust Co. v. Ford Motor Co.*, 220 N.W.2d 799 (Mich. Ct. App. 1974).

Hartman v. Remington Arms Co., CA No. 90-4074-CV-C-5 (W.D. Mo. Apr. 13, 1992) (products case; rifle) (overruling manufacturer's contention that requested documents contain "trade secret" information, the court required defendant company to produce research and development on a New Bolt Action Rifle as potentially reflecting feasibility of alternative designs. The court's order included information contained in defendant company's Customer Sales Analysis touching on alternative designs. The court's order embraced post-injury research reflecting the priority level and cost consideration of alternative designs.), *modified* Apr. 28, 1992, *further modified* May 5, 1992. *See In re Remington Arms Co.*, 952 F.2d 1029 (8th Cir. 1991).

Hotchkiss v. Sears, Roebuck & Co., 139 F.R.D. 313, 315–16, 317–18 (M.D. Pa. 1991) (products case; radial arm saw) (defendant compelled to produce (1) records pertaining to research and development of a potential guard for the saw, (2) market studies concerning saws and who used them, (3) three reports reflecting the pattern of injuries associated with the use of radial arm saws, (4) documents regarding hazards associated with the use of the subject guard on radial arm saws including follow-up interviews of purchasers of saws with the guard, (5) reports of testing performed by manufacturer on alternate guards, and (6) records of attempts to develop other types of guards for saw blade. The court found that conditions imposed by confidentiality order would adequately protect defendant's trade secret concerns.).

Sellon v. Smith, 112 F.R.D. 9, 13 (D. Del. 1986) (products case; automobile) (holding that documents relating to tests of alternative fuel systems were discoverable).

Clark v. General Motors Corp., 20 Fed. R. Serv. 2d (Callaghan) 679, 683 (D. Mass. 1975) (products case; stove) (ordering the defendant to answer interrogatories concerning whether it had ever considered marketing the product with devices other than the ones it did).

Lindberger v. General Motors Corp., 56 F.R.D. 433, 435 (W.D. Wis. 1972) (products case; front end loader) (holding that post-manufacture research was relevant to show the feasibility of alternative designs).

Hess v. Pittsburgh Steel Foundry & Mach. Co., 49 F.R.D. 271 (W.D. Pa. 1970) (products case; grinding wheel) (holding that the plaintiff was entitled to discover intercompany correspondence among four competing companies relating to all complaints and recommendations to correct conditions where grinding wheels were used).

Self v. American Home Assurance Co., 51 F.R.D. 222, 224 (N.D. Miss. 1970) (products case; bean house) (holding that information relating to other bean houses designed and built by the defendant was discoverable).

Remington Arms Co. v. Canales, 837 S.W.2d 624 (Tex. 1992) (class action regarding safety of Model 700 rifle).

Jampole v. Touchy, 673 S.W.2d 569 (Tex. 1984) (products case; fuel system integrity) (allowing plaintiff discovery of tests and studies concerning alternate fuel storage system designs).

Schelbauer v. Butler Mfg. Co., 673 P.2d 743 (Cal. 1984) (products case; roofing panels) (permitting discovery of subsequent technological developments to the extent that they indicated the existence of a feasible alternative design).

Friederichs v. Huebner, 329 N.W.2d 890 (Wis. 1983) (permitting discovery of subsequent technological developments to the extent that they indicated the existence of a feasible alternative design).

Garst v. General Motors Corp., CA No. 90-8857-NP (Wexford County, Mich. Cir. Ct. Sept. 21, 1992) (products case; rear seat, lap belt only) (Plaintiff requested (1) tests and studies reflecting the relative safety/danger to a rear seat occupant restrained by a lap belt only and/or lap/shoulder harness involved in a frontal and front angle collision and (2) reports of tests, studies and investigations, and minutes of committee meetings reflecting the basis of GM's decision to equip its vehicle with the rear seat shoulder harness. GM attempted to limit the scope of discovery to (1) its subjective and adversarial view of the facts of the particular accident, (2) the particular model year and type of vehicle involved, and (3) rear seat occupants of the same or substantially similar size as the plaintiff. The court granted plaintiff's motion to compel and ordered GM to produce the requested documents, holding that in view of the nature of the defect involved, the scope of relevant discovery extended to other year model and model types and alternate designs. The court rejected GM's attempt to limit the production of minutes of committee meetings to specified committees. The court ordered the production of post- and pre-accident documents, noting that GM had withdrawn its "time limitation objection." In response to GM's "burdensome objection" the court noted that plaintiff's counsel had expressed his willingness to go, together with his staff, to GM's facility and conduct a detailed examination of the subject documents once the material was brought together.).

§ 38.4 RESEARCH AND DEVELOPMENT

(*See also* §§ 38.2, 38.3)

Commentary

Information concerning the defendant's research and development, with respect to the operation or function of the product involved, is generally discoverable.

Secondary Sources

AMERICAN LAW OF PRODUCTS LIABILITY 3D, *supra* § 1, § 53:35.

KIELY, *supra* § 11, §§ 1.25, 1.53–1.63.

Case Law

Martell v. Boardwalk Enters., Inc., 748 F.2d 740, 747–49 (2d Cir. 1984) (holding that post-manufacture research was discoverable as relevant to defendant's failure to warn or recall).

Deitchman v. E.R. Squibb & Sons, Inc., 740 F.2d 556 (7th Cir. 1984) (allowing defendant to acquire documents from third-party university registry).

Hartman v. Remington Arms Co., CA No. 90-4074-CV-C-5 (W.D. Mo. Apr. 13, 1992) (products case; rifle) (overruling manufacturer's contention that requested documents contain "trade secret" information, the court required defendant company to produce research and development on a New Bolt Action Rifle as potentially reflecting feasibility of alternative designs. The court's order included information contained in defendant company's Customer Sales Analysis touching on alternative designs. The court's order embraced post-injury research, reflecting the priority level and cost consideration of alternative designs.), *modified* Apr. 28, 1992, *further modified* May 5, 1992. *See In re Remington Arms Co.*, 952 F.2d 1029 (8th Cir. 1991).

Snowden v. Connaught Lab., Inc., 137 F.R.D. 336, 345–46 (D. Kan.) (products case; DPT) (plaintiff sought production of pre- and post-accident research and development conducted in cooperation between parent corporation and wholly owned subsidiary; defendant objected that subject research and development constituted privileged trade secret information and that it was irrelevant; court held that the subject information was relevant and necessary concerning the feasibility of a safer alternative design and ordered the production subject to a protective order restricting dissemination), *aff'd*, 136 F.R.D. 694 (D. Kan. 1991).

Hotchkiss v. Sears, Roebuck & Co., 139 F.R.D. 313, 315–16, 317–18 (M.D. Pa. 1991) (products case; radial arm saw) (defendant compelled to produce (1) records pertaining to research and development of a potential guard for the saw, (2) market studies concerning saws and who used them, (3) three reports reflecting the pattern of injuries associated with the use of radial arm saws, (4) documents regarding hazards associated with the use of the subject guard on radial arm saws including follow-up interviews of purchasers of saws with the guard, (5) reports of testing performed by manufacturer on alternate guards, and (6) records of attempts to develop other types of guards for saw blade. Court found that conditions imposed by confidentiality order would adequately protect defendant's trade secret concerns.).

Culligan v. Yamaha Motor Corp., 110 F.R.D. 122, 125 (S.D.N.Y. 1986) (products case; ATV) (holding that post-manufacture testing data was discoverable).

Bowman v. General Motors Corp., 64 F.R.D. 62, 68 (E.D. Pa. 1974) (products case; automobile) (holding that post-manufacture research was relevant to show feasibility of alternative design that might have been utilized).

Lindberger v. General Motors Corp., 56 F.R.D. 433, 435 (W.D. Wis. 1972) (products case; front end loader) (holding that post-manufacture research was relevant to show the feasibility of alternative designs).

Hess v. Pittsburgh Steel Foundry & Mach. Co., 49 F.R.D. 271 (W.D. Pa. 1970) (products case; grinding wheel) (holding that the plaintiff was entitled to discover intercompany correspondence among four competing companies where grinding wheels were used).

Meyer v. G.D. Searle & Co., 41 F.R.D. 290 (E.D.N.Y. 1966) (products case; drug Enovid) (permitting discovery of new drug application); *see also Bristol Myers Co. v. District Court*, 422 P.2d 373 (Colo. 1967); *Snyder v. Parke, Davis & Co.*, 391 N.Y.S.2d 579 (App. Div. 1977).

Luey v. Sterling Drug, Inc., 240 F. Supp. 632 (W.D. Mich. 1965) (products case; drug Aralen) (allowing plaintiff to discover defendant's warnings to professionals, dosage determinations, and relationship to efficacy and side effects).

Eli Lilly & Co. v. Marshall, 829 S.W.2d 157 (Tex. 1992) (products case; drug Prozac) (trial court ordered defendant to produce FDA documents reflecting defendant's evaluation of drug's safety and effectiveness including clinical studies, chemical analysis, adverse reaction reports, and proposed labels. Texas Supreme Court granted mandamus and ordered trial court to hold hearing and rule on the merits of defendant's motion for a protective order under Texas rule 76a.).

Remington Arms Co. v. Canales, 837 S.W.2d 624 (Tex. 1992) (class action regarding safety of Model 700 rifle).

Procter & Gamble Co. v. Swilley, 462 So. 2d 1188, 1195–96 (Fla. Dist. Ct. App. 1985) (products case; tampons) (holding that the plaintiff was entitled to discover research from scientist whose work was funded by the defendants despite an agreement by the manufacturer not to disclose the data to third parties).

Orlich v. Helm Bros., Inc., 550 N.Y.S.2d 795, 798–99 (Sup. Ct.) (products case; automobile passive-restraint system) (holding that the plaintiff was entitled to discover all information regarding manufacturer's passive restraint research), *aff'd as modified*, 560 N.Y.S.2d 10 (App. Div. 1990).

See also

Perry v. Jeep Eagle Corp., 126 F.R.D. 542 (S.D. Ind. 1989).

In re Snyder, 115 F.R.D. 211 (D. Ariz. 1987).

Hindelang v. R.D. Werner Co., 469 N.W.2d 2 (Mich. Ct. App. 1991).

Tompkins v. Log Sys., Inc., 385 S.E.2d 545 (N.C. Ct. App. 1989), *review denied*, 389 S.E.2d 819 (N.C. 1990).

§ 39 EXAMINATIONS AND/OR TESTING (INCLUDING DESTRUCTIVE TESTING) OF SUBJECT PRODUCT

§ 39.1 GENERALLY

Commentary

FED. R. CIV. P. 34 permits "someone acting on the requestor's behalf . . . to inspect and copy, test, or sample any tangible things which constitute or contain matters within the scope of Fed. R. Civ. P. 26 . . .; or . . . to permit entry upon designated land or other property in the possession or control of the party upon whom the request is served." In the absence of a special order, however, destructive testing is not ordinarily allowed.

Rule

FED. R. CIV. P. 34.

Secondary Sources

AMERICAN LAW OF PRODUCTS LIABILITY 3D, *supra* § 1, §§ 53:35–53:36, 53:69–53:73.

Annotation, *Propriety of Discovery Order Permitting "Destructive Testing" of Chattel in Civil Case*, 11 A.L.R. 4TH 1245 (1982).

Annotation, *Right of Accused in State Courts to Have Expert Inspect, Examine, or Test Physical Evidence in Possession of Prosecution—Modern Cases*, 27 A.L.R. 4TH 1188 (1984).

Cannizzaro, Annotation, *Discovery and Inspection of Articles and Premises in Civil Actions Other Than for Personal Injury or Death the Condition of Which Is Alleged to Have Caused Personal Injury or Death*, 4 A.L.R. 3D 762 (1965).

DISCOVERY PROCEEDINGS IN FEDERAL COURT, *supra* § 2, § 7.8.

HAYDOCK & HERR, *supra* § 3, §§ 5.14–5.16.

Hursh, Annotation, *Discovery and Inspection of Article or Premises the Condition of Which Is Alleged to Have Caused Personal Injury or Death*, 13 A.L.R. 2D 657 (1950).

Ludington, Annotation, *Consumption or Destruction of Physical Evidence Due to Testing or Analysis by Prosecution's Expert as Warranting Suppression of Evidence or Dismissal of Case Against Accused in State Court*, 40 A.L.R. 4TH 594 (1985).

4A MOORE ET AL., *supra* § 1, ¶¶ 34.18, 34.19[5].

Vance, Annotation, *Discovery, Inspection, and Copying of Photographs of Article or Premises the Condition of Which Gave Rise to Instant Litigation*, 95 A.L.R. 2D 1061 (1964).

8 WRIGHT & MILLER, *supra* § 1, § 2212.

Case Law

Farnsworth v. Procter & Gamble Co., 758 F.2d 1545 (11th Cir. 1985) (products case; toxic shock) (allowing both parties to obtain copy of study conducted by Centers for Disease Control; however, court denied access to the names and addresses of study participants).

Machin v. Zuckert, 316 F.2d 336 (D.C. Cir.) (products case; Air Force crash) (holding that factual findings of Air Force report were discoverable), *cert. denied*, 375 U.S. 896 (1963).

Fine v. Facet Aerospace Prods. Co., 133 F.R.D. 439 (S.D.N.Y. 1990) (products case; aircraft) (defendant manufacturer's internal report addressing problem of water in fuel systems of its aircraft, testing done, and possible solutions were subject to discovery; court overruled defendant's objection based on attorney-client privilege; report was drafted by manufacturer's engineering department for purpose of risk management).

Ostrander v. Cone Mills, Inc., 119 F.R.D. 417 (D. Minn. 1988) (products case; flammable pajamas) (holding that the defendant was entitled to destructive testing of nightwear in question, the identical nightwear of the plaintiff's brother, and unwashed nightwear for two reasons: (1) the plaintiff could be present at the testing, and (2) the plaintiff had done its own destructive testing).

Kendall v. United Air Lines, Inc., 9 F.R.D. 702 (S.D.N.Y. 1949) (products case; airplane crash) (finding that an interrogatory was not objectionable because it called for expert opinion from engineer in defendant's employ or because it might be inadmissible at trial).

Bachner v. Pearson, 432 P.2d 525 (Alaska 1967) (products case; airplane muffler) (ordering issue preclusion concerning condition of muffler and exhaust system for defendant's failure to timely produce subject product following court order).

Lopez v. Foremost Paving, Inc., 796 S.W.2d 473 (Tex. Ct. App. 1990) (finding that the defendant failed to produce videotape simulation of defendant's version of accident until ten days before trial; introduction in evidence at trial held reversible error).

Dina v. Lutheran Medical Ctr., 548 N.Y.S.2d 541 (App. Div. 1989) (requiring defendant to produce jewitt nail for destructive testing as long as defendant's representative was allowed to be present at test).

Wierbinski v. Volkswagen A.G., CA No. A038364 (Cal. Ct. App. Dec. 30, 1988) (products case; design of suspension system causing rollover) (ordering automaker to produce accident reconstruction computer program and software for program, which defendant failed to do until middle of trial; appellate court affirmed trial court's order granting plaintiff new trial following verdict for defendant), *reprinted in* Automotive Litig. Rep. 11444-47 (Jan. 17, 1989).

§ 39.2 PLAINTIFF'S RIGHT TO BE PRESENT AT TEST/EXAMINATION

Commentary
Courts usually allow the plaintiff (or a representative) to be present during the inspection of the product.

Secondary Source
AMERICAN LAW OF PRODUCTS LIABILITY 3D, *supra* § 1, § 53:72.

Case Law
Klick v. R.D. Werner Co., 348 N.E.2d 314, 316 (Ill. App. Ct. 1976) (products case; ladder) (holding that the plaintiff had a right to be present during defendant's testing of product where object tested was basis of claim).

Salzo v. Vi-She Bottling Corp., 235 N.Y.S.2d 585, 587 (Sup. Ct. 1962) (products case; bottle) (holding that the plaintiffs had a right to be present during any examination or test of bottle which was object of the litigation).

See also

DiGiovanni v. Pepsico, Inc., 502 N.Y.S.2d 23 (App. Div. 1986).

§ 40 SUBSEQUENT REMEDIAL MEASURES IN GENERAL

(*See also* § 42)

Commentary

Information concerning the adoption of subsequent remedial measures is normally discoverable regardless of whether the information may later prove to be inadmissible as evidence.

Secondary Sources

AMERICAN LAW OF PRODUCTS LIABILITY 3D, *supra* § 1, § 53:37–53:39.

2A FRUMER & FRIEDMAN, *supra* § 36, § 17.02[3].

8 WRIGHT & MILLER, *supra* § 1, § 2009, at 75 n.49.

Case Law

Roberts v. Jeep Eagle Corp., CA No. 1:89-cv-238-HTW (N.D. Ga. Jan. 4, 1993) (products case; failure of liftgate in side impact collision) (court compelled defendant to produce (1) reports of similar incidents occurring both before and after subject claim (at 3–4); (2) requested photographs, overruling defendant's work product and attorney-client privilege on the grounds that photographs do not disclose mental impressions (at 4); (3) documents and testimony produced in other cases (at 2–3, 11); (4) tests concerning similar models (at 11); (5) information concerning profits defendant realized per vehicle during certain years pertinent to the litigation (at 12); (6) information concerning defendant's consideration of an alternative design (at 7, 12–13); and (7) information concerning defendant's consideration of a subsequent remedial measure (at 7, 12–13). The court also allowed plaintiff to depose defendant's vice president for the reason that he participated in a decision to suppress an internal memorandum concerning the defective condition of the subject liftgate (at 6–7).).

Bowman v. General Motors Corp., 64 F.R.D. 62 (E.D. Pa. 1974) (products case; fuel system integrity) (permitting plaintiff to discover information about design and testing of later models than the one involved in suit).

Lindberger v. General Motors Corp., 56 F.R.D. 433, 434 (W.D. Wis. 1972) (products case; front-end loader) (holding that post-accident changes to braking system were discoverable).

Novak v. Good Will Grange No. 127, Patrons of Husbandry, Inc., 28 F.R.D. 394, 396 (D. Conn. 1961) (slip and fall case) (holding that discovery of information regarding repairs subsequent to the accident was relevant to the subject matter of this action).

Carlson v. Chisholm-Moore Hoist Corp., 21 F.R.D. 144 (S.D.N.Y. 1957) (products case; chain hoist) (after plaintiff's injury, the hoist had been returned to defendant for testing and inspection and certain parts were replaced; reports and memoranda relating to these repairs were held discoverable, as were defendant's correspondence and reports relating to the accident), *aff'd*, 281 F.2d 766 (2d Cir.), *cert. denied*, 364 U.S. 883 (1960).

Baker v. Procter & Gamble Co., 17 Fed. R. Serv. (Callaghan) 460, 461 (S.D.N.Y. 1952) (products case; drug) (holding that discovery of post-accident modifications may lead to evidence of negligence).

Schelbauer v. Butler Mfg. Co., 673 P.2d 743 (Cal. 1984) (permitting discovery of subsequent technological developments to the extent that they indicated the existence of a feasible alternative design).

Friederichs v. Huebner, 329 N.W.2d 890 (Wis. 1983) (permitting discovery of subsequent technological developments to the extent that they indicated the existence of a feasible alternative design).

Harmon v. Ford Motor Co., 453 N.Y.S.2d 475, 476 (App. Div. 1982) (products case; automobile) (holding that the plaintiff was entitled to disclosure of post-accident design changes).

Frank v. Volkswagenwerk of Wolfsburg, Germany, 432 N.Y.S.2d 787 (Sup. Ct. 1980) (products case; automobile) (holding that the plaintiff was entitled to documents relating to post-accident design changes and to a continued examination of defendant's employee regarding those changes).

See also

Dollar v. Long Mfg., N.C., Inc., 561 F.2d 613 (5th Cir. 1977), *cert. denied*, 435 U.S. 996 (1978).

Fann v. Giant Food, Inc., 115 F.R.D. 593 (D.D.C. 1987).

Ribley v. Harsco Corp., 377 N.Y.S.2d 375 (Sup. Ct. 1975), *aff'd*, 394 N.Y.S.2d 740 (App. Div. 1977).

Contra

Reddick v. White Consol. Indus., 295 F. Supp. 243, 250–51 (S.D. Ga. 1969) (products case; gas heater) (prohibiting interrogatory seeking changes made in gas heater manual instructions as it could not lead to discovery of admissible evidence).

§ 41 POST-SALE NOTIFICATION, WARNING, RECALL, AND/OR MODIFICATION

(See also § 40)

Commentary

A service bulletin notifies the consumer of the problem with the product and gives instructions to avoid complications. Such warnings may be admissible because they may be relevant to show the nature of the defect itself, the causation (whether through defect or plaintiff misuse) of the injuries in the case, the defendant's knowledge of the defect, or the defendant's post-sale duty to its customers. These bulletins and recall notices are normally discoverable whether they are admissible in evidence at trial.

Secondary Sources

AMERICAN LAW OF PRODUCTS LIABILITY 3D, *supra* § 1, § 53:45.

Case Law

Uitts v. General Motors Corp., 62 F.R.D. 560 (E.D. Pa. 1974) (products case; spring shackle) (allowing plaintiff to discover information concerning recall campaign to correct the claimed defect).

Calo v. Ahearn, 522 N.Y.S.2d 555, 556 (App. Div. 1987) (products case; automobile) (holding that although plaintiff's vehicle had not been recalled, information concerning manufacturer's recall of vehicles of the same type and model was discoverable).

§ 42 WARRANTIES

(See also §§ 43, 44)

Commentary

The question of the existence of a warranty and/or the terms of a warranty associated with the product in question is generally discoverable.

Secondary Sources

AMERICAN LAW OF PRODUCTS LIABILITY 3D, *supra* § 1, § 53:49.

KIELY, *supra* § 11, §§ 3.37–3.43.

Case Law

Abrams v. Vaughan & Bushnell Mfg. Co., 325 N.Y.S.2d 976, 979 (App. Div. 1971) (products case; hammer) (holding that a request for production of any and all warranties pertaining to hammer in question was proper).

§ 43 ADVERTISING AND OTHER REPRESENTATIONS

(See also §§ 31, 33, 42, 44)

Commentary

The contents of advertisements and other promotional literature concerning the defendant's product may be relevant to a number of issues including (1) a claim of misrepresentation, (2) as bearing on the "reasonable expectations of the average consumer," and (3) the existence and/or terms of an express or implied warranty.

Secondary Sources

AMERICAN LAW OF PRODUCTS LIABILITY 3D, *supra* § 1, § 53:49.

KIELY, *supra* § 11, §§ 3.37–3.43.

Case Law

Roesberg v. Johns-Manville Corp., 85 F.R.D. 292, 297 (E.D. Pa. 1980) (products case; asbestos) (holding that an interrogatory seeking nature and extent of defendant's advertising was obviously relevant).

Luey v. Sterling Drug, Inc., 240 F. Supp. 632 (W.D. Mich. 1965) (products case; drug Aralen) (allowing plaintiff to discover defendant's warnings to professionals, dosage determinations, and relationship to efficacy and side effects).

Baker v. Procter & Gamble Co., 17 Fed. R. Serv. (Callaghan) 460, 461 (S.D.N.Y. 1952) (products case) (holding that interrogatories relating to advertising may be relevant to an action for breach of warranty).

Leichtamer v. American Motors Corp., 424 N.E.2d 568, 578 (Ohio 1981) (ads admissible on issue of consumer expectations).

Bikowicz v. Nedco Pharmacy, Inc., 474 N.Y.S.2d 616, 618 (App. Div. 1984).

Bleacher v. Bristol-Myers Co., 163 A.2d 526, 528 (Del. Super. Ct. 1960) (products case; deodorant) (holding that advertisements of product seen by plaintiff prior to accident were discoverable).

§ 44 MARKETING INFORMATION

(See also §§ 24, 31, 32, 33, 42, 43)

Commentary

Disputes concerning the discoverability of marketing information arise more frequently in commercial litigation than in products liability cases. Such information may be relevant to several issues that typically arise in defective product cases: (1) tracing the path of distribution of the product; (2) establishing a particular defendant's responsibility within the context of enterprise liability, concert-of-action, or a market share theory of liability; or (3) a claim for misrepresentation, breach of express or implied warranty, or failure to warn. Some of the documents covered in this topic may constitute a trade secret, justifying the entrance of an appropriate protective order limiting the dissemination of such information.

Secondary Sources

AMERICAN LAW OF PRODUCTS LIABILITY 3D, *supra* § 1, § 53:44.

KIELY, *supra* § 11, §§ 3.37–3.43.

Case Law

Hotchkiss v. Sears, Roebuck & Co., 139 F.R.D. 313, 315–16, 317–18 (M.D. Pa. 1991) (products case; radial arm saw) (defendant compelled to produce (1) records pertaining to research and development of a potential guard for the saw, (2) market studies concerning saws and who used them, (3) three reports reflecting the pattern of injuries associated with the use of radial arm saws, (4) documents regarding hazards associated with the use of the subject guard on radial arm saws including follow-up interviews of purchasers of saws with the guard, (5) reports of testing performed by manufacturer on alternate guards, and (6) records of attempts to develop other types of guards for saw blade. The court found that conditions imposed by confidentiality order would adequately protect defendant's trade secret concerns.).

Chubb Integrated Sys. Ltd. v. National Bank, 103 F.R.D. 52, 56 (D.D.C. 1984) (patent infringement action) (holding sales figures "clearly discoverable").

Luey v. Sterling Drug, Inc., 240 F. Supp. 632, 636 (W.D. Mich. 1965) (products case; drug Aralen) (holding that dollar volume and profit from sales of drug were discoverable in negligence action).

Chicago Cutlery Co. v. District Court, 568 P.2d 464, 466 (Colo. 1977) (en banc) (products case; boning knife) (holding that the customer list was discoverable).

Kaplan v. Roux Lab., Inc., 76 N.Y.S.2d 601 (App. Div. 1948).

§ 45 DISCOVERY MISCONDUCT

Commentary

The court should, in appropriate circumstances, permit discovery on the question of whether the opposing party did, in fact, abuse the discovery process.

Secondary Sources

GORELICK ET AL., DESTRUCTION OF EVIDENCE (1989 & Supp. 1991).

IMWINKELRIED & BLUMOFF, PRETRIAL DISCOVERY: STRATEGY & TACTICS §§ 8:27–8:28 (1986 & Supp. 1992).

Case Law

In re "Agent Orange" Prod. Liab. Litig., 98 F.R.D. 558, 559 (E.D.N.Y. 1983) (products case; chemical) (permitting plaintiff to depose employees of defendant company to aid in determining whether any documents relevant to the litigation were destroyed).

Mullins v. Kretchmar, CA No. 384,282 (200th Judicial Dist., Travis County, Tex. May 11, 1990) (defendants testified during court-ordered hearing concerning Honda's document destruction activities).

Blackner v. Clark Equip. Co., CA No. 2860 (Philadelphia, Pa. Ct. C.P. Nov. 7, 1983) (products case; forklift rollover).

§ 46 DOCUMENTS REVIEWED BY DEPONENT BEFORE TESTIMONY

Commentary

FED. R. EVID. 612 provides in pertinent part:

> [I]f a witness uses a writing to refresh his memory for the purpose of testifying, either—
>
> (1) while testifying, or

(2) before testifying, if the court in its discretion determines it is necessary in the interests of justice, an adverse party is entitled to have the writing produced at the hearing, to inspect it, to cross examine the witness thereon, and to introduce in evidence those portions which relate to the testimony of the witness.

Rules

FED. R. CIV. P. 26(b)(3), 26(b)(4)(A).

FED. R. EVID. 612.

Secondary Sources

Humphreys, Comment, *Whether Disclosure of Work Product to a Witness in Preparation for Testifying Waives the Protection of Federal Rule of Civil Procedure 26(b)(3)*, 76 KY. L.J. 479 (1987–1988).

Imwinkelried, *The Applicability of the Attorney-Client Privilege to Non-Testifying Experts: Reestablishing the Boundaries Between the Attorney-Client Privilege and the Work Product Protection*, 68 WASH. U. L.Q. 19 (1990).

Lewis, Note, *Discovery Under the Federal Rules of Civil Procedure of Attorney Opinion Work Product Provided to an Expert Witness*, 53 FORDHAM L. REV. 1159 (1985).

4 MOORE ET AL., *supra* § 1, ¶ 26.66[3].

Note, *Interactions Between Memory Refreshment Doctrine and Work Product Protection Under the Federal Rules*, 88 YALE L.J. 390 (1978).

Staton, Note, *Discovery of Attorney Work Product Reviewed by an Expert Witness*, 85 COLUM. L. REV. 812 (1985).

3 WEINSTEIN & BERGER, *supra* § 35, § 612[04].

Wells, Note, *Interaction Between 26(b)(3) and 26(b)(4) of the Federal Rules of Civil Procedure: Conflict and Confusion in the Federal Courts*, 9 AM. J. TRIAL ADVOC. 319 (1985).

8 WRIGHT & MILLER, *supra* § 1, §§ 2016, 2021, 2024.

Case Law

Bogosian v. Gulf Oil Corp., 738 F.2d 587 (3d Cir. 1984) (antitrust action) (holding that documents reflecting "core work product" of attorney's legal theories were not so significant to expert's testimony that protected status of documents was waived when they were shown to the expert).

William Penn Life Assurance Co. of Am. v. Brown Transfer & Storage Co., 141 F.R.D. 142, 143 (W.D. Mo. 1990) (although recognizing that opinion work product is normally entitled to a high level of protection from discovery, the court ordered the production of such material which had been shown to an expert before he formed his opinion).

Hamel v. General Motors Corp., 128 F.R.D. 281 (D. Kan. 1989) (finding that the plaintiff had made no more than a speculative showing that the subject documents might have influenced the expert's opinion, the court refused to compel the production of opinion work-product materials that defense counsel had furnished to a defense expert).

In re Joint E. & S. Dist. Asbestos Litig., 119 F.R.D. 4, 5 (E.D. & S.D.N.Y. 1988) (products case; asbestos) (determining whether providing privileged material to a witness waived the privilege involved a balancing of competing interests: "the need for full disclosure" vs. "the need to protect the integrity of the adversary system protected by the work-product rule"). To the same effect see *James Julian, Inc. v. Raytheon Co.*, 93 F.R.D. 138, 146 (D. Del. 1982) (antitrust, labor management, and state tort law action) ("[e]ach case must . . . be evaluated on its own facts").

Leybold-Heraeus Technologies, Inc. v. Midwest Instrument Co., 118 F.R.D. 609, 614–15 (E.D. Wis. 1987) (patent infringement case) (holding that a witness who reviewed privileged documents to refresh his recollection for a deposition made the documents discoverable—even if they were only partially disclosed).

North Carolina Elec. Membership Corp. v. Carolina Power & Light Co., 108 F.R.D. 283, 286 (M.D.N.C. 1985) (holding that opinion work product was privileged and nondiscoverable even when furnished to a testifying trial expert).

S & A Painting Co. v. OWB Corp., 103 F.R.D. 407 (W.D. Pa. 1984) (contract action) (a party who refreshed his recollection with materials protected by attorney-client privilege waived privilege as to those portions used and subjected examined portions to discovery.) See also *Marshall v. United States Postal Serv.*, 88 F.R.D. 348, 350 (D.D.C. 1980); *R.J. Hereley & Son Co. v. Stotler & Co.*, 87 F.R.D. 358 (N.D. Ill. 1980); *Wheeling-Pittsburgh Steel Corp. v. Underwriters Lab., Inc.*, 81 F.R.D. 8 (N.D. Ill. 1978); *Bailey v. Meister Brau, Inc.*, 57 F.R.D. 11 (N.D. Ill. 1972).

In re Comair Air Disaster Litig., 100 F.R.D. 350 (E.D. Ky. 1983) (products case; aircraft) (employee of the defendant manufacturer investigated the accident and compiled a report of his findings. That report was turned over to another of the defendant's employees for review in preparation for deposition. The court found that it was necessary in the "interests of justice" to compel production of the report. Using the balancing test, the court placed emphasis on the plaintiff's unequal access to the wreckage.).

Boring v. Keller, 97 F.R.D. 404, 407–08 (D. Colo. 1983) (medical negligence suit) (holding that document containing mental impressions could be discovered because it had been provided to defendant's expert and could arguably have influenced the expert's opinion; even the immunity afforded opinion work product was overcome if the document was used to shape or influence testimony).

Al-Rowaishan Establishment Universal Trading & Agencies, Ltd. v. Beatrice Foods Co., 92 F.R.D. 779 (S.D.N.Y. 1982) (denying request for disclosure of documents shown witness because work-product principle outweighed the values underlying rule 612).

James Julian, Inc. v. Raytheon Co., 93 F.R.D. 138, 146 (D. Del. 1982) (antitrust, labor management, and state law tort action) (holding that use of work product to refresh a witness's memory or to prepare a witness for examination waived work-product protection).

Marshall v. United States Postal Serv., 88 F.R.D. 348, 350 (D.D.C. 1980) (Fair Labor Standards Act suit) (stating, without qualification, that "once a document is used to refresh the recollection of a witness, privileges as to that document have been waived").

Berkey Photo, Inc. v. Eastman Kodak Co., 74 F.R.D. 613, 617 (S.D.N.Y. 1977) (antitrust action) (denying access to work-product documents shown to an expert witness but warning that in the future the court would force disclosure of materials used to prepare witnesses for testifying at a deposition or trial).

Quadrini v. Sikorsky Aircraft Div., 74 F.R.D. 594, 595 (D. Conn. 1977) (helicopter crash) (allowing discovery of documents prepared for expert to review).

Bailey v. Meister Brau, Inc., 57 F.R.D. 11, 13 (N.D. Ill. 1972) (holding that the plaintiff waived both attorney-client privilege and right to claim work-product immunity in documents she used to refresh witness's memory before testifying at his deposition).

§ 47 DEPOSITION OF CEO OR OPPOSING ATTORNEY

Commentary

Should a lawyer be permitted to depose an opposing party's lawyer or chief executive officer just like "any person" under Fed. R. Civ. P. 30(a)? A reading of the cases discloses two views. One view holds that it is premature to issue a protective order forbidding the deposition before the deposition is convened; thus, the lawyer or chief executive officer must attend the deposition and raise specific objections to specific questions. *See Qad, Inc. v. ALN Assocs., Inc.*, 132 F.R.D. 492 (N.D. Ill. 1990); *Hunt Int'l Resources Corp. v. Binstein*, 98 F.R.D. 689 (N.D. Ill. 1983); *Detweiler Bros., Inc. v. John Graham & Co.*, 412 F. Supp. 416, 422 (E.D. Wash. 1976); *Amherst Leasing Corp. v. Emhart Corp.*, 65 F.R.D. 121 (D. Conn. 1974); *Scovill Mfg. Co. v. Sunbeam Corp.*, 61 F.R.D. 598 (D. Del. 1973).

The other view holds that the subject attorney/deponent shows "good cause" and is entitled to a protective order precluding the deposition unless the party seeking the deposition shows: (1) deposing opposing counsel is the only means to obtain the information, (2) the information sought is relevant and nonprivileged, and (3) the information is crucial. *See Shelton v. American Motors Corp.*, 805 F.2d 1323, 1327 (8th Cir. 1986). Cases following *Shelton* include *West Peninsular Title Co. v. Palm Beach County*, 132 F.R.D. 301 (S.D. Fla. 1990); *Advance Sys., Inc. v. APV Baker PMC, Inc.*, 124 F.R.D. 200 (E.D. Wis. 1989); *Niagara Mohawk Power Corp. v. Stone & Webster Eng'g Corp.*, 125 F.R.D. 578 (N.D.N.Y. 1989); *NFA Corp. v. Riverview Narrow Fabrics, Inc.*, 117 F.R.D. 83 (M.D.N.C. 1987); *Marco Island Partners v. Oak Dev. Corp.*, 117 F.R.D. 418 (N.D. Ill. 1987).

Several cases have held that opposing counsel may not be compelled to review the names of the people he has talked to, the contents of the conversation, or the details of the interview. *Massachusetts v. First Nat'l Supermarkets, Inc.*, 112 F.R.D. 149 (D. Mass. 1986); *Board of Educ. v. Admiral Heating & Ventilating, Inc.*, 104 F.R.D. 23 (N.D. Ill. 1984); *Besly-Welles Corp. v. Balax, Inc.*, 43 F.R.D. 368 (E.D. Wis. 1968); *St. Paul Fire & Marine Ins. Co. v. King*, 45 F.R.D. 521 (W.D. Okla. 1968); *Uinta Oil Ref. Co. v. Continental*

Oil Co., 226 F. Supp. 495, 505–06 (D. Utah 1964); *see also In re Grand Jury Subpoena Dated Nov. 8, 1979*, 622 F.2d 933 (6th Cir. 1980). *See generally* 4 MOORE ET AL., *supra* § 1, ¶ 26.57[2].

Secondary Sources

Crane et al., *When the Other Side Sends You a Subpoena*, THE BRIEF, Spring 1990, at 22.

DISCOVERY PROCEEDINGS IN FEDERAL COURT, *supra* § 2, §§ 3.6–3.8.

DOMBROFF, *supra* § 3, § 12.30.

8 WRIGHT & MILLER, *supra* § 1, § 2110.

Case Law

Salter v. Upjohn Co., 593 F.2d 649, 651 (5th Cir. 1979) (upholding protective order vacating plaintiff's notice to depose defendant's president, in light of reasonable assertions that president "did not have any direct knowledge of the facts").

Roberts v. Jeep Eagle Corp., CA No. 1:89-cv-238-HTW (N.D. Ga. Jan. 4, 1993) (products case; failure of liftgate in side impact collision) (court compelled defendant to produce (1) reports of similar incidents occurring both before and after subject claim (at 3–4); (2) requested photographs, overruling defendant's work product and attorney-client privilege on the grounds that photographs do not disclose mental impressions (at 4); (3) documents and testimony produced in other cases (at 2–3, 11); (4) tests concerning other similar models (at 11); (5) information concerning profits defendant realized per vehicle during certain years pertinent to the litigation (at 12); (6) information concerning defendant's consideration of an alternative design (at 7, 12–13); and (7) information concerning defendant's consideration of a subsequent remedial measure (at pp. 7, 12–13). The court also allowed plaintiff to depose defendant's vice president for the reason that he participated in a decision to suppress an internal memorandum concerning the defective condition of the subject liftgate (at 6–7).).

M & R Amusements Corp. v. Blair, 142 F.R.D. 304 (N.D. Ill. 1992) (holding that a party must exhaust all reasonable alternatives for obtaining information before seeking to depose an adversary's attorney).

Perry v. Jeep Eagle Corp., CA No. IP 88-685-C (S.D. Ind. Apr. 27, 1989) (products case; Jeep CJ-5) (permitting deposition of assistant general counsel of Chrysler Motors).

Cooper v. Welch Foods, Inc., 105 F.R.D. 4 (W.D.N.Y. 1984) (patent infringement action) (allowing deposition of defendant's attorney and director of research and development).

Clark v. General Motors Corp., 20 Fed. R. Serv. 2d (Callaghan) 679, 688–89 (D. Mass. 1975) (products case; stove) (ordering that the deposition of corporate executive should be taken at corporation's principal place of business).

Hughes v. General Motors Corp., 18 Fed. R. Serv. 2d (Callaghan) 1249, 1250 (S.D.N.Y.

1974) (disallowing deposition of corporate president because the "information plaintiff wants is available through other employees of defendant").

Amherst Leasing Corp. v. Emhart Corp., 65 F.R.D. 121 (D. Conn. 1974) (permitting deposition of owner of corporation of antitrust action after designated spokesman proved unknowledgeable).

Colicchio v. City of New York, 581 N.Y.S.2d 36 (App. Div. 1992) (ordering examination of commissioner of transportation was abuse of discretion).

Mullins v. Kretchmar, CA No. 384,282 (Travis County, Tex. Dist. Ct. May 11, 1990) (defendants testified during court-ordered hearing concerning Honda's document-destruction activities).

See also

Marker v. Union Fidelity Life Ins. Co., 125 F.R.D. 121 (M.D.N.C. 1989).

United States v. One Parcel of Real Estate, 121 F.R.D. 439 (S.D. Fla. 1988).

First Sec. Sav. v. Kansas Bankers Sur. Co., 115 F.R.D. 181, 182–83 (D. Neb. 1987).

Dowd v. Calabrese, 101 F.R.D. 427, 439 (D.D.C. 1984).

In re Arthur Treacher's Franchisee Litig., 92 F.R.D. 429 (E.D. Pa. 1981).

Truxes v. Rolan Elec. Corp., 314 F. Supp. 752 (D.P.R. 1970).

Armstrong Cork Co. v. Niagara Mohawk Power Corp., 16 F.R.D. 389, 390 (S.D.N.Y. 1954).

Kuiper v. District Court, 632 P.2d 694 (Mont. 1981).

Hi-Plains Elevator Mach., Inc. v. Missouri Cereal Processors, 571S.W.2d 273 (Mo. Ct. App. 1978).

Contra

Shelton v. American Motors Corp., 805 F.2d 1323 (8th Cir. 1986) (products case; automobile) (disallowed deposition of opposing attorney).

Marco Island Partners v. Oak Dev. Corp., 117 F.R.D. 418, 420 (N.D. Ill. 1987) (breach of contract action) (disallowing deposition of opposing attorney where testimony could be duplicative).

N.F.A. Corp. v. Riverview Narrow Fabrics, Inc., 117 F.R.D. 83, 84–85 (M.D.N.C. 1987) (patent infringement action) (disallowed deposition of opposing attorney).

Mulvey v. Chrysler Corp., 106 F.R.D. 364 (D.R.I. 1985) (products case; automobile) (ordering that the deposition of Mr. Lee Iacocca would not proceed until written interrogatories had been propounded to him and then only if the answers warranted further testimony). *See also Colonial Capital Co. v. General Motors Corp.*, 29 F.R.D. 514, 518 (D. Conn. 1961); *cf. Mitchell v. American Tobacco Co.*, 33 F.R.D. 262, 263 (M.D. Pa. 1963).

Walker v. United Parcel Serv., 87 F.R.D. 360 (E.D. Pa. 1980) (employment discrimination action) (holding that plaintiffs did not show good cause for taking deposition of opposing attorney).

§ 48 REPORTS BY THIRD PARTIES INCLUDING GOVERNMENT AGENCY

§ 48.1 GENERALLY

(See also §§ 19, 22)

Commentary

This topic is divided into two categories, which are differentiated by who possesses the report or document in question.

The first category of third-party reports is those in the possession or control of a party to the action. The second category is reports that remain in the possession of the third party. Under the first category, the typical objection to production is the "work-product doctrine"; this objection, however, generally does not apply, and the documents should be subject to discovery.

The amendment of rule 34(c) in 1991 extends the scope of discovery to third parties. If the third party is a governmental agency, there may be a statute or regulation that limits the discoverability and/or admissibility of materials generated by the particular agency. Unless the statute or regulation expressly forbids discovery, most courts have given the limiting words of such statutes and regulations a construction that does not preclude the discovery of agency information.

The scope of the admissibility of reports rendered by government agencies was dramatically augmented by *Beech Aircraft Corp. v. Rainey*, 109 U.S. 439 (1988). In this case the Supreme Court opted for a broad interpretation of the definition of "factual findings" in rule 803(8)(c). The Court concluded that this language does not create a distinction between fact and opinion when concerning a public report.

This section also contains cases dealing with the discoverability of reports either written by or in the possession of a governmental agency. *See* § 19, *supra*.

Rules

FED. R. CIV. P. 45(c)(B)(ii).

FED. R. EVID. 803(8).

Secondary Sources

AMERICAN LAW OF PRODUCTS LIABILITY 3D, *supra* § 1, §§ 53:12, 53:16, 53:66.

Brown, Note, *Free Press, Privacy, and Privilege: Protection of Researcher-Subject Communications*, 17 GA. L. Rev. 1009 (1983).

DISCOVERY PROCEEDINGS IN FEDERAL COURT, *supra* § 2, §§ 7.9, 15.31–15.40, 16.1–16.18.

Gallagher, Annotation, *Independent Action Against Nonparty for Production of Documents and Things or Permission to Enter upon Land (Rule 34(c) of Federal Rules of Civil Procedure)*, 62 A.L.R. FED. 935 (1983).

HAYDOCK & HERR, *supra* § 3, §§ 2.5.9, 5.19.

Johnson, Annotation, *Discoverability of Traffic Accident Reports and Derivative Information*, 84 A.L.R. 4TH 15 (1991).

Kaplan & Cogan, *The Case Against Recognition of a General Academic Privilege*, 60 U. DET. J. URB. L. 205 (1983).

Kiesel, Note, *Every Man's Evidence and Ivory Tower Agencies: How May a Civil Litigant Obtain Testimony from an Employee of a Nonparty Federal Agency?*, 59 GEO. WASH. L. REV. 1647 (1991).

Krattenmaker, *Testimonial Privileges in Federal Courts: An Alternative to the Proposed Federal Rules of Evidence*, 62 GEO. L.J. 61 (1973).

Marcus, *Discovery Along the Litigation/Science Interface*, 57 BROOK. L. REV. 381 (1991).

Matherne, Note, *Forced Disclosure of Academic Research*, 37 VAND. L. REV. 585 (1984).

4 MOORE ET AL., *supra* § 1, ¶ 26.61.

4A MOORE ET AL., *supra* § 1, ¶ 34.22.

Nejelski & Lerman, *A Researcher-Subject Testimonial Privilege: What to Do Before the Subpoena Arrives*, 1971 WIS. L. REV. 1085.

O'Neil, *Scientific Research and the First Amendment: An Academic Privilege*, 16 U.C. DAVIS L. REV. 837 (1983).

2 WEINSTEIN, *supra* § 35, § 501[03].

8 WRIGHT & MILLER, *supra* § 1, §§ 2019, 2209.

Yolles et al., *Obtaining Access to Data from Government-Sponsored Medical Research*, 315 NEW ENG. J. MED. 1669 (1986).

§ 48.2 NONGOVERNMENTAL ENTITIES

Commentary

As stated previously, this section deals with reports or other documents which were generated by a third party and/or are still in the possession of that third party. These documents are usually discoverable despite the assertion of a work-product privilege.

Secondary Sources

See references cited in § 48.1, *supra*.

Flanagan, *Rejecting a General Privilege for Self-Critical Analyses*, 51 GEO. WASH. L. REV. 551 (1983).

McNab, Note, *Criticizing the Self-Criticism Privilege*, 1987 U. ILL. L. REV. 675.

Note, *The Privilege of Self-Critical Analysis*, 96 HARV. L. REV. 1083 (1983).

Case Law

University of Pa. v. EEOC, 493 U.S. 182, 188–90 (1990) (refusing to find a qualified or academic freedom privilege for peer review materials where the EEOC subpoenaed tenure files on the complainant and five other people).

Hoffman-LaRoche, Inc. v. Sperling, 493 U.S. 165 (1989) (products liability; drug Accutane) (requiring manufacturer to produce adverse drug reaction reports that included names of reporting physicians).

In re American Tobacco Co., 880 F.2d 1520 (2d Cir. 1989) (products case; cigarettes) (plaintiffs were expected to rely at trial on the research of a prominent professor at a New York medical school. The researcher and the school moved to quash the subpoena on the ground that they should be protected by a research scholar's privilege. The district court enforced the subpoena; the Second Circuit upheld without deciding the question of whether there should be a researcher's privilege.).

Deitchman v. E.R. Squibb & Sons, Inc., 740 F.2d 556 (7th Cir. 1984) (products case; DES) (defendant subpoenaed a medical registry at the University of Chicago. The records constituted the only centralized depository of data on the subject matter in dispute. The district court granted the registry custodian's motion to quash. The Seventh Circuit vacated, holding that concerns about confidentiality could be solved by some sort of redaction. Assuming that some kind of qualified privilege protecting research should be recognized, the court found that the defendant had shown sufficient necessity to justify discovery.).

In re Grand Jury Subpoena Dated Jan. 4, 1984, 750 F.2d 223 (2d Cir. 1984) (subpoena issuance) (although the district court recognized a scholar's privilege, Second Circuit reversed in part because the witness raising the issue had not made a sufficient showing of privilege), *rev'g* 583 F. Supp. 991 (E.D.N.Y. 1984).

Board of Directors, Water's Edge, Condominium Unit Owners' Ass'n v. Anden Group, 136 F.R.D. 100, 109 (E.D. Va. 1991) (products case; building material) (sanctioning party for failing to supplement its response to discovery requests by disclosing adverse test results acquired by independent experts hired by the defending party subsequent to the institute of litigation).

Hawkins v. South Plains Int'l Trucks, Inc., 139 F.R.D. 682 (D. Colo. 1991) (products case; defective hot oil unit on truck) (plaintiff's compensation insurance carrier was co-plaintiff to action. Insurance carrier served subpoena on plaintiff's employer, directing employer to produce its accident investigation file. Employer's internal claims attorney had in fact conducted an investigation within days after the incident. Employer objected on the basis that this accident file constituted privileged attorney work product. The court held that rule 26(b)(3) work-product protection does not extend to a nonparty.). *See also* 8 WRIGHT & MILLER, *supra* § 1, § 2024, at 201–02.

Fireman's Fund Ins. Co. v. ECM Motor Co., 132 F.R.D. 39 (W.D. Pa. 1990) (products case; electric motor) (holding that the plaintiff was entitled to discover Underwriters Laboratories' file concerning test done on different motor with appropriate protective order to assure confidentiality).

Solarex Corp. v. Arco Solar, Inc., 121 F.R.D. 163 (E.D.N.Y. 1988) (patent infringement action) (explicitly refusing to recognize research privilege), *aff'd*, 870 F.2d 642 (Fed. Cir. 1989).

United States v. IBM Corp., 66 F.R.D. 186, 188 (S.D.N.Y. 1974) (antitrust action) (holding that the nonexistence of the requested statements did not excuse third party from producing underlying records which would provide requested information).

Bachner v. Pearson, 432 P.2d 525 (Alaska 1967) (products case; airplane muffler) (ordering issue preclusion concerning condition of muffler and exhaust system for defendant's failure to timely produce subject product following court order).

Backlund v. General Motors Corp., 226 N.E.2d 555 (Mass. 1967).

In re Hoechst Celanese Corp., 584 N.Y.S.2d 805 (App. Div. 1992) (coverage dispute) (overruling appellant's "unduly burdensome" objection, court ordered production of documents relating to the drafting, development, and interpretation of standard-form general liability insurance policy language although appellant was not a party to the underlying action).

Neuswanger v. Ikegai Am. Corp., 582 N.E.2d 192 (Ill. App. Ct. 1991) (products case; industrial machine) (estate of worker who was killed in industrial accident sued machine manufacturer. Anticipating litigation, plaintiff's employer and workers' compensation carrier hired consulting expert who videotaped reenactment of incident. Plaintiff served subpoena seeking production of the tape. The court held that rule protecting work product of consultant expert applied only to "parties." Further, the court held that videotape was discoverable as a "tangible thing"—under Illinois rule which exempts from work-product protection tangible things which do not reveal attorney's or consultant's opinions.).

Procter & Gamble Co. v. Swilley, 462 So. 2d 1188, 1195–96 (Fla. Dist. Ct. App. 1985) (products case; tampons) (holding that the plaintiff was entitled to discover the research from scientist whose work was funded by the defendants despite an agreement by the manufacturer not to disclose the data to third parties).

§ 48.3 GOVERNMENTAL ENTITIES

(See also § 19)

Commentary

As seen in § 49, *supra*, this section deals with the situation in which a government agency has possession of the requested material. This situation is distinguished from that in § 19 where the defendant is in possession of a government report or document.

Secondary Sources

See references cited in § 48.1, *supra*.

HAYDOCK & HERR, *supra* § 3, § 2.3, at 126, §§ 2.5.9, 5.19.

Case Law

Anderson v. Cryovac, Inc., 862 F.2d 910 (1st Cir. 1988) (personal injuries related to chemical contamination of municipal water wells) (holding that a report prepared by independent testing company and filed with the EPA was discoverable), *on remand*, *Anderson v. Beatrice Foods Co.*, 127 F.R.D. 1 (D. Mass. 1989).

Farnsworth v. Procter & Gamble Co., 758 F.2d 1545 (11th Cir. 1985) (products case; toxic shock) (allowing party to obtain a copy of a study conducted by the Centers for

Disease Control; however, court denied access to the names and addresses of study participants).

Friedman v. Bache Halsey Stuart Shields, Inc., 738 F.2d 1336, 1344 (D.C. Cir. 1984) (subpoena enforcement action) (holding that § 8(a) of the Commodities Exchange Act forbidding public disclosure of certain information did not apply to the discovery process).

Freeman v. Seligson, 405 F.2d 1326, 1348–50 (D.C. Cir. 1968) (ancillary bankruptcy proceeding) (holding that § 8 of the Commodities Exchange Act did not forbid discovery in judicial proceedings).

Wechsler v. Consumer Prod. Safety Comm'n, CA No. 92-402 (S.D. Fla. Dec. 1, 1992) (FOIA proceeding) (Wechsler was the owner of an amusement park that had been sued for personal injuries in a civil action arising out of an incident that occurred on the premises. The CPSC had investigated the incident. Wechsler instituted this proceeding to obtain documentation withheld by the CPSC under FOIA exemptions. The district court upheld CPSC's claim of exemption and granted summary judgment against Wechsler.).

Scott v. Lewis, 139 F.R.D. 353, 356 (N.D. Ill. 1991) (§ 1983 action against housing authority security guards for fatal shooting) (plaintiff issued a subpoena to the director of the state agency that licensed and regulated the employment of security guards, seeking documents relating to the competence of the individual defendants and the investigative file of the subject incident. The director voluntarily furnished all the documents requested by the plaintiff with the exception of certain information (bank accounts, credit, medical and criminal histories) the disclosure of which might invade the privacy of the defendants in the civil action. The court refused to recognize a new federal common law privilege concerning communications between applicants and professional registration authorities and ordered the production of the remaining documents.).

Culligan v. Yamaha Motor Corp., U.S., 110 F.R.D. 122, 127 (S.D.N.Y. 1986) (products case; ATV) (manufacturer refused to produce certain information provided to the Consumer Product Safety Commission, arguing that 15 U.S.C. § 2055(a)(2) forbade the disclosure of trade-secret information furnished to the commission; court held that the federal statute did not prevent discovery in civil litigation).

Meyer v. G.D. Searle & Co., 41 F.R.D. 290 (E.D.N.Y. 1966) (products case; drug Enovid) (permitting discovery of new drug application); *see also Snyder v. Parke, Davis & Co.*, 391 N.Y.S.2d 579 (App. Div. 1977); *Bristol-Myers Co. v. District Court*, 422 P.2d 373 (Colo. 1967).

Baker v. Procter & Gamble Co., 17 Fed. R. Serv. (Callaghan) 460, 461 (S.D.N.Y. 1952) (products case) (holding that information about product tests made by the defendant was "clearly relevant to the issue of the exercise of due care in the manufacture and preparation of the product").

Eli Lilly & Co. v. Marshall, 829 S.W.2d 157 (Tex. 1992) (products case; drug Prozac) (trial court ordered defendant to produce FDA documents reflecting defendant's evaluation of drug's safety and effectiveness including clinical studies, chemical analysis, adverse reaction reports, and proposed labels. Texas Supreme Court granted mandamus and ordered trial court to hold hearing and rule on the merits of defendant's motion for a protective order under Texas rule 76a.).

Shannon v. Hansen, 469 N.W.2d 412 (Iowa 1991) (dram shop action) (holding that statements made by witnesses to police officer investigating motor vehicle accident in preparing official report were not protected by public-officer privilege).

Light v. State, 547 N.E.2d 1073 (Ind. 1989) (felony conviction) (holding that federal statute forbidding disclosure or use of reports in evidence did not bar pretrial discovery of Department of Transportation accident reports for portion of highway at which claimant was involved in accident).

Indiana Dep't of Transp. v. Overton, 555 N.E.2d 510 (Ind. Ct. App. 1990) (railroad crossing accident) (plaintiff sought records from state Department of Transportation relating to safety evaluations of railroad crossing; agency refused to produce, asserting 23 U.S.C. 409 and a state statute prohibiting disclosure of public records and forbidding admission of report into evidence or for use for other purposes; court held that federal law did not prohibit the discovery of state agency records relating to safety evaluations of railroad crossing).

Lamitie v. Emerson Elec. Co., 535 N.Y.S.2d 650 (App. Div. 1988) (products case; hot water heater) (holding that communications between manufacturer and consumer product safety commission were not privileged under Consumer Product Safety Act; act applied to public disclosure—not to judicial proceedings; furthermore, manufacturer failed to make a sufficient showing that communications were trade secrets; court would not adopt "critical self-analysis privilege" to protect communications), *appeal dismissed per curiam*, 540 N.E.2d 714 (N.Y. 1989).

Martinolich v. Southern Pac. Transp. Co., 532 So. 2d 435 (La. Ct. App. 1988) (vehicular collision) (holding that federal law did not prohibit discovery of state agency records but merely forbade use of records by a finder of the facts at trial), *cert. denied*, 490 U.S. 1109 (1989).

See also

Anker v. G.D. Searle & Co., 126 F.R.D. 515 (M.D.N.C. 1989).

McFadden v. Norton Co., 118 F.R.D. 625 (D. Neb. 1988).

Taroli v. General Elec. Co., 114 F.R.D. 97 (N.D. Ind. 1987), *aff'd per curiam*, 840 F.2d 920 (7th Cir. 1988).

Foster v. Heard, 757 S.W.2d 464 (Tex. Ct. App. 1988) (pipeline explosion) (holding that investigative report of incident was discoverable).

§ 49 IDENTIFICATION OF DEFENDANT'S OWN DOCUMENTS

Commentary

With growing frequency, defendant manufacturers have sought to compel plaintiffs to produce copies or a list of its own documents which plaintiffs' counsel have or may have access to from the ATLA Exchange or by virtue of counsel's membership in the AIEG.

It is significant that the documents that are the subject of this inquiry are documents that were originally created by the manufacturer and originally in the exclusive possession of the defendant manufacturer but produced to some plaintiff in some other case. The real purpose of this inquiry is to learn the identity of all documents that are "out" and available to plaintiffs' counsel. Once the defendant manufacturer knows this, it will carefully tailor its response to plaintiffs' discovery inquiries so as not to produce any new and damaging material—no matter how relevant—without fear of being caught suppressing discoverable material.

> **First Objection.** The first ground of objection is that the defendant's request for the production of its own internal documents is beyond the scope of discovery. Obviously, the defendant company does not need to "discover" its own documents. Note that there is no threat that they will be surprised by use of these documents at trial. Plaintiff will, of course, furnish the defendant with a complete list of all trial exhibits long before trial.
>
> **Second Objection.** Several cases have noted that the "opinion work-product privilege" arises and attaches to documents which counsel has selected for use in a particular case. This privilege is sometimes referred to as "the selection process" privilege and does embrace counsel in separate cases who work together in a common cause.

Rules

FED. R. CIV. P. 26(b)(1), 26(b)(3).

Secondary Sources

AMERICAN LAW OF PRODUCTS LIABILITY 3D, *supra* § 1, §§ 53:5, 53:14–53:15.

DISCOVERY PROCEEDINGS IN FEDERAL COURT, *supra* § 2, §§ 6.33–6.35, 15.45, 16.1–16.18.

DOMBROFF, *supra* § 3, §§ 2.15–2.25, 12.57.

Fromholz, *Discovery, Evidence, Confidentiality, and Security Problems Associated with the Use of Computer-Based Litigation Support Systems*, 1977 WASH. U. L.Q. 445.

HAYDOCK & HERR, *supra* § 3, §§ 1.6, 4.7.

KIELY, *supra* § 11, §§ 1.17, 1.19, 1.53–1.63, ch. 3.

McCrea, Note, *Civil Procedure—Disclosure of Attorney Work Product Under Federal Rule of Evidence 612: An Abrogation of Work Product Protection?—Sporck v. Peil*, 59 TEMP. L.Q. 1043 (1986).

4 MOORE ET AL., *supra* § 1, ¶¶ 26.63, 26.64.

Sherman & Kinnard, *The Development, Discovery and Use of Computer Support Systems in Achieving Efficiency in Litigation*, 79 COLUM. L. REV. 267 (1979).

White, *Taking the Byte Out of Discovery: Protecting Computer Information from Disclosure*, TRIAL, Mar. 1983, at 44.

8 WRIGHT & MILLER, *supra* § 1, §§ 2021–2028, 2178.

Case Law

Smith v. Bic Corp., 121 F.R.D. 235, 244 (E.D. Pa. 1988), *aff'd in part, rev'd in part*, 869 F.2d 194 (3d Cir. 1989).

Shelton v. American Motors Corp., 805 F.2d 1323, 1328–29 (8th Cir. 1986) (opposing counsel's knowledge of documents relating to subject defect was protected against deposition as work product).

Sporck v. Peil, 759 F.2d 312, 316 (3d Cir.), *cert. denied*, 474 U.S. 903 (1985).

Young v. J.I. Case Co., CA No. 3:90CV00630 (E.D. Va. Mar. 26, 1991).

Elmers v. Honda Motor Co., CA No. 90-25 ERIE (W.D. Pa. Dec. 12, 1991).

McInerney v. Suzuki Co., CA No. 90-0475-CIV-KING (S.D. Fla. June 4, 1990).

James Julian, Inc. v. Raytheon Co., 93 F.R.D. 138, 144 (D. Del. 1982).

Berkey Photo, Inc. v. Eastman Kodak Co., 74 F.R.D. 613 (S.D.N.Y. 1977).

Owens-Corning Fiberglas Corp. v. Caldwell, 818 S.W.2d 749, 751 (Tex. 1991) (holding that compilation of documents selected by attorney was entitled to work-product protection in subsequent litigation involving same issue).

Contra

Bohannon v. Honda Motor Co., 127 F.R.D. 536 (D. Kan. 1989).

§ 50 COORDINATION OF DEFENSE

Commentary

Two or more co-defendants may enter into a joint discovery agreement or a joint defense agreement that may radically affect (1) the conduct of discovery (the agreement may include provisions forbidding any defendant from voluntarily producing documents or other information adverse to a co-defendant or from conducting discovery to develop its own cross-claim casting blame on another defendant or from cross-examining witnesses where to do so might bring to light facts adverse to a co-defendant), and (2) the interest of witnesses and/or parties (such agreements contain provisions forbidding the assertion of cross-claims against co-defendants and the sharing of losses by a prearranged formula without regard to the jury's verdict). Such agreements may also forbid any settlement in the absence of an agreement by all defendants.

Joint defense agreements often include a confidentiality provision forbidding the parties to disclose the existence or the terms of the agreement either to the plaintiff or to the court. *See* Sheridan & McGraw, *A Strategy for Defending Multidefendant Lawsuits*, FOR DEF., Aug. 1983, at 18–27.

Secondary Sources

DISCOVERY PROCEEDINGS IN FEDERAL COURT, *supra* § 2, § 16.2.

HAYDOCK & HERR, *supra* § 3, § 2.5.12.

Case Law

Rastelli v. Goodyear Tire & Rubber Co., 565 N.Y.S.2d 889 (App. Div. 1991), *appeal dismissed*, 580 N.E.2d 759, *and rev'd*, 591 N.E.2d 222 (N.Y. 1992).

Williamson v. Superior Court, 582 P.2d 126 (Cal. 1978) (products case; tire and tire-changing machine) (one of the co-defendant's experts produced a report that defective design of other co-defendant's product caused plaintiff's injury. The two defendants entered into an agreement that provided that the first defendant would withdraw its expert to preclude discovery of the offending report. In return, the co-defendant would indemnify the first against any liability it might incur.).

APPENDIX 2

AUTHORITIES REGARDING THE BENEFIT OF INFORMATION SHARING[1]

This appendix contains quotes and comments regarding cases that involve discovery abuses. In places where the authors of this book have interjected their personal comments, only the first line of the paragraph is indented. Quotes and comments from other sources appear as block quotes.

A. Treatises

1. ABA Report of the Action Commission to Improve the Tort Liability System (1987).

    Recommendation No. 10

    Where information obtained under secrecy agreements (a) indicates risk of hazards to other persons, or (b) reveals evidence relevant to claims based on such hazards, courts should ordinarily permit disclosure of such information, after hearing, to other plaintiffs or to government agencies who agree to be bound by appropriate agreements or court orders to protect the confidentiality of trade secrets and sensitive proprietary information.

2. Bradley, Note, *Some Limits on the Judicial Power to Restrict Dissemination of Discovery,* 44 ME. L. REV. 417, 446–47 (1992).

    A group often excluded from receiving confidential information is other lawyers involved in similar litigation. This exclusion probably generates the greatest discomfort and disadvantage for the parties in the litigation who are restricted by the order. Plaintiffs' counsel in product liability actions involving the same or similar products are typically prevented by such protective orders from discussing the strategic significance of discovered information or interpreting for others the meaning of discovered information. In addition, counsel in similar litigation are handicapped in

---

[1] Citations have been omitted from most quotations.

their effort to determine that their discovery request was comprehensive and cannot ensure that their opponent has responded completely, consistently, and candidly to discovery requests. Particularly in product liability actions—cases that are often technically demanding—the counsel for the defendant company frequently collaborate in preparing their defenses to similar claims whereas the plaintiffs' counsel can be barred from meaningful collaboration.

These factors might not outweigh a significant public interest or some other good cause against sharing of discovery information should such public interest or good cause be shown. However, no meaningful public interest is served in most cases by restricting the sharing of confidential information among litigants in similar cases, and many courts have ruled that the risk of sharing discovery information does not constitute by itself good cause for a protective order prohibiting dissemination. Moreover, adherence to the *Seattle Times* decision does not require a restriction on the sharing of information among litigants.

Indeed, the sharing of discovery among litigants in different cases may serve the public interest. It may foster speed and minimize discovery costs in litigation, both of which fall within the goals of procedure embodied in both Maine and Federal Rule of Civil Procedure 1. One federal district court denying a protective order observed that such sharing even reduced the cost of the discovery process to the party from whom the discovery was obtained, namely, the movant for the order.

3. Bratvold, Note, *Protective Orders and the Use of Discovery Materials Following* Seattle Times, 71 MINN. L. REV. 171 (1986).

Focusing on the dissemination of discovery materials by and between legal counsel and the parties (excluding disclosure to the general public or the media), *id.* at 176 n.18, the author lists several reasons why information sharing of discovery materials would be desirable including: (1) anonymous system of verification to discourage withholding of discovery information and (2) reduction of cost associated with extensive "rediscovery." *Id.* at 174.

> *Strong policy considerations favor dissemination of discovery materials when the materials are sought for use in similar or related litigation.* The Supreme Court recognized a right to gather litigation materials in *Ex Parte Uppercu*. *Uppercu* involved an action to gain access to sealed depositions and exhibits from a resolved case. The Court granted the petitioner access to the depositions and documents, declaring a "new right" to obtain evidence. Since *Uppercu*, recognition of the right to gather litigation materials has become common in trial and appellate courts. *As a result, courts have frequently found the right dispositive in denying protective orders that prohibit either attorney collaboration or nonparty access to discovery materials.*
> [at 196–97 (emphasis added)]

Taken as a whole, the decisions which find that the right of access to litigation materials is dispositive emphasize two themes. Protective order petitions which are based on a desire to prevent access to litigation materials needed in parallel litigation will usually not be granted.

The second theme found in right to litigation materials cases suggests that justice and fair play demand dissemination to third parties when to do otherwise would leave the parties with unequal access to information relevant to the case. These inequities take many forms, for example, lack of access to limited expert witnesses, time wasted taking numerous depositions of individuals already deposed upon similar areas of inquiry, ignorance of a witness' past testimony, and the inability to match the expertise of counsel who have routinely litigated the same issues and similar facts.
[at 196 n.124 (emphasis added)]

4. *Proceedings of the Fifty-First Judicial Conference of the District of Columbia Circuit*, 134 F.R.D. 321, 389–90 (1991).

The reason it [proliferation of secrecy orders] is such a terrible problem is several-fold. First, the immediate effect that it has on the judicial system is that everybody who represents the plaintiffs has to reinvent the wheel. The defendants know this. That is why they ask for it.

The basic result is people with claims can't get into court because they can't afford the cost of discovery. Other people with claims can't get into court because they don't even know they have claims. The whole thing has been hushed up and kept secret.

Other people who have claims get into court, they do get a lawyer, they prosecute the claims; but they all recover less money than they should because each person has to pay the same cost over and over and over again of getting hold of discovery. That is just the effect of the system on specific plaintiffs.

5. Coon, Comment, *Common Law or First Amendment Right of Access to Sealed Settlement Agreements*, 54 J. AIR L. & COM. 577, 578 (1988).

[T]he right to seal records is not absolute. In fact, the right may be largely illusory and uncertain, and is often the subject of abuse.

6. Doggett & Mucchetti, *Public Access to Public Courts: Discouraging Secrecy in the Public Interest*, 69 TEX. L. REV. 643 (1991).

Concealing information when its release would enhance government accountability or avert danger to health and safety sacrifices the public interest and jeopardizes confidence in the judicial system. Unfortunately, sealing orders, protective orders, and confidentiality agreements are increasingly employed to stifle public scrutiny.
[at 644]

This support of greater access to judicial records is consistent with the broader notion of affording access to courts generally.
[at 648]

Court orders have also prevented law enforcement and regulatory agencies, as well as the public, from acquiring critical information.
[at 649]

[A]ccess to judicial records encourages greater integrity from attorneys and their clients. If documents are made public in one case, a party is less likely to deny their existence in later litigation. Even if the materials are lost, their former availability increases the likelihood of their discovery from other sources.
[at 650]

Knowledge is power. Information's free flow allows citizens to govern their fate and fortune. When its passage is arrested or reduced to a trickle, control over our lives is wrested from our hands. If the public is to make intelligent decisions about our courts, our laws and the effectiveness of those officials that enforce them, a presumption of openness should govern.
[at 655]

A party may not condition release of the documents on the return or destruction of any copies made. Because public access is mandated by the Rule, access cannot be conditioned by agreements between counsel. When making unsealed documents available to the public, opposing counsel should not be restricted by a requirement that other parties be notified of those with whom information is shared.
[at 668]

7. Durst, *Confidentiality Agreements in Product Liability Litigation*, 15 TRIAL LAW. Q. 36 (1983).

Opportunities are frequently available to share information, such as in automobile defect cases, toxic torts, and drug litigation. *Courts uniformly hold that the sharing of information between plaintiffs' attorneys furthers the purpose of the discovery rules*, avoiding duplication of effort, decreasing the cost of litigation, and promoting just determinations on the merits. This secures the just, speedy and inexpensive determination of actions in accordance with Rule 1 of the Federal Rules of Civil Procedure.
[at 37 (emphasis added)]

Minimizing discovery costs improves the accessibility and economy of justice. The evidentiary facts necessary to prove a defect in one case may be identical to that of another case, where the same defect is involved. Each plaintiff should not have to discover anew basic evidence that other plaintiffs have already uncovered.
[at 39]

8. FitzGerald, *Sealed v. Sealed: A Public Court System Going Secretly Private*, 6 J.L. & POL. 381 (1990).

   Secrecy in the judicial process is necessary in certain situations, but it greatly reduces the public's ability to monitor effectively and understand the judicial process. As a result, the political legitimacy of the courts is undermined. Unfortunately, the incidence for secrecy in the judicial process appears to be on the rise, particularly in the complex litigation area. Equally disturbing is the trend for parties to condition any pre-trial settlement on the court's granting a total sealing order covering all materials in the court's possession.
   [at 381–82]

   This desire for secrecy is in direct conflict with the information gathering purpose of discovery under the Federal Rules of Civil Procedure.
   [at 385]

   Indeed, protective orders by definition restrict the flow of information and implicate first amendment concerns.
   [at 387]

   Confidence in the system's fairness breaks down when different plaintiffs with identical causes of action receive disparate results. Judicial secrecy is an open invitation to such widely varying outcomes. Even the sealing of discovery materials can have this effect. For example, in a complex products liability suit, a particular plaintiff's counsel may not have the degree of expertise necessary to request the one "smoking gun" document out of the hundreds of thousands available. A different plaintiff's lawyer may have fortuitously requested the vital document, but he or she is often barred by a secrecy order from sharing the information with other attorneys. This may result in one plaintiff losing a case for which the other has recovered fully.
   [at 398–99]

9. Friedman, Note, *Mass Products Liability Litigation: A Proposal for Dissemination of Discovered Material Covered by a Protective Order*, 60 N.Y.U. L. REV. 1137, 1137–38 (1985).

   Despite the opportunities discovery affords to products liability plaintiffs, the discovery-related problems of expense, delay, and injustice can be severe obstacles. If the expense—often tens of thousands of dollars—exceeds the anticipated recovery, an injured party will pursue his claim only if he is willing and able to sustain a net financial loss. Even if discovery costs do not exceed the anticipated recovery, they often significantly reduce the amount of money a successful plaintiff actually receives. Further, in addition to expense, plaintiffs may be hindered by extreme delay and related injustice.

> *These problems can be ameliorated in products liability actions in which several different plaintiffs bring separate lawsuits against the same defendant alleging similar causes of action, by allowing plaintiffs to sell or share discovered materials among themselves. The practice of establishing information markets among plaintiffs has been successful in many instances, and absent evidence of bad faith or a protective order, the practice has been upheld.*
> [emphasis added]

The article analyzes the plaintiff's interest in information sharing in complex products litigation in the context of FED. R. CIV. P. 1: (1) expense, (2) time, (3) just result, and concludes, in effect, that an order forbidding the sharing of information between plaintiffs with similar causes would have a chilling effect on both the individual plaintiff and his counsel. *See id.* at 1139–42.

10. Guénégo, Note, *Trends in Protective Orders Under Federal Rule of Civil Procedure 26(c): Why Some Cases Fumble While Others Score*, 60 FORDHAM L. REV. 541, 547–48 (1991).

> These courts assert that although discovery is not a public component of civil trials, Rule 26(c) presumes public access to discovery materials unless good cause is shown. Courts and commentators further reason that cooperation among litigants in connected, albeit separate lawsuits, better promotes Rule 1 interests and therefore discovery sharing cannot constitute any part of the defendant's good cause demonstration. This practice allows parties to obtain vital information without paying the prohibitive costs associated with formal discovery.

> The time and money expended trying to compel a reluctant party to come forward with the requested information is obviated by access to previous discovery. Moreover, the party granted access to the material has the benefit of examining information that has been analyzed already by a similarly positioned party. Communication between related litigants can be established, enabling attorneys to share vital yet nondiscoverable material like the settlement value of a particular case and the availability of experts. Finally, through the use of shared discovery, potential litigants are better able to analyze the merits of their claims, presumably equipping them with sufficient information to draft pleadings more accurately.

11. Hare et al., *Confidentiality Orders in Products Liability Cases*, 13 AM. J. TRIAL ADVOC. 597 (1989).

> Since the defendant possesses infinitely superior knowledge and resources, the need for cooperation among plaintiffs' attorneys is even greater than that of defendants. The sharing of information among plaintiffs' attorneys has four main goals: (1) to minimize the advantage of the defendant and allow the plaintiff to adequately prepare his case, (2) to enhance the speed and efficacy of the discovery process, (3) to provide a mechanism for verifying the accuracy of a manufacturer's response to the plaintiff's discovery

requests, and (4) to reduce the cost of preparing each case.
[at 599–600]

Courts should refrain from granting overly restrictive confidentiality orders that deny the plaintiff access to a cooperative discovery mechanism. The needs of the victim of a defective product clearly outweigh the defendant manufacturer's unlikely speculation that the plaintiff might leak the discovered information to the defendant's competitors.
[at 612]

12. HAYDOCK & HERR, DISCOVERY PRACTICE § 1.9.3. (2d ed. 1988 & Supp. 1992).

    Distribution of discovery information to other parties engaged in similar litigation to the action in which the discovery takes place presents different issues [from the issues in *Seattle Times*] to the courts. Many defendants in multiple-claimant litigation seek to have all discovery materials produced subject to a protective order preventing dissemination of the material. *Courts are increasingly reluctant to prevent parties with similar interests from sharing information.* In one recent case [*Swenholt v. Merrell-Dow Pharmaceuticals, Inc.*, CA No. 80-2874 (D.D.C. Jan. 16, 1984)] the court noted that free dissemination of information concerning an allegedly dangerous drug would promote effective and inexpensive determination of the other actions involving the same issues, and therefore denied a protective order.
    [at 75 (emphasis added)]

13. IMWINKELRIED & BLUMOFF, PRETRIAL DISCOVERY: STRATEGY AND TACTICS §12.09 (1986 & Supp. 1992).

    Third, even when the moving party appears to have met the good cause requirement, make certain the judge is aware of the potential hidden burdens that the order may impose upon you. For example, assume you represent plaintiff in product litigation and that similar cases are being adjudicated elsewhere. The manufacturer, alleging trade secrets, wants a protective order to prohibit you from communicating with other attorneys, in effect requiring you to prepare your suit "in a vacuum." [Gilbert & Neumann, *Protective Orders: How to Counter Them*, TRIAL, Nov. 1987, at 54, 55] At the same time, defense counsel are coordinating their efforts nationwide. [Gilbert & Neumann, *Protective Orders: How to Counter Them*, TRIAL, Nov. 1987, at 54, 55; Herman, *Secrecy, Discovery Abuse Breed Unethical Conduct*, NAT'L L.J., Aug. 1, 1988, at 18, 19] Under these circumstances, one court was "convinced that the magnitude of the disparity of resources between [the] parties, plus the sophisticated and calculated exploitation of the situation by the defendant, approaches a denial of due process." [*Thayer v. Liggett & Myers Tobacco Co.*, CA No. 5314 (W.D. Mich. 1970), *quoted in* Gilbert & Neumann, *Protective Orders: How to Counter Them*, TRIAL, Nov. 1987, at 54, 56; Herman, *Secrecy, Discovery Abuse Breed Unethical Conduct*, NAT'L L.J., Aug. 1, 1988, at 18, 20, lists a number of hidden burdens that prohibitions

on document sharing impose on plaintiffs, including the need to repeat the same discovery in case after case with attending costs—and—the fact that "[c]osts to defendants are spread among claims and decrease, whereas costs to plaintiffs escalate," (corporate manufacturers') ability to form national and regional defense teams, among others]
[Supp. 1989 at 73]

14. KIELY, Preparing Products Liability Cases (1986 & Supp. 1989).

The entry of a protective order can significantly impede counsel's efforts to achieve a detailed understanding of the defendant's document generating and decision making process. The major goal of such orders is to deprive plaintiff's counsel of the opportunity to consult with more experienced lawyers. This consultation may take the form of document tutorials or the exchange of information. Corporate concern over the rippling effects of information sharing is the major factor in their routine requests for these orders.
[§ 7.21, at 224–25 (emphasis added)]

The motion for protective order has traditionally been disfavored, with the burden on the moving party to show some plainly adequate reason for the order.
[§ 7.21, at 224–25]

It is very difficult for a sole plaintiff to complete discovery in a complex products liability case when faced with a corporate opponent which has significant financial superiority and resources. Corporations should not be allowed to obtain a protective order casually without a showing of good and sufficient cause. This is particularly so when such an action is indirect conflict with the spirit of state and federal discovery rules.
[§ 7.23, at 227]

The growth of such organizations (plaintiff attorney support groups) is increasingly seen by courts as a positive factor in achieving the goal of efficient dispute resolution.
[§ 7.23, at 228]

15. Kiernan & Huttler, *More Public Access to Discovery Documents?*, LITIG., Fall 1991, at 19, 22.

[O]nly the most avid defender of confidentiality would require each new plaintiff to reinvent the wheel against a defendant that has already gathered and produced substantial litigation material.

16. Lawrence, Comment, *The Value of Copyright Law as a Deterrent to Discovery Abuse*, 138 U. PA. L. REV. 549 (1989).

The courts permit this practice [discovery sharing] in an attempt to fulfill the requirement of Federal Rule of Civil Procedure 1 that the rules "be construed to secure the just, speedy, and inexpensive determination of every action." Discovery sharing is seen as a means of reducing discovery expenses for both the plaintiff and the defendant. Furthermore, the

reduced role of the courts in various discovery proceedings conceivably promotes judicial economy.
[at 555]

A further merit of discovery sharing is its utility in detecting "stonewalling" tactics by the defendant.
[at 556]

17. Manual for Complex Litigation (Second) (1985).

Such modifications [of existing protective orders] may be needed to facilitate the discovery plans of related litigation. As discussed in § 21.422, substantial savings in time and expense may often be achieved by using information gathered in similar litigation.
[§ 21.431, at 53]

Protective orders may, of course, authorize disclosure of confidential documents to counsel in other related cases. Moreover, the terms of a protective order ordinarily do not prevent the party who furnished the confidential information from being ordered to produce the same information in another case.
[§ 21.431, at 53 n.61 (emphasis added)]

[A]voiding duplicative discovery. Techniques to coordinate discovery and avoid duplication, such as those discussed in §§ 21.422, 21.443, 21.444, and 21.465, should be considered. In particular, litigants should cooperate in conducting common discovery and establishing joint document depositories and should not be permitted to repeat interrogatories already answered or request documents already available from other sources. Notices for depositions may be filed or cross-filed in related cases to make the depositions usable in all cases. *Relevant discovery already completed should ordinarily be made available to litigants in the other cases.*
[§ 31.13, at 258 (emphasis added)]

See Wilk v. American Medical Ass'n, 635 F.2d 1295 (7th Cir. 1980). "Where an appropriate modification of a protective order can place private litigants in a position they would otherwise reach only after repetition of another's discovery, such modification can be denied only where it would tangibly prejudice substantial rights of the party opposing modification. . . . Once such prejudice is demonstrated, however, the district court has broad discretion in judging whether that injury outweighs the benefits of any possible modification of the protective order."
[§ 31.13, at 258 n.41]

18. Marcus, *Myth and Reality in Protective Order Litigation*, 69 CORNELL L. REV. 1 (1983).

By far the most important justification for granting nonparties access to discovery information is their need to use the information in other litigation. The issue generally arises when a nonparty asks the court that entered a protective order

to modify the order to permit disclosure to him. Under these circumstances, modification furthers, rather than undermines, the policies underlying rule 1.
[at 41 (emphasis added)]

After quoting from Justice Holmes's opinion in *Ex parte Uppercu*, 239 U.S. 434, 440 (1915), Professor Marcus states:

The wisdom of this approach [modification of sealing order to permit access to material produced in an earlier and similar case] is confirmed by the large number of cases granting nonparties access to discovery material pertinent to their litigation.
[at 42]

19. Marcus, *The Discovery Confidentiality Controversy*, 1991 U. ILL. L. REV. 457.

[A]rguments by plaintiffs' attorneys that confidentiality orders unduly hamper case preparation by preventing needed consultation with other attorneys provide reasons for flexibility in allowing such discussion of confidential materials obtained through discovery. Moreover, flexibility in allowing access to other plaintiffs who need the material as evidence in their cases seems to be warranted.
[at 458]

Some argue that material turned over through discovery should be public because it is disclosed as part of a judicial proceeding that is publicly created and funded. Having been unearthed through the use of the public system, they conclude, discovery information should be available to the public.
[at 470]

Courts have long recognized the validity of granting other litigants access to material obtained under protective orders when that material is relevant to their claims and properly would be discoverable in their cases.
[at 493]

Indeed, in product liability cases there is a particularly good reason for allowing some sharing of information gleaned from discovery. A prime objection to protective orders in such cases is that they cut off the ability of plaintiffs' counsel to fully prepare their cases. Noting that collaboration among counsel for defendants is frequent in such cases, plaintiffs' lawyers argue that a protective order that prohibits consultation with other plaintiffs' lawyers about the meaning and implications of material obtained through discovery interferes with their ability to prepare their own cases.
[at 495]

More generally, however, it seems that the courts continue to recognize that access for other plaintiffs should be allowed whether or not it is necessary to facilitate the preparation of the case before them because such sharing saves the courts and the litigants time and money. In addition, sharing is

consistent with a settled doctrine exempting exchange of information between litigants with a common litigation opponent from the risk that the exchange will be deemed a waiver of privileges. . . . Although the plaintiffs' bar has an understandable temptation to overstate the likelihood that later plaintiffs will be unable to uncover such misconduct without access to discovery in earlier cases, it is true that there have been instances of perjury that were unearthed by comparison of deposition testimony in different cases. [*See, e.g., Harre v. A.H. Robins Co.*, 750 F.2d 1501 (11th Cir. 1985)].
[at 496]

Concluding that other litigants often may be afforded access to material covered by a protective order does not solve some tricky problems of implementation, however, and care in the handling of access seems appropriate. As a minimum measure, a court might limit access to affiliated counsel assisting primary counsel in preparing the case for trial. A more flexible approach would permit the sharing of information with any counsel for other plaintiffs who agreed to be bound by the protective order themselves. Substantially greater dissemination would follow were the court to authorize inclusion of discovered material in data banks maintained by organizations such as the American Trial Lawyers Association.
[at 498]

20. Mathy, *Protective Orders and Third-Party Government Access to Civil Discovery: A Modest Proposal*, 9 HOFSTRA L. REV. 129 (1980–1981).

The mere fact that an opposing litigant wishes to share discovered materials with other potential or actual litigants will not justify entry of a protective order unless a movant can demonstrate that the case and the fruits of its discovery are being exploited solely to assist the related litigation.
[at 158]

After discussing *Milsen Co. v. Southland Corp.*, Professor Mathy states:

Although this holding is the strongest statement in favor of the entry of protective orders to prevent disclosure of discovered materials to nonparties, the opinion does not contain a description of the documents sought to be discovered. Since the "diversity and breadth of the documents requested" were important features of the holding, the extent of the rule is not easily ascertained, and the precedential value of the decision is thereby diminished. Further, the holding flows from an appreciation of the federal discovery rules different from that of *Johnson & Johnson* and *Johnson Foils*. The *Milsen* court concluded first, that the purpose of discovery is to enable parties to prepare their own cases and second, that the limitation in the use of documents to the case at hand could not therefore unduly hinder the plaintiff. Given the fact that a presumption of nondisclosure does not adequately reflect the policies of Rule 1 of the Federal Rules of Civil Procedure, the court's conclusion that plaintiffs will share the materials with litigating

third parties may not be sufficient reason to prevent disclosure. [citing *Milsen Co. v. Southland Corp.*, 1972 Trade Cas. (CCH) ¶ 73,865, at 91,629 (N.D. Ill. 1972)]
[at 158–59]

Professor Mathy's analysis of *Milsen* proved to be correct. The same court that originally decided *Milsen* (the Northern District of Illinois) later found that the holding should no longer be regarded as good law in light of the Seventh Circuit's opinion in *Wilk v. American Medical Ass'n*, 635 F.2d 1295 (7th Cir. 1980); *Adams v. Schmid Labs., Inc.*, No. 86 C 4783, 1987 U.S. Dist. LEXIS 2564 (N.D. Ill. Mar. 31, 1987); *see also Deford v. Schmid Prods. Co.*, 120 F.R.D. 648, 654 (D. Md. 1987).

21. Martin & Thomas, *Controlling Discovery and Guarding Confidential Data*, THE BRIEF, Winter 1988, at 48, 51.

The courts have consistently held that a plaintiff's desire to disclose documents to plaintiffs in other, similar litigation is not good cause under the rules: "in addition to the abstract virtues of sunlight as a disinfectant, access in such cases materially eases the tasks of courts and litigants and speeds up what may otherwise be a lengthy process." Thus, at least under current case law, a motion under Rule 26(c) cannot rest on such a basis.

John Martin is Associate General Counsel of the Ford Motor Co. in Dearborn, Michigan. John Thomas is a senior attorney with Ford, specializing in appellate matters. This article is based on a paper delivered at the 1987 ABA Annual Meeting in San Francisco.

22. Note, *Nonparty Access to Discovery Materials in the Federal Courts*, 94 HARV. L. REV. 1085 (1981).

[P]rotective orders that restrict an attorney's ability to consult with experts about discovered materials may unjustifiably obstruct his case preparation.
[at 1087]

Dissemination by discovering parties of fruits that are not subject to any protective order may often be efficient and desirable. [Here follows a discussion of the *Parsons v. General Motors Corp.* and *Patterson v. Ford Motor Co.* cases.] Absent a bad faith motive for litigation, most courts agree with *Parsons* and *Patterson* in allowing disclosure of discovery fruits to similarly situated litigants. Apart from the benefits to the collaborating parties, the judicial resources saved by precluding duplicative adjudication of discovery request by subsequent parties amply justify transmittal of discovery fruits to similarly situated litigants.
[at 1096–97]

Considerations that warrant second-degree discovery in general apply with even greater force to the transfer from one litigant to another of analysis derived from discovery materials. Repetitive discovery procedures are avoided by free transfer of materials. A particular advantage of second-

degree discovery is that documents and materials from first-degree discovery may have been organized by the original discoverer, thus sparing the second-degree discoverer the potentially massive expense of organizing discovery materials. *Courts should allow and encourage the transfer of such litigation support systems.*
[at 1097–98 (emphasis added)]

The footnote to the last sentence reads as follows:

The value of analyses is such that should there be a protective order preventing their transfer to similarly situated litigants, modification of the order is justified by the same considerations that generally justify modification of a protective order to accommodate litigants.
[at 1098 n.67]

23. Béchamps, Note, *Sealed Out-of-Court Settlements: When Does the Public Have a Right to Know?*, 66 NOTRE DAME L. REV. 117 (1990).

A system that limits access to court documents not on the basis of the information they contain, but on the basis of the label they bear, is not conducive to the goals of confidence, understanding, and respect. It projects an image of secrecy and distorted truth around what should be an open judicial system. A better rule would recognize a general right of access to all documents filed with the court limited by exceptions pertaining to subject matter.
[at 124]

Openness plays a significant role in the function of civil, as well as criminal, trials. It equally promotes true and accurate fact-finding by discouraging perjury and encouraging witnesses to come forward with new information.
[at 134]

Openness is an important feature of the American judicial system. Not only does it serve to check the exercise of judicial authority and to provide an understanding of how the legal system operates, but more importantly it fosters an appearance of fairness and promotes confidence in the system. When cases presented for resolution in the public forum are surrounded with secrecy, there is a natural tendency to question whether justice is being equitably administered. The public and private interests in settling cases without litigation should not be allowed to compromise the importance of a generally open judicial system. Changes are needed to halt the increasingly common practice of sealing the court records of settled cases and enforcing covenants of silence.
[at 156]

24. 2 PETERS & PETERS, AUTOMOTIVE ENGINEERING AND LITIGATION 833–34 (1991 & Supp. 1992).

The argument is often whether the proper protections in a particular case are as inclusive as those sought by the defendant. *If the idea is only to preserve competitive advantage, why is there concern over dissemination to a third-party litigator or expert whose business is not the manufacturing of products?* Is the sharing of information by attorneys and expert witnesses a legitimate basis for issuing a protective order? Numerous courts have considered the issue of whether a protective order should issue for the purpose of precluding information exchange to third parties who have no interest in the litigation, i.e., other plaintiff's attorneys. The courts have strongly stated that justice is furthered by such exchanges:

> The plaintiffs' attorneys discovery information exchange group reduces the effort and expense inflicted on all parties including Ford, by repetitive and unnecessary discovery. In this era of ever expanding litigation expense, any means of minimizing discovery costs improves the accessibility and economy of justice. If as asserted, a single design defect is then the evidentiary facts to prove it must be identical, or nearly so, in all of the cases. Each plaintiff should not have to undertake to discovery [sic] anew the basic evidence that other plaintiffs have uncovered. To do so would be tantamount to holding that each litigant who wishes to ride a taxi to court must undertake the expense of inventing the wheel. Efficient administration of justice requires that courts encourage, not hamstring, information exchanges such as that here involved. [*Ward v. Ford*, 93 F.R.D. 579 (D. Col. 1982)]

At least seven other courts have spoken with equal force and conviction about the desirability of information exchange among plaintiffs' attorney. [*Waelde v. Merck, Sharp & Dohme*, 94 F.R.D. 27, 28 (E.D. Mich. 1981); *Patterson v. Ford Motor Co.*, 85 F.R.D. 152,154 (W.D. Tex. 1980); *Upjohn Antibiotic Cleocin Prod. Liab. Litig.*, 81 F.R.D. 482, 484 (E.D. Mich. 1979), aff'd, 664 F.2d 114 (6th Cir. 1981); *Johnson Foils, Inc. v. Huyck Corp.*, 61 F.R.D. 405, 410 (N.D.N.Y. 1973); *Williams v. Johnson & Johnson*, 50 F.R.D. 31, 32 (S.D.N.Y. 1970); *Farnum v. G.D. Searle & Co.*, 339 N.W.2d 384, 389 (Iowa 1983); *Brandimarti v. Caterpillar, Inc.*, CA No. G.D. 83-12468 (Allegheny County, Pa. Ct. C.P. Oct. 8, 1985)] Far from being an inherently suspect activity, judges have welcomed the information exchange as furthering the goals of modern rules of discovery:

> Such collaboration among plaintiffs' attorneys would come squarely within the aims of the Federal Rules of Civil Procedure—to secure the just, speedy and inexpensive determination of every action . . . there is nothing inherently culpable about sharing information obtained through discovery. The availability of the discovery information may reduce time and money which must be expended in similar proceedings, and may allow for effective, speedy and efficient representation. [*Patterson v. Ford Motor Co.*, 85 F.R.D. 152, 154 (W.D. Tex. 1980)]

Even where plaintiffs' attorneys charge fees for copies of documents, courts have found the exchange is an ethical activity. "Without more, the sharing of fees between attorneys collaborating in similar cases and the collaboration itself both seem reasonable on their face." [*Williams*, 50 F.R.D. at 33]

25. Pownell, Comment, *The First Amendment and Pretrial Discovery Hearings: When Should the Public and Press Have Access?*, 36 UCLA L. REV. 609, 622 n.70 (1989).

    The Federal Rules assume that pretrial discovery is open to public scrutiny and that information obtained through the discovery processes may be freely disseminated.

26. RAEDER, FEDERAL PRETRIAL PRACTICE § 19.2, at 435 (1987).

    In fact, restrictions on the exchange of such discovery with other federal or state plaintiffs in related litigation matter are viewed as a hindrance to the appropriate dispositions of these cases, since they interfere with the formation of attorneys' information exchange groups to share discovery.

27. REPORT OF THE FEDERAL COURTS STUDY COMMITTEE 103 (Apr. 2, 1990).

    On the one hand, using protective orders to preserve the confidentiality of sensitive information (such as trade secrets) may expedite discovery by reducing concern about publicity.

28. Schultheis & Bryant, *Fighting Protective and Secrecy Orders*, in ANATOMY OF A PERSONAL INJURY LAWSUIT 139 (James S. Rogers ed., 3rd ed. 1991).

    Some reasons to resist protective orders are:

    First, if a protective order is entered, it will be virtually impossible to determine whether the defendant's discovery responses are truthful. There is no reason to assume that the defendant, who is being sued for injuring or killing people, will now be honest and thorough in responding to discovery, even when represented by honorable defense counsel.

    Second, signing a protective order will *not* enable full discovery to be obtained more quickly. The defendant will still avoid producing incriminating information. The protective order will simply make it harder to learn the truth.

    Third, a protective order will limit your ability to fully investigate facts that could help you develop your case or rebut the defendant's case. Secrecy orders can prevent the review of materials by those who may be able to impeach the defendant's witnesses, such as former employees, subcontractors, consultants, and joint or subsequent tort feasors who may not be parties in the case.

    Fourth, protective orders effectively require every victim's lawyer to reinvent the wheel. They restrict the sharing of information and, therefore, restrict effective and efficient case preparation.

    Fifth, the defendant and the defendant's insurer may lose their motivation to settle the claim expeditiously once a binding restrictive protective order has been entered.

Sixth, defendants generally draft protective orders in a way that requires plaintiffs to reveal the identity of consulting experts or other privileged work product.

For example, the order might require you to list each person who will be permitted to see and review the protected documents, a list that could include consulting, nontestifying experts. If defense counsel gives a court such a proposed order, ask for a provision that requires the defendant to reveal the same information. If any disclosure is ultimately required, it may be limited to the court only.

Seventh, protective orders inhibit your ability to prepare fact witnesses for deposition and to refresh their recollection for trial. When defense counsel asks the doctor to admit he would have prescribed drug X even if the manufacturer had warned about its side effects, it is helpful for the doctor to know what the defendant knew about these risks, the availability of a safer drug, or other facts pertinent to the answer that a treating doctor is not likely to know unless the plaintiff is free to share information with him.

Eighth, an overly broad protective order has a chilling effect on the willingness of experts to assist the plaintiff. If the expert will be bound by the protective order's terms, he may be disqualified in other cases or, worse, held in contempt. Defendants in other cases will claim that the expert witness is not at liberty to disclose all of the information forming the grounds for his opinions and that he cannot be adequately cross-examined. Or they will challenge the expert's refusal to answer certain questions, then convince an unsophisticated discovery master to impose sanctions.
[at 142–43]

Discovery sharing advances the just, efficient, and economical administration of justice, exhorted by Rule 1, while simultaneously reducing the time, effort, and expense involved in conducting discovery. . . . The need for discovery sharing is a reason to *deny* entry of a protective order, not a reason to *grant* one.
[at 156]

29. Sherman & Kinnard, *Federal Court Discovery in the 80's—Making the Rules Work*, 95 F.R.D. 245 (1983).

Protective orders can have the effect of increasing the cost of other litigation by preventing the reuse of information and requiring costly and time-consuming duplication of discovery. This can affect a significant number of suits that have common defendants or related issues or parties in such areas as anti-trust, mass disaster, product liability, the environment, securities fraud, commercial litigation, civil rights, and employment discrimination.
[at 285]

Thus, where there is, or is likely to be, other litigation involving similar issues or

parties, courts should recognize the potential savings in avoiding duplicative discovery. . . . Similarly, discovery duplication that would impose burdens on third parties such as expert witnesses would also weigh against limiting future use.
[at 287 (emphasis added)]

Referring to a case [*Litton Sys., Inc. v. AT&T Co.*, CA #76-2512 (S.D.N.Y. May 17, 1979)] in which the district court denied the government's petition for modification for the reason that expedited preparation does not by itself constitute justification for modifying a protective order, the authors comment as follows:

This decision clearly seems incorrect. Denying modification of a protective order simply because only one side in the litigation would be able to advance its pretrial preparation, when no threat to a confidentiality interest of the common defendant was shown, is contrary to the efficiency policies of Rule 1. The disposition of this case reflects a lack of judicial sensitivity both for efficiency concerns in discovery sharing and for the complications engendered by the involvement of a number of different courts in the resolution.
[at 291]

30. Smith, Note, *Anti-Dissemination Orders in Product Liability Suits*, 5 AM. J. TRIAL ADVOC. 507 (1982).

While this concealment of information does protect the defendant from adverse publicity, it is most damaging to other individuals whose claims for relief arise out of the same subject matter, but over a period of time and throughout the marketplace. Inherent in this situation is a similarity of issues which is not subject to class action or multidistrict litigation. *The restraint against the communication of this vital information requires that the various plaintiffs, who ordinarily retain different attorneys because they are located in various jurisdictions, duplicate the arduous discovery efforts necessary to provide the factual issues common to all of the other claims.*
[at 509 (emphasis added)]

Plaintiffs should be in a position to exchange information with other litigants with similar claims in order to develop their cases more fully.
[at 513]

31. Smith, *A Practical Approach to Rule 26(c) Protective Orders in Aviation Litigation*, 56 J. AIR L. & COM. 765 (1991).

A fundamental tenet of American jurisprudence is that the courts and their records are a matter of public record. Secrecy is the exception, not the rule. Furthermore, the discovery rules were designed to "make a trial less a game of blind man's buff and more a fair contest with the basic issues and facts disclosed *to the fullest practicable extent.*" [citing *United States v. Procter & Gamble Co.*, 356 U.S. 677, 682 (1958) (emphasis added)]

The Federal Rules of Civil Procedure create a statutory presumption in favor of open discovery, extending even to those materials not used at trial. A wide use of protective orders conflicts with that fundamental and important principle of openness. Consequently, the Rules limit the use of protective orders and the scope of information that should be kept from the public.
[at 768]

Thus, under the basic principles of our system, the parties should communicate in an honest effort to minimize the amount of information protected without attempting to "straight-jacket the discovery procedure . . . on the basis of speculative assumptions." [citing *Neonex Int'l Ltd. v. Norris Grain Co.*, 338 F. Supp. 845, 854 (S.D.N.Y. 1972)]
[at 768–69]

The limitations inherent in some protective orders restrict the ability of a party to pursue an action at law. The most common limitation concerns sharing the fruits of discovery with other attorneys involved in similar litigation. Sharing of data is encouraged by the courts because it is consistent with "the just, speedy, and inexpensive determination of every action." Courts have thus rejected restrictions on the sharing of information as adverse to the proper function of the judicial system. Broad protective orders that absolutely forbid such exchange of information are inconsistent with the Federal Rules of Civil Procedure and the underlying public interest in an efficient judicial system. [citing FED. R. CIV. P. 1]
[at 780–81]

32. Thomas, *Public Courts and Private Litigation: Proposed Changes to the Use of Confidentiality and Sealing Orders in Civil Cases*, 37 WAYNE L. REV. 1761 (1991).

A confidentiality order or a sealing order imposed in a civil case can affect members of the public who have been similarly injured by preventing information sharing between similarly-situated plaintiffs. It is this argument that has attracted much debate in the legal community and has led the Federal Courts Study Committee to recommend that federal courts anticipate modifying court orders to allow such information sharing between parties.

Sharing of discovery information allows plaintiffs to 1) confirm defendant's information with previously obtained materials, or 2) spare the expense of obtaining the documents themselves, or 3) use it for purposes of collateral estoppel. The federal courts have generally held that a transfer of discovery information among plaintiffs with various suits against a defendant is not improper.

* * *

Some assert that information sharing between plaintiffs is also needed to prevent deception by a defendant. The failure of defendants to turn over

relevant information appears in a number of product liability cases. The Texas Supreme Court has suggested that when companies are named in a number of suits concerning the same subject matter, the sharing of information between plaintiffs makes it more likely that the defendant will be truthful.
[at 1767 n.22]

Other interests that the courts have considered are the increased efficiency of the court system resulting from the sharing of discovery information between similarly situated plaintiffs and the specific public benefits that might arise from the release of information.
[at 1775]

The Federal Rules of Civil Procedure do not forbid the dissemination of discovery information between similarly-situated plaintiffs, and some courts have modified a protective order to allow similarly-situated plaintiffs to have access to information. In some cases, the courts have encouraged such information sharing as a means to facilitate discovery and relieve the burden on plaintiffs.
[at 1791]

33. Thompson, Note, *Protective Orders: Sword and Shield in the War of Discovery*, 12 AM. J. TRIAL ADVOC. 483, 484 (1989).

Prior to the adoption of the broad rules of discovery, civil trials were said to be "carried on in the dark." Fairness gave way to cunning and greater resources, while surprise became the trial lawyer's constant companion. Under the "sporting theory of justice," parties were forced to obtain information about their opponent's cases primarily from the pleadings or by whatever means of private investigation they could afford. As the situation worsened, it became apparent that disclosure, before trial, of all relevant information in the possession of one's adversary would best serve justice.

34. Timmins, Note, *Protective Orders in Products Liability Litigation: Striking the Proper Balance*, 48 WASH. & LEE L. REV. 1503 (1991).

Despite having the role of initiator of the legal conflict, the plaintiff is often the victim of a process that makes litigation a financial burden. Depositions, expert consultations, court reporters, exhibits, and attorneys fees make complex civil litigation a very expensive undertaking. Protective orders multiply litigation costs by forcing individual plaintiffs in similar cases to repeat the same costly discovery process to obtain the same information from the same defendant. Operating under the restriction of a protective order also forces the plaintiff to evaluate a huge amount of documents that other plaintiffs have already evaluated. Additionally, the plaintiff must take the time to consult with experts who must also analyze the documents. Challenging an umbrella protective order further complicates the plaintiff's task by imposing additional burdens on plaintiffs.

Thus, protective orders that allow information sharing can substantially reduce the burdens that the discovery process imposes on the plaintiff.

Information sharing refers to the exchange of discovery between plaintiffs involved in similar litigation, implicating both plaintiff and public interests. Collaborative mechanisms for defendants are routine in complex litigation. Moreover, plaintiffs in multidistrict or class action cases have the right to share information; plaintiffs in non-grouped cases hope that, as a matter of consistency, the courts will not burden them with additional disclosure restrictions. Protective orders that completely restrict dissemination beyond the parties block collaborative efforts that could streamline the judicial process and lower litigation costs.

Patterson v. Ford Motor Co. is the seminal products liability case in the area of information sharing and recognizes the desirable effects of information sharing. In *Patterson* the defendant moved for a restrictive protective order for the stated purpose of preventing use of the discovered information by the plaintiff's attorneys in subsequent litigation. The district court explicitly rejected the possibility of information sharing among plaintiff's attorneys as a ground for a protective order. Further, the court adopted the view that information sharing is a desirable method of reducing litigation time and cost that coincides with the three-part objective of the Federal Rules of Civil Procedure of the just, speedy, and inexpensive resolution of litigation.

In *Garcia v. Peeples*, however, the wider-reaching advantages of information sharing were achieved to a great degree. . . . The *Garcia* court reasoned that even if trade secrets existed, the court must weigh the strong public policy favoring shared discovery against the defendant's interest in preserving trade secrets. The Texas Supreme Court, therefore, required lower courts to tailor protective orders to allow information sharing. The *Garcia* court found that information sharing furthered two substantial goals: making discovery more truthful by forcing parties to be consistent in their responses, and streamlining the discovery process. Moreover, because information sharing does not diminish the value of the property, there is no significant harm in allowing such exchanges. Because substantial case law supports the position adopted by the *Garcia* court in favor of information sharing, information sharing has achieved some acceptance as a judicial policy. In Texas, for example, *Garcia* independently has created a requirement that protective orders allow information sharing among plaintiffs involved in similar litigation. The one limitation placed on the generally accepted policy of information sharing is that the plaintiff may not seek discovery merely for the purpose of assisting in the litigation of another case.

* * *

Moreover, the overwhelming support that the courts have given to information sharing as an aid to litigation in general indicates that the policy of information sharing has relatively minor disadvantages. Given the contin-

ued ability of defendants to acquire protective orders that prevent competitive losses, information sharing as a policy successfully balances the defendant's interest with the plaintiff's need to avoid expensive and duplicative litigation.
[at 1519–23]

Resistive discovery practices undermine the goals of full disclosure that the federal rules and modern case law mandate.
[at 1529]

[B]oth Rule 26(c) and Rule 5(d) enforce the proposition that absent good cause, discovery must take place in the public.
[at 1533]

[I]nformation sharing would encourage voluntary compliance because plaintiffs will be able to recognize inconsistencies in discovery responses between different cases.
[at 1538]

At the very least, however, the plaintiff involved in collateral litigation avoids the time and expense of discovery for much of the information. Moreover, the second plaintiff can use the discovery to verify compliance with his own discovery requests.
[at 1539]

Given the legitimate needs of each of the three interests involved in products litigation, only information sharing provides a stable balance. As a mechanism, information sharing avoids duplicitous discovery while maintaining the secrecy required for the defendant's competitive interests. Additionally, information sharing protects the public by allowing a limited right to disseminate information that is relevant to public welfare. In striking the correct balance, the principles embodied in *Garcia* and the policy behind the Virginia statute achieve a mutually advantageous and equitable measure of competing interests.
[at 1543]

35. Torphy-Donzella, *Products Liability Litigation and Third-Party Harm: The Ethics of Nondisclosure*, 5 GEO. J. LEGAL ETHICS 435 (1991).

A dilemma arises for the plaintiff's attorney in the products liability action because of her need to uncover as much information about the product's design, manufacture, and testing as possible in order [to] obtain concrete evidence to make her client's case. Internal documents of the defendant company such as developmental studies on design and safety of the product, research on alternative designs, risk-analysis research on the product, and quality control records are essential to the plaintiff's case and are uniquely in the control of the defendant. However, defendants will not want to release this material without a promise that the material will remain undisclosed.

The plaintiff's attorney knows that discovery is an expensive and time consuming process. Protective orders can reduce the time and expense of this process because the defendant, assured of nondisclosure of the information provided to the plaintiff, may willingly produce more internal documents requested by the plaintiff. This, in turn, saves the plaintiff dollars and time that would otherwise be expended on discovery disputes. Thus the defendant may offer to liberally provide the plaintiff the discovery sought on condition that the plaintiff stipulate to a broad umbrella protective order.

The plaintiff's attorney may privately believe that the broad shielding of the defendant manufacturer's internal documents from disclosure may not be in the best interests of society at large. For example, if the case is settled, information that might have been disclosed at trial about the dangerousness of the defendant's product could not be revealed by the plaintiff and her attorney. Thus, the media could not be provided details discovered of a latent danger in a product still on the market, nor could the appropriate regulatory agency be advised of the defect. Furthermore, the terms of the protective order, prohibiting nonparty access to the discovered materials, also prevents the plaintiff's attorney from sharing information gained in the course of the case with attorneys engaged in identical actions against the defendant. Consequently, similarly situated plaintiffs would be forced to "reinvent the discovery wheel" so to speak, each beginning at ground zero at the commencement of the action, unable to benefit from the experience of colleagues sworn to secrecy.

Thus, the plaintiff attorney's dilemma "arises out of the irrevocable conflict between the client's interest and the desire for broader public disclosure." [citing Richard Arthurs, *Defendant's* [sic] *Fight Back on Data Sharing*, LEGAL TIMES, July 16, 1984, at 1]
[at 449–51]

At minimum, no protective order should be allowed to bar a plaintiff or his attorney from disclosing potential death or substantial bodily harm from the defendant's product to the appropriate regulatory agency. Such a rule would not only ensure that the governmental bodies charged with protecting the public from injurious products were not prevented from receiving information from plaintiffs; it would also serve to spur manufacturers to report the alleged defect first.

* * *

Finally, courts should be encouraged to abandon the bipolar view of litigation in the context of protective orders over discovery and consider favorably the plaintiff's request to preserve access by other plaintiffs to discovered information. Given the limitation that future plaintiffs must agree to be bound by the terms of the protective order, parties opposing this shared use of the discovered information should be required to show [a] compel-

ling reason why this presumption in favor of access should not prevail.
[at 456–57]

36. Wilson, Note, Seattle Times: *What Effect on Discovery Sharing?*, 1985 Wis. L. Rev. 1055.

   Parties commonly share information discovered in one civil action with parties involved in similar litigation. The practice occurs most frequently in product liability or mass tort lawsuits where several plaintiffs, usually scattered across federal and state court jurisdictional boundaries, allege similar harms caused by a common defendant. Because the defendant's liability in each of these actions usually turns on identical issues, the information needs of specific plaintiffs are similar. The sharing of information therefore gives the plaintiffs an alternative source to individual discovery proceedings for the information required to construct their lawsuits.

   Federal courts which have questioned the propriety of discovery sharing have generally, and often enthusiastically, approved of the practice. Underlying this approval is the judicial perception that sharing furthers the Federal Civil Procedure Rule 1 objective of making civil actions speedy and inexpensive by eliminating duplicative use of the discovery process.
   [at 1055–56 (emphasis added)]

   Courts that have examined discovery sharing under the good cause standard generally have approved of the practice.
   [at 1060]

   The article notes that litigation support groups essentially provide the same benefits of information sharing as are provided by such procedural mechanisms as class actions, multidistrict litigation, and consolidation of cases in which all the litigants are in a position to share discovered information. *Id.* at 1055 n.1.

37. Judicial Improvements Act of 1990, 28 U.S.C. § 473(a)(4) (1990).

   The act requires each U.S. district court to consider "encouragement of cost-effective discovery through voluntary exchange of information among litigants and their attorneys and through the use of cooperative discovery devices."

B. Reported Cases

1. *Adams v. Schmid Lab., Inc.*, No. 86 C 4783, 1987 U.S. Dist. LEXIS 2564 (N.D. Ill. Mar. 31, 1987), *reprinted in* HARE, GILBERT & REMINE, CONFIDENTIALITY ORDERS app. A-7 (1988).

   Products case; IUD.

   The district court upheld the magistrate's order denying the manufacturer's motion for a restrictive confidentiality order.

   The court stated:

   Wilk's emphasis on the principles set forth in Federal Rule 1, that all of the

Federal Rules be construed to secure the just, speedy and inexpensive determination of every action, clearly indicates that the potential for disclosure of discovered materials to counsel in collateral litigation on similar issues does not constitute good cause for a protective order, as suggested by *Milsen*.

2. *In re "Agent Orange" Prod. Liab. Litig.*, 104 F.R.D. 559 (E.D.N.Y. 1985), *aff'd*, 821 F.2d 139 (2d Cir.), *cert. denied*, 484 U.S. 953 (1987).

Products case; toxic chemical.

The trial court granted a petition to unseal court records. The court stated that implicit in the *Seattle Times* analysis is the conclusion that if the movant for a protective order fails to establish good cause, then the court would not have the authority to forbid public disclosure. *See* 104 F.R.D. at 567. The court went on to note that one of the purposes of Rule 5(d) (requiring all discovery material to be filed with the court) is to provide access to "litigants similarly situated." *Id.* at 567–68.

The court of appeals expressly agreed with the district court's reading of *Seattle Times* and held that "if good cause is not shown, the discovery materials should not receive judicial protection." 821 F.2d at 145. Further, the court agreed that one of the reasons for FED. R. CIV. P. 5(d) is to provide access to "litigants similarly situated." *Id.* at 146.

3. *In re Air Crash Disaster at Detroit Metro. Airport*, 130 F.R.D. 634, 638–39 (E.D. Mich. 1989).

The Sixth Circuit Court of Appeals has stated that "[c]learly, the power of a district judge includes the power to modify a protective order." *In re Upjohn Co. Antibiotic Cleocin Products, Etc.*, 664 F.2d 114, 118 (6th Cir. 1981).

* * *

Given that proceedings should normally take place in public, imposing a good cause requirement on the party seeking modification of a protective order is unwarranted. If access to protected fruits can be granted without harm to legitimate secrecy interests, or if no such interests exist, continued judicial protection cannot be justified. In that case, access should be granted even if the need for the protected materials is minimal. When this is not the case, the court should require the party seeking modification to show why the secrecy interests deserve less protection than they did when the order was granted. Even then, however, the movant should not be saddled with a burden more onerous than explaining why his need for the materials outweighs existing privacy concerns.

* * *

[Federal Rules of Civil Procedure 27(a)(4) and 32(a)] do not address the question of whether discovery may be shared between a federal and state case on the same basis as between two federal cases. To distinguish between the two situations would be to make a distinction on the basis of citizenship, a distinction which does not appear to have been intended. Where the parties have had similar interests and motives in the various cases, then it would appear that their rights have been adequately protected and there is no reason not to make the discovered materials available. Nor can it be said that the plaintiffs in this complex litigation case have no interest in the use of multi-district discovery beyond these cases. Parties in other litigation may have knowledge of facts relevant to plaintiffs' claims. Plaintiffs should be in a position to exchange information with other litigants with similar claims in order to develop their cases more fully. *Upjohn*, 81 F.R.D. at 484.

4. *Allen v. G.D. Searle & Co.*, 122 F.R.D. 580, 582–83 (D. Or. 1988).

Products case; IUD.

The manufacturer sought a protective order forbidding the disclosure of (1) the title page of depositions taken in other similar cases and (2) a list of other similar law suits against the defendant. In denying the motion, the court held that disclosure of the title pages of depositions did not injure the privacy rights of the deponents and that a list of other similar cases was not proprietary information.

5. *American Honda Motor Co. v. Dibrell*, 736 S.W.2d 257 (Tex. Ct. App. 1987).

Products case; ATV.

The trial court denied the manufacturer's motion for a restrictive confidentiality order and adopted plaintiff's proposed order permitting information sharing under certain stated restrictions.

6. *AT&T Co. v. Grady*, 594 F.2d 594 (7th Cir. 1978), *cert. denied*, 440 U.S. 971 (1979).

Antitrust.

The Seventh Circuit upheld the district court's order granting the government's petition to modify a stipulated protective order to permit information sharing.

The court noted that "[a]s a general proposition, pretrial discovery must take place in the public unless compelling reasons exist for denying the public access to the proceedings." *Id.* at 596.

In granting the petition for modification, the Court noted: "We are impressed with the wastefulness of requiring government counsel to duplicate the analyses and discovery already made." *Id.* at 597.

7. *Baker v. Liggett Group, Inc.*, 132 F.R.D. 123, 126 (D. Mass. 1990).

Products case; cigarettes.

The district court adopted a protective order that precluded disclosure of confidential documents to the public and the media but allowed dissemination to litigants and counsel in other similar cases.

Moreover, with regard to confidential information produced in discovery, defendants have not shown good cause to preclude dissemination to litigants and lawyers in similar tobacco tort cases, subject to the protective order pertaining to confidential information being issued in this case. Such dissemination was permitted in *Cipollone*, the first of the prominent tobacco tort cases. As Judge Lee Sarokin noted in *Cipollone*, the sharing of information obtained in discovery with litigants in comparable cases is consistent with FED. R. CIV. P. 1 which provides that the Rules are to "be construed to secure the just, speedy, and inexpensive determination of every action." It is particularly appropriate that this principal be applied in tobacco tort cases in which individual plaintiffs must litigate against large, corporate defendants. Some such plaintiffs may have organized support, but many others may not. In any event, to routinely require every plaintiff in a tobacco tort case to go through a comparable, prolonged and expensive discovery process would be inappropriate. Rather, as Judge John Minor Wisdom wrote:

> Where an appropriate modification of a protective order can place private litigants in a position they would otherwise reach only after repetition of another's discovery, such modification can be denied only where it would tangibly prejudice substantial rights of the party opposing modification. *Wilk v. American Medical Association*, 635 F.2d 1295, 1299 (7th Cir. 1980).

8. *Brown v. Advantage Eng'g, Inc.*, 960 F.2d 1013, 1016 (11th Cir. 1992).

Industrial explosion.

The plaintiff in an action in the Eastern District of California sought access to pleadings and evidence that were initially openly submitted in the Northern District of Georgia but which was subsequently sealed under court monitored settlement. When the defendant refused plaintiff's offer to be bound by a blanket protective order if it would provide the requested documents, the plaintiff filed a motion for permissive intervention in the Georgia action for the purpose of unsealing the record. The Eleventh Circuit held that the district court abused its discretion in denying plaintiff's motion in the absence of compelling reasons for sealing the record, stating that "[o]nce a matter is brought before a court for resolution, it is no longer solely the parties' case, but also the public's case."

9. *Burlington City Bd. of Educ. v. United States Mineral Prods. Co.*, 115 F.R.D. 188, 190, 191 (M.D.N.C. 1987).

Products case; asbestos property damage.

The plaintiff took a video deposition of a defense expert witness. The manufacturer and the witness sought a court order forbidding the dissemination of the tape among plaintiff's lawyers in other similar cases. The court denied the motion in an opinion that recognizes the great value and benefit of information sharing among plaintiffs with similar cases.

The high cost associated with deposing expert witnesses can be curtailed

by allowing plaintiffs to share information with plaintiffs in other cases. *The courts considering the matter have overwhelmingly and decisively endorsed the sharing of discovery information among different plaintiffs, in different cases, in different courts.* Kamp Implement Co., Inc. v. J.I. Case Co., 630 F. Supp. 218 (D. Mont. 1986) (collecting cases); *Cipollone v. Liggett Group Inc.*, 106 F.R.D. 573, 586 (D.N.J. 1985) (collecting cases); *U.S. v. Hooker Chemicals & Plastics Corp.*, 90 F.R.D. 421, 426 (W.D.N.Y. 1981). The sharing of information between even diverse plaintiffs promotes speedy, efficient and inexpensive litigation by facilitating the dissemination of discovery material necessary to analyze one's case and prepare for trial. It reduces repetitious requests and depositions, thereby conserving even defendant's time and expense in having to respond or attend the deposition. It conserves judicial resources by reducing the number of discovery motions and disputes. *Permitting plaintiffs to share information helps counterbalance the effect uneven financial resources between parties might otherwise have on the discovery process, thereby protecting economically modest plaintiffs faced with financially well off defendants and improving accessibility to justice.* Defendants will not be heard to complain that sharing information will burden their defending similar type lawsuits. *U.S. v. Hooker Chemicals & Plastics Corp.*, supra. To some extent, that result is both a desired and expected consequence of the expediting and evening process which sharing produces. "[C]ollaboration among plaintiffs' attorneys . . . comes squarely within the purposes of the Federal Rules of Civil Procedure." Of course, the Court must be vigil[a]nt to prevent abuse, such as by a plaintiff's attempt to use present discovery in order to assist him or counsel in another lawsuit. *Johnson Foils, Inc. v. Huyck Corp.*, 61 F.R.D. 405, 410 (N.D.N.Y. 1973). Nevertheless, it is the party seeking the Rule 26(c) protective order who bears the burden of establishing with a specific factual showing both the need for a protective order and the harm ensuing without one, should he wish to prevent the sharing of discovery material. *Id.*; *Kamp Implement Co., Inc.*, supra. *Any protective order entered should be narrowly tailored to fit the situation and even confidential material should be shared when possible. Cipollone, supra.*
[emphasis added]

* * *

Nothing indicates plaintiff intends to use the video depositions in a nonjudicial manner or for an ulterior purpose. Nor is there anything inherently oppressive in plaintiff's contemplated use of the deposition by sharing it with plaintiffs in other cases. To the contrary, the Court would encourage all parties to share their video depositions. Without denigrating defendant's expert's natural, if not innate, aversion over the invasion of personal privacy which goes with sharing his image in a video deposition, the Court is simply not willing to sanction it. Some personal privacy necessarily must give way to the more general interest of our society in promoting better and more efficient judicial proceedings. Sharing video depositions is such an instance. Without a clear demonstration of hardship or oppression, the Court will not entertain protective orders against video depositions in order to protect a generalized concern of personal privacy.

10. *Carter-Wallace, Inc. v. Hartz Mountain Indus., Inc.*, 92 F.R.D. 67, 69–70 (S.D.N.Y. 1981).

    Antitrust.

    The plaintiff's motion requesting the defendant to produce documents from an earlier case that were under a protective order was treated as a petition for modification and was granted. The court specifically recognized that the sharing of discovery material produced in other similar litigation was within the aim and purpose of FED. R. CIV. P. 1.

11. *Chambers Dev. Co. v. Browning-Ferris Indus.*, 104 F.R.D. 133, 135–36 (W.D. Pa. 1985).

    Commercial litigation.

    The district court entered a protective order (apparently stipulated between the parties) specifically permitting the sharing of information between litigants in related cases. Note that counsel were charged with the responsibility for keeping a list of persons given access to documents subject to the order and that the list could not be disclosed except for good cause.

12. *Cipollone v. Liggett Group, Inc.*, 113 F.R.D. 86 (D.N.J. 1986), *mandamus denied*, 822 F.2d 335 (3d Cir.), *cert. denied*, 484 U.S. 976 (1987).

    Products case; tobacco.

    The magistrate entered a restrictive confidentiality order forbidding information sharing among litigants in similar cases. The district court overruled as "clearly erroneous and contrary to law" and entered an amended order specifically permitting the use of discovery materials in similar cases. The Third Circuit affirmed. Both opinions contain language strongly affirming the value of information sharing and a detailed analysis of the requirements of good cause.

    > By requiring each plaintiff in every similar action to run the same gauntlet over and over again serves no useful purpose other than to create barriers and discourage litigation against the defendants. Good cause as contemplated under Rule 26 was never intended to make other litigation more difficult, costly and less efficient.
    > [at 87]

    > Defendants' arguments are even less persuasive with regard to limiting use of discovery material in other litigation. The causal chain behind their position is as follows. Defendant's financial and competitive position may be harmed by this type of litigation; prohibiting use of *Cipollone/Haines* discovery in other litigation makes such litigation more difficult to sustain; consequently, defendant will suffer significant injury if discovery is not

confined to this litigation. Defendants' argument not only fails to substantiate a particularized and significant injury as required by Rule 26(c). *The argument also runs counter to a fundamental purpose of discovery under the Federal Rules. All of the Federal Rules are informed by the admonition of Rule 1 that they "be construed to secure the just, speedy, and inexpensive determination of every action." Acting consistent with this purpose, a number of courts have rejected requests to limit the use of discovery to the litigation in which it is initially obtained.* Their reasoning is best summarized by the opinion of Judge Wisdom in *Wilk v. American Medical Ass'n*, 635 F.2d 1295, 1299 (7th Cir. 1980), which states that the presumption of open discovery

> should operate with all the more force when litigants seek [to] use discovery in aid of collateral litigation on similar issues, for . . . access in such cases materially eases the tasks of courts and litigants and speeds up what may otherwise be a lengthy process. Particularly in litigation of this magnitude we, like the Multidistrict Panel, are impressed with the wastefulness of requiring the [collateral party] to duplicate discovery already made. . . . We therefore agree with the result reached by every other appellate court which has considered the issue, and hold that where an appropriate modification of a protective order can place private litigants in a position they would otherwise reach only after repetition of another's discovery, such modification can be denied only where it would tangibly prejudice substantial rights of the party opposing modification.

See Marcus, *Myth and Reality in Protective Order Litigation*, 69 CORNELL L. REV. 1, 41 (1983); *see also Cipollone v. Liggett Group, Inc.*, 105 F.R.D. at 585–586 (citing several cases standing for this proposition). Here, defendants' showings simply do not establish that substantial rights will be so tangibly prejudiced that injustice will result unless the discovery obtained in this litigation is limited to it. Indeed, no direct purpose can be discerned from their position except to discourage future identical actions against them by maintaining the costliness of the discovery involved to other plaintiffs. As noted by this court in its previous opinion herein,

> The court cannot ignore the might and power of the tobacco industry and its ability to resist the individual claims asserted against it and its individual members. There may be some claimants who do not have the resources or such able and dedicated counsel as in this case to pursue the thorough investigation which these cases require. To require that each and every plaintiff go through the identical long and expensive process would be ludicrous. Even from the point of view of the defendants (though they resist), it would seem that they would benefit by avoiding repetition of the same discovery in each and every case. *Cipollone*, 106 F.R.D. at 577.

So long as the initial litigation has not itself been instituted in bad faith for the purpose of obtaining documents for other actions, and so long as the

interests of those represented in the initial litigation are being fully and ethically prosecuted, the Federal Rules do not foreclose the collaborative use of discovery.
[at 90–91]

This holding was affirmed on appeal, 822 F.2d at 345.

Defendant's counsel at oral argument contended that good cause may be established by a showing that a protective order is needed "to prevent an abuse of the discovery process." Defendants' counsel explains that the sole purpose of the discovery process is to help the parties prepare for litigation. Anything that goes beyond that constitutes an abuse of the discovery process. . . ." Because dissemination to the public and use in other litigation goes beyond the "sole purpose" of discovery, the magistrate had "good cause" to enter this order to protect from that abuse.

This argument, like that concerning facilitation of discovery, ignores the language and misconstrues the purpose of Rule 26(c). The Supreme Court has stated that Rule 26(c) protective orders are designed to prevent abuse of discovery, but abuse in the sense of causing injury to particular individuals.

There is an opportunity, therefore, for litigants to obtain—incidentally or purposefully—information that not only is irrelevant but if publicly released could be damaging to reputation and privacy. The government clearly has a substantial interest in preventing this sort of abuse of its processes.

Seattle Times Co. v. Rhinehart, 467 U.S. 20, 35, 104 S. Ct. 2199, 2209 81 L.Ed.2d 17 (1984). Again, the Third Circuit's discussion of "good cause" shows that protection from injury to individuals must be the focus of a Rule 26(c) protective order. Thus, the mere fact that plaintiffs intend to use these materials outside of this litigation is not "good cause" to support the protective order, unless defendants can establish that the discovery was not procured in good faith for the purposes of this litigation. No such showing is made or claimed. Absent a showing that plaintiff's use will sufficiently injure the defendants, the magistrate had no good cause to limit use of the discovery to this case alone.

In summary, the magistrate's finding that defendants had shown good cause to support an order that nonconfidential discovery "shall be used solely for the purpose of this case" is clearly erroneous and contrary to law. To the extent that the magistrate found good cause based on embarrassment to defendants, the effect of dissemination on the fairness of trial, or the prior conduct of plaintiffs' attorney, the finding is clearly erroneous. To the extent that the magistrate found good cause based on a desire to facilitate discovery or to prevent an abuse of the discovery process, the finding is contrary to law.
[at 93]

This holding was quoted and affirmed by the Third Circuit on appeal, 822 F.2d at 341.

13. *Culligan v. Yamaha Motor Corp.*, 110 F.R.D. 122, 127 (S.D.N.Y. 1986).

Products case; ATV.

The defendant manufacturer sought a restrictive confidentiality order, which the court denied. The order adopted by the court allows the plaintiff to share information with others who agree to be bound by the order. Although the opinion notes that only some of the requested documents contain trade secret information, the court does not precisely define what particular documents actually meet the trade secrets criteria.

14. *Deford v. Schmid Prods. Co.*, 120 F.R.D. 648, 654 (D. Md. 1987).

Products case; IUD.

The defendant manufacturer sought a confidentiality order asserting barratry, trade secrets and patient privacy grounds to preclude the dissemination of its clinical studies. In overruling, the court noted the benefit and value of information sharing.

> The plaintiffs' primary argument in favor of disclosure is their desire to share information with other litigants and their counsel. This is an appropriate goal under the Federal Rules of Civil Procedure, which are intended "to secure the just, speedy, and inexpensive determination of every action." Sharing discovery materials may be particularly appropriate where multiple individual plaintiffs assert essentially the same alleged wrongs against a national manufacturer of a consumer product.

The court also noted that the holding in *Milson* is no longer good law.

15. *Earl v. Gulf & W. Mfg. Co.*, 366 N.W.2d 160, 165 (Wis. Ct. App. 1985).

Products case; machine press.

The trial court denied the manufacturer's motion for a restrictive confidentiality order. The Wisconsin appellate court upheld—noting that information sharing among litigants in similar cases "does not rise to the level of 'good cause' for a protective order."

16. *Farnum v. G.D. Searle & Co.*, 339 N.W.2d 384, 391 (Iowa 1983).

Products case; oral contraceptive.

The Iowa Supreme Court upheld the lower court's order denying the manufacturer's motion for restrictive order concerning the NDA file. The court noted that the manufacturer failed to identify specific documents and failed to establish a threat of competitive harm with particularity.

> [W]e commend the parties' efforts to cooperate in discovery on an informal basis. Efforts of this kind assist greatly in saving judicial time and in minimizing the expense to litigants that is otherwise inevitable in complex litigation.
> [emphasis added]

17. *Fidelity Bankers Life Ins. Co. v. Wedco, Inc.*, 102 F.R.D. 41, 44 (D. Nev. 1984).

The errors and omissions carrier was permitted to intervene in the principal action.

> The use of discovery obtained in one law suit in connection with other litigation accords with the purposes of the Federal Rules of Civil Procedure.

18. *Garcia v. Peeples*, 734 S.W.2d 343 (Tex. 1987).

Products case; fuel system.

The trial court granted the manufacturer's motion for a restrictive confidentiality order. The Texas Supreme Court granted the plaintiff's petition for mandamus "since the order may prohibit [the plaintiff] from effectively preparing for trial." *Id.* at 345. The court held that the entrance of a restrictive protective order was an "abuse of discretion" and remanded for the trial court to enter an order permitting the plaintiff to share discovery materials with litigants in similar cases.

> Balanced against these concerns for the confidentiality of [the defendant's] research are the public policies favoring the exchange of information.
> [at 346]

Shared discovery is an effective means to insure full and fair disclosure. Parties subject to a number of suits concerning the same subject matter are forced to be consistent in their responses by the knowledge that their opponents can compare those responses.

In addition to making discovery more truthful, shared discovery makes the system itself more efficient. The current discovery process forces similarly situated parties to go through the same discovery process time and time again, even though the issues involved are virtually identical. Benefiting from restrictions on discovery, one party facing a number of adversaries can require his opponents to duplicate another's discovery efforts, even though the opponents share similar discovery needs and will litigate similar issues. Discovery costs are no small part of the overall trial expense. *A number of courts have recognized that allowing shared discovery is far more efficient than the repetitive system now employed. Federal courts, for instance, have overwhelmingly embraced this practice in order to streamline discovery.* The Federal Judicial Center's *Manual for Complex Litigation* also suggests sharing discovery in order to avoid duplicative efforts.

The facts of this case do not justify the blanket protective order, and in rendering an overbroad order, the trial court abused its discretion. [The defendant's] interest is in protecting proprietary information from competitors while [the plaintiff] seeks to more effectively prepare for trial by exchanging information with other litigants. The public policies favoring shared information require that any protective order be carefully tailored to protect [the defendant's] proprietary interests while allowing an exchange of discovered documents.

The trial court should have balanced these competing needs and rendered an order preventing dissemination of [the defendant's] true trade secrets only to [the defendant's] competitors. There is no indication from [the defendant's] affidavits in support of the motion, nor is there any reason to believe, that [the defendant] will be harmed by the release of this information to other litigants.
[at 347–48 (emphasis added)]

In footnote 4, the court noted:

While trade secrets may be property, *allowing their release to non-competitors does nothing to diminish their value.* [The defendant's] proprietary information is valuable *only because other manufacturers lack access to it.*
[at 348 (emphasis added)]

19. *Grundberg v. Upjohn Co.*, 137 F.R.D. 372 (D. Utah 1991).

Products case; drug Halcion.

The defendant registered discovery documents as copyrighted material and then sued the plaintiffs for copyright infringement, seeking a preliminary injunction against dissemination of the material. The district court denied the defendant's claim of copyright infringement holding that the placement of documents in court files is not a publication of the material under the copyright law. The court further noted that the copyright law does not forbid disclosure of information or make nonconfidential documents confidential. Any copyrightable interest that the defendant may have in documents that are the object of discovery cannot be asserted to prevent access to them for the purpose of litigation.

20. *Johnson Foils, Inc. v. Huyck Corp.*, 61 F.R.D. 405, 409–10 (N.D.N.Y. 1973).

Patent infringement.

The plaintiff offered to agree to an order precluding disclosure of the subject documents to the defendant's competitors and the public. The defendant proposed a restrictive order. The court adopted an order permitting information sharing among litigants with similar cases.

The fact that sensitive information is involved in litigation gives a party neither an absolute nor automatic right to have the discovery process hindered.

* * *

Any protective order inhibiting liberal discovery must issue only upon a specific showing that the information in question is of the nature that its disclosure should be restricted and that the party disclosing will indeed be harmed by disclosure. Moreover, the protective order may only minimize the potential ill-effects to the party making disclosures, e.g., limiting access to certain persons or the public in general, but it should not prohibit the full disclosure of all facts necessary to the litigation. This paramount concern limits the discretion of the court to encumber the discovery process except where good judgment dictates to the contrary.

Defendant seems to have drafted this proposed order with the intent to limit plaintiff's use of the information to the instant litigation. *I find little persuasion in this position and virtually no precedent for the detailed and drastic provisions of the proposed protective order in this regard.* The liberality to be used in interpreting the federal rules mandates quite an opposite emphasis. To wit: unless it can be shown that the discovering party is exploiting the instant litigation solely to assist in other litigation before a foreign forum, federal courts do allow full use of the information in other forums. Indeed, there must be some evidence of bad faith in the institution of the suit on the part of the discovering party before a court will act to limit the discovery process. Defendant does not demonstrate in any way significant to my mind that plaintiff has used or intends to use the fruits of discovery for purposes other than as legitimate to legal actions and proceedings. This is particularly true in light of plaintiff's consent offered throughout to enter into an agreement protecting the secrecy and confidentiality of defendant's information in the traditional manner and with the customary terminology common to patent litigation.

Defendant in its proposed protective order submitted to this court in these motions also seeks to limit the number of persons, including technical experts, who may view the sensitive information. Again, defendant gives no particular reason to limit this information to a specified number of persons and *in my opinion such an order would unnecessarily hamper the progress of this litigation, and be unfair to legitimate use of the information by the plaintiff. Each party should be allowed to use all necessary consultation in preparing its litigation, consistent with a good faith effort to comply with any provisions agreed to in a protective order.*

In sum, I find the proposed protective order of the defendant limits unacceptably the use of this information in foreign litigation of a closely related nature involving what essentially are the same parties. It also unduly restricts consultation by plaintiff of this case and others by providing for an overly detailed and cumbersome protection procedure. No bad faith has been alleged against plaintiff nor is any evident to me, and in light of the voluntary consent by its attorneys to a protective order on the real concern at issue, namely, to maintain the secrecy of the information from other competitors and the general public, my conclusion is to favor their proposed order.

The able and experienced lawyers for the parties unquestionably can draft a satisfactory order in accord with the reasoning and rulings herein. The important ruling is that the discovery information obtained in this action may be used by the plaintiff in the specific litigation and proceedings identified. . . .
[emphasis added]

21. *Kamp Implement Co. v. J.I. Case Co.*, 630 F. Supp. 218, 219, 220 (D. Mont. 1986). Commercial litigation.

The district court denied the manufacturer's motion for a restrictive confidentiality order and entered an order which specifically permitted the sharing of discovery materials with plaintiff's counsel in similar cases.

Of the courts that have considered protective orders of the nature proposed by defendant, an overwhelming majority have refused to grant any type of protection from dissemination.

Citing and quoting at length from *Patterson v. Ford Motor Co.* (case no. B.31, *infra*), the court went on to say:

Decisions of other courts echo this reasoning, and most refuse to consider the possibility that plaintiff will share the fruits of discovery as any part of defendant's showing of good cause.

Defendants maintain that they are not trying to keep information from other litigants, but seek only to prevent confidential material from "freely flowing" to third parties without any safeguards. While this position has merit, the onus must be on the defendants to make a specific showing that they will be harmed by a particular disclosure. If defendants' proposed order were entered, the court would be faced with motions by litigants in other cases for modification of the order to allow the information to be released to them. This would result in duplication of time and effort in each instance where discovery is sought. Protective orders will be modified any time such modification "can place private litigants in a position they would otherwise reach only after repetition of another's discovery."

22. *Kerasotes Mich. Theatres v. National Amusements, Inc.*, 139 F.R.D. 102, 106 (E.D. Mich. 1991)

    Antitrust.

    Following a long-settled antitrust action relating to distribution of motion pictures, the plaintiff in a similar action against one of the same defendants moved to intervene for the limited purpose of modifying protective orders to obtain access to deposition transcripts. The district court held that the plaintiff would be permitted to intervene for the limited purpose of modifying protective orders entered in the settled action, subject to the restrictions of the original order. The court aptly noted that "the goal of the federal rules to seek a 'just, speedy, and inexpensive determination of every action' is . . . furthered by sharing discovery with collateral litigants."

23. *Koval v. General Motors Corp.*, 610 N.E.2d 1199, 1202 (Ohio Ct. C.P. 1990).

    Products case; fuel system.

    The trial court denied the manufacturer's motion for a restrictive confidentiality order.

    Additionally, it is apparent to the court that one of General Motors' primary concerns and reasons for its motion for a protective order is that it fears these documents might fall into the hands of a similarly situated plaintiff suing General Motors in a different forum. Based on the case law and articles written on this subject, the court is of the opinion that this is the driving force not only behind the present motion, but also behind General Motors' request that the documents be returned to it at the close of the litigation. The fact that similarly situated plaintiffs may see and even use the documents at issue in other lawsuits does not justify the issuance of a protective order. Even assuming General Motors had demonstrated that these documents were competitively valuable, which the Court finds it has not, for the reasons that follow it would not be entitled to a protective order that would preclude such information sharing or require the return of these documents.

There exists much case law supporting the sharing of discovery which General Motors so obviously abhors. *See, e.g., Garcia, Yurko,* and *Parsons*. All three of these cases involve products liability actions against automobile manufacturers in which the sharing of discovery information was approved. In *Garcia* the Texas Supreme Court, in mandamus, held that the refusal of a trial court to permit the sharing of such information was an abuse of discretion. These and other courts have noted the efficiencies, in terms of time and cost, that are created when two similarly situated litigants share discovery, and have further noted that such sharing imposes on the producing party, such as General Motors, the duty to provide full, fair and consistent disclosure of documents to each similarly situated plaintiff.

More important than any efficiency created, however, is that the public will derive an indirect benefit from a practice permitting sharing. The court notes that products have been modified and even taken off the market as a whole following the public outcry that the products are dangerous. Such revelations of a product's dangerous propensity occur mainly through litigation. Three-wheel, all-terrain vehicles, jeeps tending to roll over, and what was once called the "explode-on-impact" Pinto are all examples of products which are no longer sold due to their respective dangers.

The court concludes that this motion for a protective order has more to do with other litigation and bad publicity than with what the court finds to be but vague and conclusory allegations of competitively sensitive documents. The court "must consider the need for public dissemination, in order to alert other consumers to potential dangers posed by the product." *See Hendricks* and *United States v. Hooker Chemicals & Plastics Corp., supra*. If the sharing of discovery can possibly save lives and stop injuries such as occurred here by forcing this defendant to act, then no protective order should prohibit it. As pointed out in plaintiff's brief in opposition: "The analogous question to be asked here is whether the documents produced in the Ford Pinto Fuel tank cases should have been kept from the public." The answer there, as here, must be a resounding "No."

The court finds that the sharing of documents is beneficial, that requiring the return of these documents would hamper such practice, and, of utmost importance, that the decisions as to these matters and the denial of this motion comport with the spirit of our Civil Rules. As Civ. R. 1(B) states: "These rules shall be construed and applied to effect just results by eliminating delay, unnecessary expense and all other impediments to the expeditious administration of justice." The court can think of nothing more violative of this rule than the protective order that General Motors has proposed and argued for in this case, and, thus, its motion must be denied.

24. *Kraszewski v. State Farm Gen. Ins. Co.*, 139 F.R.D. 156 (N.D. Cal. 1991).

Sex discrimination.

The district court held that a protective order restricting discovered documents' use to a single case would be modified to permit the documents' use in other litigation in order to save repetitious discovery unless modification would tangibly prejudice substantial rights of the opposing party.

25. *LeBlanc v. Broyhill*, 123 F.R.D. 527 (W.D.N.C. 1988).

Commercial litigation.

The district court modified a stipulated protective order to provide access to materials produced in discovery in a companion case before another court.

26. *Metropolitan Life Ins. Co. v. Liberty Life Ins. Co.*, 1984-2 Trade Cas. (CCH) ¶ 66,087, at 66,066 (W.D.N.C. 1984).

Antitrust.

Three separate cases were pending before federal district courts in North Carolina, South Carolina, and Florida, all involving similar issues.

The district court in North Carolina entered an order consolidating discovery to permit information sharing "[i]n order to conserve the resources of the courts and of the parties involved, and to reduce duplicative or otherwise wasteful expenditures of time and energy. . . ."

27. *Nestle Foods Corp. v. Aetna Casualty & Sur. Co.*, 129 F.R.D. 483, 486 (D.N.J. 1990).

Contract.

Declaratory judgment action seeking money damages arising from insurance company's breach of contractual obligations to provide coverage for environmental harm.

The district court overruled the defendant's motion for a restrictive protective order in an opinion that recognized the value of information sharing.

> Moreover, if the basis for defendants' motion is to prevent information from being disseminated to other potential litigants, then defendants' application must fail. With increasing frequency, defendants, as well as other insurers, are finding themselves embroiled in litigation over whether there is coverage for property damage as a result of environmental harm. *The courts have emphatically held that a protective order cannot be issued simply because it may be detrimental to the movant in other lawsuits. Using fruits of dis-*

covery from one lawsuit in another litigation, and even in collaboration among various plaintiffs' attorneys, comes squarely within the purposes of the Federal Rules of Civil Procedure. The harm possibly emanating therefrom does not form a basis for a protective order.
[emphasis added]

28. *Olympic Ref. Co. v. Carter*, 332 F.2d 260, 264–66 (9th Cir.), *cert. denied*, 379 U.S. 900 (1964).

   Antitrust.

   This was a private civil action by Olympic against Standard Oil. Several years earlier the government settled a similar suit against the same defendant under terms that included a protective order concerning discovery materials. Olympic sought production of the discovery material produced in the earlier litigation which was covered by the earlier protective order. Standard Oil objected on the basis of the earlier protective order. Olympic moved to have it vacated. The district court denied Olympic's petition to vacate the earlier protective order. The court of appeals reversed and remanded for entry of an order modifying the confidentiality order so that materials produced in the earlier case could be used in a later case. In so doing, the Ninth Circuit stated that "pretrial proceedings are ordinarily to be conducted in public." The court noted that even if the discovery materials contained "trade secrets," that would not forbid information sharing by litigants with similar cases.

29. *Parkway Gallery Furniture, Inc. v. Kittinger/Pa. House Group, Inc.*, 121 F.R.D. 264, 268–69 (M.D.N.C. 1988).

   Commercial litigation.

   Because of time constraints and fear of noncooperation, the plaintiff agreed to a stipulated protective order that included a blanket umbrella provision. A nonparty whose deposition was taken subject to the order sought sanctions against the plaintiff for disclosing the deposition to a witness in the principal action. The district court in denying the imposition of sanctions noted the value and benefit of information sharing.

   > Even if Thomasville [the nonparty movant] had listed the purpose of the protective order as limiting the discovery information to this litigation, that would not entirely resolve the problem. Public policy disfavors such a restriction. As the Third Circuit said in *Cipollone II*, a party needs to present good cause for prohibiting the dissemination of non-confidential discovery information or from prohibiting the utilization of such discovery in other litigation. (822 F.2d at 341). *The sharing of information between the parties usually promotes efficient and inexpensive litigation, conserves judicial resources, and serves to counterbalance uneven financial resources which may otherwise deny access to justice to the more financially modest party.* Burlington Bd. of Educ. v. U.S. Mineral Prods. Co., 115 F.R.D. 188, 190 (M.D.N.C. 1987).
   > [emphasis added]

30. *Parsons v. General Motors Corp.*, 85 F.R.D. 724, 726 & n.1 (N.D. Ga. 1980).

   Products case; fuel system.

The district court denied the defendant's motion for a restrictive order covering crash tests and manufacturing information concerning the design of the product.

In responding to the defendant's charge that the plaintiff planned to share the information with other attorneys handling similar cases (which the defendant alleged was an "abuse of discovery"), the court first noted that "[t]he federal rules do not foreclose collaboration among litigants" and then held that the possibility that the plaintiff will share discovery materials with other litigants does not constitute "good cause to justify a protective order."

31. *Patterson v. Ford Motor Co.*, 85 F.R.D. 152, 153–54 (W.D. Tex. 1980).

Products case; fuel system.

The district court denied the manufacturer's motion for a restrictive order, holding that the charge that plaintiff's counsel would share information with other lawyers handling similar cases did not constitute good cause.

> To show good cause, Ford asserts that counsel for Plaintiff are members of the Texas Trial Lawyers Association and the American Trial Lawyers Association, which collect and distribute information with regard to manufacturers. *Such collaboration among plaintiffs' attorneys would come squarely within the aims of the Federal Rules of Civil Procedure—to secure the just, speedy and inexpensive determination of every action. Rule 1, F.R.C.P.* There is nothing inherently culpable about sharing information obtained through discovery. *The availability of the discovery information may reduce time and money which must be expended in similar proceedings, and may allow for effective, speedy, and efficient representation.* Unless it can be shown that the discovering party is exploiting the instant litigation solely to assist litigation in a foreign forum, federal courts allow full use of the information in other forums.
> [emphasis added]

32. *Public Citizen v. Liggett Group, Inc.*, 858 F.2d. 775, 790–92 (1st Cir. 1988), *cert. denied*, 488 U.S. 1030 (1989).

Products case; tobacco.

In this important case, a public health special interest group ("Public Citizen") petitioned the court to modify an earlier protective order forbidding disclosure of discovery materials produced by the defendant Liggett in a cancer case. The district court modified the protective order and the tobacco company appealed. The appellate court held that the public interest group had standing to intervene and upheld the modification of the protective order.

33. *Sedlock v. Bic Corp.*, 926 F.2d 757, 758, 759 (8th Cir. 1991).

Products case; cigarette lighter.

The district court ordered the defendant to produce requested documents and entered a protective order permitting dissemination of trade secret materials to other litigants in similar litigation. The court of appeals dismissed manufacturer's appeal in an opinion which recognized the benefits of information sharing even concerning discovery materials that might constitute trade secrets.

Contrary to Bic's proposal, however, the protective order allows counsel for plaintiffs in similar product liability suits against Bic access to the discovery if notice and hearing are afforded to Bic.

* * *

Bic asserts its rights will be irreparably harmed by the discovery order because the trade secrets will become public knowledge after other plaintiffs' attorneys obtain them. We disagree. The discovery materials Bic designates as trade secrets must be treated confidentially. Dissemination of the discovery is limited to other attorneys and their experts in similar cases against Bic. Other attorneys who seek the discovery must agree to be bound by the protective order's terms before access to the discovery is permitted. Thus, none of the protected discovery will become public knowledge under the terms of this order.

34. *Tosa Chrysler-Plymouth, Inc. v. Chrysler Motors Corp.*, 55 F.R.D. 41, 43 (E.D. Wis. 1972).

Antitrust.

The plaintiff agreed not to disclose the subject documents to the defendant's competitors. The court entered a protective order which permitted the plaintiff to discuss the documents with "persons, not competitors of defendant, whose aid is necessary in the preparation of the plaintiff's case."

35. *Turick v. Yamaha Motor Corp., U.S.*, 121 F.R.D. 32, 35 (S.D. N.Y. 1988).

Products case; ATV.

The district court held that (1) the defendant manufacturer failed to make the requisite showing that the subject documents (defendant's correspondence with the CPSC) met the legal criteria for a "trade secret" and (2) the defendant failed to show "good cause" to justify entrance of a protective order under rule 26(c).

The court's opinion contains an excellent discussion of the manufacturer's burden of proof.

36. *United States v. Hooker Chems. & Plastics Corp.*, 90 F.R.D. 421, 426 (W.D.N.Y. 1981).

Environmental pollution; toxic chemicals in Love Canal.

The court denied the manufacturer's motion for a restrictive confidentiality order.

Hooker also argues that the disclosure of information garnered through discovery will be detrimental to its position in parallel lawsuits. This is unquestionably true. *However, this is not a reason for a court to impose a protective order. Use of the discovery fruits disclosed in one lawsuit in connection with other litigation, and even in collaboration among plaintiffs' attorneys, comes*

squarely within the purposes of the Federal Rules of Civil Procedure. Such cooperation among litigants promotes the speedy and inexpensive determination of every action as well as conservation of judicial resources. *This is particularly the case in lawsuits where the resources available to the parties are uneven.* Individuals who are plaintiffs might have a most difficult time extracting information, whereas powerful litigants such as the United States and the State might find it relatively easier to compel production. Nor is it especially significant that the other litigants who might try to "piggy-back" their disclosure proceedings on top of federal discovery are litigants in state court. We perceive no intention in the Federal Rules that incidental benefits of liberal federal discovery should not accrue to litigants in state courts who are pursuing ancillary lawsuits, provided there is no attempt to exploit the federal litigation discovery process *solely* to assist litigation in a foreign forum.
[emphasis added]

37. *In re Upjohn Co. Antibiotic Cleocin Prods. Liab. Litig.*, 81 F.R.D. 482 (E.D. Mich. 1979), *aff'd*, 664 F.2d 114 (6th Cir. 1981).

   Products case; drug Cleocin.

   The plaintiff moved to vacate an existing protective order. The defendant manufacturer moved for an order restricting the use of discovery materials obtained in multidistrict litigation from use in other similar state court actions.

   The court permitted use of discovery materials in federal multidistrict litigation cases *and in other state cases*.

   > The two rules cited do not address the question of whether discovery may be shared between a federal and state case on the same basis as between two federal cases. To distinguish between the two situations would be to make a distinction on the basis of citizenship, a distinction which does not appear to have been intended. Where the parties have had similar interests and motives in the various cases, then it would appear that their rights have been adequately protected and there is no reason not to make the discovered materials available.
   > [at 484]

   Concerning the "trade secret" nature of the manufacturer's documents, the court noted that "[i]t cannot be argued that in a typical case the hazardous nature of a substance is properly to be regarded as a trade secret." *Id.* at 483.

   The court also rejected the defendant's "clearinghouse" and "barratry" contentions. *Id.* at 484–85.

   Interestingly, the manufacturer conceded that information released in other cases *without a protective order* was not subject to restriction. *Id.* at 483.

38. *Ex parte Uppercu*, 239 U.S. 435, 440 (1915).

   Contract.

A litigant in subsequent action petitioned the Court to modify a sealing order to permit access to materials produced in a former action. In ruling in favor of the petition, Justice Holmes recognized the value of information sharing.

> [T]he necessities of litigation and the requirements of justice found a new right of a wholly different kind. So long as the object physically exists, anyone needing it as evidence at a trial has a right to call for it, unless some exception is shown to the general rule.

It should be noted that *Uppercu* was decided before the adoption of the Federal Rules of Civil Procedure.

39. *Waelde v. Merck, Sharp & Dohme*, 94 F.R.D. 27, 29–30 (E.D. Mich. 1981).

Products case; drug Clinoril.

The court denied the manufacturer's motion for a restrictive confidentiality order. The court found that the proposed umbrella approach was too broad. The court also held that information sharing among plaintiff's counsel did not support the manufacturer's charge of a threat of "competitive" harm.

> However, this is not a case where a competitor is the party seeking the information, such as an antitrust action, where courts may be more willing to grant protective orders because of the certainty that the information would in fact be obtained by the competitor and the obvious likelihood of competitive injury. There has been no allegation in this action that plaintiff will use the fruits of discovery for other than legitimate legal proceedings. It therefore seems to this Court that the likelihood that the requested information would reach defendant's competitors is remote and the competitive damage caused by not issuing the protective order as requested is speculative at best. Moreover, as plaintiff notes, the Federal Rules do not prohibit collaboration among litigants, *and there is no merit to the position that the fruits of discovery may not be shared.*
> [emphasis added]

40. *Ward v. Ford Motor Co.*, 93 F.R.D. 579, 580 (D. Colo. 1982).

Products case; fuel system.

The district court overruled the magistrate's order granting the defendant's motion for a restrictive confidentiality order. The plaintiff had offered to agree to a protective order precluding disclosure to the defendant's competitors and the public.

> The plaintiffs' attorneys' discovery information exchange group reduces the effort and expense inflicted on all parties, including Ford, by repetitive and unnecessary discovery. In this era of ever expanding litigation expense, any means of minimizing discovery costs improves the accessibility and economy of justice. If, as asserted, a single design defect is the cause of hundreds of injuries, then the evidentiary facts to prove it must be identical, or nearly so, in all the cases. Each plaintiff should not have to under-

take to discovery [sic] anew the basic evidence that other plaintiffs have uncovered. To so require would be tantamount to holding that each litigant who wishes to ride a taxi to court must undertake the expense of inventing the wheel. Efficient administration of justice requires that courts encourage, not hamstring, information exchanges such as that here involved.

41. *Wauchop v. Domino's Pizza, Inc.*, 138 F.R.D. 539, 546–47 (N.D. Ind. 1991).

Personal injury; automobile accident.

The court overruled the defendant's motion for a restrictive protective order and instead entered an order which permitted information sharing with counsel representing plaintiffs in other similar cases.

> The risk—or in this case, the certainty—that the party receiving the discovery will share it with others does not alone constitute good cause for a protective order. Rule 1 of the Federal Rules of Civil Procedure requires that the Rules be construed so as to foster the just, speedy, and inexpensive determination of every civil action. Collaborative use of discovery material fosters that purpose; the sharing of discovery materials ultimately may further the goals of Rule 1 by eliminating the time and expense involved in "rediscovery." *See Williams v. Johnson & Johnson*, 50 F.R.D. 31, 32 (S.D.N.Y. 1970). The efficient administration of justice should encourage such practices. *Ward v. Ford Motor Co.*, 93 F.R.D. 579, 580 (D. Colo. 1982) ("Each plaintiff should not have to undertake to discovery [sic] anew the basic evidence that other plaintiffs have uncovered. To so require would be tantamount to holding that each litigant who wishes to ride a taxi to court must undertake the expense of inventing the wheel."); *accord, Baker v. Liggett Group, Inc.*, 132 F.R.D. 123, 126 (D. Mass. 1990) ("[T]o routinely require every plaintiff . . . to go through a comparable, prolonged and expensive discovery process would be inappropriate."); *Patterson v. Ford Motor Co.*, 85 F.R.D. 152, 154 (W.D. Tex. 1980) ("The availability of the discovery information may reduce time and money which must be expended in similar proceedings, and may allow for effective, speedy, and efficient representation."). Maintaining a suitably high cost of litigation for future adversaries is not a proper purpose under Rules 1 or 26. *Cipollone v. Liggett Group, Inc.*, 113 F.R.D. at 87.

As Judge Wisdom wrote in *Wilk v. American Medical Ass'n*, 635 F.2d 1295, 1301 (7th Cir. 1980): "A *bona fide* litigant is entitled to his day in court. That the expense of litigation deters many from exercising that right is no reason to erect gratuitous roadblocks in the path of a litigant who finds a trail blazed by another." That the shared information might be detrimental to Domino's in other litigation does not transform the concern into good cause:

> Hooker also argues that the disclosure of information garnered through discovery will be detrimental to its position in parallel lawsuits. This is

unquestionably true. However, this is not a reason for a court to impose a protective order. Use of the discovery fruits disclosed in one lawsuit in connection with other litigation, and even in collaboration among plaintiffs' attorneys, comes squarely within the purposes of the Federal Rules of Civil Procedure. . . . Such cooperation among litigants promotes the speedy and inexpensive determination of every action as well as conservation of judicial resources.

United States v. Hooker Chemicals & Plastics Corp., 90 F.R.D. 421, 426 (W.D.N.Y. 1981). Indeed, even Domino's might find itself spared additional rounds of disputes over what is discoverable. See *Carter-Wallace, Inc. v. Hartz Mountain Industries, Inc.*, 92 F.R.D. at 69–70.

42. *Wilk v. American Medical Ass'n*, 635 F.2d 1295, 1299–1301 (7th Cir. 1980).

Antitrust.

The court of appeals reversed the district court's denial of a petition to modify a protective order to permit information sharing.

Federal Rule of Civil Procedure 26(c) permits protective orders to be issued "for good cause shown" to protect litigants from burdensome or oppressive discovery. Yet, "[a]s a general proposition, pre-trial discovery must take place in the public [sic] unless compelling reasons exist for denying the public access to the proceedings." [citing *AT&T Co. v. Grady*, case no. B.6, supra] *This presumption should operate with all the more force when litigants seek to use discovery in aid of collateral litigation on similar issues, for in addition to the abstract virtues of sunlight as a disinfectant, access in such cases materially eases the tasks of courts and litigants and speeds up what may otherwise be a lengthy process.* Particularly in litigation of this magnitude, we, like the Multidistrict Panel, are impressed with the wastefulness of requiring the State of New York to duplicate discovery already made. Rule 1 of the Federal Rules requires the Rules to be construed "to secure the just, speedy, and inexpensive determination of every action." *We therefore agree with the result reached by every other appellate court which has considered the issue*, and hold that where an appropriate modification of a protective order can place private litigants in a position they would otherwise reach only after repetition of another's discovery, such modification can be denied only where it would tangibly prejudice substantial rights of the party opposing modification. [emphasis added]

* * *

Indeed, the only general argument advanced by the appellee for denying access is that a contrary holding might encourage others to file similar suits in hopes of obtaining a similar access to the discovery material. There is no merit whatever to this argument. A *bona fide* litigant is entitled to his day in court. That the expense of litigation deters many from exercising that right is no reason to erect gratuitous roadblocks in the path of a litigant who finds a trial blazed by another. Any legitimate interests in secrecy can be accommodated by amendment of the protective order to include the new litigants within its restrictions, rather than simply vacating it.

Much of the language above was quoted with approval in *United Nuclear Corp. v. Cranford Ins. Co.*, 905 F.2d 1424, 1428 (10th Cir. 1990), *cert. denied*, 498 U.S. 1073 (1991); *Kerasotes Mich. Theatres, Inc. v. National Amusements, Inc.*, 139 F.R.D. 102, 105 (E.D. Mich. 1991); *Kraszewski v. State Farm Gen. Ins. Co.*, 139 F.R.D. 156, 159–61 (N.D. Cal. 1991); *Phillips Petroleum Co. v. Picken*, 105 F.R.D. 545, 550–51 (N.D. Tex. 1985).

43. *Williams v. Johnson & Johnson*, 50 F.R.D. 31, 32, 33 (S.D.N.Y. 1970).

Products case; oral contraceptive.

The court denied the manufacturer's motion for a restrictive confidentiality order.

In this situation, it is at least theoretically advantageous to the attorneys for plaintiffs in the various suits to share the fruits of discovery. They thus reduce the time and money which must be expended to prepare for trial and are probably able to provide more effective, speedy and efficient representation to their clients. . . . [S]uch collaboration comes squarely within the aims laid out in the first and fundamental rule of the Federal Rules of Civil Procedure: "These rules *** shall be construed to secure the just, speedy, and inexpensive determination of every action." Rule 1, Fed. R. Civ. P. *Thus, there is no merit to the all-encompassing contention that the fruits of discovery in one case are to be used in that case only.*
[emphasis added]

* * *

The only specific allegation defendants make in this respect ["stirr[ing] up" or "promot[ing]" litigation] is that plaintiffs' attorneys may sell or may have sold the fruits of the discovery in this case with other materials and information to attorneys engaged in similar cases. Without more, the charging of fees between attorneys collaborating in similar cases and the collaboration itself both seem reasonable on their face.

44. *Wilson v. American Motors Corp.*, 759 F.2d 1568, 1571 & n.3 (11th Cir. 1985).

Products case; jeep roll-over.

The district court sealed the trial transcript as part of a settlement agreement consented to by the parties before the jury returned a verdict. Plaintiff's counsel in a similar case in California petitioned the district court to unseal the record. The district court's refusal was reversed by the Eleventh Circuit.

The defendant's desire to prevent the use of this trial record in other proceedings is simply not an adequate justification for its sealing.

* * *

Quite the contrary would appear to be true. If formal proceedings occur in one court and are relevant to issues being presented in another court, judicial economy would mandate their availability.

C. Unreported Cases

1. *Benson v. Ford Motor Co.*, No. 91-03605 (Harris County, Tex. Dist. Ct. Mar. 15, 1992) (*rev'd on procedural grounds*, 846 S.W.2d 487 (Ct. App. Tex. 1993).

    Products case; Bronco II.

    Acting under Texas Supreme Court rule 76a, the state court judge denied Ford's request for a protective order to seal discovery documents from public disclosure.

2. *Brandimarti v. Caterpillar*, CA No. G.D. 83-12468 (Allegheny County, Pa. Ct. C.P. Oct. 8, 1985), *reprinted in* HARE, GILBERT, & REMINE, CONFIDENTIALITY ORDERS, app. A-2 (1988).

    Two products cases; a forklift turnover case and an IUD case.

    The trial court denied the manufacturer's motion for a restrictive confidentiality order. Opinion specifically notes that the court might be receptive to entering an order limiting dissemination to information sharing between litigants with similar cases.

    > The attorney whose client is an alleged victim of a product defect faces many obstacles that may prevent the presentation of the client's strongest case. *The attorney may not fully understand the complicated design and engineering issues that govern his or her client's claim. The expense involved in preparing a case for trial may cause counsel to abandon the case, to settle more cheaply, or to go to trial without necessary evidence.* Inexact requests for discovery may be construed so as to avoid turning over information that would be very helpful to the party seeking discovery and would be produced if sought in a more skillful manner. Damaging information provided through discovery may be overlooked because it is presented in a manner designed to minimize its damaging aspects.

    > If a product is defective, product liability law intends that an injured party be compensated for the damages sustained from the defect. The purposes of the substantive law are thwarted if limited funds or counsel's lack of sophistication prevent the victim of a product defect from establishing the defect. *Thus, our discovery rules should not be applied in a manner that hinders the efforts of an alleged victim of a product defect to present his or her best case.*

    > If one party has been able to show that the product is defective, a second party's success should not depend upon whether he or she is able to repeat the first party's discovery. *When courts prevent successful litigants from sharing information obtained through discovery, the controlling issue is frequently not whether the product is defective but whether a party has sufficient resources and competence to discover the defect.*
    > [emphasis added]

    * * *

    > The goals of the Pennsylvania Rules of Civil Procedure are to secure the just, speedy, and inexpensive determination of every action. Pa. R. C. P.

126. Cooperation amongst attorneys representing plaintiffs with similar claims will reduce the time and money which must be expended to prepare for trial and will enable counsel to provide more effective and efficient representation. Thus, such collaboration comes squarely within the aims of the Pennsylvania Rules of Civil Procedure. *See Patterson v. Ford Motor Co.* [case no. B.31, *supra*] and *Williams v. Johnson & Johnson* [case no. B.43, *supra*].

3. *Crews v. Ford Motor Co.*, No. 90-472-Civ-Orl-19 (M.D. Fla. Jan. 8, 1991).

Products case; Bronco II.

The court denied Ford's motion for a restrictive protective order and entered an order permitting plaintiff's counsel to share confidential discovery materials with "attorneys and their experts representing plaintiffs in cases involving the same defect against this defendant who shall as a condition precedent to disclosure execute the attached agreement (Exhibit 1) which plaintiff's counsel shall maintain." *Id.* at 2.

4. *Dunshie v. General Motors Corp.*, CA No. A-136,024 (Jefferson County, Tex. Dist. Ct. Feb. 28, 1991), *appeal dismissed*, 822 S.W.2d 345 (Tex. Ct. App. 1992).

Products case; automobile.

After consideration of briefs and an evidentiary hearing, the trial court first held that GM's confidential discovery materials did not qualify for public disclosure under the provisions of rule 76a, Tex. R. Civ. P. The court then entered a protective order forbidding disclosure to any competitor of GM, holding that such a disclosure would likely result in a specific and serious harm to the defendant's interest which was not outweighed by any probable adverse effect that sealing would have upon the general public health or safety.

However, the court did permit information sharing of discovery materials between plaintiff's counsel and experts involved in similar cases [under *Garcia v. Peeples*, 734 S.W.2d 343 (Tex. 1984)] subject to certain stated conditions, including an acknowledgment by such other persons to be bound by the provisions of the court's order.

The appellate court held that the trial court did not abuse its discretion in entering the latter order.

5. *Goode v. American Honda Motor Co.*, CA No. CV 85-4033 (Jefferson County, Ala. Cir. Ct. May 27, 1987), *reprinted in* HARE, GILBERT & REMINE, CONFIDENTIALITY ORDERS app. A-6 (1988).

Products case; automobile.

The defendant manufacturer sought a restrictive confidentiality order forbidding information sharing among plaintiffs' counsel with similar cases. After extensive briefs and the evidentiary hearing, the court, without opinion, entered a protective order allowing disclosure of confidential discovery materials to "attorneys and their expert consultants representing Plaintiffs in other litigation against this Defendant involving similar products liability claims" on the condition that such persons would sign an agreement to be bound by the terms of the order and subject to the court's jurisdiction. The order further provided that the plaintiff's counsel was to maintain a copy of all the nondisclosure agreements.

6. *Go-Tane Serv. Stations, Inc. v. Ashland Oil, Inc.*, CA No. 79-C-1675 (N.D. Ill. May 5, 1980).

Antitrust.

The district court modified a restrictive confidentiality order entered by the magistrate so as to permit information sharing in other similar cases. Persons provided access were required to sign an affidavit agreeing to be bound by the order. A list of these names was kept under seal by the court.

7. *Hadfield v. Ford Motor Co.*, 7 Prod. Safety & Liab. Rep. (BNA) 905 (Nov. 16, 1979).

Products case; fuel system.

The trial court denied the manufacturer's motion for a restrictive confidentiality order.

8. *Hendricks v. Jeep Corp.*, CA No. CV-82-092 (Mont. Dist. Ct. June 4, 1986), *reprinted in* HARE, GILBERT & REMINE, CONFIDENTIALITY ORDERS 67 (1988).

Products case; jeep roll-over.

The district court wrote a special opinion upon entering a stipulated confidentiality order in which the court called attention to the burden of proof on the party seeking a protective order and the necessity for the court to consider countervailing interests affected by the order. The court noted that "[c]ooperation among litigants, through the exchange of discovered information, 'promotes the speedy and inexpensive determination of every action, as well as conservation of judicial resources.'" [citing *Hooker Chemicals* (case no. B.36, *supra*) and *Williams v. Johnson & Johnson* (case no. B.43, *supra*)]

9. *Hughes v. Honda Motor Co.*, CA No. 87-436-787-A (Victoria County, Tex. Dist. Ct. June 13, 1988).

Products case; ATV.

After months of negotiations involving this and other related cases, counsel for the plaintiff and the Honda defendants entered into an Agreed Protective Order that forbids disclosure of confidential discovery materials to the defendant's competitors but permits "plaintiffs' counsel and experts . . . to exchange information with other attorneys involved in the prosecution of similar litigation" subject to certain stated conditions including a certification that such persons agree not to disclose confidential documents except as provided in the order. *See also Oberg v. Honda Motor Co.*, CA No. A8709-05897 (Multnomah County, Or. Cir. Ct. Feb. 15, 1990).

10. *Kyle v. Stauffer Chem. Co.*, CA 89-0786-CB-C (S.D. Ala. Mar. 1, 1991).

Negligence claim; industrial explosion.

The district court denied the defendant's motion for a restrictive protective order and accepted plaintiff's proposed order which forbade dissemination of confidential discovery materials to the public or to defendant's competitors but permitted information sharing among litigants with similar cases.

On the issue of post-litigation dissemination of confidential information with other similarly situated litigants and their attorneys, the clear modern trend is to deny attempts to prohibit dissemination without specific evidence of harm, particularly if the only allegation is that the producing party will be placed in a competitive disadvantage *if* the information should make its way into the hands of a competitor.

> The courts have emphatically held that a protective order cannot be issued simply because it may be detrimental to the movant in other lawsuits. *United States v. Hooker Chems. & Plastics Corp.*, 90 F.R.D. at 426; *Kamp Implement Co., Inc. v. J.I. Case Co.*, 630 F. Supp. 218, 219 (D. Mont. 1986); *Patterson v. Ford Motor Co.*, 85 F.R.D. 152, 153 (W.D. Tex. 1980). Using fruits of discovery from one lawsuit in another litigation, and even in collaboration among various plaintiffs' attorneys, comes squarely within the purposes of the Federal Rules of Civil Procedure. *United States v. Hooker Chems. & Plastics Corp.*, 90 F.R.D. at 426. The harm possibly emanating therefrom does not form a basis for a protective order.

* * *

> Of the Courts that have considered protective orders of the nature proposed by the defendant, an overwhelming majority have refused to grant any type of protection from dissemination. *Nestle Foods Corp. v. Aetna Casualty & Sur. Co.*, 129 F.R.D. 483, 486 (D.N.J. 1990).

> The representation of documents produced for inspection by the Court clearly show that the information sought to be protected is confidential and has been treated as confidential by Akzo and its predecessor Stauffer Chemical Company. Plaintiffs do not seek an unrestricted right to disclose this information, however, they simply want to be able to use and/or share this information with future plaintiffs and their attorneys. Akzo has failed to carry its burden of persuading the Court that the granting of plaintiffs' request would likely result in economic injury or even that it is probably that competitors would be given access. Tommie Kyle is an injured employee who is seeking damages for an on-the-job accident. He is not a competitor and no motive has been shown that would indicate a willingness on his part or that of his attorneys to share confidential information with one of Akzo's competitors.

> The arguments, and facts supplied in support thereof, made by Akzo to support its position that all confidential information produced in discovery should be ordered returned after termination of this case are not sufficient to carry its burden of showing good cause for the inclusion of this specific requirement in a protective order. Accordingly, paragraph ten of the proposed protective order is rejected and plaintiffs will only be prohibited from disclosing confidential information to Akzo's competitors and the general public.

Akzo's motion for a protective order is therefore GRANTED IN PART. The Court will enter a protective order, by separate document, prohibiting the disclosure of the information contained in the documents withheld as confidential to Akzo's competitors, direct and indirect, and the general public at large, but will reserve to plaintiffs the opportunity to share the discovered information with other plaintiffs and plaintiffs' counsel. *See Cipollone v. Liggett Group, Inc.*, 113 F.R.D. 86 (D.N.J. 1986), *aff'd*, 822 F.2d 335 (3d Cir. 1987); *Deford v. Schmid Prods. Co.*, 120 F.R.D. 648 (D. Md. 1987); *Burlington City Bd. of Educ. v. United States Minerals Prods. Co.*, 115 F.R.D. 188 (M.D.N.C. 1987); *Nestles Food Corp. v. Aetna Casualty & Sur. Co.*, 129 F.R.D. 483 (D.N.J. 1990). The motion for a protective order is otherwise DENIED. [at 7-11 of Memorandum Opinion and Order]

11. *Moseley v. General Motors Corp.*, CA No. 90V6276 (Fulton County, Ga. Dist. Ct. Apr. 4, 1991).

    Products case; fuel system.

    After extensive briefs and oral arguments, the trial court denied a restrictive protective order proposed by General Motors. The court entered an order forbidding disclosure of confidential discovery materials to GM competitors but allowing plaintiffs' counsel to share such materials "with other plaintiff's attorneys and expert witnesses involved in pending fuel system integrity litigation against General Motors" on the condition that such other persons sign an attached agreement expressing their consent to be bound by the order and subject to the court's jurisdiction.

12. *Nelson v. Ford Motor Co.*, CA No. 91-698-2 (Saline County, Ark. Cir. Ct. Feb. 19, 1992).

    Products case; Bronco II.

    The trial court denied Ford's motion for a restrictive protective order and instead entered a protective order which permits information sharing among counsel representing plaintiffs in other Bronco II cases and establishes the AIEG as the clearinghouse for documents produced in the Bronco II litigation.

13. *Parker v. Kawasaki Motors Corp., U.S.*, CA No. CC10-88935 (Maricopa County, Ariz. Super. Ct. Oct. 19, 1987).

    Products case; jet ski.

    The defendant manufacturer sought a restrictive confidentiality order to forbid the plaintiff from disseminating accident data to other attorneys representing plaintiffs in similar cases.

    In an excellent opinion recognizing the value of information sharing both to plaintiff's counsel and the courts handling complex product cases, the court denied the defendant's motion.

14. *Patton v. Procter & Gamble Distrib. Co.*, CA No. A8009-05503 (Multnomah County, Or. Cir. Ct. Oct. 14, 1981).

Products case; toxic shock.

After briefs and hearing, the court denied manufacturer's motion for a restrictive protective order and entered an order forbidding disclosure of confidential documents to any competitor of the defendant; however, the order permitted "plaintiffs to otherwise consult with expert witnesses and other attorneys involved in toxic shock syndrome cases against defendant corporation" on the condition that such persons would sign a nondisclosure agreement filed under seal with the court.

15. *Peck v. General Motors Corp.*, CA No. CV-82-0249 (JM) (E.D.N.Y. Jan. 9, 1984).

Products case; heating system.

The court overruled the manufacturer's motion for a restrictive confidentiality order, finding that the defendant failed to carry its burden of showing a threat of competitive harm likely to result from information sharing among litigants in similar cases.

> Use of the discovery fruits disclosed in one lawsuit in connection with other litigation, and even in collaboration among plaintiff's attorneys, comes squarely within the purposes of the Federal Rules of Civil Procedure. Such cooperation among litigants promotes the speedy and inexpensive determination of every action as well as conservation of judicial resources (quoting from *United States v. Hooker Chems. & Plastics Corp.*).

16. *Santiago v. Sherwin-Williams Co.*, CA No. 87-2799-T (D. Mass. Oct. 4, 1989).

Products case; lead paint.

After consideration of extensive briefs and an evidentiary hearing, the court denied the manufacturer's motion for a restrictive confidentiality order. The court entered a protective order that forbade disclosure of trade secret information produced by the defendant either to the public or to the defendant's competitors but allowed information sharing with litigants in other related actions.

> The court disagrees with defendants' argument to the extent they claim that the sharing of discovery materials with other litigants constitutes an abuse of discovery.

> Numerous courts have held that the sharing of information with litigants in other related actions is not foreclosed by the federal discovery rules and indeed "promotes speedy, efficient and inexpensive litigation by facilitating the dissemination of discovery material necessary to analyze one's case and prepare for trial." *Burlington City Bd. of Educ. v. United States Mineral Prods. Co.*, 115 F.R.D. 188, 190 (M.D.N.C. 1987) (denying motion for protective order restricting the use of video depositions taken by plaintiff of defendant's expert witnesses in asbestos case). *See also Deford v. Schmid Prods. Co.*, 120 F.R.D. 648, 654 (D. Md. 1987) (sharing discovery materials with other litigants and their counsel is an "appropriate goal" under the federal discovery rules); *Cipollone II*, 113 F.R.D at 91 ("so long as the initial

litigation has not been instituted in bad faith for the purpose of obtaining documents for other actions, and so long as the interests of those represented in the initial litigation are being fully and ethically prosecuted, the Federal Rules do not foreclose the collaborative use of discovery"); *Fidelity Bankers Life Ins. Co. v. Wedco, Inc.*, 102 F.R.D. 41, 44 (D. Nev. 1984) ("[t]he use of discovery obtained in one lawsuit in connection with other litigation accords with the purposes of the Federal Rules of Civil Procedure"); *Ward v. Ford Motor Co.*, 93 F.R.D. 579, 580 (D. Colo. 1982) (plaintiffs' attorneys' exchange group promotes efficient administration of justice and courts should not "hamstring" such information exchanges); *United States v. Hooker Chems. & Plastics Corp.*, 90 F.R.D. at 426 ("[u]se of the discovery fruits disclosed in one lawsuit in connection with other litigation, and even in collaboration among plaintiffs' attorneys, comes squarely within the purposes of the Federal Rules of Civil Procedure"); *Patterson v. Ford Motor Co.*, 85 F.R.D. 152, 154 (W.D. Tex. 1980) ("[c]ollaboration among plaintiffs' attorneys would come squarely within the aims of the Federal Rules of Civil Procedure").

17. *Sieracki v. Ford Motor Co.*, CA No. 76-130 (S.D. Ill. June 6, 1978), *reprinted in* HARE, GILBERT & REMINE, CONFIDENTIALITY ORDERS, app. A-3 (1988).

Products case; fuel system.

The defendant manufacturer sought a restrictive confidentiality order for the stated purpose of precluding information sharing between plaintiff's counsel with similar cases.

In denying the manufacturer's motion for restrictive protective order, the court held that information sharing was in furtherance of Fed. R. Civ. P. 1 and found that Ford had not shown that such disclosure of their documents would result in a "competitive disadvantage."

> The primary concerns of this defendant seem to be that plaintiffs' attorney will use discovery in this case to promote further litigation involving defendants which would result in undue economic burden. This is strikingly similar to the theory rejected by the Court in *Williams v. Johnson & Johnson*, 50 F.R.D. 31 (S.D.N.Y. 1970). I cannot agree with Ford's general contention that discovery should not be communicated to anyone not a party to this litigation. *It is difficult to complete discovery in complex and time-consuming products litigation such as this.* We are concerned with specific automotive design defects which resulted in gasoline entering the passenger compartment upon impact.

* * *

> I can find no good cause or compelling reason for denying public access to this information, including access by attorneys in similar proceedings. Quite the contrary, I believe this information should be available for use in a proper case. *The availability of such discovery may reduce time and money which must be expended to prepare for trial in those cases and may allow for effective, speedy and efficient representation.*

[emphasis added]

18. *Swenholt v. Merrell-Dow Pharmaceuticals, Inc.*, CA No. 80-2874 (D.D.C. Jan. 16, 1984), *reprinted in* HARE, GILBERT & REMINE, CONFIDENTIALITY ORDERS app. A-5 (1988).

Products case; drug Thalidomide.

The district court vacated a confidentiality order entered by the magistrate requiring the parties to return discovery materials at the conclusion of the case. The case was settled. The defendant manufacturer contended that the stipulation of dismissal should include a provision requiring the plaintiff to return documents produced by the defendant.

> Dissemination will not cause substantial and serious harm; rather the free dissemination of discovery materials, especially to similar cases pending, will promote effective and inexpensive determination of the actions (citing *Hooker Chemicals* and *Patterson v. Ford Motor Co.*).

19. *Thayer v. Liggett & Myers Tobacco Co.*, CA No. 5314 (W.D. Mich. Feb. 19, 1970), *reprinted in* HARE, GILBERT & REMINE, CONFIDENTIALITY ORDERS, app. A-1 (1988).

Products case; tobacco.

The court granted the manufacturer's motion for a restrictive protective order preventing plaintiff's counsel from sharing discovery materials with attorneys handling similar cases. As to the effect of this order in the subsequent proceedings in the case, the court observed the following:

> Defendant in this case enjoyed all of the advantages that wealth naturally produces. But this was not enough. It sought, in addition, to restrict plaintiff's own flexibility in trial preparation. The success of this effort magnified the existing inequality of these parties.
>
> * * *
>
> As the total picture developed during the trial, it appeared that the protective order was serving defendant well in areas unrelated to the protection of its trade secrets or legitimate procedural rights. These indirect benefits, which were unclear to all but defendant when the order was granted, may have been the most important reason for seeking 30(b) [now Rule 26(c)(7)] protection.
>
> * * *
>
> Plaintiff's attorneys were prohibited from disclosing, discussing or referring to, with any other person, any material, privileged or not, which was furnished by defendant. Fruitful consultation between plaintiff's attorneys with similar cases in other areas was thus effectively throttled. . . . Defendant thus succeeded, to a very significant degree, in isolating plaintiff from outside assistance and advice.
>
> * * *
>
> [T]he court was somewhat puzzled by the failure of either the discovered material in the court's file or the evidence presented to reveal anything approaching a trade secret.

[F]rom the first day of the trial approximately a half dozen to a dozen defense attorneys, involved in similar cases around the country, were in constant attendance in the courtroom. These attorneys took notes, conferred with each other and conferred with defendant's counsel. By way of contrast, the breadth of defendant's protective order had effectively prohibited plaintiff from similar consultations.

* * *

To recapitulate, the court was witness to a spectacle wherein defendant, rich in resources, maintained complete freedom of association and consultation, including courtroom conferences with other attorneys experienced in the trial of similar cases, while plaintiff's counsel, already disadvantaged by the limited resources available to them, were prohibited from doing likewise by a blanket protective order obtained by defendant early in the case on grounds which later proved largely illusory.

* * *

In addition, the order prevents discovery, in future cases, of documents which normally would be public records. This, too, serves defendant well. It makes future discovery for other individual plaintiffs more difficult, more time consuming, and more expensive. It insulates data that could be used for impeachment or other evidentiary purposes.

* * *

The court is convinced that the magnitude of the impact of the disparity in resources between these parties, plus the sophisticated and calculated exploitation of the situation by the defendant approaches a denial of due process which would compel the granting of a new trial. This question, unfortunately, is now moot because plaintiff cannot afford further proceedings.

20. *Yurko v. Nissan Motor Corp., U.S.*, CA No. 756 (Lackawanna County, Pa. Ct. C.P. Jan. 26, 1984), *reprinted in* HARE, GILBERT & REMINE, CONFIDENTIALITY ORDERS app. A-4 (1988).

Products case; door lock mechanism.

The manufacturer sought a restrictive confidentiality order for design materials and drawings. The defendant specifically charged that harm would result from the plaintiff's disclosure of the documents to members of ATLA.

The court denied the manufacturer's motion for a restrictive protective order.

It is well established that it is not "inherently culpable" to share information obtained through discovery and the possibility that a party obtaining discovery will do so is not "good cause" to justify a protective order.

* * *

Rather it would be judicially prudent for attorneys to share the fruits of discovery [citing *Ward v. Ford Motor Co.*, 93 F.R.D. 579, 580 (D. Colo. 1982)].

The court noted that it would be inappropriate to limit the scope of discovery by litigants in other jurisdictions, stating that "[i]f [the defendant] requires protection in other forums, it should apply to the courts before which those cases are pending." [citing *In re Upjohn Antibiotic Cleocin Prods.*, 81 F.R.D. 482, 484 (E.D. Mich. 1979)]

The court also noted that corporations have no right of privacy.

APPENDIX 3

SUMMARY OF AUTHORITIES FOR DISCOVERY ABUSE SANCTIONS

Source of Authority	Requirement or Sanctionable Conduct	Authorized Sanctions	Sanctionable Entity	When Appealable
Fed. R. Civ. P. 16(f)	*Sanctionable Behavior:* Failure to obey a scheduling or pretrial order or to attend a pretrial conference prepared.	"Such orders as are just," which shall include reimbursement of expenses, including attorney fees.	Attorney, party, pro se litigant	*Attorney:* Immediately appealable. *Party:* Appealable upon entry of judgment or final order in the case.
Fed. R. Civ. P. 26(g)	*Requirement:* Discovery requests, responses, and objections must be signed by an attorney certifying, based on reasonable inquiry, that it is (1) consistent with the rules and warranted by existing law or a good faith argument for its extension, modification, or reversal; (2) not interposed for an improper purpose such as harassment, delay, or increased cost of litigation; and (3) not unreasonable, unduly burdensome, or expensive under the circumstances of the case. Initial and pretrial disclosures must also be signed, certifying that to the best of the signer's knowledge after reasonable inquiry, the disclosure is complete and correct at the time it is made.	Violations sanctioned by "an appropriate sanction," which may include reimbursement of expenses, including attorney fees.	Attorney, party, pro se litigant	*Attorney:* Immediately appealable. *Party:* Appealable upon entry of judgment or final order in the case.
Fed. R. Civ. P. 30(d)	*Requirement:* Impeding or delaying deposition examination.	Appropriate sanction, including reasonable costs and attorney fees.	Any person responsible, including attorney, party, nonparty witness	No case law on point. Probably immediately appealable for nonparties including attorneys and appealable on entry of judgment or final order for party.

Source of Authority	Requirement or Sanctionable Conduct	Authorized Sanctions	Sanctionable Entity	When Appealable
Fed. R. Civ. P. 30(g)	*Sanctionable Behavior:* Failure of party noticing deposition to attend or proceed; or, if the witness does not attend, failure of the noticing party to have subpoenaed the witness.	Reimbursement by noticing party of attending party's expenses, including attorney fees.	Party	Appealable upon entry of judgment or final order in the case.
Fed. R. Civ. P. 37(a)(4)	*Sanctionable Behavior:* Unsuccessfully moving for a rule 37(a) order compelling discovery or unsuccessfully opposing such a motion where such a motion or opposition is not substantially justified.	Reimbursement of prevailing party's expenses, including attorney fees.	Attorney, party, pro se litigant	*Attorney:* Immediately appealable. *Party:* Appealable upon entry of judgment or final order in the case.
Fed. R. Civ. P. 37(b)(1)	*Sanctionable Behavior:* Failure of deponent to be sworn or to answer a question after being ordered to do so.	Sanctions available for contempt of court.	Deponent	As per contempt law.
Fed. R. Civ. P. 37(b)(2)	*Sanctionable Behavior:* Failure to obey a discovery order.	"Such orders in regard to the failure which are just," including: • deeming facts established, • precluding claims or opposition to claims, • striking pleadings or portions of pleadings, • dismissal or default judgment,		

APPENDIX 3: SUMMARY OF AUTHORITIES FOR DISCOVERY ABUSE SANCTIONS

Source of Authority	Requirement or Sanctionable Conduct	Authorized Sanctions	Sanctionable Entity	When Appealable
Fed. R. Civ. P. 37(c)	*Sanctionable Behavior:* Unwarranted failure to admit, in response to a rule 36 request for admission, a matter later proven to be true.	• sanctions available for contempt of court, and • reimbursement of expenses, including attorney fees.	Attorney, party, pro se litigant	*Attorney:* Conflict of authority as to whether immediately appealable.
Fed. R. Civ. P. 37(d)	*Sanctionable Behavior:* Failure of a party to appear for properly noticed deposition, to respond to interrogatories, or to respond to a request for inspection.	Reimbursement of requesting party's expenses, including attorney fees.	Party	Appealable upon entry of judgment or final order in the case.
Fed. R. Civ. P. 37(g)	*Sanctionable Behavior:* Failure to participate in good faith in framing a rule 26(f) discovery plan.	"Such orders in regard to the failure as are just."	Attorney, party, pro se litigant	*Attorney:* Conflict of authority as to whether immediately appealable. *Party:* Appealable upon entry of judgment or final order in the case.
		Reimbursement of expenses, including attorney fees.	Attorney, party, pro se litigant	*Attorney:* Conflict of authority as to whether immediately appealable. *Party:* Appealable upon entry of judgment or final order in the case.
28 U.S.C. § 1927	*Sanctionable Behavior:* Multiplying the proceedings in any case unreasonably and vexatiously.	Reimbursements of costs, expenses, and attorney fees.	Attorney	Immediately appealable.

Source of Authority	Requirement or Sanctionable Conduct	Authorized Sanctions	Sanctionable Entity	When Appealable
Inherent Power of the Court	*Sanctionable Behavior*: Abusive litigation practices, undertaken in bad faith. Usually invoked when Fed. R. Civ. P. sanction authorities do not precisely apply.	Broad discretion of trial court to fashion appropriate sanction.	Attorney, party, pro se litigant	*Attorney*: Conflict of authority as to whether immediately appealable. *Party*: No reported cases, but presumably appealable upon entry of judgment or final order in the case.

BIBLIOGRAPHY

I. DISCOVERY, GENERAL

A. Treatises

23 AM. JUR. 2D *Depositions and Discovery* §§ 1–467 (1983 & Supp. 1992).

AMERICAN LAW OF PRODUCTS LIABILITY 3D § 53 (1987 & Supp. 1992).

BALDWIN, HARE, & MCGOVERN, *Plaintiff's Discovery, in* THE PREPARATION OF A PRODUCT LIABILITY CASE (2d ed. 1993).

DISCOVERY PROCEEDINGS IN FEDERAL COURT (Shepard's eds., 2d ed. 1991 & Supp. 1992).

DOMBROFF, DISCOVERY (1986 & Supp. 1990).

3 FRUMER & FRIEDMAN, PRODUCTS LIABILITY (rev. ed. 1992).

GLASER, PRETRIAL DISCOVERY AND THE ADVERSARY SYSTEM (1968).

GORELICK ET AL., DESTRUCTION OF EVIDENCE (1989 & Supp. 1991).

HARE, GILBERT & REMINE, CONFIDENTIALITY ORDERS (1988).

HAYDOCK & HERR, DISCOVERY PRACTICE (2d ed. 1988 & Supp. 1992).

IMWINKELRIED & BLUMOFF, PRETRIAL DISCOVERY: STRATEGY AND TACTICS (1986 & Supp. 1992).

KIELY, PREPARING PRODUCTS LIABILITY CASES (1986 & Supp. 1989).

LOWE, PRODUCTS LIABILITY LITIGATION: PRETRIAL PRACTICE (1988).

4 & 4A MOORE ET AL., MOORE'S FEDERAL PRACTICE (2d ed. 1991 & Supp. 1992).

SCHWARZER & PASAHOW, CIVIL DISCOVERY: A GUIDE TO EFFICIENT PRACTICE (1988 & Supp. 1989).

UNDERWOOD, A GUIDE TO FEDERAL DISCOVERY RULES (2d ed. 1985).

8 WRIGHT & MILLER, FEDERAL PRACTICE AND PROCEDURE (1970 & Supp. 1992).

B. Law Review Articles

Blair, *A Guide to the New Federal Discovery Practice*, 21 DRAKE L. REV. 58 (1971).

Brazil, *The Adversary Character of Civil Discovery: A Critique and Proposals for Change*, 31 VAND. L. REV. 1295 (1978).

Case Comment, *The First Amendment Right to Disseminate Discovery Materials: In re Halkin*, 92 HARV. L. REV. 1550 (1979).

Cavanagh, *The August 1, 1983 Amendments to the Federal Rules of Civil Procedure: A Critical Evaluation and a Proposal for More Effective Discovery Through Local Rules*, 30 VILL. L. REV. 767 (1985).

Chandler, *Discovery and Pre-Trial Procedure in Federal Courts*, 12 OKLA. L. REV. 321 (1959).

Civil Pretrial Discovery Symposium, 33 S.D. L. REV. 195 (1988).

Cohn, *Federal Discovery: A Survey of Local Rules and Practices in View of Proposed Changes to the Federal Rules*, 63 MINN. L. REV. 253 (1979).

Craig, *Privilege in Discovery of Documents*, 23 ALBERTA L. REV. 388 (1985).

Cutner, *Discovery—Civil Litigation's Fading Light: A Lawyer Looks at the Federal Discovery Rules After Forty Years of Use*, 52 TEMP. L.Q. 933 (1979).

Dallas, *Effective Use of Interrogatories and Depositions: Some Practical Pointers*, 45 BROOK. L. REV. 297 (1979).

Dobie, *The Federal Rules of Civil Procedure*, 25 VA. L. REV. 261(1939).

Dunlap, Comment, *Discovery Priority Rule Under the Federal Rules of Civil Procedure—Friend or Foe?*, 74 DICK. L. REV. 103 (1969).

Emfinger, Comment, *Postjudgment Use of Discovery: Recognizing the "Gap,"* 9 CUMB. L. REV. 473 (1978).

Frank, *Pretrial Conferences and Discovery—Disclosure or Surprise?*, 1965 INS. L.J. 661.

Frankel, *The Search for Truth: An Umpireal View*, 123 U. PA. L. REV. 1031 (1975).

Freedman, *Discovery as an Instrument of Justice*, 22 TEMP. L.Q. 174 (1948).

Friedenthal, *A Divided Supreme Court Adopts Discovery Amendments to the Federal Rules of Civil Procedure*, 69 CAL. L. REV. 806 (1981).

Gardner, *Privilege and Discovery: Background and Development in English and American Law*, 53 GEO. L.J. 585 (1965).

Gildin, *A Practical Guide to Taking and Defending Depositions*, 88 DICK. L. REV. 247 (1984).

Goldstein, *A Short History of Discovery*, 10 ANGLO-AM. L. REV. 257 (1981).

Heriot, Comment, *Civil Discovery of Documents Held by a Grand Jury*, 47 U. CHI. L. REV. 604 (1980).

Hoey, *Discovery Proceedings under the Federal Rules*, 9 N.Y. L.F. 517 (1963).

Holtzoff, *The Elimination of Surprise in Federal Practice*, 7 VAND. L. REV. 576 (1954).

Holtzoff, *Origin and Sources of the Federal Rules of Civil Procedure*, 30 N.Y.U. L. REV. 1057 (1955).

Joyce, Comment, *Preventing Abuse of Discovery in Federal Courts*, 30 CATH. U. L. REV. 273 (1981).

Kaminsky, *Proposed Federal Discovery Rules for Complex Civil Litigation*, 48 FORDHAM L. REV. 907 (1980).

Kaskell, *The United States and Discovery Under the Federal Rules of Civil Procedure,* 13 LOY. L. REV. 1 (1966–1967).

Kroll & Maciszewski, *Pre-Trial Discovery: Change in the Federal Rules,* 7 HAW. B.J. 48 (1970), *reprinted in* TREADWELL, NEW FEDERAL CIVIL DISCOVERY RULE SOURCE BOOK 205 (1972).

Massey, *Depositions of Corporations: Problems and Solutions—Fed. R. Civ. P. 30(b)(6),* 1986 ARIZ. ST. L.J. 81.

Matherne, Note, *Forced Disclosure of Academic Research,* 37 VAND. L. REV. 585 (1984).

Mitchell, Comment, *Federal Discovery in Concurrent Criminal and Civil Proceedings,* 52 TUL. L. REV. 769 (1978).

Mullin, Comment, *Discovery in Aid of Execution and Supplementary Proceedings: Two Weapons in the Creditor's Arsenal,* 11 VILL. L. REV. 602 (1966).

Nordenberg, *The Supreme Court and Discovery Reform: The Continuing Need for an Umpire,* 31 SYRACUSE L. REV. 543 (1980).

Note, *Developments in the Law—Discovery,* 74 HARV. L. REV. 940 (1961).

Note, *Discovery Abuse Under the Federal Rules: Causes and Cures,* 92 YALE L.J. 352 (1982).

Note, *Discovery Practice in States Adopting the Federal Rules of Civil Procedure,* 68 HARV. L. REV. 673 (1955).

Note, *Masters and Magistrates in the Federal Courts,* 88 HARV. L. REV. 779 (1975).

Note, *Nonparty Access to Discovery Materials in the Federal Courts,* 94 HARV. L. REV. 1085 (1981).

Note, *Preferential Treatment of the United States Under Federal Civil Discovery Procedures,* 13 GA. L. REV. 550 (1979).

Note, *The Use of Discovery to Obtain Jurisdictional Facts,* 59 VA. L. REV. 533 (1973).

Pike & Willis, *The New Federal Deposition-Discovery Procedure: I,* 38 COLUM. L. REV. 1179 (1938).

Randall, Comment, *Protective Orders Prohibiting Dissemination of Discovery Information: The First Amendment and Good Cause,* 1980 DUKE L.J. 766.

Roberts, *The Financial Condition and Insurance Policy Limits of a Joint Tortfeasor Wishing to Settle in Good Faith: Problems of Discovery and Confidentiality,* 26 SANTA CLARA L. REV. 63 (1986).

Rosenberg, *Sanctions to Effectuate Pretrial Discovery,* 58 COLUM. L. REV. 480 (1958).

Rosenberg & King, *Curbing Discovery Abuse in Civil Litigation: Enough Is Enough,* 1981 B.Y.U. L. REV. 579.

Savaiano, Note, *Excessive Discovery in Federal and Illinois Courts: A Tool of Harassment and Delay?,* 11 LOY. U. CHI. L.J. 807 (1980).

Savell, *Discovery Proceedings from the Defendant's Point of View,* 26 GA. B.J. 143 (1963).

Scheindlin, *Discovering the Discoverable: A Bird's Eye View of Discovery in a Complex Multidistrict Class Action Litigation,* 52 BROOK. L. REV. 397 (1986).

Schmertz, *Written Depositions Under Federal and State Rules as Cost-Effective Discovery at Home and Abroad*, 16 VILL. L. REV. 7 (1970).

Schroeder & Frank, *The Proposed Changes in Discovery Rules*, 1978 ARIZ. ST. L.J. 475.

Shapiro, *Some Problems of Discovery in an Adversary System*, 63 MINN. L. REV. 1055 (1979).

Slomanson, *Supplementation of Discovery Responses in Federal Civil Procedure*, 17 SAN DIEGO L. REV. 233 (1980).

Smith, *The Concern over Discovery*, 28 DRAKE L. REV. 51 (1978–1979).

Speck, *The Use of Discovery in United States District Courts*, 60 YALE L.J. 1132 (1951).

Sunderland, *Discovery Before Trial Under the New Federal Rules*, 15 TENN. L. REV. 737 (1939).

Sunderland, *Scope and Method of Discovery Before Trial*, 42 YALE L.J. 863 (1933).

Taine, *Discovery of Trial Preparations in the Federal Courts*, 50 COLUM. L. REV. 1026 (1950).

Uviller, *The Advocate, the Truth, and Judicial Hackles: A Reaction to Judge Frankel's Idea*, 123 U. PA. L. REV. 1067 (1975).

Welling, *Discovery of Nonparties' Tangible Things Under the Federal Rules of Civil Procedure*, 59 NOTRE DAME L. REV. 110 (1983).

Wicker, *Tactical Advantages from the Use of Discovery*, 27 TENN. L. REV. 323 (1960).

C. Other Legal Periodicals

American Bar Association, Section of Litigation, *Discovery Report of the Special Committee for the Study of Discovery Abuse*, 92 F.R.D. 149 (1982).

Barthold, *"Negligence" in Discovery: No Paper Tiger*, LITIG., Fall 1979, at 39.

Basman, *Continuing Discovery*, 6 ADVOC. Q. 23 (1985).

Blumenkopf, *Deposition Strategy and Tactics*, 5 AM. J. TRIAL ADVOC. 231 (1981).

Brazil, *Civil Discovery: How Bad Are the Problems*, 67 A.B.A. J. 450 (1981).

Brazil, *Civil Discovery: Lawyers' Views of Its Effectiveness, Its Principal Problems and Abuses*, 1980 AM. B. FOUND. RES. J. 787.

Brazil, *Improving Judicial Controls over the Pretrial Development of Civil Actions: Model Rules for Case Management and Sanctions*, 1981 AM. B. FOUND. RES. J. 873.

Brazil, *Views from the Front Lines: Observations by Chicago Lawyers about the System of Civil Discovery*, 1980 AM. B. FOUND. RES. J. 217.

Bruner, *Discovery: An Ordered Approach*, 30 FED'N INS. & CORP. COUNS. Q. 205 (1980).

Burger, *Abuses of Discovery: Judges Are Correcting the Problem*, TRIAL, Sept. 1984, at 18.

Charfoos & Christensen, *Interrogatories—How to Use Them Effectively in Personal Injury Cases*, TRIAL, June 1986, at 56.

Committee on Rules of Practice and Procedure of the Judicial Conference of the United States, FED. R. CIV. P. 26, *in Revised Preliminary Draft of Proposed Amendments* (Feb. 1979), *reprinted in* 80 F.R.D. 323 (1979), *adopted*, 85 F.R.D. 521 (1980).

Daniels, *Defending Depositions*, A.B.A. J., Oct. 1985, at 53.

Degnan, *Obtaining Witnesses and Documents (or Things)*, 108 F.R.D. 223 (1986).

Devine, *Discovery in Product Liability Cases*, 6 AM. J. TRIAL ADVOC. 241 (1982).

Dockray, *Discovery: Recent Developments*, 136 NEW L.J. 219 (1986).

Figg et al., *Uses and Limitations of Some Discovery Devices*, PRAC. LAW., Apr. 1974, at 65.

Fox, *Planning and Conducting a Discovery Program*, LITIG., Summer 1981, at 13.

Greenwald, *What You Don't Know May Hurt You: Effective Pretrial Discovery in Medical Negligence Cases*, TRIAL, July 1979, at 28.

GUYER, SURVEY OF LOCAL CIVIL DISCOVERY PROCEDURES 23–26 (Federal Judicial Ctr. ed., 1977).

Hare, *Discovery in the Products Liability Case*, TRIAL, Nov. 1980, at 42.

Hare, *Discovery: The Product Liability Case*, 1981 S.M.U. INST. PRODUCT LIABILITY § 5-1.

Hare & ReMine, *Abuse of Discovery in Product Liability Cases*, 1988 S.M.U. INST. PRODUCTS LIABILITY § 4-1.

Hellquist, *Computer Controls in Manufacturing—How Do They Affect Product Liability Litigation?*, TRIAL, Nov. 1985, at 39.

Hofeld, *Value of Discovery in a Products Liability Case*, 14 TRIAL LAW. GUIDE 501 (1970).

Jacob, *Discovery and Disclosure of Documents*, 6 CIV. JUST. Q. 293 (1987).

Johnson, *The 10 Deadly Deposition Sins*, 70 A.B.A. J., Sept. 1984, at 62.

Kornblum, *The Oral Civil Deposition: Preparation and Examination of Witnesses*, PRAC. LAW., May 1971, at 11.

Kuney, *Deposition Preparation: A Methodological Approach*, 8 AM. J. TRIAL ADVOC. 241 (1984).

Lay, *Plaintiff's Practical Uses of Discovery Techniques*, 30 PRAC. LAW. 61 (1984).

Levine, *"Abuse" of Discovery: Or Hard Work Makes Good Law*, 67 A.B.A. J. 565 (1981).

Liman, *The Quantum of Discovery vs. the Quality of Justice: More Is Less*, LITIG., Fall 1977, at 8.

Liss, *Formal Discovery from Nonparties*, LITIG., Summer 1987, at 11.

Lundquist & Schechter, *The New Relevancy: An End to Trial by Ordeal*, 64 A.B.A. J. 59 (1978).

McNamara & Sorensen, *Deposition Traps and Tactics*, LITIG., Fall 1985, at 48.

Pollack, *Discovery—Its Abuse and Correction*, 80 F.R.D. 219 (1979).

Rheingold, *Tackling Corporate Defendants in Product Cases*, 1 J. PROD. LIAB. 33 (1977).

Rheingold & Vilensky, *Discovery in the Products Case: A Checklist*, TRIAL, Nov. 1983, at 124.

Schwarzer, *Managing Civil Litigation: The Trial Judge's Role*, 61 JUDICATURE 400 (1978).

SEGAL, SURVEY OF LITERATURE ON DISCOVERY FROM 1970 TO THE PRESENT: EXPRESSED DISSATISFACTIONS AND PROPOSED REFORMS (Federal Judicial Ctr. ed., 1978).

Sherman & Kinnard, *Federal Court Discovery in the 80's—Making the Rules Work*, 95 F.R.D. 245 (1983).

Spann, *Abuse of Discovery: Some Proposed Reforms*, 25 N.C. St. B.Q. 3 (1978).

Sussman, *Strategic Discovery,* LITIG., Fall 1986, at 37.

Trine, *Product Liability—Meeting the Defenses*, TRIAL, Nov. 1985, at 22.

Umin, *Discovery Reform: A New Era or Business as Usual?*, 65 A.B.A. J. 1050 (1979).

Weinstein, *Standing Masters to Supervise Discovery in the Southern District New York*, 23 F.R.D. 36 (1959).

Wright et al., *The Practicing Attorney's View of the Utility of Discovery,* 12 F.R.D. 97 (1952).

D. Annotations

Admissibility of Deposition Under Rule 32(a)(3)(B) of Federal Rules of Civil Procedure, Where Court Finds That Witness Is More Than 100 Miles from Place of Trial or Hearing, 71 A.L.R. FED. 382 (1985).

Allen, *Statements of Parties or Witnesses as Subject of Pretrial or Other Disclosure Production, or Inspection*, 73 A.L.R. 2D 12 (1960).

Buckner, *Propriety of Discovery Interrogatories Calling for Continuing Answers*, 88 A.L.R. 2D 657 (1963).

Cannizzaro, *Discovery and Inspection of Articles and Premises in Civil Actions Other Than for Personal Injury or Death*, 4 A.L.R. 3D 762 (1965).

Crais, *Right of Prosecution to Pretrial Discovery, Inspection and Disclosure*, 96 A.L.R. 2D 1224 (1964).

Donaldson, *Application of "Discovery Rule" to Postpone Running of Limitation Against Action for Damages from Assault*, 88 A.L.R. 4TH 1063 (1991).

Donaldson, *Permissible Scope Respecting Nature of Inquiry of Demand for Admissions Under Modern State Civil Rules of Procedure*, 42 A.L.R. 4TH 489 (1985).

Dorr, *Imposition of Sanctions Under Rule 16(f), Federal Rules of Civil Procedure, for Failing to Obey Scheduling or Pretrial Order*, 90 A.L.R. FED. 157 (1988).

Dunn, *Construction and Effect of Rules 30(b), (d), 31(d) of the Federal Rules of Civil Procedure and Similar State Statutes and Rules Relating to Preventing, Limiting, or Terminating the Taking of Depositions*, 70 A.L.R. 2D 685 (1960).

Evins, *Availability of Mandamus or Prohibition to Compel or to Prevent Discovery Proceedings*, 95 A.L.R. 3D 1229 (1964).

Extension of Time for Serving Response to Request for Admissions Under Rule 36(a), as Amended, of Federal Rules of Civil Procedure, 46 A.L.R. FED. 821 (1980).

Fleming, *Propriety and Extent of State Court Protective Order Restricting Party's Right to Disclose Discovered Information to Others Engaged in Similar Litigation*, 83 A.L.R. 4TH 987 (1991).

Formal Sufficiency of Response to Request for Admissions Under State Discovery Rules, 8 A.L.R. 4TH 728 (1981).

Foster, *Time and Place, Under Pretrial Discovery Procedure, for Inspection and Copying of Opposing Litigant's Books, Records, and Papers*, 83 A.L.R. 2D 302 (1962).

Gallagher, *Independent Action Against Nonparty for Production of Documents and Things or Permission to Enter upon Land (Rule 34(c) of Federal Rules of Civil Procedure)*, 62 A.L.R. FED. 935 (1983).

Gans, *Necessity and Sufficiency Under Statutes and Rules Governing Modern Pretrial Discovery Practice of Designation of Documents, etc. in Application or Motion*, 8 A.L.R. 2D 1134 (1949).

Ghent, *Sanctions for Failure to Make Discovery Under Federal Civil Procedure Rule 37 as Affected by Defaulting Party's Good Faith Attempts to Comply*, 2 A.L.R. FED. 811 (1969).

Guarino, *Withdrawal or Amendment of Admissions Under Rule 36(b) of Federal Rules of Civil Procedure*, 64 A.L.R. FED. 746 (1983).

Gulbis, *Right of Prosecution to Discovery of Case-Related Notes, Statements, and Reports—State Cases*, 23 A.L.R. 4TH 799 (1983).

Hursh, *Discovery and Inspection of Article or Premises the Condition of Which Is Alleged to Have Caused Personal Injury or Death*, 13 A.L.R. 2D 657 (1950).

Jhong, *Discovery and Inspection of Prosecution Evidence Under Federal Rule 16 of Criminal Procedure*, 5 A.L.R. 3D 819 (1966).

Jhong, *Pretrial Examination or Discovery to Ascertain from Defendant in Action for Injury, Death or Damages, Existence and Amount of Liability Insurance and Insurer's Identity*, 13 A.L.R. 3D 822 (1967).

Jhong, *Right of Accused in State Courts to Inspection or Disclosure of Evidence in Possession of Prosecution*, 7 A.L.R. 3D 8 (1966).

Johns, *Pretrial Testimony or Disclosure on Discovery by Party to Personal Injury Action as to Nature of Injuries or Treatment as Waiver for Physician-Patient Privilege*, 25 A.L.R. 3D 1401 (1969).

Jones, *Discovery: Right to Ex Parte Interview with Injured Party's Treating Physician*, 50 A.L.R. 4TH 714 (1986).

Jovanovic, *Fraud Exception to Work Product Privilege in Federal Courts*, 64 A.L.R. FED. 470 (1983).

Karnezis, *Propriety Under 28 USCS § 1920 and Rule 54(d) of the Federal Rules of Civil Procedure of Allowing Prevailing Party Costs for Copies of Depositions*, 50 A.L.R. FED. 472 (1980).

Klein, *Discovery, in Products Liability Case, of Defendant's Knowledge as to Injury to or Complaints by Others Than Plaintiff, Related to Product*, 20 A.L.R. 3D 1430 (1968).

Klein, *Identity of Witnesses Whom Adverse Party Plans to Call to Testify at Civil Trial as Subject of Pretrial Discovery*, 19 A.L.R. 3D 1114 (1968).

Klein, *Scope of Defendant's Duty of Pretrial Discovery in Medical Malpractice Action*, 15 A.L.R. 3D 1446 (1967).

Landis, *Public Access to Records and Proceedings of Civil Actions in Federal District Courts*, 96 A.L.R. FED. 769 (1990).

Larner, *Modification of Protective Order Entered Pursuant to Rule 26(c), Federal Rules of Civil Procedure,* 85 A.L.R. FED. 538 (1987).

Lawlor, *Letters to or from Customers or Suppliers as Business Records Under Statutes Authorizing Reception of Business Records in Evidence,* 68 A.L.R. 3D 1069 (1976).

Lehmann, *Sanctions Against Defense in Criminal Case for Failure to Comply with Discovery Requirements,* 9 A.L.R. 4TH 837 (1981).

Levendusky, *Propriety of Dismissal with Prejudice Under Federal Rules of Civil Procedure upon Ground of Plaintiff's Failure to Comply with Order of Court,* 15 A.L.R. FED. 407 (1973).

Ludington, *Consumption or Destruction of Physical Evidence Due to Testing or Analysis by Prosecution's Expert as Warranting Suppression of Evidence or Dismissal of Case Against Accused in State Court,* 40 A.L.R. 4TH 594 (1985).

Ludington, *Party's Duty Under Federal Rules of Civil Procedure 36(a) and Similar State Statutes and Rules, to Respond to Requests for Admission of Facts Not Within His Personal Knowledge,* 20 A.L.R. 3D 756 (1968).

Ludington, *Protective Orders Limiting Dissemination of Financial Information Obtained by Deposition or Discovery in State Civil Actions,* 43 A.L.R. 4TH 121 (1986).

Martyn, *Discovery, in Civil Case, of Material Which Is or May Be Designed for Use in Impeachment,* 18 A.L.R. 3D 922 (1968).

McDaniel, *Right of Party in Civil Action to Obtain Disclosure Under Rule 6(e)(3)(C)(i) of the Federal Rules of Criminal Procedure, of Matters Occurring Before Grand Jury,* 71 A.L.R. FED. 10 (1985).

McLaughlin, *Necessity of Determination or Showing of Liability for Punitive Damages Before Discovery or Reception of Evidence of Defendant's Wealth,* 32 A.L.R. 4TH 432 (1984).

Neumeg, *Sanctions Available Under Rule 37, Federal Rules of Civil Procedure, for Grossly Negligent Failure to Obey Discovery Order,* 49 A.L.R. FED. 831 (1980).

Roberts, *Appealability of Discovery Order as "Final Decision" Under 28 USCS § 1291,* 36 A.L.R. FED. 763 (1978).

Roberts, *Plaintiff's Right to File Notice of Dismissal Under Rule 41(a)(1)(i) of Federal Rules of Civil Procedure,* 54 A.L.R. FED. 214 (1981).

Sarno, *Restriction on Dissemination of Information Obtained Through Pretrial Discovery Proceedings as Violating Federal Constitution's First Amendment—Federal Cases,* 81 A.L.R. FED. 471 (1987).

Swarthout, *Party's Right to Use, as Evidence in Civil Trial, His Own Testimony Given upon Interrogatories or Depositions Taken by Opponent,* 13 A.L.R. 3D 1312 (1967).

Tellier, *Names and Addresses of Witnesses to Accident or Incident as Subject of Pretrial Discovery,* 37 A.L.R. 2D 1152 (1954).

Theuman, *Dismissal of State Court Action for Failure or Refusal of Plaintiff to Appear or Answer Questions at Deposition or Oral Examination,* 32 A.L.R. 4TH 212 (1984).

Theuman, *Dismissal of State Court Action for Failure or Refusal of Plaintiff to Obey Request or Order for Production of Documents or Other Objects,* 27 A.L.R. 4TH 61 (1984).

Theuman, *Judgment in Favor of Plaintiff in State Court Action for Defendant's Failure to Obey Request or Order for Production of Documents or Other Objects*, 26 A.L.R. 4TH 849 (1983).

Theuman, *Judgment in Favor of Plaintiff in State Court Action for Defendant's Failure to Obey Request or Order to Answer Interrogatories or Other Discovery Questions*, 30 A.L.R. 4TH 9 (1984).

Trenkner, *Pretrial Discovery of Facts Known and Opinions Held by Opponent's Experts Under Rule 26(b)(4) of Federal Rules of Civil Procedure*, 33 A.L.R. FED. 403 (1977).

Vance, *Discovery, Inspection, and Copying of Photographs of Article or Premises the Condition of Which Gave Rise to Instant Litigation*, 95 A.L.R. 2D 1061 (1964).

Wagner, *Protection from Discovery of Attorney's Opinion Work Product Under Rule 26(b)(3), Federal Rules of Civil Procedure*, 84 A.L.R. FED. 779 (1987).

Wakefield, *Photographs of Civil Litigant Realized by Opponent's Surveillance as Subject to Pretrial Discovery*, 19 A.L.R. 4TH 1236 (1983).

Watson, *Discovery of Trade Secrets in State Court Action*, 75 A.L.R. 4TH 1009 (1990).

Woerner, *Pretrial Discovery to Secure Opposing Party's Private Reports or Records as to Previous Accidents or Incidents Involving the Same Place or Premises*, 74 A.L.R. 2D 876 (1960).

Zipp, *Right to Perpetuation of Testimony Under Rule 27 of Federal Rules of Civil Procedure*, 60 A.L.R. FED. 924 (1982).

Zitter, *Attorney's Conduct in Delaying or Obstructing Discovery as Basis for Contempt Proceeding*, 8 A.L.R. 4TH 1181 (1981).

II. DISCOVERY ABUSE

A. Articles

Armstrong, *Discovery Abuse and Judicial Management*, 142 NEW L.J. 927 (1992).

Asher et al., *Ex Parte Interviews with Plaintiff's Treating Physicians—The Offensive Use of the Physician-Patient Privilege*, 67 U. DET. L. REV. 501 (1990).

Austern, *Ethics, (When It Is Permissible to Destroy Client Files You No Longer Need)*, TRIAL, May 1985, at 18.

Behar, Note, *The Misuse of Inherent Powers When Imposing Sanctions for Discovery Abuse: The Exclusivity of Rule 37*, 9 CARDOZO L. REV. 1779 (1988).

Brazil, *The Adversary Character of Civil Discovery: A Critique and Proposals for Change*, 31 VAND. L. REV. 1295 (1978).

Brazil, *Civil Discovery: Lawyers' Views of Its Effectiveness, Its Principal Problems and Abuses*, 1980 AM. B. FOUND. RES. 787.

Brown, Case Comment, *Civil Procedure—In re Rinehardt: A Party's Attempt to Appeal an Interlocutory Order of Discovery by Contriving a Contempt Citation Against Its Designated Non-party Witness*, 22 MEM. ST. U. L. REV. 157 (1991).

Buchmeyer, *How to Take a Deposition: The Expose Continues* (pt. 4), 48 TEX. B.J. 1177 (1985).

Burbank, *Sanctions in the Proposed Amendments to the Federal Rules of Civil Procedure: Some Questions About Power*, 11 HOFSTRA L. REV. 997 (1983).

Burbank, *The Transformation of American Civil Procedure: The Example of Rule 11*, 137 U. PA. L. REV. 1925 (1989).

Butts-Cater, *Health Records: Prohibit Destruction, Alteration, or Falsification (Selected 1988 Georgia Legislation)*, 5 GA. ST. U. L. REV. 334 (1988).

Cadwell, Note, *The Applicability of Rule 11 Sanctions upon Removal from State to Federal Court: Imposing a Continuing Obligation*, 75 MINN. L. REV. 1731 (1991).

Cady, *Curbing Litigation Abuse and Misuse: A Judicial Approach*, 36 DRAKE L. REV. 483 (1986–1987).

Carrington, *Making Rules to Dispose of Manifestly Unfounded Assertions: An Exorcism of the Bogy of Non-Trans-Substantive Rules of Civil Procedure*, 137 U. PA. L. REV. 2067 (1989).

Cedillo & Lopez, *Document Destruction in Business Litigation from a Practitioner's Point-of-View: The Ethical Rules vs. Practical Realities*, 20 ST. MARY'S L.J. 637 (1989).

Cooper, *Dalcon Document Destruction Disputed*, NAT'L L.J., June 10, 1985, at 3.

Corboy, *Rambo-Style Discovery Common in High-Stakes Cases*, CHI. DAILY L. BULL., Aug. 6, 1990, at 2.

Councill, Note, *Civil Procedure: Discovery Sanctions—Gross Negligence in Failure to Respond to Discovery Order Sufficient Justification for Ordering Dismissal*, 53 TEMP. L.Q. 140 (1980).

Cox, *Default Ordered for Vitamin Firm's Destroying Papers: Counsel Also Criticized*, L.A. DAILY J., Sept. 11, 1984, at 1.

Daniels, Case Comment, *Discovery—Power to Impose Sanctions for Failure to Make Discovery on Jurisdictional Issues*, 13 MEM. ST. U. L. REV. 109 (1982).

Dimitriou, *Client Files: To Destroy or Not to Destroy? That Shouldn't Be the Question*, WIS. B. BULL., July 1981, at 22.

Dobbin & Lewis, *Sanctions Available Under Rules 16, 26, and 37; 28 U.S.C. Sections 1912 and 1927; and Rule 38 of Federal Rules of Appellate Procedure*, 330 PLI/LITIG. 411 (July 1, 1987).

Dudley, *Discovery Abuse Revisited: Some Specific Proposals to Amend the Federal Rules of Civil Procedure*, 26 U.S.F. L. REV. 189 (1992).

Easterbrook, *Discovery as Abuse*, 69 B.U. L. REV. 635 (1989).

EBERSOLE & BURKE, DISCOVERY PROBLEMS IN CIVIL CASES (Federal Judicial Ctr. ed., 1980).

Essig, Comment, *Preclusion: Procedural Efficiency and the Right to Defend*, 27 HOUS. L. REV. 327 (1990).

Faris, Note, Insurance Corp. of Ireland v. Compagnie des Bauxites de Guinee: *Justifying Establishment of Jurisdiction as a Discovery Sanction*, 70 CAL. L. REV. 1446 (1982).

Fedders & Guttenplan, *Document Retention and Destruction: Practical, Legal and Ethical Considerations*, 56 NOTRE DAME LAW. 5 (1980).

Feighny, *The Physician-Patient Privilege: May Defense Counsel Conduct Ex Parte Interview with Plaintiff's Treating Physician? (Kansas)*, J. KAN. B. ASS'N, Sept./Oct. 1992, at 36.

Flegal, *Introduction* to *Discovery Abuse: Causes, Effects, and Reform*, 3 REV. LITIG. 1 (1982).

Forrester, Note, Hinkle v. Sam Blanken & Co.: *Dismissals for Discovery Abuse—Toward a New Standard in the District of Columbia*, 36 CATH. U. L. REV. 761 (1987).

Foster, Comment, *Playing Hardball in Federal Court: Judicial Attempts to Referee Unsportsmanlike Conduct*, 55 J. AIR L. & COM. 223 (1989).

Goldberg, *Court OKs Case Dismissal for 1st Discovery Abuse (California)*, L.A. DAILY J., June 24, 1991, at 11.

Green & Brown, *Back to the Future: Proposals for Restructuring Civil Discovery*, 26 U.S.F. L. REV. 225 (1992).

Greene, *Reassessment of the Lawyers' Discovery Responsibilities: The Early Disclosure Provisions of the Proposed Amendments to Rule 26, Federal Rules of Civil Procedure*, 53 ALA. LAW. 278 (1992).

Halfenger, *The Attorney Misconduct Exception to the Work Product Doctrine*, 58 U. CHI. L. REV. 1079 (1991).

Hare & Gilbert, *Discovery in Products Liability Cases: The Plaintiff's Plea for Judicial Understanding*, 12 AM. J. TRIAL ADVOC. 413 (1989).

Heiderscheit, *Rule 37 Discovery Sanctions in the Ninth Circuit: The Collapse of the Deterrence Goal*, 68 OR. L. REV. 57 (1989).

Helmers, *Depositions: Objections, Instructions and Sanctions*, 33 S.D. L. REV. 272 (1987–1988).

Hildebrand, *Sanctions in Litigation and the New Model Rules*, WIS. B. BULL., Mar. 1988, at 14.

Husemoen, *A File Destruction System*, LEGAL ECON., Sept./Oct. 1982, at 21.

Inker, *Abusive Discovery Tactics in Depositions*, 26 FAM. L.Q. 27 (1992).

Ishibashi & Pettit, Note, Wong v. City and County: *Discovery Sanctions and Law of the Case Doctrine in Hawaii*, 7 U. HAW. L. REV. 473 (1985).

Jorstad, Note, *Litigation Ethics: A Niebuhrian View of the Adversarial Legal System*, 99 YALE L.J. 1089 (1990).

Joseph, *Current Issues in Discovery*, 430 PLI/LITIG. 263 (Feb. 19, 1992).

Joseph & Fabrikant, *Discovery Problems*, 367 PLI/LITIG. 93 (Dec. 1, 1988).

Kahn, *Discovery—A View from the Bench (Discovery Tactics: A Judicial Forum)*, 10 TRIAL ADVOC. Q. 18 (1991).

Kaminsky, *Proposed Federal Discovery Rules for Complex Civil Litigation*, 48 FORDHAM L. REV. 907 (1980).

Kelner & Kelner, *The Suppression of Documentary Evidence*, N.Y. L.J. Feb. 10, 1982, at 1.

Kemm, Note, *Interlocutory Appeal of Attorney Sanctions: In Search of a Standard*, 25 IND. L. REV. 919 (1992).

Kennelly, *Effective Discovery Vis-a-Vis Abuse of Discovery—Which Is Which?*, 29 TRIAL LAW. GUIDE 261 (1985).

Kilgarlin, *Sanctions for Discovery Abuse: Is the Cure Worse Than the Disease?*, 54 TEX. B.J. 658 (1991).

Kline, *Advising Clients on the Destruction of Documents Prepared and Used to Formulate Discovery Responses: Perils and Pitfalls*, 11 REV. LITIG. 47 (1991).

Latona & Klein, *Discovery Abuse: Making Piper Pay*, TRIAL, Feb. 1987, at 69.

Lawrence, Comment, *The Value of Copyright Law as a Deterrent to Discovery Abuse*, 138 U. PA. L. REV. 549 (1989).

Lempert, *Evidence Destruction Charge Boosted in Saigon Crash Case*, LEGAL TIMES, Mar. 26, 1984, at 2.

Levin & Sobel, *Achieving Balance in the Developing Law of Sanctions*, 36 CATH. U. L. REV. 587 (1987).

Lewis, *Discovery Abuse: Plaintiffs Fight Back*, TRIAL, Oct. 1990, at 70.

Linklater, *Disclosure of Confidential Information Can Destroy the Attorney-Client Privilege*, TRIAL LAW. GUIDE 178 (1985).

Lionberger, Comment, *Interference with Prospective Civil Litigation by Spoliation of Evidence: Should Texas Adopt a New Tort?*, 21 ST. MARY'S L.J. 209 (1989).

Longley & Kincaid, *Discovery and Sanctions for Discovery Abuse (Texas)*, 18 ST. MARY'S L.J. 163 (1986).

Lord, *Discovery Abuse: Appointing Special Masters*, 9 HAMLINE L. REV. 63 (1986).

Lore & Marvel, *Attorney Fined for Discovery Order Violation*, 75 J. TAX'N 99 (1991).

Lundquist & Ball, *Conclusions and Recommendations from the National Conference on Discovery Reform*, 3 REV. LITIG. 209(1982).

Lundquist & Flegal, *Discovery Abuse—Some New Views About an Old Problem*, 2 REV. LITIG. 1 (1981).

Majorie, Case Comment, Black Panther Party v. Smith: *Protecting Interrogating Parties from Concealment of Information by Organizations—A Proposed Solution*, 62 B.U. L. Rev. 1295 (1982).

Marcotte, *Judges Give Delay Causes: Discovery Abuse Tops List*, A.B.A. J., July 1, 1988, at 29.

Marshall et al., *The Use and Impact of Rule 11*, 86 NW. U. L. REV. 943 (1992).

Martin, *Do Not Burn, Shred or Mutilate; Destroying Evidence Can Ruin Cases—And Careers*, CAL. LAW., Nov. 1991, at 69.

Martin, *Third Circuit Review*, 27 VILL. L. REV. 744 (1982).

Massey, Case Comment, *Evidence: Intentionally Destroyed Medical Records Give Rise to an Irrebuttable Presumption of Malpractice*, 37 U. FLA. L. REV. 197 (1985).

Maute, *Sporting Theory of Justice: Taming Adversary Zeal with a Logical Sanctions Doctrine*, 20 CONN. L. REV. 7 (1987).

Mazurczak, Comment, *Critical Analysis of Rule 11 Sanctions in the Seventh Circuit*, 72 MARQ. L. REV. 91 (1988).

McManamon, *Is the Recent Frenzy of Civil Justice Reform a Cure-all or a Placebo? An Examination of the Plans of Two Pilot Districts*, 11 REV. LITIG. 329 (1992).

Melgaard, Note, *Spoliation of Evidence—An Independent Tort?*, 67 N.D. L. REV. 501 (1991).

Mengler, *Eliminating Abusive Discovery Through Disclosure: Is It Again Time for Reform?*, 138 F.R.D. 155 (1992).

Mokry, Note, *Discovery Sanctions Must Be "Just," as Defined by the Texas Supreme Court, Consistent with Due Process, and Are Subject to Mandamus Review:* Transamerican Natural Gas Corp. v. Powell, 811 S.W.2d 913 (Tex. 1991), 23 TEX. TECH L. REV. 617 (1992).

Mooney, *Sanctions: Prosecuting, Defending and Avoiding Malpractice Liability*, 59 DEF. COUNS. J. 554 (1992).

Mureiko, Note, *The Agency Theory of the Attorney-Client Relationship: An Improper Justification for Holding Clients Responsible for Their Attorneys' Procedural Errors*, 1988 DUKE L.J. 733.

Nance, *Missing Evidence*, 13 CARDOZO L. REV. 831 (1991).

Nelson, *Document Destruction Charge Raises Thorny Ethics Issues*, LEGAL TIMES, Feb. 24, 1986, at 7.

Note, *Discovery Abuse Under the Federal Rules: Causes and Cures*, 92 YALE L.J. 352 (1982).

Note, *Discovery—Sanctions for Refusal*, 30 DEF. L.J. 249 (1981).

Note, *Dismissal for Failure to Comply with Discovery Order*, 30 DEF. L.J. 173 (1981).

Oesterle, *A Private Litigant's Remedies for an Opponent's Inappropriate Destruction of Relevant Documents*, 61 TEX. L. REV. 1185 (1983).

Owens, Note, *Should Iowa Adopt the Tort of Intentional Spoliation of Evidence in Civil Litigation?*, 41 DRAKE L. REV. 179 (1992).

Partee, Note, 14 U. ARK. LITTLE ROCK L.J. 107 (1991).

Pepe, *Professional Responsibility in Pretrial Discovery—A Tale of Two Cities*, 64 MICH. B.J. 298 (1985).

Pines, *Sullivan & Cromwell Criticized on Discovery*, N.Y. L.J., Nov. 12, 1991, at 1.

Platt, *Trial Evidence, Civil Practice, and Effective Litigation Techniques in Federal and State Courts*, A.L.I.-A.B.A. 175 (Feb. 7–9, 1990).

Platt, *Trial Evidence, Civil Practice, and Effective Litigation Techniques in Federal and State Courts*, A.L.I.-A.B.A. 279 (July 24–26, 1991).

Polansky, Note, Taylor v. Illinois: *Supreme Court Approves Preclusion of Defense Witnesses for Discovery Violation*, 25 SAN DIEGO L. REV. 1113 (1988).

Postel, *Fraudulently Concealed Evidence*, CHI. DAILY L. BULL., May 30, 1985, at 1.

Redden & Bower, *Qualifications to the Bar of Ex Parte Contacts with Physicians*, 79 ILL. B.J. 442 (1991).

ReMine & Gilbert, *Discovery: Abuses, Sanctions, and Ethical Concerns*, TRIAL, Jan. 1987, at 53.

Renfrew, *Discovery Sanctions: A Judicial Perspective*, 2 REV. LITIG. 71 (1981).

Reske, *Rare Sanction Against Firm, Client: Judge Enters Default Judgments, Says ABC and Wilmer, Cutler Suppressed Facts*, A.B.A. J., July 1992, at 23.

Riskind, Comment, *Can a Client Be Held Liable for Attorney's Misconduct? Let the Client Beware!*, 15 T. MARSHALL L. REV. 103 (1989–1990).

Risley, Comment, *The Destruction of Subpoenaed Corporate Records*, 70 KY. L.J. 859 (1982).

Risley, *Why Texas Courts Should Not Retain the Inherent Power to Impose Sanctions*, 44 BAYLOR L. REV. 253 (1992).

Roberts, *Pre-Trial Sanctions: An Empirical Study*, 23 PAC. L.J. 1 (1991).

Robertson, *Marshalling Information Prior to Litigation: A Comment on David Schum and Peter Tiller's "Marshalling Evidence for Adversary Litigation,"* 13 CARDOZO L. REV. 705 (1991).

Rowse, Comment, *Spoliation: Civil Liability for Destruction of Evidence*, 20 U. RICH. L. REV. 191 (1985).

Sarazen, Note, *An Ethical Approach to Discovery Abuse*, 4 GEO. J. LEGAL ETHICS 459 (1990).

Schneyer, *Professional Discipline for Law Firms?*, 77 CORNELL L. REV. 1 (1991).

Schum & Tillers, *Marshalling Evidence for Adversary Litigation*, 13 CARDOZO L. REV. 657 (1991).

Schwarzer, *The Federal Rules, the Adversary Process, and Discovery Reform*, 50 U. PITT. L. REV. 703 (1989).

Schwarzer, *Slaying the Monsters of Cost and Delay: Would Disclosure Be More Effective Than Discovery?*, 74 JUDICATURE 178 (1991).

Segal, SURVEY OF LITERATURE ON DISCOVERY FROM 1970 TO THE PRESENT: EXPRESSED DISSATISFACTIONS AND PROPOSED REFORMS (Federal Judicial Ctr. ed., 1978).

Setear, *The Barrister and the Bomb: The Dynamics of Cooperation, Nuclear Deterrence, and Discovery Abuse*, 69 B.U. L. REV. 569 (1989).

Sharp, *Discovery: A View from the Appellate Bench (Discovery Tactics: A Judicial Forum)*, 10 TRIAL ADVOC. Q. 11 (1991).

Shuler, Recent Development, *Chambers v. Nasco, Inc.: Moving Beyond Rule 11 into the Uncharted Territory of Courts' Inherent Power to Sanction*, 66 TUL. L. REV. 591 (1991).

Silberberg, *Sanction for Destroying Documents (Survey of March Civil Rights Cases, Southern District of New York)*, N.Y. L.J., May 7, 1992, at 3.

Silberman, *Judicial Adjuncts Revisited: The Proliferation of Ad Hoc Procedure*, 137 U. PA. L. REV. 2131 (1989).

Sinaiko, Note, *Ex Parte Communication and the Corporate Adversary: A New Approach*, 66 N.Y.U. L. REV. 1456 (1991).

Slevin, *Fine Upheld Against Bank for Withholding Documents*, NAT'L L.J., Sept. 3, 1984, at 10.

Solovy et al., *New Dimensions in Securities Litigation: Planning and Strategies Sanctions Under Federal Rule of Civil Procedure 11*, 751 A.L.I.-A.B.A. 1 (Apr. 23, 1992).

Solovy et al., *Sanctions Under Federal Rule of Civil Procedure 11*, 351 PLI/LITIG. 507 (June 7, 1988).

Solum & Marzen, *Truth and Uncertainty: Legal Control of the Destruction of Evidence*, 36 EMORY L.J. 1085 (1987).

Soules & Wallace, *Discovery "Death Penalty" Sanctions Reviews: New "De Novo" Standard*, 55 TEX. B.J. 135 (1992).

Spears, *The Rules of Civil Procedure; 1981 Changes in Pre-Trial Discovery*, 12 ST. MARY'S L.J. 633 (1981).

Squiers, *Firm Sanctioned Again for Discovery Abuse*, N.Y. L.J., Apr. 3, 1990, at 1.

Stasney, Recent Development, 22 ST. MARY'S L.J. 1171 (1991).

Stempel, *Sanctions, Symmetry, and Safe Harbors: Limiting Misapplication of Rule 11 by Harmonizing It with Pre-Verdict Dismissal Devices*, 60 FORDHAM L. REV. 257 (1991).

Stokes, Case Note, Trubell v. Patten: *Sanctions Imposed for Failure to Supplement Interrogatories—New Teeth for the 1973 Amendment*, 20 S. TEX. L.J. 357 (1980).

Subrin, *Federal Rules, Local Rules, and State Rules: Uniformity, Divergence, and Emerging Procedural Patterns*, 137 U. PA. L. REV. 1999 (1989).

Sward, *Values, Ideology, and the Evolution of the Adversary System*, 64 IND. L.J. 301 (1988–1989).

Taylor, *Judge's Scheme to Reign in Discovery Is Overdue*, N.J. L.J., May 9, 1991, at 20.

Taylor, *Lifeline for System Drowning in Discovery*, LEGAL TIMES, Apr. 29, 1991, at 23.

Tebrugge, Case Note, 12 FLA. ST. U. L. REV. 189 (1984).

Thompson, Comment, *Spoliation of Evidence: A Troubling New Tort*, 37 U. KAN. L. REV. 563 (1989).

Thompson, Note, *Protective Orders: Sword and Shield in the War of Discovery*, 12 AM. J. TRIAL ADVOC. 483 (1989).

Trubek et al., *The Costs of Ordinary Litigation*, 31 UCLA L. REV. 72 (1983).

Twining, *Five Cheers for Schum and Tillers: A Comment on David Schum and Peter Tillers's "Marshalling Evidence for Adversary Litigation,"* 13 CARDOZO L. REV. 713 (1991).

Twitchell, *The Ethical Dilemmas of Lawyers on Teams*, 72 MINN. L. REV. 697 (1988).

Wagner, *Combatting Discovery Abuse*, 14 TRIAL DIPL. J. 197 (1991).

Wehrwein, *Were Dalkon Documents Destroyed? Testimony of Ex-Robins' Lawyer*, NAT'L L.J., Aug. 13, 1984, at 3.

Weinstein, *After Fifty Years of the Federal Rules of Civil Procedure: Are the Barriers to Justice Being Raised?*, 137 U. PA. L. REV. 1901 (1989).

Weinstein, *What Discovery Abuse? A Comment on John Setear's "The Barrister and the Bomb,"* 69 B.U. L. REV. 649 (1989).

Weissbrod, Comment, *Sanctions Under Amended Rule 26—Scalpel or Meat-Ax? The 1983 Amendments to the Federal Rules of Civil Procedure,* 46 OHIO ST. L.J. 183 (1985).

Weston, *Court-Ordered Sanctions of Attorneys: A Concept That Duplicates the Role of Attorney Disciplinary Procedures,* 94 DICK. L. REV. 897 (1990).

B. Annotations

American Bar Association Section of Litigation, *Standards and Guidelines for Practice Under Rule 11 of the Federal Rules of Civil Procedure,* 121 F.R.D. 101 (1989).

Federal Bar Council Committee on Second Circuit Courts, *A Report on the Conduct of Depositions,* 131 F.R.D. 613 (1990).

Ghent, *Sanctions for Failure to Make Discovery Under Federal Civil Procedure Rule 37 as Affected by Defaulting Party's Good Faith Attempts to Comply,* 2 A.L.R. FED. 811 (1969).

Neumeg, *Sanctions Available Under Rule 37, Federal Rules of Civil Procedure, for Grossly Negligent Failure to Obey Discovery Order,* 49 A.L.R. FED. 831 (1980).

Proceedings of the Forty-Sixth Judicial Conference of the District of Columbia Circuit, 111 F.R.D. 91 (1987).

Theuman, *Dismissal of State Court Action for Failure or Refusal of Plaintiff to Appear or Answer Questions at Deposition or Oral Examination,* 32 A.L.R. 4TH 212 (1984).

Theuman, *Dismissal of State Court Action for Failure or Refusal of Plaintiff to Obey Request or Order for Production of Documents or Other Objects,* 27 A.L.R. 4TH 61 (1984).

Theuman, *Judgment in Favor of Plaintiff in State Court Action for Defendant's Failure to Obey Request or Order for Production of Documents or Other Objects,* 26 A.L.R. 4TH 849 (1984).

Theuman, *Judgment in Favor of Plaintiff in State Court Action for Defendant's Failure to Obey Request or Order to Answer Interrogatories or Other Discovery Questions,* 30 A.L.R. 4TH 9 (1984).

Wax, *Abuse of Process Action Based on Misuse of Discovery or Deposition Procedures After Commencement of Civil Action Without Seizure of Person or Property,* 33 A.L.R. 4TH 650 (1984).

Zitter, *Attorney's Conduct in Delaying or Obstructing Discovery as Basis for Contempt Proceeding,* 8 A.L.R. 4TH 1181 (1981).

III. 1993 AMENDMENTS

Bell et al., *Automatic Disclosure in Discovery—The Rush to Reform,* 27 GA. L. REV. 1 (1992).

Brazil, *The Adversary Character of Civil Discovery: A Critique and Proposals for Change,* 31 VAND. L. REV. 1295 (1978).

Dudley, *Discovery Abuse Revisited: Some Specific Proposals to Amend the Federal Rules of Civil Procedure*, 26 U.S.F. L. REV. 189, 191 (1992).

Epstein, *English Discovery: Simpler and Cheaper*, NAT'L L.J., Nov. 28, 1988, at 17.

Federal Bar Council Committee on Second Circuit Courts, *A Report on the Conduct of Depositions*, 131 F.R.D. 613 (1990).

Ferris, *Friend or Foe?—The Proposed Amendments to Rule 26 of the Federal Rules of Civil Procedure*, 2 REGENT U. L. REV. 39 (1992).

Frankel, *Disclosure in the Federal Courts: A Cure for Discovery Ills?*, 25 ARIZ. ST. L.J. 249 (1993).

George et al., *Rule 26(g)—The "Undiscovered Rule,"* TRIAL, Aug. 1988, at 33.

Lawyers for Civil Justice Ad Hoc Committee on Procedural Reform, *Federal Rule 26 Amendments: Wrong Medicine for Discovery Problems*, 58 DEF. COUNS. J. 454, 462 (1991).

Mandelbaum, *Discovery Abuse: Some New Possibilities for Rescuing Sisyphus*, INSIDE LITIG., Dec. 1989, at 1.

Mengler, *Eliminating Abusive Discovery Through Disclosure: Is It Time Again for Reform?*, 138 F.R.D. 155 (1992).

Mills, *Practical Implication of the Zlaket Rules from a Plaintiff's Lawyer's Perspective*, 25 ARIZ. ST. L.J. 149 (1993).

Mullenix, *Hope over Experience: Mandatory Informal Discovery and the Politics of Rulemaking*, 69 N.C. L. REV. 795 (1991).

Pelham, *Civil Reform Plan Buried by Avalanche of Dissent*, N.J. L.J., Mar. 23, 1992, at 4.

Powell, *The Docket Movers: A Critique of Proposed Amendments to the Federal Rules of Civil Procedure*, 1 J. AM. BOARD TRIAL ADVOC. 1, 14 (1991).

Schwarzer, *The Federal Rules, the Adversary Process, and Discovery Reform*, 50 U. PITT. L. REV. 703 (1989).

Schwarzer, *Guidelines for Discovery, Motion Practice and Trial (1987)*, 117 F.R.D. 273 (1988).

Schwarzer, *In Defense of "Automatic Disclosure in Discovery,"* 27 GA. L. REV. 655 (1993).

Schwarzer, *Mistakes Lawyers Make in Discovery*, LITIG., Winter 1989, at 31.

Schwarzer, *New Discoveries for the Discovery Process*, LEGAL TIMES, Nov. 25, 1991, at 25.

Schwarzer, *Slaying the Monsters of Cost and Delay: Would Disclosure Be More Effective Than Discovery?*, 74 JUDICATURE 178 (1991).

SCHWARZER & PASAHOW, CIVIL DISCOVERY: A GUIDE TO EFFICIENT PRACTICE (1988 & Supp. 1989).

Simpson, *Suggestions for Change: Discovery Reform*, 55 TEX. B.J. 340 (1992).

Sugarman & Perlin, *Proposed Changes to Discovery Rules in Aid of "Tort Reform": Has the Case Been Made?*, 42 AM. U. L. REV. 1465 (1993).

Yager, *Discovery Abuse: Have the 1983 Amendments to the Federal Rules Curbed the Problem?*, 37 FED'N INS. & CORP. COUNS. Q. 399 (1987).

*In addition to the above published articles, numerous position papers and comments are on file at the:

>   Committee on Rules of Practice and Procedure
>   Judicial Conference of the United States
>   Administrative Conference of the United States Court
>   1120 Vermont Ave., N.W.
>   Room 626
>   Washington, D.C. 20544

IV. CONFIDENTIALITY ORDERS

A. Anti-Secrecy Legislation and Court Rules

1. Legislation

Sunshine in Litigation Act, FLA. STAT. ANN. § 69.081 (West Supp. 1993).

VA. CODE ANN. § 8.01–420.01 (Mitchie 1992).

2. Court Rules

SAN DIEGO COUNTY, CA., Super. Ct. R., DIV. II, GEN. CIV. LITIG. § 6.9 (1990).

DEL. SUPER. CT. R. 5(g) (Mitchie 1991); DEL. CT. CH. R. 5(g) (Mitchie 1991).

GA. UNIFORM SUPER. CT. R. 21.2 (1991) (no order limiting access may be granted "except upon a finding that the harm otherwise resulting to the privacy of the person . . . clearly outweighs the public interest").

N.Y. COMP. CODES R. & REGS. tit. 22, § 216.1 (1991).

TEX. R. CIV. P. r. 76a, 166b(5)(c) (promulgated in accordance with TEX. GOV'T CODE ANN. § 22.010 (West 1991)).

B. Congressional Materials

1. Floor Statements

135 CONG. REC. E590 (daily ed. Mar. 1, 1989) (statement of Rep. Cardiss Collins upon introducing H.R. 129, a bill to restrict courts from entering orders that prevent other litigants and government agencies from gaining access to materials).

2. Committee Hearing Statements

Hearing on Court Secrecy Before the Subcomm. on Courts and Administrative Practice of the Senate Comm. on the Judiciary, 101st Cong., 2d Sess. 5 (May 17, 1990) (testimony and prepared statement of Fredrick R. Barbee).

Hearing on Court Secrecy Before the Subcomm. on Courts and Administrative Practice of the Senate Comm. on the Judiciary, 101st Cong., 2d Sess. 55 (May 17, 1990) (testimony and prepared statement of Arthur H. Bryant of the Trial Lawyers for Public Justice).

Hearing on Court Secrecy Before the Subcomm. on Courts and Administrative Practice of the Senate Comm. on the Judiciary, 101st Cong., 2d Sess. 25 (May 17, 1990) (prepared statement of Richard P. Campbell of the Lawyers for Civil Justice).

Hearing on Court Secrecy Before the Subcomm. on Courts and Administrative Practice of the Senate Comm. on the Judiciary, 101st Cong., 2d Sess. 17 (May 17, 1990) (testimony and prepared statement of Devra Lee Davis).

Hearing on Court Secrecy Before the Subcomm. on Courts and Administrative Practice of the Senate Comm. on the Judiciary, 101st Cong., 2d Sess. 214 (May 17, 1990) (testimony and prepared statement of Justice Lloyd Doggett of the Texas Supreme Court).

Hearing on Court Secrecy Before the Subcomm. on Courts and Administrative Practice of the Senate Comm. on the Judiciary, 101st Cong., 2d Sess. 1 (May 17, 1990) (statement of Sen. Herb Kohl).

Hearing on Court Secrecy Before the Subcomm. on Courts and Administrative Practice of the Senate Comm. on the Judiciary, 101st Cong., 2d Sess. 155 (May 17, 1990) (testimony and prepared statement of Paul K. McMasters, Society of Professional Journalists).

Hearing on Court Secrecy Before the Subcomm. on Courts and Administrative Practice of the Senate Comm. on the Judiciary, 101st Cong., 2d Sess. 190 (May 17, 1990) (testimony and prepared statement of Professor Arthur Miller of the Harvard University School of Law).

Hearing on Court Secrecy Before the Subcomm. on Courts and Administrative Practice of the Senate Comm. on the Judiciary, 101st Cong., 2d Sess. 104 (May 17, 1990) (testimony and prepared statement by James W. Morris, III of the Defense Research Institute).

Hearing on Court Secrecy Before the Subcomm. on Courts and Administrative Practice of the Senate Comm. on the Judiciary, 101st Cong., 2d Sess. 118 (May 17, 1990) (testimony and prepared statement of Dianne Jay Weaver of Weaver, Weaver, and Petrio).

Hearing on Court Secrecy Before the Subcomm. on Courts and Administrative Practice of the Senate Comm. on the Judiciary, 101st Cong., 2d Sess. 136 (May 17, 1990) (testimony and prepared statement of Robert N. Weiner of Arnold & Porter).

Hearing on Court Secrecy Before the Subcomm. on Courts and Administrative Practice of the Senate Comm. on the Judiciary, 101st Cong., 2d Sess. 168 (May 17, 1990) (testimony and prepared statement of Circuit Judge Joseph F. Weis, Jr., Chairman of the Federal Courts Study Committee).

3. Committee Prints

STAFF OF THE SUBCOMM. ON OVERSIGHT & INVESTIGATIONS, HOUSE COMM. ON ENERGY & COMMERCE, 101ST CONG., 2D SESS., THE BJORK-SHILEY HEART VALVE: "EARN AS YOU LEARN" 1 (Comm. Print 101-R).

4. Congressional Research Service

CONGRESSIONAL RESEARCH SERVICE, CONFIDENTIALITY AND SECRECY ORDERS IN CIVIL CASES (Apr. 3, 1989).

C. Books

BALDWIN ET AL., THE PREPARATION OF A PRODUCT LIABILITY CASE § 5.2.5 (1981).

CAMPBELL, PROTECTIVE ORDERS AND RELATED CONSTITUTIONAL QUESTIONS, MONOGRAPH FOR THE PRODUCT LIABILITY ADVISORY COUNCIL (1987).

CLEARY, MCCORMICK ON EVIDENCE § 72 (3d ed. 1984).

DISCOVERY PROCEEDINGS IN FEDERAL PRACTICE § 11.9 (Shepard's eds., 1983).

DOMBROFF, DISCOVERY § 1.17 (1986 & Supp. 1990).

FRIEDENTHAL ET AL., CIVIL PROCEDURE § 7.15 (1985).

FRUMER & FRIEDMAN, PRODUCTS LIABILITY § 46A.06[4] (Supp. 1982).

HANDBOOK OF RECOMMENDED PROCEDURES FOR THE TRIAL OF PROTRACTED CASES, Sample Form No. 4, pt. II, para. 6 (1960), *reprinted in* 25 F.R.D. 351, 447 (1960).

HARE ET AL., CONFIDENTIALITY ORDERS (1988).

HAYDOCK & HERR, DISCOVERY PRACTICE § 1.9.1. (2d ed. 1988 & Supp. 1992).

IMWINKELRIED & BLUMOFF, PRETRIAL DISCOVERY: STRATEGY AND TACTICS § 12.01 (1986 & Supp. 1992).

KEARNEY & BENSON, *Preventing Non-Party Access to Discovery Materials in Products Liability Actions: A Defendant's Primer*, 1987 CURRENT ISSUES L. & MED. 36–44 (1987).

KIELY, PREPARING PRODUCTS LIABILITY CASES §§ 7.21, 7.23 (1986 & Supp. 1989).

MANUAL FOR COMPLEX LITIGATION §§ 2.50, 3.11 (5th ed. 1985).

MANUAL FOR COMPLEX LITIGATION, SECOND §§ 21.43, 41.36 (1985), *reprinted in* 1 MOORE ET AL., MOORE'S FEDERAL PRACTICE §§ 21.43, 41.36 (1986).

MARCUS & SHERMAN, COMPLEX LITIGATION ch. 5, § 518 (1985).

4 MOORE ET AL., MOORE'S FEDERAL PRACTICE § 26.75 (2d ed. 1991).

PAUL ET AL., *Access*, *in* 3 COMMUNICATIONS LAW 1989, ch. 5, at 621–41, 690–710 (1989).

2 PETERS & PETERS, AUTOMOTIVE ENGINEERING AND LITIGATION ch. 28, at 827 (1991 & Supp. 1992).

SCHWARZER, MANAGING ANTITRUST AND OTHER COMPLEX LITIGATION 311 (1982).

8 WRIGHT & MILLER, FEDERAL PRACTICE AND PROCEDURE § 2040 (1970 & Supp. 1992).

D. Periodicals

Almeida, *Constitutional Law—Protective Orders Prohibiting Publication of Information Obtained Through Discovery*, 32 VILL. L. REV. 813 (1987).

Almeida, *Litigation Network Links Lawyers and Insurers*, 71 A.B.A. J., Jan. 1985, at 144.

Anderson, *How to Use Protective Orders to Safeguard Confidential Information*, 32 PRAC. LAW. 23 (1986).

Anderson & Riddle, *The Risk of Public Disclosure of Confidential Discovery Documents*, 7 CIV. LITIG. REP. (C.E.B.) 233 (1988).

Angele, *Rule 26(c) Protective Orders and the First Amendment*, 80 COLUM. L. REV. 1645 (1980).

Anthony, *Safeguarding Confidential Information in ITC Injury Proceedings*, 17 LAW & POL'Y INT'L BUS. 1 (1985).

Asbestos Removal Pact Unsealed, NEWS MEDIA & L., Fall 1989, at 15.

ATLA Challenges Secrecy Order for Defective Heart Valves, Association of Trial Lawyers of America, ATLA ADVOC., May 1990, at 1.

Ballard, *Courts Defang Much Feared Rule: In Keeping Records Secret, It's Business as Usual*, TEX. LAW., Dec. 3, 1990, at 1.

Baltz, *Shhh—Confidentiality in the Courts*, CHI. LAW., Jan. 1991, at 53.

Banks, *Protective Orders: Another Episode in the Proliferation of Legal Weapons on the Frontier of Landlord-Tenant Disputes*, 32 HOW. L.J. 343 (1989).

Bates, *Secret Settlements Spur Debate*, LAW. MONTHLY, Nov. 1989, at 1.

Bauman, *Sunshine v. Secrecy in New York*, 20 TRIAL LAW. Q., Spring/Summer 1990, at 10.

Beth, *The Public's Right to Know: The Supreme Court as Pandora?*, 81 MICH. L. REV. 880 (1983) (reviewing O'BRIEN, THE PUBLIC'S RIGHT TO KNOW: THE SUPREME COURT AND THE FIRST AMENDMENT (1983)).

Brazil, *The Adversary Character of Civil Discovery: A Critique and Proposals for Change*, 31 VAND. L. REV. 1295 (1978).

Brazil, *Protecting the Confidentiality of Settlement Negotiations*, 39 HASTINGS L.J. 955 (1988).

Campbell, *The Protective Order in Products Liability Litigation: Safeguard or Misnomer?*, 31 B.C. L. REV. 771 (1990).

Campbell, *Protective Orders and the Public Right of Access to Discovery*, 11 J. PROD. LIAB. 199 (1988).

Campion, *Third Circuit Reverses Tobacco Discovery Ruling*, N.J. L.J. Mar. 20, 1986, at 3.

Carpinello, *Public Access to Court Records in Civil Proceedings: The New York Approach*, 54 ALB. L. REV. 93 (1989).

Cavten, *Discovery of Confidential Information in Complex Litigation*, FOR DEF., Jan. 1986, at 2.

Chamberlain, *Proposed Rule 76a: An Elaborate, Time-Consuming, Cumbersome Procedure*, 54 TEX. B.J. 348 (1990).

Cheh, *Judicial Supervision of Executive Secrecy: Rethinking Freedom of Expression for Government Employees and the Public Right of Access to Government Information*, 69 CORNELL L. REV. 690 (1984).

Claybrook, *Going Public About Defective Products*, TRIAL, Nov. 1989, at 34.

Coben, *Protective Orders: Manufacturers Hide Behind Them*, TRIAL, Aug. 1986, at 34.

Comment, *Common Law or First Amendment Right of Access to Sealed Settlement Agreements*, 54 J. AIR L. & COM. 577 (1988).

Comment, *The Consent Judgment as an Instrument of Compromise and Settlement*, 72 HARV. L. REV. 1314 (1959).

Comment, *Constitutional Law—Rule 26(c) Protective Orders: First Amendment Scrutiny and the Good Cause Standard*, 21 SUFFOLK U. L. REV. 909 (1987).

Comment, *The Constitutional Right to Withhold Private Information*, 77 NW. U. L. REV. 536 (1982).

Comment, *Discovery and the First Amendment*, 34 BAYLOR L. REV. 229 (1982).

Comment, *Discovery and the First Amendment*, 21 WM. & MARY L. REV. 331 (1979).

Comment, *Dissemination of Discovery Materials Is Constitutionally Protected*, 55 NOTRE DAME LAW. 424 (1980).

Comment, *An Examination of the Protective Orders Issued Under Rule 30(b)*, 15 WYO. L.J. 85 (1960).

Comment, *The First Amendment and Pretrial Discovery Hearings: When Should the Public and Press Have Access?*, 36 UCLA L. REV. 609 (1989).

Comment, *The First Amendment Right of Access to Civil Trials After* Globe Newspaper Co. v. Superior Court, 51 U. CHI. L. REV. 286 (1984).

Comment, *The First Amendment Right to Disseminate Discovery Materials: In re* Halkin, 92 HARV. L. REV. 1550 (1979).

Comment, *Indirect Gag Orders and the Doctrine of Prior Restraint*, 44 U. MIAMI L. REV. 165 (1989).

Comment, *In re* San Juan Star: *Discovery and the First Amendment*, 34 BAYLOR L. REV. 229 (1982).

Comment, *Nonparty Access to Depositions in Florida*, 39 U. MIAMI L. REV. 157 (1984).

Comment, *A Pluralistic Reading of the First Amendment and Its Relation to Public Discourse*, 99 YALE L.J. 925 (1990).

Comment, *Protecting Trade Secrets Through Copyright*, 1981 DUKE L.J. 981.

Comment, *Protective Orders Prohibiting Dissemination of Discovery Information: The First Amendment and Good Cause*, 1980 DUKE L.J. 766.

Comment, *Sealed v. Sealed: A Public Court System Going Secretly Private*, 6 J.L. & POL'Y 381 (1990).

Cortese, *Privacy Rights of Business Under Attack*, LEGAL BACKGROUNDER, Aug. 3, 1990, at 1.

Court-Approved Confidentiality Orders: Why They Are Needed, 57 DEF. COUNS. J. 89 (1990).

Court Imposes Discovery Secrecy, NEWS MEDIA & L., Spring 1986, at 36.

Courts Can't Automatically Seal Case Files, NEWS MEDIA & L., Spring 1989, at 26.

Davis, *Court-Ordered Secrecy and Public Health*, LANCET, July 21, 1990, at 168.

Davis, *Protective Orders Restricting Disclosure of Discovery in Federal Civil Proceedings*, 56 CHI.-KENT L. REV. 943 (1980).

Dayton, *Alaska's Silent Spring*, 125 NEW SCIENTIST, Mar. 24, 1990, at 25.

Defending the Right to Protective Orders, FOR DEF., July 1990, at 1.

Devine, *Litigation Support Groups,* LEADER'S PRODUCT LIABILITY NEWSL., May 1985, at 1.

Dickinson, *Safe Custody of Trade Secrets,* MED. DEVICE & DIAGNOSTIC INDUSTRY, Feb. 1990, at 26.

Discovery Documents Are Public, NEWS MEDIA & L., Summer 1987, at 13.

Discovery Document Seal Stands, NEWS MEDIA & L., Summer 1985, at 19.

Discovery; Privilege/Work Product Identification of Relevant Documents, MICH. LAW. WKLY., Apr. 1, 1991, at 12.

Discovery—Protective Orders, 33 TRIAL LAW. GUIDE, Spring 1989, at 92.

Doggett, *Keeping Court Records Open,* TRIAL, July 1990, at 62.

Doggett & Mucchetti, *Public Access to Public Courts: Discouraging Secrecy in the Public Interest,* 69 TEX. L. REV. 643 (1991).

Dore, *Confidentiality Orders—The Proper Role of the Courts in Providing Confidential Treatment for Information Disclosed Through the Pre-Trial Discovery Process,* 14 NEW ENG. L. REV. 1 (1978).

Durst, *Confidentiality Agreements in Product Liability Litigation,* 15 TRIAL L.Q. 36 (1983).

Durst, *Confidentiality Agreements: Plaintiffs' Counsel Should Resist Them,* TRIAL, Sept. 1984, at 46.

Eagles, *Disclosure of Material Obtained on Discovery,* 27 MOD. L. REV. 284 (1984).

Eccles, *The Agent Orange Case: A Flawed Interpretation of the Federal Rules of Civil Procedure Granting Pretrial Access to Discovery,* 42 STAN. L. REV. 1577 (1990).

Epstein, *Open Courts, Closed Trials,* 13 LITIG. 23 (1987).

Epstein & Levi, *Protecting Trade Secret Information: A Plan for Proactive Strategy,* 43 BUS. LAW. 887 (1988).

Fanning, *The Ultimate Paper Chase,* FORBES, May 21, 1988, at 108.

Feldman, *Protective Orders in Products Liability Cases: Plaintiff's View,* THE BRIEF, Fall 1984, at 39.

Fisher, *Disclosure of Safety and Effectiveness Data Under the Drug Price Competition and Patent Restoration Act,* 41 FOOD DRUG COSM. L.J. 268 (1986).

Formeen, *Sealing and Unsealing Wrongful Death and Minor Settlement Documents,* 13 WM. MITCHELL L. REV. 505 (1987).

Freeman & Jenner, *Just Say No: Resisting Protective Orders,* TRIAL, Mar. 1990, at 66.

Gaoliano, *Protective Orders and Commercial Information—Is Good Cause Good Enough?,* 59 ST. JOHN'S L. REV. 103 (1984).

Gilbert & Neumann, *Protective Orders: How to Counter Them,* TRIAL, Nov. 1987, at 55.

Gilfand, *"Taking" Information Property Through Discovery,* 66 WASH. U. L.Q. 703 (1988).

Gutman, *Combatting Defendant's Obstructionism in the Discovery Process,* 55 URB. L. 983 (1978).

Hagans, *Confidentiality Agreements and Orders: When Should Discoverable Materials Be Kept Secret?*, 31 S. TEX. L.J. 455 (1990).

Hare & Gilbert, *Discovery in Products Liability Cases: The Plaintiff's Plea for Judicial Understanding*, 12 AM. J. TRIAL ADVOC. 413 (1989).

Hare & Gilbert, *Resisting Confidentiality Orders*, TRIAL, Oct. 1990, at 50.

Hare, Gilbert & Ellenberger, *Confidentiality Orders in Product Liability Cases*, 12 AM. J. TRIAL ADVOC. 597 (1990).

Haynes, *The Constitutionality of Trade Secret Disclosure Pursuant to the Toxic Substances Control Act of 1976*, 27 IDEA 135 (1986).

Heidt, *The Conjurer's Circle—The Fifth Amendment Privilege in Civil Cases*, 91 YALE L.J. 1062 (1982).

Herman, *Secrecy: More Than a Kid's Game*, TRIAL, Nov. 1989, at 7.

Herring, *Sealed Court Records: Unanswered Questions and Unsolved Problems*, TEX. LAW., May 21, 1990, at 24.

Hornung, *Lawyers v. Biz in Bid to Unseal Litigation*, 14 CRAIN'S CHI. BUS., May 20, 1991, at 3, col. 2.

Hunter, *Heart Valve in Man's Chest Becomes Focus of Discovery*, TEX. LAW., Mar. 6, 1989.

Jacobson, *Protecting Discovery by Copyright*, 71 J. PAT. & TRADEMARK OFF. SOC'Y 483 (1989).

Jemison, *Discovery Problems Inherent in Products Cases*, FOR DEF., Feb. 1984, at 2.

Joslin, *Confidentiality Orders in Complex Litigation*, 4 REV. LITIG. 109 (1985).

Junker, *Protective Orders and Exclusion of Corporate Counsel from Access to Confidential Information*, 8 MD. J. INT'L L. & TRADE, Fall 1984, at 191.

Kaminsky, *Proposed Federal Discovery Rules for Complex Litigation*, 48 FORDHAM L. REV. 970 (1980).

Kearney & Benson, *Preventing Non-Party Access to Discovery Materials in Products Liability Actions: A Defendant's Primer*, 1987 CURRENT ISSUES L. & MED. 36.

Killian, *Secrecy Topic at ATLA Orlando Convention*, FLA. B. NEWS, Nov. 1, 1989, at 10.

Kirsch, *Evidence Sharing*, CAL. LAW., June 1985, at 19.

Knowles, *Limiting Discovery Through Protective Orders*, FOR DEF., Jan. 1987, at 18.

Krzton, *Due Process Concerns in Discovery: Who May Protective Orders Bind?*, 44 U. PITT. L. REV. 1081 (1983).

Larson, Case Note, *Civil Procedure—Rule 26(c) Protective Orders and the Fifth Amendment*, 63 TEMP. L.Q. 637 (1991).

Lawler, *Appellate Review of Discovery Orders in the Federal Courts*, 1980 S. ILL. U. L.J. 339.

Lawyers for Civil Justice, *Making Private Information Public*, ISSUE BRIEF, Aug. 1989.

Lawyers for Civil Justice Task Force on Protective Orders, *Court Approved Protective Orders: Why They Are Needed*, 57 DEF. COUNS. J. 89 (1990).

Legislatures Prepare for Battle on Protective Orders, FOR DEF., Sept. 1990, at 3.

Lempert, *Protective Orders: The Battle Goes On*, INSIDE LITIG., Nov. 1987, at 1.

Levin & Colliers, *Containing the Cost of Litigation*, 37 RUTGERS L. REV. 218 (1985).

Levitt, *Keeping Secrets Secret*, 13 LITIG. 10 (1986).

Liberal Modification of Protective Orders to Permit Access to Discovery Information, DEF. COUNS. J. 147 (1990).

Livingston, *Making "Good Cause" a Good Standard for Limits on Dissemination of Discovered Information*, 47 U. PITT. L. REV. 547 (1986).

Lock, *Secrecy Orders: What You Don't Know Will Hurt You*, 23 MD. B.J., Sept./Oct. 1990, at 24, col. 3.

Lowe, *How to Fight Protective Orders*, TRIAL, Apr. 1990, at 76.

Lucas, *Weighing the Price of Court-Ordered Secrecy: N.J. Pondering Prohibitions on Sealed Discovery, Settlements*, 127 N.J. L.J., Mar. 14, 1991, at 3, col. 1.

Lyons, *Leaky Seals*, 146 FORBES, Dec. 10, 1990, at 132, col. 2.

Mahar, *Legal Heartbreak? Pfizer Faces Huge Liability If It Loses a Key Lawsuit*, BARRON'S, Apr. 2, 1990, at 8.

Maher, *Court Secrecy Is a Pandora's Box*, INSIGHT, Nov. 5, 1990, at 56.

Maher, *Demolishing the Wall of Secrecy*, TRIAL, Feb. 1991, at 7.

Marcotte, *Keeping Secrets*, A.B.A. J., Nov. 1989, at 32.

Marcus, *The Discovery Confidentiality Controversy*, 1991 ILL L. REV. 457.

Marcus, *Myth and Reality in Protective Order Litigation*, 69 CORNELL L. REV. 1 (1983).

Margolies, *Kansas Lawyers Battle over Business Law*, KAN. CITY BUS. J., Mar. 8, 1991, § 1, at 8.

Martin & Thomas, *Controlling Discovery and Guarding Confidential Data*, THE BRIEF, Winter 1988, at 48.

Mason & Hare, *The Use of F.R.C.P. 26(c)(7) to Prevent or Limit the Dissemination of "Internal Documents,"* 7 J. PROD. LIAB. 1 (1984).

Mathy, *Protective Orders and Third-Party Government Access to Civil Discovery: A Modest Proposal*, 9 HOFSTRA L. REV. 129 (1980).

McElhaney & Leatherbury, *An Overview: Proposed Rule 76a*, 54 TEX. B.J. 340 (1990).

McGarity & Shapiro, *The Trade Secret Status of Health and Safety Testing Information: Reforming Agency Disclosure Policies*, 93 HARV. L. REV. 837 (1980).

McLean, *Courts Restrict Release of Discovery Information*, 65 JOURNALISM Q. 503 (1988).

Members of Congress Protest Gag Order in Toyota Suits, LIABILITY WK., Aug. 6, 1990, at 4.

Miller, *Privacy, Secrecy, and the Public Interest*, FOR DEF., Sept. 1990, at 7.

Miller, *Private Lives or Public Access? The Debate over Courthouse Confidentiality*, 77 A.B.A. J., Aug. 1991, at 64.

Mintz, *The Dangers Insurance Companies Hide*, WASH. MONTHLY, Jan./Feb. 1991, at 38.

Montgomery, *Products Liability: Eliminating Discovery Excess*, FOR DEF., Oct. 1985, at 27.

Morin, *Fighting Secrecy in the Courts*, LAW. MONTHLY, Nov. 1989, at 1.

Morrison, *Protective Orders, Plaintiffs, Defendants and Public Interest in Disclosure: Where Does the Balance Lie?*, 24 U. RICH. L. REV. 109 (1989).

Mulvey, *Modification of Protective Orders: Balancing Practical Considerations and Addressing Constitutional Rights*, 14 Suffolk U. L. REV. 1011 (1980).

Newspapers Have Right Under Common Law to See Legislator's Divorce Case File, NEWS MEDIA & L., Fall 1988, at 11.

Note, *Access to Pretrial Documents Under the First Amendment*, 85 COLUM. L. REV. 1813 (1984).

Note, *Access to Sealed Settlement Documents Granted Based on Common Law Right of Access to Judicial Proceedings*, 60 TEMP. L.Q. 1023 (1987).

Note, *All Courts Shall Be Open: The Public's Right to View Judicial Proceedings and Records*, 52 TEMP. L.Q. 331 (1979).

Note, *Anti-Dissemination Orders in Product Liability Suits*, 5 AM. J. TRIAL ADVOC. 507 (1982).

Note, *Clear Standards for Discovery Protective Orders: A Missed Opportunity in* Rhinehart v. Seattle Times Co., 8 U. PUGET SOUND L. REV. 123 (1984).

Note, *Closure of Pretrial Suppression Hearings: Resolving the Fair Trial-Free Press Conflict*, 51 FORDHAM L. REV. 1297 (1983).

Note, *The Common Law Right to Inspect and Copy Judicial Records: In Camera or on Camera*, 16 GA. L. REV. 659 (1982).

Note, *Confusion in the Courthouse: The Legacy of the Gannett and Richmond Newspapers Public Right of Access Cases*, 59 S. CAL. L. REV. 603 (1986).

Note, *Constitutional Law—Discovery—Protective Order Restraining Parties and Counsel from Disseminating Discovery Information Is an Unconstitutional Prior Restraint on Freedom of Speech*, 48 U. CIN. L. REV. 900 (1979).

Note, *Constitutional Law—Fair Trial-Free Speech—If the Issuance of a Protective Order Pursuant to Federal Rule 26(c) Would Restrain Expression, the District Court Must Determine the Order's Constitutionality Under the First Amendment*, 48 GEO. WASH. L. REV. 486 (1980).

Note, *Constitutional Standards Governing Issuance of Protective Orders Pursuant to Fed. R. Civ. P. 26(c) When Freedom of Speech Is Restrained*, 52 TEMP. L.Q. 1197 (1979).

Note, *Constructing a Public Right of Access to Pretrial Proceedings: How Sound Is the Structure?*, 66 WASH. U. L.Q. 745 (1988).

Note, *Discovery: Protective Orders* Cipollone v. Liggett Group, 30 TRIAL LAW. GUIDE 240 (1986).

Note, *Due Process Concerns in Discovery: Who May Protective Orders Bind?*, 44 U. PITT. L. REV. 1081 (1983).

Note, *First Amendment Interests in Trade Secrets, Private Materials, and Confidential Infor-*

mation: *The Use of Protective Orders in Defamation Litigation*, 69 IOWA L. REV. 1011 (1984).

Note, *A First Amendment Right of Access to Affidavits in Support of Search Warrants*, 90 COLUM. L. REV. 2216 (1990).

Note, *The First Amendment Right to Disseminate Discovery Materials: In re* Halkin, 92 HARV. L. REV. 1550 (1979).

Note, *Freedom of Speech: Discovery—Constitutional Standards Governing Issuance of Protective Orders Pursuant to Federal R. Civ. P. 26(c) When Freedom of Speech Is Restraint*, 52 TEMP. L.Q. 1197 (1979).

Note, *Justice Scalia and Judicial Restraint: A Conservative Resolution Between the Individual and State*, 62 TUL. L. REV. 225 (1987).

Note, *Mass Products Liability Litigation: A Proposal for Dissemination of Discovery Material Covered by a Protective Order*, 60 N.Y.U. L. REV. 1137 (1985).

Note, *Modification of Protective Orders: Balancing Practical Considerations and Addressing Constitutional Rights*, 14 SUFFOLK U. L. REV. 1011 (1980).

Note, *Nonparty Access to Discovery Materials in the Federal Courts*, 94 HARV. L. REV. 1085 (1981).

Note, *Protective Orders and the Use of Discovery Materials Following* Seattle Times, 71 MINN. L. REV. 171 (1986).

Note, *Protective Orders Prohibiting Dissemination of Discovery Information: The First Amendment and Good Cause*, 1980 DUKE L.J. 766.

Note, *Protective Orders Prohibiting Publication of Information Obtained Through Discovery*, 32 VILL. L. REV. 813 (1987).

Note, *Protective Orders: Sword and Shield in the War of Discovery*, 12 AM. J. TRIAL ADVOC. 483 (1989).

Note, Publicker Industries v. Cohen: *Public Access to Civil Proceedings and a Corporation's Right to Privacy*, 80 NW. U. L. REV. 1319 (1987).

Note, *Rule 26(c) Protective Orders and the First Amendment*, 80 COLUM. L. REV. 1645 (1980).

Note, *Rule 26(c) Protective Orders, First Amendment Scrutiny and the Good Cause Standard*, 21 SUFFOLK U. L. REV. 909 (1987).

Note, *Sealed Judicial Records and Infant Doe: A Proposal to Protect the Public's Right of Access*, 16 IND. L. REV. 861(1983).

Note, *Sealed Out-of-Court Settlements: When Does the Public Have a Right to Know?*, 66 NOTRE DAME L. REV. 117 (1990).

Note, Seattle Times: *What Effect on Discovery Sharing*, 1985 WIS. L. REV. 1055.

Note, Seattle Times v. Rhinehart: *Making "Good Cause" a Good Standard for Limits on Dissemination of Discovered Information*, 47 U. PITT. L. REV. 547 (1986).

Note, *Trade Secrets in Discovery: From First Amendment Disclosure to Fifth Amendment Protection*, 104 HARV. L. REV. 1330 (1991).

Note, *The Value of Copyright Law as a Deterrent to Discovery Abuse*, 138 U. PA. L. REV. 549 (1989).

Note, *Whatever Happened to the "Right to Know"?: Access to Government Controlled Information Since* Richmond Newspapers, 73 VA. L. REV. 1111 (1987).

Olson, *No Secrets*, REASONS, Feb. 1991, at 23.

O'Reilly, *Put an End to Secret Settlements*, CAL. LAW., Oct. 1990, at 128.

Osborn, *Protective Orders: The New Challenge*, FOR DEF., Mar. 1991, at 2.

Palermo, *Secrecy in the Courts*, CAL. LAW., Sept. 1989, at 32.

Parker, *Corporate Secrecy*, TRIAL, Dec. 1988, at 13.

Parnell, *The Co-Ordinated Group Defense*, FOR DEF., Nov. 1980, at 16.

Pavalon & Alvary, *Protective and Secrecy Orders: Time for Change*, TRIAL, Mar. 1991, at 110.

Perlman, *Court-Sanctioned Secrecy*, TRIAL, Sept. 1985, at 5.

Peterson, *Proposed Rule 76a: A Radical Turning Point for Trade Secrets*, 54 TEX. B.J. 344 (1990).

Pownell, *The First Amendment and Pretrial Discovery Hearings: When Should the Public and Press Have Access?*, 36 UCLA L. REV. 609 (1969).

"Protective Orders" Often Abuse Judicial System, ATLA President Charges, 116 N.J. L.J., Oct. 24, 1985, at 19, col. 1.

ReMine & Gilbert, *Discovery: Abuses, Sanctions and Ethics*, TRIAL, Jan. 1987, at 56.

Rendall, *Protective Orders Prohibiting Dissemination of Discovery Information: The First Amendment and Good Cause*, 1980 DUKE L.J. 766.

Rheingold, *The Development of Litigation Groups*, 6 AM. J. TRIAL ADVOC. 1 (1982).

Rheingold, *The MER/29 Story—An Instance of Successful Mass Disaster Litigation*, 56 CAL. L. REV. 116 (1968).

Rieders, *A New Conspiracy of Silence: Non-Publicity Clauses in Settlement Releases and Motions to Seal Settlement Petitions*, BARRISTER, Spring 1990, at 5.

Riley & Hoefer, *Protective Orders: Machiavelli Would Be Pleased*, TRIAL, Nov. 1984, at 30.

Robinson, *Defending the Right to Protective Orders*, FOR DEF., July 1990, at 1.

Rubin, *Toward a General Theory of Waiver*, 28 UCLA L. REV. 478 (1981).

Rushford, *Subpoena Challenges Court-Imposed Secrecy*, TEX. LAW., Mar. 6, 1989, at 1.

San Diego Superior Court Enacts Anti-Secrecy Rule, AUTOMOTIVE LITIG. REP. 14198 (Oct. 16, 1990).

Sargeant, *Secrecy Orders Veiling Heart Valve Defects Are Assailed*, TRIAL, May 1990, at 12.

Scheindlin, *Discovering the Discoverable: A Bird's Eye View of Discovery in a Complex Multi-District Class Action Litigation*, 52 BROOK. L. REV. 397 (1986).

Schroeder, *Heart Trouble at Pfizer*, BUS. WK., Feb. 26, 1990, at 47.

Schroeter, *Privacy Rights Can Limit Discovery*, TRIAL, Nov. 1990, at 49.

Senate Judiciary Subcommittee Looks at Court Secrecy, LIABILITY WK., May 21, 1990, at 1.

Shapiro, *Needless Papers May Haunt Manufacturers*, BUS. INS., Apr. 18, 1989, at 48.

Sherman & Kinnard, *Federal Court Discovery in the 80's—Making the Rules Work*, 95 F.R.D. 245 (1982).

Smith, *Anti-Dissemination Orders in Product Liability Suits*, 5 AM. J. TRIAL ADVOC. 507 (1982).

Smith, *A Practical Approach to Rule 26(c) Protective Orders in Aviation Litigation*, 56 J. AIR L. & COM. 765 (1991).

States Consider Limiting Discovery Material Secrecy, NEWS MEDIA & L., Spring 1989, at 28.

States That Tell Secrets, INS. REV., Sept. 1991.

Summer, *First Amendment Interests in Trade Secrets Private Materials and Confidential Information: The Use of Protective Orders in Defamation Litigation*, 69 IOWA L. REV. 1011 (1984).

Sunderland, *The New Federal Rules*, 45 W. VA. L.Q. 5 (1938).

Thacker, *Discovery of Peer Review Records—Two Competing Public Policies: The Need for Liberal Discovery Versus the Need for Confidentiality*, 53 UMKC L. REV. 663 (1985).

Thompson, *Protective Orders: Sword and Shield in War of Discovery*, 12 AM. J. TRIAL ADVOC. 483 (1989).

Thomson, *Confidentiality Orders*, TRIAL, Nov. 1979, at 12.

Tsiantar, *George Smiley Joins the Firm*, NEWSWEEK, May 2, 1988, at 46.

Wallace, *Do Not Consent to That Concealment Order*, TRIAL, Oct. 1980, at 19.

Weber, *Mass Tort Litigation: The Pot Boils Over*, 6 J. PROD. LIAB. 273 (1983).

Weiner, *Protective Orders Are Not for Dirty Little Secrets*, 125 N.J. L.J., Feb. 8, 1990, at 11.

Wheelwright, *Muzzling Science*, NEWSWEEK, Apr. 22, 1991, at 10.

Wilson, *Seattle Times: What Effect on Discovery Sharing*, 1985 WIS. L. REV. 1055.

Wittner & Campbell, *Protective Orders Under Attack*, ACCA Docket: J. AM. CORP. COUNS. ASS'N, Winter 1990, at 14.

Wobbrock, *One Effort to End Secrecy in the Courts*, TRIAL LAW. J. (Or.), Winter 1990.

E. Looseleaf Services

Cortese, *ATLA's Protective Order Campaign: Undermining Confidence in the Courts*, Toxics L. Rep. (BNA) 1497 (Apr. 24, 1991).

Honda ATV Protective Order Lifted for Certain Documents by Oregon Judge, Prod. Safety & Liab. Rep. (BNA) No. 47, at 1171 (Nov. 24, 1989).

Shenefield Predicts Carter Administration Support for Attack on Oil Industry Horizontal Integration, Antitrust & Trade Reg. Rep. (BNA) No. 834, at A-6 (Oct. 13, 1977) (interview with Assistant Attorney General John Shenefield).

Weaver, *Secrets That Can Kill Have No Place in Our Courts*, Prod. Safety & Liab. Rep. (BNA) 701 (June 14, 1991).

F. Annotations

Annotation, *Construction and Application of Provisions of Federal Rule of Civil Procedure 26(c) Providing for the Filing of Secret or Confidential Documents or Information Enclosed in Sealed Envelopes to Be Opened Only as Directed by the Court*, 19 A.L.R. FED. 970 (1974).

Annotation, *Discovery or Inspection of Trade Secrets, Formulas or the Like*, 17 A.L.R. 2D 383 (1951).

Annotation, *In Camera Trial or Hearing and Other Procedures to Safeguard Trade Secret or the Like Against Undue Disclosure in Course of Civil Action Involving Such Secret*, 62 A.L.R. 2D 501 (1958).

Annotation, *Modification of Protective Order Entered Pursuant to Rule 26(c), Federal Rules of Civil Procedure*, 85 A.L.R. FED. 538 (1987).

Annotation, *Protective Orders Limiting Dissemination of Financial Information Obtained by Deposition or Discovery in State Civil Actions*, 43 A.L.R. 4TH 121 (1986).

Annotation, *Restricting Public Access to Judicial Records of State Courts*, 84 A.L.R. 3D 598 (1978).

Annotation, *Restriction on Dissemination of Information Obtained Through Pretrial Discovery Proceedings as Violating Federal Constitution's First Amendment—Federal Cases*, 81 A.L.R. FED. 471 (1987).

Annotation, *Right of Press, in Criminal Proceedings, to Have Access to Exhibits, Transcripts, Testimony, and Communications Not Admitted in Evidence or Made Part of Public Record*, 39 A.L.R. FED. 871 (1978).

G. Newspapers

Abrahamson, *New Ruling Lifts Veil of Secrecy in Civil Cases*, L.A. TIMES (San Diego county ed.), Sept. 9, 1990, at B1, col. 5.

Alperson, *Asbestos Defendants Begin to Cooperate in Litigation*, LEGAL TIMES, Sept. 19, 1983, at 3.

Angell, *Secrecy Provisions in Litigation Become More Controversial*, L.A. DAILY J., Mar. 11, 1991, at S6, col. 2.

Arthur, *Defendants Fight Back on Data Sharing*, LEGAL TIMES, July16, 1984, at 1, col. 2.

Barrett, *Firms Use Copyright Law to Keep Documents Secret*, WALL ST. J., Aug. 31, 1988, at 27.

Barrett, *Protective Orders Come Under Attack*, WALL ST. J., Aug. 31, 1988, at 27.

Bates, *Judge Sets up DPT Library for Plaintiffs*, NAT'L L.J., Feb. 22, 1988, at 10.

Blum, *Anti-Secrecy Drive Spreads in the States*, NAT'L L.J., Jan. 14, 1991, at 3.

Blum, *ATLA Convention Filled with Activity; Protective Orders Hit*, NAT'l L.J., July 31, 1989, at 3.

Blum, *Copyright Used to Shield Discovery*, NAT'L L.J., Mar. 28, 1988, at 3.

Blum, *Drug Maker Copyrights Documents*, NAT'L L.J., Feb. 11, 1991, at 3.

Blum, *Pfizer Maneuvers to Defend Protective Order*, NAT'L L.J., Apr. 16, 1990, at 14.

Blum, *Plaintiff's Bar: Strength in Numbers*, NAT'L L.J., Nov. 21, 1988, at 1.

Blum, *Protective Orders Again Are at Issue*, NAT'L L.J, Oct. 30, 1989, at 3.

Blum, *Protective Orders Under Attack*, NAT'L L.J., May 8, 1989, at 3.

Blum, *A Public Gathering Discusses Trial Secrecy*, NAT'L L.J., May 7, 1990, at 14.

Blum, *Yamaha Loses Bid in Court*, NAT'L L.J., Nov. 19, 1990, at 9.

Cabrera, *Trial Lawyers Criticize Court Secrecy Agreements*, CHI. DAILY L. BULL., Apr. 26, 1990, at 1, col 2.

Catholic Church Is Said to Settle Molestation Suit, N.Y. TIMES, Oct. 27, 1988, at 117, col. 1.

Corboy, *Muzzled and Masked, Litigants Tell No Evil: Is This Blind Justice*, LEGAL TIMES, Jan. 8, 1990, at 27, col. 1.

Courtroom Glasnost: Laudable Ruling Means More Trial Records Will Be Open, HOUS. POST, Apr. 22, 1990, at C2, col. 1.

Dresslar, *Battle Looms over Tort Secrecy Deals*, L.A. DAILY J., Apr. 22, 1991, at 7, col. 1.

F.D.A. Is Faulted on a Heart Valve, N.Y. TIMES, Feb. 26, 1990, at B8.

Federal Judge Strikes Down Gag Rule on Complaints Against Florida Lawyers, WALL ST. J., Jan. 24, 1990, at B6.

Fox, *Lawyers, Judges Criticize Prego Settlement Secrecy*, 203 N.Y. L.J., Mar. 14, 1990, at 1, col. 3.

Fuchsburg, *The Blindfold of Justice*, 204 N.Y. L.J., Oct. 4, 1990, at 2, col 3.

Galante, *Zomax Document Release Disputed*, NAT'L L.J., Apr. 22, 1985, at 10.

Geyelin, *Plaintiffs' Lawyers Move to Preserve Exchange of Data*, WALL ST. J., July 25, 1989, at B8, col. 5.

Goldberg, *End Protective Orders in Tort Cases?*, L.A. DAILY J., Feb. 9, 1990, at 7, col. 5.

Heckelman, *Court Secrecy Bill May Be Revived*, CHI. DAILY L. BULL., June 13, 1991, at 1, col. 2.

Heckelman, *House Passes Bill to Limit Court Secrecy in Product Cases*, CHI. DAILY L. BULL., May 10, 1991, at 1, col. 2.

Heckelman, *Lawyers Debate Bill That Would Ban Secret Court Agreements*, CHI. DAILY L. BULL., Apr. 12, 1991, at 1, col. 2.

Heckelman, *Senate Committee Rejects Bill Limiting Court Secrecy*, CHI. DAILY L. BULL., Apr. 12, 1991, at 1.

Heinke, *Discovery and the First Amendment: Is a Protective Order a Prior Restraint?*, L.A. DAILY J., July 29, 1981, at 4.

Herman, *Court Cuts Civil Suit Secrecy*, HOUS. POST, Apr. 17, 1990, at A11, col. 1.

Herman, *No More Dirty Little Secrets in the Courts*, WASH. POST, Sept. 15, 1989, at A31, reprinted in ATLA ADVOC., Oct. 1989, at 4.

Herman, *Secrecy, Discovery Abuse Breed Unethical Conduct*, NAT'L L.J., Aug. 1, 1988, at 17.

Hoenig, *A New Rule on Sealing Court Records?*, 204 N.Y. L.J., July 27, 1990, at 3, col. 3.

Hoenig, *New York's Rule on Sealing Court Records*, 205 N.Y. L.J., Mar. 1, 1991, at 3, col. 1.

Hoenig, *Protective Confidentiality Orders*, 203 N.Y. L.J., Mar. 5, 1990, at 3, col. 1.

How the Plaintiff's Bar Shares Its Information, NAT'L L.J., July 23, 1984, at 1.

Hunter, *Opposition to Pfizer's Courtroom Secrecy Grows*, LEGAL TIMES, Mar. 26, 1990, at 6, col. 1.

Hyman & Wilson, *How to Bar Opponent's Impropriety*, NAT'L L.J., May 27, 1991, at 19.

Jaffe, *Public Good v. Sealed Evidence*, NEWARK STAR-LEDGER (N.J.), Sept. 2, 1990, § 3, at 1, col. 2.

Knight, *Court Business Is Public Business*, DENV. POST, Nov. 4, 1990, at 1H, col. 1.

Kolbert, *New York Bans Routine Sealing of Court Records*, N.Y. TIMES, Feb. 5, 1991, at A12, col. 1.

Kolbert, *New York's Top Judge Urges Less Secrecy in Settling Cases*, N.Y. TIMES, June 20, 1990, at A1, col. 3.

Kreindler, *The Confidentiality Order*, 202 N.Y. L.J., July 3, 1989, at 3, col. 1.

Kreindler, *Court-Entered 'Confidentiality Orders,'* 199 N.Y. L.J., June 6, 1988, at 3, col. 1.

Lawyer Cited in Document Sale, NAT'L L.J., July 18, 1983, at 10.

Legislature Should Approve Bill That Requires Hazard Disclosures, FLA. SUN-SENTINEL, May 14, 1990, at 8A, col. 2.

Lempert, *Seeds of Technology Sprout into Complex Litigation*, LEGAL TIMES, June 13, 1983, at 16, col. 1.

Lenkowsky, *Goal Is to Safeguard Confidentiality*, NAT'L L.J., May 14, 1990, at 23.

Let People Know If Danger Lurks, BATON ROUGE SUNDAY ADVOC., June 2, 1991, at 12B.

Marcus, *Firms' Secrets Are Increasingly Bared by Courts*, WALL ST. J., Feb. 4, 1991, at B1, col. 3.

Masters, *Exxon Proceeding Offers Lesson on Confidentiality*, LEGAL TIMES, Oct. 26, 1981, at 5, col. 1.

Mauro, *Court Secrecy Often Puts Public at Risk*, USA TODAY, Apr. 23, 1990, at 11A, reprinted in TRIAL, July 1990, at 65 (interview with U.S. District Judge James Carrigan).

McGonigle, *Judge Says Privacy Can Help Settle Suits*, DALLAS MORNING NEWS, Nov. 22, 1987, at 24A, col. 1.

McGonigle, *Jurist Believes Sealing Records Is Undemocratic*, DALLAS MORNING NEWS, Nov. 22, 1987, at 25A, col. 1.

McGonigle, *Sealed Lawsuits Deal with Poisonings, Sex, Surgery*, DALLAS MORNING NEWS, Nov. 23, 1987, at 1A, col. 5.

McGonigle, *Secret Lawsuits Shelter Wealthy, Influential*, DALLAS MORNING NEWS, Nov. 22, 1987, at 1A, col. 1.

Middleton, *Should a Court Keep Secrets*, NAT'L L.J., Oct. 17, 1988, at 22.

Moran, *Texans Should Be Worried When Judges Seek Secrecy*, HOUS. CHRON., May 27, 1990, at 4F, col. 2.

Moskowitz, *Fighting Orders for Secrecy*, WASH. POST, Oct. 31, 1988, at WB 18C.

Moskowitz, *States Try to Bar Secrecy Pacts in Settlements*, WASH. POST, Apr. 1, 1991, at F12.

No Contradiction, NAT'L L.J., May 27, 1991, at 14.

N.Y. Panel Curtails Sealing of Court Records, NAT'L L.J., Feb. 18, 1991, at 6.

On Court Secrecy, NAT'L L.J., Nov. 6, 1989, at 12.

Open Court, LEGAL TIMES, Oct. 23, 1989, at 17.

Ostrow, *Secrecy Accords in Product Liability Lawsuits Debated*, L.A. TIMES, Apr. 26, 1990, at A16, col. 1.

Pavalon & Haralson, *How to Challenge and Remove Protective Orders*, CHI. DAILY L. BULL., Mar. 19, 1990.

Pelman, *Reagan Deposition to Spawn Battle Over Access*, LEGAL TIMES, Feb. 12, 1990, at 10.

Postal, *Protective Orders of Courts*, CHI. DAILY L. BULL., Oct. 16, 1986, at 1, col. 1.

Price & Thompson, *Girlfriends Aided Probe of Vogel*, WASH. POST, Sept. 29, 1990, at B1, col. 2.

Protective Order to Be Considered for Confidentiality, 10 PA. L. J. R., Nov. 23, 1987, at 11, col. 4.

Public Hazards Can't Be Concealed by a Court Order Under New Florida Law, WALL ST. J., June 4, 1990, at B8, col. 2.

Quinn, *Stipulated Protective Orders Respecting Confidential Information*, L.A. DAILY J., June 2, 1981, at 4.

Rae-Dupree, *Groups Seek Release of Mobil Plant Documents*, L.A. TIMES, Mar. 1, 1991, at B3, col. 4.

Rae-Dupree, *Newspapers Seek Access to Mobil Documents*, L.A. TIMES, Mar. 1, 1991, at B3, col. 1.

Ranii, *How the Plaintiffs' Bar Shares Its Information*, NAT'L L.J., July 23, 1984, at 1.

Reardon, *Court Confidentiality Debate's Rhetoric*, 204 N.Y. L.J., Oct. 16, 1990, at 2, col. 3.

Reynolds, *"If Only We Had Known," Say Victims of Secrecy*, USA TODAY, Apr. 23, 1990, at 11A.

Rich, *Defendant's Fight Back on Data Sharing*, LEGAL TIMES, July 16, 1984, at 1.

Riley, *Secret Tobacco Documents Stay Secret*, NAT'L L.J., Mar. 24, 1986, at 3.

Riley, *Tobacco Companies Fight Data Release*, NAT'L L.J., Oct. 14, 1985, at 13.

Robb, *Admissibility of Prior Accidents Can Be a Key Evidentiary Issue*, NAT'L L.J., July 10, 1989, at 18.

Rushford, *Legal, Political Fallout from Secret Valve Study*, LEGAL TIMES, Feb. 6, 1989, at 1, col. 3.

Rushford, *Pfizer Fires Opening Salvo in Its Public Defense*, LEGAL TIMES, Mar. 3, 1990, at 7.

Rushford, *Pfizer's Telltale Heart Valve*, LEGAL TIMES, Feb. 26, 1990, at 1, col. 2.

Rushford, *Subpoena Quickens Beat of Heart-Valve Fight*, LEGAL TIMES, Mar. 6, 1989, at 5, col. 1.

Sablatura, *Sealed Court Records Shroud Williams' Business Practices*, HOUS. CHRON., Aug. 26, 1990, at 1A, col. 5.

Schwaneberg, *Proposals Aim to Ban Court Secrecy Agreements on Dangerous Products*, NEWARK STAR-LEDGER (N.J.), Nov. 25, 1990, §1.

Secrecy, Continued, NAT'L L.J., Mar. 26, 1990, at 12.

Secrecy Rules Hide Dangers, DALLAS TIMES HERALD, Oct. 23, 1988, at A1.

Siegel, *Dilemmas of Settling in Secret: Companies Offer Hefty Sums in Exchange for Keeping the Details of Public Hazard Lawsuits Quiet*, L.A. TIMES, Apr. 5, 1991, at A1, col. 1.

Sinclair, *Protective Orders: How Much Protection Do They Really Offer?*, NAT'L L.J., Mar. 2, 1981, at 1.

Spencer, *State Bar Votes to Oppose Court Rule on Sealing Files*, N.Y. L.J., Jan. 28, 1991, at 1.

Squiers, *Documents OK'd for RICO Use*, NAT'L L.J., Oct. 29, 1990, at 13.

Suit Against GM to Test New Texas Rules Limiting Protective Orders, WALL ST. J., Nov. 26, 1990, at B3.

Sullivan, *ATLA Concerned About Protective Orders*, CHI. DAILY L. BULL., Sept. 28, 1989, at 1, col. 2.

Sullivan, *Ban on Secrecy Shatters Privacy Rights (Settlements in the Sunshine?)*, L.A. DAILY J., May 30, 1991, at 6, col. 5.

Sullivan, *In Lawsuits, How Much Should the Courts Keep Secret*, N.Y. TIMES, March 3, 1991, § 4, at 6, col. 1.

Sullivan, *Sealed Court Files Face Threat*, L.A. DAILY J., Mar. 9, 1991, at 14.

Sullivan, *Trial Lawyers Campaign Against Protective Orders*, CHI. DAILY LAW BULL., Oct 13, 1989, at 1, col. 5.

Sunshine Act for the Courtroom, THE TIMES-PICAYUNE (NEW ORLEANS), June 16, 1991, at B8.

Templin, *Ford Settles Big Lap-Belt Injury Suit*, WALL ST. J., Apr. 5, 1990, at B1.

Texas High Court Cuts into Secrecy in Civil Suits, N.Y. TIMES, Apr. 23, 1990, at A17.

Torry, *Texas Supreme Court Curbs Secrecy of Lawsuit Records*, WASH. POST, Apr. 21, 1990, at A2, col. 5.

Unseal Court Records, MIAMI HERALD, Apr. 17, 1990, at 10A.

Wagner, *Secrecy Betrays Justice*, NAT'L L.J., July 24, 1989, at 17.

Walpin & Lange, *Confidentiality Pacts—Handling Sensitive Materials*, NAT'L L.J., July 29, 1985, at 15.

Walsh, *Rising Secrecy in Civil Cases Prompts Legislative Backlash*, WASH. POST, Feb. 20, 1989, at B1, col. 2.

Walsh, *Secrecy Limits in Civil Cases Approved*, WASH. POST, Feb. 22, 1989, at B5.

Walsh, *Va. Firms Seek Veto of Disclosure Bill*, WASH. POST, Mar. 26, 1989, at C6.

Walsh & Weiser, *Judge Had Case Records Destroyed After Settlement; '87 Hearing Involved Mine Worker's Safety Complaint*, WASH. POST, Dec. 24, 1988, at A2, col. 5.

Walsh & Weiser, *Public Courts, Private Justice: Court Secrecy Masks Safety Issues*, WASH. POST, Oct. 23, 1988, at A1, col. 3.

Walsh & Weiser, *Public Courts, Private Justice: Hundreds of Cases Shrouded in Secrecy*, WASH. POST, Oct. 24, 1988, at A1, col. 1.

Walsh & Weiser, *Va. Moves to Limit Lawsuit Secrecy*, WASH. POST, Feb. 6, 1989, at D3, col. 1.

Weiner, *Keeping Confidences: Protective Orders Not for Dirty Little Secrets*, LEGAL TIMES, Jan. 29, 1990, at 25.

Weiser, *D.C. Hospital Sued in Surgical Death: Conspiracy to Conceal Report on Doctor's Performance Alleged*, WASH. POST, Oct. 6, 1989, at A50, col. 1.

Weiser, *Lawyers Launch Fight Against Court Secrecy*, WASH. POST, Oct. 31, 1989, at D5, col. 1.

Weiser, *Playtex Hired Opponent's Lawyer in Toxic Shock Lawsuits*, WASH. POST, Oct. 16, 1989, at A1, col. 1.

Weiser, *Public Courts, Private Justice: Forging a "Covenant of Silence,"* WASH. POST, Mar. 13, 1989, at A1, col. 1.

Weiser, *Release of Sealed Records Ordered in Xerox Toxic Chemical Case*, WASH. POST, Aug. 17, 1989, at A24, col. 1.

Weiser, *Secrecy in Toxic-Spill Case Assailed*, WASH. POST, Mar. 22, 1989, at A16, col. 1.

Weiser, *Secrecy Rules Eases in Md. Cancer Lawsuits*, WASH. POST, Aug. 14, 1989, at E2, col. 1.

Weiser & Walsh, *Public Courts, Private Justice: Drug Firm's Strategy: Avoid Trial, Ask Secrecy*, WASH. POST, Oct. 25, 1988, at A1, col. 1.

Weiser & Walsh, *Public Courts, Private Justice: Settlements Kept Former Drug Salesman's Story Under Wraps*, WASH. POST, Oct. 25, 1988, at A13, col. 1.

Weiser & Walsh, *Secret Filing, Settlement Hide Surgeon's Record*, WASH. POST, Oct. 26, 1988, at A1, col. 1.

Wise, *Abrams Advocates Government Access to Court-Sealed Files*, N.Y. L.J., April 12, 1991, at 1.

Wise, *Comments Sought on Proposed Ban on Sealing Records*, N.Y. L.J., Sept. 12, 1990, at 1.

Wise, *Court Rule Adopted on Sealing Records*, N.Y. L.J., Feb. 5, 1991, at 1, col. 6.

Wise, *Hearing Set on Disclosure of Agent Orange Documents*, N.Y. L.J., Jan. 7, 1985, at 1., col. 3.

Wise, *Judge Refuses to Seal File in Doctor's Suit*, N.Y. L.J., Oct. 29, 1990, at 1.

Wise, *Opinion Sharply Divided on Sealing Rule*, N.Y. L.J., Dec. 10, 1990, at 1.

Wise, *Proposal Endorsed on Sealing Records*, N.Y. L.J., July 27, 1990, at 1.

Wise, *Realtor Ordered to Yield Records in Suit for Bias: Protective Order Directed at Helmsley-Spear*, N.Y. L.J., Nov. 4, 1983, at 1.

Wise, *Sealed Transcripts Unnerve Lawyers*, N.Y. L.J., Mar. 21, 1989, at 1.

Wise, *Sealing of Records Stirs Action*, N.Y. L.J., Apr. 30, 1990, at 1.

Ziegler, *Judges Sit in the Eye of the Secrecy Storm*, S.F. DAILY J., Oct. 30, 1990, at 1, col. 2.

Ziegler, *Letting 'Sunshine' In: California Joins Trend to Strip Secrecy from Court Files*, S.F. DAILY J., Oct. 29, 1990, at 1, col. 2.

Ziegler, *Trend in States Seems to Favor Allowing a Little 'Sunshine' In*, S.F. DAILY J., Oct. 29, 1990, at 9, col. 1.

H. ATLA Convention and Seminar Materials

Association of Trial Lawyers of America Board of Governors, Resolution on Protective Orders, May 6, 1989.

Bryant, Fighting Federal Preemption and Protection Orders in Toxic Tort Cases (ATLA Winter Convention paper, 1990).

Bryant, Working Together to Oppose Secrecy in the Courts (ATLA Winter Convention paper, 1990).

Gievers, Duking It Out on the Line of Scrimmage: Protective Orders, Confidentiality (ATLA seminar paper, Aug. 1990).

Gilbert & Hare, Confidentiality Orders in Products Liability Cases (ATLA Winter Convention paper, 1990).

Gilbert & Neumann, Protective Orders in Product Liability Litigation (ATLA seminar paper, Oct. 1987).

Habush, How to Fight and Remove Protective and Secrecy Orders in Your Cases (ATLA Winter Convention paper, 1990).

Hare, Points and Authorities Concerning Confidentiality Orders in Product Liability Cases (ATLA seminar paper, Sept. 1989).

Hitchcock, How to Fight and Remove Protective and Secrecy Orders in Other Cases, (ATLA Winter Convention paper, 1990).

Lowe, How to Fight and Remove Protective and Secrecy Orders (ATLA Winter Convention paper, 1990).

Pavalon & Haralson, How to Fight and Remove Protective and Secrecy Orders in Other Cases (ATLA Winter Convention paper, 1990) (handout that was not included in the convention materials).

ReMine, Protective Orders in Product Liability Litigation (ATLA seminar paper, May 1987).

Thomas, Confidentiality Orders and Sealing Orders: Legislative Options (ATLA Winter Convention paper, 1990).

Weaver, The Inappropriate Use of Rule 26(c) of the Federal Rules of Civil Procedure for the Issuance of Protective Orders in Products Liability Cases (ATLA Winter Convention paper, 1990).

Weaver, The People's Right to Know: Secrecy and Protective Orders (ATLA Annual Convention paper, 1991).

Weiser, How Protective and Secrecy Orders Hurt the Public (Winter Convention paper, 1990).

I. Miscellaneous Materials

All Things Considered (National Public Radio broadcast, Mar. 16, 1988) (transcript on file with the public education department, Association of Trial Lawyers of America).

American Bar Association, Media Access to Pre-Trial Discovery: Is Anything Private? (Fourteenth Annual Fall Meeting, Litigation Section, Oct. 6, 1989).

American Bar Association, Report of the Action Commission to Improve the Tort Liability System 30 (1987).

Bowman & Greene, The Uses and Abuses of Pre-Trial Discovery—The Most Dangerous Discovery Issues Facing the Defense (Eighth Annual Symposium on Products Liability, Southern Methodist University, Apr. 9–10, 1987, at G1).

Curtis, Confidentiality Orders: Cover-Ups and Consequences (June 1989) (paper presented at the 25th Annual Convention of the North Carolina Academy of Trial Lawyers).

Dombroff, Document Retention Programs and Protective Orders: Preventing Litigation (Eighth Annual Symposium on Products Liability, Southern Methodist University, Apr. 9–10, 1987, at B1).

Edwards, Protection of In-House Personnel and Documents During the Discovery Phase (Defense Research Institute, Products Liability Seminar, Feb. 1, 1990, 917C, at K1).

Florida Academy of Trial Lawyers, Information Packet on Secrecy, Apr. 1990.

Grange, *Media Join Other Groups to Keep Legal Fights on the Record*, FOI (1989–1990 Report of the Society of Professional Journalists, at 7).

Grange, *Public Left in Dark by New Legal Trend Toward Secret Justice*, FOI (1989–1990 Report of the Society of Professional Journalists, at 7).

Hare, An Analysis of and Response to the Defendants' Use of FRCP 26(c)(7) to Forbid the Dissemination of Internal Documents Among Plaintiff's Counsel in Design Defect Litigation (Eighth Annual Symposium on Products Liability, Southern Methodist University, Apr. 9–10, 1987, at C1).

Hare, Points and Authorities Concerning Confidentiality Orders in Product Liability Cases (paper presented to TIPS section, American Bar Association, Annual Meeting, Aug. 12, 1988).

Judicial Conference of the District of Columbia, proceedings regarding confidentiality orders (May 17, 1990).

Judicial Conference of the U.S., Report of the Federal Courts Study Comm. 102–03 (1990).

Lawyers for Civil Justice, Position Paper: Court Confidentiality Relating to Protective Orders (approx. June 1991).

Lawyers for Civil Justice, Practical Considerations Relating to Protective Orders (approx. June 1991).

Lawyers for Civil Justice, Protective Orders, Court Seals and Confidentiality: Points and Counterpoints (approx. June 1991).

McHam, Secrecy in the Public Domain: A Report on Discovery, Protective Orders and Sealed Records (Texas Policy Research Forum, Mar. 9, 1990).

Miller, Memorandum on New York Civil Practice Law and Rules Regarding a Right to Public Access to Information Produced in Litigation (submitted to the New York Advisory Committee on Civil Practice, June 15, 1990).

Miller, Memorandum to the New York State Office of Court Administration on Proposed Rule 216.1 Regarding the Sealing of Court Records (Dec. 10, 1990).

Miltenberg, Steelworkers for Democracy v. United Steelworkers of America and U.S. Steel Corp. (unpublished paper, on file at the Association of Trial Lawyers of America).

Olender, Malpractice and the Shroud of Secrecy (unpublished paper) (excerpts from an address at the National Mental Health Project National Conference, Washington, D.C., Apr. 14, 1989).

Protective Orders Balance the Access to Documents Afforded by the Discovery Rules (unpublished position paper made available by attorney Victor Schwartz).

Rutgers Center for Negotiation and Conflict Resolution, Secrecy in Settlement: Privacy v. Public Access (transcript of conference sponsored by Media/Bench/Bar Dialogues of the Rutgers Law School—Newark and the Rutgers Center, Feb. 27, 1991).

Seitz, Motions for a Protective Order (Annual Meeting of the American Bar Association's Litigation Section).

Sinclair, Federal Protective Orders for Confidential Data (ALI-ABA Course Materials, Oct. 1981, at 67).

Society of Professional Journalists & Ass'n of Trial Lawyers of Am., Keeping Secrets: Justice on Trial (1990).

Statements of Frederick Barbee, Devra Lee Davis, James Miller, and Ed Keller from "Keeping Secrets: Justice on Trial," the joint conference sponsored by ATLA and the Society of Professional Journalists, Apr. 25, 1990 (prepared statements on file at the Association of Trial Lawyers of America).

World News Tonight: Court Secrecy (ABC television broadcast, July 25, 1990).

INDEX BY JURISDICTION

This index lists case citations in this book according to jurisdiction. The index is divided into two sections: the first section refers to specific footnotes within the book's *chapters*, and the second section refers to numbered locations within the book's *appendices*. Please note that when a footnote contains more than one case citation for the same jurisdiction, the footnote number will be repeated for each citation.

INDEX TO CHAPTERS

Federal Courts

	Chapter	Footnotes
Supreme Court	1	2, 5, 8, 9, 17, 27, 29, 30, 65
	2	62
	3	7, 28, 28, 42, 53, 53, 62
	5	167, 168, 169, 175
	6	52
	8	71, 87, 101, 102, 103, 104, 105
	10	1, 2, 4, 6, 9, 11, 16, 23, 66, 67, 68, 70, 70, 76, 77, 80, 82, 83, 85, 85, 91, 92, 92, 95, 104, 113, 113, 128, 137, 157, 157, 161, 187
1st Circuit	Intro.	5, 5
	1	44, 47, 78, 99
	2	10, 10, 30, 31, 37, 44, 46, 51, 59, 59, 60, 78, 94
	4	8, 13
	5	1, 55, 94, 96, 112, 120, 121, 147, 153
	6	2, 2, 2, 19, 23, 29, 29, 29, 32, 32, 34, 36, 37, 38, 40, 42, 44, 49, 49, 49, 52, 53, 54, 59
	7	25, 27, 62
	8	55, 106

Federal Courts, continued

	Chapter	Footnotes
1st Circuit, continued	9	3, 3
	10	93, 94, 119, 134, 150, 152, 159, 159, 166
2d Circuit	Intro.	5, 5, 5
	1	10, 21, 21, 22, 39, 46, 52, 58, 76, 96, 100, 109
	2	28, 38, 39, 41, 45, 50, 55, 55, 57, 57, 58, 58, 61, 61, 62, 63, 71, 79, 93, 94, 104, 107, 111, 119, 132, 134
	3	37
	4	12, 13
	5	16, 16, 18, 23, 55, 56, 70, 70, 103, 105, 118, 125, 127, 131, 134, 134, 140, 141, 147, 148, 165, 172, 174, 176
	6	2, 2, 18, 20, 22, 26, 34, 34, 40, 42, 49, 53, 92, 94, 95
	7	14, 17, 18, 20, 23, 33
	8	27, 55, 58, 58, 59, 59, 60, 63, 63, 67, 68, 69, 78, 78, 78, 78, 80, 81, 106
	9	3, 3, 8, 12
	10	16, 18, 19, 20, 24, 29, 41, 44, 45, 58, 58, 62, 64, 73, 80, 86, 97, 132, 150, 151
3d Circuit	Intro.	2, 2, 4, 7
	1	21, 27, 35, 36, 46, 52, 76, 82, 83, 93, 100, 100, 110
	2	10, 27, 27, 35, 38, 50, 55, 55, 55, 55, 56, 58, 58, 58, 62, 71, 79, 102, 104, 105, 107, 107, 107, 107, 110, 112, 118, 118, 119, 122, 124, 132
	4	7, 12, 12, 12, 13
	5	6, 7, 8, 9, 13, 14, 15, 15, 24, 24, 28, 29, 41, 42, 94, 131, 134, 137, 149, 149, 152, 161, 172, 172, 172, 179

	Chapter	Footnotes
	6	2, 2, 3, 15, 23, 25, 26, 31, 33, 34, 35, 39, 42, 46, 46, 49, 49, 50, 51, 53, 53, 53, 55, 55, 84
	7	44, 65
	8	42, 61, 68, 70, 78, 78, 79, 79, 81, 81, 82, 84, 86, 86, 107
	10	34, 42, 47, 50, 59, 60, 101, 108, 122, 138, 146, 151, 152, 160, 186
4th Circuit	Intro.	4, 4
	1	10, 10, 20, 21, 52, 73, 83, 85, 90, 113
	2	18, 55, 63, 63, 87, 134
	5	1, 48, 88, 90, 103, 103, 121, 130, 131, 134, 172, 175, 179
	6	2, 2, 18, 24, 29, 30, 38, 46, 49, 51, 51, 55, 61, 82
	7	6, 6, 7, 8, 9
	8	27, 68, 80
	10	97, 99, 111, 132, 133, 141, 142, 143, 144, 186
5th Circuit	Intro.	1, 5, 5
	1	15, 15, 35, 79, 100
	2	14, 15, 33, 47, 52, 69, 79, 80, 94, 104, 107, 124, 126
	4	12
	5	10, 15, 30, 31, 55, 90, 90, 106, 107, 132, 135, 146, 148, 155, 172
	6	33, 38, 40, 50, 55
	7	30, 52, 58, 61
	8	45, 46, 46, 54
	9	11
	10	20, 25, 43, 58, 63, 73, 100, 102, 107, 110, 139, 140, 145, 147, 177, 179, 186
6th Circuit	1	35, 77, 87, 87, 104, 111
	2	19, 32, 59, 102, 124, 124

Federal Courts, continued

	Chapter	Footnotes
6th Circuit, continued	5	18, 18, 43, 55, 55, 120, 120, 131, 170, 172, 175
	6	51, 53, 58, 59, 61, 86, 87
	7	34, 41, 45, 45, 61
	8	24, 61, 68, 69, 71, 75, 77, 95
	9	4
	10	48, 87, 122, 186
7th Circuit	Intro.	5
	1	29, 34, 43, 85, 110
	2	27, 28, 30, 32, 43, 49, 50, 55, 55, 56, 61, 63, 71, 91, 93, 102, 102, 104, 105, 107, 118, 119, 119, 124, 126, 126
	5	6, 22, 55, 57, 90, 90, 90, 103, 104, 120, 130, 131, 131, 131, 149, 174, 174
	6	2, 3, 22, 38, 42, 48, 50, 51, 51, 55, 58, 59, 61
	7	14, 20, 23, 23, 24, 30, 30, 52, 57, 61, 61, 62, 65
	10	16, 22, 22, 25, 86, 88, 97, 103, 109, 129, 148, 149, 149, 158, 186
8th Circuit	Intro.	1, 5, 6, 6
	1	76, 83, 85, 88
	2	19, 35, 39, 49, 51, 69, 72, 75, 80
	3	24, 25, 26
	5	2, 3, 4, 6, 23, 27, 40, 45, 49, 70, 76, 77, 95, 96, 97, 98, 99, 100, 101, 102, 103, 104, 113, 114, 115, 141, 149, 149, 165, 172, 172, 175
	6	22, 32, 34, 49
	7	14, 15, 23, 24, 26, 26, 41, 42, 43, 44, 44, 57, 67
	8	25, 46, 57, 63
	9	3, 5, 6

	Chapter	Footnotes
	10	14, 21, 21, 71, 72, 79, 83, 96, 104, 172, 173, 186
9th Circuit	Intro.	4, 4
	1	18, 43, 43
	2	23, 46, 57, 58, 62, 68, 84, 94, 98
	5	1, 1, 1, 1, 78, 101, 109, 110, 118, 153, 174, 175, 176
	6	2, 18, 33, 49, 53
	7	10, 13, 19, 22, 23, 23, 23, 33, 41, 48, 49, 57, 76
	8	55, 78, 114
	9	3
	10	17, 24, 34, 39, 47, 50, 61, 70, 71, 71, 71, 80, 81, 84, 86, 93, 97, 130, 131, 136, 153
10th Circuit	1	34, 43, 48, 57, 75, 82, 85, 88, 90, 91, 111, 117
	2	15, 27, 30, 32, 58, 58, 64, 71, 94, 105, 113, 121, 124, 124
	4	7
	5	10, 18, 18, 58, 70, 92, 93, 96, 103, 105, 108, 111, 149, 153, 174, 177, 180, 182
	6	2, 18, 23, 36, 42, 48, 54, 54, 55, 55, 96, 97, 98, 99, 100, 101, 102
	7	11, 26, 57
	8	16, 27, 29
	9	4
	10	16, 36, 40, 48, 48, 49, 50, 74, 78, 95, 109, 113, 113, 114, 114, 118, 147, 152, 157, 161, 161, 186
11th Circuit	Intro.	4, 5
	1	40, 58, 99
	2	38, 57, 57, 59, 107, 107, 124
	3	37
	4	13

Federal Courts, continued

	Chapter	Footnotes
11th Circuit, continued	5	1, 1, 1, 1, 18, 31, 32, 33, 34, 36, 37, 55, 68, 70, 96, 103, 103, 112, 120, 127, 133, 174, 174, 179, 184
	6	2, 30, 34, 34, 36, 52, 59, 82, 84, 90
	7	14, 15, 20, 26, 34, 41, 45, 57, 57
	8	6, 25, 27, 27, 80
	9	3, 3, 9
	10	2, 4, 5, 10, 16, 23, 57, 86, 97, 113, 115, 146, 172
District of Columbia Circuit	1	15, 30, 42, 44, 52, 52, 56
	2	57, 62, 71, 75, 92
	5	1, 125, 130, 163, 165, 176
	6	23, 53, 55
	7	21, 63
	8	78, 87
	10	16, 58, 70, 75, 101, 157, 171, 186
Federal Circuit	2	88, 89, 90
	10	21, 22, 113
Court of Claims	10	42

State Courts

	Chapter	Footnotes
Alabama	1	15
	2	37, 48
	5	70, 112
Alaska	Intro.	4
	1	76
	2	42
	4	7, 10
	5	1, 70, 72, 145, 145
	7	11, 75, 76
	10	117
Arizona	1	15, 35
	5	145
	7	83

	Chapter	Footnotes
Arkansas	6	104
California	Intro.	5
	2	56, 58
	4	4, 10
	5	1, 48, 56, 70, 70, 79, 80, 87, 91, 91, 149
	7	1, 1, 15, 71, 72, 73, 74, 81, 81
	8	8
	10	101, 186
Colorado	5	86, 146, 147, 148
	7	51
	8	111
	10	122
Connecticut	5	146, 147
Delaware	5	145, 148
District of Columbia	2	76, 76, 79, 79, 79, 80
	7	64, 64
Florida	Intro.	4, 5
	2	55
	5	53, 71, 72, 74, 96, 101, 112, 131, 147, 160, 172, 173, 183
	7	16, 26, 29, 54, 60, 77, 78, 79, 80, 87, 88
	10	116, 126, 127
Georgia	5	81, 82, 83, 118
	10	130
Hawaii	4	10
	7	16
Idaho	5	148
Illinois	Intro.	1, 2, 3
	1	10, 35
	2	51, 69, 71
	5	1, 56, 66, 67, 68, 90, 90, 108, 122, 123, 125, 146, 146, 147, 147, 148, 155

State Courts, continued

	Chapter	Footnotes
Illinois, continued	7	5, 16, 51, 52, 52, 59, 68, 69
	8	44
	10	164, 178, 180, 181, 184, 186
Indiana	7	82
Iowa	Intro.	1, 5
	2	71
	7	23
	8	69
	10	175, 176, 186
Kansas	2	75
	5	112
	7	82
Kentucky		
Louisiana		
Maine	Intro.	3
	6	78
Maryland	7	62, 83
Massachusetts	5	70
	7	50
Michigan	Intro.	1
	1	35
	2	71
	7	82
	8	46
	10	172, 174
Minnesota	5	179
Mississippi	4	10
	7	64
Missouri	5	146
	6	85
	7	66
Montana	2	71

	Chapter	Footnotes
	5	1, 145, 148, 148, 149
Nebraska	4	10
Nevada		
New Hampshire		
New Jersey	2	130
	7	84, 85, 86
New Mexico	1	29, 33, 100
	2	57, 107
	4	12, 13
	5	18, 60, 70, 118, 119
New York	1	26, 35, 35, 47
	2	27, 54, 93
	5	44, 55, 70, 112, 127, 147, 183, 183, 183
	6	52
	7	16, 17, 21, 23, 83
North Carolina		
North Dakota		
Ohio	Intro.	1
	5	54, 91, 103, 146, 148
	10	182
Oklahoma		
Oregon	6	72, 73, 74, 105
Pennsylvania	5	147
	7	58, 61
	8	50
Rhode Island	7	14, 57
South Carolina	5	51, 52
South Dakota		
Tennessee		
Texas	Intro.	2, 4, 4, 5
	1	10, 10, 10, 40, 76, 100
	2	67, 68, 75

State Courts, continued

	Chapter	Footnotes
Texas, continued	4	12
	5	1, 1, 1, 72, 84, 84, 84, 88, 90, 90, 102, 102, 103, 103, 112, 125, 125, 145, 145, 145, 146, 146, 148, 148
	6	48, 58, 61, 62, 63, 66
	7	16, 57
	8	64, 76, 95, 110, 111
	10	2, 11, 125, 172, 183
Utah		
Vermont		
Virginia		
Washington	Intro.	5, 5
	1	100
	2	71, 107
	4	12
	5	15, 50, 61, 62, 63, 64, 65, 155
	8	43
	10	186, 186
West Virginia		
Wisconsin	8	9, 10, 25, 56
Wyoming	5	75

INDEX TO APPENDICES

Federal Courts

	Appendix	Location
Supreme Court	1	§1, §17.2, §20, §22.2, §23.2, §48.2, §48.2
	2	A18, A31, B12, B38
1st Circuit	1	§8, §11, §12, §15.1, §15.1, §16.3, §16.4, §17.3, §19, §20, §22.2, §22.4, §22.4,
		§22.5, §22.5, §23.3, §28, §33, §35, §36, §36, §36, §36, §37, §38.1, §38.1, §38.1, §38.2, §38.2, §38.3, §47, §47, §47, §47, §48.3
	2	B7, B32, B41, C16

	Appendix	Location
2d Circuit	1	§1, §1, §3, §4, §5.1, §5.1, §5.1, §5.2, §5.2, §6, §6, §6, §8, §11, §13, §15.2, §15.3, §16.3, §16.3, §16.4, §16.4, §16.4, §18.2, §18.3, §19, §19, §19, §20, §22.3, §22.3, §22.4, §22.5, §22.5, §23.4, §26, §34, §35, §36, §36, §37, §37, §38.1, §38.1, §38.1, §38.2, §38.4, §38.4, §38.4, §39.1, §39.1, §40, §40, §40, §43, §45, §46, §46, §46, §46, §47, §47, §47, §47, §47, §48.2, §48.2, §48.2, §48.2, §48.3, §48.3, §48.3, §49
	2	A24, A24, A24, A29, A31, B2, B9, B9, B13, B20, B22, B35, B36, B41, B41, B41, B43, C8, C8, C10, C10, C15, C15, C16, C17, C18
3d Circuit	1	§2, §3, §3, §3, §4, §5.2, §5.2, §8, §9.4, §12, §15.1, §15.1, §15.1, §16.3, §16.3, §16.4, §17.1, §17.1, §17.1, §17.1, §17.2, §17.2, §17.7, §17.7, §18.1, §18.2, §19, §22.2, §22.4, §22.5, §26, §28, §28, §32, §33, §33, §35, §36, §36, §36, §36, §36, §36, §36, §37, §37, §37, §37, §37, §37, §38.1, §38.1, §38.1, §38.2, §38.2, §38.2, §38.2, §38.2, §38.3, §38.3, §38.3, §38.4, §38.4, §38.4, §40, §41, §43, §44, §46, §46, §46, §47, §47, §47, §48.2, §49, §49, §49, §49
	2	B9, B9, B10, B11, B12, B12, B27, B29, B41, C10, C10, C10, C16
4th Circuit	1	§2, §3, §4, §5.1, §6, §6, §9.4, §11, §15.1, §15.2, §15.2, §15.3, §16.3, §16.3, §16.3, §16.4, §16.4, §17.1, §17.2, §18.1, §18.1, §18.2, §18.2, §22.2, §22.3, §22.3, §22.5, §34, §34, §34, §35, §36, §46, §47, §47, §47, §48.2, §48.3, §49
	2	A20, B9, B14, B25, B26, B29, B29, C10, C10, C16, C16
5th Circuit	1	§2, §4, §5.2, §6, §6, §15.1, §15.2, §15.3, §15.3, §16.3, §16.4, §16.4, §16.4, §16.4, §16.4, §17.2, §18.1,

Federal Courts, continued

	Appendix	Location
5th Circuit, continued		§18.1, §18.1, §18.2, §22.2, §22.5, §22.5, §23.4, §26, §35, §36, §36, §36, §37, §38.2, §38.3, §38.3, §40, §47
	2	A24, A24, B21, B23, B31, B41, B42, C10, C16
6th Circuit	1	§6, §9.1, §10, §16.3, §16.3, §16.4, §18.1, §18.2, §18.2, §19, §19, §19, §20, §22.3, §22.4, §22.4, §33, §34, §35, §36, §36, §36, §37, §37, §37, §38.2, §38.2, §38.2, §38.4, §43, §44, §46, §47
	2	A13, A24, A24, B3, B22, B37, B39, B42, C19, C20
7th Circuit	1	§2, §4, §7, §8, §8, §16.4, §16.4, §16.4, §16.4, §16.4, §17.2, §18.1, §18.2, §20, §22.2, §22.3, §22.3, §22.5, §34, §36, §38.1, §38.2, §38.2, §38.3, §38.4, §38.4, §38.4, §40, §46, §46, §47, §47, §47, §47, §47, §47, §47, §47, §48.2, §48.3, §48.3
	2	A17, A20, A20, A20, B1, B6, B7, B12, B34, B41, B41, B42, B42, C6, C17
8th Circuit	1	§3, §4, §9.1, §9.1, §9.1, §9.4, §12, §15.1, §15.3, §16.4, §16.4, §17.1, §17.2, §17.2, §17.3, §18.1, §18.3, §19, §22.3, §22.4, §22.4, §22.5, §23.1, §23.3, §28, §35, §36, §36, §36, §37, §38.1, §38.1, §38.2, §38.2, §38.3, §38.4, §39.1, §46, §47, §47, §47, §48.3, §49
	2	B33
9th Circuit	1	§5.2, §8, §16.4, §16.4, §16.4, §18.1, §18.2, §18.3, §20, §20, §22.3, §22.3, §22.4, §22.5, §22.5, §34, §34, §35, §35, §38.4, §47
	2	B4, B9, B9, B17, B21, B24, B28, B42, C8, C10, C16
10th Circuit	1	§6, §8, §15.3, §15.3, §16.3, §16.3, §16.3, §16.4, §17.1, §17.2,

	Appendix	Location
		§17.2, §18.2, §18.2, §18.3, §20, §20, §22.3, §22.4, §22.5, §34, §36, §38.1, §38.4, §46, §46, §47, §47, §48.2, §49
	2	A24, B19, B40, B41, B42, C16, C20
11th Circuit	1	§1, §1, §4, §5.1, §6, §15.1, §15.1, §15.2, §16.3, §17.1, §17.3, §17.5, §18.1, §18.1, §18.1, §18.1, §18.2, §18.2, §19, §19, §19, §20, §22.3, §22.4, §22.4, §22.5, §22.5, §26, §28, §34, §34, §35, §35, §35, §36, §36, §36, §36, §36, §36, §37, §38.1, §38.1, §38.1, §38.2, §38.2, §39.1, §40, §40, §47, §47, §47, §48.3, §48.3, §49
	2	A19, B8, B23, B30, B44, C3, C10
District of Columbia Circuit	1	§1, §16.4, §16.4, §19, §20, §22.4, §22.5, §23.4, §36, §36, §36, §39.1, §40, §44, §46, §47, §48.3, §48.3
	2	A12, C18
Federal Circuit	1	§16.4, §22.3, §22.5, §35
State Courts		
Alabama	1	§4, §5.1, §8, §10, §16.3, §16.3, §16.3, §18.1, §18.1, §18.2, §22.4, §22.5
	2	C5
Alaska	1	§2, §39.1, §48.2
Arizona	1	§36, §37
	2	C13
Arkansas	2	C12
California	1	§5.1, §10, §15.2, §16.4, §18.1, §18.2, §22.2, §22.4, §22.4, §22.5, §22.5, §22.5, §36, §36, §37, §38.3, §39.1, §40, §50
Colorado	1	§36, §37, §38.3, §44
Connecticut	1	§5.2
Delaware	1	§28, §36, §37, §37, §43
District of Columbia		

State Courts, continued

	Appendix	Location
Florida	1	§1, §4, §5.1, §5.1, §5.2, §16.3, §16.3, §16.3, §22.4, §35, §38.4, §48.2
Georgia	1	§18.1
	2	C11
Hawaii		
Idaho		
Illinois	1	§16.3, §16.4, §19, §22.4, §22.5, §35, §36, §37, §39.2, §48.2
Indiana	1	§16.4, §22.2, §22.3, §22.4, §22.4, §22.5, §48.3, §48.3
Iowa	1	§19, §22.2, §48.3
	2	A24, B16
Kansas		
Kentucky		
Louisiana	1	§5.2, §15.2, §15.2, §37, §48.3
Maine		
Maryland	1	§5.2
Massachusetts	1	§48.2
Michigan	1	§21, §33, §36, §36, §37, §38.1, §38.2, §38.2, §38.3, §38.3, §38.4
Minnesota	1	§5.2, §9.2
Mississippi	1	§5.1
Missouri	1	§37, §47
Montana	1	§16.4, §22.2, §36, §47
Nebraska	1	§15.1
Nevada	1	§36
New Hampshire	1	§28, §36, §37
New Jersey	1	§15.1, §15.2, §22.2, §36
New Mexico		
New York	1	§1, §5.2, §5.2, §9.1, §9.1, §13, §15.1, §16.3, §17.2, §17.2, §19, §19, §21, §22.3, §22.3, §22.4, §22.4, §22.5, §22.5, §23.3, §24, §31, §32, §33, §33, §35, §36, §36,

	Appendix	Location
		§36, §36, §36, §36, §37, §37, §37, §37, §38.1, §38.1, §38.2, §38.3, §38.4, §39.1, §39.2, §39.2, §40, §40, §40, §41, §42, §43, §44, §47, §48.2, §48.3, §50
North Carolina	1	§38.1, §38.2, §38.4
North Dakota		
Ohio	1	§15.1, §43
	2	B23
Oklahoma		
Oregon	1	§17.1, §22.4
	2	C9, C14
Pennsylvania	1	§11, §12, §15.2, §16.2, §17.2, §17.4, §18.1, §18.2, §23.1, §36, §36, §36, §38.1, §45
	2	A24, C2, C20
Rhode Island	1	§1, §5.2
South Carolina		
South Dakota		
Tennessee	1	§15.1, §36
Texas	1	§5.1, §15.1, §16.2, §16.3, §16.4, §16.4, §17.2, §17.2, §18.1, §18.1, §18.1, §18.1, §19, §19, §20, §22.3, §22.4, §22.4, §22.4, §22.4, §22.4, §22.5, §28, §28, §36, §38.1, §38.1, §38.1, §38.2, §38.2, §38.2, §38.2, §39.1, §45, §47, §48.3, §48.3, §49
	2	B5, B18, C1, C4, C9
Utah		
Virginia		
Washington	1	§15.2, §15.2, §36, §36, §37
West Virginia		
Wisconsin	1	§5.2, §23.3, §36, §38.3, §40
	2	B15
Wyoming	1	§22.5